THE GARDEN OF JOY

A PRIMER FOR THE PRAIRIE PROVINCES AND ROCKY MOUNTAIN EMPIRE

REVISED EDITION

———————————

BY JAMES D. SEARLES

AMERICAN & WORLD GEOGRAPHIC PUBLISHING
HELENA, MONTANA

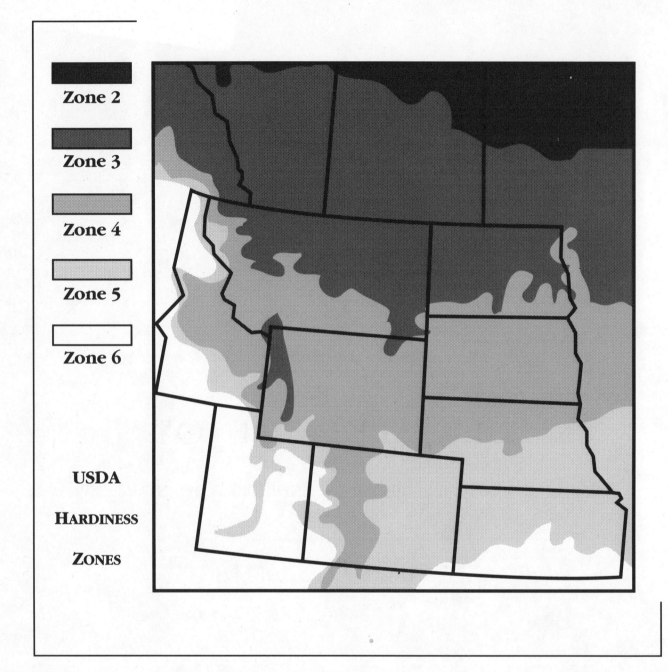

Zone 2

Zone 3

Zone 4

Zone 5

Zone 6

USDA

HARDINESS

ZONES

 Text printed on recycled paper

ISBN 1-56037-018-1
© 1992 American & World Geographic Publishing
P.O. Box 5630, Helena, Montana 59604

Text © 1992 Estate of James D. Searles,
Karl J. Donovan, Personal Representative

Library of Congress Cataloging-in-Publication Data

Searles, James D.
    The garden of joy : a primer for the prairie provinces
and Rocky Mountain empire / by James D. Searles. -- Rev.
ed.
        p.   cm.
    Includes bibliographical references and index.
    ISBN 1-56037-018-1
    1. Gardening--Great Plains.   2. Gardening--Rocky Moun-
tains region.   3. Plants, Cultivated--Great Plains.   4. Plants,
Cultivated--Rocky Mountains Region.   I. Title
SB453.2.G74S43   1992
635.9'5178--dc20   92-17470

CONTENTS

Virtually no plant can be expected to survive if it is positioned outside the perimeters of its needs or without human care and love. So, too, is man's gentle spirit. Hold carefully to the sight and sound that you are blessed with...

Love Your Garden
Look to this day, for it is life.
For yesterday is already a dream
and tomorrow is only a vision.
But today, well lived, makes every
yesterday a dream of happiness,
and every tomorrow a vision of hope.
—*Sanskrit proverb*

SHAPING & NURTURING THE GARDEN

Every place in the world is special and original, but the areas along the Rocky Mountains subject to warm, dry winter chinook winds are particularly unique. There is a kind of electric excitement in a chinook wind. We revel in the sudden break from cold winter temperatures, if only for a few days. The snow melts off, and grazing animals have an easier time finding food. People shed their heavy outerwear and wander outside with big smiles.

But while we're enjoying the chinook winds, plants are being stressed to their limits. Radical temperature fluctuations are very stressful for interior plant cells, and only a special group of plants can withstand the rigors of our northern winters combined with warm chinook winds. USDA zones set useful parameters for selecting plants for our area of North America, but the chinook winds eliminate many plants that will cheerfully grow in the same USDA zone as ours.

This book will help you plan and maintain a successful landscape in the chinook zone. Learn about microclimates, sun and shade areas, drought-tolerance, and basic landscape principles for pleasing designs.

Then try the step-by-step guide to planning your landscape, complete with ground covers, trees, play areas and lawns. Learn how to enrich your soil, reduce watering needs, and deal with insect pests. Then you can delve into ideas for specific interest areas such as rock gardens, perennial gardens, water gardens, native plants, and vegetable gardens.

Finally the species-by-species guide to chinook-hardy plants provides much useful information regarding their needs and preferences, as well as personal tips from my own experience in gardening with these plants.

Gardening can be very easy with the proper selection of plants for specific growing areas. If you are a beginning or busy gardener, I heartily advise you to utilize the many plants in this book marked "easy." Then, as you gain experience, and as your knowledge of soil quality and watering techniques increases, you can experiment with other varieties.

This guide is intended to supplement other gardening books. Specifically, I recommend *Easy Gardening* by Time/Life Books, *The Wild Garden: Making Natural Gardens Using Wild and Native Plants* by Violet Stevenson, and *Gardening on the Prairies: A Guide to Canadian Home Gardening* by Rodger Vick.

THE GARDEN OF JOY

The interaction of plants and humans has been widely documented in newspapers, on television and in books. Most striking of all has been the Findhorn Community's astonishing garden on the northern tip of Scotland. There, plants were grown to such monstrous proportions and unexplainable hardiness that they could not be ignored by confounded experts. Simply put, the Findhorn Community employed love, and cooperation with the spirits of nature.

"The radiations put out by every gardener contribute to the growth of the garden and these emotional and mental forces are transmuted by the nature forces and can add to plant growth. Certain people stimulate plant growth, others depress it and even draw from the plant. When our forces are consciously focused towards adding to plant health, this produces a still greater effect. Like children, gardens need tender loving care. In turn, children and happiness are very good for plants. Human affirmative thought protects and feeds plants, as it does all of life. Our separative thought jars Nature's patterns. Flavor is improved in vegetables grown in a harmonious atmosphere. Our thanks and appreciation unite us with the life of whatever we are thankful for and appreciative for, making a compatible blend of forces to help development on various levels, including the physical. As positive thoughts and emotion influence the plant, the resulting higher quality food that we eat influences us positively— an ascending spiral."

To Hear The Angels Sing,
Dorothy MacLean

To illustrate how this could be applied to your own gardening, try a simple but intriguing exercise. First, plant two identical groups of seeds (corn works well for this). With one of the groups hold it lovingly, and verbally encourage it on a daily basis. The other is just a control and is to be given water only. You will soon see for yourself the difference that love makes.

One can gain an astonishing gardening ability by listening to plants. In my own experience, I began this lesson by learning to let my houseplants ask me for water. Nothing extraordinary happened, I merely would become aware of a particular plant and know that it needed water. I do a pleasant variation of this by sitting quietly in my night garden, savoring its peace. Shortly, I begin to feel a sense of the earth and even, perhaps, the movement of plant roots growing. Then I become aware of the garden as a whole, feeling each plant's presence and needs. In yet another method, some people enjoy meditating in their garden with fingers pressed gently into the soil. This can provide a wonderful feeling of oneness. Less noticeably, many other people quietly enjoy this same loving oneness when hand-watering or walking in the rain. Not to be overlooked is the importance of a sense of affection that a loving person creates when caressing a plant's leaves. This is much the same as the way one would stroke a beloved pet or fellow human.

Become more and more aware
Of the things that really matter in life
The things that gladden the heart
Refresh the spirit
And lift the consciousness.

The more beauty you absorb
The more beauty you can reflect.
The more love you absorb
The more love you have to give.
The world needs more and more love,
Beauty
Harmony and understanding
And you are the ones to give it forth.

Why not open your hearts now
And do it
Foundations of Findhorn
by Eileen Caddy

THE CHINOOK ZONE

Dry, warm winds called chinooks pound specific areas in Montana and Alberta. Although keenly appreciated by people, these dramatic warm winds push plants to the limits of their tolerance. The foremost danger is the rapid temperature change inside plant cells as the thermometer mercury shoots up or down. Water in the plant cells expands as it freezes, rupturing cell walls. Stressed to their limits, the tissues of less-tolerant plants are shredded as they expand and contract with temperature fluctuations.

The other critical danger is the "False Spring Effect" during our notoriously hot and cold winters. If a plant ends its dormancy by running sap and swelling its buds, it may not survive later frosts. These demands of climate foster a need for a special group of plants.

HARDY PLANTS

The word "hardy" used in most gardening books is relatively meaningless for our area. One such example is by the Hardy Plant Society of England, whose far limit of cold tolerance would be equivalent to Seattle's climate. Furthermore, plants hardy to Nepal, Tibet and the Himalayas are not usually suitable for us either. Though these plants endure tremendous cold, they will not tolerate the Northern Plains' alkaline soil, hot summers or lack of snow cover. And most perplexing of all are those plants that would be cold-tolerant enough, but require snowcover. In the chinook zone, the treacherous lack of snow and freeze/thaw periods wreak havoc on such plants.

In short, many factors influence a "hardy" plant's tolerance of the chinook zone climate. They include:

1. a tolerance for abrupt temperature changes;
2. general vigor—a weak plant will be less hardy;
3. acceptable soil pH or drainage;
4. adequate potassium for hardening off;
5. susceptibility to die-back (does it bloom on old wood?);
6. tolerance for dry winter wind damage.

In Canada particularly, much testing has been done to see what will grow in the chinook zone. One major difficulty has been the vast quantity of plants to test. Even beyond the endless numbers of species, the hybrids boggle the mind because of their unpredictable hardiness. They can be more or less cold-tolerant than their parents. To add to the confusion, local gardeners can breed hardier plants themselves by saving and planting the seeds of acclimatized plants. These offspring are usually much hardier than their parents. That is why finding a local source for acclimatized plants is so important.

HARDINESS ZONES

To this confusing realm of considerations, add the problem of maps zoned for hardiness rating. Nature simply has no use for such climate lines, preferring instead a subtle blending of microclimates. Although widely criticized for accuracy, the USDA and Agriculture Canada zone maps are still the best around.

Many of this guide's zone ratings are based on the plants successfully grown in Olds, Calgary or Brooks, Alberta; Great Falls, Helena or Bozeman, Montana. On the USDA map ratings, Great Falls and central Montana are in Zone 4. Northeastern Montana and southern Alberta are in Zone 3. Calgary and northern parts of the chinook zone are on the southern edge of USDA Zone 2. Edmonton and the areas of central Alberta outside the chinook zone have a distinctly different gardening climate due to predictable snow cover.

LANDSCAPE PRINCIPLES

Much unnecessary maintenance and frustration can be eliminated right at the start, with proper planning. This is the secret to a garden that "effortlessly" churns out an endless show of apparent magic. A carefully planned landscape will surprise you with how easy gardening can be.

The choices of landscape design encompass many broad areas: energy factors, special usage needs, watering reduction and the special problems and needs of trees. This all has to be cleverly balanced with the paramount characteristic of year-round garden interest. You have many choices and will have to base your decision on their relative importance to you and your personal style.

IT ALL BEGINS ON PAPER

The two main considerations for most people seem be: first, the ability of a design to provide a secure sense of privacy or refuge; and secondly, the ability of a site to afford a view of the surrounding area (sometimes referred to as borrowed scenery). Do your best to accentuate one or both of these. To begin, map out the factors affecting your area. This important step is critical for becoming what will seem like a magical gardener.

1. Take a very large sheet of paper and list the compass directions around the paper's edge, with north at the top. Then draw the boundaries of your property.

2. Add to this the outlines of buildings, walks, driveways, nearby roads and alleys, play areas, storage or work areas, seating areas, fences or walls, hose faucets, septic tank, drain field or sewer lines, utility powerline right-of-ways, water drainage problem areas and/or creekbeds.

3. Then, draw dotted-line circles to show existing trees and shrubs, approximating their eventual spread.

4. Next, use colored pencils to mark the views you would like to keep and other views you would like to hide. Do this around your map's edge.

5. Look for the routes of mail carriers and delivery people—and, most importantly, the shortcuts of children and dogs. Plan either foot paths or barrier plantings for these areas.

6. Consider your willingness and ability to water. Before selecting any plants that are not drought-tolerant, you should reflect carefully on their distance from patios, house entrances and water outlets. A rule of thumb is that the farther a plant is from your door, the less water it will receive. The relative importance of such a plant will be quickly tested in this manner.

7. Draw arrows from the north showing cold winter winds that rob your house of heat. Then, for the chinook zone, draw gusty southwest winds. Keep in mind that these winds pound your heated home from a second direction.

8. Remember to consider storage, work, play and seating areas.

MICROCLIMATES

A very important concept to understand is microclimates. These are the ways that man and nature alter the overall climate to create varied zones of protection and exposure.

While your home may be located in a specific USDA hardiness zone, various factors can combine to make your neighborhood, or even an area of your property, an exception to the general zone map. Solid bar-

riers like a fence or a structure at the bottom of a hill may trap down-flowing cold air and create a very cold pocket of still air. Conversely, a dark-colored south-facing wall can trap heat during the day and create an unusually warm pocket of air, followed by very cold nights when the warm air rises and leaves the area.

These microclimates affect the growing conditions in specific areas around your property. In general, you can expect the microclimate zone to change to an adjacent zone, either warmer or colder. For example, a gardener in Zone 3 may have a sheltered microclimate between the house and garage that simulates conditions in Zone 4; or a portion of that same property may be exposed to especially harsh winter winds, and have microclimates that support only Zone 2 plants.

The most dramatic effects of microclimate involve frost pockets. Initially, it may help you to think of cold air flow as similiar to water drainage, sliding down into low areas and getting caught behind low walls and hedges. In areas near canyon bottoms and mountains, this effect is especially pronounced and should be noted carefully so that you can control it. You may want to accumulate cold air in some areas to minimize early thawing. Alternately, you may want to divert this frigid effect in other areas to reduce late frost damage and create warm areas earlier in the year. Such are the choices provided by microclimates.

SUN AND SHADE ZONES

Move outside and orient yourself to the four directions with a compass. Now that you have done this, you will be able to guess the path of the sun as it rises approximately due east, arches in the sky at noon (due south) and finally sets to the west. Attempt to figure the height of the sun's midday arch, which is highest overhead in midsummer, and near the horizon in midwinter. During the growing season, this alteration will affect 3 to 4 feet on the edge of shade zones. Becoming aware of the sun's usual arch will teach you to automatically see full sun, half-sun, half-shade, and deep shade areas. While standing outside, pay close attention to gaps or holes in the tree canopy, as these create relatively brighter shade areas. All growing zones are preferred by one or another type of plant. Learn to position plants in their best locations for maximum growth, an invaluable skill for the magic gardener.

Half-shade refers to a location receiving a few hours of dappled or reflected sun each day. Half shade is often located under a lone tree. A light-colored house wall can reflect light and may support plants that need half-shade.

Half-sun refers to a location receiving three to five hours of sunshine each day. Morning sun is less intense than afternoon sun, so plants needing half-sun will respond differently if their allotment is morning sun or intense afternoon sun.

Full shade means exactly that. No direct sunlight reaches the area. This is usually an area under a closed canopy of trees, where the leaves don't reflect any sunlight. It may also be the north side of a dark-colored structure or wall.

Full sun refers to a location receiving six or more hours of sun each day.

MAPPING YOUR MICROCLIMATES

Look for deep shade areas north of buildings, walls and trees. These are problem areas where few plants survive. You might consider these for cool, seating areas. Lightly mark these areas on your map. Next, look for full sun zones exposed to the south and unshaded by trees or buildings. These areas tend to bake dry in the summer and require excessive water . The areas east and west of buildings and trees will vary between half-sun, half-shade,and full shade.

COOLING AND WARMING

For many gardeners, the energy factors of landscaping can become quite an insatiable study. To start with, an astonishing quantity of natural cooling in summer can be accomplished merely through the placement of trees or vines. Deciduous trees are most commonly used for this purpose. They require little maintenance and lose their leaves in the fall, allowing the sun's warmth in during the winter. For a dense canopy of leaves and limbs, try elms *(Ulmus),* linden trees *(Tilia),* and maples *(Acer).* Kentucky coffee tree *(Gymnocladus),* honey locust *(Gleditsia)* and Manchurian walnut *(Juglans)* provide slightly less shade in summer, but allow much more sun in during the winter. Small trees create almost no usable shade. Another choice is using vines that grow quickly, offering the advantage of fast effect, particularly the annual vines: ornamental hops *(Humulus),* moonvine *(Ipomoea)* and scarlet runner beans. You should also plant for the long-term effect of perennial vines, though they require a year or two to become established. In addition, ground covers and lawns help by reducing heat accumulation and reflection.

Equally important is the winter season, when attention is centered on the placement of wind protection. Sheltering trees and dense hedges can help protect the warmth of your dwelling in winter. Once effectively located, these barriers create air pockets that buffer cold winds. Unfortunately, wind complicates this situation by deflecting and channeling into odd directions between buildings and walls. However, an observant gardener can determine wind patterns by watching cloth strips tied to tall stakes, snow drift patterns and smoke from a chimney. Once this is done, you can create effective wind shields using dense evergreens such as Colorado blue spruce or tall junipers.

CONSIDER THE TREE...

Be aware that trees have their own problems and needs best solved in the planning stage. Most, if not all, of these problems are easily avoided by considering a tree's ultimate height and natural shape. Far too often, large trees are planted next to buildings, powerlines, other trees or, worst of all, planted on hillsides with views. Pruning should never be considered a corrective measure for a badly positioned tree (removal is quite often the best and only alternative). To repeat, remember to allow room for a tree's normal spread as well as height while in the planning stage. Naturally large plants cannot be pruned smaller in any practical manner.

Another difficult tree problem is that of "messy" trees placed near patios, driveways, parking spaces and swimming pools. Silver maples, cottonwoods, poplars, ashes and willows are notoriously brittle trees that grow quickly and continually sluff off older limbs. You will always find downed branches under these trees after a wind storm. Two additional problems you may encounter are the sap-dripping foliage of birches and the dangerously large buckeye seedpods that drop in the fall. Not suprisingly, these problems can be avoided with planning.

Remember, when planting shelterbelts it is important to plant a variety of species and to avoid unbroken straight lines. Trees and shrubs planted in attractive grove-like clumps are optimally effective at diffusing wind and providing cover for wildlife. But best of all, they make attractive scenery for people. Please be considerate of the fact that row-like hedges are a powerful visual disturbance on a landscape.

Now, with completed map in hand, you have a powerful tool for making clear decisions. At this point, it is hard to believe the number of saved steps and the miraculous effects of winter and low-maintenance gardening now possible. Your future success in using this garden guide hinges primarily on whether you made such a map. If you have not done so already, go back and do it now.

DROUGHT-TOLERANT LANDSCAPING

Here in the arid West, nearly all of our water is deposited as snow during the winter and melts into the water table in spring and early summer. During May and June, most areas receive rain. However, by July, the gift of water from the sky ends and the land begins its normal dry period, which lasts until the snows of early fall. These are the parameters of nature. Common sense dictates that first consideration in landscaping choices be given to climatically-adapted plants.

However, in any garden the following care will make it more drought tolerant:

1. Correctly identify the light exposure (sun, half-sun, half-shade, shade) as well as the drying wind exposure of the site. This helps you select the most adapted plants. Quite suprisingly, most drought-tolerant plants require full sun. Only a very few plants can tolerate both shade and drought.

2. Double-dig your garden soil and add organic material. This makes the soil more water retentive.

3. Water deeply and avoid run-off.

4. Eliminate weed and grass competition. Weeds consume large quantities of nutrients and water, in addition to choking out sunlight.

5. Plants labeled as drought-tolerant usually need water until they are established (annuals for the first month, perennials and shrubs for the first year). During very dry spells, even established drought-tolerant plants benefit from occasional water.

JOY OF GARDENING

Once your plan is completed on paper, you can delve into the pleasures of creating an interesting year-round garden. Basically, you want to promote an endless parade of beauty in tune with the seasons.

To begin, try to become aware of your garden's show of color during its seasons. Some people merely list which of their flowers bloom each month. But for others, a more complete map is essential. When doing this, pay attention to finding gaps. A common gap is the interval in June between the spring flowers and the summer flowers. Fortunately, this is easily filled with peonies *(Paeonia)*, daylilies *(Hemerocallis)*, or early shrub roses *(Rosa)*. Another gap often exists in the early fall when a garden should be filled with the exuberance of the late autumn flowers—asters, boltonia, chrysanthemums, colchicums, and goldenrod *(Solidago)*. Finish rounding out the year with suggestions from the "Montana Winter Gardening" section of this guide.

Next, start looking for an essence or feeling to use as a focus. Stop for a moment and consider nearby themes, particularly your house's style, or area dramatic accents. This can lead to some pleasant discoveries. Try to encourage a harmonious sense of unity with the area surrounding your landscaped space.

Color choices in the garden add a whole new realm of mood play. While the warm tones—reds, pinks, oranges and yellows—energize and brighten, the cool tones—blues, purples and greens—soothe and relax. Subtle tones such as brown and dark green create an earthy mood. And most dramatically, white, the aristocrat of the garden, splashes a sense of uplift. Oddly enough, choosing fewer colors can create more interest, while a kaleidoscope color scheme can blur a garden's impact.

An intriguingly easy design method is to make photographs of the areas being developed, and simply draw your ideas on a clear plastic overlay with colored markers. The beauty of this method is the immediate vision of the finished plan and the possibility of uncovering potential problems. You can have a lot of fun designing and redesigning your landscape. Go for it!

Night lighting a garden further enhances colors and accents, while adding a mood of its own. Try using spot lighting to illuminate dramatic trees, specimen plantings, lacy or silvery foliage plants or even statuary. Side or back lighting is the most dramatic. Be sure to conceal the light source. For the best choices for colored lighting, try light blue to accent natural moonlight or else use amber or light green. Consider the possibilities of including several small diffuse lights at a distance. And remember, night lighting allows you to hide less attractive areas by simply leaving them dark. In all uses of night lighting, be conscientious of your neighbors. Shielding a light is always a basic consideration.

A new realm of possibilities exists with the addition of soothing sounds. Consider splashing water, and other pleasant random noises such as wind drones. How about weather-proof speakers connected to a sound system? Have you ever noticed that at night a garden has its own characteristic sound quality in quiet moments? You may discover that each plant makes its own characteristic rustles and rubbing sounds.

Equally important, do you need to mask street sounds? The most effective choices are solid fences and artificial hill mounds. Other choices include dense plantings of hedges or trees.

Allow yourself to fully consider the inviting possibilities of the following suggestions.

1. A swing for a quiet corner in your backyard.
2. A play area for adults or that tree-house denied you as a child.
3. A suntrap (a warm sunny area) well protected from the wind for winter, spring and fall use. For a moment, you might even entertain the possibility of a relaxing hot tub fantasy.
4. Then, for the heat of summer, consider a cool patio in deep shade or even a simulated cave grotto complete with ferns and dripping water. Such sitting areas quickly become exercises in nature worship.

In your designs, always use comfortable seats of natural wood. Marble or concrete benches can be very uncomfortable and cold.

A FEW INCIDENTAL ACCENTS

1. Use the striking combination of ferns and partially unearthed large rocks, as well as the natural drama of water and large trees. One fascinating combination is a grass lawn surrounded by a dark forest-like planting.

2. People living on street corners and road curves have a particular responsibility to maintain showy landscapes. These are the areas that many people see.
3. Plant accents of daylilies, peonies or yarrow at the base of lampposts, gates or birdbaths.
4. For best visual impact, avoid solitary plants. Instead, repeat flower patterns throughout the garden for maximum continuity.
5. In most plantings, small or delicate plants belong in the foreground, and tall or bold plants are more to scale in the background.
6. Try to blend plantings so lines are less noticeable.
7. For greatest visual impact, use a healthy dose of prudent simplicity.
8. Label plants with names to lend a sense of adventure for visitors.
9. The theme garden ideas beginning on page 20 will help you create a garden with a specific focus. But your most important first step is to stress winter landscaping. Choose from the large number of plants noted for winter interest before choosing any others.

OF DIGGING AND DIRT

One of the first things to understand in gardening is that complex mixture of compounds called soil.

In general, the character of one's soil depends on its distance from floodplains. Because most of the northern Great Plains was at one time or another covered with lakes or oceans, most areas have rich deposits of silt and clay (sometimes called gumbo) in a deep layer of topsoil. Usually this soil contains little organic material and its pH is alkaline. However, if a site was previously forested, then its soil is probably less alkaline and contains more humus.

For the most part, gardeners can best enrich their

soil by double-digging and adding compost, manure and peat. Optimally, this formula should also include bone and blood meal and spare quantities of wood ashes.

Double-digging with organic material is the very best thing you can do for your soil. To dig a bed in this manner, you first remove a row of topsoil one spadeful deep and place it in a wheelbarrow. Then loosen the subsoil with a spading fork (or shovel) and mix in compost, manure, peat, blood and bone meal, kelp meal, and trace element mixtures. Next move the topsoil from the adjacent row onto the loosened row, and work the exposed subsoil as before. Continue this procedure to the last row in the bed where you finish by adding the topsoil from the wheelbarrow. Attempt to mix evenly the subsoil, topsoil and organic additions.

From this method you can expect benefits of
1. amazingly productive plants with a deep and large root structure;
2. increased water absorption;
3. more oxygen in the soil;
4. improved water drainage;
5. a more neutral pH.

Additionally, the organic nutrients' gradual breakdown supports beneficial earthworms and soil microorganisms.

To avoid compacting double-dug soil, do not walk on these beds. Instead use boards or stones for paths. A word to the wise is: plan garden beds two arm-reaches wide, with foot paths on either side. Narrow rows or scattered plantings work well in such beds. The problem with conventionally-wide garden rows is that they waste space and become compacted from the walkways between rows.

Alkaline-induced chlorosis, or yellowing of leaves, is a common soil problem in the Northern Plains. This problem is caused by a high-alkaline soil locking up the iron in the soil, making it unavailable to plants. Generally, this problem shows up in plants native to acidic forest soils (oaks, maples, spirea, roses and some pines). This iron-deficiency causes a characteristic yellowish color in new growth. A similar problem, also caused by an alkaline pH, is phosphorus deficiency. This shows itself as a characteristic purplish-green color in the early spring growth. In mild cases, alkaline pH can be easily buffered by adding peat or manure (but be careful of high-salt manure from feedlot cows) and watering deeply. Sulphur compounds are a short-term solution but become damaging in long-term usage. In areas of extreme alkalinity, select plants listed as being the most alkaline tolerant. An excellent article on this subject is in the January 1986 Rodale's *Organic Gardening* magazine.

Soil testing is an excellent means to identify one's soil makeup. In addition to pH and soil quality, you will see what levels of nitrogen, phosphorus, potassium, iron and essential trace elements are already in your soil. This helps immensely in knowing what to and what not to add. Many gardening books list which organic materials contain what nutrients. Generally, however, homemade compost contains a little of everything needed for good soil.

Chemical fertilizers and amendments are a hotly contested issue. Due to their "white sugar" effect of accelerating weak plant growth and their long-term depletion of the soil, I urge you to use them sparingly. Until more is known of their cumulative effect on earthworms, microorganisms, and fungus interrelationships, their role in the garden should be minimized.

"What is dirt but the very substance of this planet refined through aeons of time, the seed bed of life at the disposal of all and every life, not keeping itself to itself but free and removable for all. That immense purity you feel in us is most applicable to earth."
To Hear the Angels Sing, Dorothy MacLean

COMPOST

Compost is organic matter in a state of decay. While nature is constantly breaking down organic materials into more usable compounds, a tended compost pile speeds up this natural process by promoting an optimal ratio of nitrogen and phosphorus to carbon, and controlling humidity and temperature. Remember to incorporate air shafts or you will need to physically turn the pile so it can breathe. For additional information I refer you to an excellent work on the subject, a small booklet called *Make Compost in 14 Days,* which can be obtained by writing Rodale's *Organic Gardening* magazine.

Green manure is similar to composting, but is much simpler. Basically, this method consists of planting an unused piece of ground with any of the following plants: winter rye, buckwheat, annual rye, mustard or rape. Also, legumes (soybeans, vetches, cowpeas and various clovers) work well as a green manure, and additionally contribute the benefits of their nitrogen-fixing root nodes. Just before the green manure crop flowers, turn it under and it will decompose into organic nutrients.

SOIL DEFICIENCIES

A lack of certain soil nutrients causes predictable symptoms. The nutrients and their deficiencies listed below may help identify a problem. However, soil testing is the most reliable means for complete identification of such problems. This descriptive list is taken from *Diseases of Small Fruits in Alberta* published by the Alberta Horticultural Research Centre, Brooks, Alberta in 1981.
DEFICIENCY IN:
Boron—Bases of young leaves of terminal buds become light green and finally break down. Stems and leaves become distorted. Fruit may crack on the surface or rot in the center.

Calcium—Young leaves become distorted with the tips hooked back and the margins curled. New leaves may fail to unroll. Often the leaves are irregular in shape and ragged with brown scorching or spotting at the margins. Terminal buds eventually die if the deficiency is severe. Affected plants have poor root systems.

Copper—Younger leaves become pale green with red areas between the veins. A pronounced red discoloration may develop in the stems and leaf petioles of strawberries.

Magnesium—Older leaves are thin. The younger ones become mottled or chlorotic, followed by reddening and occasional appearance of necrotic, or dead, spots. The tips and margins of leaves may turn downward and inward so that the leaves appear cupped. Defoliation may follow.

Manganese—Leaf symptoms are similar to copper deficiency except that small leaves are apt to become crinkled. This deficiency is most common on high-pH soils.

Nitrogen—Plants grow poorly and usually are light-green in color. Lower leaves turn yellow or light brown and the stems are short and slender. In strawberries, older leaves may develop a red color at the leaf serrations.

Phosphorus—Young leaves are bluish-green with purple tints. The lower leaves sometimes turn light bronze with purple or brown spots. Shoots are short and thin, upright and spindly.

Potassium—Plants have thin shoots. Dieback may occur in severe cases. Older leaves may show slight chlorosis with typical browning of the tips, scorching of the margins and many brown spots, usually near the margins. Leaves may gradually roll upward and inward.

Sulphur—Plants have pale green or light yellow young leaves without spot formation. Symptoms may resemble those of nitrogen deficiency.

Zinc—Leaves may initially show intervenal chlorosis, then later develop necrotic areas and show purple pigmentation. Leaves are few and small, with short internodes. Poor fruit production is a common symptom of zinc deficiency.

WATER

Proper attention to watering can reduce the biggest share of garden maintenance. You can eliminate needless work by planting drought-tolerant plants in distant garden beds and under thirsty trees. To this basic advice, I would like to add a few hints:

1. Water only when necessary. Soil dryness can be felt by inserting a finger into the top 2 to 3 inches of dirt. Moist soil has a clinging sense of life about it, while dry soil feels drawing or powdery. This method is preferable to waiting for plants to weaken and wilt. Testing the soil often in this manner will rapidly develop one's internal sense of plant needs.

2. Always water deeply, using a slow-drench method to avoid runoff. Drip irrigation is especially good for this. If watering with sprinklers, you can set out cans or bowls to determine the quantity of water sprinkled. Be sure to water until one to two inches accumulates in the can. Shallow waterings require more frequent waterings and encourage plants to become shallow-rooted. Hand-watering is also an effective method. But be sure not to merely wet the surface of the ground. Drench an area, move on to another area, and then come back to resoak the first area again.

3. Dig out catch basins around the base of large plants to hold rain and irrigation water. These should be about six inches deep and sized proportionally to the plant.

4. Weed your garden areas regularly. Weeds compete aggressively not only for soil moisture but also for nutrients and light.

5. Use automatic water timers to shut off sprinklers, precisely controlling water usage.

6. Snap-on hose couplings eliminate the frustrating wristwork of normal screw-on hose fittings.

Pay careful attention to watering in the fall. This time of year is normally hot and dry, and many parched plants, especially evergreens, need water to survive the winter. However, take care not to overwater and thus encourage frost-tender new growth. Conversely, many annual flowers and vegetables will bloom and grow well into the early winter if they are watered. These include sweet alyssum, violas and pansies, beets, and cabbage. In the fall, use just enough water to keep things healthy. But if you start seeing new growth, hold back a bit.

MULCH

Mulch is the gardener's best friend. In addition to retaining precious soil moisture, it effectively controls weeds, protects the plants' roots from heat and cold, provides organic nutrients and protects the soil from compaction and erosion. In forests, this layer of fallen leaves and debris is nature's way of protecting the soil. However, man often carelessly removes this important protection thinking it needs to be "cleaned up." As you become familiar with mulch, unprotected soil will seem naked to you.

Many materials work well for mulch, providing they can be penetrated by water and will eventually turn into humus. Plastic mulch fails on both accounts and eventually creates a large disposal problem. In general, most any organic material makes a usable mulch. You can use grass clippings, but have to be careful of their source because of the herbicides used on lawns. Indeed, compost that is naturally-broken-down organic material makes another exceptional mulch. Another material that makes an attractive yet functional mulch is pine needles. Their biggest advantage is their strongly acidic pH, which helps buffer alkaline soils. Another variation is a stone mulch used mostly around evergreen trees and in rock gardens. It is a layer of small, light-colored rock used to deflect heat and cool the soil. Mulching may begin to seem as essential as watering.

One other important kind of cover is called winter mulch. Here in the chinook zone, this winter mulch is of critical importance for some plants because of our unpredictable snowcover. Usually this mulch consists of evergreen boughs, peat or straw placed on plants in December after the ground has frozen, and removed in March or April. This is not to keep the plant warm, but to protect it from thawing. This is in addition to providing cover from sun scald and wind burn. In fact, for an experienced gardener, this technique allows one to grow all sorts of extraordinary half-hardy plants. But these must be low enough to be protected with a covered mound or with an enclosed snow fence filled with leaves. This is a trick that experienced gardeners use for growing just about anything they want.

LAWNS AND GROUND COVERS

GRASS

To most people, it is no surprise that grass is the dominant vegetative species of our area. What is startling, however, are the surprising difficulties encountered here in the care of a basic lawn. Traditional lawns began in rainy damp England, where a short, green lawn is ridiculously easy to care for. But here in the baked-dry Plains states, that same green lawn is out of place, and artificially dependent on tremendous outlays of energy. Many people are discovering other choices. This section covers some of these.

To start with, it must be conceded that a regular lawn has many advantages as well as disadvantages. First and foremost, a green grass lawn is highly resistant to foot traffic, an attribute no other ground cover can replace. This attribute will continue to inspire its cultivation. Second, many people enjoy sitting and walking on a lawn's cool velvety texture. And finally, the other plus for lawns is that the act of mowing it tends to eliminate the most aggressive range weeds.

However, these advantages carry a very high price. One of the highest is its critical demand for water in the heat of summer. On a personal level this means weekly and daily attention to irrigation. But on a larger level, the guarded water resources of the arid West must be considered. To many people, this excessive use of

precious water for such a frivolous purpose is unconscionable. Likewise, a similar consideration is the squandering of petroleum in the weekly mowings, not to mention the petroleum-based fertilizers. Of equal concern are the untold amounts of harsh, damaging herbicides and pesticides applied to that same green lawn. These chemicals spread destruction to birds, insects and plants far beyond their targeted pests. Because of these problems, many people are now asking "What else is there?"

To begin with, one can still choose a regular green grass lawn. An excellent book called *Lawn Beauty, The Organic Way* by Glen Johns will help tremendously to reduce the work and environmental impact of lawn care. Additionally, more drought-tolerant grass varieties can be chosen. Although these require far less care, they do tend to be less lushly green. Some choices for these drought-tolerant lawns include buffalo grass (the best one), as well as western wheatgrass, bluebunch wheatgrass, streambank wheatgrass, thickspike wheatgrass, and green needlegrass.

HERBAL LAWNS

An herbal lawn is an alternative with many advantages over a grass lawn. Basically, it requires less water, mowing and fertilizer. In addition, it is lushly green and tolerates moderate foot traffic, unlike other ground covers. But for most people, the greatest benefit is its flower color as it blooms throughout the summer, and its pleasant herbal fragrance, most noticeable as you walk or sit on it. This old fashioned herb lawn has a history dating back to Tudor England, the peak of its popularity. To this day, many English estates (Buckingham Palace among them) proudly maintain their herbal lawns.

To create an herbal lawn, you must first carefully remove the grass sod already there and replant with plant sets of chamomile, thyme, and a special low yarrow. But for areas receiving less footwear, you may also include pussytoes, *armeria, aubrieta, scilla, sedum acre* and *Veronica prostrata*. These creeping plants quickly grow together to form an everblooming, fragrant carpet of color.

For care, the majority of the work involved is a twice-a-summer weeding and mowing to keep it clean-looking and even. For the first couple of years, water deeply at least once a month until the planting is established and no longer needs water. Its drawback is the preparation step requiring removal of the existing ground cover. In this kind of lawn, grass suddenly becomes a difficult weed.

GROUND COVERS

Dramatic beds of low maintenance ground covers are another choice. These are singly planted areas, most commonly using snow on the mountain, juniper, Virginia creeper, creeping sumac, and *vinca minor*. Besides suppressing grass and weed growth, these plants also tolerate extreme conditions. They require practically no care and are well suited to the needs of elderly or handicapped gardeners. But for additional color, seasonal interest and fragrance, a number of others are listed here as useful. However, these tolerate less weed competition and less drought, and may require varying degrees of ground preparation. Most unfortunately all of these ground covers will not tolerate even moderate foot traffic and you must consider adding walkways in such areas. In shady spots, consider using native wildflowers as a ground cover.

Similar to a ground cover planting is the moss garden ground cover, which stays green throughout the winter and mats so tightly that weed seeds cannot reach the soil. Unfortunately this lawn is especially sensitive to even light foot traffic, and requires a knowledge of native moss species and their tolerance to drought and sun. One other problem is the three to four years required for a moss ground cover to fill in an area without gaps. But those people who have experienced the cool serenity of a moss-carpeted Japanese garden know there is no substitute. Another equally showy usage is in a fern-filled grove of majestic trees. For more information, see the listing under Moss in the descriptive plant listings.

WILDFLOWERS

In sunny areas, one can also consider the ambitious alternative of using large-scale plantings of wildflowers. However, like the last choice, these flowers will not tolerate more than light foot traffic. To plant wildflowers, remove the grass cover, fallow the soil to eliminate weed seeds, and sow the wildflower mixture. Long-term maintenance involves occasional weeding and some watering for the first couple years. Unfortunately, the greatest disadvantage to this method is the scrupulous detail with which you must cultivate (fallow) the land to remove hidden weed seeds. Best started in fall, this process requires turning the soil for one or two seasons before the wildflower planting can start. If this is not

properly done, the hidden weeds will grow and quickly obliterate the desired planting.

The second step is selecting appropriate wildflowers. You would be best advised to seek professional advice for optimal results, though it is not essential. Avoid using any mix which contains either ox-eye daisy or rapacious bellflower. One other hint is to first select perennials for continuous bloom and drought tolerance, then mix in a few showy annuals for the first year's bloom. Follow the instructions on page 22 for Prairie Plantings.

COVERUPS

A final alternative is the black plastic and decorative bark cover used commonly by landscapers. The black plastic eliminates weeds, while the decorative bark or rock cover hides and protects the plastic from weather-induced breakdown. Its drawback is the eventual brittleness of the plastic and resulting invasion of weeds. Another problem is its disruption by water runoff in heavy rainstorms.

Considering the advantages and disadvantages of the above choices, I give you my preferred solution: the gradual reduction of lawn areas into flower and vegetable gardens. Eventually, paving and ground cover will replace the last bit of grass. Having seen the alternatives and their problems, you can now make an informed choice about your needs.

PLANT BREEDING

If you want a new apricot that blooms later or has better-tasting fruit, or if you want daisies of a different color, you can breed them yourself. The catch is the time it takes. Plant breeding is not difficult in technique, but it requires patience spread over many years. Every time a flower mixes male pollen with a receptive female organ, a new seed is formed. This act of mixing two different cells into one creates the potential for evolving better, newer forms. Anyone can use nature's ways to create a desired new plant. It is as easy as planting the seeds of successful seedlings over and over again. Many breeders also control pollination between specific plants. Less scientific breeders can work equally spectacular results by allowing bees to haphazardly perform the pollination. The trick is the time it takes for a selected seedling to flower and seed, and then for its offspring to flower and seed. This is repeated many generations to get results.

But there is always a high element of chance to this game. In plant breeding, it may take one cross or 10,000 crosses to gain one desired variation, such as a new flower color. But this is the area where hard science fades, and the theories and results of unorthodox breeders fill the void. Many exceptional plant wizards such as Luther Burbank believed deeply that plants were capable of understanding human requests and, the other side of the coin, human threats. Luther Burbank wrote several books about his unusual breeding methods, and how he asked his plants to give him the results he wanted. At the end of the season, he built a bonfire and burned the plants that refused. His life achievements demonstrate the vast potential plants are capable of.

Annuals and many perennial flowers are the simplest to breed because these plants flower and set seed in one or two years. But trees that require up to 20 years for a single plant to reach flowering maturity require a short-cut technique. To speed up this whole cycle, buds are grafted from promising seedlings onto full-grown trees. These usually flower and fruit the following year, allowing selection of the best varieties for continued propagation. Once a desired trait has been established, it is often "fixed" into the variety by subsequently growing several generations of offspring in which each year's offspring holds the desired trait. However, this step is not necessary for plants that can be propagated by division or grafting.

BUGS

"...most small gardens, left alone with natural controls, function quite well with minimum care."
The Natural Way to Pest Free Gardening,
Jack Kramer

One of the greatest advantages of our rigorously harsh climate is the relative scarcity of destructive insects. In general, all that really needs to be known about insect control are the organic methods that promote predatory bug populations, and the combined use of trap and repellent plants. The use of pesticides increases long-term problems by weakening plants (disruptive bugs prefer weak plants) and eliminating the natural enemies of such insect pests. In general, what I practice is an ecosystem approach to bugs. I encourage a great number of insects and other lifeforms in my garden. Praying mantis, a common control elsewhere, is not winter hardy here. However, predatory wasps exist here and can be attracted to a garden simply by planting a food source for them. These tiny wasps live on flower nectar, but lay their parasitic eggs on all sorts of insects. Their favorite flowers are those of the *Umbelliferae* family which include carrots, dill, Queen Anne's lace, caraway, parsley, coriander, fennel and lovage. Other insect predators to encourage are ladybugs, spiders, toads, frogs and birds. For more information see "Attracting Wildlife."

Companion plant protection falls into three broad areas. Of the most obvious help are the trap crops (like nasturtiums or radishes) that attract bugs to them and away from the others. Repellent plants are companion plants which repel bugs by smell; some good examples are garlic, marigolds or mint. And finally, there are some plants (like chamomile) that help other plants to grow strong overall and resist insect attacks. Try to include plants from each category throughout your garden—the more, the merrier.

To plains gardeners, just a few bugs present the greatest challenges. First and foremost are grasshoppers. Some years there are few, other years they are a deadly scourge. One powerful yet safe alternative is the use of grasshopper spore disease, called Grasshopper Attack, a commercially available control that kills grasshoppers but no other creature. This defense must be applied to the garden foliage very early in May so that the young grasshoppers will contract this disease early. Because it takes a while to affect the population, it is critical to apply it early and be patient. The supply of this product can be extended by grinding up diseased grasshoppers in a blender and spreading the resulting mixture over one's garden.

Other enemy bugs include the Colorado potato beetle, a scourge of potatoes, peppers, and eggplants. Hand-picking the somewhat large black-and-orange striped beetles is very effective, especially if started early. White cabbage moths are naturalized invaders from Europe. You may find yourself going to extreme lengths to protect broccoli, cauliflower, cabbage and mustard from these insidious green worms. Other bugs that attact these cabbage family vegetables are flea beetles—particularly near heavily-sprayed agricultural areas—and root maggots. For ideas on dealing with these pests, see the plant listing for broccoli. Tent caterpillars on trees can be bad. One method is to burn the tents at night when the worms are sleeping. Another method is to encourage birds in your area.

WEEDS

There is nothing more unnerving than to see a new garden robbed of life under a cover of weeds. A few simple hints will help eliminate this problem in new gardens.

First thing, when starting a garden, search carefully for any signs of rapacious bellflower. Look for its heart-shaped foliage (very similar to violet leaves) and its attractive flower stalk of bluebell-like flowers that bloom mainly in June and flower sparcely on to August. This is a dangerously insidious weed because its white, tuberous roots hide four to six inches underground. If you merely weed the surface, these roots send up new shoots for several years. Untold numbers of frustrated gardeners have dug up and replanted whole gardens simply because they ignored this common weed.

Use a double-fallow method to destroy such annual

weeds as chickweed and mustards. In this process, a bed is cultivated and watered to allow surface weed seeds to sprout. After the weeds have emerged, turning the soil will destroy them. In heavily infested areas, do this a couple of times.

When digging garden beds, edge the boundaries with plastic or aluminum grass guards to fence out spreading grass and weed roots. This step alone substantially reduces weeding. If you skip this step, you'll be sorry later when the grass has completely invaded your garden.

And finally, in established garden plantings, always use a mulch to smother weeds. A proper mulch should be at least two to three inches deep, and will benefit the garden throughout the entire growing season. Planting ground covers in unused areas also reduces weed growth. But note that a mulch will slow soil warming in the spring. Cold soil slows plant and seed growth.

ATTRACTING WILDLIFE

For many people, no aspect of gardening merits as much interest as wildlife, particularly for children and those adults able to spend time at home during daytime hours. Most of the creatures listed below can be killed by pesticides and herbicides. If you value wildlife, please be careful of your use of garden poisons.

BIRDS

Birds of many, many varieties are quite common throughout the Plains. To many people, the best-of-life experiences are watching the humorous antics, and identifying the characteristics of, birds. This is an all-year sport, with quite a number of winter sightings. For a full list of locally sighted species contact the local Audubon Society or wildlife refuge.

To encourage birds to visit your garden, simply provide food, water and protective cover. Food varies according to the type of bird you wish to attract. Water needs are met by providing a year-round birdbath. Be sure to select a design that allows for the expansion of freezing water, as well as being easily cleanable. From a bird's point of view, this area should be visibly out of a cat's range. For real bird lovers, a water-misting system is essential. It is also a good idea to allow some of your flowers and vegetables to go to seed. The most convenient place to watch birds is your own backyard. That is the reason many people choose to create a natural preserve by planting bird-attracting landscaping.

The problem of birds raiding people's favorite fruit is quite overblown. There are three alternatives that satisfactorily eliminate this problem. The first one is to interplant fruit that birds prefer among the human-preferred fruit. Some examples of bird-preferred fruit are bird cherry, chokecherry, hawthorn and crabapple. Researchers have shown that birds prefer these to domesticated fruit. A second alternative is to attract purple martins or house wrens to your garden. These birds do not eat fruit, and they fiercely defend their claimed territory from other birds. The final solution is to use netting draped over fruit. This method is the most effective for the bird-favored fruits of pie cherry and elderberry.

TOADS & SUCH

Most valuable of all wildlife in the garden is the toad. This happy creature will joyfully adapt to a home in an upturned flower pot and live there for years, ridding your garden of destructive bugs. They need an occasional source of water and a small strip of unmowed grass. You might consider checking around to buy native toads commercially. The native toads are the western toad (*Bufo borealis* of the Rocky Mountains), the Great Plains toad (*Bufo cognatus* of the Northern Plains) and Woodhouse's toad (*Bufo woodhousei*). In addition, there is the western spadefoot (*Scaphiopus bombifrons*) of the plains. Those people who have a water garden or natural pond may consider including two other natives: painted turtles (*Chrysemys picta*) or boreal chorus frogs (*Pseudacris triseriata*). Besides eating insects, these colorful creatures are quite an attraction to observers.

BEES & BUTTERFLIES

Another useful creature to encourage is the bee. Unjustly maligned for their sting, these gentle insects are loathe to attack unless provoked. The fear of bees is a very unneccessary problem. Watching bees at work can stir a deep love for these fascinating creatures.

Among other insects of interest are the butterflies. Books on native species include *Guide to Rocky Mountain Butterflies* and *Guide to Western Butterflies*. Also, an association of butterfly enthusiasts with members everywhere is the Lepidopteris Society, c/o Julian P. Donahue, Dept of Entomology, LA County Museum of Natural History, 900 Exposition Blvd, Los Angeles, CA 90007.

To attract butterflies and moths into your garden, you would do best to include many plants which feed them. Beds of these plants are far more attractive to butterflies than are individual plants. Determined enthusiasts will attempt to plant specific food sources accord-

ing to the kind of butterfly desired. For moths, add night lighting in black light colors. Shallow water with tiny stepping stones will also attract them as well as myriad other fascinating bugs.

At the far extreme of this avocation, one might consider a greenhouse used solely for raising tropical butterflies. There are excellent books on this subject: *The Butterfly Garden* by Matthew Tekulsky, and a British book *The Butterfly Gardener* by Miriam Rothchilds. The December 1985 issue of Rodale's *Organic Gardening*

magazine has a fascinating article taken from Matthew Tekulsky's book.

A few other insects deserve more attention for their beauty. These are dragonflies, scarab beetles and tiger beetles. Many people study these creatures just as avidly as butterflies. When you open your eyes and heart, the world is a jungle of fascination. Highly recommended books are *Wildlife in Your Garden* by Gene Logsdon, *The Prairie World* by David Costello and, surprisingly, *The Natural Way to Pest-free Gardening* by Jack Kramer.

TREES

"Those who reach out to us we lift. When you are in our aura and reach into your being, you are lifted because we are in a rhythm of harmony. In fact, we can aid humans to achieve an inward peace. There should always be large areas where trees reign supreme and undisturbed, where we can give solace to you. Such areas would ultimately do much for the healing of nations."

To Hear The Angels Sing, Dorothy MacLean

"The trees along our avenues and streets and in your parks are already the city's greatest asset. No municipal work of Great Falls can compare in value with planting and maintaining trees within its limits, and the thing never to be slighted is the maintaining of trees ev-

erywhere within our borders. The last injunction I would give to my fellow citizens before leaving Great Falls, would be to continue the planting of trees and to never neglect them under any circumstances."

Quoted from a 1912 speech by Paris Gibson, founder of Great Falls, Montana, and avid supporter of public parks and gardens

WHAT TREES DO

1. The leaves, canopy and roots create food and shelter for birds, insects and myriad other life.
2. Slow the impact of rain, increase absorption, reduce erosion, and protect soil cover.
3. Raise the ground water level.
4. Reduce wind speed and damage.
5. Create warmer microclimates in wind-protected areas of large trees.
6. Raise the humidity in dry summer weather.
7. Create varied zones of shading.
8. Produce a fall crop of leaves for mulch or compost.

COMMON CHINOOK-ZONE TREES

The beauty of trees can be found in the varied texture of their foliage, seasonal gifts of flowers, fruit and fall color. But to many people the grandest aspects of trees are both their symmetry of form and their rich bark texture that enlivens the bleakness of winter.

When you begin to experience the character of tree forms and their variations, a new world of fascination opens. Suddenly a tree is no longer just a tree. Tree species can be easily distinguished by their unmistakable pattern:

1. Tall, symmetrical spreading canopies are created by elms, honey locust, and walnuts.
2. Semi-large, round, full shapes are created by apple and crabapple, hawthorn, pear, and mountain ash. These trees can exhibit a timeless oriental beauty with expert pruning.
3. A romantic ideal of a strong impressive trunk with weeping branches is created by golden willow.
4. Cottonwood and poplar love to grow in groves as tall, narrow, awe-inspiring trees. These trees constantly sluff off lower limbs, which creates a tall canopy with stark dead branches below.
5. Lindens have a dramatically symmetrical branch structure. Viewed at a distance, their oval or pyramidal form is quite moving.
6. Oaks reach straight for the sun; their outstreched limbs seem almost an afterthought.
7. Maples and buckeyes are large rounded trees with a nice degree of balanced form.
8. Green ash trees have an absence of symmetrical form. They grow quickly and have a brittle messy nature.
9. Weeping birches show off a striking dream-like beauty, especially in early spring when they are budding out.
10. A mature ponderosa pine, Montana's state tree, shows its true regal character, summer or winter. It has a gently rounded crown and a majestic cinnamon-colored bark.

"Trees, rooted guardians of the surface, converters of the higher forces to Earth through the ground, have a special gift for man in this age of speed and drive and busy-ness. We are calmness, strength, endurance, praise, and fine attunement, all of which are greatly needed in this world. We are more than that. We are expressions of the love of the Creator for his abundant, unique and related life. Come to our side whenever you can, and lift your consciousness."

Foundations of Findhorn, Eileen Caddy

PRUNING CARE

No tree requires pruning; most of them manage well on their own. But this is not to downplay the dramatic beauty and strength that careful pruning develops over a period of time. The best pruners seek to accentuate the natural form, strength and inherent beauty unique to each individual tree. The goal is not to "round" or "shape" a tree, but to correct individual problems of form. This perspective will greatly advance your tree care ability.

The first step is to examine the tree. What kind of tree is it? What is its shape: pyramidal, oval, rounded, upright—spreading, columnar or pendulous? What will its shape be at maturity—will that be different? Try to find a mature specimen of the tree to get a mental image for yourself. This step will help you avoid irreparably disfiguring a tree's form through ignorance.

Next, look for branches that need correction. Are there any branches lower than seven feet from the ground? These should be removed to protect people from walking into the limbs. This also opens up the area under the tree. If lower limbs are removed when the tree is young, the smaller scars will heal quickly and reduce the chance of infection.

Are there any branches that cross over other branches? Such limbs give a tree a tangled appearance and rub together in wind storms. These occasional wild branches should be removed.

In spring or summer when the leaves are out, check for dead wood. It is important to remove those branches before a storm brings them down—fast and hard. In most trees there will only be a few such limbs. However, fast-growing, brittle trees such as cottonwood, ash or willow usually have a large number of them.

While examining your tree, see if any limbs extend over a rooftop or powerline.

THE ALDER.

Although they may seem strong, these should be removed to eliminate the possibility of their coming down and damaging property. This last consideration is called lateral pruning. Like all other pruning work, it is best to do this when the limb is young, so that the tree can heal more easily. If the limb is very large, you must call a professional tree trimmer.

For those who are attempting a do-it-yourself pruning job, here are several valuable tips:

1. Cut each branch back to the main trunk, never leave a stub sticking out.

2. Before starting any cut, make a shallow cut all the way through the bark on the extreme lower side of the limb. Then remove the branch. This simple precaution protects the tree's bark from being stripped off when the branch falls.

3. Always sterilize cutting tools after each use and between trees. This step is critical to avoid spreading common viral and bacterial infections from one tree to another. But sterilize your tools before and after each cut when removing obviously diseased branches, particularly the burned-looking branch tips of a fire blight outbreak. Sterilization can be done easily by wiping or dipping tool blades with rubbing alcohol.

One pruning technique is called drop-crotching. Very few trees need drop-crotching. Those that do are primarily apple trees, ornamental crabapples and plum trees. These trees, if left alone, tend to grow overly tall and straggly. This process is best started on five- to ten-year-old trees that are begining to show their form. To begin, the highest major crotch (or fork) near the top of the tree is removed down to a lower branch crotch. It is important that this lower crotch is of an inside branch as opposed to a outwardly spreading branch. This is both to preserve the tree's attractive form and to avoid the problem of a large upper limb shading out lower branches. This process spurs new growth lower in the tree and avoids obvious pruning cuts.

For any tree, you should establish a pruning schedule that begins with a first pruning when it becomes established at three to four years after planting. Then again as the tree nears the stage of being half-grown, around eight to ten years old. And it should be pruned again as it reaches early maturity, around twenty years old. Newly planted young trees and fully mature trees should never be pruned unless done by a very knowledgeable expert. On an older tree, few methods are useful if the tree has simply outgrown its location. There is some potential for reshaping by removing the largest and outermost branches. But for the most part, there are only two choices for an overgrown tree: leave the tree as it is, or remove it.

TREE CARE PROFESSIONALS

For larger projects, you should not hesitate to call in a professional tree trimmer, primarily for large limbs that must be lowered in sections. This is very dangerous work, which professionals are trained to do in a safe manner. Other pruning work requires a detailed eye for the intricacies of tree shape. This work is best done by a professional.

A professional tree trimmer can be compared to a car mechanic. While you might know the basics, the professional tree care expert often sees things that you might not notice. It is this whole view of the tree which enables him or her to do a better job.

The following suggestions will help you select a reputable tree care professional:

1) Avoid, at all cost, pruners who advertise that they do topping.

2) Make sure anyone who works on your trees is insured. Otherwise, you as the homeowner may end up liable for damages or injuries that occur on your property. Some authorities even recommend contacting the insurer before work starts, to confirm coverage. This is the most important reason you should avoid the door-to-door tree trimmers.

3) Make sure that anyone who works on your trees knows what kind of trees they are and, most importantly, their natural habit of growth.

4) Ask why undisturbed branch tips are so important. A professional should tell you that the branch tips make the tree's shape and that removing them permanently disfigures the tree. If the pruner does not understand this, then find another pruner. Just this step alone will help ensure the safety of your tree.

5) Ask which limbs will be removed and why.

6) Discreetly watch his technique on the first cuts. All cuts should be made flush to the trunk, leaving no stubs. He should undercut each limb before removing it, as mentioned earlier, and lower large limbs in sections. If you see him damaging your tree in any way, stop him immediately.

Among the many jobs a professional should be called for are those that require a careful eye for tree growth. On such jobs calling in a trained professional is far more practical than attempting to do it yourself. One of these jobs is opening up the interior structure by removing some of the inside limbs. This lightens the tree's wind load and creates a dramatic silhouette against the sky.

A WORD OF WARNING

It seems so simple, to cut the branch ends to shape a tree. But few things around us are as permanently ugly as the visual disturbance and damage of a bad pruning job. A few years ago, my grandparents decided to trim their beautiful tall willows. When I first saw the result, I was nauseated. The trees had been denuded of branches and the tops stubbed off ruthlessly. When questioned, the professional pruner replied, "They're willows, and you can't kill 'em." If this initial shock wasn't enough, the worst was the regrowth of tangled suckers. Following this, I began to see many other stubbed trees. A particular tragedy is the common destruction of crabapple trees, whose tips have been trimmed to make them more rounded.

"Making many saw cuts throughout the tops of trees without considering branch points is called stubbing. Stubbing is not an approved pruning method. Arborists refer to stubbing as butchery."
Pruning Handbook, Sunset Editors

"Topping is the indiscriminate removal of a tree's crown, leaving large branch stubs vulnerable to decay and resulting in a profusion of adventitious branches. The reasons for such improper pruning are based largely on the fear that during storms tall trees will fall on houses or other property. Topping has been done often enough also so that it appears to be the correct thing to do. However, it is a tragedy of many cities and towns that large sums are expended on topping in this misguided belief. This belief is often encouraged by contractors who either know no better practices or find topping the most profitable."
Urban Forestry, Gene Gray

"The healthier a tree, the fuller its crown and vice versa. We have seen that the crown with its leaves is the workshop of the tree and the source of all beneficial effects to man. Regular pruning of a tree crown, therefore, is always wrong. It weakens the vitality of the tree as a whole because an essential part of its productive faculties is taken away. The more frequent and severe the pruning, the more wounds occur, giving access to thousands of fungi and bacteria. As little pruning as possible will keep the tree healthy."
Tree Ecology and Preservation, A. Bernatzky

"Routine topping, as advocated by the quacks of the tree-service industry, usually results in dead trees or large branches that cannot callus over their horrible wounds. These huge stubs begin to rot while small sucker sprouts begin to grow around the edge. As the rot gets more serious, the sprouts get heavier and finally crash to the ground when the rotten wood can no longer support their weight."

Steve Sandfort and Edwin C. Butcher, "How To Hire A Tree-Care Pro," *American Forests*, Oct 1985

Dr. Ed Burke, Professor of Forestry at the University of Montana referred to tree topping as a "utility company crewcut" and expounded on the damage it does to the trees involved. First, he stated that it introduces airborne fungus and bacteria and spreads viral contamination from unsterilized pruning tools into the tree. Second, it stunts and weakens the vigor of the tree. Third, the resulting tangled watershoots create dangerously weak branch crotches which often break in windstorms. Then he added that this hedge-like mass acts like a wind-wall, very similar to the sail on a ship. This adds a tremendous stress to the tree's windload. He urged that topping not be done to large shade trees and in his opinion there was no use for this practice at all.

The lesson in all this is that a tall tree will always be a tall tree and, if it is "topped," will attempt to regrow to the exact same height and shape, forever retaining a mutilated form. Not knowing this, many people assume that topped trees will become bushy and fill in like a tomato when pinched. Then, without realizing the expensive mistake they are getting into, they turn grand, beautiful trees into monuments to ignorance. Especially in winter, when leafless, these tragic mutilations add a particular bleakness. We must educate people that not all trees are round and bushy like architects' models. And, most of all, that you cannot change a tree's natural shape by cutting the branch tips. Other terms for topping are stubbing, dehorning, pollarding—all referring to the same practice.

Power Lines. Most of the topped trees you see are usually under power lines. Attempting to clear line right-of-ways, local utilities often use the unsatisfactory method of topping. In addition to the permanent visual damage, this method produces a dense hedge-like regrowth that becomes more difficult to control later. The only real solution is to remove tall trees directly under power line right-of-ways. A tall tree will always struggle to be a tall tree regardless of how rigorously or often it is pruned.

Tree Pollarding. The second biggest motivation for topping trees is the image of an architect's model of a ball-shaped tree. You should be forewarned of the considerable expense and work involved in the process of permanently altering and stunting a tree to make it ball-shaped. Every city has examples of such shaped trees, that have been trained annually to create an artificial image. Each year, in a time-consuming and expensive process, the watershoots and ingrown interior structure must be carefully removed. What few people realize is that these trees can never return to their natural form. Without annual pruning, they quickly grow into a permanent tangle of watershoots. Obviously, tree pollarding is not a one-shot deal. The problem is that many people see these topped trees and never realize this.

No trees are naturally lollipop-shaped, but there are some bushy and round trees (eg. Hawthorn-*Crataegus,*

Sorbus pohuaensis, Prince Georges Crabapple-*Malus,* Apricot-*Prunus armeniaca,* and Buckeyes-*Aesculus).* All trees have a unique shape which is natural to their species. Some shapes are tall and narrow (Cottonwoods), some are upright and spreading (Elms) and some are pyramidal (Lindens). But few people realize that tall trees take less ground space and create shade to sit under. Short, bushy trees occupy all their ground space and provide no useable shade.

Problem Trees. There are distinct situations where trees are notably out of place and are best removed. On hillsides with views, tall trees and evergreens such as Colorado blue spruce and Douglas fir are an unfailing issue with the neighbors. Please use courtesy and common sense to remove existing tall trees and plant low-growing landscaping materials.

One further problem requiring proper planning, or else later tree removal, is the misplacement of messy trees over car parking areas. Birch trees drip a sticky sap in summer, buckeyes drop large thorny seedpods in the fall, and the common ash constantly drops limbs and twigs. To amend the situation, either remove the trees or eliminate the parking spaces.

Take Action. Tell your friends and neighbors about the dangers of tree topping. Show them pictures, or point out badly miscut trees as you drive around. If there is an especially nice tree in your neighborhood, go talk to the owner and politely mention the dangers of topping. Likewise, if someone you know has a previously topped tree, suggest its removal. There is simply no reason why everyone must learn this lesson by destroying their trees. Education about topping is the best way to keep more trees from being permanently mutilated.

IF YOU SEE A TREE BEING TOPPED

1. Find out what company the pruner is working for and show them pictures of top-pruned trees.

2. Most importantly, find the tree owner and show him or her pictures of topped trees. Usually they simply don't know the expensive mistake they are making.

Pictures of topped trees and the resulting regrowth are a direct and effective teaching tool for this.

Protect yourself and your neighborhood from topping. The fault rests not with tree pruners, but with an uninformed public. Door-to-door tree men would prefer you to believe that pruning is carelessly easy. They will try to tell you "Any fool can cut a tree." There will probably always be people selling tree trimming jobs, especially in spring, the worst time to prune most trees.

GARDEN THEMES

WINTER GARDENING

Winter gardening consists primarily of ornamental landscaping for winter color and interest. A closely related area is that of creating a protected microclimate to dramatically lengthen the growing season, as with cold frames and cloches. And finally, there is indoor forcing of flowers, an interesting sideline.

Far too often, the subject of winter gardening is neglected in gardening books. But this crisp time of snow and ice can be just as adventurous as any other season. With just a little attention to winter gardening, our area could easily become a spectacular paradise year-round.

To start, let us create an imaginary winter garden, and experience the breathtaking beauty of its majestic trees, its statuary and austere rocks. Winter carries such a garden to its essence of character, holding its feeling starkly. Now begin to look at the details of brightly colored berries on the trees and shrubs. And look down to see the dried flower ghosts of an oregano clump, sedum 'autumn joy' and baby's breath. Clumps of ornamental grass hold their beauty throughout the winter also. And finally, in among these, there is scattered evergreen color from sedums, sempervivums, blue fescue grass, dwarf conifers, and junipers. This is the elegant beauty that a winter garden can hold. Doesn't it make sense to plan your garden for the eight months of winter as well as the four months of summer? Listed throughout the plant descriptions are notes on the many plants offering winter interest. All gardeners are encouraged to include some of these plants throughout their normal garden beds for midwinter greenery, as well as for late fall and early spring flowers.

WINTER MICROCLIMATES

For advanced gardeners, there is the challenge of creating precocious mid-winter greenery and flowers

from a protected microclimate. Such displays never fail to bowl over friends and astound local newspapers.

The working of winter miracles starts with the microclimate. If one can control the wind, the chinook zone is a particularly advantageous location for winter gardening because of its distance from mountains and their cold night air. While the rest of the continent languishes in winter, chinook zone gardeners can count on early flower displays. To do this, a small special garden area just for winter gardening is easiest to control and most dramatic to experience. The previously wind-protected, sun-pocket seating area is ideal for such usage.

The first consideration is maximum sun exposure, ideally including eastern exposure. The second most essential ingredient is the effective use of cold air diverters for wind protection. Use combinations of building sides, garden walls and tight shelterbelt plantings to do this. These wind diverters work to create a warm niche where paving, large buried rocks and terraced stone ledgework are placed to trap and hold heat. Moreover, the terraced ledgework provides the advantage of quick-draining soil that warms fastest in the sun. In general, soil composition should be a quick-draining, rocky mixture similar to rock-gardening soil. This is to guard against winter root rot.

Another aspect of winter gardening is the imaginative usage of cold frames and cloches. These protect plants the way snow cover does in other areas. In particular, these unheated devices actually protect plants from frost burn, rapid temperature drops and drying wind. Their uses include:

1) dramatically extending the fall and spring growing seasons;

2) protecting seedlings from late spring frosts;

3) hardening nursery plants;

4) growing mid-winter vegetables (spinach, lettuce, radishes, bok choy, etc). In short, they can quickly become essential to a determined gardener.

WINTER BLOOMS

And then there is the drama of indoor forced blooms from many common flowering shrubs and bulbs in mid-winter. Bulbs can be forced to bloom at any time of the year. But forcing twigs from shrubs and trees requires that they be picked after the proper amount of winter exposure. Consequently, starting a branch closest to its natural bloom time is the safest procedure. Once cut, the twig ends should be split or smashed, wrapped in wet newspapers or soaked in a large tub, and left in a cool dark place. After four to six weeks, the buds should be swollen and ready to flower. When brought into a warm room, these branches will burst forth with flowers within days. For prolonging bloom, keep flowers away from direct sun, and preferably in a cool, humid area. Treat potted bulbs in a very similar manner.

Once you see how easy it is to force flowers, you will never again suffer through the long days of winter without colorful and fragrant relief. Forcing mid-winter flowers could become a lucrative business selling to local restaurants for their tables, and stores for their window displays.

Plants suitable for forcing are: chokecherry, crabapple, double flowering almond, forsythia, lilac, Mayday tree, plum, saskatoon, serviceberry, spiraea, Ussurian pear, and winter honeysuckle.

PRAIRIE PLANTINGS

Prairie planting is a finely tuned art form. While being the most challenging to create, the prairie complex holds the greatest variety of interest and is the most stable to maintain. Basically, it is the controlled and knowledgeable re-establishment of the original Plains ecosystem using both grasses and wildflowers. For many people, this labor of love is a long term accomplishment.

"There is something warm and good about creating a bit of nature where native plants can grow wild and free, something that makes the endless miles of neon signs, overgrazed range land, herbicide-sprayed roadsides, eroding agricultural fields and other modern blights somehow less threatening and more tolerable," said Richard Clinebell in his article about prairie from the book *Alpines of the Americas.* The biggest advantage to prairie-keeping is the way it changes a gardener's perspective toward the inner workings and essential balance of the Great Plains environment. Your experience of a grassy panorama will forever be altered.

RESTORATION & CARE

Oddly enough, the restoration of prairie is not accomplished merely by allowing nature to take over. The problem is that introduced (non-native) weeds are extremely aggressive and will take over very quickly. Indeed, these range weeds cause the number-one difficulty in establishing a prairie planting. For until the sod is established, you will fight a constant battle in the form of fallowing soil preparation, selective weeding and an annual spring burning. In particular, the following weeds fight at every inch for a niche in the system: yellow and curly dock, dandelions, wild morning glory (also called bindweed), thistles, leafy spurge, wild oats, and crested wheatgrass. It is these ruthless plants that have prompted most cities to adopt weed-control ordinances. Although such laws were created to protect our neighborhoods, some question exists over whether they apply to native plants. Some checking on legality should be done within any city limits.

Equally important, you should be concerned with neighbors' attitudes toward landscaping. This is because the borderline between prairie plantings and conventional lawns can be a site of conflict. One very effective solution is to maintain a mowed strip between a prairie planting and a neighbor's lawn. A width of ten feet will buffer any problems.

For care, an established prairie does not need water, fertilizer, spraying or mowing, but it does need an occasional spring burn. This must be done the second year after planting and in alternate years down the line. Basically, what this does is destroy weeds, and return nutrients to the soil, all without damaging the prairie plants. However, if burning is not possible, then substitute an annual mowing, raking and reseeding.

ESTABLISHING A PRAIRIE PLANTING

To start a prairie, first determine your soil type (clay, loam or sand). Then consider whether to classify it as wet (still green in late summer), mesic (defined as midway-wet in spring, dry in summer), or dry (such as on a slope). Each of these zones supports an entirely different system of plants. At this point you would be best served by consulting a prairie expert or landscape architect. These professionals can steer a beginner through the complexities of choosing a mix with the correct percentage of prairie wildflowers (occasionally called forbs), legumes for their soil-enriching ability, and grasses to support the whole system. Just as important is the first year's protective cover crop. Try to include a few showy annuals for the first year's bloom. Some suggestions are bachelor buttons, *gaillardia,* annual phlox, *dianthus chinensis, gypsophillia, coreopsis tinctoria, godetia,* and Shirley poppies. Avoid using any commercial mix that contains either ox-eye daisy or rapacious bellflower.

Grass, a critically important aspect of a prairie, must be in a correct ratio with wildflowers in the original mix. Richard Clinebell states that "grass is like the mold that forms and supports the prairie." The aesthetic attributes of grass are its dried winter beauty and its variety of flowering grassheads in spring and summer. Additionally, grass provides the fuel to support the spring burn.

Unfortunately, the greatest disadvantage to establishing a prairie planting is the scrupulous detail with which you must remove hidden weed seeds from the soil. If this is not properly done, the hidden weeds will grow and quickly obliterate your seed planting. The most common method is to cultivate the land for a season before planting. This is called fallowing. Best started in fall, this process requires turning the soil for one or two seasons before the planting is started. There are also chemical sprays that can kill hidden seeds in the soil. If your area is badly infested with weeds, cheat and quack grass being the worst, then you should consider spraying. These sprays have not been proven to be destructive to a prairie planting in the long run. However, they do kill the beneficial soil insects and fungus when first applied.

You can use either seeds or sets. Though less expensive, seeds are more difficult as they must contact the soil and also be hidden from birds. To sow large areas most effectively, consider mechanical seeding equipment (such as a Truax drill). To hand sow, mix your seeds with sand. Scatter the seed evenly, walk in north-south lines, then crisscross the area again walking east-west. Follow this with raking and rolling. Finish by adding a fine mulch over the area. Later when the plants are up and growing, add more mulch. Once a basic prairie system is started, you can add more diversity with plant sets. These can be simply plugged into the ground and watered for their first season. Once established, the sets will self-sow new plants around them.

For added beauty, plan "drifts" of plants that naturally occur together, remembering their size and eventual spread. Preferably, prairie plants should not come too close to buildings because of the need for a spring burn. Try to keep tall plants near the edges of the design, but away from buildings. Several additional hints:

1. cold-treat those seeds requiring cold dormancies;
2. plan a prairie planting only in full sun;
3. expect to wait at least two to three years for a prairie to establish (a long time to wait while looking at what appears to be just weeds.;
4. start with a small area in the beginning…you can always enlarge it later;
5. use primarily plants and seed from a site similar to yours;
6. do not transplant native plants. You should either buy nursery-propagated plants or gather and start your own seed.

PRAIRIE GARDEN RESOURCES

Earthly Delights, Rosalyn Creasy
The Prairie World, David Costello
Restoring the Earth, John Berger
Wildflower Gardening, Time-Life Books
Prairie Wildflowers: An Illustrated Manual of Species Suitable for Cultivation and Grassland Restoration, R. Currah, A. Smrecia, and M. Van Dyk, published by Friends of the Devonian Botanic Garden, University of Alberta, Edmonton

Restoration and Management Notes, Journal Division, University of Wisconsin Press, 114 N. Murray St, Madison WI, 53715. This is a fascinating scientific journal on prairie restoration. Subscription is $11 per year
The Prairie Garden: 70 Native Plants You Can Grow in Town or Country, J. Robert and Beatrice Smith
Landscaping with Wildflowers and Native Plants, William Wilson, Ortho Books
Directory to Resources on Wildflower Propagation, Missouri Botanic Gardens
Flora of Montana part I—Grasses; part II—Flowers, Booth
Flora of the Rocky Mountains and Adjacent Plains, Rydberg
Prairie Restoration for the Beginner: Fifty Questions and Answers, available from the Prairie Seed Source, Box 83, North Lake, Wisconsin, 53064
Native plant societies; see the Resource Directory.
The local office of the state Soil Conservation District
Aullwood Audubon Center and Farm, 1000 Aullwood Rd, Dayton, OH, 45414
A large network of prairie enthusiasts and specialized nurseries exists in the midwestern states. Although the plants of their tall grass prairie are quite different from our short grass prairie, these people are a tremendous resource for inspiration and experience. However, do not use midwestern tall grass prairie plants here; they are poorly adapted to our arid climate.

WATER GARDENS

"It scarcely seems necessary to sing the praises of water in the garden. We have all felt the lazy pleasure of sitting beside a sunny pond or the quiet refreshment and tranquillity of a shady pool. Water's power to evoke strong moods in us is unmatched. Indeed, man's first-known gardens, in ancient Babylon and Egypt, were water gardens. An oasis of water, shade and flower, away from the desert's piercing heat. Gertrude Jekyll has most simply and eloquently called them, 'The soul of the garden'."

quoted from the Magic Garden catalog

Every garden's uplifting joy should be centered in the union of earth and water. Consider the way that a pool of water brings in the colors of the sky as it reflects the beauty all around it. At its simplest level is a bowl filled with a few plants and perhaps goldfish. Other tempting pursuits are a sparkling fountain surrounded by ferns, or a complete bog habitat for water plants.

Water creates life. Unfortunately, this is a basic problem when dealing with a water garden. Even a cupful of water creates many

problems if left unattended. First there are mosquitoes—anxiously seeking water to nurse their young larvae into adulthood. Secondly, there is the ever-present algae—always waiting, summer or winter, to fill any container with colorful slime. These are your opponents. Your allies are snails and fish—which require special care. Snails eat algae and generally clean up their habitat. The best kind are commercially available aquarium snails, which must be introduced into the pond every spring. Wild snails do not stay in the water, and will venture out to eat your garden plants.

Fish require a science of their own. Their primary purpose is to eat mosquito larvae. You must establish them each year, provide oxygenating plants, and offer sheltering cover from birds, cats, and raccoons. Goldfish work well and look appealing in a pond.

The final major concern is the structural destruction by frost. All water must be completely drained from any pipes and other man-made structures for winter. To this end, a drain is usually installed at a low point in the system. However, for pools designed to hold water during the winter, the shape is very important. Open rounded shapes work the best. Areas that are the most vulnerable to damage from expanding ice are constrictions, or necks in the design. Automobile antifreeze is never used because it is dangerously poisonous to both water plants and pets.

BOWLS, BATHTUBS & FOUNTAINS

The easiest water garden to maintain is a bowl. It is simply a large container filled with water in the summer and emptied at season's end. Beautiful plants can be set in the dish, as well as live fish. Suitable for this use are large Oriental ceramic bowls, oak barrels or other large containers not treated with a poisonous preservative. This choice is recommended for beginners, because it is so easy to maintain and inexpensive to start.

A full-size pond is an ambitious project. A water-holding structure and a source of water are prerequisites. One such garden used an old bathtub, the edges carefully concealed, to make the pond. An overflow area planned into the design created a bog habitat. Water level was maintained by hand-watering every couple days, but an automatic water refill system could have been included.

In all water lines and the pool itself, fall drainage is essential. A natural earthen-bottomed pond requires no winter drainage, but it requires vigilant care to maintain its ecosystem from mosquitoes and algae. The same problems apply to combination swimming pools and water gardens. Chlorine and plants are incompatible. A swimming pool without chlorine must have some other control for algae, bacteria and other nuisance water-life.

Clearly the most dramatic accent is a fountain. If no plants are to be included, then chemicals can be used to keep the water algae-free. A simple pump with a leaf filter on its intake, a fountain kit and perhaps lights are all that is required. However, the inclusion of plants and goldfish makes a considerable leap in the complexity of the system. There must be adequate screening to protect fish from the recirculating pump. The system must clean itself with a more complex filtering device. And finally, winter-proofing the whole thing becomes a serious venture—fish and plants removed, everything carefully drained.

With all this trouble to maintain, why do it? Because water breathes life into an area. The sound of a rock overhang dripping water, or the sight of a moist vertical wall covered with bog plants and ferns is simply without substitute. In the parched heat of summer, a deep pool surrounded by tall trees satisfies a primeval hunger.

An unusual diversion would be to create a fountain for use in the winter. Because of the chinook zone's season of eight months of winter and four months of summer, I often fantasize about the possibility of an ice fountain designed to spray water into sculptures. The variety of wind patterns and freezing conditions would create a nearly limitless range of possibilities. Letting imagination soar, I see ordinary suburban lawns transformed into wonderlands of ice and fantasy. Mountains rise for children to play on. Crystalline caves and castle spires glisten in the sunlight. I think we have been neglecting this part of winter fun too long.

CONTAINER GARDENING

Potted plants can be a beautiful asset to a patio. They eliminate problems of lack of soil and create alcoves of color and fragrance. These suggestions barely scratch the surface of the endless possibilities.

Windowboxes make a pleasant frame for a window

view and decorate a house's exterior. Use a lightweight soil mix of perlite, peat and compost. Recommended are fragrant plants, especially annuals because they require less root space. Vines can be trained up to frame the entire window.

Wheelbarrow planters are quite decorative and, best of all, easy to move around. Be sure to drill drainage holes in the bottom.

Hanging planters have the advantage of bringing flowers up to eye level and fragrance closer to the nose. However, a suspended pot requires slightly more watering than one on the ground.

Raised planter beds elevate plants to a better working level for people who find bending difficult. This method protects the beds from human and animal foot traffic, increases drainage, and eliminates the spread of grass by roots. But best of all, raised beds can complement any type of architecture. Walls for planter beds can be constructed of masonry, cast concrete, redwood or treated wood. For a really showy version, create a dry wall of stacked and unmortared flat rocks. Then, you can plant amazingly dainty rock garden plants in the dirt-filled cracks between rock slabs. Surprisingly, the most difficult and spectacular rock garden plants, such as *Campanula portenschlagiana* and bitterroot thrive in such spartan crevices.

Screens for balconies or indoor room dividers can be made from long planters with attractive plantings. Light exposure will determine plant selection. In optimally bright light, the choices include many flowering vines. To avoid water spills, plan ahead for necessary drainage.

Patio containers should be thought of as moveable art. Clay pots, flue tiles of varied heights, even large tin cans can be used as is or hidden inside decorator pots. Ideally, one should strive to maintain a continuous bloom show from early spring to late fall, even into winter if possible. Wooden tubs, half barrels and concrete urns are less moveable, but will hold larger plants. But be sure all containers have drainage holes, and use liners to catch drips. Avoid leaving small containers outside in winter, as the freeze/thaw cycles can crack them.

Container plants have three special needs:
1. regular water and fertilizer;
2. good drainage; and
3. protection from excessive heat or cold. A mulch, even a decorative stone mulch, will help slow water loss. The soil mix, a crucial consideration for a potted plant, must be fast draining, lightweight, and loose. Unfortunately, regular dirt by itself simply does not work. Here are some basic potting mixes:

• Regular mix—humus (peat, leaf mold, worm castings), perlite (or vermiculite), sand, traces of composted manure, bonemeal and other fertilizers.

• Humusor acid-loving plants—use the basic mix recipe with slightly less perlite and sand, but more humus.

• Rock garden or cactus mix—use the basic mix recipe with less humus and fertilizer, but more perlite and sand.

When planting or arranging containers, avoid rows or lines. Indeed, you want to try to space them in naturalistic groups or in odd numbers for best visual impact. When plants are grouped together, they help conserve each other's moisture.

A hint to conserve water is to plug the pot's bottom hole (with a rubber stopper or cork) before watering it. Then drench it, and let it soak for 15 minutes, remembering to open the drainage hole afterward. This little bit of extra work will drastically reduce watering needs.

Annuals often work best in the shallow root space of pots. Perennials will need to be protected differently according to whether they can be left out or must be cold-stored (such as in a garage). Ornamental grasses in a freeze-proof urn look spectacular in midwinter.

ROCK GARDENS

Rock gardens are a real treat to experience and are started quite easily.

Here are some hints:
1. When designing a rock garden, always strive to create a maximum of different habitats varying from full sun to shade, and hot to cool areas.
2. Carefully bury rocks of similiar appearance, mak-

ing sure their strata lines (or grain) are running in the same direction. The desired result should resemble a natural outcropping.

3. All rocks should appear as though the bulk of their surface remained buried. This is an important consideration too often neglected.

4. Rocky, well drained soil is essential for many rock garden plants. In nature the freeze/thaw process breaks down rocks into a top layer of large gravel with smaller gravel below. Under this is heavier soil. Strive to create these layers for your rock garden.

5. Finish by dressing the garden with an attractive mulch of light-colored rock. Primarily, this reduces heat damage to roots, while at the same time minimizing water loss in the soil and suppressing weed growth. For many choice rock garden gems, this is an essential item.

6. Many evergreen plants need a location where they will be protected from winter sun (try north or northeast exposure).

7. Most importantly, stay ahead of the persistent danger of weeds, especially grasses. These aggressive plants can be difficult to remove once they begin to take over the garden. The root competition and shading they produce can kill many rock garden plants.

8. For beginners or small collections, use troughs or deep pans with proper drainage. These are easier to construct and just as attractive as a whole garden bed.

When selecting plants, use those native to the North American plains and foothills, the Siberian steppes, or the mountains of Asia Minor. A recommended book is *Jewels of the Plains* by Claude Barr. Also, two other tremendous resources exist for local enthusiasts: the Rock Gardens at the University of Alberta's Devonian Gardens (near Edmonton), and the Rock Garden Section at the Denver Botanic Garden. Both are becoming world renowned.

CHILDREN'S GARDENS

"Truly, I say to you, unless you turn and become like children you will never enter the kingdom of heaven."
Matthew 18:3

Re-exploring childhood roots can return your perspective to an appropriately knee-high sense of wonder. Children are really teachers who show us what it is to marvel, and to smell and taste; in short, the really extraordinary drama it is to be alive. Occasionally we need to leave our stale, rational ways and find flight in re-childizing the adult. Children and gardens together can be enthusiastic guides, reopening our vision of how important play and fun are. So, if you have children, can borrow some children, or really have the courage to "be as children," then try some of the following ideas designed to be fun and a bit crazy.

Most kids prefer the adventure of bushes, vines, tall grass and wildflowers to the seemingly sterile environment of grass lawns and concrete.

PLANTS TO GROW

Odd plants. Burning bush, baby's breath, globe amaranth, gourds, lamb's ears, love lies bleeding, obedience plant, sea holly.

Edible Plants. Strawberries, raspberries, plums, apples, sugar peas, cherry tomatoes, wheat, corn, zucchinis, Brussels sprouts (very unusual-looking plants), popcorn and pumpkins.

Edible flowers. Nasturtiums, borage and violas.

Miniature flowers. *Iris reticulata,* miniature roses, *Tulipa kaufmaniana* or *T. gregii,* dwarf marigolds, snapdragons (Magic Carpet), *linaria* (Fairy Bouquet), zinnia (Tom Thumb variety).

Catnip for cats. You can watch them roll around in it. For a beloved toy, fill a cloth bag with dried catnip.

Plants that attract butterflies or birds.

Write names by seeding letters with sweet alyssum. You will need to trim the top and sides as it grows to make it most readable.

Late fall garden: ornamental cabbage, pansies.

Make a rainbow from plants of similar heights (red salvia, orange and yellow marigolds, green carrot foliage, light and dark blue lobelia, and purple petunias), then border it with white or purple sweet alyssum.

Don't grow: daffodils and other poisonous plants.

Be sure to include some bedding plants for instant interest.

PLAYTIME

• Tunnel frame covered with bean vines, morning glories, etc.

• Tipi made from corn stalks.

• Maze made from permanent hedges or temporary annual plants. The most complex designs have confusing identical curves and sitting benches.

• May Day baskets (place a basket of flowers on a neighbor's door, ring the bell and hide).

• Leis made by stringing flowers together with needle and thread. Marigolds and portulaca last well.

• Hedge a play area with tithonia, sunflowers or heliopsis.

• Make a scarecrow.

• Arrange dried flowers for Christmas gifts (see index under Everlastings).

• Make dolls from hollyhock flowers.

• Create jewelry by stringing together green pumpkin seeds or rosehips.

• Bake poppyseed cakes from the seed of Shirley poppies.

• Make crystalilzed rose petals or rose petal jam.

• Drive into the high mountains in mid-July to see the wildflowers.

WHEN YOU'RE STUCK INSIDE

• Force bulbs and twigs to flower mid-winter (for directions, see the Winter Gardening section).

• Start a luxuriant sweet potato vine by propping a tuber up in a jar, one third of it above water. Try to avoid grocery store tubers sprayed with sprout retardant.

• Grow clipped-off vegetable tops in saucers of water (carrots, beets, parsnips, turnips).

• Root houseplant cuttings in glasses of water (mint, watercress, wandering Jew, Swedish ivy).

• An onion potted in soil and placed in a sunny window will grow and eventually bloom.

KEY TO DESCRIPTIVE LISTINGS

annual—a plant that completes its life cycle in a year or less. The plant germinates, grows, blossoms, fruits, and dies all in the same year.

basal clump—a low clump of ground-hugging foliage. The leaves are often arranged symmetrically in a rosette pattern.

biennial—a plant that completes its life cycle in two years. Generally, they produce leaves the first year, and bloom, fruit, and die the second year. Self-sowing biennials must be planted two years in a row to avoid a later gap in blooming.

bloom—bloom time is based on observations in Great Falls, Montana, located in Zone 4. Flower bloom time depends on many factors. Usually, the early spring and late summer bloom times are most easily distorted by climate, topography, and other factors, while the mid-summer (June and July) bloom times are most accurate. For far northern areas of Canada, allow a week or two leeway when estimating your area's bloom time.

botanical name—the first name is the genus and the second name is the species. Common names are included in plant descriptions, and in the index. But common names for the same plant often vary by geographic region, and using the botanical name ensures accuracy. The botanic plant names are based on *Hortus III*. When botanical names change, the old name is listed in parentheses.

culture—refers to the general ease or difficulty of successfully growing a plant in the chinook zone.

deciduous—a plant with foliage that dies and falls off at the end of the growing season.

dry—refers to the moisture needs of a plant. These are plants that grow best when allowed to dry out between waterings. A general rule of thumb is to provide an inch of water to the plant when the top three inches of soil feel dry and powdery to the touch. This may be once every two to four weeks in very hot weather.

evergreen—a plant with foliage that stays fully green throughout the year.

fire blight—a disease that attacks and kills apple trees, and occasionally kills hawthorns, pears, and saskatoons. An outbreak first shows on a flowering branch tip shortly after the flowering period. The individual branch tip wilts and appears to have been burned with fire.

germination—to sprout from a seed. Seeds germinate most successfully under either cold, warm, light, or dark conditions, or some combination of those conditions. **Cold** refers to keeping the planted seeds at about 50 to 60 degrees F. until the seeds have sprouted and formed seedlings. **Warm** refers to keeping the seeds at about 70 to 80 degrees until they germinate. Some seedlings require bright **light** to germinate. Others must be kept in a **dark**ened place until the seedlings are up (and then move them to a bright area). There are excellent booklets available with more specific information on successfully germinating seeds.

half-shade—refers to a location receiving a few hours of dappled or reflected sun each day. Half shade is often located under a lone tree. A light-colored house wall can reflect light and may support plants that need half-shade.

half-sun—refers to a location receiving three to five hours of sunshine each day. Morning sun is less intense than afternoon sun, so plants needing half-sun will respond differently if their allotment is morning sun or intense afternoon sun.

hardwood cuttings—propagating a plant by cutting the wood from the previous season's growth. This is best done during dormancy, between autumn and winter.

height—refers to the approximate height of the plant. Site conditions and variety differences affect a plant's height.

likes—refers to the conditions in which the plant will best thrive. See the specific terms defined in this key.

moist—refers to the moisture needs of a plant. In general, plants that like moist conditions need an inch or two of water a week, and cannot tolerate drying out at all. The soil should form a ball when squeezed, but not drip. Mulch heavily to conserve soil moisture.

perennial—a plant that lives longer than two years.

pinching—removing the plant's growing tips, to promote bushiness and stagger the flowering period.

propagation—starting new plants. Propagation may be from seeds, from sets, or from cuttings, budding, or grafting. Never dig wild plants or buy from unscrupulous nurseries that transplant wild plants. Rare native plants are in danger of extinction, and scenic wild areas are left with potholes by these collectors. Buy plants propagated in the nursery.

pruning—cutting parts of the plant to modify its growth or remove dead wood.

root suckering—refers to plants which spread weedy new plants from their roots.

self-sowing—refers to the ability of some plants to seed new plants around them with no help from you.

semidry—refers to the moisture needs of a plant. Semidry conditions allow the plant to dry out slightly between deep waterings. In general, provide an inch of water when the top two inches of soil have dried out and are powdery to touch. This may mean watering about once every two weeks.

semi-evergreen—a plant with foliage that remains partially green throughout the winter.

semi-hardwood cuttings—stem cuttings of the growth tip, usually taken after the growth flush in mid-summer or early fall.

sets—young plants that are started in pots, and later transplanted.

shade—means exactly that. No direct sunlight reaches the area. This is usually an area under a closed canopy of trees, where the leaves don't reflect any sunlight. It may also be the north side of a dark-colored structure or wall.

shrub, bush—terms are used interchangeably to describe a small, usually multi-stemmed, woody plant.

soft-hardwood cuttings—stem cuttings of the soft, flexible growth tip, best taken during the active growing season in spring and early summer. Also referred to as semi-hardwood cuttings.

sun—refers to a location receiving six or more hours of sun each day.

tolerates—growing conditions the plant will survive, but blossoming or growth rate may be slow.

variety—the word variety is used to describe cultivated varities, natural varieties, and hybrid varieties. While botanists use those specific terms to describe genetic characteristics, such terms have little usefulness to a home gardener. It may take local nurseries several years to catch up with all the varieties listed in this guide. It is my hope that you will be patient and buy locally when possible. If you cannot wait for a local source, then try the mail order catalogues listed in this book.

white to pink flowers—refers to the way some flowers change color, starting as the first color and aging to the second.

winter mulch—refers to a covering of mulch, straw, evergreen boughs, peat, leaves, or other substances to protect a plant from sun, drying winds, temperature extremes, or from thawing too early in the spring. It is important that the mulch is light enough to permit some light and air movement to the plant.

zone—refers to USDA hardiness zones. All plants in this book are hardy to Zone 2, 3, or 4. Plants marked Zone 4-5 are marginally hardy in the chinook zone, and probably require extra attention and protection.

HARDY CHINOOK-ZONE PLANTS

ABIES BALSAMEA, Balsam Fir, dwarf varieties only. Perennial to Zone 2.
Height: 10 inches.
Shape: globe-shaped dwarf conifer.
Likes: moist.
Tolerates: sun/half-sun/semidry.
Propagation: sets (hardwood cuttings in winter).
Comments: requires good drainage in winter; prefers cool summer areas or mid-day shade; must be protected from wind and winter sun in exposed areas.

'Hudsonia,' compact globe shape, needles are arranged flatly and evenly on either side of each branch.

'Nana,' irregular globe shape, needles radiate in whorls around each branch.

A. LASIOCARPA, Alpine Fir. Native to alpine areas of the Rocky Mountains from Alaska to Arizona. Perennial to Zone 2.
Height: 10 feet.
Shape: showy compact evergreen tree.
Likes: sun/half-sun/semidry/moist.
Propagation: sets or seeds.

ABRONIA FRAGRANS, Sand Verbena. Native to sandy areas of the Great Plains and Rocky Mountains. Perennial.
Height: 1 foot.
Bloom: fragrant white rounded flower clusters, blooms from end May to end June, flowers seem more visible in the evening.
Foliage: low basal clump.
Likes: sun/half-sun/dry/semidry/sandy, well-drained soil.
Propagation: sets or seeds.

ACER GINNALA, Amur Maple. Perennial to Zone 3.
Height: 15 feet.
Shape: dense shrubby tree.
Bloom: tiny fragrant creamy-white flowers before leaves appear in late April; showy red-winged seeds in August.
Foliage: bright orange-red color in early fall.
Culture: easy.
Likes: sun/moist.

Alpine Fir, Abies lasiocarpa

Tolerates: half-sun/half-shade/semidry.
Propagation: sets or seeds. Buy only sets with their terminal bud tip intact; softwood cuttings in summer.
Comments: may become chlorotic in highly alkaline soil, remedy with chelated iron or water leaching of soil; this plant can be trained as a large multi-stemmed shrub or pruned annually to be a single trunk tree. Prune only in late summer to early fall or it bleeds to death. There are varieties of *Acer ginnala* with an especially compact growth habit, 'Compacta' and 'Durand Dwarf,' and other varieties with redder seeds. 'Flame' is a variety selected for its vivid red seeds that color the tree throughout the late summer. However, a new selection with red seeds, improved fall color, and increased hardiness is called either 'V N Strain' (V N Stands for Valley Nursery, Helena) or *'Bergiana'* (named for Clayton Berg, owner of Valley Nursery). A tree similar to this species is *Acer tataricum.*

A. PLATANOIDES 'EMERALD LUSTER,' Norway Maple. Perennial to Zone 3-4.
Height: 40 feet.
Shape: rounded tree.
Foliage: showy dark green; yellow fall color.
Likes: moist.
Tolerates: sun/half-sun/semidry/alkaline soil.
Propagation: sets.
Comments: this variety of Norway Maple is the hardiest, and less sensitive to alkalinity than any of the other varieties. 'Emerald Luster' was introduced by Bailley's Nursery, St. Paul, Minnesota, in 1979. For gamblers, there are two redleaf varieties, 'Crimson King' and *'Schwedleri,'* which could be attempted in a forest-like microclimate if given abundant water.

A. RUBRUM, Red Maple. Perennial to Zone 3 (protected areas only).

Height: 40 feet.
Shape: oval-shaped in youth, becoming rounded with age.
Foliage: rich scarlet-red fall color.
Likes: moist/humus-rich soil.
Tolerates: sun/half-sun/semidry.
Propagation: sets.
Comments: very sensitive to alkalinity; needs lots of water. Two hardy varieties of note are 'Firedance' and 'Northwood.'

A. SACCHARINUM, Silver Maple. Perennial to Zone 2.
Height: 60 feet.
Shape: fast-growing upright tree which becomes rounded with age.
Foliage: poor fall color.
Likes: sun/half-sun/dry/semidry/moist/humus-rich soil.
Propagation: sets.

A. SACCHARUM, Sugar Maple. Perennial to Zone 4.
Height: 60 feet.
Shape: upright rounded tree.
Foliage: long-lasting, vivid orange-red fall color.
Likes: moist/humus-rich soil.
Tolerates: sun/half-sun/semidry.
Propagation: sets or seed.
Comments: sensitive to alkalinity; needs lots of water. Surprisingly, this tree is more tolerant of our climate than one might expect. Established trees exist in Great Falls and Big Sandy, Montana. There is also a subspecies *Nigrum,* called the Black Maple, which may be more alkali- and drought-tolerant.

A. TATARICUM, Tartarian Maple. Perennial to Zone 3.
Height: 25 feet.

Tartarian Maple, Acer tataricum

Shape: showy small V-shaped tree.
Foliage: red or yellow fall color depending on variety, showy red seeds.
Culture: easy.
Likes: sun/moist.
Tolerates: half-sun/half-shade/semi-dry.
Propagation: sets or seeds.
Comments: may become chlorotic in highly alkaline soil, remedy with chelated iron or water leaching of soil. This tree is appealing because of its beautiful V-shaped form. Its natural fall color is a poor yellow, so try to plant varieties such as *'Rubrum,'* which is propagated for its red fall color.

ACHILLEA AGERATIFOLIA. Perennial to Zone 2.
Height: 6 inches.
Bloom: small white daisy-like flowers on stalks; blooms from May to June (long season).
Foliage: silvery-white finely-divided foliage (semi-evergreen in winter).
Culture: easy.
Likes: sun/semidry.
Tolerates: half-sun/dry/moist.
Propagation: sets or seeds.

A. CLAVENNAE, Perennial to Zone 2.
Height: 4 inches.
Bloom: white flower clusters from May to June.
Foliage: white woolly mat of foliage; semi-evergreen in winter.
Culture: easy.
Likes: sun/semidry.
Tolerates: dry.
Propagation: sets or seeds.

A. FILIPENDULINA, Yarrow. Perennial to Zone 1.
Height: 3 feet.
Bloom: large yellow flat-topped flowers from July to September (very long season).
Foliage: semi-evergreen in winter.
Culture: easy.
Likes: sun/moist.
Tolerates: half-sun/dry.
Propagation: sets or seeds. (Seed germination: needs light.) Can be planted outside before the frost-free date.
Comments: spreading clump habit. Besides being showy in the garden, flowers make both good cut flowers and dried everlastings.

A. MILLEFOLIUM, Yarrow, native circumpolar. Perennial to Zone 1.
Height: 2 feet.

Bloom: red, pink, yellow or white flat-topped flower clusters from July to September (long season).
Foliage: finely-divided, semi-evergreen.

Yarrow, *Achillea milleflorium*

Culture: easy.
Likes: sun/moist.
Tolerates: half-sun/dry.
Propagation: Sets or seeds. (Seed germination: needs light.) Can be planted outside before the frost-free date.
Comments: invasive by root spreading. Besides being showy in the garden, flowers make good cut flowers and dried everlastings. Two exceptional new varieties from Germany are 'The Beacon' ('Fanny') with scarlet-red flowers, and 'Great Expectations' ('Hoofing') with yellow flowers. Yarrow is an excellent companion for broccoli and cabbage because it repels pests. Yarrow is often planted near herbs because it seems to strengthen the aromatic properties of their volatile oils. The name *millefolium* means 'thousand leaves' in Latin and refers to the finely-divided foliage.

A. PTARMICA. Perennial to Zone 1.
Height: 2 feet.
Bloom: white flower clusters from June to frost (long season).
Foliage: finely-divided foliage; semi-evergreen in winter.
Culture: easy.
Likes: sun/moist.
Tolerates: half-sun/dry.
Propagation: sets or seeds.
Comments: invasive due to self-sown seeds, but extra plants are easily removed. Varieties of note

Achillea ptarmica

are 'Angel Tears,' 'The Pearl' and 'Ballerina.'

A. TAYGETEA. Perennial to Zone 4.
Height: 2 feet.
Bloom: primrose-yellow flat-topped flower clusters from June to August (long season).
Foliage: finely-divided gray-green foliage; semi-evergreen in winter.
Culture: easy.
Likes: sun/semidry.
Tolerates: moist.
Propagation: sets.
Comments: this species is similar in appearance to *Achillea millefolium,* but is less invasive. The variety 'Moonshine' has blue-gray foliage and profuse light yellow flowers.

A. TOMENTOSA, Dwarf Woolly Yarrow. Perennial to Zone 1.
Height: 8 inches.
Bloom: yellow flower clusters on stalks, blooms from June to July (long season).
Foliage: woolly finely-divided gray-green foliage clustered in a mat; semi-evergreen in winter.
Culture: easy.
Likes: sun/semidry.
Tolerates: half-sun/dry/moist.
Propagation: sets.
Comments: spreading low clump. This is a great lawn substitute which can be mowed to 2 inches tall. Runners slowly spread plants and tolerate light foot traffic. Much less invasive than *Achillea millefolium.* It is also excellent in the front of the garden.

ACONITUM CARMICHAELII (A. fischeri), Monkshood. Perennial to Zone 2.
Height: 4 feet.
Bloom: rich blue-purple flowers on stalks, blooms from August to September.
Foliage: attractive dark green glossy foliage.
Likes: half-sun/moist.
Tolerates: half-shade.
Propagation: sets or seeds. (Seed germination: cold treatment.)
Comments: upright clump; flower stalks may need to be windstaked in exposed areas. For best vigor, this plant should be transplanted into new soil every 3 to 5 years. This is an excellent companion plant for late blooming Asiatic Lily Hybrids. The variety *'wilsonii'* is much taller than the species form.

Ernest 'Chinese' Wilson introduced this plant. Native to the Kamtschatka area of Asia. All parts of this plant are poisonous.

A. JAPONICUM, Japanese Wolfbane. Perennial to Zone 1.
Height: 3 feet.
Bloom: dark blue-purple flowers on a stalk, blooms from August to late September (late season).
Foliage: light green foliage which turns an attractive yellow in the fall.
Likes: half-sun/moist.
Tolerates: half-shade.
Propagation: sets or seeds. (Seed germination: cold treatment.)
Comments: upright clump; flower stalks may need to be windstaked in exposed areas.

A. NAPELLUS, Common Monkshood, Wolfbane. Perennial to Zone 1.
Height: 4 feet.
Bloom: blue-purple flowers on a stalk, blooms from July to August.
Foliage: attractive.
Likes: half-sun/half-shade/moist.
Tolerates: sun/wet.
Propagation: sets or seeds. (Seed germination: cold treatment.)
Comments: upright clump. For best vigor, this plant should be transplanted every 3 to 5 years. 'Bicolor' is an attractive variety with blue and white flowers. There are also white flowering and pink flowering varieties. All parts of this plant are poisonous. The name wolfbane comes from the use of this plant's root to poison meat for killing wolves. There is a legend that it was also used on werewolves.

ADONIS AMURENSIS 'PLENA,' Amur Adonis. Perennial to Zone 2.
Height: 8 inches.
Bloom: showy yellow flowers with green centers, blooms from early to late April.
Foliage: attractive finely-divided foliage which goes dormant and disappears in mid-summer.
Likes: sun/half-sun/moist
Propagation: sets or seeds.
Comments: prefers a humus-rich soil. The variety 'plena' has a double number of petals.

A. VERNALIS, Spring Adonis. Perennial to Zone 2.
Height: 1 foot.
Bloom: yellow daisy flowers from mid-April to early May.
Foliage: attractive finely-divided foliage which goes dormant and disappears in midsummer.
Likes: sun/half-sun/moist.

AEGOPODIUM PODAGRARIA 'VARIEGATUM,' Goutweed, Snow on the Mountain. Perennial to Zone 1.
Height: 1 foot.
Foliage: spreading clump of variegated green and white foliage.

Culture: easy.
Likes: half-sun/semidry
Tolerates: shade/dry.
Propagation: sets.
Comments: spreading clump. Very invasive due to root spreading (easily contained by concrete sidewalks).

Snow on the Mountain, Aegopodium podagraria

This makes an aggressive ground cover plant that tolerates shade.

AESCULUS GLABRA, Ohio Buckeye Tree; state tree of Ohio. Perennial to Zone 2.
Height: 30 feet.

Ohio Buckeye Tree, Aesculus glabra

Bloom: white flower clusters in May.
Shape: rounded tree in youth which becomes a tall spreading tree at maturity.
Foliage: orange fall color.
Likes: sun/half-sun/semidry/moist.
Propagation: sets or seeds (buy only sets with their terminal bud tip intact).
Comments: prune to accentuate its

tall-growing wide-spreading form. This tree grows slowly when young or in an extremely adverse site. Another species is *Aesculus hippocastanum* (Horse Chestnut), which has locally selected varieties that are hardy to Zones 3-4. This species has showy white flower clusters in the spring and a yellow fall color. Seed pods of all species are poisonous.

AGASTACHE FOENICULUM, Anise Hyssop, native to moist grass areas and forest openings in the Great Plains and foothills, north to the parklands. Perennial to Zone 1.
Height: 2 feet.
Bloom: purple flowers on stalks, blooms from June to frost.
Foliage: aromatic.
Likes: sun/semidry.
Tolerates: half-sun/moist/wet.
Propagation: sets or seeds.
Comments: clump habit.

AGERATUM HOUSTONIANUM, Flossflower. Annual.
Height: 8 inches.
Bloom: blue or white flower clusters, blooms from May to September.
Likes: half-shade/moist.
Tolerates: sun/shade/semidry.
Propagation: sets or seeds. (Seed germination: light, warm.)
Comments: this plant is excellent in pots or containers. The name *Ageratum* means 'to old age' in Latin, and refers to its unending bloom season.

AGROPYRON SPICATUM, Bluebunch Wheat Grass, official state grass of Montana. Native to the Great Plains and Rocky Mountains. Perennial to Zone 2.
Height: 3 feet.
Foliage: tufted non-spreading bunch habit, attractive segmented (or chain-like) grassheads are most dramatic in fall and winter when they turn a reddish-bronze color.
Culture: easy.
Likes: sun/half-sun/dry/semidry.
Propagation: sets or seed (self-sows somewhat but is not invasive).
Comments: this is a nice ornamental grass for winter interest. The poorest soils produce the most attractively delicate plants.

AGROSTIS NEBULOSA, Cloud Grass. Annual.
Height: 1 foot.
Bloom: showy cloud-like grass-

heads in July.
Likes: sun/semidry.
Tolerates: half-sun/moist.
Propagation: sets.
Comments: besides being showy in the garden, it can be used in containers, and as a cut flower in arrangements.

ALCEA ROSEA (Althea rosea), Hollyhock. Biennial to Zone 1.
Height: 4 feet.
Bloom: red, pink, yellow, white, purple or black flower spikes from late June to July (long season).
Foliage: semi-evergreen in winter.
Culture: easy.
Likes: sun/semidry.
Tolerates: half-sun/dry.
Propagation: sets or seeds.
Comments: seed can be planted outside in the spring, or late summer. Seed tolerates cool soil and can be planted in late fall. Plant seed very shallowly. Try to plant a few new seeds each year. This plant was associated with the crusaders who brought it to Europe to be used as a prized vegetable. They named it hollyhock meaning 'holy vegetable.' This plant has been grown experimentally by Montana State University as a fiber for fine paper. The common variety called 'Powderpuff' was created in Edmonton, Alberta. Shepherd's Garden Seeds offers a European variety 'Chater's Choice' which has double flowers in a color range of dark pink, light pink, soft yellow, white and lavender. Three other closely related plants that resemble Hollyhock are listed in this guide. They are *Lavatera, Malope* and *Malva.*

Hollyhock, Alcea rosea

ALLIUM, Onion.
Bloom: nearly all have sphere-like flowers on a stalk.
Foliage: aromatic from volatile sulfur compounds (though noticeable only if foliage is crushed).
Likes: sun/semidry.

Tolerates: half-sun/dry/moist.
Propagation: bulbs (bury small bulbs 3-4 inches deep and large bulbs 5-6 inches deep) or seeds. (Seed germination: cold treatment.)
Comments: prefers good drainage. Many species are invasive by self-sown seeds. On these species, simply remove seedheads after bloom to eliminate this problem. Other species produce tiny bulblets near the soil surface that slowly spread new plants. Most alliums make excellent long-lasting cut flowers and can also be used as dried everlastings. Hostas make a good combination with Alliums.

Order of bloom: *Allium zebdanense* (May); *A. aflatunense* (late May to early June); *A. textile*—Prairie Onion (late May to early June); *A. karataviense*—Turkestan Allium (early to mid-June); *A. schoenoprasum*—Chives (June); *A. cernuum*—Nodding Purple Onion (mid- June to July); *A. ostrowskianum* (mid-June to early July); *A. christophii*—Star of Persia (late June); *A. senescens* (late June); *A. cyanthophorum* (late June to July); *A. giganteum*—Globe Allium (late June to July); *A. narcissiflorum* (late June to July); *A. caeruleum* (early to mid-July); *A. hymenorrhizum* (early to mid-July); *A. moly*—Golden Garlic (early to mid-July); *A. obliguum* (July); *A. flavum*—Nodding Yellow Onion (mid-to late July); *A. nutans*—Steppes Onion (mid-July to August); *A. ramosum*—Siberian Fragrant Onion (mid-July to August); *A. sphaerocephalum*—Drumstick Allium (mid-July to August); *A. stellatum* (August); *A. tuberosum*—Garlic Chives (August to September).

A. AFLATUNENSE. Perennial to Zone 3-4.
Height: 3 feet.
Bloom: globe-like lavender flower clusters (3 inches across), blooms from late May to early June.
Foliage: strap-like.
Comments: invasive by self-sown seeds. This flower closely resembles *Allium giganteum* but is slightly shorter, and blooms a month earlier. It is showy in the garden as well as being excellent for either fresh cut flowers or dried everlastings. An improved variety is 'Purple Sensa-

tion' which has showy red-purple flowers. Native to Aflatum, an area of central Asia.

A. CAERULEUM (A. azureum). Perennial to Zone 1.
Height: 2 feet.
Bloom: showy sky-blue globe-shaped flower clusters, blooms from early to mid-July.
Foliage: grass-like.
Comments: very invasive by self-sown seeds and bulblets. This plant is summer dormant: it comes up in the fall and lives through the winter, then goes dormant and dies to the ground in early summer. After the foliage has disappeared in mid-summer, the flowers magically appear. This flower holds its color extremely well once dried and thus makes a good dried everlasting. It also makes excellent fresh cut flowers. Native to Siberia and west Turkestan. This species has the bluest flowers of any listed Alliums.

A. CERNUUM, Nodding Purple Onion, native to all of western North America. Perennial to Zone 1.
Height: 1 foot.
Bloom: nodding pinkish-white to lavender onion flowers from mid-June to July.
Foliage: grass-like foliage emerges early in the spring.
Comments: interesting dried seedheads. Dried flowerheads are useful in arrangements. The name 'cernuum' means crooked or bent and refers to the crooked neck of the flower stalk. This was an Indian food that Lewis and Clark mentioned enjoying. The onion smell of this bulb is an important method used by the Indians for distinguishing it from the deadly poisonous Death Camas (*Zygadenus gramineus*). The Nodding Onion is an excellent candidate for selective breeding. Its flower color varies from rich red-purples in its range in the southern Rockies to the pale lavenders in the Northern Plains and Rocky Mountains.

A. CHRISTOPHII (A. albopilosum), Star of Persia. Perennial to Zone 4.
Height: 2 feet.
Bloom: open globe-like cluster of star-like lavender flowers with a metallic sheen, blooms in late June.
Comments: This makes excellent cut flowers or dried everlastings.

A. CYANTHOPHORUM. Perennial to Zone 3.
Height: 8 inches.
Bloom: deep purple nodding flowers from late June to July.
Foliage: grass-like.
Comments: non-invasive. Native to China.

A. FISTULOSUM, Welsh Onion. Perennial to Zone 3.
Height: 1½ feet.
Bloom: small insignificant white flowers.
Foliage: onion-like foliage is used like green onions.
Comments: very invasive by self-sown seeds. Native to Siberia.

A. FLAVUM, Yellow Nodding Onion. Perennial to Zone 3.
Height: 1½ feet.
Bloom: nodding yellow flowers from mid- to late July.
Foliage: chive-like.
Comments: somewhat invasive by self-sown seeds. Native to southern Europe, from France to Greece. There is a particularly showy dwarf variety called 'Nanum' that grows to 6 inches tall.

A. GIGANTEUM, Globe Allium. Perennial to Zone 4.
Height: 3 feet.
Bloom: dramatically large purple globe flowers from late June to July.
Foliage: onion-like foliage.
Comments: non-invasive. This flower makes a good cut flower. Because it is originally native to the Himalayas, it prefers a humus-rich soil.

A. HYMENORRHIZUM. Perennial to Zone 3.
Height: 2 feet.
Bloom: very attractive rosy-pink flowers from early to mid-July.
Foliage: grass-like.
Comments: very invasive by self-sown seeds.

A. KARATAVIENSE, Turkestan Allium. Perennial to Zone 3.
Height: 5 inches.
Bloom: pinkish-lavender flowers in globes (3 inches across), blooms from early to mid-June.
Foliage: distinctive tulip-like foliage.
Comments: this dramatic-looking plant is appealing for its showy foliage, flowers, and seedheads. Native to the Kara Tau mountain range of Kazakhstan.

A. MOLY, Golden Garlic. Perennial to Zone 3-4.
Height: 1 foot.
Bloom: bright yellow globe flowers (2 inches across), blooms from early to mid-July.
Foliage: narrow, tulip-like.
Comments: non-invasive. In the *Odyssey,* Homer states that this plant protected Ulysses' head from being transformed into a pig head.

A. NARCISSIFLORUM. Perennial to Zone 3.
Height: 1 foot.
Bloom: very showy bell-shaped pink flowers; flowers are nodding at first, later becoming erect; blooms from late June to July.
Foliage: flattened.
Comments: native to limestone scree in the Alps of France and Italy.

A. NUTANS, Steppes Onion. Perennial to Zone 2.
Height: 2 feet.
Bloom: large pinkish-lavender or white drumstick-like flower clusters on a stalk, blooms from mid-July to August.
Foliage: clump of attractive flat leaves.
Comments: very invasive by self-sown seeds.

A. OBLIGUUM. Perennial to Zone 3.
Height: 3 feet.
Bloom: small yellow flowers in July.
Foliage: resembles a miniature corn plant.
Comments: very invasive by self-sown seeds.

A. OSTROWSKIANUM. Perennial to Zone 3.
Height: 6 inches.
Bloom: pink flowerheads from mid-June to early July.
Foliage: grass-like.
Comments: not invasive by self-sown seeds, but produces bulblets.

A. RAMOSUM, Siberian Fragrant Onion. Perennial to Zone 3.
Height: 2 feet.
Bloom: very fragrant grayish-white flat-topped flower clusters, blooms from mid-July to August.
Foliage: strap-like.
Comments: very invasive due to self-sown seeds.

A. SCHOENOPRASUM, Chives, culinary herb. Perennial to Zone 1.
Height: 1 foot.

Bloom: showy small lavender flowerheads in June.
Foliage: showy clumps of grass-like foliage that greens up very early in the spring.
Comments: Use the chopped foliage in sour cream mixtures and herb butters. Additionally, the flowers

Chives, Allium schoenoprasum

can be used in salads. As an ornamental, this plant is excellent for dramatic edged borders. There are sterile varieties of this plant which do not self-sow. These are the best to use. It can also be grown in pots indoors during the winter.

A. SENESCENS. Perennial to Zone 3.
Height: 3 feet.
Bloom: pinkish-lavender flowers in late June.
Foliage: flattened.
Comments: this species is similar to *Allium nutans.*

A. SPHAEROCEPHALUM, Drumstick Allium. Perennial to Zone 3.
Height: 2 feet.
Bloom: dense sphere-shaped red-purple flowers from mid-July to August.
Foliage: narrow, rounded.
Comments: non-invasive by self-sown seeds, but produces bulblets. Native to Europe.

Drumstick Allium, A. sphaerocephalum

A. STELLATUM. Perennial to Zone 3.
Height: 1 foot.
Bloom: pink flowers in August.
Foliage: grass-like.
Comments: non-invasive. Similar to *Allium cernuum* except it blooms later and its flowers are erect, rather than nodding. Native from

Saskatchewan to Texas.

A. TEXTILE, Prairie Onion, native to the Great Plains. Perennial to Zone 2.
Height: 6 inches.
Bloom: attractive white flowers from late May to early June.
Foliage: grass-like foliage.
Comments: scattered clump habit; non-invasive. The flower petals turn papery and dry on the flowerhead to protect the seeds. There are two other hardy *Allium* species: *Allium geyeri,* native to the Rocky Mountains and isolated mountains of the plains, has delicate pink flowerheads; and *Allium perdulce,* native to South Dakota and the central plains, has strongly fragrant rose-pink flowers.

A. TUBEROSUM, Garlic Chives, culinary herb. Perennial to Zone 3.
Height: 2 feet.
Bloom: showy fragrant white flowers with a violet-like scent, blooms August to September.
Foliage: flattened grass-like.
Comments: very invasive by self-sown seeds.

A. ZEBDANENSE. Perennial to Zone 3.
Height: 1 foot.
Bloom: showy white flowers in May.

AMARANTHUS CAUDATUS, Love-Lies-Bleeding. Annual.
Height: 2 feet.
Bloom: hanging red-tasseled spikes from July to frost (very long season).
Culture: easy.
Likes: sun/moist.
Tolerates: half-sun/dry/semidry/ very poor soil.
Propagation: sets or seeds. (Seed germination: warm.)
Comments: there are also attractive green tasseled varieties. The name *Amaranthus* means 'unfading' and refers to the unfading color of the tasseled seed spike.

A. MELANCHOLICUS, Amaranth, *Amaranthus melancholicus.* Annual vegetable.
Height: 2 feet.
Description: red or green, large fuzzy seedheads.
Culture: easy.
Likes: moist.
Tolerates: sun/half-sun/dry/semidry/poor soil.
Propagation: sets or seeds. (Seed germination: warm.)
Harvest tips: seed is easily cleaned by pouring it from bowl to bowl in a mild wind.
Comments: may be pinched when young for a more compact plant. The red-foliaged seed varieties are very showy in a garden. Edible seed varieties were heavily used by many Indian tribes. In fact, the Aztec Empire used this grain as an article of taxation. The tall attractive seedheads are best grown eight inches apart for wind support. The foliage of amaranth can be eaten either raw or cooked, as well as used as a garnish. It contains abundant vitamins and minerals including calcium and iron. See also the listing under 'Spinach—Warm Season' for Tampala (*Amaranthus gangeticus*)—a spinach-like green. The name *amaranthus* means "unfading," referring to the long-lasting color of the seedhead.

A. TRICOLOR, Amaranth. Annual.
Height: 2 feet.
Bloom: red, orange, yellow and green multicolored foliage from July to frost (very long season).
Culture: easy.
Likes: half-sun/moist.
Tolerates: sun/dry/semidry/poor soil.
Propagation: sets or seeds. (Seed germination: warm.)
Comments: may be pinched when young for a more compact plant. 'Illumination' is a scarlet-red variety with a molten yellow center. Two related plants are *Amaranth,* used for its edible seed, and Spinach-Warm Season (*Tampala*).

AMELANCHIER ALNIFOLIA, Saskatoon, Serviceberry. Native to the plains, foothills and mountains. Perennial to Zone 1.
Height: 13 feet.
Shape: narrow shrubby tree.
Bloom: white flower clusters from early to late May, delicious edible fruit in July and August.
Culture: easy.
Likes: half-sun/moist.
Tolerates: sun/half-shade/semidry.
Pests: occasionally susceptible to fireblight; rust may attack this plant if there are native junipers (*J. scorpulorum*) nearby.
Propagation: sets or seeds. (Seed germination: cold treatment for 100 days; root suckers or softwood cuttings in spring or summer.)
Comments: somewhat invasive due to root suckering; for best fruit, prune out oldest stems in the center of the shrub and the lowest branches, and maintain shrub height at 6-10 feet. This plant is self-pollinating.

Berries were an important staple of the Indian diet and an essential ingredient in pemmican. Alex Johnston states in his book *Plants and the Blackfoot* that pemmican was made from dried lean meat that was smoked and pounded into powder. This was mixed with equal proportions of the two kinds of buffalo fat—soft rich-flavored back fat, and grease-like hard fat—which were melted at a low temperature. The final ingredients were dried Saskatoon berries, chokecherries, and occasionally wild mint. This mixture was formed into cakes and packed into skin bags. It would stay good for years.

The wood of this plant was commonly used for arrow shafts and teepee stakes.

Today, the berries are primarily used for pies, preserves, and wine. Kim Williams stated that this is one of the few berries that can be eaten fresh in large quantities without any chance of stomach ache. Be forewarned: birds love this fruit, even though many other kinds of fruit are ripe at the same time.

Recommended varieties:

'Altaglow,' a tall ornamental variety with sparse white fruit and spectacular fall color including purple, vivid red, and yellow. For best fruit production, it must be cross-pollinated by a different variety. It was introduced by Brooks Research Station in 1960.

'Honeywood,' a variety with dramatically large berries in large clusters. It bears fruit at a young age. Introduced by Bert Porter of the Honeywood Nursery of Parkside, Saskatchewan.

'Pembina,' a variety less prone to root suckering. Introduced in 1953 by the Beaverlodge Experimental Farm in Alberta. John Wallace selected this variety from the wild near the Pembina River. This variety is considered to be the best for

*Ameliancher
alnifolia*

home gardeners because of its lack of root suckering.

'Regent,' a dwarf variety selected for both its profuse fruit yield and its ornamental attractiveness. Discovered by J. Candrian of Regent, North Dakota.

'Smoky,' selected from the grounds of the Beaverlodge Experimental Farm near the Smoky River in the Peace Country of Alberta. Introduced in 1953 by the Beaverlodge Experimental Farm in Alberta. Because of its profuse root suckering, it is considered the best variety for commercial farmers.

'Thiessen,' selected for its large fruit size, prolonged season of ripening, and columnar form. Discovered by Issak Thiessen of Langham, Saskatchewan. Introduced in 1976.

A. GRANDIFLORA, Serviceberry bush, perennial to Zone 3.
Height: 15 feet.
Shape: gracefully spreading shrubby tree.
Bloom: white flower clusters in early May.
Foliage: red fall color, edible fruit
Culture: easy.
Likes: sun/half-sun/half-shade/semidry/moist.
Propagation: sets or seeds (buy only sets with their terminal bud tips intact).
Comments: the new variety 'Princess Diana' was selected for its exceptionally long-lasting pinkish-red fall color, but its hardiness on the plains is yet unknown.

A. LAEVIS, Eastern Serviceberry. Perennial to Zone 3.

Height: 25 feet.
Shape: narrow shrubby tree.
Bloom: white flower clusters in late April; edible berries.
Foliage: new foliage is purplish in spring and then turns green in early summer; yellow fall color.
Culture: easy.
Likes: moist.
Tolerates: sun/half-sun/semidry.
Propagation: sets or seeds (buy only sets with their terminal bud tips intact).
Comments: prune only to accentuate its dramatic upright growth.

AMMOBIUM ALATUM, Winged Everlasting. Annual.
Height: 2 feet.
Bloom: papery white daisy flowers with a yellow center, blooms from late July to August.
Likes: sun/semidry/rich sandy soil.
Tolerates: moist.
Propagation: sets.
Comments: the plant itself is rather bizarre-looking. The commonly available species form has very small flowers. The variety 'Grandiflorum' has much improved larger flowers. This flower can be used as a cut flower or dried like a strawflower. Cut before buds open.

AMSONIA TABERNAEMONTANA, Blue Star. Perennial to Zone 3.
Height: 3 feet.
Bloom: light blue star-like flowers May to June.
Foliage: willow-like.
Likes: half-shade/moist/humus-rich soil.
Tolerates: sun/half-sun/semidry.
Propagation: sets or seeds. (Propagation: divisions in spring.)
Comments: upright clump.

ANCHUSA AZUREA, Alkanet, Bugloss. Perennial to Zone 3.
Height: 3 feet.
Bloom: blue flowers from June to August.
Likes: sun/moist.
Tolerates: sun/half-shade.
Propagation: sets or seeds.
Comments: the variety 'Loddon Royalist' has cobalt blue flowers.

A. CAPENSIS. Annual.
Height: 1 foot.
Bloom: blue flowers from May to July.
Likes: sun/moist.
Tolerates: half-shade.
Propagation: sets or seeds.

Comments: shear back after flowering for a rebloom; dies back in midsummer (plan to fill in the resulting bare spot).

ANDROMEDA POLIFOLIA 'NANA,' Dwarf Bog Rosemary, native to the boggy areas of the subarctic and boreal forest and Arctic tundra of North America. Perennial to Zone 4 (protected areas only).
Height: 8 inches.
Bloom: creeping heather-like shrub with bell-shaped pink flowers in early May.
Foliage: evergreen rosemary-like foliage.
Culture: difficult.
Likes: sun/moist.
Tolerates: half-sun/semidry.
Propagation: sets.
Comments: requires humus-rich acidic soil; requires light winter mulch to protect it from winter sun and wind. The dwarf variety *'nana'* is hardier than the species. All parts of this plant are poisonous.

*Bog
Rosemary,
Andromeda
polifolia*

ANDROPOGON SCOPARIUS (Schizachyrium scoparium), Little Bluestem. Native to dry-to-moist hillsides in the Great Plains. Perennial.
Height: 2 feet.
Foliage: tufted bunch habit, odd-looking fuzzy white seedheads, foliage turns showy reddish-brown color after the first frost and remains attractive throughout the winter.
Likes: sun/half-sun/dry/semidry/moist/sandy soils rich in calcium.
Propagation: sets or seeds.
Comments: the name bluestem refers to its blue-green stem bases in the spring. During the winter, the persistent fuzzy seedheads are a valuable food source for the few small birds that overwinter on the open prairie. The proper botanical name is *Schizachyrium scoparium*. But there has been so much resistance to this recent renaming that it may get its old name back.

ANEMONE CANADENSIS. Native to moist grassy areas and wooded low

areas of the Great Plains. Perennial.
Height: 2 feet.
Bloom: flat-topped white flower clusters from early May to early June.
Foliage: upright clump, finely divided.
Likes: sun/half-sun/half-shade/semidry/moist.
Propagation: sets or seeds.
Comments: very invasive by root spreading; tolerates southern exposure. Because this plant loves to grow in patches, it would do well in an aggressive ground cover mixture.

Anemone canadensis

A. HUPENHENSIS, Hardy Fall Anemone. Perennial to Zone 1.
Height: 3 feet.
Bloom: pink to white flowers from August to September (late season).
Culture: difficult.
Likes: half-sun/moist.
Tolerates: half-shade/shade.
Propagation: sets or seeds.
Comments: clump habit. Requires humus-rich soil; requires winter mulch in exposed areas.

A. MULTIFIDA, Ball Anemone. Native to north-facing grassy slopes and open woods of the Great Plains and foothills. Perennial.
Height: 2 feet.
Bloom: pink, cream or purple flowers on a stalk (also, some blue and green varieties), blooms from end May to early June, round cottony white seedheads.
Foliage: stiffly upright clump of attractive silky-hairy finely-divided foliage.
Likes: semidry/sandy soil.
Tolerates: sun/half-sun/half-shade/moist.
Propagation: sets or seeds.
Comments: let it self-sow in your garden and come up everywhere. Extra plants can be removed easily.

A. OCCIDENTALIS, White Pasque Flower, Chalice Flower. Native to hillsides in the high mountains. Perennial.
Height: 10 inches.
Bloom: waxy white flowers in May (brief season in low altitudes).

Foliage: silky-hairy stalks, finely-divided green leaves, attractive fuzzy seedheads on elongated stalks.
Culture: difficult.
Likes: half-sun/semidry/moist/good drainage.
Propagation: sets or seeds.
Comments: requires scree conditions (underground watering and good drainage); must have winter mulch in areas without predictable snowcover. This attractive but brief flower should be attempted only by experienced gardeners.

A. PATENS (Pulsatilla patens), Pasque Flower, Prairie Crocus; official state flower of South Dakota and official floral emblem of Manitoba. Native to dry grassy areas of the plains and foothills. Perennial to Zone 1.
Height: 4 inches.
Bloom: smoky-purple flowers which blow in the wind from early April to early May; attractive fuzzy seedheads on elongated stalks.
Foliage: silky foliage appears after bloom.
Likes: sun.
Tolerates: half-sun/dry/semidry/poor soil.
Propagation: sets (transplants best when dormant from mid- to late summer—move carefully as a root ball) or seeds (germinates best with cold treatment).
Comments: plant several patches of this flower in both hot sun and cool shade exposures for the longest display of blooms. The name *patens* means "spreading."

A. SYLVESTRIS, Snowdrop Anemone. Perennial to Zone 1.
Height: 1 foot.
Bloom: fragrant large nodding white flowers, blooms from late April to July (very long season).
Foliage: attractive finely-divided.
Likes: half-sun/moist.
Tolerates: half-shade/shade.
Propagation: sets or seeds (may self-sow in favorable location).
Comments: clump habit, requires humus-rich soil; requires winter mulch in exposed areas. There is a showy hybrid variety called *'x lesseri'* which has profuse rose-carmine flowers in June and sporadically throughout the rest of the summer. Native to Siberia. This mildly aggressive plant makes an excellent ground cover.

ANETHUM GRAVEOLENS, Dill, culinary herb. Annual.
Height: 3 feet.
Bloom: yellow-green flowerheads from July to August.
Foliage: finely-divided.
Culture: easy.
Likes: sun/moist.
Tolerates: half-sun/dry/semidry.
Propagation: sets or seeds. (Seed germination: light.) Can be planted outside a month before the frost-free date.
Comments: upright clump, prefers to be crowded. The word *dill* comes from an Anglo-Saxon word meaning 'to lull or calm' referring to the sedative properties of the seeds. Dill seed or chopped foliage is tasty with baked fish and adds sparkle to tuna, chicken, or egg salad sandwiches. Additionally, it can be added to salads, cottage cheese, potatoes, and dill bread. The dried flowers are showy in arrangements.

ANGELICA ARCHANGELICA, Angelica. Perennial to Zone 3.
Height: 5 feet.
Bloom: greenish-white flower clusters in July.
Foliage: attractive, finely-divided.
Likes: half-sun.
Tolerates: half-shade/moist.
Propagation: sets or seeds.
Comments: upright clump. Plant dies after seeds ripen unless the spent flowerheads are removed after bloom. Stems can be used fresh like celery or candied as a cake decoration.

A. ARGUTA, Lyall's Angelica. Native to moist grassy areas and stream banks in the Rocky Mountains. Perennial.
Height: 4 feet.
Bloom: very showy white flat-topped flower clusters from the end of June to early July; showy, reddish-purple seedheads.
Foliage: aromatic fern-like foliage.
Likes: moist.
Tolerates: sun/half-sun.
Propagation: sets or seeds.
Comments: established plants resent transplanting. This plant closely resembles the poisonous Water Hemlock (*Cicuta maculata*). Angelica can be distinguished by its winged seeds. Additionally, when split lengthwise, the root of Angelica is solid, while the root of Water Hem-

lock is chambered.

ANTENNARIA, Pussytoes. Perennial to Zone 2.
Bloom: creeping plants with unusual fuzzy flower heads on stalks.
Culture: easy.
Likes: sun/moist.
Tolerates: half-sun/dry/semidry.
Propagation: sets or seeds.
Comments: for best appearance, shear off spent flowers after bloom.

    A. ANAPHALOIDES. Native to the foothills and Rocky Mountains.
Height: 1 foot.
Bloom: white flowers on stalks (some red varieties).
Foliage: long gray-green leaves.
Comments: unlike the other mat-forming *Antennarias,* this plant tends to grow as an individual plant habit or in small tufts to 4 inches across.

    A. AROMATICA. Native to areas of the Rocky Mountains.
Bloom: yellowish flowers on stalks.
Comments: tight clump habit. Requires rock garden soil.

    A. CORYMBOSA. Native to moist meadows of the northern Rockies.
Height: 10 inches.
Bloom: tall whitish flowers.
Foliage: spreading mat-like habit.

    A. DIMORPHA, Dwarf Pussytoes. Native to dry open areas of the Great Plains and foothills.
Height: 1 inch.
Bloom: stalkless yellow flowers from April to early May.
Foliage: tiny woolly gray clump that resembles lichen, goes dormant and shrivels up in late summer or fall.

    A. PARVIFOLIA. Native to dry areas of the Great Plains and foothills of the northern Rockies.
Height: 3 inches.
Bloom: nodding white flowers (some pinkish varieties); seeds become fluffy and blow away.
Foliage: carpet-like habit, low clump of silvery-white woolly foliage.
Comments: this species is somewhat similar to *Antennaria microphylla.* The name *parvifolia* means "small leaves." This species is much more attractive than the commonly available *Antennaria rosea,* which tends to die out in the middle of its clump.

    A. ROSEA. Native to grasslands in the Great Plains and Rocky Mountains.
Height: 6 inches.
Bloom: variable flower color from pink to cream to white, blooms from May to June.
Foliage: tufted spreading clump, gray woolly foliage.
Comments: the center of the plant tends to die as edges grow outward. Alex Johnston in his book *Plants and the Blackfoot* states that "the leaves were sometimes used in the tobacco mixture, and were chewed by children for the flavor."

ANTHEMIS TINCTORIA, Dyer's Chamomile, Golden Marguerite. Perennial to Zone 2.
Height: 2 feet.
Bloom: yellow daisy flowers from June to frost (long season if spent flowers are removed).
Foliage: very showy finely-divided foliage.
Culture: easy.
Likes: sun/semidry.
Tolerates: half-sun/dry/moist.
Propagation: sets or seeds.
Comments: spreading upright clump. Requires division every couple of years for best appearance. This plant closely resembles a yellow daisy-like chrysanthemum.

Golden Marguerite, Anthemis tinctoria

ANTHRISCUS CEREFOLIUM, Chervil, culinary herb. Annual.
Height: 1-2 feet.
Bloom: attractive white flat-topped flower clusters from August to frost.
Foliage: attractive finely-divided foliage with anise-like scent.
Likes: half-sun/moist.
Tolerates: sun/half-shade/semidry.
Propagation: sets or seeds. (Seeds are slow to germinate; see the listing for Carrots for additional information.)
Comments: clump habit. Established plants resent transplanting. This easy-to-grow plant attracts beneficial insects to your garden. As a seasoning, Chervil is excellent with eggs and in salads.

ANTIRRHINUM MAJUS, Snapdragon. Annual.
Height: 1-2 feet.
Bloom: red, pink, yellow, white or purple flowers from June to frost (very long season if spent flowers are removed).
Likes: sun/moist/humus-rich soil.
Tolerates: half-sun/semidry/poor soil.
Propagation: sets or seeds. (Seed germination: light, warm.) Seeds can be planted outside in either the late fall or spring.
Comments: can be pinched for more flowers and a compact form; shear back plant after bloom for a rebloom. Besides being used in the garden, this flower is also showy in pots or containers. It makes excellent cut flowers, too.

Snapdragon, Antirrhinum majus

AQUILEGIA SPECIES, Columbine. The name comes from *'aquila,'* which in Latin means eagle.

    A. CAERULEA, Rocky Mountain Columbine, native to the central and northern Rockies; official state flower of Colorado. Perennial to Zone 1.
Height: 2 feet.
Bloom: blue and white flowers from May to June (long season if spent flowers are removed).
Foliage: attractive, lacy.
Likes: half-sun/semidry.
Tolerates: half-shade/moist.
Propagation: sets or seeds. (Seed germination: light, cold treatment.)
Comments: Encourage it to self-sow throughout your garden. It also makes a good cut flower.

    A. CANADENSIS, Canadian Columbine. Perennial to Zone 1.
Height: 2 feet.
Bloom: small red and yellow flowers from May to June (long season if spent flowers are removed).
Foliage: attractive, lacy.
Likes: half-sun/semidry (prefers cool summer areas).
Tolerates: half-shade/moist.
Propagation: sets or seeds. (Seed germination: cold treatment.)
Comments: It makes both a good cut flower and a great garden plant.

Plains Indians ground this plant's seeds along with *Lomatium, Lobelia cardinalis* and Wild Ginseng to make a treasured fragrance used in love potions.

A. CHRYSANTHA, Golden Columbine. Perennial to Zone 3.
Height: 3 feet.
Bloom: bright yellow flowers in May to June (long season if spent flowers are removed).
Foliage: attractive.
Likes: half-sun/semidry.
Tolerates: sun/moist.
Propagation: sets or seeds. (Seed germination: light, cold treatment.)
Comments: bushy clump. It makes both a good cut flower and a great garden plant.

A. FLAVESCENS, Yellow Columbine. Native of low to high elevation open-wooded areas in the Rocky Mountains. Perennial.
Height: 1 foot.
Bloom: yellow nodding flowers from end of May to mid-June.
Foliage: clump habit, attractive foliage.
Comments: this plant is normally found in the mildly acidic soil of aspen forests.

A. JONESII. Native to limestone talus areas, found only east of the Continental Divide of Montana, northwestern Wyoming and southwestern Alberta. Short-lived perennial.
Height: 3 inches.
Bloom: dramatic single blue-purple flowers in May.
Foliage: compact clump habit, showy miniature columbine foliage.
Culture: difficult.
Likes: half-sun/half-shade/well-drained rocky soil.
Propagation: sets or seeds.
Comments: requires scree conditions (underground watering and good drainage). Those rock gardeners who have had success getting this plant to flower use a deep layer (3 feet) of crushed rock to imitate its native talus conditions.

AQUILEGIA HYBRIDS. Perennial to Zone 1.
Height: 2 feet.
Bloom: red, orange, yellow, white or blue flowers, blooms from May to June (long season if spent flowers are removed).

Canadian Columbine, Aquilegia canadensis

Foliage: attractive.
Likes: half-sun/moist.
Tolerates: sun/half-shade/semidry.
Propagation: sets only.
Comments: these flowers make both good cut flowers, and great garden plants. 'Dragonfly' and 'McKana' are the most common varieties. 'Silver Queen' is an exceptionally vigorous long-blooming variety with white flowers. Shepherd's Garden Seeds offer a European variety, 'Langdon's Rainbow,' with a color range of pink, yellow, white, purple and blue. 'Biedermeier' and 'Fairyland' are excellent dwarf varieties.

ARABIS ALPINA, Alpine Rock Cress. Perennial to Zone 1.
Height: 5 inches.
Bloom: white or pink flowers from late April to May.
Likes: half-sun/semidry/well-drained soil).
Propagation: sets or seeds. (Seed germination: light.)
Comments: mound-like habit, requires winter mulch in areas without snow cover.

A. CAUCASICA, Common Rock Cress. Perennial to Zone 3.
Height: 7 inches.
Bloom: red, pink or white flowers from late April to May.
Foliage: greenish-white, hairy.
Likes: half-sun/semidry.
Propagation: sets or seeds. (Seed germination: light, warm.)
Comments: upright mounds; may need winter mulch in exposed areas. This plant makes an excellent companion for primroses, and is an attractive edging for the front of the garden as well as a cascading plant to hang over a wall. Two varieties of note are the following: 'Corfe Castle,' which has vivid magenta red flowers, (selected by Bruce and

Gill Corfe of England); and 'Rosabella,' which has pink flowers.

A. NUTTALLII, Nuttall's Rock Cress. Native to areas in the Rocky Mountains. Perennial.
Height: 10 inches.
Bloom: white flowers.
Foliage: sprawling clump.
Likes: sun/half-sun/semidry/moist/well drained, rocky soil.
Propagation: sets or seeds.
Comments: requires mid-day shade in hot summer areas. This species is considered the best native *Arabis* for the garden because its flower stalks do not elongate and become messy looking.

ARCTOSTAPHYLOS UVA-URSI, Kinnikinnick, Bearberry, native to western North America. Perennial to Zone 1.
Height: 6 inches.
Bloom: insignificant white flowers, red berries.
Foliage: trailing mat of evergreen.
Likes: half-sun/semidry.
Tolerates: sun/dry/moist.
Propagation: sets.
Comments: this plant is commonly used as a ground cover. An improved variety named 'Massachusetts' has profuse flowering. It was developed in western Oregon from seed sent from Massachusetts. Another improved variety is 'Vulcan's Peak.' It has profuse flowering and berries. There is commercial potential for marketing this plant as a Christmas decoration. *Arctostaphylos* is the genus name for all Manzanitas. The species name *uva-ursi* translates from Latin to mean 'bear berry.' These berries are edible, but mealy and poor-tasting. In the wild they are eaten by birds, rodents, and bears. The Indians used this plant to buffer the harsh taste of their local tobaccos. The Indian name kinnikinnick means 'that which is mixed.'

ARCTOTIS HYBRIDS, African Daisy. Annual.
Height: 1 foot.
Bloom: red, orange, yellow, white, or purple daisy flowers on stalks, blooms from July to frost (very long season).
Foliage: gray.
Culture: easy.
Likes: half-sun/semidry.
Tolerates: sun/dry/moist.

Propagation: sets.

Comments: besides being a good garden plant, it makes good cut flowers. But, most unusual, the cut flowers close at night and open in the morning.

ARGEMONE POLYANTHEMOS (A. intermedia), Prickly Poppy. Native to dry rocky soil in the Great Plains. Perennial.

Prickly Poppy, Argemone polyanthemos

Height: 2 feet.
Bloom: dramatically large white poppy flowers with showy yellow stamens in the center, blooms from early July to end of August.
Foliage: coarse thistle-like clump, prickly leaves are a silvery blue-green color and covered with a waxy bloom.
Likes: sun/dry/semidry/rocky well-drained soil.
Propagation: sets or seeds.
Comments: established plants resent transplanting. Its cycle is that of a short-lived perennial. The first year, it blooms late in the summer if at all. It blooms best the second year, and may bloom a third year before dying. Because of its prickles and sticky yellow sap, this plant is never eaten by animals.

ARISTOLOCHIA MANSHURIENSIS, Manchurian Dutchman's Pipe. Perennial to Zone 1.
Height: Vine to 15 feet.
Bloom: insignificant flowers.
Foliage: dramatically large leaves.
Likes: moist.
Tolerates: sun/half-sun/semidry.
Propagation: sets or seeds.

Manchurian Dutchman's Pipe, Aristolochia manshuriensis

Comments: beautiful tropical-looking vine.

ARMERIA MARITIMA, Sea Pink, Sea Thrift. Perennial to Zone 3.
Height: 8 inches.
Bloom: vivid pink flowerheads from May to June (long season).
Culture: very easy.
Likes: sun/dry/semidry.
Propagation: sets or seeds. (Seed germination: soak seeds overnight before planting.)
Comments: semi-evergreen grass-like mound. This plant makes an attractive edging for the front of the garden. Additionally, the flowers can be used either fresh or dried. The white variety *'alba'* is especially showy. Another variety 'Dusseldorf Pride' has blood-red flowers.

ARTEMISIA ABROTANUM, Wormwood, Southernwood. Perennial to Zone 1.
Height: 3 feet.
Foliage: green finely-divided foliage.
Culture: easy.
Likes: sun/dry/well-drained poor soil.
Tolerates: half-sun/semidry.
Propagation: sets.
Comments: for most attractive compact form, prune out oldest wood in winter. A low hedge of this plant tends to repel cats and dogs from a garden. Fox Hill Farm lists two exceptional varieties, one with camphor-scented foliage and the other with tangerine-scented foliage.

A. ARBUSCULA. Native to the Rocky Mountains. Perennial.
Height: 1 foot.
Bloom: dramatic yellowish-green flower spikes from June to July.
Foliage: low upright clump of gray foliage.
Likes: sun/half-sun/semidry/moist.
Propagation: sets or seeds.

A. DRACUNCULUS, Tarragon, culinary herb. Perennial to Zone 3.
Height: 2 feet.
Bloom: insignificant white flowers in July.
Foliage: green aromatic foliage.
Culture: easy.
Likes: sun/semidry.
Tolerates: half-sun/dry/poor soil.
Propagation: sets.
Comments: may need winter mulch. The French variety has the most refined flavor but is less hardy than the coarser tasting Russian Tarragon variety.

A. FRIGIDA, Fringed Sage, Woman Sage. Native to a wide area of the Great Plains and northern Rockies. Perennial to Zone 2.
Height: 1 foot.
Bloom: upright bloom stalks from early July to August.
Foliage: fuzzy silvery-blue clump, aromatic foliage.

Wormwood, Artemisia abrotanum

Culture: easy.
Likes: sun.
Tolerates: dry/semidry.
Propagation: sets or seeds.
Comments: for greatest attractiveness, shear off flower stalks after bloom. The Indians had many sacred uses for this plant. The smell of this sage species burning has a haunting, mind-clearing quality you never forget.

A. LACTIFLORA, White Mugwort. Perennial to Zone 3.
Height: 4 feet.
Bloom: showy white flower spikes in August.
Foliage: attractive dark green foliage.
Culture: easy.
Likes: sun/semidry/humus-rich soil.
Tolerates: half-sun/dry/moist.
Propagation: sets.
Comments: invasive by root spreading. The flowers make both good cut flowers and dried everlastings. A hedge of this plant tends to repel dogs and cats from a garden. This plant was introduced from China.

A. LONGIFOLIUM, Longleaf Sagebrush. Native to alkaline areas of the Great Plains. Perennial.
Height: 2 feet.
Bloom: yellow flower spikes from June to July.
Foliage: showy long and narrow silvery-white woolly leaves.
Likes: sun/half-sun/semidry.
Propagation: sets or seeds.
Comments: upright woody clump. This plant is extremely alkaline tolerant.

A. LUDOVICIANA, Cudweed Sage, Man Sage. Native to a wide area of the Great Plains and Rocky Mountains. Perennial to Zone 1.
Height: 5 inches.
Foliage: silvery-white.
Culture: easy.
Likes: sun/dry/semidry.
Tolerates: any well-drained poor soil.
Propagation: sets.
Comments: tends to invade lawns, particularly dry ones. This plant was very sacred to the Indians.

A. PONTICA, Roman Wormwood. Perennial to Zone 4.
Height: 1 foot.
Foliage: very finely-divided gray foliage.
Culture: easy.
Likes: sun/semidry/well-drained soil.
Tolerates: half-sun/dry/moist.
Propagation: sets.
Comments: for most attractive compact form, prune out oldest wood in winter. A low hedge of this plant tends to repel pets from a garden.

A. SCHMIDTIANA 'NANA,' Silvermound. Perennial to Zone 1.
Height: 1 foot.
Bloom: flowers are not showy and are best removed.
Foliage: finely-divided silver-gray foliage.
Culture: easy.
Likes: sun/semidry/poor well-drained soil.
Tolerates: half-sun/dry.
Propagation: sets.
Comments: mound-like clump. A low hedge of this plant tends to repel pets from a garden.

ARUNCUS DIOICUS (A. sylvester), Goat's Beard. Perennial to Zone 2.
Height: 3 feet.
Bloom: showy smoke-like white flower plumes from late June to July (flowers dry up and stay attractive on plant until fall).
Foliage: showy finely-divided.
Likes: half-shade.
Tolerates: half-sun/shade/moist.
Propagation: sets or seeds.
Comments: spreading clump, requires a winter mulch in areas without dependable snowcover. This plant closely resembles the less hardy plant called Astilbe. The variety 'Kneiffii' has improved dark green foliage.

ASPARAGUS, Asparagus officinalis. Perennial vegetable to Zone 1.
Height: 3 feet.
Description: attractive finely-divided foliage.
Culture: easy.
Likes: half-sun/moist/potassium-rich soil.
Tolerates: semidry/mildly alkaline soil, but not heavy clay.
Propagation: plant either roots or seeds. Roots should be spread horizontally like wheel spokes when planting. Plan to give this plant plenty of room. Seeds are easy to start if soaked overnight before planting.
Growing tips: the immature shoots are eaten as a vegetable. To use as a vegetable, do not cut the spears for the first three years after planting to allow the roots to build strength. To do so will damage roots, lowering future harvests. Follow the 2-4-8 rule for harvesting. On the third year after planting, cut stalks for two weeks, the fourth year cut stalks for four weeks, and in following years cut for eight weeks. For vegetable use, remove the female plants that produce red berries and smaller stalks. This way you also eliminate the seedlings that tend to crowd established plants.
Harvest tips: to harvest, cut spears when 6 inches tall (cut off spear an inch underground). Do not harvest spears off a plant for more than 6 weeks.
Comments: plants are either male or female (only female plants produce the showy red berries). Add potassium-rich wood ashes when first planting. Tolerates drought well but prefers cool, moist conditions. Plant only rust-resistant varieties. Weed and mulch the patch carefully the first year.

It was originally named "Sparrow Grass" because small birds would nest in its foliage. This plant is native to central Asia east of the Caspian Sea. Asparagus was grown throughout Eurasia before recorded history. It was popular with the Romans. Introduced to North America by settlers, birds have spread wild plants across the continent. Now it is commonly found everywhere in brushy areas near water.

Asparagus can be eaten either raw or cooked. It can also be preserved by blanching, freezing, canning, or pickling. Asparagus spears pickled with garlic are so tasty, they could become the basis of a cottage industry. However if using asparagus for florist greenery, do the opposite; cut spears repeatedly when partially extended until spindly shoots appear. Asparagus foliage could be a good commercial crop for local growers. Again, female plants with red berries are preferred for arrangements.

It also makes a showy ornamental planted next to a house foundation or the back of a flower bed; female plants with red berries are the showiest.

ASTER SPECIES. In Greek, 'aster' means star.

A. ALPINUS, native Alpine Aster. Perennial to Zone 1.
Height: 10 inches.
Bloom: violet-blue daisy flowers on stalks, blooms from May to June.
Foliage: low basal clump.
Culture: easy.
Likes: half-sun/moist.
Tolerates: sun/half-shade/semidry.
Propagation: sets.
Comments: 'Beechwood' is a refined variety with pinkish-lavender flowers. This plant can also be used as a cut flower.

A. AMELLUS, Italian Aster. Perennial to Zone 3.
Height: 2 feet.
Bloom: profuse pink, white, blue, or purple flowers in August (long season).
Culture: easy.
Likes: half-sun/semidry.
Tolerates: sun/half-shade/moist.
Propagation: sets or seeds. (Seed germination: warm.)
Comments: compact mounded habit. This plant can be used as either a garden plant or as a cut flower. It is showy in pots or containers. For longest season of bloom, use this plant in combination with *Aster novae-angliae* or *A. novae-belgii,* which bloom later.

A. CONSPICUUS, Showy Aster. Native to the foothills and Rocky Mountains. Perennial to Zone 2.
Height: 2 feet.
Bloom: large clusters of purple flowers in August.
Foliage: tends to put out more foliage than flowers.
Likes: sun/half-sun/semidry/moist.

Propagation: sets or seeds.
Comments: this plant is relished by livestock.

A. ERICOIDES, Many-Flowered Aster. Native to grasslands, disturbed areas and lawns. Perennial to Zone 2.
Height: 1 foot.
Bloom: profuse small white flowers from August to frost (long season).
Likes: sun/half-sun/dry/semidry.
Propagation: sets or seeds (tends to self-sow).
Comments: nearly prostrate sprawling habit. This plant would be excellent in an aggressive ground cover mixture.

A. LAEVIS (A. geyeri). Native to the isolated mountains of the Great Plains. Perennial.
Height: 3 feet.
Bloom: attractive soft blue daisy flowers with a yellow center, blooms from July to August.
Foliage: attractive dark green foliage.
Likes: half-sun/dry/semidry.
Propagation: sets or seeds.
Comments: slow-growing clump habit; somewhat invasive through self-sown seeds. This plant is relished by livestock. Claude Barr selected a variety with large powder-blue flowers which he named 'Black Hills.'

A. NOVAE-ANGLIAE, New England Aster, Michaelmas Daisy. Perennial to Zone 3.
Height: 2 feet.
Bloom: deep pink or purple flowers from late August to September (long season).
Culture: easy.
Likes: half-sun/moist.
Tolerates: sun/half-shade/semidry.
Propagation: sets or seeds. (Seed germination: warm.)
Comments: small upright habit. This plant can also be used as a cut flower. This species and the following one are both native to the northeastern forests of North America.

A. NOVAE-BELGII, New York Aster, Michaelmas Daisy. Perennial to Zone 3.
Height: 2 feet.
Bloom: red, pink, white,

Many-Flowered Aster, Aster ericoides

blue, or purple flowers from late August to September (long season).
Culture: easy.
Likes: half-sun/moist.
Tolerates: half-shade/dry/semidry.
Propagation: sets or seeds. (Seed

Michael-mas Daisy, Aster novae-angliae

germination: warm.)
Comments: small upright habit. This plant makes an excellent trouble-free garden plant and can also be used as a cut flower. Two superior varieties are 'Harrington's Pink' with pink flowers, and 'Professor Kippenburg' with near-blue flowers.

A. SCOPULORUM, Rock Aster. Native to dry mid-elevation areas in the Rocky Mountains. Perennial to Zone 2.
Height: 6 inches.
Bloom: profuse light purple flowers borne singly, blooms from end of June to July.
Foliage: rigidly upright clump of woolly gray-green foliage.
Likes: sun/half-sun/dry/semidry.
Propagation: sets or seeds.

A. STENOMERES. Native to medium elevations in the foothills. Perennial to Zone 2.
Height: 1 foot.
Bloom: large light-purple flowers.
Foliage: erect clump.
Likes: sun/half-sun/semidry/moist.
Propagation: sets or seeds.

ASTRAGALUS, Milkvetch; a

very large group of showy prairie and foothill plants. *Astragalus* is closely related to *Oxytropis;* they are separated by their minutely differing flower structures. *Oxytropis* has a pointed beak and *Astragalus* has a rounded beak on the keel of the flower. One other difference between the two is that *Astragalus* has leaves on the flowering stalks and *Oxytropis* does not. For more information, see listing for *Oxytropis*.

Astragalus plants are mostly tap-rooted and can be transplanted only when very young. There are fungal interactions needed by these plants. For best results, you may wish to transplant an intact clump of soil from near an established *Astragalus* or *Oxytropis* to introduce beneficial native fungi into your garden. Seed germination is improved by cold treatment.

A. ABORIGINUM, Indian Milkvetch. Native to hillsides in the Great Plains, foothills and Rocky Mountains. Perennial.
Height: 10 inches.
Bloom: white flowers with purple tips; showy nodding pods on stalks (in late summer and fall).
Foliage: silver-green foliage.
Likes: sun/half-sun/half-shade/semidry/moist.
Propagation: sets or seeds.
Comments: Mr. A. C. Bud states that the long roots were harvested as food by the Indians. The species name *aboriginum* refers to the Indians' usage of this plant.

A. ADSURGENS, Standing Milkvetch. Native to moist grassy areas of the Great Plains and foothills. Perennial.
Height: 1 foot.
Bloom: lavender-blue flowers from early June to mid-July; seedheads on elongated stalks.
Foliage: silvery-green foliage.
Likes: sun.
Tolerates: half-sun/dry/semidry.
Propagation: sets or seeds.

A. AGRESTIS, Purple Field Milkvetch. Native to moist bottomlands of the Great Plains and foothills. Perennial.
Height: 1 foot.
Bloom: dense blue-purple flower heads, smooth green foliage.
Likes: sun/half-sun/moist.
Propagation: sets or seeds.

A. ARETIOIDES, Sweetwater Milk-

vetch. Native to dry hills in the Great Plains. Perennial.
Height: 1 inch.
Bloom: tiny stalkless blue-purple flowers turn yellow with age.
Foliage: moss-like clump of silvery-gray foliage.

Likes: sun.
Tolerates: half-sun/dry/semidry.
Propagation: sets or seeds.
Comments: this plant is rare and should never be dug from the wild.

A. ARGO-PHYLLUS, Silverleaf Milkvetch. Native to moist soil along streams in submontane areas. Perennial.
Height: 4 inches.
Bloom: large stemless blue-purple flowers.

Astragalus

Foliage: tufted clump of showy silvery-gray foliage.
Likes: half-sun/moist.
Propagation: sets or seeds.

A. BARRII, Barr's Milkvetch. Native to hilltops in the Great Plains. Perennial.
Height: 2 inches.
Bloom: stemless pinkish-purple flowers in May.
Foliage: tufted clump of gray-green woolly foliage.
Likes: sun.
Tolerates: half-sun/dry/semidry.
Propagation: sets or seeds.
Comments: this rare native is named for the much beloved South Dakota native plant grower, Claude Barr. It is similar to *Astragalus gilviflorus,* differing mainly by flower color.

A. BISULCATUS, Two-Grooved Milkvetch. Native to bottomlands in the Great Plains and Rocky Mountains. Perennial.
Height: 1½ feet.
Bloom: showy magenta-purple flowers from early June to July.
Foliage: large upright clump of fern-like green foliage which gets weedy-looking in late summer.
Likes: sun/half-sun/semidry/moist.

Propagation: sets or seeds.
Comments: the common name refers to the two grooves on the top side of the seed pod. This species is a selenium accumulator, which makes it poisonous to livestock.

A. CERAMICUS, Painted Milkvetch. Native to sandy areas of the Great Plains. Perennial.
Height: 8 inches.
Bloom: insignificant yellowish flowers; showy red, yellow, and brown mottled seedpods which look as if they were painted.
Foliage: delicate grass-like gray-green foliage.
Likes: sun/sandy soil.
Tolerates: half-sun/dry/semidry.
Propagation: sets or seeds.

A. CRASSICARPUS, Buffalo Ground Plum. Native to Great Plains and foothills. Perennial.
Height: 4 inches.
Bloom: attractive cream-white flowers with a purple center from early June to July (long season); plum-red and green fruit-like seed pods which turn brown and persist through the winter.
Foliage: semi-erect clump of fern-like foliage.
Likes: sun/half-sun/dry/semidry.
Propagation: sets or seeds.
Comments: the name *crassicarpus* means "thick fruit." Indians occasionally made use of this watery and bland-tasting fruit, eating it raw or boiling it.

A. DRUMMONDII, Drummond Milkvetch. Native to sandy clay soils of the Great Plains and foothills. Perennial.
Height: 2 feet.
Bloom: creamy-white flower heads from June to early July.
Foliage: upright clump of smooth green foliage with a woolly underside.
Likes: sun/half-sun/semidry/moist.
Propagation: sets or seeds.

A. GILVIFLORUS (A. triphyllus), Three-leaved Milkvetch. Native to dry rocky slopes and eroded areas in the Great Plains and foothills. Perennial.
Height: 2 inches.
Bloom: stalkless creamy-white flowers from early May to end of May; woolly seedpods on short stalks.
Foliage: tufted moss-like clump of silver-gray foliage.

Likes: sun.
Tolerates: half-sun/dry/semidry.
Propagation: sets or seeds.
Comments: this tends to be a common plant in the Missouri River breaks and dry hillsides in north-central Montana. Claude Barr, a noted plains hor-

Astragalus crassicarpus seedpod

ticulturist, mentioned pink and purple tinged varieties in his book *Jewels of the Great Plains.*

A. GLAREOSUS. Perennial.
Height: 4 inches.
Bloom: blue-purple flowers; fuzzy seedpods.
Foliage: tufted clump of silver-green foliage.
Propagation: sets or seeds.

A. HYALINUS. Native to the Great Plains. Perennial.
Height: 4 inches.
Bloom: insignificant colorless flowers in July.
Foliage: attractive tightly matted clump of silver-white foliage.
Likes: sun/dry/semidry.
Propagation: sets or seeds.
Comments: this is a rare native that should never be dug from the wild.

A. INFLEXUS. Native to the Great Plains as well as river bottomlands in the Rocky Mountains. Perennial.
Height: 1 foot.
Bloom: deep blue-purple flowers.
Foliage: upright clump of gray-green woolly foliage.
Likes: sun/half-sun/semidry/moist.
Propagation: sets or seeds.

A. KENTROPHYTA, Prickly Milkvetch. Native to dry sandy areas of the Great Plains. Perennial.
Height: 3 inches.
Bloom: insignificant small creamy-white flowers with a purplish tinge, flowers bloom on plant tips from mid-June to mid-July.
Foliage: mat-like clump of moss-like foliage with spiny tips.
Likes: sun/sandy soil.
Tolerates: half-sun/dry/semidry.
Propagation: sets or seeds.

A. MICROCYSTIS. Native to sandy areas in the foothills. Perennial.
Height: 8 inches.
Foliage: semi-erect mat-like creeper, silver-gray foliage, woolly seed pods.
Bloom: showy reddish-purple flowers.
Likes: sun/sandy soil.
Tolerates: half-sun/dry/semidry.
Propagation: sets or seeds.
Comments: this plant closely resembles *Oxytropis besseyi*.

A. MISSOURIENSIS, Missouri Milkvetch. Native to eroded hillsides and disturbed areas in the Great Plains; short-lived perennial.
Height: 4 inches.
Bloom: blue-purple flowers on stalks, blooms from late May to mid-June, small gray woolly seedpods.
Foliage: rosette-like clump to 1 foot wide, silky silver-gray foliage.
Likes: sun/half-sun/dry/semidry.
Propagation: sets or seeds; self-sows moderately in favorable locations.

A. PECTINATUS, Narrowleaf Milkvetch. Native to dry sandy soils in Great Plains and foothill areas. Perennial.
Height: 1½ feet.
Bloom: whitish-yellow flowers from May to early June.
Foliage: vigorous upright clump of finely-divided foliage that resembles grass.
Likes: sun.
Tolerates: half-sun/dry/semidry.
Propagation: sets or seeds.

A. PURSHII, Woolly Pod Milkvetch. Native to dry eroded areas of the Great Plains and foothills areas. Perennial.
Height: 2 inches.
Bloom: purple or white flowers; woolly seedpods.
Foliage: clump of showy gray-green woolly foliage.
Likes: sun.
Tolerates: half-sun/dry/semidry.
Propagation: sets or seeds.

A. SPATULATUS, Draba Milkvetch. Native to dry hills in the Great Plains; long-lived perennial.
Height: 3 inches.
Bloom: profuse pink-purple flowers on stalks, blooms from end April to May.
Foliage: cushion-like tuft of silky silver-green foliage.
Likes: sun/half-sun/dry/semidry/

rocky limestone soil with a little added humus.
Propagation: sets or seeds.

A. VEXILLIFLEXUS, Bent-flowered Milkvetch. Native to the foothills and mountains. Perennial.
Height: 10 inches.
Bloom: blue-purple flowers.
Foliage: semi-erect clump of gray-green woolly foliage.
Likes: sun/half-sun/semidry/moist.
Propagation: sets or seeds.
Comments: selections should be made for improved flower color.

ASTRANTIA MAJOR, Masterwort. Perennial to Zone 2.
Height: 2 feet.
Bloom: white star-like papery flowers from June to July.
Foliage: showy delphinium-like.
Likes: half-shade/wet (a bog plant).
Tolerates: half-sun/moist.
Propagation: sets only (seeds are not true to variety).
Comments: prefers cool summer areas or mid-day shade (too much sun results in smaller flowers). There are new varieties with improved pure white flowers—search for these. The older variety called 'Margery Fish' has been propagated by seed and has become a poor quality variety. There is also a murky-red variety called 'Rubra.'

AUBRIETA DELTOIDEA, Purple Rock Cress. Perennial to Zone 3.
Height: 6 inches.
Bloom: profuse pink, white, lavender, or purple flowers from April to May (long season).
Culture: easy.
Likes: half-sun/moist.
Tolerates: half-shade/dry/semidry.
Propagation: sets or seeds. (Seed germination: warm.)
Comments: spreading mound. An excellent cover for the early spring bulbs. This plant is great as a front edging in the garden or planted in a pot or container. Varieties of note are the following: 'Dr. Mules,' an exceptional old variety with rich purple flowers and a good rebloom; 'Joan Allen' with double scarlet-red flowers; 'Maurice Prichard,' a light pink variety; 'Triumphant,' a blue-purple variety considered to be the closest to true blue.

AURINA SAXATILIS (Alyssum saxatile), Basket of Gold. Perennial to Zone 3.

Height: 8 inches.
Bloom: bright sulphur-yellow flowers from early May to early June (reblooms if spent flowers are removed).
Culture: easy.
Likes: sun/semidry (prefers extreme full sun).
Tolerates: half-sun/dry.
Propagation: sets or seeds.
Comments: ragged semi-upright form. Shear back plant after bloom for best appearance. Established plants resent transplanting. 'Citrina' has attractive pale yellow flowers.

BAPTISIA AUSTRALIS, Blue False Indigo. Perennial to Zone 4.
Height: 3 feet.
Bloom: blue-purple lupine-like flowers in June, interesting seed pods (useful in dried arrangements).
Foliage: attractive.
Culture: easy.
Likes: sun/semidry.
Tolerates: half-shade/dry.
Propagation: sets or seeds. (Seed germination: nick seed coat and soak overnight before planting.)
Comments: upright bushy clump. Established plants resent transplanting. This plant can also be used as a cut flower. Removing spent flowers prolongs bloom and increases vigor the following year.

BALSAMORHIZA INCANA, Hoary Balsamroot. Native to exposed grassy areas of the foothills and Rocky Mountains. Perennial.
Height: 4 inches.
Bloom: showy yellow daisy flowers on short stalks in May and June.
Foliage: dramatic basal clump of woolly silvery-green fern-like foliage.
Likes: sun/semidry/moist.
Propagation: sets or seeds.
Comments: established plants resent transplanting.

B. SAGITTATA, Arrowleaf Balsamroot, Vaseline-root. Native to the foothills and Great Plains. Perennial.
Height: 2 foot.
Bloom: yellow sunflower-like blossoms in June.
Foliage: coarse rounded clump of floppy big leaves, dull gray-green foliage which gets messy-looking in late summer.
Likes: sun.

Tolerates: half-sun/dry/semidry.
Propagation: sets or seeds.
Comments: peeled roots are greasy and scented with a strong balsam-like smell. Indians ate the young shoots in the spring. The large tap-roots were baked, the core fibers pounded out and the remaining root eaten. The roots were also burned as incense. The large coarse leaves were used between layers of camas roots when baking in a pit.

BEANS, *Phaseolus* hybrids. There are many types of beans: listed here are pole and bush beans. Listed separately are Faba Beans. Annual vegetable.
Height: pole beans vine to 15 feet tall; bush beans form a clump up to 3 feet tall.
Climbing habit: climbs by twining tips and leaf stems—give pole beans something to climb on.
Bloom: white flowers from June to frost.
Culture: easy.
Likes: sun/moist/humus-rich soil/moderately warm weather/humidity.
Tolerates: half-sun/half-shade/semidry.
Pests: bothered mostly by grasshoppers and Colorado Potato Beetles (watch for small holes in the leaves) and blight disease, which is spread by contact when leaves are wet—thus you should harvest or cultivate around this plant only when vines are dry.
Propagation: sets or seeds. (Seed germination: plant outside at the frost-free date or start inside; seeds start better with warm soil. In cool soil, root rot diseases attack the seeds. Stagger plantings monthly through the spring and summer to prolong harvest. Do not soak seeds overnight before planting because even moisture is critical to their germination.)
Harvest tips: edible green beans best picked young before pod bulges; in peak season, harvest every third day. But harvest dried beans after seeds swell the pod and it dries.
Comments: benefits from legume inoculant in the soil; does not like being root crowded by other plants.

Green beans can be used raw, cooked, and can be preserved either canned, frozen, or best of all, pickled with garlic. Beans pickled with garlic are so tasty they could become the basis of a cottage industry. Preserve beans by canning or freezing after blanching. The best way to cook dried beans is to soak them in a refrigerator for 2 days and then slow cook them for 8 hours.

Beans, Phaseolus

This long preparation produces very tender bean dishes. Onions are added in the last hour to preserve their crisp texture and sweet taste.

Lettuce enjoys the shade under bean vines and is a good companion plant in the garden for beans. Potatoes also make good neighbors. However, beans should not be planted near onions, garlic or chives. Bean vines are an excellent choice for growing in shady areas or under trees. They produce fewer pods in the shade, but still do acceptably well in an otherwise unusable area.

The beans we are familiar with were native to the New World and cultivated by the Indians before the Europeans arrived. Previously, the only beans known in Europe were Cow Peas and Faba Beans. *Phaseolus* is the ancient Latin name for these beans. Today, a majority of the planet's human population survives on a diet that includes either beans or cowpeas.

Originally native to Central America, beans have been cultivated and bred for so many centuries that today thousands of bean varieties exist. One showy variety is 'Royal Burgundy,' which has attractive purple pods that turn green when cooked.

Another useful variety is the Scarlet Runner Bean. Besides producing an abundance of tasty beans, this plant is often grown as an attractive ornamental vine. It is native to the Andes Mountains of South America where it is grown for its tubers as well as its bean pods. Hummingbirds are attracted to Scarlet Runner Bean flowers but don't stay for the nectar.

BEETS, Beta vulgaris. Biennial to Zone 1 (usually grown as an annual).
Height: 1 foot; attractive clump habit, semi-evergreen foliage with red stems, grown primarily for its dark red root.
Culture: easy.
Likes: sun/moist/humus-rich, deeply dug soil/trace minerals such as boron and calcium in its soil.
Tolerates: half-sun/half-shade/moderate alkalinity.
Propagation: seeds. Plant in place from very early spring to early August—stagger planting if you prefer to harvest small tender beets. Soak seed overnight before planting.) Each seed is actually a multiple seed fruit—so you usually have to thin plantings. Now there are a few varieties with monogerm seeds which do not need thinning. Plan to eventually thin beets to 3 inches apart. When planting during hot summer weather, shade the plot and keep it moist until seeds germinate.
Harvest tips: beets can be harvested once they are the size of a quarter.
Comments: requires regular water; tolerates slight shade well. This vegetable can tolerate light frosts but not heavy freezes. Roots can be stored in the ground through the fall if loosened and buried shallowly, but hard freezes ruin them by making them tough. The root dies when its top is cut off, so leave a little bit of stem on, or twist it off leaving the shoulder intact. For best winter storage, store cool and moist in a root cellar.

Beet roots are cooked and eaten fresh, or preserved by canning, freezing, or pickling. Additionally, the foliage can be used fresh as a cooked green, or preserved by either canning or freezing. Beets tend to be rich in iron.

Beet, Beta vulgaris

This plant is actually quite ornamental in the front of a flower bed or in a dramatic formal strip along both sides of a sidewalk. 'Victoria' is an especially showy ornamental variety. 'Golden' is an orange-yellow beet. 'Albino' is a white beet. The name *beta* refers to the second letter of the Greek alphabet. This vegetable was bred during the 16th century.

BEGONIA HYBRIDS. Annual.
Height: 1 foot.
Bloom: attractive red, pink, orange, yellow, or white flowers from June to frost.
Foliage: some varieties are grown for their unusual foliage.
Likes: half-shade/moist/protection from extreme wind.
Tolerates: half-sun/semidry.
Propagation: sets or bulbs.
Comments: prefers to dry out slightly between waterings. The first frost will kill this plant, but it can be potted and brought inside at the end of summer. It is also a good plant for pots or containers.

BERBERIS KOREANA, Korean Barberry. Perennial to Zone 1.
Height: 6 feet.
Shape: attractively rounded wide-spreading shrub (give it lots of room).
Bloom: yellow flower clusters in May; clusters of red berries which hang on bush until the birds eat them in late winter.
Foliage: red fall color.
Culture: easy.
Likes: semidry.
Tolerates: sun/half-sun/dry/moist.
Propagation: sets.
Comments: root suckers some. This spiny shrub makes an excellent barrier plant, but it gets very big. This plant has proven to be immune to the Blackstem Rust Disease, and it can be sold legally in the United States. However, it is illegal to propagate, sell, or transport this species in Canada.

B. THUNBERGII 'ATROPURPUREA,' Purple-leaf Barberry. Perennial to Zone 1.
Height: 3 feet.
Shape: decorative bush with sharp spines; red berries held throughout the winter (fruit is edible, but dry and tasteless).
Foliage: attractive red-purple *foliage* throughout the spring and summer; bright red fall color.
Culture: easy.
Likes: sun/half-sun/semidry/moist.

Begonia

Propagation: sets.
Comments: protect from extreme wind exposure; in severe winters there may be some twig die-back. An excellent combination can be achieved by planting a blue-flowering vine, such as *Clematis macropetala* 'Bluebird' under it. This small spiny shrub makes an excellent barrier plant. Like the Korean Barberry described above, this species is also immune to blackstem rust disease. In the United States it is sold legally, but in Canada it is illegal to sell this plant. Native to Japan, it was introduced to North America in 1864.
'Crimson Pygmy,' a dwarf plant with crimson foliage.
'Dart's Red Lady,' a dwarf plant with nearly black foliage, good red fall color.
'Gold Ring,' red-purple foliage edged with a yellow margin.
'Helmond Pillar,' a striking pillar-like plant, purple foliage.
'Kobold,' a dwarf plant with green foliage, good fall color.

Korean Barberry, Berberis koreana

'Rosy Glow,' foliage starts in spring as rose red and changes to dark maroon.
'Silver Beauty,' green foliage variegated with white and pink.

BERGENIA CORDIFOLIA, Bergenia. Perennial to Zone 1.
Height: 1 foot.
Bloom: pink flowers on a stalk from late April to June.
Foliage: rather large leathery leaves which turn bronzy-purple in the winter.
Culture: very easy.
Likes: half-shade/moist.
Tolerates: half-sun/semidry/poor soil.
Propagation: sets.
Comments: spreading clump. Established plants resent transplanting. *Bergenia crassifolia,* another species, is similar in nearly every way.

BESSEYA WYOMINGENSIS (B. cinerea), Kittentails. Native to dry rocky hillsides of the Great Plains and foothills. Perennial.
Height: 10 inches.
Bloom: unusual-looking woolly pink-purple flower spikes, blooms from end April to mid-May.
Foliage: long-stemmed woolly gray leaves which go dormant and disappear in July.
Likes: sun/dry/semidry.
Propagation: sets or seeds (division after flowering).
Comments: seeds are best planted in the fall. The related species *Besseya rubra* has dull red flowers on a low spike.

BETULA OCCIDENTALIS (B. fontinalis), Water Birch. Native to the Rocky Mountains. Perennial to Zone 2.
Height: 25 feet.
Shape: showy vase-shaped clump with multiple trunks; shiny smooth dark brown bark becomes ruffled with age.
Foliage: light yellow fall color.
Likes: moist/humus-rich soil.
Tolerates: sun/half-sun/semidry.
Propagation: sets or seeds.
Comments: sensitive to alkalinity. Rarely needs pruning, and then only prune in late summer or early fall. If pruned in winter or spring, it can bleed to death. This plant's most notable attribute is its dramatic V-shaped clump.

B. PENDULA 'GRACILIS,' European

Cut-leaf Birch, Weeping Birch. Perennial to Zone 1.
Height: 50 feet.
Shape: weeping tree form.
Foliage: showy in the spring when first leafing out and later in the fall when it turns yellow; the white bark is most spectacular in winter.
Likes: sun/moist/humus-rich soil.
Tolerates: half-sun/semidry.
Propagation: sets (buy only sets with their terminal bud tips intact).
Pests: Birch borer (defoliates the tree in late summer) is a problem in some areas.
Comments: may suffer chlorosis in highly alkaline soil. Prune only in late summer or early fall to remove dead wood and accentuate its weeping form. If pruned in winter or spring, it can bleed to death. It

Weeping birch, Betula pendula

rarely needs any other pruning. Never plant this tree over driveways, streets, or parking spots because it drips sticky sap from its foliage all summer. If the white bark is vandalized or carved, it will show for a long, long time. An interesting commercial use is to make wall hangings and floral displays from birch twigs that have been stripped and twisted together. Dried everlasting flowers are added for color. Outstanding varieties are the following:
  'Aurea,' a yellow foliage variety with marginal hardiness.
  'Fastigiata,' a tall columnar form—ideal for narrow spaces.
  'Golden Cloud,' a vivid yellow foliage variety with marginal hardiness.
  'Trost's Dwarf,' a dramatic-looking 4-foot-tall dwarf whose finely-divided foliage resembles a Japanese Maple.
  'Youngii,' a dwarf tree with a dra-

matically irregular umbrella-like form (it must be staked upright).

  B. PLATYPHYLLA VAR. MANDSCHURICA, Manchurian Birch. Perennial to Zone 2.
Height: 40 feet.
Shape: strong sturdy tree with ruffled brown bark.
Foliage: yellow fall color.
Likes: sun/moist/humus-rich soil.
Tolerates: half-sun/semidry.
Propagation: sets (buy only sets with their terminal bud tip intact).
Comments: may suffer chlorosis in highly alkaline soil. Rarely needs pruning, and then only prune in late summer or early fall or it bleeds to death. This tree is fast gaining popularity because of its resistance to the birch borer.

BLUEBERRY, *Vaccinium* species. Perennial to Zone 3.
Height: 2 feet.
Description: delicate shrub, urn-shaped white flowers in May, delicious blueberries, spectacular scarlet fall color.
Culture: difficult.
Likes: wet/well-drained damp soil such as humus-rich bog covered with several inches of sand (for surface drainage).
Tolerates: sun/half-sun/moist.
Propagation: sets.
Comments: requires an acidic soil—use liberal amounts of peat and composted pine needles (or aluminum sulfate in moderation). Must be winter mulched in exposed areas; blueberries are self-fertile but produce better when two varieties cross-pollinate each other. The varieties 'Northblue,' 'North Country,' and 'Northsky' are the hardiest. The latter variety is dwarf and most suitable for growing in containers.

BOK CHOY, Brassica chinensis. Cool-season annual.
Height: 1 foot.
Description: upright clump habit, primarily grown for its thick fleshy foliage and succulent celery-like stems, bolts quickly into mustard-like yellow flowers on long stalks in moderately warm weather.
Culture: easy.
Likes: sun/half-sun/half-shade/moist/manure.
Tolerates: nitrogen-poor soil.
Propagation: sets (transplants well) or seeds (plant from July through

August for a fall crop—it will tolerate light frost. Spring plantings tend to bolt into flower before harvest).
Pests: flea beetles, root maggots and white cabbage moths.
Growing tips: Achillea, chives, garlic or onions are good companion plants.
Harvest tips: for best flavor harvest before flowering.
Comments: this vegetable (along with spinach) is excellent grown through the winter in a cold frame. In fact, Alberta farmers are discovering this is a profitable use for an unheated greenhouse. The main advantage of winter cultivation is the lack of insect pests, as well as a profitable crop during a normally slow season. Take care not to overwater if grown in cold soil during the winter.
  Both the leaves and stem are used in stir-fry cooking; the raw leaves have a mild mustard-like flavor that is tasty in salads and sandwiches. An exceptional variety, 'Mei Qing Choi,' is noted for its tenderness.

BOLTONIA ASTEROIDES, Prairie Aster. Native to the eastern plains and northern parklands. Perennial to Zone 2.
Height: 3 feet.
Bloom: white or lilac flower clusters from late July to August (long season).
Likes: sun/semidry.
Tolerates: half-sun/dry/moist.
Propagation: sets or seeds.
Comments: 'Snowbank' is a very tall and showy variety which starts blooming in late August. This variety's stems are stronger and more wind tolerant than the species form.

BORAGO OFFICINALIS, Borage, Beeplant. Culinary herb. Annual.
Height: 2 feet.
Bloom: true blue star-like flowers on pinkish stems from June to frost (very long season).
Foliage: unusual fuzzy foliage.
Culture: easy.
Likes: half-sun/moist.
Tolerates: sun/half-shade/semidry.
Propagation: sets or seeds. (Seed germination: dark, warm.)
Comments: established plants resent being transplanted. Leaves and flowers are eaten for their cucumber-like flavor. They are a rich

source of potassium. Flowers can be candied, frozen in ice cubes, or floated as a garnish in a punch-bowl. *Girad's Herbal* written in the 16th century states that borage is 'used everywhere for the comfort of the heart, for driving away sorrow, and increasing the joy of the mind.' Flowers attract honeybees. Native to the Mediterranean area.

BOUTELOUA CURTIPENDULA, Sideoats Grama Grass. Native to the northern Great Plains. Perennial to Zone 3.
Height: 2 feet.
Foliage: tufted bunch habit of nodding oat-like seeds held only on one side of the stalk; grassheads are attractive from mid-summer to the end of winter, plant is light red color in fall and winter.
Culture: easy.
Likes: sun.
Tolerates: half-sun/dry/semidry.
Propagation: sets or seeds; clump spreads but is not invasive.
Comments: this grass grows in the spring and fall but goes dormant during the heat of mid-summer.

B. GRACILIS, Blue Grama Grass. Native to the northern Great Plains. Perennial.
Height: 10 inches.
Foliage: ground-hugging mat of foliage; dense sod-forming clump; attractive reddish-purple comb-like seedheads held at an angle to the stem; seedheads are held from mid-June through winter.

Borage, Borago officinalis

Likes: sun/half-sun/very dry/semidry.
Propagation: sets or seeds.
Comments: growth occurs in May to July, then the plant goes dormant in the dry summer months. This delicate and attractive grass was one of the dominant species of the Short Grass Prairie. It is impossible to confuse the comb-like seedheads of this grass with any others. In a native garden, this grass fills in and protects the soil between other plants.

BRASSICA OLERACEA, Ornamental Kale. Annual.
Height: 1 foot.
Foliage: rosy-pink, white, green, or purple multicolored foliage; some varieties have a lacy texture.
Likes: half-sun/moist.
Tolerates: sun/half-shade/semidry.
Propagation: sets or seeds.
Comments: this plant is excellent for planting in mid-summer for color during the late summer and early winter (usually up to Christmas). It is showiest when grown as an accent plant in either the garden or in a pot or container. Additionally, it is edible and can be used as an edible garnish. This kale was bred to be ornamental. See also the Kale listing.

BROCCOLI, Brassica oleracea, botrytis group. Cool-season annual.
Height: 2 feet.
Description: clump habit; primarily grown for its edible flower clusters; attractive blue-green foliage which can tolerate heavy frosts.
Likes: moist/humus-rich soil/manure.
Tolerates: sun/half-sun/half-shade/semidry.
Propagation: sets (transplants well) or seeds. Broccoli sets started inside can be planted in a cold frame in January, or without a cold frame in April; they will tolerate harsh cold if protected by snow. These early plants have the advantage of beating the onslaught of the white cabbage moth. Seeds can be started early inside as sets a couple weeks before outdoor planting or planted in the ground several weeks before the frost-free date. For a fall harvest, plant in late June or July.
Pests: flea beetles, root maggots, and white cabbage moth.
Bacterial spore disease must be applied early. The best and most difficult solution is to cover the entire broccoli clump with shear gauze curtains. Cover immediately when sets are put in the garden, and cover the curtain edges with soil to keep bugs out. Water and sun penetrates the curtains well, but flea beetles and white cabbage moth cannot.
Growing tips: shallow rooted (avoid disturbing soil under plants); prefers to be closely packed together with

other broccoli plants in a clump (this conserves water and protects the soil from compression); tolerates slight shade well; rotating broccoli crops to different soil each year reduces pest problems; prefers to be slightly crowded, but not shaded.

Companion-plant with wasp-attracting flowers of the carrot family nearby (carrots, chervil, coriander, dill, fennel or lovage); other companion plants are onions, garlic, chives, leeks, or *achillea*.
Harvest tips: because it tolerates heavy frosts, it can be harvested into early winter. Harvest first flower stalk with 4 inches of stem, second flower stalk with 2 inches of stem, and then use the profuse small side shoots the rest of the season.
Comments: use broccoli either fresh or cooked. It can be preserved by freezing. An outstanding and showy variety is 'Romanesco,' which has unusual light green flowerheads. 'Violet Queen' is a showy rose-purple variety. It is purple when raw and changes to green when cooked.

Broccoli was originally bred in Denmark. Because of its attractive blue-green foliage, some gardeners enjoy growing broccoli in their flower beds just for its beauty.

BRIZA MAJOR, Quaking Grass. Annual.
Height: 18 inches.
Bloom: nodding grassheads (they resemble hop flowers), blooms in July.
Likes: sun.
Tolerates: half-sun/semidry/moist/poor soil.
Propagation: Seeds.
Comments: this plant can be used either as an attractive garden plant, as a cut flower, or dried as an everlasting. Cut before heads open fully and dry them quickly. It has commercial potential for selling to florists. There are three species of *Briza: Briza major, B. media,* and *B. minor.* The main difference between them is size.

BRODIAEA GRANDIFLORA. Native to the southern and central Rocky Mountains. Perennial.
Height: 1 foot.
Bloom: rich dark blue flowers on stalks.

Foliage: grass-like.
Propagation: bulbs.
Comments: prefers to dry out in late summer. This bulb is edible, but it closely resembles the deadly poisonous Death Camas *(Zygadenus)* when out of bloom.

BROMUS BRIZIFORMIS, Brome Grass. Annual.
Height: 1 foot.
Bloom: graceful delicate nodding grassheads from July to August.
Likes: sun/half-sun/semidry/moist.
Propagation: Seeds.
Comments: clump habit. This plant has larger grassheads than *Briza* (Quaking Grass) and is a more refined and shapely plant. This plant can used either as an attractive garden plant, as a cut flower, or dried as an everlasting. Cut before heads open fully and dry them quickly. This plant is a showier garden subject in overall plant form than *Briza.*

BROWALLIA AMERICANA, Browallia, Blue Stars. Annual.
Height: 1 foot.
Bloom: showy star-like blue-purple flowers, blooms from June to frost.
Likes: half-shade.
Tolerates: half-sun/shade/moist.
Propagation: sets or seeds. (Seed germination: light. Seeds are easy but slow requiring 3 weeks to germinate.)
Comments: this elfin-like shade plant should be more commonly used as a garden plant, as well as in pots and containers. In addition, it makes a good cut flower. It is very attractive in combination with *Impatiens*

Brodiaea grandiflora

and *Lobelia,* but give *Browallia* extra room in the planting because it is less aggressive than the other two plants. In the fall, plants can be potted (with fertilizer) and brought inside to bloom in the winter. An exceptional variety is 'Sapphire,' which has blue flowers and a white eye.

BRUSSELS SPROUTS, Brassica oleracea, gemmifera group. Cool-season annual which requires a long growing season.
Height: 3 feet.
Description: large upright plant grown for its tasty buds produced on the stalk.
Likes: sun/half-sun/half-shade/moist/humus-rich soil/manure.
Propagation: start seeds either indoors (it transplants well) or plant seeds in place outdoors several weeks before the frost-free date.
Pests: flea beetles, root maggots, and white cabbage moth; rotate crops to new soil each year to reduce insect pests. You can companion plant wasp-attracting flowers of the carrot family (carrot, chervil, coriander, dill, fennel, or lovage) to reduce pest problems.
Growing tips: hot summer areas of Zones 3 and 4 should only attempt fall crops; plant in mid-summer and give it mid-day shade. In cool summer areas, plant in staggered intervals in the spring and harvest throughout the summer and fall.

Good companion plants are *achillea,* onions, garlic, or chives.

Remove lower leaves early in the season to encourage a tall stalk; in late August or early September, remove the tip of the stalk to encourage plant to form sprouts. Do this when lowest sprouts are 1 inch across.

Prefers mid-day shade in hot summer areas; shallow rooted (avoid disturbing soil near plant). This is a large plant; give it lots of room.
Harvest tips: they are most tender when harvested small, but flavor is sweetest after light frosts. Buds can be harvested in the fall and early winter. This plant tolerates heavy frost.
Comments: this plant was once a major crop grown near Brussels, Belgium, and thus acquired its common name. The head-like sprouts are cooked and seasoned with butter or a white sauce. They can be preserved by blanching and freezing.

BRUNNERA MACROPHYLLA, Siberian Forget-me-not. Perennial to Zone 3.

Brussels Sprouts, Brassica oleracea

Height: 1 foot.
Bloom: blue flowers from May to June (long season).
Foliage: bold heart-shaped foliage (use it in the background so you can hide it when it dies down in late summer).
Likes: half-sun/moist.
Tolerates: half-shade/wet.
Propagation: sets or seeds.
Comments: may need light winter mulch in exposed areas. The English have bred three distinctively different white variegated forms of this plant. The commonly available variety *'variegata'* is the least valuable and the most difficult to grow. Preferred choices are 'Haden's Cream,' which has exceptional creamy-white mottled foliage, and 'Lantrees,' with its green foliage distinctively marked with metallic silver spots.

BUCHLOE DACTYLOIDES, native Buffalo Grass. Perennial to Zone 2.
Height: 6 inches.
Culture: easy.
Likes: sun/dry/semidry.
Propagation: sets or seeds; best germination if seed is commercially treated.
Comments: running rhizomes form a thick sod; it is very useful for a drought-tolerant lawn; can be mowed to a height of 3 inches. Its main disadvantage to most gardeners is its determined preference to turn brown in late summer. Best watered deeply once in July and twice in August. Water heavily to keep it green. This grass is at its northern limit in Montana. Rarely is it found in Alberta. Its common

name refers to the fact that buffalo relished this forage above all others. Oddly enough, male and female flowers exist on separate plants.

BULBOCODIUM VERNUM, Pink Crocus. Perennial to Zone 2.
Height: 6 inches.
Bloom: pink crocus-like flowers in April.
Culture: easy.
Likes: half-sun/moist/well-drained soil.
Tolerates: sun/half-shade/semidry.
Propagation: bulbs.
Comments: this pink flowering crocus is a real surprise in the early spring garden.

BUPLEURUM AMERICANUM, Thorough-wax. Native to rocky areas of the Rocky Mountains. Perennial.
Height: 10 inches.
Bloom: unusual-looking yellowish-orange flowers in dense clusters.
Foliage: upright clump.
Propagation: seeds.
Likes: sun/half-sun/semidry/moist.
Comments: tap-rooted established plants resent transplanting. This plant is fairly rare and should never be disturbed in the wild.

BUXUS MICROPHYLLA KOREANA, Korean Boxwood. Perennial to Zone 3.
Height: 1 foot.
Shape: shrub.
Foliage: evergreen broadleaf.
Culture: difficult.
Likes: half-sun/moist.
Tolerates: sun/half-shade/semidry.
Propagation: sets (softwood cuttings or soft-hardwood cuttings in spring, summer or fall).
Comments: must be watered carefully in the late summer and fall—not enough water and it will suddenly die from drought, but too much water will force tender new growth. Requires careful protection from winter sun and winter wind (either plant it in a protected location or cover it with evergreen branches during the winter). This is one of the very few broad-leafed evergreen plants that survive in our area. Even with careful winter protection, there may be some dieback of the branches; therefore, it is recommended that you prune it informally so that occasional gaps do not show. Its natural form is a showy, soft, billowy shape. Buy this

plant only from a reputable local source, preferably as far north as possible. This plant is native to Korea. It was introduced to North America in 1919. The variety 'Wintergreen' is a newer variety.

CABBAGE, Brassica oleracea, capitata group. Cool-season annual vegetable.
Height: 2 feet.
Description: large rounded clump of either blue-green, green, or red-purple leaves.
Likes: humus-rich soil/moist/manure and fertilizer.
Tolerates: half-sun/half-shade/heavy clay soil.
Propagation: sets (transplants well) or start seeds in place outdoors several weeks before the frost-free date for a summer crop, or in early June for a fall crop.
Pests: flea beetles and root maggots, but white cabbage moths are the worst. Companion plant liberally with *achillea,* garlic, onions or chives and use bacterial spore disease early to kill young moth larva. Additionally, the wasp-attracting flowers of the carrot family (carrots, chervil, coriander, dill, fennel, or lovage) can reduce pest problems. As a final solution, read about the gauze curtain method mentioned in the Broccoli section.
Growing tips: prefers midday shade in hot summer areas; shallow rooted (avoid disturbing soil near plant); must be rotated to new soil each year. Has heavy water requirements. Watering is critical; must have even moist conditions or the heads will split.
Harvest tips: harvest when the head is firm to the touch. When the head is nearly ready, some gardeners push a spade in the ground on one side of the plant to cut off a part of the roots. This eliminates the chance of the head splitting from getting too much water.
Comments: tolerates heavy frost well. This plant requires 70-120 days (depending on variety) to form a head. Many gardeners plant cabbage in their flower beds as a bold accent plant, the Savoy and Red varieties are especially showy. For best appearance, crowd cabbage with other plants.

This plant was developed in northern Europe three centuries ago. A similar plant which thrives during the hot summer weather is Collards, also called Non-heading Cabbage.

CABBAGE, CHINESE, Brassica rapa, pekinensis group. Cool season annual vegetable.
Height: 1 foot.
Description: upright clump of deeply ruffled leaves.
Likes: half-sun/half-shade/semidry/moist/humus-rich soil without excessive nitrogen.
Propagation: sets or seeds (start seeds either indoors or plant in place in the garden a month before the frost-free date).

Cabbage, Brassica oleracea

Pests: flea beetles, root maggots, and white cabbage moth. Companion plant with *achillea,* chives, garlic, onions or carrot family flowers (to draw predatory wasps) or use the gauze curtain method described in the Broccoli section.
Comments: in hot weather, this plant bolts a flowerstalk quickly and turns bitter. Because seeds tolerate cool soil and light frost, it can be grown either in the early spring (put out hardened-off sets in mid-April); or for an early fall crop, plant in mid-summer. It is also a prime candidate for winter cultivation in cold frames.

This plant seems like a cross between bok choy and cabbage. Its mildly flavored leaves are more tender and easily digested than cabbage. For an even softer texture, Chinese cabbage can be briefly dipped in boiling water and rechilled. This vegetable is used primarily in stir-fry cooking and Korean kim chee, but it is also excellent in salads and sandwiches. It stores well if cool and dry.

CALAMAGROSTIS CANADENSIS, Bluejoint, Marsh Reed Grass. Native to

moist grasslands and marshes of the plains and foothills north to the sub-arctic. Perennial.
Height: 4 feet.
Bloom: attractive plumy seed head appears in mid-July, then at the first frost seedheads turn a showy, tawny-brown color.
Likes: sun/half-sun/moist/wet (a bog plant).
Propagation: sets or seeds.
Comments: creeping clump habit, roots are somewhat invasive but plant in general is not aggressive. The new growth of this grass is relished by wildlife and livestock. This long-lived plant has been known to live as long as 100 years. It tolerates petroleum spills and has been used for reclaiming such areas in Alaska. A related ornamental grass is *Calamagrostis arundinacea* 'Karl Forrester,' which forms a showy narrow clump and attractive seedheads.

CALENDULA OFFICINALIS, Calendula, Pot Marigold. Annual.
Height: 1 foot.
Bloom: orange or yellow flowers from May-October (long season).
Culture: easy.
Likes: half-sun/moist/humus-rich soil.
Propagation: sets or seeds. (Seed germination: dark, warm.) Seeds can also be planted in the fall.
Comments: prefers cool summers and lots of water. Besides being used in the garden, this flower can be planted in pots or containers, or used as a fresh cut flower. Additionally, *Calendula* petals can be used to dye food a saffron-yellow color. The variety 'Apricot Sherbet' is more heat tolerant than other varieties.

Pot Marigold, Calendula officinalis

CALLIRHOE INVOLUCRATA, Purple Mallow. Native to sandy areas of the central Great Plains. Perennial to Zone 4.
Height: 6 inches by 24 inches wide.
Bloom: very fragrant, showy, purple poppy-like flowers with yellow stamens, blooms from May to July (longer if given water in late summer).
Foliage: sprawling mound of attractive finely-divided foliage, edible parsnip-like roots.
Likes: semidry.
Tolerates: sun/half-sun/dry/moist.
Propagation: sets, roots or seeds.
Comments: besides the large edible roots, the leaves can be used to thicken soups. The name *callirhoe* comes from "kallirrhoos" meaning "beautiful flowering."

CALLISTEPHUS CHINENSIS, China Aster. Annual.
Height: 1 foot.
Bloom: red, pink, white, blue, or purple flowers from late July-November (long season if seed planting is staggered).
Culture: easy.
Likes: sun/moist.
Tolerates: half-sun/semidry.
Propagation: sets or seeds.

China Aster, Callistephus chinesis

Comments: tall varieties need to be windstaked with a brush-type support. Do not plant this flower in the same place year after year because the soil becomes infected with Aster Yellows disease. Fortunately, this disease does not affect any plants other than *Callistephus*. This flower is excellent in the garden, in pots, or as a cut flower. The name *callistephus* means 'beautiful crown' in Greek and refers to the shape of the flowers.

CALOCHORTUS GUNNISONI, Prairie Mariposa Lily, Sego Lily, official state flower of Utah. Native to the foothills and Rocky Mountains. Perennial.
Height: 1 foot.
Bloom: creamy-white flowers with purple markings in the center, blooms in mid-June.
Foliage: scattered clump habit; grass-like foliage.
Likes: sun/half-sun/dry/semidry.
Propagation: bulbs.
Comments: named the state flower of Utah because early Mormon settlers survived the first hard years at Salt Lake by eating these sweet edible bulbs. Indians roasted and dried the bulbs, then ground them to make bread. The seeds were eaten also. Unfortunately when out of bloom, this plant closely resembles the deadly poisonous Death Camas. The name *Calochortus* means "beautiful grass" in Greek. Other species, *C. apiculatus, C. elegan, C. macrocarpus* and *C. nuttalii,* are found in northwest Montana and in wide areas of the Great Basin.

CAMASSIA CUSICKII, Camas. Native to a wide area of the Rocky Mountains and east to the Cascades. Perennial to Zone 4.
Height: 3 feet.
Bloom: blue star-like flowers on a stalk, blooms from end May to June.
Foliage: grass-like.
Likes: sun/half-sun/moist/wet (a bog plant).
Propagation: bulbs; self-sows in a favorable location.
Comments: Indians harvested the bulbs when the lowest flowers on the stalk started to form seeds in June. They lined a pit with layers of camas, separated by layers of leaves. On top, a slow fire was maintained for three days to cook the bulbs. Properly cooked bulbs turn black and stay preserved for a couple of years. Kim Williams tried cooking bulbs for a couple of hours in

Camas, Camassia cusickii

an oven. She said they were gummy and bland. She thought the longer cooking method of the Indians would convert more of the starch to sugar. The deadly poisonous Death Camas (*Zygadenus elegans*) is completely identical, except that it has white flowers and white seeds.

CAMPANULA SPECIES, Bellflower; all prefer well-drained soil, bright sun exposure, cool roots and careful mulching. *Campanula* means 'bell-like' in Latin and refers to the flower shape.

C. CARPATICA, Carpathian Bell-flower. Perennial to Zone 2.

*Carpathian Bellflower,
Campanula carpatica*

Height: 8 inches.
Bloom: white or lavender-blue flowers from July to August (long season if spent flowers are removed).
Culture: easy.
Likes: half-sun/semidry.
Tolerates: half-shade/dry/moist.
Propagation: sets.
Comments: low spreading clump. This plant is useful for the front of the garden. Three varieties of note are 'Chewton Joy,' which has a late, but long bloom season; 'Isobel,' which has dark blue flowers; and 'Nana,' which is a compact dwarf variety.

C. COCHLEARIFOLIA, Moss Campanula. Perennial to Zone 2.
Height: 2 inches.
Bloom: extremely profuse sky-blue flowers from early to mid-June.
Likes: half-sun/moist.
Tolerates: half-shade/semidry.
Propagation: sets or seeds.
Comments: moss-like creeper. May need winter mulch in exposed locations. The variety 'Oakington Blue' has large dark blue flowers. There are also white varieties.

C. GLOMERATA, Clustered Bell-flower. Perennial to Zone 1.
Height: 3 feet.
Bloom: clump habit, blue, white, or purple flower spikes from June to July.
Culture: easy.

Likes: sun/semidry.
Tolerates: half-sun/half-shade/dry/moist.
Propagation: sets or seeds.
Comments: 'Crown of Snow' is an attractive white variety.

C. MEDIUM, Canterbury Bells. Biennial to Zone 3 with winter protection.
Height: 3 feet.
Bloom: dramatic pink, white or blue flower stalks in July.
Foliage: basal clump of coarse hairy foliage.
Likes: sun/moist/humus-rich soil.
Tolerates: half-sun/wet.
Propagation: sets.
Comments: requires careful winter mulch.

C. PERSICIFOLIA, Peachleaf Bell-flower. Perennial to Zone 3.
Height: 2 feet.
Bloom: airy clusters of blue or white flowers on stalks, blooms from late June to July.
Foliage: attractive peachleaf-like.
Culture: easy.
Likes: half-sun/moist/rich soil.
Tolerates: half-shade/semidry.
Propagation: sets.
Comments: the variety 'Pride of Exmouth' has exceptional light blue flowers.

C. PORTENSCHLAGIANA (C. muralis). Perennial to Zone 4.
Height: 6 inches.
Bloom: blue-purple flowers from May to June.
Foliage: shiny low mound.
Culture: difficult.
Likes: half-shade/semidry.
Tolerates: half-sun/moist.
Propagation: sets or seeds.
Comments: low spreading clump, spectacular rock garden plant, requires good drainage. This plant is most successful if grown in crevices in a wall or in a rock garden.

C. PYRAMIDALIS, Chimney Bell-flower. Perennial to Zone 4.
Height: 4 feet.
Bloom: dramatic large white or lavender-purple flower stalks from late July to frost.
Foliage: basal clump.
Culture: easy.
Likes: sun/moist.
Tolerates: half-sun.
Propagation: sets or seeds.
Comments: flower stalks need windstaking. May need winter

mulch in exposed areas. This dramatic stalk of flowers rises to 4 feet tall and blooms for months. It is best used in the back of a flower bed.

C. ROTUNDIFOLIA, Harebell, Blue-bell of Scotland. Native throughout the Northern Temperate Zone. Perennial to Zone 1.
Height: 8 inches.
Bloom: delicate nodding blue flowers on stalks, blooms from late June to July (shear back after bloom for a rebloom).
Culture: very easy.
Likes: sun/semidry.
Tolerates: half-sun/very dry/moist.
Propagation: sets or seeds. Self-sows in favorable location.
Comments: low clump habit. This plant loves to self-sow into the cracks of a rock wall.

*Harebell,
Campanula
rotundifolia*

CAMPSIS RADICANS, Scarlet Trumpet Vine. Perennial to Zone 4-5.
Height: dense vine to 25 feet.
Bloom: orange-scarlet trumpet flowers from August to September.
Climbing habit: climbs by self-clinging rootlets, but needs a strong support in windy areas.
Likes: sun/semidry/humus-rich soil.
Tolerates: half-sun/dry/moist.
Propagation: sets.
Comments: may occasionally winterkill and regrow from roots. Needs its top pruned back when it becomes too heavy. Flowers attract hummingbirds.

CARAGANA ARBORESCENS, Siberian Pea-Shrub. Perennial to Zone 1.
Height: 12 feet.
Bloom: insignificant yellow flowers in May.
Shape: thorny shrub.
Likes: sun/half-sun/dry/semidry.
Propagation: sets or seeds.
Comments: prune out oldest wood after bloom. This plant was originally collected in the Altai Mountains of Russia. This spiny plant is excellent as a barrier planting or as a hedge. Seeds are edible and can be eaten cooked like cowpeas; howev-

er, some people are allergic to them. Chickens also relish these seeds.

Varieties of note:

'Lorbergi,' Fernleaf Pea-shrub; height 7 feet. Has showy finely-divided foliage. This variety closely resembles a tamarix in texture and form.

'Pendula' is a weeping form. It can be grown on a standard such as 'Sutherland' or used as a ground cover.

'Plume' has showy fine textured foliage on semi-pendulous branches.

'Sutherland,' height 16 feet with narrow columnar form. It was introduced in 1945 by Sutherland Forest Nursery Station, Sutherland, Saskatchewan.

'Walker' is a fine textured weeping form, which can be grafted onto a tree standard or used as a ground cover.

C. FRUTEX 'GLOBOSA,' Globe Pea-Shrub. Perennial to Zone 1.
Height: 4 feet.
Shape: compact rounded form, branches are spineless.
Foliage: apple-green foliage throughout the summer.
Culture: easy.
Likes: sun/half-sun/dry/semidry.
Propagation: sets or seeds.
Comments: root suckers some. This plant was introduced by Dr. Frank Skinner, Dropmore, Manitoba, in 1949. It makes a good hedge.

C. MAXIMOWICZIANA. Perennial to Zone 1.
Height: 3 feet.
Bloom: yellow flowers in May.
Shape: densely branched spreading habit.
Culture: easy.
Likes: sun/half-sun/dry/semidry.
Propagation: sets or seeds.

C. MICROPHYLLA, Little Leaf Pea-Shrub. Perennial to Zone 1.
Height: 6 feet.
Shape: attractive rounded clump.
Culture: easy.
Likes: sun/half-sun/dry/semidry.
Propagation: sets or seeds.

C. PYGMAEA, Pygmy Caragana. Perennial to Zone 1.
Height: 4 feet.
Shape: slender arching form.
Foliage: tiny foliage, thorny branches.

Culture: easy.
Likes: sun/half-sun/dry/semidry.
Propagation: sets or seeds.
Comments: does not root sucker. This plant makes an excellent clipped border for a formal garden with the advantage of being an effective windbreak. The related species *Caragana aurantiaca* is similar but has a more upright shape, which makes it particularly good for hedges.

CARROT, Daucus carota. Biennial vegetable usually grown as an annual.

Carrot, Daucus carota

Description: upright clump of showy finely-divided foliage grown primarily for its sweet orange root; the second year's growth produces showy white flowers on 3-foot stalks.
Likes: sun/moist/deeply dug, humus-rich soil.
Tolerates: half-sun/half-shade/semidry.
Propagation: seeds. (Planting can be staggered from late April to late summer if you like a constant supply of young carrots). Germinating carrot seeds is a science of its own. In general, always use fresh seed and plant it shallowly.

Seeds can be planted in either the fall or spring. When planting in the fall, plant after frosts start, use extra seed, and do not water at planting time. Fall planting has proved successful as far north as central Alberta.

For spring and summer plantings,

cover a freshly planted carrot patch with gunny bags for two weeks, then remove them. Give it frequent light waterings to maintain a moist soil surface; this is critical during germination. The gunny bags slow the weed seeds giving the slow-germinating carrots an advantage and protecting important surface moisture.

Another method is to start seeds in a rolled up moist paper towel. When roots start to show in several days, then plant the seeds outside in moist soil. This should be started 2-4 weeks before the frost-free date.
Pests: companion plant with onion family plants to avoid root maggots.
Growing tips: it is very important to thin the patch in late spring once the tiny plants have three leaves.
Harvest tips: harvest carrots from mid-summer on. Because they tolerate light frost well and grow late into the fall, carrots can be harvested into the fall and early winter. Before the ground freezes, loosen the carrot bed and cover thickly with straw. Thus prepared, carrots can be harvested throughout the late fall and early winter. Though freezing dramatically increases carrots' sugar content, a hard winter freeze ruins their texture for eating. Root cellars that are cool and moist are the best method for storing carrots through the winter. Always leave a bit of the green growth tip on roots or else twist off the top. After this tip is removed, the carrot and its natural flavor dies. That is why store-bought carrots often taste so foul. The living tip has been removed and they are dead.

Carrot Flower

Comments: in general, carrots have heavy water requirements; and tolerate slight shade well. Carrots can be eaten raw or cooked, or preserved by either freezing, canning, or pickling.

Varieties of note are 'Scarlet Nantes' and 'Touchon,' both bred for their excellent flavor and sweetness. The variety 'Royal Chantenay' has excellent flavor and stores particularly well.

Many gardeners grow second-year carrot flowers both as an ornamental flower and to attract predatory wasps and other beneficial insect life. Watching the life on these tall refreshment stands is quite a thrill. Carrot flowers are also appealing for their old-fashioned appearance in a garden. These flowers are very easy to start by simply planting carrot roots into a garden—they will bloom the same year.

Originally, carrots were bred in northern Europe during the 13th century from Queen Anne's Lace *(Daucus carota)*. Queen Anne's Lace spread to North America and became a common introduced weed.

CARUM CARVI, Caraway, culinary herb. Biennial to Zone 3.
Height: 2 feet.
Bloom: white flower clusters from late June to July.
Foliage: finely-divided, semi-evergreen in winter.
Culture: easy.
Likes sun/heat.
Tolerates: half-sun/semidry/moist.
Propagation: seeds.
Comments: upright clump, prefers a low nitrogen soil. Because it is tap-rooted, it is best seeded into place or transplanted carefully when young in either fall or early spring. Seeds are used to flavor rye bread, cheese, or cakes. Young shoots are used as salad herb, or as a seasoning in meat or vegetable dishes. Native to Asia Mi-

Caraway, Carum carvi

nor. The name caraway comes from its Arabic name *'karaawya.'*

CATALPA SPECIOSA, Catalpa. Perennial to Zone 4-5 (protected areas only).
Height: 30 feet.
Bloom: showy large clusters of white flowers in early July; long bean-like seedpods.
Shape: narrowly upright tree.

Catalpa speciosa

Foliage: large distinctive leaves.
Likes: sun/moist/humus-rich soil.
Tolerates: half-sun/semidry.
Propagation: sets or seeds.
Comments: sensitive to alkalinity.

CAULIFLOWER, Brassica oleracea, botrytis group. Cool-season annual vegetable.
Height: 2 feet.
Description: rounded leafy clump, grown for its edible flowerheads.
Likes sun/half-sun/half-shade/moist/humus-rich soil/manure.
Tolerates: slight shade.
Propagation: sets (transplants well and tolerates light frost) or seeds (because it tolerates cool soil, start first planting several weeks before frost-free date and stagger plantings up to early June).
Pests: flea beetle, root maggot, white cabbage moth. Strategies include bacterial spore disease (apply it very early), companion planting with *achillea,* chives, garlic, onions or carrot family flowers (to attract predatory wasps) or most effective—use the gauze curtain method described in the Broccoli section.
Growing tips: shallow rooted (avoid disturbing soil near plant); prefers evenly moist soil; must be moved to new soil each year; prefers mid-day shade in hot summer areas. Prefers to be slightly crowded, but not shaded. This plant is very finicky about its conditions in hot summer areas. It takes a lot of room and produces little crop.

When the head starts forming, lower leaves must be tied together (or clothespinned) up around the head to blanch it. Head rots quickly if leaves are tied too tightly.
Harvest tips: harvest about a week

after tying, when head is firm. When overripe, heads become uneven or ricey. There are new self-blanching varieties that do not require tying.
Comments: tolerates a light frost but not a heavy freeze. This vegetable is eaten either raw or cooked. It is often served with a butter or cheese sauce. Cauliflower can be preserved by freezing or else stored in a cool, moist root cellar. Most people who have eaten store-bought cauliflower have no idea what a delightful flavor and aroma this vegetable has when harvested fresh from a garden.

Some gardeners enjoy growing this showy plant as an ornamental in their flower beds. The bold textured foliage and ornamental colors have much appeal amongst flowers.

CELASTRUS SCANDENS, Bittersweet. Native to eastern North America. Perennial to Zone 2.
Height: vine to 20 feet.
Bloom: a somewhat wild-looking vine with scarlet-orange berries from early fall through the winter.
Climbing habit: climbs by twining vine tip—needs wire or lattice to climb.
Culture: easy.
Likes: sun/moist/humus-rich soil.
Tolerates: half-sun/semidry.
Propagation: sets or seeds.
Comments: you must have both male and female plants to produce fruit—plant 3 or 4 plants and eliminate all but one male (identified by its lack of fruit). Showy fruit can be used in winter flower arrangements. Its common name "bittersweet" refers to the season of early fall when the seedpods open.

CELERIAC, CELERY ROOT, Apium graveolens var. rapaceum. Annual vegetable.
Height: 2 feet.
Description: upright clump of celery-like foliage, large thickened root used for its celery-like flavor in soups and salads.
Likes: half-sun/moist/humus-rich soil/regular fertilizing during the summer.
Tolerates: sun/half-shade/heavy soil if well drained.
Propagation: sets only. This vegetable requires a long season and must be started very early indoors in Fe-

buary. Because it tolerates light frost, sets can be put out in late April if hardened off.

Pests: celery worm, which is the larva of the swallowtail butterfly.

Growing tips: prefers mid-day shade in hot summer areas. For best bulb-root growth, remove side shoots and withered lower leaves.

Harvest tips: several weeks before harvest, dig down to expose the top half of the bulb and break off the fine roots by hand. Then re-bury the whole bulb carefully under soil to blanch it.

Comments: this vegetable is easier to grow and requires less space than celery. Stalks and foliage are strong tasting but can be used sparingly in place of celery. This vegetable is particularly tasty in potato salad and mashed potatoes. Steam it until cooked before cutting or mashing it. It can also be used raw in salads or pickled.

CELERY, Apium graveolens. Cool season annual vegetable.

*Celery,
Apium
graveolens*

Height: 1½ feet.

Description: upright clump of celery foliage.

Likes: half-sun/evenly moist, humus-rich soil/manure and trace minerals (magnesium and calcium both help prevent diseases).

Tolerates: half-sun/half-shade.

Propagation: sets or seeds. (Seed is slow to germinate. Start seed indoors in Febuary. Seed must be fresh and soil must be cool for best germination; soak it overnight before planting).

Pests: celery worm, the larva of the swallowtail butterfly. It is important to clean up dead foliage carefully after harvesting plant; this eliminates many insect pests.

Growing tips: prefers mid-day shade in hot summer areas; give it frequent light waterings; prefers to be crowded with other celery plants (this increases moisture and eliminates soil compaction for this shallow rooted plant). Sets will bolt to flower if frosted when first put outside, so wait until frost-free date to put outside.

This vegetable is easier to grow in evenly cool and moist areas. But it bolts if soil is too cold or wet. Plant tolerates light frost, but not heavy freezes in the fall.

Harvest tips: older varieties require being blanched by soil mounding for best taste and texture. Two other methods of blanching are either using milk cartons or crowding plants close together. Newer varieties have a less bitter taste and can be grown without blanching. Harvest whenever stalks are large enough for use. However, a light frost improves sweetness.

Comments: the plant as we know it was bred during the 15th century. In its native conditions, it is a swamp plant. Besides using the celery stalks, the leaves are rich in vitamins and flavor. Store it cool and moist. Many people dry the leaves and seeds for use as a seasoning.

CELOSIA CRISTATA, Cockscomb Celosia. Annual.

Height: 1-2 feet.

Bloom: velvety red, orange, yellow, or purple flower clusters that resemble a rooster's comb, blooms from June to frost (long season).

Culture: easy.

Likes: sun/heat/semidry.

Tolerates: half-sun/dry/moist/poor soil.

Propagation: sets or seeds. (Seed germination: warm.) Blooms moderately quickly from seed.

Comments: multi-branched upright clump. In the garden, this flower is most attractive when mass planted by itself. Also it makes an excellent pot or container plant. Additionally, taller varieties can be used either as fresh cut flowers or dried everlastings. There are tall growing varieties and dwarf compact varieties.

C. PLUMOSA, Plumed Celosia. Annual.

Height: 2-3 feet.

Bloom: red, orange, yellow, or pink plume-like flower clusters, blooms from June to frost (long season).

Culture: easy.

Likes: sun/heat/semidry.

Tolerates: half-sun/dry/moist/poor soil.

Propagation: sets or seeds. (Seed germination: warm. Blooms moderately quickly from seed.)

Comments: spike-like upright habit. In the garden, this plant combines spectacularly well with most other flowers. It also makes an excellent pot or container plant. Taller varieties can be used as either fresh cut flowers or dried everlastings.

CELTIS OCCIDENTALIS, Hackberry. Native to eastern North America. Perennial to Zone 2.

Height: 50 feet.

Shape: unattractive shrubby tree in youth, eventually maturing into a bland-looking tall tree, no other ornamental features.

Likes: sun.

Tolerates: half-sun/dry/semidry/moist/alkaline soil.

Propagation: sets or seeds.

Comments: for greatest attractiveness prune to remove shrubby lower branches.

CELTUCE, Lactuca sativa var. asparagina. Cool-season annual vegetable.

Height: 10 inches.

Description: an upright clump which resembles leaf lettuce; leaves and stems have a unique taste similar to both cucumber and zucchini.

Likes: half-sun/evenly moist, humus-rich soil.

Tolerates: sun/half-shade.

Propagation: sets or seed. (Seed germination: seed must be fresh for best germination.) Because seed tolerates cool soil, plant outside in mid- to late April.

Growing tips: this plant prefers evenly cool and moist areas and mid-day shade in hot summer areas; does not like to be crowded (give it as much space as head lettuce).

Harvest tips: the flowering stalk is used like celery (but peel off the bitter skin first). Harvest stalk when it is one inch thick—it gets bitter when flowering starts. Young leaves are used in salads.

Comments: introduced in 1938 from western China.

CENTAUREA CYANUS, Bachelor's Buttons, Cornflower. Annual.
Height: 2 feet.
Bloom: pink, white, or blue flowers from late May to frost (long season if seed planting is staggered and spent flowers are removed).
Culture: easy.
Likes: sun/semidry.
Tolerates: half-sun/half-shade/very dry.
Propagation: sets or seeds. (Seed germination: dark. Can be planted in early spring long before the frost-free date.)
Comments: solitary plant habit. Besides being used in the garden, this plant makes good cut flowers. It was decreed by Kaiser Wilhelm I as the Floral Emblem of the German Imperial Family. The story says that when Napoleon invaded Berlin, Kaiser Wilhelm I's mother hid her family in a cornfield and made garlands for her children from this flower.

C. DEALBATA, Persian Centaurea. Perennial to Zone 3.
Height: 2 feet.
Bloom: reddish-purple flowers from late June to August (long season).
Culture: easy.
Likes: sun/moist.
Tolerates: half-sun/semidry.
Propagation: sets or seeds. (Seed germination: dark, warm.)
Comments: rounded mound. 'Steenbergii' has showier flowers than the species, and gray-green foliage.

C. MONTANA, Mountain Bluet. Perennial to Zone 1.
Height: 1 foot.
Bloom: deep true-blue flowers from late May to June (long season if spent flowers are removed).
Culture: easy.
Likes: sun/semidry.
Tolerates: half-sun/half-shade/dry/moist.
Propagation: sets or seeds.
Comments: sprawling clump habit, may need winter mulch in extremely exposed areas.

C. MACROCEPHALA. Perennial to Zone 1 (with winter protection).
Height: 4 feet.
Bloom: sparse yellow powderpuff-like flowers from July to frost.
Foliage: bushy clump of coarse foliage.
Likes: sun/semidry.

Tolerates: half-sun/moist.
Propagation: sets or seeds.
Comments: this flower makes good cut flowers and dried everlastings, but it is not a particularly showy garden plant.

C. MOSCHATA, Sweet Sultan. Annual.
Height: 2 feet.
Bloom: fragrant yellow powderpuff-like flowers (very regal-looking) from July to August (long season).
Foliage: finely-divided foliage.
Likes: sun/moist/humus-rich soil.
Tolerates: half-sun/semidry.
Propagation: sets or seeds.
Comments: this makes a good cut flower, as well as an attractive garden plant.

CERASTIUM TOMENTOSUM, Snow in Summer. Perennial to Zone 1.
Height: 6 inches.
Bloom: white flowers from late May to June.
Foliage: semi-evergreen silver foliage.
Culture: easy.
Likes: sun/moist.
Tolerates: half-sun/very dry/semidry.
Propagation: sets or seeds.
Comments: fast-spreading mat, invasive due to stem rooting.

CERATOIDES LANATA (Eurotia lanata), Winterfat. Native to dry hillsides of the Great Plains and foothills. Perennial.

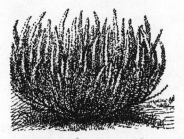
Winterfat, Ceratoides lanata

Height: 1 foot.
Bloom: insignificant flowers.
Foliage: irregular bushy clump of showy blue-gray woolly foliage in both summer and winter.
Likes: sun.
Tolerates: half-sun/dry/semidry.
Propagation: sets or seeds (young plants transplant easily.)
Comments: this accent plant is particularly showy throughout the winter and can be considered a low

maintenance plant. Every couple of years (when the plant gets leggy), cut it to the ground for best appearance. In winter, it contains a high protein content and thus provides excellent browse for livestock and wild animals. The Indians made tea from the leaves. The name *lanata* means "woolly."

CERCOCARPUS LEDIFOLIUS, Curl-leaf Mountain Mahogany. Native to the central Rocky Mountains and Great Basin area. Perennial to Zone 3.
Height: 4 feet.
Shape: irregularly shaped shrub.
Foliage: evergreen gray-green foliage (winter interest); unusual-looking fuzzy seeds.
Likes: sun/semidry.
Tolerates: very dry/poor soil/exposed locations.

Cercocarpus ledifolius

Propagation: sets or seed.
Comments: established plants resent transplanting. This plant is included because of its evergreen foliage. It should be selected and bred for improved winter foliage color. The wood of this plant burns intensely hot. Indians used the wood for making tools and war clubs, and the inner bark for a purple dye. It was described by Thomas Nuttall in southern Idaho in 1838.

CHAMAEMELUM NOBILE (Anthemis nobilis), Roman Chamomile. Perennial to Zone 3.
Height: 6 inches.
Bloom: small white daisies with yellow centers, blooms from July to Aug.
Foliage: finely-divided, aromatic.
Culture: easy.
Likes: sun/moist/humus-rich soil.
Tolerates: half-sun/dry/semidry.
Propagation: sets or seeds.
Comments: low-growing clump. This herb make a soothing and healing herbal tea. Use 3-5 flower heads and let it steep 15 minutes (a long time). Used as a rinse, Chamomile brings out gold highlights in blond and brown hair. As an aromatic herbal lawn, this plant tolerates considerable foot traffic.

'Fleuro plena' has double flowers; 'Treneague' is a non-flowering spreading variety with a compact habit used as a ground cover.

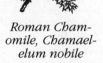

Roman Chamomile, Chamaelelum nobile

CHEILANTHES GRACILLIMA, Rock Fern. Native to dry rocky areas in the foothills and Rocky Mountains, perennial to Zone 3.
Height: 6 inches.
Foliage: dainty-looking (but tough) evergreen fern.
Culture: difficult.
Likes: half-sun/dry/semidry (never wet)/rock garden soil.
Propagation: buy sets—never transplant wild plants.
Comments: the related species *Cheilanthes feei* is a subalpine species occurring only in limestone cliffs. It is difficult to grow but is especially showy.

CHICKPEA, *Cicer arietinum.* Warm season annual vegetable.
Height: 2 feet.
Description: squat bushy plant with bean-like seedpods.
Likes: sun/moist well-drained soil.
Propagation: sets or seeds (plant outside after frost-free date).
Comments: requires a hot summer season to ripen seed pods. Native to China, and cultivated before recorded history.

CHIONODOXA SPECIES, Glory-of-the-Snow.

C. LUCILLIAE. Perennial to Zone 2.
Height: 4 inches.
Bloom: lavender-blue star-like flowers with a white eye, blooms from mid- to late April.
Foliage: grass-like.
Culture: easy.
Likes: sun/half-sun/semidry.
Propagation: bulbs (bury 3 inches deep) or seeds.
Comments: there are occasionally pink or white variations. An outstanding horticultural variety is *'Gigantea,'* which has large flowers and a vigorous habit. Native to Crete and Asia Minor.

C. SARDENSIS. Perennial to Zone 2.
Height: 4 inches.
Bloom: intense gentian blue star-like flowers with a white eye, blooms from mid- to late April (same time as early tulips).
Foliage: grass-like.
Culture: easy.
Likes: sun/half-sun/semidry.
Propagation: bulbs (bury 3 inches deep) or seeds.
Comments: this species is less available than *Chionodoxa lucilliae,* but its rich blue color is far more spectacular. Native to Crete and Asia Minor.

CHRYSANTHEMUM CARINATUM (C. segetum), Annual Chrysanthemum, Crown Daisy, Garland Chrysanthemum. Annual.
Height: 2 feet.
Bloom: showy daisy-like flowers, a color range of red, orange, yellow, white, or maroon, flowers have a red or yellow band and a dark brown center, blooms from July to frost (very long season).
Foliage: finely-divided.
Culture: easy.
Likes: sun/semidry.
Tolerates: half-sun/moist.
Propagation: sets or seeds.
Comments: mound habit. This makes both a good garden flower and an excellent cut flower. It can also be grown in either pots or containers.

C. CINERARIFOLIUM, Dalmatian Pyrethrum. Perennial to Zone 2.
Height: 1 foot.
Bloom: white or pink daisy flowers from June to August, silvery foliage.
Likes: sun/semidry/humus-rich soil.
Tolerates: half-sun/moist.
Propagation: sets or seeds.
Comments: This flower's petals are used to make the insecticide called Pyrethrum.

C. COCCINE-UM, Pyrethrum Daisy, Painted Daisy. Perennial to Zone 3.
Height: 2 feet.
Bloom: vivid red, pink or white daisy flowers from late June to July (long season if spent

Painted Daisy, Chrysanthemum coccineum

flowers removed).
Foliage: finely-divided.
Culture: easy.
Likes: sun/moist/humus-rich soil.
Tolerates: half-sun/semidry.
Propagation: sets only (seedlings do not come true to color).
Comments: this flower was once the mainstay of the European florist industry. It makes a good garden plant, with the advantage of also being an excellent long-lasting cut flower.

C. CORONARIUM, Shungiku, Edible Chrysanthemum. See listing under Chrysanthemum, Edible.

C. FRUTESCENS, Marguerite, Paris Daisy. Annual.
Height: 2 feet.
Bloom: pink, yellow or white daisies from June to frost (very long season).
Foliage: finely-divided foliage.
Culture: easy.
Likes: half-sun/moist/humus and fertilizer-rich soil.
Tolerates: sun/semidry.
Propagation: sets.
Comments: this plant is best displayed as an accent plant in a pot or container, though it can be used throughout the garden as well.

C. LEUCANTHEMUM, Common Ox-eye Daisy. Perennial to Zone 1.
Height: 1 foot.
Bloom: white daisy flowers with yellow center, blooms from mid-May to late June.
Foliage: scalloped leaves.
Likes: sun/half-shade/dry/moist.
Comments: very invasive; low spreading mound habit. This plant is a noxious weed that spread from Asia to Europe, then from the Eastern Seaboard of North America across to the West Coast. Do not buy any wildflower mix containing this plant. On the other hand, this cheerful and showy flower already exists in nearly every lawn and can be allowed to bloom briefly, then mowed down before it makes seeds. The trick is to cut the lawn the first time in the spring a couple weeks later than usual. By then the low clumps of scalloped foliage and emerging flowerheads are clearly visible and can be avoided when mowing. After flowering, mow down the daisies before they start dispersing seeds. The name *leucan-*

themum means 'white flower.'

C. X MORIFOLIUM, Garden Chrysanthemum. Perennial to Zone 3.
Height: 2 feet.
Bloom: flowers in all colors except blue and black; the hardiest varieties are the single, double (called decorative), and pompon forms; flowers bloom from August to September (long season with mixed early to late varieties). Choose varieties which bloom no later than mid-September to avoid frost damage to buds.
Likes: half-sun/moist/humus and fertilizer-rich soil.
Tolerates: sun/semidry.
Propagation: sets (easily propagated by cuttings).
Comments: requires winter mulch in exposed areas. For best flowering, plants should be divided and replanted in new soil every two years; windstake with brush support. Plants should be pinched at three intervals (late May, late June and mid-July) to promote best flowering and most compact form, but pinch no later than mid- to late July. The Morden varieties are the hardiest. For the longest lasting cut flowers, cut just as flowers openand crush stem ends. In Japan,this flow-

Garden Chrysanthemum, Chrysanthemum x morifolium

er was allowed to be cultivated only by the emperor and nobility. There is a National Chrysanthemum Society in the U.S. and a Canadian Chrysanthemum Society. Their addresses are listed in the Resource Directory. Chrysanthemums make excellent cut flowers, as well as good garden flowers.

C. PARTHENIUM, Feverfew. Perennial to Zone 3.
Height: 2 feet.
Bloom: clusters of small white daisy-like flowers from July to frost (long season).
Foliage: attractive bright green foliage

(semi-evergreen in winter).
Culture: easy.
Likes: half-sun/semidry.
Tolerates: sun/moist.
Propagation: sets or seeds. (Seed germination: light, warm.)
Comments: this plant was very popular in Victorian times. A row of it makes a showy formal edging along a walkway. Additionally, it makes a good cut flower.

C. X SUPERBUM (C. maximum), Shasta Daisy. Perennial to Zone 3.
Height: 2 feet.
Bloom: white daisy with a yellow center, blooms from July to September (very long season if spent flowers are removed).
Foliage: basal clump of shiny dark green foliage.
Culture: easy.
Likes: sun/moist.
Tolerates: half-sun/wet/heavy soil.
Propagation: sets or seeds. (Seed germination: light.)
Comments: one of the many flowers nominated for U.S. National Flower. Best divided often. This garden plant also makes a good cut flower. 'King Edward VII' and 'Sedgewick' are the hardiest varieties. The Shasta Daisy was originally created by Luther Burbank, but his one hundred different flower forms and colors including blue, pink, and orange varieties have been lost. The one Burbank variety that survives is the white variety 'Chiffon.' *Shasta* is an Indian word meaning 'white.'

CHRYSANTHEMUM, EDIBLE, Shungiku Chrysanthemum, C. coronarium. Annual.
Height: 2 feet.
Description: attractive yellow daisies in June to September (very long season), peppery-tasting leaves are used in oriental cooking and salads. Its primary use is in Oriental stir-fry.
Culture: easy.
Likes: sun/half-sun/

Edible Chrysanthemum, Chrysanthemum coronarium

moist/humus and fertilizer-rich soil.
Propagation: sets or seeds. Seeds tolerate cool soil; plant outside in mid- to late April.
Comments: not only can you use leaves in salads and cooking, but you can enjoy its showy yellow daisy flowers as an ornamental accent in your garden. Furthermore, this plant makes long-lasting cut flowers for arrangements.

CHRYSOPSIS VILLOSA (Heterotheca villosa), Golden Aster. Native to dry sandy hillsides of the Great Plains and foothills. Perennial to Zone 2.
Height: 1 foot.
Bloom: showy yellow aster-like flowers from mid-July to frost.
Foliage: coarse semi-erect clump of gray-green foliage, coarsely hairy stiff stems.
Likes: sun/half-sun/dry/semidry/moist.
Propagation: sets or seeds. (Seed germination: cold treatment.)

Golden Aster, Chrysopsis villosa

Comments: regular water and pinching the tips in early summer will cause later and more profuse flowering. This plant is better known in Europe than in North America, where it is native. Its name *chrysopsis* means "gold-like," referring to the flower color, and *villosa* means "softly hairy," referring to the foliage texture.

CHRYSOTHAMNUS NAUSEOSUS, Rubber Rabbit Bush, Golden Sagebrush, native to dry, poor-soil areas of the Great Plains and foothills. Perennial to Zone 2.
Height: 2 feet.
Bloom: bright yellow flowers from August to September.
Likes: sun/dry.
Tolerates: half-sun/semidry/poor soil.
Propagation: sets or seeds.
Comments: upright loose clump. With age this plant resembles the twisted and gnarled form of sagebrush, *Artemisia tridentata*. The name *chrysothamnus* means 'gold-

en bush' and the name *nauseosus* means 'heavy scented,' referring to the taste of the foliage. The common name refers to the fact that this plant's white juice contains natural rubber. Even so, it is used for winter forage by antelope, deer, elk, and rabbits.

CIMICIFUGA RACEMOSA, Black Cohosh, Snakeroot. Perennial to Zone 2.
Height: 6 feet.
Bloom: narrow white flower spikes from July to early August.
Foliage: attractive finely-divided foliage.
Likes: half-sun/moist/humus-rich soil.
Tolerates: half-shade/wet.
Propagation: sets or seeds.
Comments: low clump; may require winter mulch in exposed areas; established plants resent transplanting. The variety *'Atropurpurea'* has strikingly beautiful bronzy-purple foliage. The root of this plant is a commercial herb which deadens pain and causes a heavy drowsiness. Pioneers used it to treat rattlesnake bite, and thus its common name snakeroot.

C. SIMPLEX 'WHITE PEARL,' Kamchatcha Bugbane. Perennial to Zone 2.
Height: 3 feet.
Bloom: very showy white flowers which resemble arched bottle brushes from July to early August.
Likes: half-sun/moist/humus-rich soil.
Tolerates: half-shade/wet.
Propagation: sets or seeds.
Comments: may require winter mulch in exposed areas; established plants resent transplanting.

CLAYTONIA LANCEOLATA, Spring Beauty, Groundnut, Fairy Spud. Native to damp areas on the edges of forest in the foothills and Rocky Mountains. Perennial.
Height: 4 inches.
Bloom: delicate light pink flowers with deep pink lines, blooms from end April to end May.
Foliage: spreading clump habit of thick succulent foliage; closely resembles heart-shaped Miner's Lettuce (a closely related plant).
Likes: sun/half-sun/half-shade/semidry/moist.
Propagation: bulbs.
Comments: plant goes dormant and

disappears in mid-summer. The edible bulb of this plant was an important foodstuff for the Indians.

CLEMATIS SPECIES. Every house or garden should have at least one clematis. In a preferred location, this vine (which belongs to the *Ranunculaceae* or Buttercup Family) is exceptionally easy to grow.
Likes: sun/moist.
Climbing habit: clematis attach themselves by twisting the leaf stalk (petiole) around any object that is small enough. Give it a support such as small tree branches, shrubs, a latticework, or chicken wire around a tree. In the smaller herbaceous types, the climbing habit is absent.
Propagation: seeds, or softwood or semi-hardwood cuttings in summer. (Seed germination: cold.)
Comments: most varieties prefer an eastern or northern exposure, with optimal growth in full sun and cool roots (best achieved by overplanting with a ground cover, or mulched with grass clippings, old manure, or stone mulch). Mix different varieties for longest bloom season, especially the large-flowering types. Some varieties require several years to become established and produce full bloom. In severe climates, the large-flowering clematis may be successfully grown by planting near the warm basement of a house, and providing plenty of mulch as winter protection.

Clematis are divided into small-flowering and large-flowering classes. To assist the gardener in culture and pruning techniques, all listed clematis are assigned one of the following type classifications.

Type One: These clematis provide clusters of flowers from May to June on stems produced the previous season. Basic pruning requirements are the following: First year of planting, cut back all stems to 1 foot in early spring. Second year, in early spring cut back all stems to 3 feet. Third and subsequent years, cut out any weak or dead stems after flowering; or if the plant gets out of hand, prune back hard to 2-3 feet above ground directly after flowering or in early spring.

Type Two: These produce their flowers on the old or previous season's stems. A single flower is borne

on each stem; flowering usually starts before the end of June on old wood, and again on current season's stems in July and August. Basic pruning requirements: First year, cut back all stems to 1 foot in early spring. Second year, cut back all stems to 3 feet in early spring. Third and subsequent years, cut back all stems to a strong pair of buds in early spring and tie the stems onto their support. One should not leave all stems the same length; variation in length will give a well balanced flowering plant.

Type Three: These clematis produce flowers on new stems each year, usually from July on, with several flowers to each stem. The previous season's top growth often becomes useless and dies away naturally each winter. This growth must be removed to allow the current season's stems room to grow to maturity. Basic pruning requirements: First year, in early spring cut back all stems to 1 foot (or near ground level in severe climates). Second and subsequent years, reduce all stems to just above the base of the previous season's growth above soil level (or near ground level in severe climates).

SMALL-FLOWERING CLEMATIS

C. AETHUSIFOLI. Native to Mongolia and Manchuria. Perennial to Zone 1.
Height: vine to 6 feet.
Bloom: yellow bell-shaped, nodding solitary flowers.
Foliage: finely-divided foliage, a rather elegant and pretty plant.
Likes: half-sun.
Tolerates: sun/half-shade/semidry/moist (water well in hot weather).
Propagation: seeds, cuttings, layering.
Pruning requirements: Type 3.
Comments: dies to the ground in severe climates. Rare in cultivation.

C. ALPINA, Alpine Virgin's Bower; native in the Alps from southeastern France to Austria, the Apennines of northern Italy, and the Carpathian and Northern Balkan mountains from Czechoslovakia to northwestern Bulgaria. Perennial to Zone 1.
Height: vine to 10 feet.
Bloom: single nodding, four-sepaled, violet-blue flowers from late May to June on old wood, and

again with less profuse bloom in August, followed by silky, fluffy seed heads.

Foliage: leaflets, evenly and rather finely toothed.

Likes: sun/half-sun/half-shade/semidry/-moist.

Pruning requirements: Type 1.

Propagation: seeds, cuttings, layering.

Comments: cool north exposure is ideal; water well in hot weather; prefers shelter from drying winter winds; best grown on a tree, shrub, fence, or a trellis.

The variety *sibirica* (once considered a separate species) has white flowers and more coarsely and irregularly toothed foliage. It is distinguished by its narrower, tapered sepals and is native from northern Norway and Finland to eastern Siberia, and south to the Ural Mountains, the Tien-Shan Mountains, and Manchuria.

Another variety, *ochotensis,* has broader, blunter flowers than the species form. It is native from Korea and central Honshu, Japan, north to eastern Siberia, Sakhalin, and Kamtchatka. Some notable cultivars of *Clematis alpina* are 'Pamela Jackman' with deep azure-blue flowers; 'Ruby' with soft purplish-red flowers; and 'Columbine' with long pointed lavender-blue flowers.

C. 'BETTY CORNING' (a hybrid of *C. crispa* and *C. viticella).* Perennial to Zone 1.

Height: vigorous vine to 10 feet

Bloom: profuse fragrant violet-blue, bell-shaped blooms from June to late September.

Likes: sun/half-sun/half-shade/semidry/moist.

Pruning requirements: Type 3 (prune to ground level in severe climates, less so in milder areas).

Propagation: cuttings, layering, or division.

Comments: water well in hot weather. This variety is thought to be the first hybrid clematis introduction of American origin; apparently a naturally occurring hybrid found by Mrs. Betty Corning II (for whom the hybrid is named) growing in a garden in Albany, New York in 1932. She perpetuated it in her own and other gardens for years, until it finally found its way into commerce.

C. COLUMBIANA, Rocky Mountain Clematis. Native to the northern Rocky Mountains. Perennial to Zone 1.

Height: sprawling vine to 3-6 feet.

Climbing habit: prefers to climb on trees, shrubs, or a trellis.

Bloom: delicate four-sepaled, nodding violet-blue flowers from late May to June, occasional flowers are produced through August.

Likes: half-sun/half-shade/semidry/moist.

Rocky Mountain Clematis, Clematis columbiana

Pruning requirements: Type 1 (except for the dwarf forms of *tenuiloba,* which may not require pruning at all).

Propagation: seeds or cuttings.

Comments: rare in commerce. An interesting novelty form *tenuiloba* has aerial stem portions consisting of small dense tufts less than an inch high, with occasional plants elongating to 3 feet. This plant offers tremendous potential for hybridization and selection of new horticultural varieties. Grows in more exposed, drier habitats; native to the northern Rockies and isolated mountain ranges and hills east of the Rockies in Montana and the Dakotas.

C. GLAUCA, Perennial to Zone 1.

Height: slender stemmed vine to 10 feet.

Bloom: orange-yellow flowers, up to 2 inches across, on slender stalks from late July to September.

Climbing habit: prefers to climb over rocks, along walls, or on trellises in fairly exposed garden sites.

Foliage: divided blue-green leaflets.

Likes: sun/half-sun/semidry/moist.

Pruning requirements: Type 3 for severe climates, or prune to thin in early spring for milder areas.

Propagation: seeds, suckers, or layering.

Comments: rare in commerce. The variety *akebioides* has orange-yellow and purple flowers, blooms somewhat earlier, and is followed by silvery seed heads. This is a lovely garden plant. Native to Western China and Siberia.

C. HERACLEIFOLIA (C. tubulosa), Perennial to Zone 1.

Height: sprawling semi-shrub to 10 feet long.

Bloom: fragrant tubular blue flowers in short dense clusters, blooms from August to September, rather coarse trilobed leaves.

Climbing habit: needs support to climb.

Likes: half-sun/half-shade/semidry/moist.

Propagation: seeds (hybrids will produce variable seedlings), cuttings, layering, and root division.

Pruning requirements: Type 3. Prune to the ground in fall or winter.

Comments: improved varieties are *davidiana,* which has deep indigo-blue flowers and a taller growing habit, and 'Wyevale,' which has larger and darker blue flowers. Hybrids of note are 'Jouiniana,' a vigorous climber to 12 feet with white to lavender-blue flowers from August to September; and 'Mrs. Robert Brydon,' another vigorous climber with pale blue flowers. These plants are best seen cascading over something, covering tree stumps or garden eye-sores. Native to northern China and Mongolia.

C. HIRSUTISSIMA, Vase Flower, Sugar Bowls; native in the Dakotas, Montana, Washington, and southern British Columbia. Perennial to Zone 1.

Height: 2 feet.

Bloom: showy violet-blue to purple bell-shaped flowers, blooms from May to June.

Foliage: upright clump of hairy finely-divided foliage which goes dormant and disappears in late summer.

Likes: half-sun/well-drained, humus-rich, sandy, loam soil.

Tolerates: sun/half-shade/semidry.

Propagation: sets or seeds (division in summer when dormant).
Pruning requirements: prune to the ground in late summer or fall.
Comments: prefers to dry out when dormant in late summer. Rare in commerce. The name *hirsutissima* means "the hairiest," and refers to the woolly hairs on the stems and flowers. This plant is a spectacular native on which breeding work needs to be done to develop horticultural varieties more tolerant of garden conditions. The variety *scottii* has mauve to pink blooms.

C. INTEGRIFOLIA, Solitary Clematis. Perennial to Zone 1.
Height: 2 feet.
Bloom: single, nodding, bell-shaped, indigo-blue flowers with a velvety texture, blooms from June to August.
Climbing habit: prefers to grow on small shrubs for support, be tied to a low trellis, or allowed to sprawl amongst low-growing flowering perennials.
Likes: sun/half-sun/half-shade/semi-dry/moist.
Pruning requirements: Type 3.
Propagation: seeds, cuttings or division.
Comments: native to southern Europe. The semi-woody stems die to the ground each winter, regrowing each spring from the hardy roots. A white form *alba* and a pink form *rosea* are occasionally seen in cultivation. Improved hybrids of this species are 'Blueboy' from the cross *C. integrifolia x C. viticella,* a selection bred by Dr. Frank Skinner of Dropmore, Manitoba. It grows to 8 feet, producing an abundance of flat, outward-facing, bluish-violet flowers which measure two inches across, blooming in mid-summer on new wood for well over two months. Two other hybrids from a similar cross, which both bloom July to September, are *Hendersoni,* which has large violet-blue flowers and grows to 6 feet; and *Eriostemon,* which has deep blue flowers and grows to 6 feet. Another hybrid *Durandii,* from the cross *C. integrifolia x C. x jackmanii,* climbs to well over 6 feet and has dark violet-blue flowers borne freely from June to September. All of these hybrids die back in the winter and have the same pruning requirements as the species.

C. KOREANA, Korean Clematis. Perennial to Zone 1.
Climbing habit: a sprawling woody vine that can be trained to climb.
Bloom: single nodding bell-shaped flowers, reddish to dull violet (clear yellow in variety *lutea),* from June into the summer.
Likes: sun/half-sun/half-shade/semi-dry/moist.
Propagation: seeds, cuttings, layering.
Pruning requirements: Type 3.
Comments: water well in hot weather. Native to northern Korea and Manchuria.

C. LIGUSTICIFOLIA, Traveler's Joy, Western White Clematis. Native to western North America. Perennial to Zone 1.
Height: vigorous climber to 35 feet or more.
Bloom: fragrant clusters of small star-like flowers from July to August.
Likes: semidry.
Tolerates: sun/half-sun/dry.
Pruning requirements: Type 3.
Propagation: seeds, cuttings, layering.
Comments: This species seems aggressive and weedy when used in home landscaping, so locate it where it will not become a problem (i.e., use it to cover up eyesores in your yard, or let it grow into trees or on trellises attached to electrical poles, etc.). An improved variety is 'Prairie Traveler's Joy,' bred a cross of *C. ligusticifolia x C. virginiana* and superior to both parents. It is a more restrained and floriferous vine with larger flower clusters and a heavy dark green foliage. It was bred in 1962 by Dr. Frank Skinner. The Indians used this native plant's stem fibers for making snares and carrying-nets.

C. MACROPETALA, Downy Clematis. Perennial to Zone 1.
Height: showy woody vine to over 10 feet.
Bloom: nodding flowers are typically violet-blue, occasionally pinkish-violet or white, the flowers are "double," made up of a double row of pointed sepals with an inner ring of petal-like staminodia in the center, usually blooms from late May to June on old wood, and again less profusely in August on new wood, followed by interesting fuzzy seedheads in the fall.
Climbing habit: best displayed when trained onto a small shrub, tree, or trellis, fence, etc.
Likes: sun/half-sun/half-shade/semi-dry/moist.
Propagation: seeds (hybrids will produce variable seedlings with different colors), cuttings, and layering.
Pruning requirements: Type 1.
Comments: water well during hot weather. A good companion plant is *Lonicera heckrottii,* Goldflame Honeysuckle Vine. This species is similar to *C. alpina,* but the flower structure differs markedly. One of the most noteworthy cultivar selections is 'Markham's Pink,' a 1935 introduction from England with lovely double, nodding flowers of a lavender-pink with greenish-white centers. Dr. Frank Skinner of Dropmore, Manitoba, bred and introduced three notable selections: 'Blue Bird,' which has large purple-blue flowers with white centers 3 inches across, introduced in 1965 (this variety makes an excellent combination with Purple-leaf Barberry [*Berberis thunbergii*]); 'Rosy O'Grady,' which has large rosy-pink flowers with white centers 3 inches across, introduced in 1964; and 'White Swan,' which has very large white flowers up to 5 inches across. Native to northern China and eastern Siberia.

C. MAXIMOWICZIANA (C. paniculata), Sweet Autumn Clematis, Japanese Virgin's Bower. Perennial to Zone 4-5 (though root hardy to Zone 3 if adequately winter-mulched or grown near a warm house basement).
Height: vigorous vine to over 30 feet.
Bloom: profuse clusters of fragrant white star-like flowers (a dry hawthorn-like scent) from late July to September.
Climbing habit: best grown trailing down a bank or trained on a trellis—give it lots of room.
Likes: sun/half-sun/half-shade/semi-dry/moist.
Propagation: cuttings, seeds, or layering.

Sweet Autumn Clematis,
Clematis maximowicziana

Pruning requirements: Type 3.
Comments: Water well in hot weather. This species is closely related to *Clematis recta.* A good companion plant is *Lonicera heckrottii,* Goldflame Honeysuckle Vine. Native to Japan.

C. OCCIDENTALIS, Native Blue Clematis. Native across all of North America. Perennial to Zone 1.
Height: size varies by variety.
Bloom: bell-shaped, reddish-violet flowers from May to early June.
Likes: half-shade.
Tolerates: half-sun/shade/moist.
Pruning requirements: Type 1.
Comments: bright northern exposure is ideal. The variety *'grosseserrata,'* native to northern Alberta and southwestern Yukon, has elongated violet-blue, rarely white, flowers which are bell-shaped at first and with age spread to almost flat. Another variety of note is *'dissecta,'* native only to the Wenatchee Range of Washington. It has short vines 3 feet long, showy finely-divided foliage, and reddish-violet, occasionally blue-violet, flowers on short tufted stems. These two varieties offer tremendous breeding potential for crosses with *C. alpina* and *C. macropetala.*

C. SERRATIFOLIA, Cut-leaf Clematis, Perennial to Zone 1.
Height: vigorous vine to 10 feet.
Bloom: pale yellow nodding bell-shaped flowers with purple stamens from August to September, followed by attractive silky seed heads that persist throughout the winter.
Likes: sun/half-sun/semidry/moist.
Propagation: seeds, cuttings, or layerings.
Pruning requirements: Type 3 (dies to the ground in severest climates).
Comments: native to Korea. Some root suckering (try to confine the roots). Makes a good ground cover or trellis climber, but give it lots of room; a good companion plant is *Lonicera heckrottii,* Goldflame Honeysuckle Vine. Closely related to *C. tangutica,* but with smaller flowers than that species.

C. TANGUTICA, Golden Clematis. Perennial to Zone 1.
Height: vine to 10 feet.
Climbing habit: A delightful species for roving over rocks or through trees and shrubs in the rock garden, or on a trellis, fence, or pole.
Bloom: charming, single, nodding, bell-shaped, bright yellow flowers from August to September, followed by silky fuzzy seedheads which persist throughout the winter. Native of western Mongolia and northwestern China.
Likes: sun-half-sun/semidry-moist.
Pruning requirements: Type 3.
Propagation: seeds, cuttings, or layering.
Comments: give it lots of room. Some potential for becoming a weed if allowed to escape from the garden. A good companion is *Lonicera heckrottii,* Goldflame Honeysuckle Vine. Varieties to look for are *obtusiuscula,* which is later blooming and a larger vine; and 'Gravetye Variety,' an improved horticultural variety.

C. TEXENSIS, Scarlet Clematis, perennial to Zone 3-4 (with winter mulch).
Height: vine to 5 feet.
Bloom: nodding flowers are bell-shaped or pitcher-shaped with thick substance, colors vary from red to pink-purple, blooms from July to frost.
Likes: sun/half-sun/half-shade/regular water.

Propagation: seeds, cuttings, layerings.
Pruning requirements: Type 3 (most years, the vine will die to the ground and bloom from new wood).
Comments: native of Texas. Varieties of note are the following: 'Duchess of Albany,' which has pink flowers; 'Etoile Rose,' which also has pink flowers; and 'Gravetye Beauty,' which has red flowers. Dr. Frank Skinner produced a profusely free-flowering hybrid between this plant and *Clematis integrifolia.* It had bell-shaped, rosy-purple flowers, and unfortunately has been lost to cultivation.

LARGE-FLOWERING HYBRID CLEMATIS

This is a complex group which is composed of hybrids from various species or hybrid combinations. The gardener, in making a choice for his or her particular hardiness zone, should check the zone recommended for each clematis cultivar. If, for example, a cultivar is placed in Zone 1, then it will undoubtedly be root hardy in all warmer areas, making the choice quite easy. It must be remembered, however, that all of these clematis will benefit considerably if planted near the warm basement of a house (especially in the colder areas), and given adequate mulch of peat moss, dry leaves, wood chips, etc. as insulation against winter cold. In areas with plenty of snowfall, heaping snow over this mulch further ensures survival. In addition, to assist the gardener, pruning requirements are grouped in Type 1, 2, or 3, as explained in the introductory section on Clematis.

To provide the gardener with further information, the large-flowering clematis are categorized into several groups. This is simply to give an insight into how these cultivars came to be; each group is given a capital designation, i.e. "F" for Florida Group, followed by the hardiness zone, with both the designation letter and zone bracketed ("F"; Zone 3) as for Clematis 'Duchess of Edinburgh.'

This exceptional section on clematis was written by Stanley Zubrowski of Prairie River, Saskatchewan. He is a prairie plant breeder, particularly concerned with breeding hardy clematis. We will be grateful for decades for the work of this man.

Clematis Groups

Designated "F," *Clematis florida,* native of China, comprises the Florida Group (Pruning: Type 2). These double and semi-double cultivars owe their existence to the blood of some early Japanese cultivars that belonged, it is believed, to the *C. florida x C. patens* group. Sometimes both double, semi-double, and single flowers will appear at the same time on a plant. Young plants from this section usually produce the much sought after double flowers only after two or three years of establishing themselves. 'Vyvyan Pennell' is a typical example.

Designated 'J,' the Jackmanii Group (Pruning: Type 3) includes the famous *C. x jackmanii* raised in 1858 by the Jackman family of Woking, England. The clematis in this group were raised from hybrids that came about by crossing C. lanuginosa and C. viticella and intercrossing some of the early hybrids between the two clematis. *C. x jackmanii* has given rise to other large late-flowering cultivars such as 'Victoria,' 'Star of India,' and 'Perle D'Azur.'

Designated 'L,' the Lanuginosa Group (Pruning: Type 2 or 3) includes some of our loveliest hybrids that have been developed with *Clematis lanuginosa,* a large-flowered Chinese species, as one of the parents. This species has been crossed with several other species, including *C. patens* and *C. florida.* Generally clematis in this group cannot be considered free flowering, but there are exceptions to this rule, namely *Henryi* and 'Marie Boisselot.'

Designated 'P,' the Patens Group (Pruning: Type 2) are derived from *Clematis patens,* a Japanese species. These large-flowered cultivars have been bred from *C. patens x C. lanuginosa* and early Chinese and Japanese cultivars, and also *C. florida. C. patens* gave the genes to create early flowering hybrids such as 'Nelly Moser,' 'the President,' 'Dr. Ruppel,' 'Lincoln Star,' and 'Carnaby,' to name a few.

Designated 'V,' the Viticella Group (Pruning: Type 3) is derived from *Clematis viticella,* a native of southern Europe. *C. viticella* was the first clematis species to be introduced into England from Europe in the mid-16th century. This species has given rise to many small-flowered hybrids in a great range of colors, and even a double form. *Clematis viticella purpurea plena elegans* has delightful two inch wide, fully double flowers of a violet-purple shade. *C. viticella* gave the genes to create *C. x jackmanii* and other late, large-flowered cultivars, although other small-flowered, free-flowering hybrids are more typical of *C. viticella.* Cultivars 'Minuet' and 'Royal Velours' are typical examples.

All the above groups prefer full sun to partial shade, with regular watering during hot weather, and a cool root run. All require a trellis to climb. The more vigorous varieties look best planted with different vines that bloom at the same time, or at other seasons. All the following clematis are available commercially either in Canada or the U.S. Others not listed can be located through the International Clematis Society, which is listed in the Resource Directory.

Blue and Purple Clematis Varieties

'Alice Fisk' ("P x L"; Zone 3); light wisteria-blue flowers, sepals long-pointed, stamens dark brown, blooms from May to June and September; pruning Type 2.

'Annabel' ("L"; Zone 3); mid-blue flowers with white stamens, blooms from May to June, pruning Type 2.

'Azure Skies.' See 'Sho-Un' below.

'Barbara Dibley' ("P x L"; Zone 3); pansy-violet with deep carmine bars, stamens dark, blooms from May to June and September; pruning Type 2. Suitable for cut flowers.

'Barbara Jackman' ("P x L"; Zone 3); vivid bluish-purple flowers with a wide crimson bar and creamy stamens, May to June and September bloom; pruning Type 2. Suitable for cut flowers.

'Beauty of Worcester' ("J x F"; Zone 3); deep violet-blue with white stamens, June to September bloom, early bloom double, late bloom single; pruning Type 2. Suit-able for cut flowers.

'Belle Nantaise' ("P x L"; Zone 3); large delicate grayish-lavender-blue flowers, sepals long-pointed, stamens creamy white, June to September bloom, pruning Type 2.

'Belle of Woking' ("F"; Zone 4-5); soft blue with silvery overtones, stamens creamy white, June to July and September bloom; pruning Type 2.

'Blue Gem' ("P x L"; Zone 3); light lavender-blue, darker center-base and darker veins, stamens dark, May to September bloom; pruning Type 2.

'Count of Lovelace' ("F"; Zone 4-5); double rosette-shaped bluish-violet flowers in spring, single flowers later on new wood, stamens white, June to September bloom; pruning Type 2.

'C W Dowman' ("P x L"; Zone 3); lavender flowers with purplish-pink shading and a vivid scarlet bar, stamens golden, June to September bloom; pruning Type 2.

'Edo Murasaki' ("P x L"; Zone 3); broad overlapping deep violet-blue flowers with striking white-tipped stamens, May to June and September bloom; pruning Type 2.

'Elsa Spath' ("J x F"; Zone 2); deep bluish-violet flowers with purple shadings, stamens dark, June to September bloom; pruning Type 2.

'Empress of India' ("P x L"; Zone 3); light violet-purple flowers, deepening in center, stamens white, July to August bloom; pruning Type 2.

'Etoile Violette' ("V"; Zone 1); deep purplish-violet flowers with yellow stamens, very vigorous and free-flowering from July to September; pruning Type 3.

'Fair Rosamund' ("P x F"; Zone 3); bluish-white flowers with wine-red bars and purple stamens, slightly scented, June to September bloom; pruning Type 2.

'Fuji Musume' ("P x L"; Zone 3); large blue flowers with golden stamens, flowering June to September; pruning Type 2.

'Gabrielle' ("P x L"; Zone 3); light blue flowers, May to June bloom; pruning Type 2.

'General Sikorski' ("P x L"; Zone 3); striking lavender-blue flowers with red tint in center, stamens creamy-white; June to September bloom; pruning Type 2.

'Gipsy Queen' ("J"; Zone 1); deep violet-purple flowers with a velvety sheen, stamens reddish-purple, bloom July to September continuously; pruning Type 3.

'Haku Ookan' ("P x L"; Zone 3); lustrous violet flowers with striking white stamens, May to June and September bloom; pruning Type 2. A cultivar from Japan, the name means "white royal crown."

'H F Young' ("P x L"; Zone 3); mid-blue color, widely overlapping sepals with creamy stamens, May to June and September bloom; pruning Type 2. Suitable for cut flowers.

'Horn of Plenty' ("P x L"; Zone 3); rosy-purple overlapping sepals with deeper bar, stamens reddish-purple, June to September bloom; pruning Type 2. Suitable for cut flowers.

'Jackmanii' ("J"; Zone 1); violet-blue flowers, June to September continuous bloom, very vigorous; pruning Type 3.

'Jackmanii Superba' ("J"; Zone 1); deep purplish-violet flowers with broader sepals than 'Jackmanii', continuous bloom June to September; pruning Type 3.

'Joan Picton' ("P x L"; Zone 3); flowers are a beautiful shade of old lilac with a white bar and brown stamens, May to June and September bloom; pruning Type 2.

'Kathleen Durnford' ("P x L"; Zone 3); deep rosy-purple flowers with deeper bar, early blooms semi-double, later are single, stamens golden, May to June and September bloom; pruning Type 2.

'Kathleen Wheeler' ("P x L"; Zone 3); very large purplish-violet flowers with striking golden stamens, profuse bloom June to September; pruning Type 2. Suitable for cut flowers.

'King Edward VII' ("P x L"; Zone 3); soft violet flowers with pale crimson bar and brown stamens, June to August bloom; pruning Type 2. Suitable for cut flowers.

'Lady Betty Balfour' ("J"; Zone 2); vivid deep violet-blue flowers with yellow stamens, profuse bloom August to September, needs full sun as it is late-flowering; pruning Type 3.

'Lady Caroline Nevill' ("P x L x F"; Zone 4-5); bluish-mauve flowers with beige stamens, single flowers, sometimes double early in the season, June to September bloom; pruning Type 2. Suitable for cut flowers.

'Lady Northcliffe' ("P x L"; Zone 3); deep Wedgwood-blue broad overlapping sepals with white stamens, June to September bloom; pruning Type 2.

'Lasurstern' ("P x L"; Zone 3); ultramarine-blue flowers with striking white stamens, overlapping broad sepals with a wavy margin, May to June and September bloom; pruning Type 2.

'Lawsoniana' ("L x F"; Zone 4-5); sepals broad, overlapping, purplish-blue with a rosy tint, stamens pale brown, June to August bloom; pruning Type 2.

'Lord Nevill' ("P x L"; Zone 3); intense ultramarine-blue flowers with a wavy edge, purple stamens, May to June and September bloom; pruning Type 2. Suitable for cut flowers.

'Marcel Moser' ("P x L"; Zone 3); soft bluish-violet flowers with deep carmine bars and reddish-purple stamens, May to June and September bloom; pruning Type 2.

'Maureen' ("J"; Zone 1); rich purplish-violet flowers with velvety sheen, yellow stamens, profuse bloom June to September; pruning Type 2 or 3.

'Miriam Markham' ("P x L"; Zone 3); rich lavender flowers, earliest blooms are double, later ones are single, bloom May to June and September; pruning Type 2. Suitable for cut flowers.

'Mrs. Bush' ("P x L"; Zone 3); rich lavender-blue flowers, bloom June to September; pruning Type 2.

'Mrs. Cholmondeley' ("F x J"; Zone 2); light lavender-blue flowers with long-pointed sepals and brown stamens, profuse bloom May to September; pruning Type 2.

'Mrs. N. Thompson' ("P x L"; Zone 3); violet-purple flowers with vivid red bar down center of each sepal, stamens striking deep red, bloom May to June and September; pruning Type 2.

'Mrs. B Truax' ("P x L"; Zone 3); medium to light blue flowers with yellow stamens, bloom May to June and September; pruning Type 2.

'Perle D'Azur' ("J"; Zone 1); light sky-blue flowers with purplish tinge, stamens green, blooms June to September continuously; pruning Type 3. This variety is best viewed from underneath.

'Perrin's Pride' ("J"; Zone 1); an improved purple Jackmanii with a more rounded flower.

'Picadilly' ("J"; Zone 1); rich blue flowers with contrasting creamy-white stamens, satiny texture, blooms June to September continuously; pruning Type 3.

'Prince Philip' ("P x L"; Zone 3); rich purplish-blue flowers with a cast of crimson, large pointed wavy-edged sepals with white stamens, bloom June to August; pruning Type 2.

'Prins Hendrik' ("P x L"; Zone 3); lavender-blue flowers, large fine-pointed sepals with attractive crimped edges, stamens purple, bloom June to August; pruning Type 2. "Prins" is the Dutch spelling for prince.

'Mrs. P. T. James' ("P x L x F"; Zone 4-5); deep blue flowers, semi-double in the spring, and single in late summer, blooms May to June and September; pruning Type 2.

'Ramona' (syn C. 'Sieboldia')("P x L"; Zone 3); light lavender-blue flowers with dark stamens, blooms June to September; pruning Type 2.

'Richard Pennell' (P x L x F"; Zone 4-5); plum or rosy-purple flowers with striking gold and maroon center, sepals saucer-shaped, overlapping, blooms May to June and September; pruning Type 2.

'Royal Velours' ("V"; Zone 1); deep velvety-purple flowers with black stamens, blooms July to September; pruning Type 3. This variety has the deepest color of the viticella group.

'Sally Cadge' ("P x L"; Zone 3); mid-blue flowers with deep carmine bars, very profuse bloom May to June and September; pruning Type 2.

'Serenata' ("J"; Zone 1); deep velvety violet-purple flowers with contrasting yellow stamens, profuse bloom May to September; pruning Type 3. Suitable for cut flowers.

'Sho-Un' ('Azure Skies') ("P x L"; Zone 3); soft lavender to sky-blue flowers, sepals broad and overlapping with deep veins, stamens white, blooms June to September; pruning Type 2.

'Sir Garnet Wolseley' ("P x L"; Zone 3); velvety purple flowers fading to mauve blue, pale purplish bars, stamens dark, blooms May to June and August; pruning Type 2. Suitable for cut flowers.

'Star of India' ("J"; Zone 1); deep bluish-violet flowers with broad red bars, blooms July to September; pruning Type 3. This is a very tropical-looking flower.

'Teshio' ("P x L x F"; Zone 4-5); light lavender flowers, fully double rosette-shaped blooms, creamy-white stamens, blooms June to September; pruning Type 2.

'The President' ("P x L"; Zone 3); deep bluish-purple flowers with silvery undersides, dark purple stamens, blooms June to September continuously; pruning Type 2. Suitable for cut flowers. This variety doesn't fade in sun.

'Tillicum' ("P x L"; Zone 3); large delicate blue flowers with deep purple stamens, blooms June to September; pruning Type 2.

'Velutina Purpurea' ("J"; Zone 1); rich blackish-purple flowers with greenish stamens, blooms July to September; pruning Type 3.

'Victoria' ("J"; Zone 1); light purplish-violet flowers, beige stamens, profuse bloom June to September; pruning Type 3.

'Violet Charm' ("P x L"; Zone 3); deep violet flowers with long-pointed sepals attractively crimped, stamens beige, blooms June to September; pruning Type 2.

'Vyvyan Pennell' ("F"; Zone 4-5); purplish-lavender flowers, double rosette-shaped flowers in spring, single in late summer, blooms May to June and September; pruning Type 2. Suitable for cut flowers.

'W E Gladstone' ("P x L"; Zone 3); lavender-blue flowers with prominent purple stamens, blooms June to September; pruning Type 2. This variety has the largest flowers of any clematis. Suitable for cut flowers.

'Will Goodwin' ("P x L"; Zone 3); lavender-blue flowers, overlapping wavy-edged sepals with golden stamens, blooms June to September; pruning Type 2.

'William Kennett' ("P x L"; Zone 3); deep lavender-blue flowers with dark purple stamens, blooms June to September, needs full sun exposure; pruning Type 2. Suitable for cut flowers.

Red, Pink and Mauve Clematis Varieties

'Allanah' ("J"; Zone 1); bright ruby-red flowers with dark brown stamens, blooms from June to September; pruning Type 3.

'Beauty of Richmond' ("P x L"; Zone 3); pale lavender-mauve with darker bar, June to August bloom; pruning Type 2. Suitable for cut flowers.

'Bee's Jubilee' ("P x L"; Zone 3); mauve-pink with deep carmine-rose bars, stamens golden, May to June and August bloom; pruning Type 2.

'Capitaine Thuilleaux' ("P x L"; Zone 3); broad strawberry-pink bars on a creamy background, sepals pointed, stamens golden-brown, May to June and September bloom; pruning Type 2.

'Charissima' ("P x L"; Zone 3); large bright pink flowers with dark pink bar and delicate veining, sepals pointed, stamens maroon, June to September bloom; pruning Type 2.

'Comtesse de Bouchard' ("J"; Zone 1); mauve-pink flowers with creamy white stamens, satiny-textured, blooms June to September continuously, somewhat bushy habit; pruning Type 3. This variety needs several years to establish before blooming fully.

'Corona' (P x L"; Zone 3); purplish-red flowers with dark red stamens, velvety texture, May to June and August bloom; pruning Type 2.

'Crimson King' ("J"; Zone 1); bright rosy-red flowers paling down the center, stamens yellow-brown, July to August bloom; pruning Type 2.

'Dawn' ("P x L"; Zone 3); soft pearly to pink flowers maturing to white, purple stamens, May to June and September bloom; for best coloring, this clematis should be grown out of direct sunlight; pruning Type 2.

'Dr. Ruppel' ("P x L"; Zone 3); mauve-pink flowers with deeper bars, stamens golden, May to June and September bloom; pruning Type 2.

'Duchess of Sutherland' ("P x L x F"; Zone 3); carmine or wine-red flowers with a lighter bar, early flowers double, later flowers are single, June to September bloom; pruning Type 2.

'Ernest Markham' ("J"; Zone 1); vivid red flowers with golden stamens, flowering from July to September continuously, needs full sun to flower properly; pruning Type 3.

'Guiding Star' ("J"; Zone 1); crimson-purple flowers from July to September; pruning Type 3.

'Hagley Hybrid' ("J"; Zone 2); light pink flowers, stamens brown, blooms June to September continuously, compact vine habit; pruning Type 3.

'Jackmanii Rubra' ("J"; Zone 1); velvety crimson flowers with creamy stamens, early bloom semi-double, later bloom single, blooms June to September continuously; pruning Type 3.

'John Warren' ("P x L"; Zone 3); soft pink flowers edged in carmine, with central carmine bars and red stamens, blooms June to September continuously; pruning Type 2. Suitable for cut flowers.

'Kasugyama' ("P x L"; Zone 3); delicate pink flowers with slight overcasting of soft lavender, stamens contrasting deep purple, June to September bloom; pruning Type 2.

'King George V' ("P x L"; Zone 3); pale pink saucer-shaped flowers with bright pink bars, stamens brown, June to September bloom, plant in southern exposure; pruning Type 2.

'Lady Londesborough' ("P"; Zone 4-5); mauve flowers fading to silvery mauve, prominent dark stamens, June to September bloom; pruning Type 2.

'Lincoln Star' ("P x L"; Zone 3); raspberry-pink flowers with paler edges and maroon stamens, May to June and September bloom; pruning Type 2. Suitable for cut flowers.

'Louise Rowe' ("P x L x F"; Zone 4-5); attractive pale mauve flowers with golden stamens, produces single, semi-double, and double blooms, June to July and September; pruning Type 2.

'Margaret Hunt' ("J"; Zone 1); lavender-pink flowers with brown stamens, blooms June to September continuously; pruning Type 3.

'Miss Crawshay' ("P x L x F"; Zone 4-5); semi-double soft mauve-pink flowers with pale fawn stamens, single blooms in late summer, May to June and September bloom; pruning Type 2.

'Mme. Baron Veillard' ("J"; Zone 1); lilac-pink flowers with pointed sepals, blooms late July to September continuously; pruning Type 3. Suitable for cut flowers.

'Mme. Edouard Andre' ("J"; Zone 1); deep wine-red flowers with pointed sepals and creamy white stamens, blooms June to September continuously; pruning Type 3. Suitable for cut flowers.

'Mme. Grange' ("J"; Zone 1); deep reddish-purple flowers, velvety texture, incurving sepals reveal a silvery reverse, stamens dark, August to September bloom; pruning Type 3.

'Mme. Julia Correvon' ("V"; Zone 1); deep wine-red spaced sepals which are slightly twisted, stamens yellow, blooms June to September continuously; pruning Type 3.

'Nelly Moser' ("P x L"; Zone 3); pale mauve-pink flowers with deep carmine bar, bloom May to June and September; for best color, this clematis should be grown away from hot sun; pruning Type 2.

'Niobe' ("J"; Zone 1); deep ruby-red flowers, almost black on opening, velvety texture, stamens golden, free-flowering June to September; pruning Type 3. This remarkable clematis originated in Poland.

'Percy Picton' ("P x L"; Zone 3); rich mauve or rosy-purple flowers with dark stamens, paler blooms in late summer, bloom May to June and September; pruning Type 2.

'Pink Fantasy' ("J"; Zone 1); shell-pink flowers with deep bar and attractive wavy sepals, stamens brown, blooms June to September continuously; pruning Type 3.

'Proteus' ("P x L x F"; Zone 4-5); mauve flowers with yellow stamens, flower form is semi-double in the spring, and single in late summer, blooms May to June and September; pruning Type 2.

'Rouge Cardinal' ('Red Cardinal') ("J"; Zone 1); rich crimson with brown stamens, blooms June to September continuously; pruning Type 3. This is considered the very best of the red clematis.

'Ruby Glow' ("P x L"; Zone 3); glowing ruby-red flowers with

pointed sepals and dark stamens, blooms June to September; pruning Type 3. This variety is a Canadian introduction.

'Sunset' ("J"; Zone 1); velvety-red flowers with dark purple blush on outer edge, blooms May to frost; pruning Type 3.

'Twilight' ("J"; Zone 1); deep rosy-mauve flowers with yellow stamens, bloom July to September; pruning Type 3.

'Ville de Lyon' ("J"; Zone 1); carmine-red flowers shading to deep crimson at the edges of the sepals, stamens are striking golden, bloom June to September continuously, prefers a west or east exposure; pruning Type 3.

'Volucea' ("J"; Zone 1); rosy-red flowers with yellow stamens, free-flowering bloom June to September; pruning Type 3.

'Walter Pennell' ("F"; Zone 4-5); deep pink flowers with a mauve tinge, flowers are double in spring, and single in late summer, blooms May to June and September; pruning Type 2.

White and Pale-Colored Clematis Varieties

'Carnaby' ("P x L"; Zone 3); white flowers with red bars, chocolate-red stamens, May to June and September bloom; pruning Type 2.

'Duchess of Edinburgh' ("F"; Zone 2); double white flowers, rosette-shaped blooms, stamens yellow, May to June and September bloom; pruning Type 2.

'Edith' ("P x L"; Zone 3); pure white flowers with contrasting dark red stamens, free-flowering from May to September; pruning Type 2. Suitable for cut flowers.

'Fairy Queen' ("P x L"; Zone 3); white flowers with rose pink bars, stamens dark, June to August bloom; for best color, this clematis should be grown out of direct hot sun; pruning Type 2. Suitable for cut flowers.

Florida 'Sieboldiana' (C. florida bicolor)("F"; Zone 4-5); creamy-white flowers with rosette-shaped center of rich violet-purple petaloid stamens, June to September bloom; pruning Type 3.

'Gillian Blades' ("P x L"; Zone 3); pure white flowers with frilled edges, stamens golden, May to June

and September bloom; pruning Type 2.

'Henryi' ("L x F"; Zone 3); creamy-white flowers with dark stamens, June to September bloom; pruning Type 2. Suitable for cut flowers.

'Huldine' ("J"; Zone 1); pearly to white flowers with pale mauve bars on the reverse of sepals, bloom July to September continuously; pruning Type 3. Suitable for cut flowers.

'Jackmanii Alba' ("J"; Zone 1); white flowers with brown stamens, early blooms semi-double, blooms June to September continuously; pruning Type 2 or 3.

'John Huxstable' ("J"; Zone 2); clear white flowers from June to September; pruning Type 3. This variety makes a good contrast with darker varieties.

'John Paul II' ("P x L"; Zone 3); creamy-white flowers with pink trails which sometimes become pink bars in summmer, May to June and September bloom; pruning Type 2.

'Margaret Wood' ("P x L"; Zone 3); ivory-white flowers with striking dark purple stamens, May to June and September bloom; pruning Type 2.

'Marie Boisselot' (Mme Le Coultre) ("L"; Zone 3); pure white, waxy overlapping sepals, stamens pale yellow, June to September bloom; pruning Type 2. Suitable for cut flowers.

'Minuet' ("V"; Zone 1); medium-size cream-colored flowers edged with lavender, profuse bloom July to September; pruning Type 3.

'Miss Bateman' ("P x L x F"; Zone 4-5); creamy white flowers with attractive chocolate-red stamens, profuse bloom from May to June and September; pruning Type 2. Suitable for cut flowers.

'Mme. Le Coultre.' See 'Marie Boisselot.'

'Mrs. George Jackman' ("P x L x F"; Zone 4-5); satiny white flowers with a cream bar down the middle of overlapping sepals, stamens brown, early blooms, single in late summer, bloom May to June and September; pruning Type 2. Suitable for cut flowers.

'Silver Moon' ("L"; Zone 4-5); mother-of-pearl grey flowers with yellow stamens, profuse bloom from June to September; an outstanding performer in heavy shade; pruning Type 2.

'Snow Queen' ("P x L"; Zone 3); snow-white flowers with a blue tint, stamens brown, pink bar may appear in September, blooms May to June and September; pruning Type 2.

'Star Fish' ("P x L"; Zone 3); light white flowers with a pinkish cast, blooms May to June; pruning Type 2.

'Sylvia Denny' ("P x L x F"; Zone 4-5); white semi-double flowers with golden stamens, blooms May to June and September; pruning Type 2.

'Wadd's Primrose' ("P"; Zone 4-5); primrose yellow flowers with deeper cream bars and yellow stamens, blooms June to September; pruning Type 2.

CLEOME SERRULATA, Prairie Cleome, Rocky Mountain Beeplant. Native to sandy and disturbed areas of the Great Plains. Annual.
Height: 3 feet.
Bloom: showy pink flowers from end June to September (long season).
Foliage: rounded shrubby habit of showy dark green three-lobed foliage.
Culture: easy.
Likes: sun/moist.
Tolerates: half-sun/dry/semidry.
Propagation: sets or seeds.
Comments: bees are attracted to this plant. The Indians boiled the leaves and flowers as a vegetable, and ground the seeds for flour. Some tribes used this plant to obtain a black pottery dye. There is also a rare yellow-flowering species, *Cleome lutea*. It has lupine-like foliage and blooms from mid-May to early June.

C. SPINOSA, Cleome, Spider Flower. Annual.
Height: 3 feet.
Bloom: red, pink, white, or violet-purple flowers from July to frost.
Foliage: attractive five-lobed (palmate) leaves, insignificant thorns on stems.
Culture: easy.
Likes: sun/semidry/heat.
Tolerates: dry.
Propagation: sets or seeds; plant seed only in warm soil.
Comments: individual clump habit. For showiest compact plants, water sparingly. Besides being attractive in a border, this flower also makes

good cut flowers. Named varieties are commonly available. 'Violet Queen' is a showy purple-pink variety. 'Helen Campbell' is a pure white variety.

COIX LACRYMA-JOBI, Job's Tears. Annual.
Height: 3 feet.
Bloom: large pearl-like seeds which droop from stems.
Foliage: grassy clump of reed-like foliage.
Culture: easy.
Likes: sun/half-sun/semidry/moist.
Propagation: sets or seeds.
Comments: these hard shiny seeds have a natural hole through the middle for stringing, but they come only in drab colors of lavender, white, and gray. Seed stalks are also useful in flower arrangements. A corresponding Bible verse is Job 16:16.

COLCHICUM AUTUMNALE, Autumn Crocus. Perennial to Zone 4.
Height: 4 inches.
Bloom: pink, white or purple water-lily-like flowers in September.
Foliage: strap-like.
Culture: easy.
Likes: sun/moist.
Tolerates: half-shade/dry.
Propagation: bulbs.
Comments: foliage grows in the spring, then goes dormant and disappears in July. It is most attractive planted under a hedge or as an edging along a wall. All parts of this plant are extremely poisonous. Colchincine, obtained from this plant, is used by plant breeders to double a plant's chromosome count for diploids and tetraploids. The white variety is called 'Album.' There is a similar species *C. agrippinum*, which is hardy to Zone 3.

COLEUS HYBRIDUS, Coleus. Annual.
Height: 1 foot.
Bloom: insignificant flowers.
Foliage: red, pink, yellow, green, and white multicolored foliage from May to frost (very long season).
Culture: easy.
Likes: half-sun/moist.
Tolerates: half-shade/shade/wet.
Propagation: sets or seed. (Seed germination: light, warm.)
Comments: individual clump habit. This is a good plant for either flower borders or containers. Its vivid color makes it a good accent plant.

Additionally it can be grown indoors as a house plant.

COLLARDS, Non-heading Cabbage. Brassica oleracea, acephala group. Warm-season annual vegetable.
Height: 3 feet.
Description: rounded clump of smooth thickened foliage on a stalk, grown primarily for its summer and fall crop of cabbage-flavored leaves.
Likes: half-sun/half-shade/semidry/moist/humus-rich soil.
Propagation: sets or seeds. Because its seeds tolerate cool soil, they can be planted anytime between mid-April to July; stagger plantings for prolonged harvest.
Pests: flea beetles, root maggots and white cabbage moth (see strategies for control in the Broccoli section).
Harvest tips: harvest individual leaves, or the whole head can be harvested throughout the season.
Comments: light frosts sweeten the flavor. The main advantage of this plant is that its cabbage-like leaves are produced during the heat of summer and fall. Low in calories, high in vitamins, it is used raw in salads or cooked as a potherb. It is closely related to kale, differing mainly in its season of growth.

COLUTEA ARBORESCENS, Bladder Senna. Perennial to Zone 2.
Height: 4 feet.
Shape: irregularly shaped bush.
Bloom: yellow pea flowers from May to frost; odd-looking red seedpods.
Foliage: vicious thorns.
Culture: easy.
Likes: sun/half-sun/dry/semidry.
Tolerates: poor soil.
Propagation: sets or seeds.
Comments: occasionally winterkills to the ground but regrows quickly from its roots. In general this is not a showy plant, but it makes a good barrier plant.

CONSOLIDA AMBIGUA (Delphinium ajacis), Annual Delphinium, Larkspur. Annual.
Height: 3 feet.
Bloom: pink, white, or blue-purple flower spikes from June to early August.
Foliage: attractive finely-divided foliage.
Culture: easy.
Likes: sun/moist/humus-rich soil.
Tolerates: half-sun/semidry.
Propagation: sets or seeds. (Seed

germination: dark. Use fresh seed only.) Can be seeded outside a month before frost-free date.
Comments: individual plant habit; remove flowers after bloom for re-bloom. Though it has a brief bloom season, it is beautiful in a flower border. It also makes good cut flowers.

CONVALLARIA MAJALIS, Lily-of-the-Valley. Perennial to Zone 1.
Height: 6 inches.
Bloom: waxy white bell-like flowers in early May.
Culture: very easy.
Likes: half-shade/moist.
Tolerates: half-shade/shade/semi-dry.
Propagation: plant roots in the fall or potted sets in the spring.
Comments: foliage comes up in late winter to early spring. Pink-flowering varieties are especially attractive and are fragrant as well. All parts of this plant are extremely poisonous.

CONVOLVULUS TRICOLOR, Dwarf Morning-glory Bush. Annual.
Height: 1 foot tall by 2 feet wide.
Bloom: red, pink, white, or blue flowers from June to frost (long season).
Culture: easy.
Likes: sun/moist.
Tolerates: half-sun/semidry/wet.
Propagation: seeds (nick seed coat or soak overnight before planting in warm soil.)
Comments: creeping mound. Flowers tend to have three different colors in them, hence the species name tricolor.

COREOPSIS GRANDIFLORA, Coreopsis. Perennial to Zone 4.
Height: 2 feet.
Bloom: bright yellow flowers from June to frost (long season if spent flowers removed).
Culture: easy.
Likes: sun/dry/semidry.
Propagation: sets or seeds. Because seeds tolerate cool soil, they can be seeded outside a month before frost-free date.
Comments: this makes both a good garden plant and a good cut flower.

C. LANCEOLATA, Coreopsis. Native to eastern North America. Perennial to Zone 4.
Height: 2 feet.
Bloom: bright yellow flowers from June to frost (long season if spent flowers removed).

Culture: easy.
Likes: sun/dry/semidry.
Propagation: sets or seeds.
Comments: this makes both a good garden plant and a good cut flower.

C. TINCTORIA, Annual Coreopsis, Caliopsis, native to the southern and central plains. Annual.
Height: 2 feet.
Bloom: red, yellow, or reddish-brown flowers from June to frost (long season if spent flowers removed).
Culture: easy.
Likes: sun/very dry/semidry.
Propagation: sets or seeds. Because seeds tolerate cool soil, they can be seeded outside a month before frost-free date.

Caliopsis, Coreopsis tinctoria

Comments: windstake with brush support in exposed areas. This flower is showy if planted in masses or sprinkled throughout a flower bed. It also makes an excellent cut flower.

C. VERTICILLATA, Threadleaf Coreopsis. Perennial to Zone 3.
Height: 2 feet.
Bloom: bright yellow daisy flowers from July to frost (long season if spent flowers removed).
Foliage: attractive, finely-divided.
Culture: easy.
Likes: sun/very dry/semidry.
Propagation: sets or seeds
Comments: good for growing as an accent plant in the garden or in containers. It can also be used for cut flowers. The award-winning variety 'Moonbeam' has profuse light yellow flowers, distinctive gray foliage, and is disease resistant.

CORIANDRUM SATIVUM, Coriander, Cilantro, culinary herb. Perennial to Zone 3.
Height: 3 feet.
Bloom: tiny white flowers in flat-topped clusters, blooms from July to August.

Cilantro, Coriander, Coriandrum sativum

Foliage: attractive foliage which somewhat resembles parsley, flat-topped seed clusters.
Culture: easy.
Likes: sun/moist/heat.
Tolerates: half-sun/semidry/moist.
Propagation: seeds. (Seed germination: dark, warm.)
Comments: upright habit; established plants resent transplanting. The foliage is used as the seasoning called Cilantro. It is an important seasoning in Mexican salsas. It is also a characteristic taste in Thai and Vietnamese cooking. The seeds are the spice called Coriander. There are two main varieties: the one used for its foliage is slow to bolt; the other used for its seeds, bolts and ripens its seed early. Additionally, this easily grown ornamental plant can be used to loosen soil deeply with its powerful roots. Native to the eastern Mediterranean and Asia and cultivated since ancient times.

CORN, Sweet Corn, *Zea mays.* Warm-season annual grain.
Height: 4 to 10 feet.
Description: a coarse leafy plant which bears ears of grain on its stalks.
Culture: easy.
Likes: sun/very rich, very deeply dug soil with humus, nitrogen (use manure), phosphorus (use bone-meal) and trace minerals.
Tolerates: moist.
Propagation: sets (transplants well) or seeds. Seed must be fresh for best germination; soak seed over-

night before planting; plant shallowly and maintain critical moisture while seed is germinating. Seed requires warm soil to germinate. Supersweet corn varieties are particularly sensitive to soil moisture while germinating. Plant outside after the frost-free date.

Pests: Colorado potato beetle and corn borer worm. Suckers naturally form at the base of the plant. It is not necessary to remove them.

Growing tips: heavy water requirements, particularly during seed germination and during silk stage of fruiting. Burying dead fish below seed level at planting time is an excellent fertilizer source.

Harvest tips: test for ripeness in the garden by peeling husks and piercing a kernel; if juice is clear, corn is not yet ripe; if juice is milky, corn is ripe; if juice is thick, corn is overripe.

Comments: corn has an amazing double set of deep and shallow underground roots. Fo best cross-pollination, always plant corn in clumps of three or more plants.

For longest season, plant both early and late ripening varieties in hot summer areas. In cool season areas, plant both early and mid-season varieties. Short varieties tend to be early ripening.

In the garden, corn can be used for mid-day shade for lettuce, mustard, radish and spinach. An excellent companion plant for corn is pumpkin, which seems to thrive in the shade of the corn patch. Beans and squash are

Corn, Zea mays

also planted with corn. But do not plant corn and popcorn near each other because they will hybridize together and produce strange tasting corn and popcorn. For more information, see the listing for Popcorn.

This plant has been cultivated since antiquity by the native peoples of Central and South America

as a dried grain to be ground into flour. North American breeders of the last century have been responsible for the development of the sweet eating varieties.

Hybrid varieties have the best vigor, productivity, and resistance to disease. A regular variety of corn (as opposed to a supersweet variety) has its sweetest taste if cooked seconds after being picked. Otherwise, natural enzymes convert sugars into less digestible starches. However, supersweet corn varieties were bred to retain their sugar content even through days of storage. In fact, some people pick supersweet corn a day before using it so that it is less sweet. Recommended varieties are 'Northern Supersweet' and 'Extra-early Supersweet'.

Corn can be easily preserved by freezing if it is blanched briefly to inactivate the enzymes before being frozen. Wise cooks know to carefully chill the inner core thoroughly in an ice bath. This is more crucial and difficult than it sounds because the cob takes surprisingly long to cool. If this step is not done properly, the resulting frozen corn will have a cob-like off-taste. Corn can be cut off the cob and either canned, dried, or frozen. Additionally, cornstalks can be fed to livestock.

A seed saving note: Because all corn varieties will cross-pollinate and hybridize with each other, special isolation techniques must be used for true-to-variety seeds. In general, hybrid varieties are useless for saving seeds.

Popcorn is grown exactly like corn, but it requires a longer season to ripen its ears.

CORN SALAD, Mache, Lamb's Lettuce, Valerianella olitoria. Cool-season annual vegetable.

Height: 6 inches.

Description: low clump of tender foliage, subtle delicate flavor and tender succulent texture.

Culture: easy.

Likes: half-sun/humus-rich soil/cool temperatures.

Tolerates: sun/half-shade/moist.

Propagation: sets or seeds. Germinates easily, tolerates cold soil extremely well.

Comments: plant in late summer to harvest in the fall; plant in early fall

and give it light mulch for a winter and spring crop; plant in mid-winter for a spring crop.

This is a prime candidate for winter cultivation in a cold frame. Named Corn Salad because it appears in European cornfields during the winter.

Shepherd's Garden Seeds lists an exceptional French variety 'Verte de Cambrai'. They recommend tossing the leaves with "a simple vinaigrette dressing and sieve a hard-boiled egg over the leaves."

CORNUS ALBA, Dogwood. Perennial to Zone 1.

Dogwood, Cornus alba

Height: 5 feet.

Bloom: white flower clusters in May.

Shape: attractive rounded shrub with reddish bark on twigs.

Culture: easy.

Likes: half-sun/moist/wet.

Tolerates: sun/half-shade/semidry.

Propagation: sets (softwood cuttings or soft-hardwood cuttings in summer).

Comments: protect from extreme winter sun exposure. Prune out oldest wood only in late summer or early fall, or it will bleed profusely. The showy ornamental varieties of this beautiful shrub make an excellent untrimmed hedge. In a border it combines dramatically with red foliage plants such as Redleaf Rose *(Rosa rubrifolia),* Thunderchild Crabapple *(Malus),* Schubert Chokecherry *(Prunus virginiana 'Schubert'),* or Purpleleaf Barberry *(Berberis thunbergii).* Showy varieties are the following: *'Argenteo-marginata,'* which has white, pink, and green variegated foliage and red stems; *'Aurea,'* which has bright yellow foliage (it must have protection from extreme sun and wind exposure, while still getting moderately bright sun exposure);

'Gouchaultii,' which has yellow and green variegated foliage and red stems; and 'Spathii,' which has soft yellow foliage and red stems. The branches of these dogwoods can be used for slingshots, as well as campfire cooking racks and kettle hangers.

C. ALTERNIFOLIA, Pagoda Dogwood. Perennial to Zone 3.
Height: 10 feet.
Bloom: white flower clusters in May, blue-black berry clusters in the fall.
Shape: tree-like shrub, showy oriental-looking form.
Culture: easy.
Likes: moist.
Tolerates: half-sun/half-shade/semidry.
Propagation: sets (buy only sets with their buds intact).
Comments: prune only to accentuate its tier-like branch structure; prune only in late summer or early fall, or it will bleed to death. This shrub is native to the eastern forests of North America as far north as Manitoba.

C. SERICEA 'WHITE GOLD,' Variegated Red Osier Dogwood. Perennial to Zone 2.
Height: 5 feet.
Bloom: small white flowers from May to June.
Shape: irregularly rounded shrub with yellow stems.
Foliage: dramatic white variegated foliage.
Culture: easy.
Likes: half-sun/moist/wet.
Tolerates: sun/half-shade/semidry.
Propagation: sets.
Comments: this remarkably beautiful shrub is similar to *Cornus alba* 'Argenteo-marginata.'

CORYLUS HYBRIDS, Hazelnut. Native to both the forest and prairie, north to the parklands. Perennial to Zone 1.
Height: 6 feet.
Bloom: attractive yellow catkins late winter into spring; delicious edible hazelnuts.
Shape: graceful multi-trunked shrub with an irregular habit.
Culture: easy.
Likes: half-sun/moist.

Corylus Hybrid, Hazelnut

Tolerates: half-shade/semidry.
Comments: established plants resent transplanting. Prune out 2- to 3-year-old wood each winter. For best nut production, plant two for cross-pollination sets only (buy hardy hybrid varieties of crossed European and American parentage, occasionally called 'Filazel'). The two North American hazelnuts, *Corylus americana* and *C. cornuta,* are much hardier than the European ones. As an ornamental, this plant is very attractive in an informal or wild landscaping theme garden. The nuts provide excellent winter forage for many wild animals.

CORYPHANTHA MISSOURIENSIS (Neobesseya missouriensis), Ball Cactus. Native to dry hillsides in the Great Plains and foothills. Perennial to Zone 3.
Height: 2 inches.
Bloom: straw-colored flowers in June.
Likes: very dry.
Tolerates: sun/semidry.
Propagation: sets or seeds.

C. VIVIPARA, Cushion Cactus. Native to dry hillsides in the Great Plains and foothills from the Canadian border south to Colorado. Perennial to Zone 3.
Height: 3 inches.
Bloom: magenta-purple flowers in mid-June (brief season); fruit ripens in August.
Propagation: buy only nursery-grown plants, wild ones reproduce slowly.
Likes: very dry.
Tolerates: sun/semidry.
Comments: the tiny fruit of this plant was relished by the Indians and early explorers.

COSMOS ATROPURPUREA, Chocolate Cosmos. Annual (frost-tender dahlia-like rhizome).
Height: 2 feet.
Bloom: rich red-brown flowers with an unforgettable cocoa scent, blooms from June to frost (long season if spent flowers removed).
Foliage: attractive foliage, dramatic dark brown stems.
Likes: half-sun/humus-rich soil.
Tolerates: moist.
Comments: clump habit; dahlia-like root must be dug up and stored cool and dry each year like dahlias. There is no other flower on earth which is chocolate-scented.

C. BIPINNATUS, Cosmos. Annual.
Height: 3 feet.
Bloom: red, pink, and white flowers from July to frost (very long season).
Foliage: finely-divided.
Culture: easy.
Likes: sun/semidry/heat.
Tolerates: half-sun/dry.
Propagation: sets or seeds. (Seed germination: warm.)
Comments: windstake with brush or hoop support in exposed areas; can be pinched when young for a bushier compact shape. This plant is spectacular in mass plantings, sprinkled amongst other flowers in a bed, in containers, or used for cut flowers. Try to find more attractive varieties than the plain pink, purple and white mix. One dramatic variety, 'Versailles,' has pink flowers with red centers.

Cosmos, Cosmos bipinnatus

C. SULPHUREUS, Cosmos. Annual.
Height: 3 feet.
Bloom: vivid red, orange, or yellow marigold-like flowers from July to frost (very long season).
Foliage: finely-divided.
Culture: easy.
Likes: sun/semidry/heat.
Tolerates: half-sun/dry.
Propagation: sets or seeds.
Comments: windstake with brush support in exposed areas. This plant is spectacular in mass plantings, sprinkled throughout a flower bed, grown in containers, or used as cut flowers.

COTONEASTER ACUTIFOLIUS, Peking Cotoneaster. Perennial to Zone 3, this is an over-planted hedge plant with little ornamental value beyond its brief fall color and black berries.

C. HORIZONTALIS PERPUSILLA, Dwarf Rockspray. Perennial to Zone 3.
Height: 1 foot.
Bloom: red berries in the fall and winter.
Foliage: showy dark green foliage

in summer and red fall color.
Culture: easy.
Likes: sun/moist.
Tolerates: half-sun/semidry.
Propagation: sets. (softwood cuttings or soft-hardwood cuttings in summer.)
Pruning: prune only to accentuate natural cascading form, remove oldest branches at ground level.
Comments: dwarf creeper; herringbone branch pattern; may need light winter mulch in exposed areas. The dwarf variety *'perpusilla,'* mentioned here, is much hardier than the species form and can be used in a rock garden. This plant also makes a particularly showy edging with its winter display of red berries.

C. MULTIFLORUS. Perennial to Zone 3.
Height: 8 feet.
Bloom: spiraea-like white flowers in mid-May; showy red berries held until early winter.
Shape: large bush with upright arching habit (give it lots of room for its wide-spreading nature).
Foliage: attractive gray-green foliage.
Culture: easy.
Likes: sun/moist.
Tolerates: half-sun/dry/semidry.
Propagation: sets or seeds (softwood cuttings or soft-hardwood cuttings in summer).
Comments: this plant is slightly susceptible to fireblight (see the listing for *Malus* for more information). Native to western China, it was first introduced in 1854.

C. RACEMIFLORUS SOONGORICUS, Sungari Red Bead Cotoneaster. Perennial to Zone 1.
Height: 8 feet.
Bloom: white flowers in early June; profuse pinkish-red fruit in fall and winter.
Shape: large wide-spreading bush with upright arching habit (give it lots of room).
Foliage: rounded gray-green leaves.
Culture: easy.
Likes: sun/moist.
Tolerates: half-sun/dry/semidry.
Propagation: sets or seeds (softwood cuttings or soft-hardwood cuttings in summer.)

CRATAEGUS CRUS-GALLI, Cockspur Hawthorn. Perennial to Zone 1.

Height: 30 feet.
Bloom: slightly fragrant white flowers from early to mid-May; profuse red berries held through fall and early winter.
Shape: nicely shaped rounded tree.
Foliage: dark green foliage, orange-red fall color; very large and dangerous thorns about the size of cockspurs.
Culture: easy.
Likes: semidry.
Tolerates: sun/dry.
Propagation: sets (buy only sets with their terminal bud tips intact; softwood cuttings or hardwood cuttings in summer or winter).
Pests: occasionally susceptible to fireblight.
Comments: prune very little and only after bloom (it watershoots easily). There is a thornless variety of this plant called 'Inermis.' Kim Williams mentioned using the thorns as survival fishhooks and the berries for making syrup. She says to cook the berries in water and strain out the seeds, then mix the juice with other fruit for best flavor. Hawthorns must be cross-pollinated to produce large amounts of fruit.

C. MOLLIS, Red Haw, Hawthorn tree, state flower of Missouri. Perennial to Zone 3.

Hawthorn, Crataegus

Height: 30 feet.
Bloom: white flowers from early to mid-May, large red berries in fall and winter (useful for jelly).
Shape: showy wide-spreading tree; large thorns.
Culture: easy.
Likes: sun/semidry.
Tolerates: half-sun/half-shade/dry/moist.
Propagation: sets (buy only sets

with their terminal buds intact; softwood cuttings or hardwood cuttings in summer or winter).
Comments: prune very little and only after bloom.

C. X MORDENENSIS. Perennial to Zone 3.
Height: 12 feet.
Bloom: white or pink flowers, sparse red berries from August to November.
Foliage: long-lasting orange-red fall color.
Culture: easy.
Likes: sun/semidry.
Tolerates: half-sun/dry/moist.
Propagation: sets.
Comments: prune very little and only after bloom. 'Snowbird' is an upright spreading tree with double white flowers in May, discovered as a seedling of 'Toba.' It tends to be a better tree form and hardier than its parent. 'Toba' is a small slow-growing tree that blooms in May with fragrant double white flowers aging to pink. People seem to really notice and enjoy the color change. This dwarf size variety closely resembles an English hawthorn except for its small size. It was bred by Morden Research Station, Manitoba (in 1949), as a cross between 'Paul's Scarlet' and a native plains hawthorn (*Crataegus succulenta*).

CROCUS SPECIES. Perennial to Zone 3.
Height: 3 inches.
Bloom: dramatic flowers in very early spring.
Culture: easy.
Likes: sun/half-shade/moist/semidry.
Propagation: bulbs or seeds.
Comments: The god Mercury created this flower from the blood of Crocus, the son of Europa, who was struck and killed while the two played a game of quoits.

Order of bloom: *ancyrensis* (early April); *imperati* (early April); *sieberi* (early to mid-April); *chrysanthus* (early to mid-April); *flavus* (mid-April); *tomasinianus* (mid- to late April); Dutch hybrids (mid- to late April). Species crocus bloom earlier than the hybrids, so mix them together for the longest season.

C. ANCYRENSIS, Golden Bunch Crocus—orange-yellow flowers in early April, clustered habit. This is the very earliest crocus to bloom.

Plant it if you want your picture in the newspaper as the gardener with the earliest crocus in town.

C. CHRYSANTHUS—fragrant orange, yellow, white, or blue flowers in early to mid-April.
Comments: 'Bluebird' has soft blue flowers. 'Cream Beauty' has creamy-white flowers which darken at the base. 'Ladykiller' has heart-stopping white and gray-black flowers with symmetrical markings. 'Snowbunting' is a fragrant white variety.

C. FLAVUS (C. aureus), Dutch Yellow Crocus—orange-yellow flowers in mid-April.

C. IMPERATI—fragrant regal-looking purple flowers with an orange throat, blooms in early April.
Propagation: may self-sow.

C. SIEBERI—purple, white, and lilac flowers with a yellow-orange throat in early to mid-April.
Comments: 'Atticus' is an early purple variety with a yellow throat. 'Firefly' has warm lavender petals and vivid orange stamens in the center. 'Versicolor' is a fragrant striped variety.

C. TOMASINIANUS—fragrant purple and pale violet flowers in mid- to late April.
Propagation: may self-sow.

C. HYBRIDS, Dutch Crocus—yellow, white, lilac, and purple flowers in mid- to late April, usually a larger flower size than the species Crocus. The variety 'Pickwick' has lavender flowers with dark purple stripes.

CRYPTANTHA INTERRUPTA, Miner's Candle. Native to dry areas of the Great Plains and Rocky Mountains; short-lived perennial.
Height: 10 inches.
Bloom: fragrant candle-like white flower stalk blooms from mid-May to end June, but dries up and remains attractive throughout the summer, fall, and winter.
Foliage: insignificant hairy gray basal foliage disappears in early summer.
Likes: sun/half-sun/dry/semidry.
Propagation: sets or seeds.
Comments: the species C. celosioides has a drumstick-like flower form, while C. interrupta has a tiered flower structure.

CUCUMBER, *Cucumis sativus.* Warm-season annual vegetable.

Description: sprawling vine to 8 feet; attractive plant with distinct lobed foliage and oblong-shaped fruit, vining habit which climbs with twining tendrils.
Culture: easy.
Likes: sun/moist/humus-rich soil/compost.
Propagation: sets (start inside and plant out after frost-free date; its sensitive roots transplant easier with a treatment of B1—Thiamine) or seeds (because it requires warm soil, plant seed outside after frost-free date; soak seed overnight before planting).
Growing tips: loves heat (for maximum heat retention in soil, use a clear plastic layer over a black plastic mulch); for best growth, give it wind protection and moderate humidity; does not like to be crowded for light; shallow rooted (avoid disturbing soil near plant); prefers to be thickly mulched; carefully remove dead foliage in the fall to reduce disease and insect pests; requires lots of water or fruit gets bitter; prefers monthly feedings of fertilizer and manure tea.

Good companion plants for cucumbers are radishes and tall sunflowers; however, do not plant melons in the same soil as cucumbers because they can share diseases; for best fruit set, plant at least two for cross pollination and encourage bees or hand pollinate.
Comments: to save space, regular climbing cucumbers can be allowed to climb up a lattice or net support. Bush varieties require less space in a garden, but produce less fruit.

Cultivated since before recorded history in the tropics, it probably originated in India.

One of the very best traditional varieties is the Armenian Cucumber, which has an extremely tender skin and is never bitter. In general, seedless varieties are taking over the market because they are easier to grow, produce larger cucumbers, and have more fruit per plant. For extremely short season areas, two very early varieties are 'Early Russian' and 'Morden Early.'

Cucumber,
Cucumis sativus

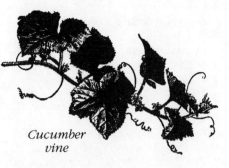
Cucumber vine

CYNOGLOSSUM AMABILE, Chinese Forget-me-not. Annual.
Height: 1 foot.
Bloom: sky-blue flowers, blooms continuously from June to frost (longest season if seed planting is staggered).
Culture: easy.
Likes: half-sun/moist.
Tolerates: sun/half-shade/dry/semidry.
Propagation: sets or seeds. (Seed germination: dark.)
Comments: This flower is showiest when sprinkled throughout a flower bed.

CYTISUS NIGRICANS, Black Broom. Perennial to Zone 3.
Height: 3 feet.
Bloom: bright yellow and white pea-like flowers from mid-June to early July.
Foliage: very dark green foliage contrasts well with other plants.
Culture: easy.
Likes: sun/semidry.
Tolerates: dry/poor soil.
Propagation: sets only (soft-hardwood cuttins or hardwood cuttings in summer or winter.)
Comments: small bush-like habit; winter kills to the ground each year and grows back from its roots. Other hardy broom species are Cytisus elongatus (yellow flowers); Cytisus glaber (yellow flowers); Cytisus purpurea (sparse light purple flowers); Cytisus ratisbonensis (brief yellow flowers on a showy symmetrically rounded mound). These plants are far more restrained than the weedy brooms (C. scoparius), which cause trouble on the Pacific Coast. See also listing for Genista.

DAHLIA HYBRIDS, Dahlia. Annual.
Height: 1-4 feet.
Bloom: red, pink, orange, yellow, white, or purple flowers from July to frost.
Likes: intense sun/heat/well fertilized humus-rich soil.
Tolerates: sun/moist.
Propagation: root is dug and saved each year (it is critically important that each root has an inch of stem attached and is planted right side up). Plant one week before frost-free date.
Comments: must be wind staked for eventual height at the time root is planted. Upright bush-like form. The miniature varieties start flowering the earliest and make the best show in our area. Collarette and Single Form varieties are particularly showy. Additionally, they make excellent cut flowers. The large flowering varieties should not be attempted except in hot summer areas. Store roots during the winter in a dry cool condition. Do not let them freeze.

DELOSPERMA NUBIGENUM, Ice Plant. Perennial to Zone 4.
Bloom: showy yellow daisy flowers from June to August (long season).
Foliage: succulent bright green leaves in summer, reddish winter color.
Likes: sun/semidry.
Tolerates: half-sun/dry.
Propagation: sets or seeds. Stems root and spread slowly.
Comments: mat-like habit; requires light winter mulch in exposed areas. This plant is native to high areas in the mountains of Lesotho, South Africa. There is a similar plant, *Delosperma cooperi,* which has pink flowers.

DELPHINIUM AJACIS. See *Consolida ambigua,* Larkspur.

D. BICOLOR, Low Larkspur. Native to grassy hills of the Great Plains, foothills and Rocky Mountains. Perennial.
Height: 10 inches.
Bloom: intoxicating blue-violet flowers on stalks from end of April to May.
Foliage: low basal clump of attractive delphinium-like foliage.
Likes: sun/half-sun/semidry/moist.
Propagation: sets or seeds.
Comments: when this plant is young, its foliage resembles the native Geranium. By midsummer, this plant goes dormant and disappears. A showy related species is the 1-foot-tall *Delphinium geyeri,* which is native to the Great Basin. It also has intoxicating rich blue flowers and low basal foliage. Delphiniums, in general, are responsible for a great deal of cattle poisonings.

D. GRANDIFLORUM (D. chinensis), Siberian Larkspur. Perennial to Zone 1.
Height: 2 feet.
Bloom: white or gentian-blue flower spikes from July to August (long season if spent flowers removed).
Foliage: very showy, finely-divided.
Likes: sun/humus-rich soil.
Tolerates: half-sun/moist.
Propagation: sets or seeds. (Seed germination: dark.) Use fresh seed only. Can be seeded outside a month before frost-free date.
Comments: windstake with brush support; remove spent flowers for rebloom. This plant makes an excellent companion for coolness-loving plants like *Salpiglossis.* It is also a good cut flower.

D. ELATUM HYBRIDS, Garden Delphinium. Perennial to Zone 1.
Height: 5 feet.
Bloom: showy pink, white, blue, or purple flower spikes from June to July (long season).
Likes: half-sun/moist/well-drained humus-rich soil/regular water.
Tolerates: half-shade.
Propagation: sets.
Comments: windstake individual flower spikes; remove spent flowers before they set seeds for best

Low Larkspur, Delphinium bicolor

plant vigor. For longest-lasting cut flowers, cut when flowers are open and crush stem ends. These flower stalks can also be dried for use in dried floral arrangements. Additionally, the dried seedpods are also attractive in arrangements. The hybrid varieties known as 'Pacific Giants' are world-renowned. There is an International Delphinium Society in England (address listed in the Resource Directory).

D. TATSIENENSE, Tatsien Larkspur. Annual (self-sowing).
Height: 2 feet.
Bloom: vivid rich blue flowers from July to frost.
Likes: sun/semidry.
Tolerates: half-sun/moist.
Propagation: sets or seeds (stagger seed planting from April to June.) Encourage it to self-sow.
Comments: upright clump. Individual plants die after setting seeds, but it will come back year after year from self-sown seeds. This species is native to the snow-capped Tatsien or Celestial Mountains of western China's Gobi Desert.

DESCHAMPSIA CAESPITOSA, Tufted Hair Grass. Native to moist grassy meadows of the Rocky Mountains and the boreal forest (and occasionally found in wet areas of the plains). Perennial to Zone 4.
Height: 3 feet.
Bloom: tufted clump of dramatically delicate airy seedheads from July to September which dry and persist until winter.
Foliage: dark green foliage.
Likes: sun/semidry/moist.
Propagation: sets or seeds. Self-sows moderately in favorable location.
Comments: basal clump; roots are non-invasive. This attractive plant can be used as an ornamental accent; however, it tends to be short-lived. Luckily it self-sows new plants. There are horticultural varieties with gold-colored foliage.

DIANTHUS BARBATUS, Sweet William. Biennial to Zone 3 (with protection).
Height: 1 foot.
Bloom: red, pink, and white multicolored flowers from June to July.
Likes: half-shade/moist/humus-rich soil.
Tolerates: half-sun.
Propagation: sets or seeds. Tolerates cool soil and can be seeded outside before frost-free date.
Comments: requires light winter mulch. This plant is an excellent choice for a partial shade location. But unfortunately, very few hybrids

are fragrant. The original species form is intensely fragrant. This plant is used in pots or containers as well as for long-lasting cut flowers.

D. CARYOPHYLLUS, Carnation. Ohio's official state flower is the Scarlet Carnation; most varieties hardy only with winter protection.
Height: 1 foot.
Bloom: very fragrant red, yellow, white, or purple flowers from June to August.
Likes: sun/moist/humus-rich soil.
Tolerates: half-sun/semidry.
Propagation: sets (usually propagated by cuttings).
Comments: requires winter mulch of evergreen branches that hold snowcover and yet let in light. Besides being very colorful in the garden, this plant makes a long-lasting cut flower. In a sunny location, it can be grown in a pot or container. 'Marguerite' is an annual variety with quick growth, an extra long bloom season, and fragrance; other fragrant varieties are **'Baby,'** 'Camellia-flowered,' 'Clove Beauty,' 'Dwarf Bouquet,' 'Dwarf Grenadin,' 'Dwarf Vienna' (coral red), 'Enfant de Nice,' and 'Fragrance.'

D. CHINENSIS, China Pinks. Annual.
Height: 8 inches.
Bloom: red, pink, and white multicolored flowers with fringed petals, from July to frost (long season).
Likes: sun/moist.
Tolerates: half-sun/semidry.
Propagation: sets or seeds. Can be seeded outside before frost-free date. Seeds can be saved and replanted year to year.
Comments: This showy annual should be more commonly grown. It is best displayed in mass plantings. Some varieties are fragrant.

D. DELTOIDES, Maiden Pinks. Perennial to Zone 1.
Height: 6 inches.
Bloom: red or pink flowers on stalks from late May to June.
Foliage: low mat of grass-like foliage.
Likes: half-sun/moist/well-drained soil.
Tolerates: sun/dry/semidry.
Propagation: sets. May self-sow and spread slowly.
Comments: in exposed areas may require light winter mulch. If grass

Maiden Pinks,
Dianthus deltoides

invades the clump, it can be very difficult to remove. This plant is excellent for the front of the garden.

D. GRATIANOPOLITANUS, Cheddar Pinks. Perennial to Zone 3.
Height: 6 inches.
Bloom: fragrant fringed pink flowers on stalks from June to July.
Foliage: dense blue-gray grass-like mat.
Likes: half-sun/semidry/well-drained soil.
Tolerates: sun/dry/moist.
Propagation: sets.
Comments: in exposed areas may need light winter mulch; shear back after bloom. Sometimes other non-fragrant plants such as *Dianthus deltoides* are sold under this name. There are many named varieties of this plant in white and pink colors; double varieties tend to be the most fragrant. This plant is excellent for the front of the garden or as a formal edging. It makes an excellent small cut flower or an edible garnish.

D. PLUMARIUS, Cottage or Scotch Pinks. Perennial to Zone 1 (with winter protection).
Height: 10 inches.

Cottage Pink, Dianthus plumarius

Bloom: very fragrant fringed flowers in multicolors of red, pink, and white, from May to June.
Foliage: grass-like semi-evergreen clump.
Likes: half-sun/moist/well-drained soil.
Tolerates: sun/dry/semidry.
Propagation: sets or seeds.
Comments: must have light winter mulch of evergreen branches to survive harsh winters, but varieties differ in hardiness. Most varieties require windstaking with hoop support. This spectacular and well-loved plant is excellent for the front of the garden and also as a cover for bulbs. It makes an excellent small cut flower or an edible garnish. The group called Laced Pinks are fragrant and have showy banded petals. Some extremely choice varieties which ought to be more available outside of England are 'Paisley Gem,' 'Rainbow Loveliness,' and 'Allspice.' Allwood varieties such as 'Doris' are also very valuable.

The vast majority of breeding work on this plant was done in England and Scotland from the 17th to 19th centuries. Allwood hybrids were bred in the early part of this century and are considered modern hybrids. Originally the word 'pink' meant fringed edges (such as pinking shears) and not a color. However through the association of the name 'pinks' with this flower, the usage of the word 'pink' as a color evolved.

DICENTRA SPECTABILIS, Bleeding Heart. Perennial to Zone 3.
Height: 3 feet.
Bloom: red or white heart-shaped flowers from May to June.
Foliage: attractive fern-like foliage.
Likes: half-shade/semidry.
Tolerates: shade/moist.
Propagation: sets or seeds. (Seed germination: cold treatment.)
Comments: leafy upright clump; requires water in late summer. Besides being irreplaceable in the shade garden, this plant produces good cut flowers. The species spectabilis was introduced from China. In coldest areas use *Dicentra formosa,* the native Rocky Mountain Bleeding Heart, hardy to Zone 1. It has a wild look that appeals to

many gardeners, and blooms in the spring. The Eastern Bleeding Heart (*Dicentra eximia*) is hardy in the chinook zone if winter mulched. Its advantage is a long bloom season from mid- to late summer. The varieties of this species 'Bountiful' and 'Luxuriant' have showy red-pink flowers and a long bloom season from mid- to late summer.

DICTAMNUS ALBUS, Gas Plant, Burning Bush. Perennial to Zone 1.
Height: 3 feet.
Bloom: showy white or pink flowers from June to July, ornamental seed pods.
Foliage: glossy, leathery leaves give off a pleasant lemon-like scent.
Culture: easy.
Likes: sun/semidry/humus-rich soil.
Tolerates: half-sun/dry.
Propagation: sets or seeds. (Seed germination: cold.)
Comments: rounded bush-like habit; established plants resent transplanting. This is the 'Burning Bush' plant, whose glossy leathery foliage can be briefly ignited in mid-summer without injury to the plant. A low maintenance plant once established. The white variety is particularly showy, especially at night. The pink variety is less vigorous, but its flowers are a soft clear tone of pink.

DIGITALIS PURPUREA, Foxglove. Biennial.
Height: 4 feet.
Bloom: narrow flower stalk with purple or white bell-like flowers, blooms from July to August.
Foliage: attractive basal foliage.
Likes: half-sun/moist.
Tolerates: sun/half-shade/semidry.
Propagation: sets or seeds.
Comments: the first year this is an attractive clump of foliage; the bloom stalk grows the second year. Requires winter protection in areas without predictable snowcover. This plant is the source of the heart drug digitalis. All parts of this plant are deadly poisonous (a mouthful of foliage can kill). Because it closely resembles Borage whose leaves are eaten in salads, do not plant these two plants in the same garden. Varieties of interest are 'Excelsior,' which is a pleasing mix of purples and whites, and 'Foxy,' an annual flowering variety. Additionally, there are extremely attractive yellow flowering hybrids, which unfortunately are less hardy.

DIMORPHOTHECA PLUVIALIS (D. Annua), African Daisy. Annual.
Height: 1 foot.
Bloom: white daisy with a yellow center and a purple underside, blooms from June to frost (very long season); flowers close at night.
Likes: sun/semidry/heat.
Tolerates: half-sun/dry.
Propagation: sets or seeds. (Seed germination: use fresh seed only.)
Comments: requires nine weeks from seed to flowering. Besides being showy in the garden, this also makes a good cut flower.

D. SINUATA (D. aurantiaca). Annual.
Height: 1 foot.
Bloom: orange, yellow, and white flowers from June to frost (very long season). Flowers close at night.
Likes: sun/semidry/heat.
Tolerates: half-sun/dry.
Propagation: sets or seeds. (Seed germination: use fresh seed only.)
Comments: requires nine weeks from seed to flowering. Besides being showy in the garden, this also makes a good cut flower.

DIOSCEREA BATATAS, Cinnamon Vine, Chinese Yam. Annual.
Height: vine to 10 feet.
Bloom: cinnamon-scented flowers (inconspicuous appearance) from late July to frost.
Climbing habit: twining.
Likes: sun/moist/well-fertilized, humus-rich soil/heat.
Tolerates: half-sun.
Comments: this attractive plant makes a fast-screening effect, and its unusual cinnamon-like scent is a pleasant novelty. Its hardiness is variable; a few plants are known to have survived mild winters in the ground in Great Falls, Montana. Yam-like roots can be harvested after frost kills vine. They can be eaten or saved for next year's vine.

DODECATHEON CONJUGENS, Shooting Star. Native to western North America. Perennial to Zone 3.
Height: 8 inches.
Bloom: multicolored purplish-pink, white, and yellow shooting star flowers, blooms from late April to early June (long season).
Foliage: attractive basal clump.
Likes: half-sun/moist.

Shooting Star, Dodecatheon conjugens

Tolerates: half-shade/wet.
Propagation: sets or seeds. (Seed germination: cold treatment.)
Comments: this plant tends to go dormant and disappear by mid-summer. A high elevation mountain species, *Dodecatheon pulchella*, requires constant moisture (such as a bog), but it blooms longer and has a peppermint-like scent.

DORONICUM CAUCASICUM, Leopardbane. Perennial to Zone 4.
Height: 2 feet.
Bloom: yellow daisy flowers with darker yellow centers, blooms from early May to late June.
Foliage: heart-shaped leaves go dormant and disappear in mid-summer.
Likes: half-sun/half-shade/moist.
Propagation: sets or seeds.
Comments: may require winter protection in exposed areas. Useful for cut flowers. The variety 'Magnificum' has larger flowers. Native to the Caucasus Mountains of southeastern Europe. The common name refers to its use for poisoning large cats such as leopards and lions.

DOROTHEANTHUS BELLIDIFORMIS, Ice Plant, Livingstone Daisy. Annual.
Height: 4 inches.
Bloom: vividly intense pinkish-red, white, or pinkish-purple flowers, blooms from June to frost (long season).
Foliage: succulent green foliage appears covered with ice or dew, red stems.
Culture: easy.
Likes: intense sun/heat.
Tolerates: sun/dry/scmidry/very poor soil.
Propagation: sets or seeds. Flowers

in 45 days from seed; plant seed only in warm soil.

Comments: semi-upright sprawling habit. This plant is attractive as an edging or in a rock garden. For a perennial species, see *Delosperma nubigenum.*

DOUGLASIA MONTANA. Native to dry foothills and Rocky Mountains (often found in combination with *Juni-*

Douglasia montana

perus horizontalis). Perennial.
Height: 1 inch.
Bloom: tiny, profuse stemless pink flowers, blooms from April to early May.
Foliage: tufted clump of green moss-like foliage.
Likes: sun/half-sun/semidry/moist.
Propagation: sets or seeds.
Comments: does not tolerate weed or grass competition. This plant is commonly confused with other moss-like plants: *Eritrichium nanum* (blue flowers), *Phlox hoodii* (pink or white flowers), *Saxifraga oppositifolia* (purple flowers), and *Silene acaulis* (reddish-purple flowers).

DRABA INCERTA, Yellowstone Draba. Native to rocky ridges in the foothills and alpine mountain areas. Perennial.
Height: 3 inches.
Bloom: attractive yellow flowers on stalks from mid-April to May.
Foliage: loosely tufted clump of tiny bright green leaves.
Likes: sun/rocky soil.
Propagation: sets or seeds.
Tolerates: half-sun/dry/semidry.

D. PAYSONII. Native to dry slopes of foothills and Rocky Mountains (often found in combination with *Juniperus horizontalis).* Perennial.

Height: 2 inches.
Bloom: light yellow flowers from early May to June.
Foliage: dense mat-like habit of woolly semi-evergreen leaves.
Likes: sun.
Tolerates: half-sun/dry/semidry.
Propagation: sets or seeds.

DRACOCEPHALUM NUTTALLII, False Dragonhead. Native to streambanks and bogs in the Great Plains, foothills and Rocky Mountains. Perennial.
Height: 2 feet.
Bloom: showy pinkish-purple flower spikes from June to July.
Foliage: upright clump.
Propagation: sets (transplants easily) or seeds.
Likes: sun/half-sun/moist/wet (a bog plant).
Comments: invasive. The name *dracocephalum* translates literally to "dragonhead." This plant closely resembles *Physostegia virginiana,* the Obedience Plant, a common garden flower.

DRYAS DRUMMONDII. Native to gravelly floodplains in the foothills and Rocky Mountains. Perennial.
Height: 6 inches.
Bloom: showy, nodding, creamy-white, rose-like flowers from May to June; flowers never fully open; interesting long-twisted seedpods on stalks.
Foliage: dense mat-like creeper; attractive basal foliage is green on top and densely woolly silver-gray underneath.
Likes: sun/semidry/moist/mildly alkaline limestone soil.
Propagation: sets or seeds.
Comments: cannot tolerate any

Dryas octopetala

shade; prefers scree conditions with underground watering and good drainage. This plant has the interesting characteristic of being the very first plant to colonize rocky soil left by glaciers. It can tolerate this extremely nitrogen-poor soil because its root nodules contain a fungus that fixes nitrogen from the air. A showier but more difficult rock garden gem is the related species, *Dryas octopetala.* It is native to alpine scree areas, and has showy fully opened creamy-white flowers and crinkled green foliage.

Purple Coneflower, Echinacea purpurea

ECHINACEA PURPUREA, Purple Coneflower. Native to dry foothills in the plains. Perennial to Zone 3.
Height: 3 feet.
Bloom: mauve-purple daisy flowers from July to frost (long season).
Culture: easy.
Likes: sun/semidry.
Tolerates: half-sun/dry.
Propagation: sets or seeds. (Seed germination: cold treatment.)
Comments: besides being an attractive garden plant, the dried flower heads are useful in the winter garden. Varieties of note are the following: 'Bressingham Hybrids,' an attractive color mix; and 'Luster,' a showy white variety. The Indians had many medicinal uses for this plant. Today, this plant is used as an important infection fighter in herbal medicine.

ECHINOPS EXALTATUS, Tall Globe Thistle. Perennial to Zone 2.
Height: 4 feet.
Bloom: steel-blue thistle flowers from July to August (long season).
Culture: easy.
Likes: sun/semidry.
Tolerates: half-sun/dry.
Propagation: sets or seeds.

Comments: established plants resent transplanting. This flower can be used as a cut flower or dried like a strawflower. Cut before flowers open.

E. RITRO, Small Globe Thistle. Perennial to Zone 1.
Height: 2 feet.
Bloom: steel-blue thistle-like flowers from August to September (long season).
Culture: easy.
Likes: sun/semidry.
Tolerates: half-sun/dry.
Propagation: sets or seeds.
Comments: 'Taplow Blue' is a variety with the best flower color. In Zones 1 and 2, this species acts like a biennial.

EGGPLANT, Aubergine (Solanum melongena). Warm-season annual vegetable.
Height: 2 feet.
Description: upright plant, dramatically beautiful blackish-purple flowers, showy thick green foliage with black stems, blackish purple fruit (also red, white, green or yellow-fruited varieties).
Likes: sun/moist/deeply dug, humus-rich soil/trace minerals and

Eggplant, Solanum melongena

regular fertilization in mid-summer for optimal vigor.
Propagation: sets or seeds. (Start seeds inside 6-7 weeks before the frost-free date. They transplant easily).
Growing tips: requires maximum heat and sun exposure (for extra heat retention in soil use a clear plastic layer over a black plastic mulch). For best growth, give it wind protection and moderate humidity; windstake stems when young to avoid damage from heavy fruit set. Prefers frequent deep waterings (it has heavy water requirements) but must dry out slightly between waterings.
Pests: Colorado potato beetle. Never plant eggplants near tomatoes or peppers because they are related and share diseases. Blossom end rot (characterized by a depressed greyish spot on the blossom end of fruit) is caused by either inconsistent watering or a lack of calcium in the soil.
Harvest tips: when harvesting fruit, cut the stem to reduce damage to the plant. Fruit is ready for harvesting when the skin turns shiny. Blossoms should be thinned at the end of summer to allow last fruit to ripen before frost.
Comments: eggplant is much more sensitive to cold than are tomatoes. Do not set out eggplants until a week or two after the tomatoes. Small fruiting Japanese varieties produce more fruit and ripen better in our growing season than the large fruited varieties.

Use eggplant in stir-fry, paté-like pastes, and casseroles. It can be preserved by either freezing or canning.

Eggplant, as well as potatoes and tomatoes, should be rotated to different areas of the garden each year. This plant can also be used in the garden as an ornamental for the beauty of its flowers and fruit.

Probably native to India, it has been grown as a vegetable in the Middle East and Asia for centuries. There are many varieties not yet introduced from China and Thailand.

ELAEAGNUS ANGUSTIFOLIA, Russian Olive Tree. Perennial to Zone 3-4.
Height: 30 feet.
Bloom: insignificant fragrant yellow flowers; inconspicuous cherry-size green fruit.
Shape: oriental-looking shrubby tree; gray-brown bark.
Foliage: showy silvery-gray foliage held attractively until early winter.
Culture: easy.
Likes: sun.
Tolerates: half-sun/very dry/semidry.
Propagation: sets or seeds. (Hardwood cuttings in winter; Seed germination: cold.)
Pests: this tree suffers many diseases which do not kill the tree but constantly kill the oldest branches.
Comments: prune annually to remove dead wood and accentuate the twisted oriental features in its form. Though mainly grown as a tree, this plant can also be pruned into a good hedge. Frank Meyer of the USDA discovered a highly ornamental form with orange-red fruit in Chinese Tashkent and again in Sinkiang, but these were lost in shipping. However, the USDA still has the variety he sent from Tbilisi, Georgia, in Russia. It has large fruits which were eaten fresh, dried, or stewed in milk and sugar.

EMILIA SAGITTATA (Cacalia coccinea), Tassel flower. Annual.
Height: 1 foot.
Bloom: showy nodding clusters of red or yellow flowers, blooms from late June to frost.
Culture: easy.
Likes: sun/half-sun/semidry.
Propagation: sets or seeds. Besides being a beautiful flower in the garden, this plant can be used for cut flowers and dried everlastings.

EQUISETUM SCIRPOIDES, Horsetail. Native to medium elevation forests of the Northern Temperate Zone. Perennial to Zone 2.
Height: 6 inches.
Foliage: carpet-like tufts of very delicate horsetail foliage.
Likes: half-sun/half-shade/shade/moist/wet (a bog plant).
Propagation: sets only.
Comments: this species is easier to control and much more attractive than the common weedy species *Equisetum arvense*. Another useful and attractive garden species is *Equisetum sylvaticum*, which grows to 3 feet tall and resembles a forest of small trees. This unusual plant is exceptionally attractive in planters or in a water garden. This genus was one of the dominant plants during the time of the dinosaurs. The Indians used this plant for scouring pots and for pol-

Horsetail, Equisetum scirpoides

ishing carved wood.

ERIGERON SPECIES, Fleabane. Perennial to Zone 2.
Height: 1 foot.
Bloom: small blue-lavender daisy flowers from July to August.
Culture: easy.
Likes: sun/semidry.
Tolerates: half-sun/dry.
Propagation: sets.
Comments: varieties of note are the following: 'Amity' grows to 2 feet, considered one of the best; 'Charity;' 'Darkest of All,' a dark violet-purple variety; 'Pink Jewel,' a tall variety with bright pink flowers with yellow centers; and 'Rote Schoonhert.' For native species, see the list of native plants. Most species of *Erigeron* closely resemble each other; notable exceptions are mentioned below. The name *Erigeron* means "soon becoming old," referring to the short life of individual flowers. The name fleabane refers to this plant's usage as a flea repellent.

E. CAESPITOSUS. Native to dry rocky hillsides in the Great Plains, foothills and Rocky Mountains. Perennial.
Height: 6 inches.
Bloom: daisy flowers on stalks, usually bluish-lavender, but there are also natural pink and white varieties; blooms from early June-July.
Foliage: tufted habit of woolly gray-green foliage.
Likes: sun.
Tolerates: half-sun/dry/semidry.
Propagation: sets or seeds.

E. FILIFOLIUS. Native to sandy areas of the Great Plains and foothills.
Height: 1½ feet.
Bloom: blue or white daisy flowers.
Foliage: large symmetrical clump of narrow linear foliage.
Likes: sun/half-sun/semidry/moist.
Propagation: sets or seeds.

E. GLABELLUS. Native to moist areas of the Great Plains, parklands and boreal forest. Perennial.
Height: 1 foot.
Bloom: blue daisy flowers on stalks,

blooms from end June to August.
Foliage: tufted clump habit of narrow smooth foliage.
Likes: sun/half-sun/moist.
Propagation: sets or seeds.
Comments: full sun tends to fade the flower color.

E. OCHROLEUCUS, Bluff Fleabane. Native to rocky hillsides in the Great Plains, foothills and high mountains.
Height: 8 inches.
Bloom: profuse yellowish-white or blue-purple flowers in June.
Foliage: tufted habit, narrow foliage that stays near the ground.
Likes: sun.
Propagation: sets or seeds.
Tolerates: half-sun/dry/semidry.

E. PUMILUS, Shaggy Fleabane. Native to dry sandy Great Plains areas; short-lived perennial.
Height: 6 inches.
Bloom: showy light blue or white flowers from mid-May to June.
Foliage: clump habit, unusual-looking hairy leaves.
Likes: sun.
Tolerates: half-sun/dry/semidry.
Propagation: sets or seeds.
Comments: the name *pumilus* means "small" and refers to the plant size. The flowers seem large by contrast.

E. TWEEDYI. Native to dry slopes in the Rocky Mountains.
Height: 6 inches.
Bloom: light blue flowers (occasionally blue-purple or white flowers), blooms from Aug-Sept (late season).
Foliage: attractive sprawling clump habit, gray foliage.
Likes: sun-half-sun/dry-semidry.
Propagation: sets or seeds.

ERIOGONUM, Wild Buckwheat.
Likes: extreme full sun/rocky well-drained, moderately alkaline soil.
Propagation: sets or seeds; seed germinates poorly unless cold treated.
Comments: all are extremely drought tolerant. Plants tend to self-sow in favorable locations. Estab-

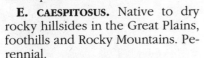

Fleabane, Erigeron

lished plants resent transplanting. Most species hold their dried rust-red flowers attractively in winter. The tap root on old plants can become very large and was eaten as a starvation survival food by the Indians.

E. ACAULE, Stemless Eriogonum. Perennial.
Bloom: stemless yellow flowers.
Foliage: silver-gray clump.

E. ANNUM, Annual Eriogonum. Native to dry hills in the Great Plains. Annual or biennial.
Height: 2 feet.
Bloom: pinkish-white flowers in loose open clusters in August.
Foliage: loose clump habit, silvery-gray woolly foliage and stems.

E. CAESPITOSUM, Tufted Eriogonum. Native to dry rocky hills in the Great Plains and Great Basin. Perennial.
Height: 3 inches.
Bloom: tiny yellow to orange-red flowers, blooms from May to June.
Foliage: tiny silver-white clump of woolly foliage.
Comments: this rare plant should not be dug from the wild.

E. FLAVUM, Yellow Eriogonum. Native to dry exposed ridges of the Great Plains and foothills. Perennial.
Height: 8 inches.
Bloom: medium-large yellow flower clusters on stalks from early June to end of June, flower color darkens as they age, dead dried flowers are an undesirable brown color.
Foliage: upright basal clump of thick green foliage with a woolly gray underside.

Wild Buckwheat, Eriogonum

E. MANCUM. Native to sagebrush slopes in the foothills. Perennial.
Height: 3 inches.
Bloom: small yellow or pinkish-red rounded flower clusters.
Foliage: silvery-green woolly mat-like foliage clump.

E. OVALIFOLIUM, Oval-leaf Eriogonum. Native to dry slopes of the Great Plains and foothills. Perennial.
Height: 8 inches.
Bloom: medium-size rounded light yellow flowers on stalks, blooms from June to July.
Foliage: oval or rounded silvery-gray woolly foliage in basal clump.
Comments: Claude Barr also mentioned white and pink flowered varieties.

E. UMBELLATUM, Sulphur Flower. Native to rocky dry areas of the foothills and Rocky Mountains. Perennial.
Height: 8 inches.
Bloom: creamy white to yellow flat-topped flower clusters on stalks, blooms from June to early July.
Foliage: dense ground-hugging clump of gray-green foliage, leaves are smooth on top, and woolly underneath.
Comments: the rare natural variety *aureum* has the most vividly attractive yellow flower color. Siskiyou Rare Plant Nursery lists a dwarf form with purple winter foliage. The name Sulphur Flower refers to the vivid yellow flower color. However, other species such as *Eriogonum flavum* have more desirable true-tone yellow flowers.

ERIOPHORUM ANGUSTIFOLIUM, Northern Cotton Grass, native to bog areas of the boreal forest and arctic tundra. Perennial to Zone 1.
Height: 10 inches.
Bloom: insignificant green flowers, dramatic white silky cottonheads that persist through the late summer and fall.
Foliage: grass-like leaves.
Likes: half-sun/wet (a bog plant).
Propagation: sets or seeds.

Northern Cotton Grass, Eriophorum angustifolium

Comments: tufted clump. This attractive plant is included for use in a bog garden.

ERIOPHYLLUM LANATUM, Woolly Yellow Daisy, Oregon Sunshine. Native to dry rocky (talus) areas of the foothills and Rocky Mountains. Perennial.
Height: 1 foot.
Bloom: yellow daisy flowers from June to early July.
Foliage: upright rounded clump, attractive woolly white foliage.
Likes: sun.
Tolerates: half-sun/dry/semidry.
Propagation: sets or seeds.
Comments: this plant tends to transplant easily. The name *eriophyllum* means "woolly leaf," and the name *lanatum* means "woolly." The foliage can be used as an accent in drought-tolerant planters.

Oregon Sunshine, Eriophyllum lanatum

ERITRICHIUM HOWARDII, Foothills Forget-Me-Not. Native to dry foothill areas; short-lived perennial.
Height: 3 inches.
Bloom: hauntingly unforgettable, tiny dark blue flowers on tiny stalks, blooms in April to May.
Foliage: moss-like clump of showy gray-green foliage.
Comments: this plant is considered to be challengingly difficult even for experienced rock gardeners.

E. NANUM, Alpine Forget-Me-Not. Native to alpine scree areas of the northern Rockies. Perennial.
Height: 2 inches.
Bloom: profuse, stalkless, tiny single baby-blue flowers, blooms from May to June.
Foliage: moss-like mat of gray-green foliage.
Likes: half-sun.
Propagation: sets or seeds. (Seed germination: cold treatment.)
Comments: requires scree conditions (underground watering and good drainage); requires mid-day shade in hot summer areas. This

plant is one of the most highly esteemed rock garden plants in the world.

ERYNGIUM PLANUM, Sea Holly. Perennial to Zone 1.
Height: 2 feet.
Bloom: small blue thistle-like coneflowers from July to August (long season).
Foliage: blue heart-shaped foliage.
Culture: easy.
Likes: sun/semidry.
Tolerates: half-sun/half-shade/dry/moist.
Propagation: sets or seeds.
Comments: this species is better used as a cutting flower than for a garden specimen. Established plants resent transplanting. Native to Eastern Europe. A showy combination with this prickly steel-blue flower is the soft pink-flowered *Lavatera*. It is said that Sappho wore *Eryngium* to attract her lover. This plant is a common ingredient in love potions. *Eryngium alpinum* (Alpine Sea Holly) is a much showier plant but is difficult to grow in the chinook zone. It needs cool summers and a predictable winter snow-cover.

ERYSIMUM ASPERUM, Western Wallflower, Siberian Wallflower. Native to dry sandy plains and foothills of North America. Biennial to Zone 3.
Height: 1 foot.
Bloom: fragrant bright red, orange, and yellow flowers with a charming spicy scent, blooms from early May to late June (long season).
Culture: easy.
Likes: sun/semidry.
Tolerates: half-sun/dry/moist.
Propagation: sets or seeds; self-sows.
Comments: shear off spent flowers for a rebloom; best planted in place and overwintered with light winter mulch.

Sea Holly, Eryngium planum

ESCHSCHOLZIA CALIFORNICA, California Poppy, official state flower of California. Annual.

Western Wallflower,
Erysimum asperum

Height: 8 inches.
Bloom: red, orange, yellow, creamy-white, or purple poppy flowers, blooms from June to frost (long season if seed pods are removed).
Foliage: finely-divided gray-green foliage.
Culture: easy.
Likes: sun/semidry.
Tolerates: half-sun/very dry.
Propagation: sets or seeds (transplant carefully.)
Comments: This plant can be grown either in a flower bed, creeping amongst a rock garden, or growing out of a crack in a wall. It can also be used as a cut flower if the stem is seared with a match immediately after being cut. The commonly available variety 'Mission Bells' has attractive bright colors.

EUONYMUS ALATA, Burning Bush. Perennial to Zone 3.
Height: 10 feet.
Bloom: unusual-looking fruit attracts birds which eat it.
Shape: shrub with horizontal branching pattern.
Foliage: vivid bright red foliage color in early fall.
Culture: easy.
Likes: sun.
Tolerates: half-sun/dry/semidry/moist/poor soil.
Propagation: sets or seeds.
Comments: 'Compacta' (rated to Zone 4) is a dwarf form about 4 feet

California Poppy,
Eschscholzia californica

tall (it makes a good hedge). There is a Korean strain of this species which is even more hardy.

E. MAACKII. Perennial to Zone 2.
Height: 10 feet.
Shape: multi-stemmed tree-like shrub.
Foliage: broad leaves, fall color is pink mottled with red and creamy-white; attractive pinkish-red fruit is showy in the fall and winter.
Culture: easy.
Likes: sun.
Tolerates: half-sun/dry/semidry/moist.
Propagation: sets.
Comments: fruit is useful for arrangements. This plant was first introduced by Frank Skinner, Dropmore, Manitoba.

E. NANA 'TURKESTAN,' Turkestan Euonymus. Perennial to Zone 2.
Height: 3 feet.
Shape: low shrubby habit.
Foliage: semi-evergreen fine textured narrow leaves, orange and pink fruit.
Likes: sun/semidry.
Tolerates: half-sun/half-shade/shade/dry.
Propagation: sets (soft-hardwood cuttings in summer).
Comments: requires protection from winter sun; prefers wind protection in exposed areas. This plant makes a good ground cover. However, it should be selected and bred for improved winter color. Some confusion exists over the name: *Euonymus nana* is a larger plant than the smaller, more compact *Euonymus nana* 'Turkestan.'

E. VERRUCOSA. Perennial to Zone 2.
Height: 3 feet.
Bloom: attractive unusual-looking pink flowers in May.
Shape: showy globe-like shrub.
Foliage: dull green foliage which turns an attractive orangish-pink color in the fall.
Likes: sun.
Tolerates: half-sun/semidry/moist.
Propagation: sets or seed.
Comments: other *Euonymus* considered hardy are *Euonymus europaeus* (a large tree-like shrub), *E. obovatus* (a low creeping ground cover), and *E. sachalinensis* (a very showy tree-like shrub).

EVERLASTINGS. See *Ammobium ala-*

tum (Winged Everlasting), *Briza major* (Quaking Oats), *Bromus briziformis* (Brome Grass), *Goniolimon tataricum* (German Statice), *Gypsophilla elegans* (Baby's Breath), *Helichrysum bracteatum* (Strawflower), *Helipterum, Lagurus ovatus* (Rabbit Tail Grass), *Limonium* (Statice), *Nigella damascena,* and *Xeranthemum annuum* (Common Immortelle).

FABA BEAN, Broad Bean, Vicia faba. Cool-season annual vegetable.
Height: 2 feet.
Description: bushy clump, white flowers in the spring, large flat beanpods.
Likes: sun/semidry/moist.
Tolerates: half-sun.
Propagation: sets or seeds. Start seed indoors in a moist rolled-up paper towel. Start seeds in August for fall crops. Plant outside when roots first start to show. Because it tolerates cold soil, seeds can be set out in early to mid-April.
Harvest tips: harvest when seeds inside pod are juicy and tender.
Comments: this crop has been grown for five thousand years by the Chinese. This extremely frost-hardy plant prefers to have cool weather for setting its fruit. Hot summer areas should choose the dwarf fast-maturing varieties for early spring and fall crops. Cook them fresh or dry them for storage.

FESTUCA OVINA 'GLAUCA,' Blue Fescue Grass. Perennial to Zone 2.
Height: 8 inches.
Foliage: silver-blue grass that holds its color throughout the winter.
Culture: easy.
Likes: intense sun/semidry.
Tolerates: half-sun/dry/moist.
Propagation: sets.
Comments: densely rounded clump. For best foliage color, shear to two inches tall in the spring. This is a great plant for rocky dry slopes.

FILIPENDULA CAMTSHATICA, Kamchatka Filipendula. Perennial to Zone 1 (with protection).
Height: 5 feet.
Bloom: spectacular clump of large plumy white flowers from mid- to late June.
Foliage: large tropical-looking leaves.
Likes: half-shade/wet/humus-rich soil.

Tolerates: half-sun/shade/moist.
Propagation: sets or seeds.
Comments: requires winter mulch in exposed areas of Zones 3 and 4 and in all areas of Zone 2. This showy plant must have a favorable site and lots of water. It is a dramatically large accent plant that tolerates light shade.

F. ALMATA, Siberian Meadowsweet. Perennial to Zone 4.
Height: 2 feet.
Bloom: plumy pink to white flowers from July to August (long season).
Foliage: attractive bold foliage.
Likes: half-sun/wet/humus-rich soil.
Tolerates: half-shade/moist.
Propagation: sets or seeds.
Comments: may require winter mulch in exposed areas. There is a less hardy Japanese species (*F. purpurea*) sometimes sold under this name.

F. RUBRA, Queen of the Prairies. Native to the eastern tall-grass prairies. Perennial to Zone 3.
Height: 4 feet.
Bloom: dense plumes of pink flowers from July to August (long season).
Foliage: attractive bold foliage.
Likes: half-sun/moist/humus-rich soil.
Tolerates: half-shade/wet.
Propagation: sets or seeds.
Comments: prefers, but does not require, cool summers; may require winter mulch in exposed areas; established plants resent being moved. This plant is useful in the garden, as well as making a good cut flower. *'Venusta'* has the showiest red-pink flower color. This variety makes an excellent accent plant.

F. ULMARIA, Queen of the Meadows. Perennial to Zone 1.
Height: 3 feet.
Bloom: showy and fragrant cream-white flower clusters, blooms from July to August.
Foliage: attractive, bold, with subtle silvery-green color tone.
Likes: half-sun/wet.
Tolerates: half-shade/moist.
Propagation: sets or seeds.
Comments: established plants resent being moved. *Flore pleno* is an attractive double white form. *Aurea* has yellow foliage. There is also an attractive variegated form of this plant.

FOENICULUM VULGARE, Fennel, Fennelroot, used three ways: as a root-vegetable, as a culinary spice—both foliage and seeds, and as a showy ornamental. Annual.
Height: 4 feet.
Bloom: greenish-yellow flat-topped flowers from July to August.
Foliage: semi-evergreen, finely-divided.
Culture: easy.
Likes: half-sun/semidry.
Tolerates: sun/dry.
Propagation: seeds.
Comments: established plants resent transplanting. Flowers in two months from seed. It is attractive in any type of garden, with the added advantage that it attracts

Fennel, Foeniculum vulgare

beneficial predatory wasps to the garden. Seeds are used for their flavor in many kinds of cooking. Additionally, foliage can be baked under a fish. Fennel seeds are used for their anise-like seasoning in cookies and cakes. Chewing a few fennel seeds brings immediate relief from internal gas (flatulence). Special varieties are grown for their delicious roots, which have a celery-anise taste.

Harvest them in the fall, slice, and cook in butter. Shepherd's Garden Seeds lists an Italian root variety 'Fennel Fino' that is bolt resistant. There is a showy ornamental variety with bronze-colored foliage and stems. In Greek mythology Prometheus brought fire to man in a hollow fennel stalk.

FORESTIERA NEOMEXICANA, Desert Olive. Perennial to Zone 3.
Height: 9 feet.
Shape: multi-stemmed shrub.
Foliage: narrow green leaves.
Bloom: insignificant small black fruit.
Culture: easy.
Likes: sun.
Tolerates: half-sun/dry/semidry/

poor soil/alkalinity.
Propagation: sets or seeds.
Comments: this plant makes a fast-growing hedge. Native to the southwest U.S.

FORSYTHIA 'NORTHERN GOLD.' Perennial to Zone 2-3.
Height: 6 feet.
Bloom: showy display of vivid yellow flowers from mid- to late April.
Foliage: light green.
Culture: easy.
Likes: sun/half-sun/moist.
Propagation: sets only (softwood cuttings or hardwood cuttings in summer or winter).
Comments: prune out oldest wood in fall. This variety was developed in 1962 by Mr. D. R. Sampson of the Ottawa Research Station. Flower buds are undamaged to temperatures of -35° F. A similar variety, 'Meadowlark,' originated in 1936 in the Arnold Arboretum. There is great commercial potential for growers to force branches in mid-winter and sell them to restaurants, florists, etc. Plant this shrub in the background because Forsythia has little ornamental value once its bloom is over. Grape Hyacinth (*Muscari*) makes an attractive combination.

FRAGARIA VIRGINIANA, Wild Strawberry. Native to moist shrubby areas of the plains and forests of the mountains. Perennial to Zone 2.
Height: 5 inches.
Bloom: dainty white flowers from early May to early July.
Foliage: delicate serrated-edge foliage turns bright red in the fall and early winter.
Likes: half-sun/moist/nitrogen-poor, humus-rich soil for best fruit.
Tolerates: sun/half-shade/shade/semidry.
Propagation: sets.
Comments: fast-spreading invasive plant through runners—but they are so cute. Rare to occasional tiny strawberries with an exceptionally vivid sweet flavor, fruit ripens from early June to July. This plant makes a good ground cover. The Indians made intensive use of this native fruit.

FRAXINUS MANDSHURICA 'MANCANA,' Manchurian Ash. Perennial to Zone 3.
Height: 40 feet.
Shape: oval form in youth, maturing

into a rounded form.

Foliage: attractive large leaves composed of many leaflets, yellow fall color.

Culture: easy.

Likes: sun/moist.

Tolerates: semidry.

Propagation: sets.

Pests: susceptible to ash bark beetle and ash borer, which causes individual limbs to die and fall off. They do not kill the whole tree, just limbs here and there.

Comments: requires regular water when young. This tree tends to drop large amounts of both large and small branches throughout the year. The variety 'Mancana' is a seedless male variety introduced by Morden Research Station.

F. NIGRA 'FALL GOLD,' Black Ash. Perennial to Zone 3.

Height: 40 feet tall, somewhat graceful form.

Foliage: yellow foliage color in the early fall.

Likes: sun/moist.

Tolerates: semidry.

Propagation: sets.

Pests: susceptible to ash bark beetle and ash borer.

Comments: requires regular water when young. This tree tends to drop large amounts of both large and small branches throughout the year. 'Fall Gold' is a seedless male variety introduced by Morden Research Station.

F. PENNSYLVANICA, Green Ash. Perennial to Zone 3-4.

Height: 50 feet.

Shape: commonly available seedling trees are horribly shapeless, but named varieties listed below are selected for their superior form.

Likes: sun.

Tolerates: dry/semidry.

Propagation: sets.

Pests: susceptible to ash bark beetle and ash borer.

Comments: this tree is drought-tolerant. It seeds profusely, and its wildlings become weeds everywhere. Two seedless male varieties selected for improved form at North Dakota State University are 'Centennial,' with its wide-spreading rounded form, and 'Prairie Spire,' with its tall narrow form.

FRITILLARIA ATROPURPUREA, Leopard Lily. Native to rich grasslands and open woods in the foothills of the Rocky Mountains. Perennial to Zone 3.

Height: 1½ feet.

Bloom: nodding dull brown flowers spotted with yellow and white, blooms from late April to early May.

Foliage: narrow, lance-like.

Likes: half-sun/moist/well-drained humus-rich soil.

Tolerates: sun/semidry.

Propagation: bulbs. Bulb offsets can be divided in July.

Comments: prefers to dry out and go dormant in late summer. The tiny rice-like bulblets are edible and were a foodstuff for native peoples. Unfortunately when out of bloom, this plant resembles the deadly poisonous Death Camas, *Zygadenus.*

F. IMPERIALIS, Crown Imperial. Perennial to Zone 3-4.

Height: 3 feet.

Bloom: red, orange, or yellow pineapple-like flowers on a stalk in May, tulip-like foliage.

Likes: half-sun/moist/well-drained humus-rich soil.

Tolerates: sun/half-shade/semidry.

Propagation: bulbs.

Comments: out of the soil these bulbs dry out and die quickly. When planting, bury them 6 inches deep. There is also a variegated form of this plant with white edging on the leaves.

F. MELEAGRIS, Checkered Lily. Perennial to Zone 4.

Bloom: checkered bronze, gray, purple, or white flowers in May.

Likes: half-sun/moist/well-drained humus-rich soil.

Propagation: bulbs.

Comments: grass-like clump. This species is native to Europe including England. Other hardy species are *Fritillaria palidiflora,* which has pale yellow flowers (native to Siberia), and

Checkered Lily,
*Fritiliaria
meleagris*

Fritillaria ruthenica, which has dark purple bell-shaped flowers (native to the Ruthenia area of Russia).

F. PUDICA, Yellow Bells, Yellow Snowdrops. Native to moist hillside areas in the foothills and Rocky Mountains; short-lived perennial to Zone 3.

Height: 8 inches.

Bloom: sparse nodding bright yellow flowers, blooms from early to late April, flower color darkens with age.

Foliage: gray-green, lance-like.

Likes: half-sun/semidry.

Tolerates: sun/moist.

Propagation: bulbs.

Comments: scattered clump habit; prefers to dry out and go dormant in late summer. Like *F. atropurpurea,* the tiny rice-like bulblets are edible and were a foodstuff for native peoples.

GAILLARDIA ARISTATA, Blanketflower. Native to a wide area of the central and northern plains and Rocky Mountains. Perennial to Zone 2.

Height: 2 feet.

Bloom: large yellow daisy flowers with dark orangish-red centers, blooms from mid-June to early August.

Foliage: coarse hairy green leaves, interesting seedpods

Likes: sun/semidry.

Tolerates: half-sun/dry.

Propagation: sets or seeds; tends to self-sow.

Comments: loose upright habit. This native plant is best grown in a regular garden where its self-sowing nature and sparse foliage can be appreciated. Its common name refers to a time when it once covered the landscape like a vividly colored blanket.

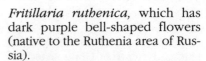

*Blanketflower,
Gaillardia
aristata*

G. GRANDIFLORA, Blanketflower. Perennial to Zone 2.

Height: 2 feet.
Bloom: yellow daisy flowers with dark orangish-red centers, blooms from July to frost (long season if spent flowers removed).
Foliage: somewhat coarse foliage.
Culture: easy.
Likes: sun/semidry.
Tolerates: half-sun/dry.
Propagation: sets or seeds. (Seed germination: warm, light.)
Comments: this plant is attractive in the garden and also makes a short-lasting cut flower.

G. PULCHELLA, Annual Gaillardia. Annual.
Height: 2 feet.
Bloom: vividly colored red, yellow, and bronze daisy flowers, blooms from July to frost (long season if spent flowers removed).
Culture: easy.
Likes: sun/semidry.
Tolerates: half-sun/dry.
Propagation: sets or seeds. (Seed germination: warm.) Self-sows some.

GALIUM ODORATUM, Sweet Woodruff. Perennial to Zone 3-4.
Height: 6 inches.
Bloom: white star-like flowers from May to early June (long bloom season starts at the same time as mid- to late tulips).
Foliage: attractive six-pointed foliage whorled around the stem.
Culture: easy.
Likes: half-shade/moist.
Tolerates: half-sun/shade/dry-semidry.
Propagation: sets or seeds (self-sows).
Comments: invasive by self-sown seed. Use this plant for edging the front of a shade garden or covering bulb areas. Sweet Woodruff is an essential flavoring in May wine.

GARLIC, Allium sativum, culinary herb. Perennial vegetable to Zone 4.
Height: 1 foot.
Description: white flowers in August; semi-evergreen onion-like foliage.
Culture: easy.
Likes: moist/humus-rich, sandy soil.
Tolerates: sun/half-sun/dry/semidry/cold soil.
Propagation: plant seeds or bulbs in the fall or early spring.
Growing tips: reduce watering in late summer to allow foliage to die down. Plants should be thinned to 6 inches apart. An excellent companion plant for roses, all root crops, and brassicas (broccoli, cabbage, kohlrabi, etc). However, do not plant it near beans or peas. Remove occasional flowerheads for best underground bulb development.
Harvest tips: harvest in the early fall when its foliage dies back.
Comments: bulbs last up to a year if dried thoroughly, and stored cool and dry. It is best not to refrigerate garlic because this breaks its dormancy and it starts to sprout. An excellent way to store garlic is to put peeled cloves in a jar and cover them with oil. The cloves will keep for months, and the oil acquires a delicious flavor.

The large size elephant garlic has an extremely mild flavor. It is tasty when roasted whole with a pot roast and eaten as a vegetable. It is less hardy than regular garlic, and must be planted only in the early spring.

GAZANIA RINGENS, Gazania. Annual.
Height: 6 inches.
Bloom: red, pink, orange, yellow, or white daisy flowers with black center band, blooms from May to frost (very long season if spent flowers are removed), flowers close at night.
Culture: easy.
Likes: sun/heat/semidry.
Tolerates: dry.
Propagation: sets.
Comments: this plant is excellent either in the front of a sunny garden or in a container.

GENISTA PILLOSA, Broom. Perennial to Zone 3 (with protection).
Height: 6 inches.
Bloom: bright yellow flowers from mid- to late June.
Foliage: semi-evergreen.
Likes: sun/semidry.
Tolerates: half-sun/dry/very poor soil.
Propagation: sets or seeds.
Comments: slow creeping habit; established plants transplant poorly. This plant is excellent in a rock garden or spilling down a rock wall. The variety 'Vancouver Gold' is particularly free-blooming.

G. TINCTORIA, Dyer's Greenweed. Perennial to Zone 3.
Height: 2 feet.
Bloom: bright yellow flowers from mid- to late June.
Likes: sun/semidry.
Tolerates: half-sun/dry/moist/poor soil.
Propagation: sets or seeds.
Comments: fast-spreading clump; somewhat invasive due to root spreading; established plants transplant poorly. Other hardy species of *Genista* are *Genista lydia* (an upright rounded form), and *G. ovata.* See also the listing under *Cytisus.*

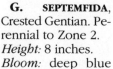

Dyer's Greenweed, Genista tinctoria

G. SEPTEMFIDA, Crested Gentian. Perennial to Zone 2.
Height: 8 inches.
Bloom: deep blue flowers in early August.
Likes: sun/half-sun/semidry/moist/humus-rich soil.
Propagation: sets only, seeds are not true to color.
Comments: semi-erect circular clump. This gentian species is tolerant of moderate heat and easy to grow, but its color is not the legendary gentian blue. Furthermore, its circular fairy-ring style of growth is rather strange. For a hardy cobalt-blue species, try *Gentiana sino-ornata.* It requires cool summers, acidic soil and winter mulch. Obviously, this plant will be difficult to grow in hot plains areas.

GENTIANA AFFINIS, Prairie Gentian. Native to sandy areas and moist grasslands of the Great Plains, foothills and parklands. Perennial.
Height: 1 foot.
Foliage: gracefully shaped upright habit when supported by grass.
Bloom: clear deep blue flowers in July; an unforgettable realization of perfect form and true rich blue color.
Likes: sun/half-sun/semidry/moist/slightly alkaline soil.
Propagation: sets or seeds.
Comments: established plants resent transplanting. Other useful species are *Gentiana amarella,* an annual blue or white flowered species, and

a rare species *Gentiana puberulenta*, Downy Gentian, found in sedge meadows. The gentians, in general, are difficult to maintain and should be left for the most experienced gardeners.

GERANIUM SPECIES, Hardy Geranium, Cranesbill. Perennial to Zone 1.
Height: 2 feet.
Bloom: small purple, red, pink, white, or blue flowers; odd-looking cranebill-like seedpods.

Gentian

Foliage: attractive foliage.
Likes: half-sun/moist.
Tolerates: sun/half-shade/semidry.
Propagation: sets or seeds. (Seed germination: use fresh seed only.)
Comments: rounded mound habit; must have lots of water to prolong bloom in July and August. *Geranium macrorrhizum* has purple, red, or white flowers from late May to July; *Geranium pratense* has white or blue flowers from June to August. Two noteworthy varieties of this species are *'Coeruleum plenum'* with double light blue flowers and *'Plenum'* with double bluish-mauve flowers. *Geranium sanguineum* has red, pink, or white flowers from June to July. A variety of note is *'Lancastriense splendens'* with showy rose-pink flowers. These plants are most attractive grown in combination with ornamental grasses of the same height. Low geraniums are excellent for the front edging of the garden. Taller geraniums are excellent in com-

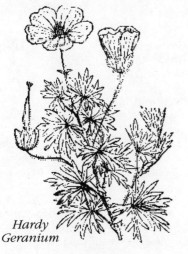

Hardy Geranium

bination with Hostas.

GEUM TRIFLORUM, Prairie Smoke. Native to grassy areas of the Great Plains and Rocky Mountains. Perennial.
Height: 10 inches.
Bloom: soft pinkish-red flowers with a fuzzy texture, blooms from mid-April to June; interesting fuzzy seedheads on elongated stalks.
Foliage: basal clump of fern-like hairy foliage which appears in March to April and goes dormant in mid-summer.
Likes: sun/half-sun/half-shade/dry/semidry/moist.
Propagation: sets or seeds.
Comments: this plant is very common throughout its range. The Indians ground up ripe seeds to use as perfume. The name Prairie Smoke refers to the seedheads, which look a bit like smoke. The seedheads of this plant and *Anemone patens* are very similar.

GILIA RUBRA, Scarlet Gilia. Native to the central Great Plains, central and northern Rockies and the Great Basin, but not the northern Great Plains. Perennial to Zone 4.
Height: 2 feet.
Bloom: vivid scarlet flowers on a loose flower stalk from end of June to the end of July.
Foliage: finely-divided.
Likes: sun/dry/semidry.
Propagation: sets or seed (self-sows into patches in a favorable location.)
Comments: this is a showy plant to include in a prairie planting. Hummingbirds love this flower. Possibly, this wild native could be domesticated to life in a regular garden. A closely related species is *Gilia aggregata*. It is a biennial with either scarlet-red flowers or occasional varieties having white flowers with pink spots. The genus *Gilia* was named for the 18th century Spanish botanist Felipe Gil.

GLADIOLUS HORTULANUS, Gladiolus. Annual.
Height: 2 feet.
Bloom: red, pink, orange, yellow, white, green or purple flowers on a stalk.
Foliage: iris-like foliage that dies down at the end of summer.
Likes: sun/moist/well fertilized humus-rich soil.

Tolerates: half-sun/semidry.
Propagation: bulbs (plant two weeks before frost-free date).
Comments: cool summer areas should plant only early and mid-season varieties. In the garden, this flower blooms much longer than it does as a cut flower. The name *gladiolus* means 'little sword' and refers to the flower stalk. Luther Burbank bred a spectacular hyacinth-flowering gladiolus that was lost shortly after his death. The bulbs had been sent to Ontario and were not dug up one winter.

GLEDITSIA TRIACANTHOS 'INERMIS,' Thornless Honey Locust. Perennial to Zone 4.
Height: 50 feet.
Shape: fast-growing attractive tree.
Foliage: fine-textured with feathery lacy appearance, insignificant yellow fall color.
Culture: easy.
Likes: sun/semidry.
Tolerates: dry/moist.
Propagation: sets (buy only sets with their terminal bud tip intact; hardwood cuttings in winter.)
Pests: occasionally this tree is attacked by canker disease.
Comments: prune only to accentuate natural open shape. This tree leafs out late in the spring and drops its leaves very early in the fall; its delicate branches cast almost no shade in winter. These factors are useful for passive solar heating and cooling. Its drought and pollution tolerance make this a preferred tree for busy streets. The two best varieties are 'Imperial' with a rounded form and 'Skyline' with a dramatically beautiful upright form. The yellow-foliaged variety 'Sunburst' is marginally hardy in Zone 4.

GODETIA AMOENA, Farewell-to-Spring. Native to the Cascade Range and Rocky Mountains. Annual.
Height: 1-3 feet.
Bloom: showy reddish-pink flowers from early- to late June.
Likes: half-sun.
Tolerates: half-shade/moist.
Propagation: sets or seeds. Plant seed in either the fall or early spring.
Comments: clump habit; requires wind protection in exposed locations. For prolonged bloom, stagger seed planting to June.

G. GRANDIFLORA, Satin Flower. Annual.
Height: 1 foot.
Bloom: showy profuse red, pink or white flowers, blooms from June to frost (long season).
Likes: half-sun.
Tolerates: half-shade/moist.
Propagation: sets or seeds.
Comments: requires wind protection in exposed locations. This old-fashioned flower makes a beautiful show in the garden.

GOMPHRENA GLOBOSA, Globe Amaranth. Annual.
Height: 2 feet.
Bloom: pink, white or purple clover-like flowers, blooms from July to frost (long season).
Culture: easy.
Likes: sun/semidry/heat.
Tolerates: half-sun/dry.
Propagation: sets.
Comments: small bush habit. This plant is primarily used for long-lasting cut flowers, as well as dried everlastings.

GONIOLIMON TARTARICUM (Limonium tartaricum), German Statice. Perennial to Zone 2.
Height: 1 foot.
Bloom: white airy clusters from late June to August (long season).
Foliage: basal clump of foliage.
Culture: easy.
Likes: half-sun/semidry/humus-rich soil.
Tolerates: sun/dry/moist.
Propagation: sets or seeds.
Comments: established plants resent transplanting; flowers can be left on plant for winter interest. This plant looks attractive in the garden from late summer to early winter. Additionally, it can be used as either a cut flower or a dried everlasting. This statice lends itself to particularly showy store window displays.

GOOD KING HENRY, Chenopodium bonus-henricus. Cool-season annual vegetable.
Height: 1 foot.
Description: sprawling clump of green arrow-shaped foliage, insignicant green flowers.
Culture: easy.
Likes: moist.
Tolerates: sun/half-sun/half-shade/semidry.
Propagation: sets or seeds.
Comments: these tender and vitamin-rich leaves are used as a cooked green. This wonderful spinach-like plant should be better known.

GOURDS, many species and hybrids of *Curcurbitaceae*—Squash family. Warm-season annual vegetable.
Height: 1 foot by 4 feet wide.
Description: sprawling vine with coarse leaves, small ornamental fruit.
Culture: very easy.
Likes: sun/moist/humus-rich soil.

Gourd, Curcurbitaceae

Propagation: sets (set outside after frost-free date) or seeds (very easy).
Growing tips: heavy water user.
Comments: gourds produce ornamental hard fruit. In many parts of the world, gourds are used to make scoops, cups, and culinary tools. Additionally, gourds can be used to make rattles.

GUTIERREZIA SAROTHRAE (Xanthocephalum sarothrae), Broom Snakeweed. Native to dry poor hillside areas of Great Plains and foothills. Perennial.
Height: 1 foot.
Bloom: showy flat-topped yellow flower clusters from end of July to frost.
Foliage: many-stemmed woody upright clump, narrow green foliage.
Likes: sun.
Tolerates: half-sun/dry/semidry.
Propagation: sets or seeds.
Comments: this plant is often confused with the taller *Chrysothamnus nauseosus*, Rubber Rabbit Bush, which grows in precisely the same areas. Indians used this plant as a broom.

GYMNOCLADUS DIOICA, Kentucky Coffee Tree. Perennial to Zone 4.
Height: 60 feet.
Bloom: insignificant greenish flower clusters, brown seedpods in fall.
Shape: oblong upright shape when young, growing slowly into a large spreading rounded form; attractive gray bark.
Foliage: fine-textured foliage that somewhat resembles the tropical jacaranda tree.
Likes: sun.
Tolerates: half-sun/dry/semidry/moist.
Propagation: sets (buy only sets with their terminal bud tips intact).
Comments: disease and pest resistant. Prune minimally. This tree often suffers transplant shock. It is best moved when young. This tree drops its large compound leaves in the fall and assumes a strikingly beautiful, austere branch form. Because of this habit, this tree would be a prime solar usage tree (dense shade in summer and minimum of branches in the winter). This choice tree should be much more widely planted as a street tree and in parks. It is native to eastern North America. The Indians roasted the seeds like chestnuts. The early settlers used the roasted seeds as a coffee substitute,

Kentucky Coffee Tree, Gymnocladus dioica

and thus the common name.

GYPSOPHILA ELEGANS, Baby's Breath. Annual.
Height: 2 feet.
Bloom: white or pink airy clusters from mid-June to mid-July (longer season if seed planting is staggered).
Culture: very easy.
Likes: sun/semidry.
Tolerates: half-sun/very dry/poor soil.
Propagation: seeds. (Seed germination: plant in the fall or early spring, sow seed into a clump.)
Comments: established plants resent

transplanting. Flowers can be either left on plant for winter interest, used as a fresh cut flower or dried as an everlasting. This is the commercial baby's breath that florists use. It has naturalized in sandy areas of the West. This plant makes a showy contrast when planted with shrub or hybrid tea roses.

G. PANICULATA, Perennial Baby's Breath. Perennial to Zone 1.
Height: 3 feet.
Bloom: white or pink airy clusters from mid-July to August.
Culture: easy.
Likes: sun/semidry.
Tolerates: half-sun/moist.
Propagation: sets or seeds. (Seed germination: warm.)
Comments: established plants resent being transplanted; windstake with brush support. An exceptional variety *'Compacta plena'* has double white flowers and a compact habit.

G. REPENS, Creeping Baby's Breath. Perennial to Zone 3.
Height: 4 inches.
Bloom: white or pink airy flowers from June to late July (long season).
Culture: easy.
Likes: sun/dry/semidry.
Propagation: sets or seeds. (Seed germination: warm.)
Comments: low creeping mound; requires a winter mulch in exposed locations. This plant makes an excellent edging in a garden, as well as a good bulb cover. Native to the European Alps. *'Monstrosa'* is a vigorous 1 foot tall variety. 'Rosy Veil' is a showy pink variety.

HAPLOPAPPUS LANUGINOSUS, Goldenweed. Native to moist areas of the rocky areas of the Rocky Mountains. Perennial.
Height: 1 foot.
Bloom: large yellow flowers from July to August.
Foliage: densely compact tufted habit, basal rosette of lance-shaped dark green leaves.
Likes: sun/half-sun/dry/semidry.
Propagation: sets (division in spring) or seeds.
Comments: established plants resent transplanting. Some varieties have very woolly foliage and others are smooth textured.

H. SPINULOSUS, Spiny Goldenweed. Native to dry ridges and disturbed areas of the Great Plains and foothills. Perennial.
Height: 6 inches.
Bloom: profuse showy yellow aster-like flowers from July to August; fuzzy seedheads produced at the same time as the new flowers.
Foliage: spreading semi-erect clump, attractive fern-like gray-green foliage with prickles at the tips.
Likes: sun.
Tolerates: half-sun/dry/semidry.
Propagation: sets or seeds (seed germination: cold treatment).
Comments: established plants resent transplanting.

H. SUBFRUTICOSUS, Woody Goldenweed. Native to rocky areas in medium to high elevation Rocky Mountains. Perennial.
Height: 2 feet.
Bloom: yellow aster-like flowers in July to August.
Foliage: upright shrub-like habit, interesting semi-curled foliage.
Likes: sun/half-sun/dry/semidry.
Propagation: sets or seeds.
Comments: established plants resent transplanting.

HELENIUM AUTUMNALE, Sneezeweed, native to stream banks and moist areas in the plains and mountain valleys. Perennial to Zone 2.
Height: 2 feet.
Bloom: red, orange, yellow, or brown daisy flowers with brown-black centers, blooms from early August to frost.
Foliage: slightly toothed lance-shaped leaves.
Likes: half-sun/moist/nitrogen-rich, humus-rich soil.
Tolerates: sun/wet.
Propagation: sets or seeds.
Comments: upright clump; requires winter mulch in areas without predictable snowcover; prefers annual division in the spring for best bloom. Besides being showy in the garden, this plant also makes good cut flowers. The botanical name refers to Helen of Troy. The common name refers to the fact that the Indians dried the petal, and crushed them into a powder. This snuff-like powder was inhaled to stop sneezing caused by allergies, thus the common name, Sneezeweed. Two varieties of note are 'Brilliant,' which has small red, orange, yellow, and brown flowers, a late, long bloom season, and strong flower

stalks; and 'Bruno,' which has reddish-brown flowers.

HELIANTHUS ANNUUS, Sunflower; official state flower of Kansas, one of the many flowers nominated for U.S. national flower. Annual.
Height: 4-8 feet.
Bloom: yellow or white flowers with dark centers from late July to frost (long season).

Sunflower,
Helianthus annuus

Culture: easy.
Likes: sun/moist/humus and fertilizer-rich soil.
Tolerates: half-sun/dry/semidry.
Propagation: sets or seeds. (Requires warm soil. Start inside in April or outside after the frost-free date.)
Comments: forms either a bush or a tall single stalk depending on variety. The variety 'Taiyo' makes a particularly long-lasting cut flower. A native species, *Helianthus petiolaris,* has small yellow flowers and is showy in a winter garden.

H. DECAPETALUS. Perennial to Zone 4.
Height: 4 feet.
Bloom: double yellow flowers from July to frost (long season if spent flowers are removed).
Culture: easy.
Likes: sun/semidry.
Tolerates: half-sun/half-shade/dry.
Propagation: sets or seeds.
Comments: bush habit.

H. X MULTIFLORUS, Bush Sunflower. Annual.
Height: 5 feet.
Bloom: showy yellow flowers from July to frost (long season).
Culture: easy.
Likes: sun/semidry.
Tolerates: half-sun/dry/moist.
Propagation: sets only (this hybrid's seed is sterile).
Comments: rounded bush.

H. TUBEROSUS, Jerusalem Artichoke. See Jerusalem Artichoke entry.

HELICHRYSUM BRACTEATUM, Strawflower. Annual.
Height: 2 feet.
Bloom: red, pink, coppery-brown, yellow or white long-lasting flowers with a papery texture, blooms from late July to frost (long season).
Likes: sun/heat.
Tolerates: half-sun/moist.
Propagation: sets or seeds. (Seed germination: light, warm.)
Comments: needs either a wind support or to be thickly seeded in a clump. This is the main strawflower sold commercially. Besides being showy in the garden, it can be used as either cut flowers or dried everlastings. Cut just before flowers open and thread stem with florist's wire. An improved variety is *'Monstrosum'* which has larger flowers. Native to Australia.

HELIOPSIS HELIANTHOIDES 'SCABRA.' Perennial to Zone 1.
Height: 4 feet.
Bloom: showy yellow flowers from July to frost.
Culture: easy.
Likes: sun/moist.
Tolerates: half-sun/dry.
Propagation: sets or seeds.
Comments: rounded bush-like clump. This plant is showy in a garden as well as producing good cut flowers. Three varieties of note: 'Golden Plume' is a dwarf size plant with profuse yellow flowers; *'Incomparabilis'* has a refined color and form; 'Summer sun' has extra large flowers.

HELIOTROPIUM ARBORESCENS, Heliotrope. Annual.
Height: 1 foot.
Bloom: very fragrant purple or white flowers from June to frost (very long season).
Foliage: attractive crinkled foliage.
Likes: half-sun/moist/humus-rich soil.
Tolerates: half-shade.
Propagation: sets or seeds. (Seed germination: warm, slow to flower from seed.)
Comments: very slow-growing habit; pinching young plant delays bloom, but produces a bushier form. The white flowering varieties have the most soothing vanilla-like scent. This is a spectacular plant for an old urn. It is a good plant for pots or containers with the advantage that you can bring it inside for the winter. In Greek mythology, the water nymph Clytie was so in love with Apollo that all she could do all day was watch him cross the sky. Eventually, she rooted to the spot and became a flower that turned to face the sun throughout the day. Unfortunately, in this case the name is misleading. This flower does not move at all.

HELIPTERUM HUMBOLDTIANUM, Strawflower. Annual.
Height: 1 foot.
Bloom: papery yellow flower clusters from August to frost (long season).
Likes: sun/dry/sandy soil/heat.
Tolerates: half-sun/semidry.
Propagation: sets.
Comments: This flower is used primarily as either a fresh cut flower or dried everlasting. Cut when flowers are fully open.

H. MANGLESII (Rhodanthe manglesii), Swan River Everlasting. Annual.
Height: 1 foot.
Bloom: delicate-looking red, pink, or white daisy flowers with a papery texture, blooms from August to frost (long season).
Foliage: spindly odd-looking foliage.
Likes: sun/dry/sandy soil/heat.
Tolerates: half-sun/semidry.
Propagation: sets.
Comments: this flower makes a showy fresh cut flower, but cannot be used as a dried everlasting unless its thin stem is wired for support. For cut flowers, cut when flower buds first begin to open.

H. ROSEUM, Acroclinum. Annual.
Height: 2 feet.
Bloom: white to pink daisy flowers from August to frost (long season).
Foliage: attractive, grass-like.
Likes: sun/dry/sandy soil.
Tolerates: half-sun/semidry.
Propagation: sets.
Comments: this flower makes an excellent cut flower or dried everlasting. Cut just as flower buds begin to open. Shepherd's Garden Seeds offers a Dutch variety, 'Mixed Palette,' with flowers in a color range of cherry red, dark pink, light pink, and white.

HEMEROCALLIS CITRINA, Night-blooming Daylily. Perennial to Zone 2.
Height: 3 feet.
Bloom: yellow flowers in early July, flowers are fragrant only at night (they open in the evening and are wilted by noon the next day).
Foliage: basal clump of daylily foliage.
Likes: half-sun/half-shade/moist.
Propagation: roots or seeds. (Seed germination: cold treatment.)
Comments: prefers cool summers areas or mid-day shade. This plant makes good cut flowers as well as being an attractive garden plant.

H. DUMORTIERI. Perennial to Zone 2.
Height: 2 feet.
Bloom: yellow-orange flowers with a brown underside and a jasmine- or honeysuckle-like scent in mid-May (extremely short bloom season).
Likes: half-sun/half-shade/moist.
Propagation: roots or seeds. (Seed germination: cold treatment.)
Comments: this plant makes good cut flowers as well as being an attractive garden plant.

H. FULVA AND HYBRIDS, Common Daylily. Perennial to Zone 1.
Height: 3 feet.
Bloom: a color range of red, pink, orange, yellow, near-white, green, purple, and near-black flowers. There are no blue or true white col-

Common Daylily,
Hemerocallis fulva

ors. Blooms from June to August (long season with mixed early and late varieties).
Culture: very easy.
Likes: sun/moist/well-drained soil.
Tolerates: half-shade/very dry/semidry/wet.
Comments: tolerates tree roots and

grass competition well; remove seedpods as they form for best vigor the following year; prefers to be fertilized in the spring with a low nitrogen fertilizer; roots can be planted at any time; used both as a garden plant and as a cut flower. This plant makes a good combination with Jacob's Ladder *(Polemonium)*. Some varieties are fragrant; try to choose these. One tall fragrant variety is 'Gaiety,' which grows 4 feet tall, with lemon yellow flowers.

There are also dwarf varieties which are very charming in a small garden. One of these, the variety 'Stella d'Oro,' is especially recommended for its extremely long and profuse bloom season. It occupies very little space and blooms heavily for a long time. Avoid evergreen varieties because they are less hardy than the deciduous ones. It is important to remove dead foliage in mid-winter. This disposes of many insect pests. There is an American Hemerocallis Society (address is listed in the Resource Directory).

H. LILIOASPHODELUS (H. flava), Lemon Lily. Perennial to Zone 4.
Height: 3 feet.
Bloom: yellow flowers with a heavy lily-like scent from late May to early June.
Likes: sun/moist.
Tolerates: shade/semidry/wet.
Comments: roots can be planted at any time. This plant makes good cut flowers as well as being an attractive garden plant.

H. MIDDENDORFII. Perennial to Zone 1.
Height: 2 foot.
Bloom: showy butterscotch-orange flowers from mid-May to early June, small size but very fragrant.
Likes: sun.
Tolerates: half-sun/semidry/moist.
Propagation: roots or seeds. (Seed germination: cold treatment.)
Comments: this is the very first Daylily to bloom. This plant makes good cut flowers as well as being an attractive garden plant.

H. THUNBERGII. Perennial to Zone 3-4.
Height: 3 feet.
Bloom: yellow flowers in June, flowers are fragrant only at night (they open in late afternoon and are closed by noon the next day).

Likes: half-sun/moist.
Tolerates: sun/half-shade/semidry-wet.
Propagation: roots.
Comments: this plant makes good cut flowers as well as being an attractive garden plant.

HERACLEUM LANATUM, Cow Parsnip. Native to moist areas of the Northern Temperate Zone. Perennial to Zone 2.
Height: 4 feet.
Bloom: very large flat-topped white flower clusters from end of June to August.
Foliage: large coarse leaves, attractive dried seedheads that persist throughout the fall and winter.
Culture: easy.
Likes: half-sun/half-shade/moist/wet (a bog plant).
Propagation: sets or seeds.
Comments: established plants resent transplanting. This plant was named for Hercules. Many winged insects feed on the nectar of the Cow Parsnip, and many birds feed on the seeds. Do not confuse this obviously coarse-leafed plant with the extremely poisonous Water Hemlock *(Cicuta douglasii)*, which has finely-divided leaves and a chambered root if cut open lengthwise. They both grow in exactly the same habitat. This plant was the "sacred rhubarb" used in the Blackfoot Sun Dance Ceremony. Its shoots were commonly eaten in the spring. They were either boiled or roasted over coals. The stems were eaten later in the year, but they must be peeled to remove the tiny hairs. Kim Williams commented that they taste poor to our modern taste buds. Shoots are also eaten by livestock, bears, elk, and marmots.

HESPERIS MATRONALIS, Sweet Rocket. Biennial to Zone 1.
Height: 2 feet.
Bloom: lilac, white, or purple phlox-like flowers in May to June (long season); flowers have an intensely powerful spicy fragrance only at night.
Foliage: strikingly evergreen during the plant's first winter (winter interest).
Culture: very easy.
Likes: half-sun/moist.
Tolerates: sun/half-shade/dry/semidry.

Propagation: seeds. (Seed germination: light.)
Comments: seeds are invasive, but extra plants are easily removed. This plant has naturalized in our area as a much loved weed; there are also many named horticultural varieties. The name *matronalis* refers to the elderly women of the Roman Empire who grew this flower.

HEUCHERA SANGUINEA, Coral Bells. Perennial to Zone 2.
Height: 2 feet.
Bloom: red, pink, white or green airy flower clusters from June to July (long season if spent blooms are removed).
Likes: half-shade/semidry/humus-rich soil.
Tolerates: half-sun/moist.
Propagation: sets or seeds.
Comments: attractive low clump; may need winter mulch in exposed areas. 'Brandon Glow' (deep pink flowers), 'Brandon Pink' (light pink flowers), and 'Northern Fire' (red flowers) are especially hardy varieties. These were developed jointly by Brandon Agricultural Station and Morden Research Station, both in Manitoba. For Zone 4 and warmer zones, there is a dramatic variety called 'Firefly.' It has brick-red flowers and vivid yellow centers. *Heuchera richardsonii,* native to the northern Rocky Mountains, has evergreen foliage (winter interest) and insignificant green flowers in June.

HOLODISCUS DISCOLOR, Mountain Spray Bush, Ocean Spray. Native to dry forested areas of the foothills and mountains, west to the Pacific Ocean. Perennial to Zone 3.
Height: 10 feet.
Shape: irregularly shaped native shrub.
Bloom: showy sprays of cream-colored flowers which darken with age, blooms from July to late August; dried flower clusters remain on plant through most of the winter.
Foliage: attractive spiraea-like foliage.
Likes: semidry/humus-rich soil.
Tolerates: half-sun/dry/moist.
Propagation: sets or seeds.
Comments: prefers wind-protected location. This showy native bush is

best suited for an informal forest-like garden or background plant.

HORSERADISH, Armoracia rusticana. Perennial vegetable to Zone 1.
Height: 2 feet.
Description: long coarse foliage, primarily grown for its sharply flavored taproot.
Likes: sun/half-sun/half-shade/dry/semidry.
Propagation: sets (it is important that the root is planted right side up).

Horseradish, Armoracia rusticana
Comments: very invasive by root spreading; this plant can be very difficult to remove from a garden. If the main root is pulled, tiny rootlets stay in the ground and start new plants.

For use as a condiment, peel the roots and grind them in a blender. Place in a jar, cover with vinegar to prevent discoloration, and refrigerate. Excellent served with beef.

HOSTA SPECIES. Perennial to Zone 1.
Height: 1 foot.
Bloom: white or lavender flower spikes from June to August (long season with mixed early to late flowering species).
Foliage: showy bold foliage in colors of green, blue, gold and white; leaf sizes vary from very tiny (1 inch across) to very large (1 foot across); leaf forms include oval, round, lance-shaped, heart-shaped or cup-shaped; textures vary from smooth, puckered, corrugated, seersuckered to waffled.
Culture: easy.
Likes: half-shade/moist/low nitrogen fertilizer.
Tolerates: half-sun/shade/semidry (gold foliage varieties require half-sun to maintain color, and blue foliage varieties tolerate the most shade).
Propagation: sets.
Comments: prefers but does not require humus-rich soil. Most can be used as cut flowers. Low varieties are excellent for edging the front of the garden or as a ground cover. Hostas combine well either with ornamental alliums or hardy geraniums. There is a Hosta Society listed in the Resource Directory.

Varieties of Note:

'August Moon'—crinkled yellow foliage.
'Blue Skies'—dramatic blue foliage, tidy rosette habit, excellent for use in the front of a shady garden.
'Frances Williams'—large blue-green leaves trimmed with an irregular gold border.
'Gold Edger'—small gold leaves and a tidy habit. Excellent for the front of the garden.
'Gold Standard'—large gold leaves edged with green, tolerates shade well.
'Great Expectations'—leaves have a yellow midrib with light and dark green sides, a very dramatic looking variety.
'Honeybells'—fragrant lavender flowers, blooms in July, foliage is green.
'Krossa Regal'—large frosty-green leaves.
H. montana 'Aureo-Marginata'—dramatic green leaves edged irregularly with yellow.
'Northern Halo'—rich blue leaves with a puckered texture and white edge.
H. plantaginea 'Grandiflora'—fragrant white flowers, blooms in August, foliage is plain green.

Hosta

'Royal Standard'—fragrant white flowers, blooms in August, attractive light green foliage.
'Sun Power'—bright yellow foliage with an undulating edge.
H. ventricosa—showy large purple flowers, blooms from late July to August, foliage is green.
H. venusta—purple flowers, light green foliage, and tolerates shade well.

HUMULUS LUPULUS 'AUREUS,' Ornamental Golden Hops, vine. Perennial to Zone 2.
Height: fast-growing vine to 20 feet.
Bloom: female plants have greenish hop flowers with an odd fragrance that some people enjoy, blooms in August.
Climbing habit: climbs by twining tips, needs a lattice or wire support to climb.
Foliage: gold variegated foliage.
Culture: easy.
Likes: sun/moist.
Tolerates: half-sun/semidry/wet.
Propagation: seeds.
Comments: hops flowers are often used in tea or in dream pillows to induce relaxation and sleep.

Ornamental Golden Hops, Humulus lupulus 'aureus'

H. JAPONICUS 'VARIEGATUS,' Annual Ornamental Hops. Annual.
Height: fast-growing vine to 20 feet.
Climbing habit: climbs by twining tip, needs a support to climb.
Foliage: showy white and green foliage with red stems.
Culture: easy.
Likes: sun/moist/humus-rich soil.
Tolerates: half-sun/wet. This vine makes a fast screen.

Propagation: seeds.

HUNNEMANNIA FUMERIFOLIA, Mexican Tulip Poppy. Annual.
Height: 2 feet.
Bloom: bright yellow poppy-like flowers (large size—3 inches across), blooms from mid-summer to frost.
Likes: sun/dry/semidry.
Propagation: sets or seeds.
Comments: tolerates drought well.

HYACINTHUS ORIENTALIS, Hyacinth. Perennial to Zone 3-4.
Height: 8 inches.
Bloom: fragrant red, pink, yellow, white, blue, or black flowers in mid-April.
Likes: sun/semidry/humus-rich soil.
Tolerates: half-sun/moist.
Propagation: bulbs (bury 4 inches deep).
Comments: best grown near the warm wall of house. This flower blooms in every color of the rainbow except green. In Greek mythology it grew from Hyakinthos, a mortal man loved by Apollo, the god of the sun. One day while the two were playing quoits, Zephyrus, god of the west wind, became so jealous of the mortal man's beauty, that he caused Apollo's throw to strike and kill Hyakinthos. Apollo created this sweet-scented flower from the blood of his beautiful lover.

HYDRANGEA ARBORESCENS 'GRANDIFLORA,' Hills of Snow. Perennial to Zone 2.
Height: 6 feet.
SBloom: dramatically large snowball-like flower clusters; flowers start out white and age to a greenish color; blooms from late June to July.
hape: rounded shrub.
Foliage: attractive large rounded leaves.
Likes: half-sun.
Tolerates: sun/half-shade/moist.
Propagation: sets.
Comments: prune this shrub to the ground in the spring in alternate years for best compact habit and vigorous flowering. Another variety 'Annabelle' is also considered choice.

H. PANICULATA 'GRANDIFLORA,' Pee Gee Hydrangea. Perennial to Zone 2.
Height: 15 feet.
Shape: attractive large shrub, white

Hills of Snow, Hydrangea arborescens

elongated flower clusters from late July to August.
Culture: easy.
Likes: sun/half-sun/half-shade/moist.
Propagation: sets.
Comments: plan to give this large shrub lots of room.

HYMENOXYS ACAULIS, Butte Marigold. Native to dry rocky hillsides in the Great Plains. Perennial.
Height: 6 inches.
Bloom: large golden-yellow daisy flowers with orange veins on stalks, blooms from mid-May to mid-June (occasional sparse rebloom in the fall).
Foliage: low basal clump of silky gray-green foliage.
Likes: sun.
Tolerates: half-sun/dry/semidry.
Propagation: sets or seeds.
Comments: tends to be easy to grow in a rock garden. The name *acaulis* means "stalkless" and refers to the lack of stem on the leaves. The flowers, however, are borne on 6 inches tall stalks.

H. RICHARDSONII, Colorado Rubber Plant. Native to dry hilltops and disturbed areas in the Great Plains. Perennial.
Height: 10 inches.
Bloom: bright yellow daisy flowers on stalks, blooms from May to June.
Foliage: clump habit of finely-divided foliage.
Likes: sun.
Tolerates: half-sun/dry/semidry.
Propagation: sets or seeds.
Comments: the roots contain a milky-white latex sap, which once

was considered as a substitute for rubber.

HYSSOPUS OFFICINALIS, Hyssop. Perennial to Zone 3.
Height: 1 foot.
Bloom: profuse blue flowers (there are also pink and white varieties) from July to September (long season).
Foliage: dark green narrow foliage in low shrubby clump.
Culture: easy.
Likes: sun/semidry/poor or alkaline soil.
Tolerates: half-sun/moist.
Propagation: sets or seeds.
Comments: requires winter mulch in areas without predictable snow-cover. This plant can also be trimmed into a low hedge or border. Its name comes from the Hebrew word *azob* meaning 'Holy Plant.' Native to southern Europe and Asia. The plant called anise hyssop (*Agastashe foeniculum*) is not related to this plant.

IBERIS PINNATA (I. affinis), Annual Candytuft. Annual.
Height: 1 foot.
Bloom: fragrant white flowers from June to July (longer season if seed planting is staggered).
Culture: easy.
Likes: half-sun/semidry.
Tolerates: sun/half-shade/moist.
Propagation: sets or seeds. (Seed germination: can be seeded outside a month before the frost-free date.)
Comments: pinched plants have a bushier habit as well as a more profuse bloom. This plant is excellent in garden beds and containers as well as used as a cut flower. 'Purity' is a profusely flowering variety.

I. SEMPERVIRENS, Perennial Candytuft, perennial to Zone 4-5.
Height: 8 inches.
Bloom: white flowers from early to late May.
Likes: half-sun/semidry.
Tolerates: half-shade/dry/moist.
Propagation: sets or seed. (Can be seeded outside a month before the frost-free date.)
Comments: difficult in areas without snow cover as foliage tends to turn brown and die. Requires light winter mulch to protect foliage; shear to four inches tall after bloom for compact form; pinch out half of the flower buds in early spring to stag-

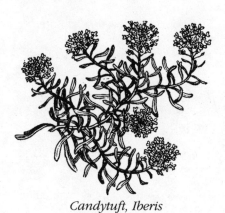

*Candytuft, Iberis
sempervirens*

ger bloom. A dwarf variety that may prove better adapted to the chinook zone is '*Pygmea*,' which grows to only 4 inches tall.

I. UMBELLATA, Annual Candytuft. Annual.
Height: 1 foot.
Bloom: red, pink, white, or purple flowers from June to July (longer season if seed planting is staggered).
Culture: easy.
Likes: half-sun.
Tolerates: sun/moist.
Propagation: sets (must be transplanted carefully) or seeds.
Comments: clump habit; pinch when young for bushier form and more profuse flowering.

ILEX VERTICILLATA, Dogwood Holly. Perennial to Zone 2.
Height: 10 feet.
Shape: graceful open shrub.
Bloom: insignificant flowers; red berries.
Foliage: attractive dogwood-like leaves which drop in the fall.
Likes: sun/half-sun/semidry/moist.
Propagation: sets or seeds.
Comments: two varieties of note are 'Xmas Cheer' and 'Winter Red,' which have showy red berries held until spring. Individual plants are either male or female. A male plant must be nearby for a female plant to have berries. Unpruned, this plant makes a showy landscaping shrub, and with pruning can be used as a hedge. This shrub is a species of holly, but it bears no resemblance whatsoever to the evergreen plant.

ILIAMNA RIVULARIS, Streambank Mallow. Native to stream banks in the Great Plains and Rocky Mountains

and disturbed areas. Perennial.
Height: 4 feet.
Bloom: small showy pink hollyhock flowers on stalks from June to July.
Foliage: large coarse clump, malva-like foliage.
Likes: sun/half-sun/moist/wet.
Propagation: sets or seeds.
Comments: the name *rivularis* means "of the brookside." The plant is closely related to Hollyhock *(Alcea rosea)*.

IMPATIENS BALSAMINA, Balsam-rose. Annual.
Height: 1 foot.
Bloom: red, pink, white, or lavender rose-like flowers with a waxy texture, blooms from June to frost.
Culture: easy.
Likes: half-sun/moist/mid-day shade in hot summer areas.
Tolerates: half-shade/semidry.

*Balsam-rose,
Impatiens balsamina*

Propagation: sets or seeds. (Seed germination: light, warm.)
Comments: clump habit. This attractive old-fashioned plant should be more commonly grown. Besides being attractive in the garden, it is also excellent in pots or containers.

I. BIFLORA, Jewel Weed. Native to stream banks in the Great Plains. Annual.
Height: 3 feet.
Bloom: small orange flowers marked with small red-brown spots; blooms from July to frost.
Foliage: multi-branched upright clump, odd-looking succulent stems.
Likes: sun/half-sun/moist/wet (a bog plant).
Propagation: sets or seeds.
Comments: Indians used this plant for treatment of any rash. Today, this plant is an important treatment

for poison ivy rash.

I. GLANDULIFERA, Bush Impatiens, Poor Man's Orchid. Annual.
Height: 4 feet.
Bloom: pink, white or lavender flowers from July to frost.
Likes: half-sun in hot summer areas/ full sun in cool summer areas/ moist.
Propagation: sets or seeds. Self-sows. (Seed germination: light, warm.)
Comments: multi-branched shrub-like plant. This dramatically tall tropical plant is quite striking planted in beds.

I. WALLERIANA, Impatiens. Annual.
Height: 1 foot.
Bloom: red, pink, orange, white or purple flowers from May to frost (very long season).
Foliage: some varieties have attractive variegated foliage.
Culture: easy.
Likes: half-shade/moist.
Tolerates: shade.
Propagation: sets. (Seed germination: light, warm.)
Comments: clump habit; pinch tips back for bushier plants when young. This plant is especially showy planted with sweet alyssum *(Lobularia maritima)* or *lobelia*, but plant them in brighter sun exposure than normal for them. It is attractive as a border edging, a mass planting in a shady area, as well as in pots or containers. In the fall, it can be brought inside for a winter houseplant.

IPOMOEA ALBA (Calonyction aculeatum), Moon Flower Vine. Annual.
Height: vine to 20 feet.
Bloom: large white fragrant morning-glory flowers which open at sunset (spectacular to watch) from July to frost (long season).
Climbing habit: climbs by twining tips, needs a support to climb.
Likes: sun/moist/humus-rich, fertilizer-rich soil/lots of heat.
Tolerates: wet.
Propagation: sets (must be transplanted carefully) or seeds. (Seed germination: warm, nick seeds or soak overnight before planting.)

I. BATATAS, Sweet Potato. Annual.
Height: attractive fast-growing vine to 6 feet.
Foliage: bold heart-shaped leaves, edible tubers.

Likes: sun/moist/well-drained, humus-rich soil.

Propagation: tuber planted after frost-free date, but can be started indoors in water.

Comments: requires maximum heat and sun; likes deeply dug soil. Low-nitrogen soil and an extremely long, hot growing season will produce tubers. However, nitrogen-rich soil produces a showy fast-growing vine and no tubers. This plant rarely flowers and it makes few tubers in our short season, but it makes a showy ornamental vine. Native to the Caribbean. True yams belong to a different genus, *Dioscorea*.

I. PURPUREA, Morning Glory. Annual.

Height: fast-growing vine to 10 feet.

Climbing habit: climbs by twining tips, needs a support to climb.

Bloom: red, white, blue, or purple flowers from July to frost (long season).

Propagation: sets (must be transplanted carefully) or seeds. (Seed germination: warm, nick seeds or soak overnight before planting.)

Likes: half-sun/heat.

Tolerates: sun/half-shade/moist.

Comments: Named Morning Glory because its flowers are open only until noon.

IRIS. This is the official city flower of Great Falls, Montana, and the official state flower of Tennessee. In mythology, the goddess Iris was Juno's personal messenger and her path was the rainbow. Besides being showy garden plants, all of the iris genus can be used as cut flowers. The roots of all species are so poisonous that a tincture of Iris versicolor is an effective remedy for athlete's foot fungus. There are plant societies devoted to Species Iris, Siberian Iris, Median Iris, and more general groups like the American Iris Society and the Canadian Iris Society. Addresses for these are listed in the Resource Directory.

Order of bloom: Reticulata species (early to late April), Juno species (early May), Dwarf Bearded (early May), Median Bearded (mid-May), *Flavissima* (late May), Miniature Tall Bearded (late May), Border Bearded (late May), Tall Bearded (late May), *Graminea* (late May), *Pallida* (early June), *Missouriensis*

(mid-June), *Pseudacorus* (mid-June), Versicolor (mid-June), Siberian Group (late June), *Spuria* (late June to early July), *Ensata* (early to mid-July), *Dichotoma* (late July to frost).

Bearded Iris Hybrids. Perennial to Zone 1 (except for some of the less hardy modern hybrids of Tall Bearded Iris).

Bloom: flowers bloom in every color of the rainbow, including green.

Culture: very easy.

Likes: sun/moist.

Tolerates: half-shade/shade.

Comments: roots can be planted anytime except late fall and midwinter (plant shallowly so that the roots can bake in the summer sun). It is important to remove dead foliage in winter; this disposes of many insect problems.

The group classified as Miniature Dwarfs (less than 8 inches tall) blooms in early May; Standard Dwarfs (12 inches tall) bloom in mid-May; and three types (Intermediate Bearded, Border Bearded and Tall Bearded Iris) bloom from late May to June. The old varieties of Tall Bearded Iris are much hardier than new varieties. Many collectors prefer the older varieties for their smaller flowers, branched flower stalks, and absence of ruffled edges on the petals. *Iris germanica* and *Iris florentina* are in such a category, and both have a refreshing fragrance. It is recommended that you search out varieties with true deep blue color such as the following:

'Banbury Ruffles'—Dwarf Bearded, rich deep blue.

'Blue Denim'—Dwarf Bearded, mid-blue.

'Crystal Blue'—Tall Bearded, light glacier blue.

'Night Owl'—Tall Bearded, dark navy blue.

'Pacific Panorama'—Tall Bearded, a

Tall Bearded Iris

haunting blue-purple color, fragrant.

I. DICHOTOMA, Vesper Iris. Perennial to Zone 3.

Height: 2 feet.

Bloom: small white, blue, or purple butterfly-like flowers on multi-branched stalks from late July to September; each flower opens in the late afternoon and closes at midnight.

Foliage: fan-like foliage is sparse-looking (not a showy plant by itself).

Likes: sun/semidry.

Tolerates: half-sun/moist.

Propagation: sets.

Comments: must have water in late summer while blooming. This plant is a short-lived perennial. It seems to bloom itself to death. Try to hand pollinate flowers and save seed each year to propagate new plants.

I. ENSATA (I. kaempferi), Japanese Iris. Perennial to Zone 3-4.

Height: 3 feet.

Bloom: pink, white, blue, or purple flowers from June to July.

Culture: difficult.

Likes: half-sun/wet/acidic humus-rich soil/composted manure.

Tolerates: sun/half-shade/moist.

Propagation: roots.

Comments: requires winter mulch. This iris is rather difficult for beginning gardeners. However, in Germany, breeding work is being done to create a Japanese Iris that can tolerate alkaline soil, drought, and cold. Dr. Frank Skinner bred a hardy variety called 'Smoky.'

I. FLAVISSIMA, Goldbeard Iris, a regelia species. Perennial to Zone 3.

Height: 4 inches.

Bloom: vivid bright yellow flowers with orange-gold beards in early May.

Foliage: goes dormant and disappears in mid-summer.

Culture: easy.

Likes: sun/dry/well drained rock garden soil.

Tolerates: half-sun/semidry.
Propagation: sets.
Comments: Because it is a Regelia Iris species, it must have well-drained soil, and is best suited for a rock garden, drought tolerant garden, or native plant collection. The name *flavissima* means 'the yellowest.'

I. GRAMINEA, Grass Iris. Perennial to Zone 3.
Height: 1 foot.
Bloom: spectacular plum-scented flowers in multicolors of white, yellow, blue, or purple; flowers bloom in mid-May and are usually completely hidden in the foliage.
Foliage: clump of attractive grass-like foliage.
Likes: sun.
Tolerates: half-sun/semidry/moist.
Propagation: sets.
Comments: prefers being divided and moved to new rich soil every couple of years for best flowering. The fragrance of the flowers is most pronounced in hot weather. Some people describe the scent as similar to ripe peaches. However, there is a variety named *'pseudocyperus'* that has slightly larger flowers and lacks fragrance. As you might imagine, the fragrant and nonfragrant varieties are sometimes confused in commerce. So, ask questions at the nursery if you want a fragrant one. For cut flowers, cut when the buds show color. This flower has tremendous commercial value for sales to florists as a small size cut flower.

I. JUNO. Perennial to Zone 4.
Height: 1-2 feet.
Bloom: yellow, white, or light blue Iris-like flowers (some are powerfully fragrant) from late April to May.
Foliage: resembles a small corn plant in the spring, and in mid-summer it goes dormant and disappears.
Likes: half-sun/semidry/well-drained soil.
Tolerates: sun/half-shade/dry/moist.
Propagation: bulbs.
Comments: must dry out in mid-summer. The critically important rootlets underneath the bulb are brittle and must be moved very carefully. If they are broken off, the plant will be unnecessarily set back. Juno Irises are commonly sold as individual species. Look for *Iris bucharica* (white and yellow flowers bearing an intensely powerful violet-like scent).

I. MISSOURIENSIS (I. montana), Rocky Mountain Iris, native to both the plains and the Rockies. Perennial to Zone 1.
Height: 1 foot.
Bloom: delicate-looking pale blue flowers in early June; interesting seedpods.

Rocky Mountain Iris, Iris missouriensis

Foliage: grass-like foliage.
Likes: half-sun/semidry.
Tolerates: sun/very dry/semidry.
Propagation: sets or seeds. (Seed germination: cold.)
Comments: roots are best transplanted in spring before or during bloom. This flower is an excellent candidate for breeding work. Even though it will not cross breed with other irises, work can be done to select native plants with the best color, form, and plant shape. Its flower color varies from white to bright blue to bright purple. Seeds of these color varieties are available from the SIGNA seed exchange (see address in Resource Directory). Kim Williams stated that Indians used this plant to make poison arrowheads. They ground the roots, mixed them with animal bile, put it all in a gall bladder and heated the mixture slowly for several days.

I. PALLIDA, Sweet Iris. Perennial to Zone 3.
Height: 2 feet.
Bloom: fragrant lavender-blue flowers in early June.
Culture: easy.
Likes: half-sun/moist.
Tolerates: sun/half-shade/dry/semidry.
Propagation: roots.
Comments: 'Dalmatica' is considered the most fragrant variety; 'Ze-bra' has showy yellow variegated foliage, but it flowers sparsely.

I. PSEUDACORUS, Yellow Water Iris. Perennial to Zone 1.
Height: 2 feet.
Bloom: yellow flowers from late May to June.
Likes: half-sun/wet (a bog plant).
Tolerates: sun/half-shade.
Propagation: invasive by self-sown seed; roots.
Comments: remove seedpods or it will spread quickly. It has potential to become a weed in areas near water. Breeding work has produced several interesting varieties of this plant in colors of greenish yellow, light yellow, and yellow with brown markings.

I. PUMILA, Dwarf Iris. Perennial to Zone 1.
Height: 4 inches.
Bloom: flowers in every color (except red) in early May.
Culture: easy.
Likes: half-sun/semidry.
Tolerates: sun/half-shade/dry/moist.
Propagation: roots.
Comments: this plant closely resembles a Miniature Dwarf Bearded Iris.

RETICULATA IRIS GROUP. Perennial to Zone 3.
Height: 6 inches.
Bloom: yellow or blue flowers (some very fragrant) in early to mid-April.
Culture: easy.
Likes: half-sun/semidry/well-drained humus-rich soil.
Tolerates: sun/half-shade/dry/moist.
Propagation: bulbs (bury 4 inches deep).
Comments: Iris danfordiae, a yellow species, blooms the very earliest in the spring (late March to early April). It was introduced by a Mrs. Danford in 1876 from the Taurus Mountains of Turkey. *Iris histrioides 'major'* also blooms very early in the spring and is an exotic tropical blue color. The species *Iris reticulata* and *Iris bakeriana* are the most fragrant of the group. The name *reticulata* means 'netted' and refers to the bulb's fibrous covering. All of these species are excellent for forcing.

SIBERIAN IRIS GROUP. Perennial to Zone 1.
Height: 3 feet.
Bloom: red, yellow, white, blue,

and purple flowers from mid- to late June, interesting seedpods.

Likes: sun/moist/humus-rich soil.

Tolerates: half-sun/half-shade/semi-dry/wet.

Propagation: roots.

Comments: the famous Canadian plant breeder Isabella Preston named all of her Siberian hybrids after Canadian rivers. These varieties are the hardiest Siberians. Siberian Irises are showy in the garden and also make good cut flowers. The seedpods of Siberian Iris are attractive in dried arrangements. This Iris makes attractive combinations with Peonies (Paeonia), Echinacea, or Shasta Daisy *(Chrysanthemun x superbum).*

Varieties of Note:

'Alice Mae Cox'—deep blue flowers (available from Borbeleta Gardens).

'Harbormist'—mid-blue flowers.

'Mountain Lake'—clear mid-blue flowers.

'Orville Fay'—rich dark blue; because it is a tetraploid the flowers and foliage are large and heavily textured.

'Ottawa'—light blue flowers.

'Papillon'—soft-looking light blue flowers.

'Perry's Pygmy'—mid-blue flowers, dwarf size plant.

'Ruffled Velvet'—purple flowers with black and gold markings, late bloom season.

'Sea Shadows'—blue and blue-green color.

'Tropic Night'—blackish-purple flowers.

SPURIA IRIS GROUP. Perennial to Zone 3.

Height: 2 feet.

Bloom: bronze-red, yellow, white, blue, lavender, or purple flowers from late June to early July (long season with early to late varieties).

Culture: easy.

Likes: sun/semidry/humus-rich soil.

Tolerates: half-sun/dry/moist/poor soil.

Comments: prefers to dry out in late summer. Roots resent being transplanted and are best moved into place in the spring (if they are planted in the fall, use heavy winter mulch the first year). This is a spectacular cut flower with tremendous commercial potential to florists in our area; cut as soon as the buds show color (like gladiolus).

Outstanding varieties are the following:

'Dawn Candle'—flowers have white standards, yellow falls, and an excellent flower form.

'Eleanor Hill'—violet and yellow flowers.

'Elixir'—vivid orange-yellow flowers, though not a heavy bloomer.

'Ethic'—dark blue and brown flowers.

'Evening Dress'—very dark blackish-purple flowers, a new variety.

'Fort Ridge'—excellent blue color with profuse flowering.

'Forty Carats'—rich yellow flowers, excellent flower form.

'Happy Choice'—flowers are a combination of blue, white and yellow.

'Imperial Bronze'—an excellent bronze color.

'Marilyn Holloway'—soft lavender and yellow flowers, a strikingly showy variety.

'Pink Candles'—good pink color, though not a heavy bloomer.

'Red Oak'—one of the very best red spurias.

'Social Circle'—white and yellow flowers, included because it is an early variety.

Blue Water Iris, Iris versicolor

I. VERSICOLOR, Blue Water Iris. Perennial to Zone 1.

Height: 2 feet.

Bloom: deep blue flowers (also red and pink varieties) in June.

Likes: half-sun/wet (a bog plant).

Tolerates: sun/half-shade.

Propagation: roots.

Comments: the blue species form was immortalized in Van Gogh's paintings. A spectacularly beautiful variety is 'Kermesima,' which has wine-red flowers with yellow and white markings.

JERUSALEM ARTICHOKE, Sunroot, Tuberous Sunflower (Helianthus tuberosus), native to the eastern plains of North America and north as far as the parklands. Perennial vegetable to Zone 3.

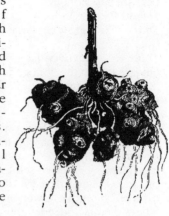

Jerusalem Artichoke, Helianthus tuberosus

Height: 5 to 10 feet.

Culture: easy.

Likes: sun/dry/semidry/moist/nitrogen-poor, humus-rich soil.

Propagation: tubers.

Growing tips: best grown in same area year after year. Jerusalem artichokes and potatoes should not be planted near each other because they seem to stunt each others growth.

Harvest tips: harvest these roots from the late fall to early spring until the new growth starts.

Comments: this plant has insignificant flowers. It is grown mostly for its edible tubers. It can also be used for a fast-growing instant hedge (fastest growth if planted thickly in humus-rich soil).

Because they need high humidity, they keep best either in the ground or sealed in a plastic bag in damp peat moss in a refrigerator.

The roots were cultivated by the Indians, who roasted them slowly for 2-3 days to break down their starch and fiber content.

Be forewarned, mice and other rodents love to dig in the garden for these roots. This plant is an excellent candidate for use in sustainable agriculture. Roots can be eaten peeled or unpeeled. One suggestion for their water chestnut-like texture is using them thinly sliced in a winter salad. Montana author Kim Williams, in her book *Eating Wild Plants,* suggested boiling the roots or cooking them with a roast in a slow oven. Diabetics find this root valuable because of the starch insulin.

JUGLANS CINEREA, Butternut Tree. Perennial to Zone 3.
Height: 75 feet.
Shape: slow-growing large showy tree.
Foliage: attractive large leaves emerge late in the spring; delicious hard-shelled nuts.
Culture: easy.
Likes: sun/dry/semidry.
Propagation: sets (buy only sets with their terminal bud tip intact).
Comments: established plants resent transplanting. Though self-fertile, it produces better if cross-pollinated by wind. Remove lower branches when young and encourage it to form an attractive open canopy. This tree often suffers transplant shock. It is best moved when young. Being a hardwood, this tree almost never drops large branches. Try to find varieties with easy to crack nuts such as 'Chamberlin,' 'Craxeasy,' 'Kinneyglen' or 'Love.' Another hint is that nuts crack more easily if covered with boiling water and soaked for 15 minutes. Butternut trees do not poison nearby plants with a root gas the way black walnut trees do.

Black Walnut, Juglans nigra

J. NIGRA, Black Walnut. Perennial to Zone 3.
Height: 75 feet.
Shape: slow-growing large tree.
Foliage: yellow fall color.
Culture: easy.
Likes: sun/dry/semidry.

Propagation: sets (buy only sets with their terminal bud tips intact).
Comments: delicious nuts. Has no pests; established plants resent transplanting; never needs pruning. Though self-fertile, walnuts produce better if cross-pollinated (plant them close together for wind pollination). This tree often suffers transplant shock. It is best moved when young. Being a hardwood, this tree almost never drops large branches. Some improved nut-producing varieties are 'Ohio' and 'John.' An ornamental cutleaf variety is *'Laciniata.'* Uncollected nuts tend to stain sidewalks or driveways. Black walnuts also have the unfortunate tendency to kill or stunt some plants growing near their roots. Avoid planting tomatoes, beets, lettuce, scarlet sage and many other plants near black walnut trees. Manchurian walnut and butternut do not stain sidewalks or stunt nearby plants.

J. MANDSHURICA, Manchurian Walnut. Perennial to Zone 3.
Height: 60 feet.
Shape: moderately fast-growing ornamental tree with attractive weaving branches and an open canopy.
Foliage: showy large leaves that turn yellow early in the fall.
Propagation: sets (buy only sets with their terminal bud tip intact).
Likes: sun/dry/semidry.
Comments: tasty edible nuts similar to butternuts. Established plants resent transplanting. Remove lower branches when young and encourage it to form an attractive open canopy. This tree often suffers transplant shock. It is best moved when young. This species is the very first tree to drop its leaves in the fall, which makes it a good tree in front of solar heating panels. Being a hardwood, this tree almost never drops large branches. Native to the Amur River area of Siberia.

JUNIPERUS. Evergreen shrub, many colors and forms.
Culture: very easy.
Likes: sun/half-sun/very dry/semidry.
Tolerates: alkaline soil.
Propagation: sets.
Comments: though drought-tolerant, junipers appreciate one deep watering in the early fall just before the ground freezes. The berries of

all varieties can be used as a flavoring. The following varieties are arranged by species (*Juniperus chinensis, J. communis, J. horizontalis, J. procumbens, J. sabina, J. scopulorum, J. virginiana*) and are all hardy to Zone 2, unless otherwise noted.

J. CHINENSIS. 'Columnaris Glauca,' height 8 feet. *Shape:* irregular upright form which closely resembles the beautifully twisted Hollywood Juniper.
'Gold Tip Pfitzer,' 2 feet tall by 6 feet wide, foliage tips are gold colored, older foliage is light green. This variety is hardy only to Zone 3.
'Green Pfitzer,' 3 feet tall by 6 feet wide, a basic green juniper included here because it tolerates light shade. This variety is hardy only to Zone 4.
'Hetzii,' 3 feet tall by 6 feet wide, showy blue-green color.
'Maneyi,' 5 feet tall by 8 feet wide, attractive large V shape, green color.
'Mint Julep,' height 4 feet; low irregular form; dramatic sea-green color.
'Saybrook Gold,' a new variety hardy to Zone 4. Its foliage looks like someone sprinkled gold dust all over it.
'Shimpaku,' 1 foot tall by 3 feet wide, slow-growing irregular form, very unusual-looking delicate green foliage.

J. COMMUNIS. Native circumpolar in rocky areas:
'Depressa Aurea,' 1 foot tall by 4 feet wide; foliage tips are bright yellow and contrast with the older green foliage, semi-erect arched habit.
'Vase,' 4 feet tall by 3 feet wide, blue-green foliage, very dramatic large vase-like shape.

J. HORIZONTALIS, Carpet Juniper. Native to dry rocky slopes circumpolar:
'Blue Chip,' 6 inches tall by 4 feet wide, warm blue-gray color, compact habit which unfortunately mounds up with age.
'Emerald Spreader,' 4 inches tall by 4 feet wide, showy dark emerald color, loose mat habit.
'Jade River,' 3 inches tall by 4 feet wide, showy bluish-green color, carpet-like form which does not mound with age.

'Minimus,' 4 inches tall by 4 feet wide, blue-gray feathery appearance, tightly compact habit without bare spots.

'Plumosa Compacta,' 6 inches tall by 4 feet wide, unusual soft off-green color, never gets a bare spot in the middle. The older variety 'Plumosa' is less showy in form and color.

'Prince of Wales,' 6 inches tall by 4 feet wide; green ground-hugging creeper; in winter its foliage turns an attractive bronzy-plum color; each branch radiates from the center to form a star-like pattern. This plant was discovered near High River, Alberta, and introduced by Morden Research Station, Manitoba.

'Wisconsin,' 3 inches tall by 4 feet wide; carpet-like form which does not mound with age, attractive gray-green color. This is perhaps the most evenly carpet-like variety of the species.

'Yukon Belle,' 6 inches tall by 4 feet wide, a showy silvery-blue ground-hugging creeper. Unfortunately, this variety does not mat tightly and occasionally burns in exposed areas.

J. PROCUMBENS, Japanese Garden Juniper; height 1 foot; low creeping form; attractive delicate green foliage which is very prickly. This species does not mound with age.

J. SABINA. Native circumpolar.

'Buffalo,' 2 feet tall by 6 feet wide, upright spreading form, basic green color, attractive slow-growing habit, blue-green berry-like fruit. This variety is an improvement over the common 'Tam' juniper.

'Calgary Carpet,' 6 inches tall by 4 feet wide, creeping form, distinctive lacy green foliage, creeping arched form with a depressed center. This beautiful variety should be more commonly planted.

'Scandia,' 2 feet tall by 4 feet wide; upright spreading form; green color; branch tips arch gracefully at an angle to the plant. This variety is an improvement over 'Arcadia.'

'Von Ehren,' 3 feet tall by 6 feet wide; rounded vase-like shape, attractive dull green color. Its unusual height and soothing color are the appealing reasons to include this variety.

J. SCOPULORUM, Rocky Mountain Juniper. Native to dry slopes in the Rocky Mountains and Black Hills.
Height: 15 feet.
Shape: tall broadly rounded shrub.
Comments: this species is just beginning to be selected and bred. In coming years, there will be many new varieties to choose from. It is suggested that breeders consider selecting tree-shaped varieties. These symmetrically rounded lollipop-shaped evergreen trees might become very popular in home and commercial landscaping. A pest concern, though rarely a major problem, is that this species is an alternate host to cedar-apple rust, which affects a few susceptible varieties of crabapples, apples, and hawthorns. For more information about this disease and susceptible apple varieties, see *Malus*. The name *scopulorum* means 'of the rocks.'

'Blue Heaven' (or 'Blue Haven'); broad pyramidal upright shrub, loose habit, attractive blue-gray color. This variety is less hardy than other varieties in extremely exposed locations.

'Extra Blue,' low-growing creeper; 1 foot tall by 8 feet wide; dramatic steel-blue color with a sheen. This variety was selected west of Augusta, Montana.

'Green Spire,' narrow form, soft dull green color.

'Gray Gleam,' broadly pyramidal upright shrub, compact habit, vivid silvery-gray color, slow-growing habit.

'Grizzly Bear,' broadly rounded shrub, new foliage is gray, and old foliage is green, producing a two-tone effect. This old variety is extremely hardy.

'Lori,' broadly pyramidal, semi-compact habit, attractive sea-green color.

'McFarland,' pillar-shaped shrub, loose habit, gray-green color.

'Medora,' showy semi-narrow co-lumnar form, very dense habit, soft green color. This variety was selected in the Badlands near Medora, North Dakota, in 1956.

'Moonglow,' broadly pyramidal shrub, very open habit, blue-gray color.

'Pathfinder,' pyramidal shrub, compact habit, attractive steel-blue color.

'Platinum,' vivid silvery-white color.

'Sneed's Columnar,' the most narrowly columnar variety, gray-green color; unfortunately this variety gets bare at its base with age.

'Spartan,' broadly rounded form with an attractive irregular look; 8 feet tall; showy dark green color. A good background plant.

'Table Top Blue,' irregular semi-upright shape. Four feet tall by 6 feet wide, blue color, irregular vase-like shape. When young this plant has a loose vase shape, but with age it fills densely and develops a distinct flat top. Plan to give this variety enough room to get large.

'Tolleson's Weeping Juniper,' rounded shrub. Fifteen feet tall; a spectacularly dramatic plant which somewhat

Rocky Mountain Juniper,
Juniperus scopulorum

resembles a densely compact weeping birch. Blue varieties are more reliably hardy than the green varieties. For best appearance, protect from extreme wind exposure, which damages the hanging foliage.

'Welchii,' broadly pyramidal shrub, blue-green color.

'Wichita Blue,' broadly pyramidal shrub, very irregular loose habit, attractive vivid blue-gray color.

'Winter Blue,' low-growing spreading shrub. Two feet tall by 4 feet wide, showy soft blue color, low-spreading arched form, extremely tough and durable. This plant was introduced by Clayton Berg of Helena's Valley Nursery.

J. VIRGINIANA. This species is well known as an alternate host for cedar-apple rust. Be careful planting this species near susceptible apple varieties. 'Skyrocket' is a dramatically narrow columnar variety. Fifteen feet tall with attractive blue-gray color. Stake tree when it gets tall or else heavy snowfalls will break it.

KALE, Brassica oleracea, acephala group. Cool-season annual vegetable.
Height: 2 feet.
Description: clump of thick blue-

Kale, Brassica oleracea

green lacy foliage with a slightly bitter, cabbage-like flavor.
Culture: easy.
Likes: half-sun/half-shade/semidry/moist/humus- and fertilizer-rich soil.
Propagation: sets or seeds. Because its seeds tolerate cool soil and germinate easily, plant as early as mid-April.
Pests: flea beetles, root maggots, and white cabbage moth—though these are less of a problem during the cool months when kale is grown.
Harvest tips: harvest the lowest leaves or the whole plant for salad greens, cooked greens, or for garnishes.
Comments: this plant is extremely frost tolerant. It can be grown outside unprotected through most of the winter. Then during the harshest part of December, January, and Febuary, protect it with a mulch or a cold frame. Additionally, it is attractive enough to be grown in a winter garden as an ornamental.

Historically, this plant was cultivated by the ancient Greeks and Romans. The two commonly available varieties are 'Scotch,' which is

earliest, and 'Siberian,' which is slightly more heat tolerant. Shepherd's Garden Seeds Catalog lists a superior Dutch variety called 'Westlandse'. It is a winter-type kale which must be grown in the winter in a coldframe.

KALE, ORNAMENTAL, see *Brassica oleracea*.

KELSEYA UNIFLORA, official emblem of the Montana Native Plant Society, a rare native found only in certain limestone cliffs in Montana, Wyoming, and Idaho. Perennial.
Height: 1 inch.
Bloom: showy red stalkless flowers.
Foliage: heavy moss-like clump of silky, hairy, green foliage.
Likes: sun/half-sun/dry/semidry.
Propagation: sets or seeds.
Comments: the habitat of this slow-growing plant can be easily damaged by wild plant collectors. Buy only propagated plants, never dig or buy wild plants. Named for Rev. F. D. Kelsey, an early Helena, Montana naturalist.

KOELERIA CRISTATA, June Grass. Native to the Great Plains and foothills. Perennial to Zone 2.

Height: 6-10 inches (height depends on soil moisture).
Bloom: erect candle-like flower spikes in early June.
Likes: sun/half-sun/dry/semidry.
Propagation: sets or seeds. Self-sows in favorable location.
Comments: small tufted habit; roots are non-invasive; plant turns golden-yellow and remains attractive

June Grass, Koeleria cristata

throughout the winter. This attractive grass prefers to self-sow in spaced intervals all over your garden. In the heat of summer this plant stops growing and goes dormant. It is excellent for its attractive winter appearance. Because it is not

an aggressive grass, it should be encouraged to self-sow throughout the garden for its gift of winter interest.

KOHLRABI, Brassica oleracea var. gongylodes. Annual vegetable.
Height: 1 foot.
Description: leafy upright plant with an enlarged edible stem.
Culture: easy.
Likes: sun/half-sun/half-shade/moist/humus- and fertilizer-rich soil/manure.
Propagation: sets (transplants very easily, and if hardened off, it can be set out a month before the frost-free date, and will be ready for harvest 40 days from transplant), or seeds (germinates very easily and can be planted in cool soil in early to mid-April). Stagger plantings every two weeks throughout spring and summer for longest harvest; plant as late as early August for a fall crop, which can be harvested 60 days from seed planting.
Pests: flea beetles, root maggots, and white cabbage moth. Companion plant with *achillea,* chives, garlic, onions or carrot family flowers (to attract wasps).
Growing tips: tolerates slight shade well; prefers an evenly moist soil; shallow rooted (avoid disturbing soil near plant); space plants 4 inches apart; crowd it slightly, which also gives it some wind support.
Harvest tips: the enlarged stem is the part that is eaten.
Comments: it can be sliced into strips and eaten either raw or steamed until tender. When steaming strips, leave on the skin. The foliage is also edible raw or cooked.

There are white, green, and purple varieties to choose from, all of which are moderately heat tolerant. This vegetable was first recorded as being grown in Italy in the 1500s. It is a good substitute for turnips in areas with severe root maggot problems.

LAGURUS OVATUS, Rabbit-Tail Grass. Annual.
Height: 2 feet.
Bloom: tuft-like grass heads (ticklers) from July to August.
Likes: sun/half-sun/moist.
Propagation: seeds.
Comments: established plants resent transplanting; plant seeds in natural-

looking clumps. These are the 'tickler' grassheads sold by florists. They can be used either fresh as a cut flower or dried as an everlasting. The plant itself is moderately attractive in the garden.

LAMIUM MACULATUM, Dead Nettle. Perennial to Zone 2.
Height: 1 foot.
Bloom: tiny whitish-pink flowers.
Foliage: grown primarily for its white and green variegated foliage.
Likes: half-shade.
Tolerates: shade/semidry/moist.
Propagation: sets only.
Comments: vigorously spreading clump; invasive by fast-spreading roots. 'White Princess' is a new variety with especially attractive white foliage.

LARIX LARICINA. Native Rocky Mountain Larch; not included because of poor adaptation to the plains climate.

L. SIBIRICA, Siberian Larch, Tamarack. Perennial to Zone 1.
Height: 50 feet.
Shape: somewhat irregular pyramidal tree.
Foliage: bright gold fall color, drops needles in early winter, fresh new green growth in early spring.

Rocky Mountain Larch, Larix sibirica

Culture: easy.
Likes: sun/dry/semidry.
Propagation: sets (fall planting is particularly successful with this tree).
Comments: this variety has the best form and richest fall color in the larch species. It was introduced by Frank Meyer in 1913 from Russia's St. Petersburg Botanic Garden.

LATHYRUS LATIFOLIA, Perennial Pea. Perennial to Zone 4-5.
Height: vine to 6 feet.
Bloom: non-fragrant pink flowers from late June to August.
Climbing habit: climbs by twining tendrils.
Likes: half-sun.
Tolerates: sun/moist/heat.
Propagation: Seeds (soak seeds before planting).

Perennial Pea, Lathyrus latifolia

Comments: established plants transplant poorly. There are named horticultural varieties of this plant. In the milder and wetter climates of the mountains, this plant can become a weed, but on the arid plains it remains a good garden subject. Besides being used as a garden plant, it can be used as a cut flower, too.

L. ODORATUS, Sweet Pea. Annual.
Height: vine to 5 feet.
Bloom: very fragrant red, pink, white, blue, purple, and black flowers from May to frost (long season if spent flowers removed).
Climbing habit: climbs by twining tendrils.
Likes: half-sun/deeply dug, humus-rich soil.
Tolerates: sun/half-shade/moist.
Propagation: sets or seeds (soak it before planting).
Comments: protect from mid-day heat. Can be started inside in early spring and planted out after germination, pea seeds germinate only when the soil is warm. Grow this either in the garden or best of all in a hanging pot. This plant can also be used as a cut flower.
Pests: include aphids and red spider mites. Varieties described as being pre-Spencer, Grandiflora, or Sicilian have the greatest fragrance and heat tolerance. These old varieties are fast regaining popularity. Spencer varieties were developed in England by Princess Diana's ancestors. They have a frilled petal edge and will not tolerate heat. However, Spencer varieties tend to be the ones most commonly available.

There is an active Sweet Pea Society in England. Its address is listed in the Resource Directory. Until recently, Alberta had its own Sweet Pea Society. Bozeman, Montana, has a Sweet Pea Festival each August, which is a revival of a regionally-popular event from the early part of this century.

LAVATERA TRIMESTRIS, Tree Mallow. Annual.
Height: 4 feet.
Bloom: large satiny pink or white flowers, blooms from July to frost (bloom is more profuse if spent flowers are removed).
Likes: sun/semidry.
Tolerates: half-sun/dry/moist.
Propagation: sets or seeds.
Comments: densely rounded shrubby clump. Try to find named varieties with improved flower color. Besides being a showy garden plant, it also produces good cut flowers. This plant makes a showy instant hedge or background plant in a garden—give it lots of room. It is also attractive in combination with Eryngium, Sea Holly. Other closely related plants are *Alcea rosea* (Hollyhock), *Lavatera, Malope,* and *Malva.*

LAYIA PLATYGLOSSA (L. elegans), Tidytips. Annual.
Height: 1 foot.
Bloom: yellow daisies from July to frost (long season).
Foliage: yellow petals have white tips.
Likes: sun/semidry.
Tolerates: half-sun/dry.
Propagation: seeds.
Comments: established plants resent transplanting. This is an extremely long-lasting cut flower that should be sold more commonly. Native to the Central Valley of California.

LEEK, Allium ampeloprasum var. porrum. Annual or perennial vegetable.
Height: 1 foot.
Description: onion-like plant with a thickened stem.
Likes: sun/half-sun/half-shade/moist, well drained soil/humus and fertilizer-rich soil (loves manure!).
Tolerates: slight shade.
Propagation: bulbs or seeds. Plant either bulbs or tiny offset bulblets in fall. Because seeds tolerate cool soil, they can be planted in early to mid-April. Seed must be fresh for best germination.
Growing tips: requires a long sea-

son in cool summer areas. Plant leeks in a trench so that you can mound up the soil to whiten the stems. Thin to 4 inches apart.

Harvest tips: harvest any time after mid-summer, but frost makes them sweeter. Dig out the roots, don't pull them.

Comments: this plant tolerates heavy frost and can be left in place and used through the winter. However, you should loosen the soil and mulch heavily for easier harvesting in mid-winter.

The main popularity of leeks is due to their mild onion flavor. It is excellent in potato soup.

Leeks are native to southern Europe. Emperor Nero was know as 'leek-throated' for his daily consumption of leeks to clear his throat. Leeks are the historic emblem of Wales; they are worn by all Welsh fighters.

LEONTOPODIUM ALPINUM, Edelweiss. Perennial to Zone 2.

Height: 6 inches.

Bloom: irregular star-shaped flowers whose texture resembles white flannel, blooms in June.

Likes: sun/semidry/well drained rock garden soil.

Tolerates: half-sun/moist.

Propagation: sets or seeds.

Comments: low clump habit; does not tolerate crowding by other plants. This plant makes an unusual-looking garden flower. It also makes excellent cut flowers and dried everlastings. Native to the Alps of Europe.

LESQUERELLA ALPINA, Alkaline Bladderpod. Native to rocky hillsides in the Great Plains and Rocky Mountains. Perennial.

Height: 4 inches.

Bloom: showy yellow flowers at the end of May; yellowish-green inflated pods remain on plant in late summer and fall.

Foliage: tufted clump, finely textured silver-gray foliage.

Likes: sun/half-sun/dry/semidry/sandy, rocky soil.

Propagation: sets or seeds.

LETTUCE, *Lactuca sativa.* Annual vegetable.

Height: 1 foot.

Description: upright clump.

Culture: easy.

Likes: sun/half-sun/half-shade/ma-

nure/moist, well-drained, deeply dug humus-rich soil best prepared by a green manure crop the previous year.

Propagation: sets (because it tolerates light frost, hardened off sets can be safely put outside two weeks before the frost-free date; transplants well) or seeds (fresh seed germinates best). Because lettuce prefers cool soil, plant in either the fall or very early spring. When planting in the fall, use extra seeds. Plant seed shallowly. For plantings

Lettuce, Lactuca sativa

in hot weather, soak seed overnight, and dry briefly before planting.

Pests: lots of them: grasshoppers, slugs, and aphids are the worst. Companion plant with nasturtiums to draw off the aphids, or under bean vines for their cooling shade.

Growing tips: in hot summer areas, give it mid-day shade; prefers moderately hot days and cool evenings. Give it a regular dose of manure in mid-season. For best lettuce, grow plants rapidly with maximum fertilizer, abundant water and cool night temperatures. Shallow rooted (avoid disturbing soil near plants); prefers adequate space between plants or it bolts into flower early; give it a careful mulching which holds moisture, cools the soil, and unfortunately harbors slugs.

Harvest tips: for the longest season of harvest, stagger planting monthly from early spring to early August. Harvest individual leaves or whole plant anytime during the summer and late fall. Cold slows growth, but lettuce tolerates light frosts well.

Comments: there are many varieties, which fall into three main categories: leaf lettuce, head lettuce and romaine lettuce. Oakleaf lettuce, a leaf lettuce, is not common, but is especially attractive. Recommended

is Romaine for hot weather and Buttercrunch for cool weather. Red Leaf Lettuce is also good for hot weather. It is tender and extremely attractive, and can be used as a showy red garnish. Leaf lettuce, in general, is ornamental enough to plant in the front of a flower bed. Lettuce contains Vitamins A and C, calcium and iron.

Originally, lettuce was native to the Middle East and Asia. Its name comes from an old French word *laitues* meaning "milky" referring to the sap.

LEUCOCRINUM MONTANUM, Prairie Star Lily. Native to dry Great Plains areas. Perennial.

Height: 6 inches.

Bloom: spectacular white star-like flowers from end of April to May.

Foliage: slow-growing multiple clump habit, thickened narrow foliage.

Likes: sun/half-sun/dry/semidry/moist/clay soil mixed with sand or gravel.

Propagation: seeds or sets.

Comments: seeds form below the ground and can be dug out with a narrow spoon. They tend to germinate easily. This plant's root seems to transplant well from the wild. However, native stands can be easily damaged by collectors. Please start with seeds or nursery grown sets. This amazingly easy native can be grown in any dry garden area or containers. The name *leucocrinum* means "white lily."

LEVISTICUM OFFICINALE, Lovage, culinary herb. Perennial to Zone 1.

Height: 3 feet.

Bloom: profuse flat-topped flowers in early July.

Foliage: attractive celery-like foliage.

Likes: sun/moist.

Tolerates: half-sun/half-shade.

Propagation: sets (transplant carefully) or seeds.

Comments: since this plant acts as a short-lived perennial, start new plants every couple of years. The stems and leaves of this plant are similar to celery in flavor and use. Native to Europe.

LEWISIA PYGMAEA, Pygmy Bitterroot. Native to moist scree areas of high elevation Rocky Mountains of the central and northern Rockies. Perennial.

Height: 2 inches.
Bloom: tiny pink waterlily-like flowers in June.
Foliage: appears in mid-winter.
Culture: difficult.
Likes: dry/well-weeded rock garden soil.
Tolerates: sun/half-sun.
Propagation: sets or seeds. (Seed germination: cold.)
Comments: requires scree conditions—underground watering and good drainage; must have light winter mulch in areas without snow cover.

L. REDIVIVA. Native Bitterroot, official state flower of Montana. Native to rocky areas in the foothills and Rocky Mountains. Perennial to Zone 3.
Height: 3 inches.
Bloom: pink waterlily-like flowers from June to early July.
Foliage: evergreen foliage appears in mid-winter and disappears in early spring before flowers bloom.
Culture: difficult.
Likes: dry/well-weeded rock garden soil.
Tolerates: sun.
Propagation: sets or seeds (self-sows). (Seed germination: cold treatment.)
Comments: in its natural habitat, this plant prefers a rocky well-drained sunny slope with a minimum of competition from other plants. Claude Barr states that seedlings are best started in a lathhous. Never dig this plant from the wild; it is illegal to do so in Montana. Siskiyou Rare Plant Nursery lists a white flowering variety. The Indians harvested this plant's root in the early spring when flower buds first appeared. It was boiled and the skin slipped off to reveal a clear spaghetti-like mass. Even if cooking water is changed, a slight bitter taste remains. Some people chew a tiny piece of the dried root for its health benefits.

LIATRIS PUNCTATA, Liatris. Native to dry areas of the Great Plains and foothills. Perennial to Zone 1.
Height: 1 foot.
Bloom: magenta-purple spikes from late July to frost.
Culture: easy.
Likes: sun/semidry.
Tolerates: half-sun/dry.

Propagation: sets or seeds; seed germinates easily.
Comments: established plants transplant poorly. The potato-sized root is edible, but very fibrous. The name *punctata* refers to the white dots on the underside of the leaves. *Liatris ligulistylis* is another attractive native species.

L. PYCNOSTACHYA, Kansas Gay-feather. Perennial to Zone 4.
Height: 3 feet.
Bloom: showy purple spikes from August to September.
Culture: easy.
Likes: semidry.
Tolerates: sun/dry.
Propagation: sets or seeds.
Comments: this species is native to the eastern tall-grass prairie. For best appearance, crowd this plant slightly.

L. SCARIOSA, Tall Gay-feather. Perennial to Zone 4.
Height: 4 feet.
Bloom: purple flower spikes in September.
Culture: easy.
Likes: sun/semidry.
Tolerates: dry.
Propagation: sets or seeds.
Comments: windstake with brush in exposed areas. This plant looks best if slightly crowded.

L. SPICATA. Perennial to Zone 3.
Height: 3 feet.
Bloom: purple spikes in July.
Culture: easy.
Likes: sun/moist.
Tolerates: wet.
Propagation: sets or seeds.
Comments: this species is native to meadows of eastern North America. This plant looks best if slightly crowded.

LIGULARIA PRZEWALSKII. Perennial to Zone 2.
Height: 4 feet.
Bloom: dramatic yellow flower spikes in July.
Foliage: showy unusual-looking toothed leaves, purple-black stems.
Likes: half-sun/wet/humus and fertilizer-rich soil (a bog plant).
Tolerates: moist.
Propagation: sets or seeds.
Comments: a variety called 'The Rocket' has flower spikes 5 feet tall in August. May need winter mulch in exposed areas.

L. VEITCHIANA. Perennial to Zone 2.

Height: 5 feet.
Bloom: showy yellow flowers from late July to August.
Foliage: very large tropical-looking leaves.
Likes: half-sun/wet/humus and fertilizer-rich soil (a bog plant).
Tolerates: half-shade/moist.
Propagation: sets or seeds.
Comments: may need winter mulch in exposed areas. Dried flowers can be used in arrangements.

LILIUM SPECIES AND HYBRIDS, Lily. A true aristocrat of the garden. Some lilies are easy and are recommended for first time growers (*Lilium amabile, L. bulbiferum, L. henryi, L. pumilum,* Asiatic hybrids, and Martagon hybrids).

Things to know about lilies in general:

1. Full sun is preferred, but some slight shade can be tolerated. A low growing ground cover cools the soil and adds visual attractiveness to somewhat top-heavy lily plants. Suggested ground covers are Baby's Breath (*Gypsophila*), Balloonflower (*Platycodon*—for Aurelian Hybrids), *Campanula persicafolia,* Columbine (*Aquilegia*), Delphinium—for Aurelian Hybrids, Impatiens, Ostrich Fern—for Martagon Lilies only, Phlox sublata, Salpiglossis, Silvermound (*Artemisia schmidtiana*), Sweet Allysum (*Lobularia*), *Thalictrum*—for Aurelian Hybrids, Veronica, Vinca minor, Violas, Violets.

2. Drainage conditions are of utmost consideration. First, locate lilies on a slight slope. Second, create a raised bed (or even individual hills) to move water away from the bulb. Test soil for difficult species by digging a hole, filling it with half a pail of water and rechecking in a half hour to see if it has drained away. If drainage is poor, choose another area. Marginal areas can be improved by mixing more sand and humus into soil. However, this should be done in large beds, not individual holes.

3. Most lilies can tolerate slight drought, but prefer to have regular water throughout the summer. Because the bulb really never goes dormant, lilies require water until late in the fall. The best way to water lilies is to simply leave a hose

running to flood them and move it from place to place. This keeps water off the foliage and reduces evaporative losses. A soaker hose is excellent for the same reasons. Finally, be sure to mulch carefully—all lilies appreciate mulch.

4. Lilies love humus. You can use peat moss, leaf mold, well-rotted compost, or any other disease-free organic material. Particularly in areas with heavy clay soil, you must add generous quantities of humus to the soil. Lilies also love bonemeal. In highly alkaline soil, add pelleted sulfur. High pH can interfere with the availability of micronutrients. Fertilize with chemical fertilizer each year right around flowering.

5. Manure carries root rot diseases and must not touch the bulb. However, well-rotted manure can be used as a mulch on the soil surface where it will feed the lilies' stem roots without any problems.

6. Always, always, always mulch lilies to cool the soil, hold in moisture, and suppress weed competition. Some acceptable mulches are grass clippings, straw, leaf mold, compost, manure, peat moss, or a layer of evergreen needles. Add a little nitrogen fertilizer to a grass clipping or straw mulch, or else the decomposition process robs the lilies of nitrogen.

7. Disease problems are a demon for lily growers in other parts of the country. However, we who live in the arid West have a definite advantage of reduced disease problems. For most species labeled 'difficult,' disease susceptibility is often the cause for their short life.

Good air circulation between plants is very important for preventing mildew and botrytis. To avoid mildew problems, water only early in the day, never in the evening or best of all use a soaker hose. Botrytis is a soil fungus whose spores start by killing the lower leaves and move up the plant. The best preventative measure is to carefully remove all dead lily foliage every year in the fall and discourage excess humidity by never watering in the evening. Another method is to maintain good air circulation around particularly susceptible plants by not planting them too closely together. Fungicide sprays can be used early in

Madonna Lily, Lilium candidum

the season, but only if you catch the problem early.

One of the worst problems is viral diseases spread by a number of agents, mainly aphids and leaf hoppers. Two surprising sources of viral infection are Rembrandt Tulips and Tiger Lilies, both of which can carry viruses without showing signs of infection. A virus-infected lily showing symptoms will have stunted size, lose its vigor, and the leaves become twisted or mottled. It must be pulled out and destroyed before it spreads the disease to healthy plants nearby. One way to avoid this problem is to grow lilies, including Tiger Lilies, from seeds. They will be reliably free of virus.

8. Some lilies should be windstaked so that the top-heavy flowers will not fall over while in full bloom. This is particularly important in exposed areas and areas with violent summer hailstorms. Be careful not to pierce the bulb when placing the stake. The best solution is to bury a deep marking stake when the bulb is first planted. Then in mid-summer, the marking stake is removed and a suitably tall windstake is placed in its hole. Replace the marking stake in the fall.

9. Bulbs are usually planted in the fall and winter mulched carefully the first year. Spring planting is also acceptable, but must be done very, very early. Bulbs need to be stored carefully prior to planting. Protect them from drying, and refrigerate if long storage is needed. Plant small bulbs 3 inches deep and large bulbs 5 inches deep. They need rich soil both below the bulb for the basal roots, and above the bulb for the stem roots. The one exception is the Madonna Lily *(L. candidum)*. It must be planted no more than 1-2 inches deep. Water bulbs deeply immediately after planting, and don't forget to label them.

10. For maximum vigor, remove spent flowers before seeds form. And like other bulbs, the foliage must ripen and die naturally to store energy for the following year.

11. Winter mulch plants to keep them evenly cold, slowing their early spring growth. Lilies often start growing too early and are damaged by late frosts. Asiatic hybrids are the exception to this rule. They are extremely cold-hardy.

12. The clump should be divided when stems become crowded together and flowering vigor is reduced. In September, separate bulbs and replant them 6 to 12 inches apart. Depending on variety, this should be done every 3 to 6 years.

13. Many varieties of Asiatic and Aurelian hybrids can be grown in pots. The trick is to use a deep enough pot so that the lily has room for basal roots below the bulb, and stem roots above the bulb. They require humus-rich potting soil, full sun, and lots of water.

Once growth appears above the soil, start regular fertilizings. They require approximately 3½ months from planting to flowering.

14. There is a North American Lily Society. Its address is listed in the Resource Directory. It is composed of smaller regional organizations spread across the U.S. and Canada.

Order of bloom: *Lilium pumilum* (late May to June), *L. monadelphum* (mid-June), *L. philadelphicum* (June to July), *L. martagon* (June), *L. abile* (late June), *L. cernuum* (late June to July), *L. concolor* (late June to early July), Asiatic hybrids (late June to July), *L. candidum* (late June to July), *L. dauricum* (late June to early July), *L. bulbiferum* (early to mid-July), *L. davidii* (early to mid-July), *L. centifolium* (mid- to late July), *L. lancifolium* (mid- to late July), *L. leichtlinii* (late July), *L. regale* (July), Oriental hybrids (late July to August), *L. michiganese* (early to mid-August), *L. speciosum* (early to mid-August), *L. wilsonii* (late August), *L. henryi* (late August), Aurelian hybrids (late August).

L. AMABILE, Korean Lily. Perennial to Zone 1.
Height: 3 feet.
Bloom: red-orange flowers in late June; flowers have an odd, somewhat unpleasant smell.
Culture: easy (this is a good species lily for beginners).
Likes: sun/half-sun/moist (less water in fall)/humus-rich soil.
Tolerates: alkaline soil.
Propagation: bulbs, bulblets, or seeds.
Comments: bulblets are the cluster of tiny bulbs produced just below the soil surface next to the stems. There is a showy yellow variety called *luteum.*

L. BULBIFERUM. Perennial to Zone 2.
Height: 1-4 feet.
Bloom: upfacing flowers with an umbel cluster of one to six blooms, bright orange petals deepening to red at the tips and centers, dark red-brown spots decorate the raised papillae, blooms in early to mid-July.
Culture: easy (this is a good lily for beginners).
Likes: sun/half-sun/moist/humus-rich soil.
Tolerates: half-shade/mild alkalinity.

Propagation: seeds, bulbs, bulbils (produced in leaf axils on the stems), or bulblets (produced just below the soil surface next to the stem).
Comments: this plant can be propagated very quickly with the multitude of bulblets and bulbils. There are varieties with deep gold to amber colored flowers. Native to the Alps and Pyrenees of Europe.

L. CALLOSUM. Perennial to Zone 2.
Height: 4 feet.
Bloom: turk's-cap flowers are red on the outside and orange on the inside, lightly spotted, blooms in mid-August.
Foliage: narrow slender plant with sparse foliage.
Culture: easy.
Likes: sun/half-sun/moist (less water in the fall)/slightly acidic humus-rich soil.
Tolerates: mild alkalinity.
Propagation: bulbs or seeds.
Comments: may require windstaking in exposed locations. Native to the coast of China, Japan and Manchuria. This plant is similar to the Siberian Coral Lily (*L. pumilum*). There is also a showy yellow unspotted variety named *'flaviflorum.'*

L. CANDIDUM, Madonna Lily. Perennial to Zone 4-5.
Height: 3 feet.
Bloom: very fragrant, pure white flowers from late June to July.
Likes: sun/half-sun/moist (less water in fall)/humus-rich soil.
Tolerates: clay soil and alkalinity.
Propagation: bulbs (plant shallowly—two inches deep, with the tip of the bulb at ground level).
Comments: plant it in late summer to early fall soon after flowering. One of the main difficulties in growing this plant is its tendency to send up foliage in the late fall to get a start on spring. Winter mulch it carefully; protect its tiny new foliage from early spring warmth, which makes it grow too early and then winter burn. The second main difficulty in growing this plant is its extreme susceptibility to virus disease. For this reason, do not grow it near other lilies. This lily has been cultivated since antiquity in the Mediterranean.

L. CENTIFOLIUM. Perennial to Zone 3.

Height: 6 feet.
Bloom: extremely large flower stalk from mid- to late July, upfacing trumpet flowers are whitish-green inside and purplish-brown on the outside.
Likes: sun/half-sun/moist (less water in the fall)/humus-rich soil.
Tolerates: mild alkalinity.
Propagation: bulbs.
Comments: requires winter mulch in exposed areas. This species requires several years to fully establish itself. Native to China.

L. CERNUUM. Perennial to Zone 2.
Height: 2 feet.
Bloom: showy, nodding, fragrant, rosy-purple flowers from late June to July.
Culture: Easy.
Likes: sun/half-sun/moist (less water in the fall)/humus-rich soil.
Propagation: bulbs or seeds.
Comments: requires winter mulch in exposed areas. To avoid basal root rot, plant bulb on top of several inches of pea gravel. Because it is so susceptible to a number of diseases, it tends to be a short-lived perennial. Native to Korea and Manchuria. This species was used to hybridize the pink forms of the Asiatic hybrids.

L. CONCOLOR. Perennial to Zone 2.
Height: 2 feet.
Bloom: showy rounded clump of upfacing flowers, bright orange-red star-shaped flowers which open nearly flat, attractively spotted, blooms in late June to early July.
Foliage: sparse at the top of the stem.
Culture: easy.
Likes: sun/half-sun/moist/humus-rich soil.
Tolerates: alkalinity well.
Propagation: bulb (a small size bulb) or seeds.

L. DAURICUM. Perennial to Zone 2.
Height: 2 feet.
Bloom: upfacing yellow-orange flowers (3 inches across) in an umbel-type cluster, blooms in late June to early July.
Propagation: bulbs or seeds.
Comments: this species requires an acidic humus-rich soil. Native to Northern Russia, China, and Korea.

L. DAVIDII WILLMOTTIAE. Perennial to Zone 2.
Height: 3 feet.

Bloom: turk's-cap flowers (2 inches across) are dark red and lightly spotted, blooms in early to mid-July.
Foliage: narrow dark green foliage.
Culture: easy.
Likes: sun/half-sun/moist/humus-rich soil.
Tolerates: mild alkalinity.
Propagation: bulbs (bulblets are produces along its stoloniferous root) or seeds.
Comments: showy arching form, stems come out of the ground at a slant and continue to arch in a graceful curve. May need windstaking with a hoop support in exposed areas. Somewhat disease resistant. Native to the mountains of western China. It was introduced by Duchartre. There are also named hybrids of this plant. The bulb is edible and has been cultivated in Asia as a foodstuff since antiquity.

L. DUCHARTREI. Perennial to Zone 2.
Height: 2 feet.
Bloom: dainty umbels of milky-white turk's-cap flowers streaked with vivid purple, these flowers are powerfully fragrant, blooms in early to mid-July.
Foliage: willowy narrow stems and foliage.
Culture: easy.
Likes: half-sun/low nitrogen, humus-rich, mildly alkaline, well-drained soil.
Tolerates: sun/half-shade (prefers mid-day shade in hot summer areas)/moist.
Propagation: bulbs (bulbs are small and white, creates new bulblets along its stoloniferous stem which can creep far away from the mother plant) or seeds.
Comments: requires mulching to cool its roots in summer. Native to limestone alpine meadows in central China. Introduced in 1915 by Mr. Franchet from Gansu, China. It is closely similar to *L. martagon*.

L. HENRYI. Perennial to Zone 2.
Height: 5 feet.
Bloom: large orange turk's-cap flowers (4 inches across) which are fragrant, some varieties are spotted, dramatically long stamens give this downfacing flower a look of distinction, blooms in late August.
Foliage: shiny dark green.
Culture: easy (this is a good lily for

beginners).
Likes: sun/half-sun/moist/humus-rich soil.
Tolerates: alkalinity.
Propagation: bulbs (normal bulbs are large and yellow, additional small bulblets are produced just below the soil surface on the stem) or seeds.
Comments: very large arching shape; windstake with hoop support or plant where it can grow through the stems of a shrub. Moderately resistant to virus infection. Extreme full sun can fade petal color. Named for Augustine Henry, who collected it in limestone gorges on the Yangtze River. This species lily is one of the original parents of the Aurelian hybrids.

L. LANCIFOLIUM (L. tigrinum), Tiger Lily. Perennial to Zone 1.
Height: 3 feet.
Bloom: orange-red or yellow flowers in mid- to late July.
Culture: easy.
Likes: sun/half-sun/semidry/moist/humus-rich soil.
Tolerates: poor soil.
Propagation: bulbs, bulbils (produced in leaf axils on the stems), bulblets (produced just below soil surface next to the stem), or seeds.
Comments: occasionally needs to be divided and moved to rich new soil. This plant can be propagated very quickly with the multitude of bulblets and bulbils. Unfortunately,

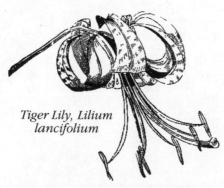

Tiger Lily, Lilium lancifolium

this lily often carries viral diseases without showing symptoms. In this aspect it is a kind of Trojan horse infecting the other lilies in the garden. However, Tiger Lilies grown from seed are reliably free of virus. This lily has been cultivated as a foodstuff in China and Japan since antiquity.

L. LEICHTILINII MAXIMOWICZII. Perennial to Zone 2.
Height: 5 feet.
Bloom: orange-red turk's-cap flowers with purple spots, blooms in late July.
Likes: sun/half-sun/moist/light sandy soil.
Propagation: bulbs.
Comments: may require windstaking in exposed areas. In general, this lily is very similar to the Tiger Lily (*L. lancifolium*). The variety *'maximowiczii'* is more commonly available because of its studier stems. The species type of *L. leichtlinii* is more delicate-looking and has heavily spotted yellow flowers. Native to northern China and Manchuria.

L. MARTAGON, Turk's-cap Lily. Perennial to Zone 1.
Height: 3 feet.
Bloom: lightly pink-purple turk's-cap flowers clustered on a stalk in June, flowers have an unpleasant smell, leaves arranged in whorls around the stem.
Culture: easy (this is a good lily for beginners).
Likes: sun/half-sun/half-shade/moist (less water in the fall)/humus-rich soil.
Tolerates: alkalinity.
Propagation: bulbs or seeds.
Comments: this species and its hybrids tolerate shade better than other lilies. Windstake individual flower stalks. Hybrids of this species seem to be nearly resistant to virus disease. Bulbs can be slow to establish—the first year after planting they may refuse to send up top growth. Then the second year, growth and flowering will be normal. Starting from seed is easy but slow—up to 7 years. 'Album' is a natural white variety. Native to a wide area from Portugal to Mongolia. There is also a yellow variety. Frank Skinner of Dropmore, Manitoba created several spectacular hybrid varieties. These are 'Black Prince' (dark red, almost black, 1961), 'Juanita' (creamy-white and pink, 1954), and 'Rosalinda' (large pink flowers, 1955). Other hybrids are 'Brocade,' 'Nepera,' and 'Terrace City.' The *'Dalhansonii'* hybrid belongs in this section. It has chestnut-brown petals marked with gold

spots, and grows up to 4 feet tall.

L. MICHIGANENSE, native from Ontario to Oklahoma and west to Minnesota. Perennial to Zone 2.
Height: 5 feet.
Bloom: downfacing blooms begin as funnels, and later turn into reflexed pendants, petals are orange-red with a golden center, spotting is heavy on inner part of petals, blooms in early to mid-August.
Foliage: whorled foliage is an unusual gray-blue-green color.
Culture: easy.
Likes: sun/half-sun/moist/acidic humus-rich soil.
Tolerates: mild alkalinity.
Propagation: bulbs.
Comments: heart-stoppingly beautiful upright plant. Buy only small white bulbs, because large yellow ones are old and dying; bulblets are produced by stoloniferous roots. Requires windstaking for best appearance.

L. MONADELPHUM. Perennial to Zone 2.
Height: 5 feet.
Bloom: rich yellow downfacing bell-like flowers (4 inches across), petals are reflexed with light spotting, blooms in mid-June.
Foliage: thick foliage is large, bold and very glossy.
Likes: sun/humus-rich soil.
Tolerates: moist/alkaline soil.
Propagation: bulbs.
Comments: strikingly dramatic upright habit. Transplants best as small young bulbs, then be patient—expect to wait 5 to 7 years before plant is fully established. Because of the dramatic flowers and foliage of this plant, it makes an excellent accent plant. Native to the Caucasus Mountains of Russia.

Lilium michiganense

L. PHILADELPHICUM. Native Western Orange Cup, Prairie Lily; official floral emblem of Saskatchewan. Perennial to Zone 1.
Height: 3 feet.
Bloom: scarlet-orange upfacing cup flowers from June to July.
Foliage: leaves are arranged both in whorls and scattered around the stem.
Culture: difficult.
Likes: sun/half-sun/semidry/moist (less water in fall)/moderately acidic soil.
Propagation: bulbs (best moved in the fall) or seeds. (Seed germination: cold.).
Comments: careful winter mulching is critical in areas without reliable snow-cover; often suffers botrytis in gardens. Seed can be collected in early fall when it is ripe. There is also a rare yellow flowering form. These roots were once an important Indian food widely spread throughout the northern plains. There was a time when patches of this vivid wildflower bloomed in large masses, filling early settlers' hearts with rapture. Now, however, it has been obliterated in almost all of its range due to plowing and the collection of plants from the wild. For this reason, wild plants should not be moved from the wild. Dr. Frank Skinner bred hybrids of this plant with *Lilium bulbiferum,* and *L. dauricum.*

Prairie Lily, Lilium philadelphicum

L. PUMILUM (L. tenuifolium), Siberian Coral Lily. Perennial to Zone 1.
Height: 2 feet.
Bloom: fragrant coral-red down-facing turk's-cap flowers from late May to June.
Foliage: narrow grass-like leaves.
Culture: easy (this is a good lily for beginners).
Likes: sun/half-sun/moist (less water in fall)/humus-rich soil.

Propagation: bulbs or seed.
Comments: there are also orange varieties. Native to a wide area of northern Russia, China, and Korea.

L. REGALE, Regal Lily. Perennial to Zone 3.
Height: 4 feet.
Bloom: powerfully fragrant trumpet flowers (inside color is white and outside color is dark purple) in July.
Likes: sun/half-sun/half-shade/semidry/moist/humus-rich, slightly acidic soil.
Tolerates: mild alkalinity.
Propagation: bulbs or seeds (often blooms the second year from seed).
Comments: windstake individual flower stalks. Doesn't like fertilizer-rich soil. This plant was found by plant hunter Ernest 'Chinese' Wilson on a remote mountain in the Szechwan Province of China. This was the famous trip in which an avalanche broke his leg, and he was forced by the narrow trail to lie on the road while an entire mule caravan was guided over him. There are few outstanding hybrids of this species because its genes are distinctly dominant in any cross. The main varieties are 'Black Dragon' and 'Pink Perfection.'

L. SPECIOSUM, Japanese Showy Lily. Perennial to Zone 4.
Height: 3 feet.
Bloom: red, pink or white flowers with pink markings and an intensely powerful sweet scent, blooms in early to mid-August. *Likes:* sun/half-sun/moist

Japanese Showy Lily, Lilium speciosum

(less water in fall)/humus-rich soil.
Propagation: bulbs.
Comments: this species requires an acidic pH—give it lots of extra humus; windstake individual flower stalks; requires winter mulch; susceptible to virus diseases. This plant is more cold-hardy than Zone 4, but it requires a very long season to ripen before winter. In Zone 3, it dies off slowly, getting smaller and less vigorous each year. The name 'ru-

brum' applies to any red or pink *Lilium speciosum*.

L. TSINGTAUENSE. Perennial to Zone 2.
Height: 2 feet.
Bloom: dainty clump, vividly bright orange upfacing flowers (2 inches across), showy narrow petals.
Foliage: whorled around the stem; young foliage may be mottled.
Likes: sun/half-sun/half-shade/moist/slightly acidic humus-rich soil.
Propagation: bulbs.
Comments: In appearance, this lily is similar to *L. philadelphicum*. Named for the port of Qingdao (Tsingtau) on the Shandong Coast of China. Native to the coasts of China and Korea.

L. WILSONII. Perennial to Zone 2.
Height: 3 feet.
Bloom: large upfacing apricot-orange or pale yellow flowers (6 inches across) which open nearly flat, each petal has a golden-amber band and showy heavy spotting, blooms in late August.
Likes: sun/half-sun/moist.
Propagation: bulbs (bulblets are produced by stoloniferous roots).
Comments: upright form. Other hardy lilies are *Lilium columbianum*, *L. distichum*, *L. elegans*, *L. hansonii*, *L. parryi*, *L. pyrenaicum*, *L. sachalinensis*, *L. wardii*.

LILIUM ASIATIC HYBRIDS. Perennial to Zone 1.
Height: 1-4 feet (depending on variety).
Bloom: upfacing, outfacing or pendant flowers in red, pink, orange, yellow, white and blackish-red; many are pastels or bicolors, blooms from late June to July.
Culture: easy (these are good lilies for beginners).
Likes: sun/half-sun/moist (less water in the fall)/humus-rich soil.
Tolerates: mild alkalinity.
Propagation: bulbs or seeds.
Comments: windstake the tallest varieties—especially in windy areas. Unfortunately most are non-fragrant.
Varieties of Note:
'Apple Blossom'—a pink and cream bicolor.
'Aroma'—a good white variety.
'Black Butterfly'—dark red, downfacing flowers.

'Brushmark Hybrids'—red, orange, yellow, or white upfacing flowers with a bright splash of color on each petal.
'Connecticut King'—golden orange-yellow upfacing flowers. This exceptional variety is one of the Piedmont Lilies bred by David Stone and Henry Payne of Piedmont, Connecticut in 1967. It makes an excellent cut flower. But be sure to leave at least a third of the stalk and leaves to grow next year's bulb.
'Delicious'—orange upfacing variety, slightly fragrant. Introduced by Honeywood Nursery, Parkside, Saskatchewan.
'Earlibird'—apricot-colored outfacing flowers. This is an older variety from Honeywood Nursery, Parkside, Saskatchewan. It is disease-resistant and of a vigorous habit.
'Embarrassment'—soft pink outfacing flowers with dark spots, tall growing habit. This is considered one of the best pink varieties.
'Enchantment'—vivid red-orange upfacing flowers with black spots, excellent vigor. This is a good variety for beginners. Introduced as a Mid-Century Hybrid in 1947 by the famous lily breeder January de Graaff in Sandy, Oregon. This is a vigorous and reliable variety.
'Faberge Strain'—the most fragrant of the Asiatic lilies. Because they are slow to establish, it is best to plant small bulbs and be patient. Varieties are: 'Gypsy Queen,' red with a yellow throat; 'Czar,' yellow with red spots; 'Nutcracker,' pinkish-red with yellow throat. These varieties were bred from *Lilium monadelphum* by Len Marshall of Casper, Wyoming, and propagated by Judith McRae of Gresham, Oregon. They sell their lilies under the name Columbia-Platte Hybrids.
'Firebright'—vivid red outfacing flowers. A Canadian hybrid.
'Honey Pink'—warm pink downfacing flowers, disease resistant. A recent introduction by Mr. F. Fellner of Vermilion, Alberta.
'Kismet'—orange upfacing flowers.
'Matterhorn' ('White Sail')—a good white variety lightly spotted with black.
'Maxwill'—extra vigorous dark red-orange pendulous flowers, 30

to 40 flowers per stem. This tremendously showy variety was bred from *Lilium davidii* by Dr. Frank Skinner, Dropmore, Manitoba. It is a very stately plant.
'Mount Blanc'—a good white upfacing variety lightly spotted with brown in the center.
'Red Velvet'—velvety red outfacing flowers. This vigorous variety is a triploid, which makes the stems, foliage, and petals stronger and thicker.
'Sterling Star'—a good white upfacing variety with black spots.
'Yellow Blaze'—vivid yellow upfacing flowers with blackish-brown spots, blooms at the end of the Asiatic season, extra-vigorous. This is another exceptional variety of the Piedmont Lilies by Stone and Payne.

LILIUM AURELIAN HYBRIDS. Perennial to Zone 3 (with protection).
Height: 2-5 feet.
Bloom: color range of pink, orange, yellow, white, or purple; blooms in August; most of these hybrids have a powerful fragrance.
Likes: sun/half-sun/moist (less water in the fall)/humus-rich soil.
Tolerates: mild alkalinity.
Propagation: bulbs.
Comments: requires careful winter mulching. Flower stalks must be windstaked. Many varieties have an arching form due to their *Lilium henryi* parentage. These varieties were originally created by crossing *Lilium henryi* and *Lilium sargentiae*.
Varieties of note:
'Gold Eagle'—lemon-yellow flowers with dark spots, hardier than most Aurelian hybrids.
'Golden Splendor'—rich golden flowers with maroon stripes on outside of petals, very fragrant.
'Purple Majesty'—rich majestic purple with yellow throat, very fragrant. Bred by Leslie Woodriff of McKinleyville, California in 1983.
'White *Henryi*'—bold white flowers with a golden-yellow throat and cinnamon-brown flecks, petals reflex attractively, hardier than most Aurelian hybrids. Introduced by Leslie Woodriff in 1945.

LILIUM TETRAPLOID HYBRIDS. Perennial to Zone 1.
Height: 3-6 feet.
Bloom: very large, long-lasting red, pink, or orange flowers, blooms

from late July to late August, petals are very thick and succulent.
Foliage: extremely thick foliage and stems.
Likes: sun/half-sun/moist (less water in the fall)/humus and fertilizer-rich soil.
Propagation: bulbs.
Comments: vigorous and disease resistant nature. For decades, many breeders have been working toward the elusive goal of creating tetraploids by doubling the chromosome count. The following varieties are creations of LeVern Freimann of Bellingham, Washington. Now being propagated by tissue cloning, these varieties will create a stir when finally offered to the public during the 1990s.

    'Apricot Supreme'—apricot color.
    'Catherine Walton'—deep scarlet red.
    'Lady Marion'—clear light pink.
    'Scarlet Delight'—scarlet red.
One of the other main hybridizers of Tetraploid Lilies is Mr. Strasser of West Germany, whose varieties are not yet available in North America.

LIMONIUM LATIFOLIUM, Perennial Statice. Perennial to Zone 1, height 2 feet.
Bloom: showy purple-blue or white mist-like flower clusters from July to August.
Culture: easy.
Likes: sun/dry/semidry/moist/deeply dug, well-drained, humus-rich soil.
Propagation: sets or seeds.
Comments: established plants resent transplanting. Flowers can be dried as an everlasting or left on plant for winter interest. 'Violetta' has deep lavender-blue flowers that hold their color particularly well after drying.

  L. SINUATUM, Florist's Statice. Annual.
Height: 2 feet.
Bloom: red, pink, white, or blue-purple flowers, blooms from July to frost (very long season).

Perennial Statice, Limonium latifolium

Culture: easy.
Likes: sun/moist.
Tolerates: half-sun/dry/semidry.
Propagation: sets (tolerates light frost. Plant hardened-off sets two weeks before the frost-free date.)
Comments: flowers can be dried as an everlasting or left on the plant for winter interest. This is the statice sold commercially by florists. In the garden, it is valuable for its amazingly long bloom. Additionally it can be used as either a long-lasting cut flower or dried as an everlasting. A small cottage industry could harvest this plant through the summer and sell dried bouquets, wreaths, and car dash decorations during the rest of the year. Shepherd's Garden Seeds lists the variety 'Rainbow Custom Colors' with a color range of pink, apricot, white, light lavender-blue, and dark blue-purple. Breeding work needs to be done to create better blue varieties. The varieties 'True Blue' and 'Kampf's Blue' are at best a blue-purple color, not a true blue.

LINANTHUS SEPTENTRIONALIS. Native to disturbed sandy areas of the Great Plains. Annual.
Height: 8 inches.
Bloom: white flowers on stalks.
Foliage: fine textured clump, very finely-divided foliage best described as thread-like.
Likes: sun/half-sun/dry/semidry.
Propagation: sets or seeds.

LINARIA ALPINA, Alpine Toadflax. Annual.
Height: 6 inches.
Bloom: showy multicolored flowers in red, pink, yellow, blue, and purple; blooms from June to frost.
Culture: easy.
Likes: moist.
Tolerates: sun/half-sun/semidry.
Propagation: sets or seeds. Self-sows moderately.
Comments: creeping clump habit. This easy-to-grow annual looks most dramatic planted in cracks in a wall or in a rock garden. It also does well in pots or containers.

LINUM GRANDIFLORUM, Red Flax. Annual.
Height: 1 foot.
Bloom: scarlet-red flowers from June to frost (long season).
Foliage: delicate-looking.
Culture: easy.

Likes: sun.
Tolerates: half-sun/semidry/moist.
Propagation: sets (transplant carefully) or seeds.

  L. PERENNE, Blue Flax. Perennial to Zone 2.
Height: 1 foot.
Bloom: delicate blue flowers from late June to July (long season).
Foliage: attractive, fine-textured.
Culture: easy.
Likes: sun/half-sun/dry/semidry.
Propagation: sets (transplant carefully) or seeds (self-sows some).
Comments: dried flower stalks are attractive in arrangements. Closely related is the native flax *Linum perenne ssp. lewisii* named for Capt. Meriwether Lewis. He mentioned seeing fields of this flower along the Missouri River from the Great Falls portage camp to the Gates of the Mountains. The Indians ground and ate the seeds.

LINUM PERENNE SUBSPECIES LEWISII, Blue Flax. Perennial.
Height: 1 foot.
Bloom: delicate-looking blue flowers and foliage from early June to July (long season); dried flower stalks are attractive and can be used as a dried flower.
Culture: easy.
Likes: sun/semidry.
Tolerates: half-sun/dry.
Propagation: sets (transplant carefully) or seeds (self-sows some).
Comments: this native plant is closely related to the Common Blue Garden Flax *(Linum perenne).* This native subspecies was named for Captain Meriwether Lewis of the Lewis and Clark Expedition. He mentioned seeing fields of this flower along the Missouri River from the Great Falls portage camp to the Gates of the Rocky Mountains. The Indians cooked the seeds of this plant. There is also a native yellow flax, *Linum rigidum,* an annual, which flowers later in the summer from late June to August.

  L. USITATISSIMUM, Commercial Flax. Annual.
Height: 2 feet.
Bloom: light blue flowers from July to August.
Culture: easy.
Likes: semidry.
Tolerates: sun/half-sun/dry/moist.
Propagation: seeds (self-sows some).

LISIANTHUS RUSSELIANUS (Eustoma grandiflorum), Prairie Gentian, native to the central plains. Annual.
Bloom: upright clump, purple, pink, or white poppy-like flowers.
Likes: sun/semidry.
Tolerates: half-sun/dry/drought.
Propagation: sets or seeds.
Comments: this flower makes a long-lasting cut flower.

LITHOPHRAGMA TENELLA, Prairie Star. Native to rocky hillsides in the foothills. Perennial.
Height: 5 inches.
Bloom: delicate white star-like flowers on elongating stalks, blooms from end of April to May.
Foliage: individual plants may form an attractive mat-like clump of attractive dark green foliage.
Likes: sun/half-sun/semidry.
Propagation: bulbs.
Comments: plant goes dormant and disappears in mid-summer. The other species *Lithophragma bulbifera* and *L. parviflora* are also especially attractive.

LOBELIA ERINUS, Edging Lobelia. Annual.
Height: 4 inches.
Bloom: delicate-looking mound of red, white, blue or purple flowers from May to frost (very long season).
Culture: easy.
Likes: half-sun/half-shade/moist/humus-rich soil.
Propagation: sets or seeds. (Seed germination: warm. Flowers 8 weeks from seed.)
Comments: this annual makes a showy edging at the front of the garden or under a rose bed. 'Red Cascade' has beautiful reddish-violet flowers; 'Kobalt Blue' has exceptional pure gentian-blue flowers.

LOBULARIA MARITIMA, Sweet Alyssum. Annual.
Height: 4 inches.
Bloom: spreading mound of pink,

Prairie Star, Lithophragma tenella

white, or purple flowers from May to November (very long season if watered in the fall).
Culture: easy.
Likes: half-sun/moist.
Tolerates: sun/half-shade/dry/semidry.
Propagation: sets or seeds. (Seed germination: can be planted out a month before frost-free date. Flowers from seed in 4 weeks.)
Comments: white varieties are cold hardiest. This plant is very attractive as a carpet under Hybrid Tea Roses or in cracks in a stairway. Additionally, it can be used as an edging at the front of the garden or planted in a pot or container.

LOMATIUM DISSECTUM, Desert Parsley. Native to dry rocky slopes and cliff bases in the foothills. Perennial.
Height: 3 feet.
Bloom: light yellow (and occasionally purplish-black) flower clusters in May; unusual seedheads in June.
Foliage: upright clump, attractive large hairy carrot-like foliage which emerges in early April.
Likes: sun/dry/semidry.
Comments: this plant's taproot was used heavily by the Indians for food. The poisonous Water Hemlock (*Cicuta maculata*) resembles many of the *Lomatiums,* but only when the foliage is emerging in the early spring. The Water Hemlock's root is chambered while the *Lomatium's* root is solid.

L. MACROCARPUM, Long-fruited Prairie Parsley. Native to dry and rocky exposed hillsides in the Great Plains and foothills. Perennial.
Height: 1 foot.
Bloom: white (or occasionally yellow) flower clusters on stalks; blooms from early to end of May; unusual-looking papery seedheads from June to July.
Foliage: densely hairy, silvery-white fernlike foliage on short stalks, foliage emerges in mid-April.
Likes: sun.
Tolerates: dry/semidry.
Comments: large taproot makes this plant difficult to transplant. A closely related plant is *Musineon divaricatum,* Leafy Musineon, which is similar except for its shiny smooth green foliage and very early yellow flowers.

L. VILLOSUM (L. foeniculaceum),

Yellow Prairie Parsley, Biscuit Root, Parsley Dill. Native to dry creek beds and clay soil areas of the Great Plains. Perennial.
Height: 4-10 inches.
Bloom: showy yellow flower clusters from mid-April to May; unusual seedheads from June to July.
Foliage: densely hairy gray-green fernlike foliage which emerges in early April.
Likes: semidry.
Tolerates: sun/dry.
Propagation: root cuttings in spring or fall. (Seed germination: cold treatment.)
Comments: plant goes dormant and disappears by mid-summer; this plant has a large taproot, which makes it difficult to transplant. The roots of primarily *Lomatium cous,* but also *L. ambiguum, L. dissectum, L. macrocarpum,* and *L. villosum* were heavily harvested by the Indians, who dried the roots, and pounded them into flour which they mixed with water and baked into flat cakes. Lewis and Clark traded with the Indians for this food stuff. After leaving hibernation in the spring, bears seek out this root which they locate by smell.

LONICERA HECKROTTII, Goldflame Honeysuckle Vine. Perennial to Zone 4.
Height: vine to 15 feet.
Climbing habit: vine tip twines; loose climbing habit.
Bloom: tubular two-tone pink and yellow flowers (fragrant only at night) in June (long season).
Likes: half-sun/moist.
Propagation: sets, seeds, softwood or hardwood cuttings in summer or winter.
Comments: may be winter-killed to ground, but will regrow quickly from its roots. This vine is an excellent combination with an equally aggressive Clematis variety.

L. MAACKII, Amur Honeysuckle. Perennial to Zone 2.
Height: 15 feet.
Bloom: fragrant white flowers in early June, showy long-lasting red berries.
Shape: coarse upright bush with horizontal branches.
Foliage: In the fall, coarse textured foliage stays green until November (early winter interest).

Likes: semidry.
Tolerates: sun/half-sun/dry/moist.
Propagation: sets or seeds (softwood cuttings or hardwood cuttings in summer or winter).
Comments: protect from extreme wind exposure for best appearance. The variety 'Podocarpa' holds its foliage the longest. Native to the Amur River area of Manchuria.

L. PERICLYMENUM, Woodbine Vine. Perennial to Zone 4-5 (protected areas only).
Height: vine to 20 feet.
Bloom: yellowish-white flowers (fragrant only at night) from June to August (long season), red fruit.
Likes: half-sun/moist.
Tolerates: half-shade/semidry.
Propagation: sets or seeds.
Comments: common name refers to its twining habit's ability to strangle trees. *Belgica* has an early bloom season, and *Serotina* has a mid- to late season (plant these two together for the longest bloom season).

L. STANDISHII, Winter Honeysuckle. Perennial to Zone 4 (protected areas only).
Height: 5 feet.
Bloom: intensely fragrant white flowers appear with new leaves from early April to May (same time as the crocus flowers).
Shape: bush.
Likes: half-sun/semidry/moist.
Propagation: sets or seeds.
Comments: best grown in a protected location or near a house wall. This is an extremely early, fragrant shrub. If you want to have the very first fragrant shrub on your block, this is it. Should be more commonly planted. Makes an attractive combination with Grape Hyacinth (*Muscari*).

L. SYRINGANTHA, Lilac Honeysuckle Bush. Perennial to Zone 4.
Height: 5 feet.
Bloom: fragrant lilac-scented purple flowers in May, red fruit.
Shape: flattened mound (give it lots of room).

Woodbine Vine, Lonicera periclymenum

Foliage: gray-green, willow-like.
Propagation: sets or seeds.
Culture: easy.
Likes: half-sun/semidry/moist.
Comments: This plant was introduced from China.

L. TATARICA. Perennial to Zone 1.
Height: 10 feet.
Shape: upright bush.
Bloom: non-fragrant sparse pink flowers in May, orange-red fruit in June.
Culture: easy.
Likes: half-sun/moist.
Tolerates: half-shade/dry/semidry.
Propagation: sets or seeds.
Pests: aphids are a devastating problem.
Comments: this plant makes a good hedge. There are varieties with either white, pink, or red flowers. Of these, 'Arnold' (red flowers, red fruit) is the preferred selection for its showy flowers, long bloom season, and total resistance to aphids. 'Bella Dropmore,' a Skinner hybrid of 1941, produces such a massive berry display that its branches arch to the ground. Give it lots of room. The original species form of this plant was collected in the Altai mountains of Russia.

L. THIBETICA, Tibet Honeysuckle Bush. Perennial to Zone 4.
Height: 4 feet.
Bloom: fragrant purple flowers in May; red fruit.
Shape: sprawling mounded clump.
Foliage: shiny foliage which stays green until late fall.
Culture: easy.
Likes: half-sun/semidry/moist.
Propagation: sets or seeds.
Comments: this plant is best displayed cascading down a rocky slope or wall.

L. X BROWNII 'DROPMORE SCARLET TRUMPET,' Honeysuckle Vine. Perennial to Zone 2.
Height: vine to 10 feet.
Bloom: non-fragrant coral-orange flowers from early June to September (long season).
Climbing habit: vine tip twines, needs a wire or lattice to climb.
Foliage: light green.
Culture: easy.
Likes: sun/half-sun/semidry/moist.
Propagation: sets, softwood or hardwood cuttings in summer or winter.

Dropmore Scarlet Trumpet, Lonicera x brownii

Comments: this hybrid of *Lonicera hirsuta* and *Lonicera sempervirens* was introduced by Frank Skinner of Dropmore, Manitoba, in 1950. In Zone 2, plant on a sheltered wall, or south or east-facing exposure.

This will provide the longest bloom season and least amount of winter dieback. Mr. Robert Simonet of Edmonton has produced hybrids similar to Skinner's hybrid, except that they are much hardier in the extreme northern areas. Unfortunately, these were never named or released into the horticultural trade.

L. X XYLOSTEOIDES, Hedge Honeysuckle. Perennial to Zone 3.
Height: 4 feet.
Bloom: insignificant flowers, red berries.
Shape: compact shrub.
Foliage: blue-green.
Culture: easy.
Propagation: sets.
Likes: half-sun.
Tolerates: sun/half-shade/semidry/moist.
Comments: prune minimally. 'Hedge King,' hardy only to Zone 3, is a narrowly upright form bred for hedges. 'Minniglobe' is a dwarf mound-shaped shrub that grows to 2 feet tall, leafs out very early in the spring, and requires little pruning. It is a fairly recent introduction by Wilbert Ronald, previously at Morden Research Station.

LUPINUS LEPIDUS, Mountain Dwarf Lupine. Native to the western Great Plains and Rocky Mountains. Perennial.
Height: 1 foot.
Bloom: dark blue-purple flowers from June to July.
Foliage: attractive tightly compact clump of silvery-green foliage.
Likes: sun/half-sun/semidry/moist.
Propagation: sets (plants are best transplanted only in the spring) or seeds (seeds germinate best if boil-

ing water is poured on seeds and soaked overnight).

Comments: established plants resent transplanting. Use a legume inoculant when planting. This species is particularly showy because of its low compact habit. For longest lasting cut flowers, crush stem ends. Foliage and roots are poisonous.

L. SUBCARNOSUS, Texas Blue Bonnet; official state flower of Texas. Annual.
Height: 1 foot.
Bloom: blue flower stalks in July.
Culture: easy.
Likes: sun/semidry.
Tolerates: half-sun/dry/moist.
Propagation: sets (must be transplanted carefully) or seeds.

LUPINUS HYBRIDS. Perennial to Zone 1.
Height: 4 feet.
Bloom: red, pink, orange, yellow, white, blue, and purple flowers (many bicolored) from mid-June to mid-July.
Foliage: attractive foliage.
Likes: sun/moist/humus-rich soil/thick mulch.
Tolerates: half-sun.
Propagation: sets.
Comments: clump habit; prefers cool summer areas or mid-day shade; needs even moisture throughout summer; prefers not to be crowded. There are exceptional gentian-blue varieties—search for these. The common variety 'Russell Hybrids' is a hodgepodge mix of old named varieties. Foliage and roots are poisonous.

LYCHNIS ALPINA (Viscaria alpina), Arctic Campion. Perennial to Zone 1.
Height: 4 inches.
Bloom: magenta flowers, blooms at end of May.
Foliage: cushion-like mound.
Culture: difficult.
Likes: half-sun/rock garden soil.
Tolerates: sun/half-shade/semidry.
Propagation: sets or seeds.
Comments: prefers cool summer areas or mid-day shade in hot summer areas. The name *lychnis* means "lamp" in Greek and refers to the genus' vividly bright flower colors.

L. CHALCEDONICA, Maltese Cross. Perennial to Zone 2.
Height: 2 feet.
Bloom: coral-scarlet flowers from June to July (long season).

Likes: half-sun/moist.
Tolerates: half-shade/semidry/wet.
Propagation: sets or seeds. (Seed germination: warm.)
Comments: two hybrid varieties 'arkwrightii' and 'haageana' have larger flowers than the species, and the latter has dark bronze-green foliage. There is a pink variety called 'rosea' with salmon-on-pink flowers. The name 'lychnis' means 'lamp' in Greek and refers to the genus' vividly bright flower colors.

L. CORONARIA, Mullein Pink. Perennial to Zone 2.
Height: 3 feet.
Bloom: magenta-pink flowers from June to frost (long season if spent flowers removed).
Foliage: grayish-white.
Culture: easy.
Likes: half-sun.
Tolerates: sun/dry/semidry/moist.
Propagation: sets or seeds.
Comments: invasive by self-sown seed, though extra plants are easily weeded out. The rare white variety is particularly attractive.

LYGODESMIA JUNCEA, Rush Skeletonweed, Prairie Pink. Native to dry sandy grassland and eroded areas of the Great Plains. Perennial.
Height: 1 foot.
Bloom: delicate five-petaled pink flowers from early July to early August.
Foliage: small inconspicuous foliage.
Likes: sun/dry/semidry/sandy soil.
Propagation: sets or seeds. (Seed germination: cold treatment.)
Comments: established plants resent transplanting. Dramatically rigid multi-branched clump; unusual-looking stems can become nearly as thick as pencils; could be described as skeleton-like in appearance. The small pink flowers closely resemble Pinks *(Dianthus)* to which this plant is not related. Two other species also of interest are *Lygodesmia*

Maltese Cross, Lychnis chalcedonica

grandiflora, native to Wyoming and Colorado, which has large attractive flowers; and *Lygodesmia rostrata,* which is an annual with wire-like leaves tipped with spines and pink flowers. The Indians dried the milky sap of these species to make chewing gum.

LYSIMACHIA NUMMULARIA 'AUREA,' Golden Moneywort, Golden Creeping Jenny. Perennial to Zone 2.
Height: 2 inches.
Bloom: fragrant yellow flowers from June to July.
Foliage: rounded, bright yellow leaves.
Culture: easy.
Likes: sun/half-sun/half-shade/semidry/moist.
Propagation: sets or seeds.
Comments: fast-spreading creeper, invasive by stem rooting. This aggressive plant can be used as a ground cover, an edging at the front of the border, or in a hanging pot. It is most attractive cascading off the side of a container. However, it is too invasive for use in a rock garden. The round leaves resemble coins, thus the common name 'moneywort.' This plant can be used in shady areas as a ground cover, but loses its beautiful yellow foliage color if grown in too much shade.

LYTHRUM VIRGATUM, Purple Loosestrife. Perennial to Zone 1.
Height: 4 feet.
Bloom: red, pink, or purple flower spikes from late July to August (long season).
Culture: easy.
Likes: sun/moist.
Tolerates: half-sun/semidry/wet.
Propagation: sets.
Comments: invasive by roots and self-sown seed. This European native has escaped cultivation and is causing extreme problems to wildlife habitat across North America. 'Dropmore Purple' has rich purple flowers (bred by Dr. Skinner in 1942). 'Morden Gleam' has bright carmine flowers and red fall foliage (bred by Mr. Bert Harp of Morden Research Station in 1954). 'Morden Pink' has deep pink flowers (bred by Morden Research Station in 1937). 'Rose Queen' has soft pink flowers.

**MAACKIA AMU-
RENSIS.** Perenni-
al to Zone 3.
Height: 30 feet.
Shape: attractive
vase-shaped
tree, attractive
light brown
bark.
Bloom: insignif-
icant white
flowers.
Foliage: dull
green.
Likes: sun.
Tolerates: half-
sun/semidry/
moist.
Propagation:
sets or seeds.

*Loosestrife,
Lythrum virgatum*

Comments: this slow-growing small
tree has little appeal beyond its attractive shape and the fact that few
horticulturists can identify it. Unfortunately, the more attractive *Maackia chinensis* is not hardy here.

MACHAERANTHERA TANACETIFOLIA,
Tahoka Daisy. Native to sandy areas
of the central and northern Great
Plains. Annual.
Height: 1 foot.
Bloom: profuse small blue-purple
aster-like flowers with golden yel-
low center from July to frost.
Foliage: rounded clump of showy
fernlike foliage.
Likes: sun/half-sun/semidry.

Propagation: sets.
Comments: two re-
lated native peren-
nial species are
*Machaeranthera
canescens* and *M.
glabriuscula.*

**MAHONIA AQUIFOLI-
UM,** Oregon Grape,
Holly Grape, official
state flower of Ore-
gon, native to moun-
tain forests. Perenni-
al to Zone 3.
Height: 2 feet.

*Tahoka Daisy,
Machae-
ranthera
tanacetifolia*

Bloom: showy yel-
low flower clusters
from late April to
early May; sparse
but attractive dark
blue fruit clusters
hidden in the leaves from August to
late winter.
Foliage: glossy holly-like leaves that

are dark green in summer and
bronzy-red in winter.
Likes: half-sun/half-shade/dry/semi-
dry/moist.
Propagation: sets or seeds (transplants easily when young.)
Comments: loose sprawling habit;
prefers either light mid-day shade
from a tree or a bright northern exposure; requires wind protection in
exposed areas. This plant is valued
for its reddish evergreen foliage and
dark blue berries. The sour grape-
like fruit is best harvested after
frosts. It makes a tasty jelly. This
plant can be used in a moderately
aggressive ground cover mix. The
peeled yellow wood was often
used in Mexico to make crucifixes.
As an ornamental, this plant should
be selected for larger and showier
blue fruit. Then it would become a
more popular landscaping plant. A
related plant, native to Rocky
Mountain forests, *Mahonia repens*

*Oregon Grape,
Mahonia aquifolium*

(holly grape, Oregon grape), has a
less showy creeping form.

MALCOLMIA MARITIMA, Virginia
Stock. Annual.
Height: 1 foot.
Bloom: pink, yellow, white, or purple stock-like flowers, blooms from
June to frost (long season).
Likes: sun/half-sun/moist/humus-
rich soil.
Propagation: sets or seed. (Seed
germination: flowers 45 days from
seed.)
Comments: upright clump. This
plant resembles Stock (*Matthiola
incana*) but is non-fragrant. It is an
excellent cover for bulbs.

MALOPE TRIFIDA. Annual.
Height: 3 feet.
Bloom: large pinkish-red or pinkish-
purple hollyhock flowers on a stalk,
blooms from July to frost.
Foliage: attractive mallow-like
leaves.
Likes: sun/humus-rich soil.
Tolerates: half-sun/semidry/moist.
Propagation: sets (transplants poorly) or seeds (plant in place two
weeks before the frost-free date).
Comments: upright bushy plant;
leaves mutilated by rust disease in
late summer. This plant is closely
related to *Alcea rosea* (Hollyhocks),
Lavatera (Tree Mallow), and *Malva*—all listed in this guide.

MALUS, Apple and Crabapple; state
flower of Arkansas and Michigan.
The most beautiful and long-lived
trees result from rarely pruning
them and never cutting the grass
underneath them. The tall grass also
breaks the fall of apples. Prune
trees by drop-crotching outermost
branches (best done professionally
and in early summer after bloom);
never top or stub the branch tips
because the damage is irreversible.
For the same reason, buy only sets
with their terminal bud tips intact.
Suckers should be removed from
the base of the tree. For more information on proper pruning, see the
Tree Care Section.

All varieties listed here are resistant
to fire blight unless noted otherwise.
Research has indicated that susceptible
trees tend to suffer less fire blight in nitrogen-poor soil. Apple scab disease is
not a problem in arid areas of the
northern Great Plains. However, varieties which are susceptible to apple
scab have been noted for gardeners of
the mountain areas where it is a problem. Cedar-apple rust is a mild problem for some apples if a Rocky Mountain Juniper (*Juniperus scopulorum*) or
Eastern Juniper (*Juniperus virginiana*)
is planted within 300 yards. Cedar-apple rust is rarely a devastating problem.
Varieties particularly sensitive to this
problem are noted.

Apple trees prefer humus-rich soil
and may suffer chlorosis in highly
alkaline soil. Germinate apple seeds
after cold treatment; propagate apple varieties with either layering,
grafting or budding.

There is an International Ornamental Crabapple Society. Its address is listed in the Resource Directory.

Gardeners in mountain areas can choose from many more varieties than those listed here. The plains climate is particularly harsh for apple varieties.

The Eating Apple Section begins on page 111. The following varieties are considered suitable for plains gardeners.

ORNAMENTAL VARIETIES

'Almey.' Perennial to Zone 1.
Height: 20 feet.
Shape: large upright tree.
Bloom: purplish-red buds which open into clusters of pink flowers in early May, vivid crimson fruit ripens in the fall and is held throughout the winter.
Foliage: reddish-purple.
Comments: this variety is extremely

Flowering Crabapple, Malus

susceptible to apple scab, but in the Great Plains areas this is not a problem. This Rosybloom Crabapple tree was introduced in 1945 by Morden Research Station, Manitoba. In 1967, it was selected as Canada's Centennial Tree.

M. baccata, Siberian Crabapple Tree. Perennial to Zone 1.
Height: 40 feet.
Bloom: fragrant white flowers from late April to early May, red or yellow fruit which hangs on the tree until birds eat it.
Shape: large wide-spreading tree.
Foliage: red fall color.
Culture: easy.
Likes: sun/dry/semidry.
Propagation: sets or seeds.
Comments: 'Gracilis' grows to a height of 30 feet; graceful semi-pendulous form slowly grows into a large spreading tree; fragrant white flowers. 'Mandshurica' is a broadly-spreading large tree 30 feet tall;

with fragrant white flowers in mid-April. It is the very first crabapple to bloom. 'Rosthern' has a showy pyramidal shape, white flowers, and an extremely beautiful display of small red fruit held on the tree until eaten by birds.

'Brandywine.' Perennial to Zone 4-5 (protected areas only).
Height: 15 feet.
Bloom: very showy fragrant double pink flowers, fruit hangs on tree throughout the winter.
Shape: small rounded tree.
Foliage: wine-red cast to the foliage, reddish-brown fall color.
Comments: this variety is severely susceptible to cedar-apple rust. Do not plant it in the vicinity of a Rocky Mountain Juniper or Eastern Juniper.

'Centurion.' Perennial to Zone 3.
Height: 20 feet.
Bloom: deep pink flowers in mid-May, showy profuse red fruit held on the tree until eaten by birds.
Shape: upright rounded form.
Comments: this variety has the unfortunate habit of blooming only on the branch tips. It originated with Robert C. Simpson.

'Dolgo,' attractive large tree with dramatic flower show. It is listed in the Eating Apple Section.

'Katherine.' Perennial to Zone 4-5 (protected areas only).
Height: 12 feet.
Bloom: profuse pink to white large double flowers in mid-May; red fruit which the birds quickly eat. This tree flowers at an early age.
Shape: semi-shrub with a showy upright-spreading irregular shape.

'Kelsey.' Perennial to Zone 1.
Height: 15 feet.
Bloom: profuse semi-double purplish-red flowers in early May, purplish-red fruit which is somewhat messy in the fall.
Shape: low-branching rounded tree similar in form to a Hopa Crabapple.
Foliage: has reddish cast in the spring, but it becomes green in the summer.
Comments: Dr. William Cummings of Morden Research Station, Manitoba, introduced this variety in 1970. This was Manitoba's official Centennial Tree; it was named for Henry Kelsey, who was the first white man to cross Hudson's Bay

and see Manitoba. The Western Canadian Society for Horticulture gave this variety their Award of Merit in 1973.

'Kerr,' attractive flower display.

'Liset.' Perennial to Zone 4-5 (protected areas only).
Height: 12 feet.
Bloom: deep red flowers in early May, showy dull red fruit held until eaten by birds.
Shape: rounded upright tree.
Foliage: purplish foliage in early spring which turns green in summer.

'Pink Spires.' Perennial to Zone 3.
Height: 20 feet.
Bloom: pink flowers in mid-May, profuse red fruit held until eaten by the birds.
Shape: very showy symmetrical upright tree.
Foliage: purple-red foliage in the spring turns to a bronzy-green in summer, spectacular red-orange fall color.
Comments: this tree is a real asset for its beautiful form, pink flowers, and superior fall color. Selected by W. L. Kerr of Sutherland, Saskatchewan.

'Prince Georges.' Perennial to Zone 4-5 (protected areas only).
Height: 20 feet.
Bloom: very large double pink flowers with rose-like scent in late May, does not produce fruit.
Shape: upright rounded tree, low-branched form.
Comments: this attractive tree produces a naturally rounded lollipop-shaped tree. This variety is susceptible to cedar-apple rust.

'Radiant.' Perennial to Zone 2.
Height: 25 feet.
Bloom: deep red buds open into very showy pinkish-red flowers in mid-May; profuse bright red fruit hangs on the tree until eaten by birds.
Foliage: reddish foliage in spring turns to green in the summer.
Comments: the name refers to the luminous color of the flowers. This variety is susceptible to apple scab in mountain areas where this is a problem. Introduced by the University of Minnesota in 1957.

'Red Jade.' Perennial to Zone 4.
Height: 15 feet.
Shape: graceful pendulous tree (eventually reaching to the ground).

Bloom: pink to white flowers in mid-May; scarlet-red fruit is held throughout the winter (an excellent specimen tree).
Comments: requires full sun, moderately susceptible to fire blight and apple scab. Because of its weeping form, do not plan to use the space below this tree. Introduced by the Brooklyn Botanical Garden.

'Red Splendor.' Perennial to Zone 3.
Height: 25 feet.
Bloom: pink flowers in late May; showy profuse crimson fruit which hangs on tree until birds eat it.
Shape: upright form.
Foliage: bronzy-green foliage color, attractive fall color.
Comments: occasionally, though rarely, this tree gets fire blight. Developed by Melvin Bergeson, Fertile, Minnesota. Introduced by the University of Minnesota.

M. sargentii, Sargent Crab. Perennial to Zone 3.
Height: 6 feet.
Bloom: fragrant white flowers from red buds in mid-May; small scarlet fruit hangs on tree throughout the winter.
Shape: spreading dense shrub-like form.
Comments: there exists some question over its hardiness, but Alberta sources claim success with a hardy rootstock such as *Malus columbiana.* There is also a dwarf variety 'Tina.' This tree is moderately susceptible to fire blight. Named for Charles S. Sargent of Harvard's Arnold Arboreteum who introduced it from Japan in 1892.

'Selkirk.' Perennial to Zone 1.
Height: 20 feet.
Bloom: deep pink flowers; very showy dull red fruit becomes somewhat messy.
Shape: large rounded upright tree.
Comments: this Rosybloom Crabapple was introduced in 1963 by Morden Research Station, Manitoba. Named for Lord Selkirk who encouraged the migration of Scottish farmers into the Red River Valley of Manitoba. This variety is susceptible to apple scab in mountain areas.

'Spring Snow.' Perennial to Zone 1.
Height: 18 feet.
Bloom: fragrant white flowers; because it is a sterile hybrid, this variety does not set fruit.

Shape: distinctly oval-shaped form in youth becoming an upright rounded form at maturity.
Comments: mildly susceptible to apple scab in mountain areas.

'Thunderchild.' Perennial to Zone 1.
Height: 20 feet.
Bloom: deep red flowers while new foliage is green, sparse dark red fruit which hangs on tree until the birds eat it in the fall.
Shape: upright spreading tree.
Foliage: turns red-purple in summer.
Comments: this beautiful tree was selected (by Percy H. Wright, Saskatoon, Saskatchewan) not only for its colorful dark foliage, but also for its resistance to Fire Blight.

'Vanguard.' Perennial to Zone 3.
Height: 20 feet.
Bloom: deep rose-red flowers in late May, red fruit is held on tree until eaten by the birds.
Shape: appealing vase-shaped tree in youth becoming rounded with age.
Foliage: purple-red foliage in spring becoming dark green in summer.
Comments: introduced by the University of Minnesota.

EATING APPLE VARIETIES

The only difference between crabapples, apple-crabs, and apples is fruit size. To avoid these terms, the following apple varieties are noted

Apple, Malus

as small, medium, and large sizes. Individual taste preference varies widely from tart to sweet; most people simply don't know what they like best. It is recommended that you taste several varieties of apples and plant your favorite ones.

To produce well, apples must be cross-pollinated by a different variety that blooms at the same time. Wind does not carry the pollen

well, which makes bees important pollinators. However, you should give each tree ample space so that its roots are not competing with other apple trees. In extremely exposed areas, it is recommended that you plant four apple trees in a clump. Two of the trees are hardy and are used for a windbreak; the other two trees are less hardy and are protected from the wind. Additionally, shrubby windbreaks on the north side and avoidance of frost pockets will also help.

When pruning, avoid leaving any weak V-crotches which tend to break from a fruit load. U-shaped crotches are much stronger. Furthermore, new apple pruning techniques recommend leaving lower branches intact as low as two feet above the ground. *Rodale's Organic Gardening Magazine* had an excellent article on apple pruning in their December 1987 issue.

Some people leave the grass long beneath an established tree to soften the landing of falling ripe apples. These trees with uncut grass below them produce smaller harvests, but live longer and are more disease-resistant. Possibly there is a microrhizal relationship with soil fungus.

Apples can be used for fresh eating, garnishes, apple pies, applesauce, jams and jellies, dried, canned, or cider (hard or soft). It is noteworthy to point out that apple trees cannot be grown in the tropics. And thus a cottage industry could form around the global marketing of apple products in the tropics. Because of apple's natural pectin, Kim Williams suggested juicing apples and freezing the juice to use for next year's strawberry and raspberry jam. She also suggested making fruit leather from a combination of tart and sweet apple varieties.

SEASON OF RIPENING: It is recommended that you plant varieties which ripen their fruit at different times.

EARLY SEASON—'Carroll,' 'Dolgo,' 'Heyer #12,' 'Norland,' 'Oriole,' 'Red Astrachan,' and 'Rescue.'

EARLY to MID-SEASON—'Colette,' 'Duchess of Oldenburg,' 'Lubst Queen,' and 'Patterson.'

MID-SEASON—'Dakota,' 'Brookland,' 'Fameuse,' 'Mandan,' 'Norda,' 'Parkland,' 'Shafer,' 'Sunnybrook,' 'Trailman,' and 'Westland.'

MID- TO LATE SEASON—'Breakey,' 'Chestnut,' 'Goodland,' 'Kerr,' and 'Rosybrook.'

LATE SEASON—'Carlos Queen,' 'Cortland,' 'Fall Red,' 'Fireside,' 'Haralson,' 'Hazen,' 'Keepsake,' 'Macoun,' 'McIntosh,' 'Prairie Spy,' and 'September Ruby.'

QUALITY GRADING SCALE: excellent, good, fair, poor.

'Adanac.' Perennial to Zone 2; good for eating; good for cooking; fair keeper; medium size; fruit color: red stripes over a green base; flesh bruises easily; good resistance to fire blight. Introduced by John Lloyd. It is a cross of 'Battleford' and 'Heyer #12.'

'Breakey.' Perennial to Zone 2-3; excellent for eating—one of the best; fair for cooking; fair to good keeper; medium to large size (apple-crab); fruit color: yellowish-green base with bright red stripes; soft sweet flesh with a greenish-yellow color; ripens mid- to late season; good resistance to Fire Blight; considered to be one of the best apples developed at Morden Research Station. It was developed from a seedling of 'Blushed Calville' and introduced in 1935, but now it is being replaced by a superior Morden variety called 'Fall Red.'

'Brookland.' Perennial to Zone 1; fair to good for eating and cooking; medium size (apple-crab); fruit color: greenish-yellow base with red stripes; crisp flesh; ripens early to mid-season. Some susceptibility to fire blight. This is a 1979 introduction from Brooks Horticultural Station in Brooks, Alberta. It was bred from a cross of 'Haralson' and 'Heyer #12.'

'Carlos Queen.' Perennial to Zone 1; good for eating (its taste is very similar to a Granny Smith apple); good for cooking; good keeper, large size; fruit color: red blush over a green base; ripens late season. Selected by Robert Erskine of Rocky Mountain House, Alberta.

'Carroll.' Perennial to Zone 3; good to excellent for eating and cooking; good for cider and apple-sauce; fair keeper; large size; fruit color: red markings on a green base; crisp and juicy flesh; ripens

early. Tree is a small to medium size. Introduced in 1961 by the Morden Research Station; it was the official fruit tree for Manitoba's Centennial in 1970. This variety came from a cross between 'Moscow Pear' and 'Melba.'

Apple Tree, Malus

'Chestnut.' Perennial to Zone 1-2; excellent for eating; good for cooking; good keeper; ripens mid- to late season; small-medium size (crabapple); fruit color: red blush over a green base; very disease-resistant. Named for its fruit's chestnut-like flavor. Introduced in 1946 by the University of Minnesota.

'Collet.' Perennial to Zone 3; good for eating; excellent for cooking; good keeper; ripens mid-season; medium to large size; fruit color: creamy-green with red stripes. Some susceptibility to fire blight. Introduced by Morden Research Station in 1948, it was discovered by Albert Collet of Notre Dame de Lourdes, Manitoba.

'Cortland.' Perennial to Zone 4-5 (protected areas only); excellent eating and cooking apple; good for cider base; good in salads; good keeper; large size; fruit color: dark red; its white flesh doesn't brown in the air which makes it an excellent apple for salads or cider; ripens late season. This variety is a cross of 'Ben Davis' and 'McIntosh.'

'Dakota.' Perennial to Zone 3; good apple for fresh use or cooking; fair to good keeper; medium size (apple-crab); fruit color: red and yellow skin; ripens mid-season.

'Discovery.' Perennial to Zone 4; excellent eating apple; excellent for cooking; poor keeper; medium size

(applecrab); fruit color: red; attractive tree but may not be hardy in exposed areas. Ripens early mid-season. Introduced from England.

'Dolgo.' Perennial to Zone 1; excellent for jelly (superb tart flavor and no need to add extra pectin); fair to good for eating; good cider; poor keeper; ripens early season; fruit color: small shiny red oblong fruit (crabapple); height 30 feet; attractively rounded upright tree; white flowers. Unfortunately, this variety is moderately susceptible to fire blight. Its name means 'long' in Russian and refers to the oblong shape of the fruit. This variety was obtained from Russia in 1897 and released by Dr. N. E. Hansen, Brookings Station, South Dakota, in 1917 under the name 'Dolgo.'

'Duchess of Oldenburg' (also called 'Duchess' and 'Oldenburg'). Perennial to Zone 3; good for eating, jelly and cooking; also a good cider apple; large size; fruit color: red, aromatic flesh; ripens early to mid-season. This variety makes a large spreading tree. Introduced from Russia in the 1830s.

'Exeter.' Perennial to Zone 2; used for its high quality juice; poor keeper; large size; fruit color: mostly red. Introduced by the University of Saskatchewan, Saskatoon, Saskatchewan, in 1959.

'Fall Red.' Perennial to Zone 2; excellent for eating (considered one of the best); fair to good for cooking; good keeper; ripens late season; fruit color: red blush over green base; flesh is very juicy; medium to large size. Selected by the University of Alberta in Edmonton, it is a cross of 'Duchess of Oldenburg' and 'Haralson.' It was introduced by Morden Research Station in 1986.

'Fameuse' (or Snow Apple). Perennial to Zone 3; fair to good eating apple (somewhat tart); good for cooking or cider; medium to large size; fruit color: beautiful dark red; its skin is rather tough; snow-white aromatic flesh; ripens late mid-season. This is an old apple variety discovered in Canada in 1739. It is a parent of 'McIntosh.'

'Fireside.' Perennial to Zone 4-5 (protected areas only); poor eating apple (very tart); excellent cooking apple; fair keeper; fruit color: green;

must have hot summers to ripen fruit; ripens very late season (pick fruit after several hard frosts). Introduced by Charles Haralson of the University of Minnesota Fruit Breeding Farm in 1943.

'Goodland.' Perennial to Zone 3 (requires sheltered location in exposed areas); an excellent eating apple; excellent for cooking; good for cider; good keeper; ripens mid- to late season; medium to large size; fruit color: red blush over a creamy-green base. Moderately susceptible to fire blight. This variety is a seedling of 'Patten Greening' selected by Morden Research Station, Manitoba, and introduced in 1955.

'Haralson.' Perennial to Zone 2; fair for eating; fair to good for cooking; good to excellent keeper; fruit color: nearly red over a greenish-yellow base; large size; ripens very late season; a very hardy eating apple. This tree tends to bear heavily. Fruit must be thinned for best size. Introduced in 1923. Named for Charles Haralson, Superintendent of the University of Minnesota Fruit Breeding Farm. It is a cross of 'Malinda' and 'Ben Davis.'

'Hazen.' Perennial to Zone 3; good for eating; fair for cooking; fair keeper; ripens late season; large size; fruit color: red skin. Tree is small to medium size. This Delicious-type apple was introduced from North Dakota. It is a cross of 'Duchess of Oldenburg' and 'Starking Delicious.'

'Heyer #12.' Perennial to Zone 1; a fair eating apple; excellent for cooking and applesauce; poor keeper; ripens very early, large size; fruit color: green to yellow skin. Best harvested before ripening and while still green. Named for Adolph Heyer of Neville, Saskatchewan. This variety was originally introduced to replace the fire-blight-afflicted 'Transparent' apple. Now 'Heyer #12' is being superseded by a superior variety 'Westland.'

'Keepsake.' Perennial to Zone 4 (protected areas only); good eating apple; good for cooking; excellent keeper; small to medium size fruit (crabapple); fruit color: red; crisp, hard-textured aromatic yellow flesh; ripens very late season. It is a cross of 'Malinda' and 'Northern Spy.'

'Kerr.' Perennial to Zone 1-2; good to excellent for eating or cooking (especially for canning); good for cider and jelly; excellent keeper; ripens mid- to late season; fruit color: dark purple-red; small to medium size (crabapple). Good resistance to fire blight. This variety has an especially attractive flower show in the spring and starts to fruit at a young age. The tree form is an attractive upright arching habit. Introduced by Morden Research Station, Manitoba, in 1952. Named for Les Kerr, who crossed 'Dolgo' and 'Haralson' to produce this variety in 1938.

'Lubst Queen.' Perennial to Zone 4 (protected areas); good eating and cooking (tart flavor); fair to good keeper; fruit color: very showy red and pink markings on a porcelain-white base; white flesh; large size; ripens early to mid-season. Introduced from Russia between 1879 and 1885.

'Macoun.' Perennial to Zone 4-5 (protected areas); an outstandingly excellent eating apple; fair for cooking; poor keeper; resembles 'McIntosh' but exceeds it in flavor and aroma; fruit color: red; sweet juicy white flesh; ripens late season; tends to be somewhat of an alternate bearer. Named for Mr. W. T. Macoun of Ottawa's Central Experimental Farm; introduced in 1923. This variety is a cross of 'Jersey Black' and 'McIntosh.'

'Mandan.' Perennial to Zone 3; good eating quality; fair to good for cooking; fair to good keeper; ripens mid-season; medium size; fruit color: red.

'McIntosh.' Perennial to Zone 4-5 (protected areas); excellent eating apple; fair for cooking; poor keeper; fruit color: red; juicy snow-white flesh; ripens late season. Moderately susceptible to fire blight, highly susceptible to apple scab, which is not a problem on the plains. This is a seedling of 'Fameuse,' the Snow Apple. It was discovered in Dundela, Ontario.

Apple Blossom, Malus

'Norda.' Perennial to Zone 1; good for eating; good for cooking; moderately good keeper; small-medium size; fruit color: red stripes on a yellowish-green base; ripens mid-season; upright small-sized tree; tends to bear heavily. This variety is considered one of the best extremely hardy ones. Introduced by the Beaverlodge Research Station in 1975, as a cross between 'Rosilda' and 'Rescue.'

'Oriole.' Perennial to Zone 3; fair to good for eating; excellent for cooking; poor keeper; large size; fruit color: yellow and red; ripens early season; vigorous upright tree; heavy producer. Moderately susceptible to fire blight. Introduced in 1949 by the University of Minnesota.

'Parkland.' Perennial to Zone 2-3; fair to good for eating; excellent for cooking; fair to good keeper; fruit color: greenish yellow with light red blush; medium size; resistant to fire blight; tends to bear heavily in alternate years. This variety is very similar to Norland and has replaced it because of its resistance to fire blight. Selected by the Lacombe Research Station, Lacombe, Alberta, in 1978. It is a cross of 'Red Melba' and 'Rescue.'

'Patterson.' Perennial to Zone 2; fair quality for eating; good to excellent for cooking; good for cider; good keeper; ripens early mid-season; fruit color: greenish-yellow base with sparse red striping. Resistant to fire blight. This variety tolerates wind, heat, cold, and drought better than most apple varieties. It is also a heavy bearer. Named in memory of Dr. C. F. Patterson of the University of Saskatchewan. Introduced in 1960. A similar variety is called 'Mclean.'

'Prairie Spy.' Perennial to Zone 3-4 (protected areas only); good to excellent eating apple; good keeper; large size; fruit color: red markings on a greenish-yellow base; ripens late season. Introduced in 1940 by the University of Minnesota.

'Red Astrachan.' Perennial to Zone 3; excellent for eating, cooking and cider; extremely poor keeper; medium to large size; fruit color: red and yellow skin, which adds a natural pink color to applesauce or jelly; white flesh; ripens the earliest of any apple variety; fruit ripens unevenly on the tree. It is best to pick this variety slightly green before fruit turns mealy on tree; medium-sized tree; somewhat alternate bearer. Introduced from Russia in 1935.

'Rescue.' Perennial to Zone 1; a good eating apple; good for cooking; good for cider; poor keeper; ripens early season; fruit color: nearly red over a yellow base; crisp white flesh; medium to small size (applecrab). This variety is a heavy bearer. Susceptible to apple scab, which is not a problem on the plains. Mildly susceptible to fire blight. It is a seedling of 'Blushed Calville,' introduced in 1936 by the Scott Experimental Farm of Scott, Saskatchewan. The name 'Rescue' refers to the fact that the original tree was destroyed by children raiding fruit, but John Lloyd rescued some budwood for grafting. From this budwood, the variety was discovered. This variety is being superseded by the newer variety 'Trailman.'

'Rosybrook.' Perennial to Zone 2; good to excellent for eating; good for cooking; excellent for canning; fair to good keeper; fruit color: mainly red; small to medium size (applecrab); ripens mid- to late season. This productive variety is a naturally small-sized tree which bears fruit at a young age. Introduced by Brooks Horticultural Station, in 1979. It is a cross of 'Trail' and 'Rescue.'

'September Ruby.' Perennial to Zone 2; good for eating; good for cooking; good keeper; ripens late season; medium size; fruit color: red blush on green skin; vigorously upright tree which requires some pruning. Introduced by Morden Research Station, Manitoba, in 1986. It is a cross between 'Haralson' and 'Rescue.'

'Shafer.' Perennial to Zone 2; good for eating; fair for cooking; excellent for canning; excellent for cider; fair keeper; ripens mid-season; fruit color: orange-yellow base blushed with red; small size (crabapple). Produced by Shafer's Nursery of Poplar Point, Manitoba, this variety is a cross between 'Rescue' and 'Trail.' Introduced by Morden Research Station, Manitoba, in 1963.

'Spartan.' Perennial to Zone 4-5 (protected areas only); an excellent eating apple; good keeper; fruit color: red skin; crisp flesh; medium size. Introduced by Summerland Station, BC, in 1936. This variety is a cross of 'McIntosh' and 'Newton Pippin.'

'Sunnybrook.' Perennial to Zone 1; good for eating (but only briefly); good for cooking (especially good for pies); fair keeper; ripens mid-season; large size; fruit color: yellow skin with bright red stripes. Tree has an upright form with a spreading head. A Brooks Horticultural Station introduction of 1979, it is a cross of 'Heyer 12' and a Morden selection 'M359.'

'Trailman.' Perennial to Zone 1; good for eating; excellent for cooking and canning; excellent keeper; ripens mid-season; small to medium size; fruit color: yellow-green skin with dull red blush; crisp golden-yellow flesh. Resistant to fire blight, this variety bears fruit at an early age. Introduced by John Wallace of the Beaverlodge Nursery, Beaverlodge, Alberta, in 1973. It is a cross of 'Osman' and 'Trail.' This variety is replacing the fire-blight-afflicted 'Rescue.' Children are particularly fond of this variety, and thus it is a good candidate for edible landscaping and municipal plantings.

'Westland.' Perennial to Zone 2-3; fair for eating (tart apple); good to excellent for cooking; good keeper; ripens early to mid-season; fruit color: yellow-green skin with red blush; medium to large size. Tree is particularly hardy and somewhat drought tolerant. A good replacement for 'Heyer #12' and 'Transparent' apple varieties. A Brooks Horticultural Station introduction of 1979. It is a cross of 'Heyer #12' and 'Dr. Bill.'

MALVA ALCEA 'FASTIGIATA,' Hollyhock Mallow. Perennial to Zone 4.
Height: 4 feet.
Bloom: profuse soft pink flowers 2

Hollyhock Mallow, Malva alcea 'fastigiata'

inches across, blooms from July to frost (long season).
Foliage: attractive mallow-like foliage.
Likes: sun.
Tolerates: half-sun/ semidry/ moist.
Propagation: sets or seeds.
Comments: upright bushy clump. This plant is attractive both in garden beds and as a cut flower. It resembles a small bushy hollyhock in both foliage and flowers. It is closely related to Hollyhock (*Alcea rosea*) and Tree Mallow (*Lavatera trimestris*).

MARRUBIUM VULGARE, Horehound, herb. Perennial to Zone 4.
Height: 1 foot.
Bloom: greenish flowers from late July to August.
Foliage: aromatic woolly gray-green foliage.
Culture: easy.
Likes: sun/half-sun/half-shade/dry/semidry/moist.
Tolerates: poor soil.
Propagation: sets or seeds.

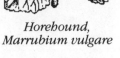

Horehound, Marrubium vulgare

Comments: fast-spreading clump; very invasive by root spreading and self-sown seed. Foliage is most aromatic when grown on dry poor soil. Native to southern Europe and Asia, and naturalized as a weed throughout North America. This herb is often used as a flavoring in cough syrups.

MARTYNIA PROBOSCIOLEA, Unicorn Plant. Annual.

Height: 2 feet tall.
Bloom: showy clusters of yellow, white, or purple flowers in June, mainly grown for its unusual seed pods which, when ripe, resemble birds.
Likes: sun.
Tolerates: half-sun/semidry/moist.
Propagation: sets or seeds.
Comments: immature seedpods can be pickled like cucumbers. Mature seedpods are dried and painted to resemble birds.

MATTEUCCIA STRUTHIOPTERIS, Ostrich Fern. Perennial to Zone 1.
Height: 3 feet.
Bloom: upright plume-like fronds.
Likes: half-shade/moist/humus-rich soil/bonemeal.
Tolerates: half-sun/shade/semidry/wet.
Propagation: sets.
Comments: this easy-to-care-for fern makes a great foundation planting, but place it where it will be easy to water. The hardiest variety of this fern is the one native to Saskatchewan and Manitoba. Crullers (also called fiddlenecks) can be boiled and eaten in the spring.

MATTHIOLA INCANA, Stock. Annual.
Height: 1 foot.
Bloom: very fragrant pink, white, lavender,

Stock, *Matthiola incana*

or purple flowers from May to late frost (very long season)
Likes: half-sun/humus-rich soil.
Tolerates: half-shade/moist.
Propagation: sets or seeds.
Comments: windstake with brush or hoop support in exposed areas; prefers cool summer areas. This plant is very frost tolerant. Hardened off sets can be planted outside 2 weeks before the frost-free date. Seeds can also be planted outside well before frost-free date. This fragrant flower is often used in gardens, in containers, and as a long-lasting cut flower. For longest-lasting cut flowers, crush stem ends. 'Trysomic Varieties' are less fragrant, but more heat tolerant.

M. LONGIPETALA, Night-scented Stock. Annual.
Height: 1 foot.
Bloom: dull purple flowers which are powerfully fragrant in the evening, blooms from May to frost (very long season).
Foliage: a weak spindly-looking plant (try to hide it among other flowers—like Baby's Breath, *Gypsophilia elegans*).
Likes: half-sun/humus-rich soil.
Tolerates: half-shade/moist.
Propagation: sets or seeds (stagger seed planting for longest season).
Comments: prefers but does not require cool summer areas. Once you try this flower, you will always want it scenting the air around your garden. Its powerful spicy scent resembles a combination of carnation and jasmine, but it is fragrant only at night.

MECONOPSIS BETONICIFOLIA, Himalayan Blue Poppy. Perennial to Zone 2.
Height: 2 feet.
Bloom: haunting azure-blue downfacing poppies on a tall flower stalk, blooms from June to July.
Foliage: basal rosette of hairy foliage.
Culture: difficult.
Likes: half-sun/moist/humus-rich soil/acidic pH.
Tolerates: half-shade/wet.
Propagation: sets (this is a short-lived perennial) or seeds (fresh seed germinates best).
Comments: prefers cool summer areas (requires protection from midday heat in hot summer areas); must be protected from wind; requires winter mulch. Because it is tap-rooted, young plants must be transplanted carefully and established plants cannot be transplanted. Obviously, this is not an easy plant to grow in the chinook zone. Cool summer areas with predictable snowcover will find this plant most adapted to their climate. However, this poppy is so unforgettable that once you see one, you will want one. *Meconopsis grandis* is a much more difficult plant with rich dark blue flowers. There are also yellow and orange flowering species.

MELICA SPECTABILIS, Purple Onion Grass, native to moist grassy areas of the plains and mountains. Perennial to Zone 2.
Height: 2 feet.
Bloom: showy purple and white grassheads from June to frost.
Culture: easy.
Likes: sun.
Tolerates: half-sun/semidry/moist.
Propagation: bulbs.
Comments: slow spreading clump. This attractive ornamental grass is showy in the garden. It is not invasive. The grassheads of this plant make excellent cut flowers and dried everlastings.

MELLISSA OFFICINALIS, Lemon Balm. Perennial to Zone 3.
Height: 2 feet.
Bloom: insignificant green flowers.
Foliage: rounded clump of aromatic green foliage.
Likes: sun/half-sun/semidry/moist.
Propagation: sets or seeds.
Comments: invasive by root spreading. The lemon-scented foliage of this herb can be used in salads and soups. It can be dried for use in potpourris and herb teas. This plant's crinkled foliage and unusual light green color make it almost an ornamental, too.

MENTHA SPECIES, Mint. In Greek mythology, the nymph Mentha was Pluto's mistress. However, his captive queen Persephone was not pleased and trampled Mentha to death. So Pluto changed Mentha's body into a plant which is fragrant when trod on.

M. AQUATICA, River Mint. Native near water throughout North America. Perennial to Zone 1.
Height: 1 foot.
Bloom: insignificant purple flowers from June to frost.
Foliage: aromatic.
Culture: easy.
Likes: wet.
Tolerates: half-sun/half-shade/shade/moist.
Propagation: sets.
Comments: fast-spreading clump, very

River Mint, *Mentha aquatica*

*Pennyroyal,
Mentha pulegium*

invasive by root spreading. Indians boiled this native mint with their traps to destroy any human scent.

M. PULEGIUM, Pennyroyal. Perennial to Zone 3.
Height: 1 foot.
Bloom: insignificant reddish-purple flowers in August.
Foliage: aromatic.
Culture: easy.
Likes: half-sun/half-shade/shade/moist.
Propagation: sets.
Comments: spreading clump, very invasive by root spreading. Once commonly used to rid houses of fleas and lice, this plant was brought to America by the Pilgrims.

M. SPICATA, Spearmint. Perennial to Zone 1.
Height: 1 foot.
Foliage: aromatic.
Culture: easy.
Likes: half-sun/half-shade/shade/moist.
Propagation: sets.
Comments: fast-spreading clump, very invasive. Plants vary in quality, choose one with the best clean, fruity scent. Spearmint makes a good herb tea combination with the following: strawberry leaves, raspberry leaves, clover, nettle, rose hips, watercress, or violet leaves. The variety called 'Ginger Mint' has gold variegated foliage and needs at least half-sun for best color. Fox Hill Farm lists 17 different varieties of mint including Blue Balsam Mint and Candy Mint. Mints are best grown in a pot buried in the ground and positioned to catch faucet drips.

M. SUAVEOLENS, Apple Mint. Perennial to Zone 2.
Height: 1 foot.
Foliage: an apple-green color.
Culture: easy.
Likes: half-sun/half-shade/shade/moist.

Comments: spreading clump, very invasive by root spreading sets. The variety called 'Pineapple Mint' (or *'variegata'*) has variegated white and green foliage with a pineapple scent.

M. X PIPERITA, Peppermint. Perennial to Zone 1.
Height: 1 foot.
Foliage: aromatic.
Culture: easy.
Likes: moist.
Tolerates: half-sun/half-shade/shade/wet.

Peppermint, Mentha x piperita

Propagation: sets.
Comments: fast-spreading clump, very invasive by root spreading. Plants vary in quality, choose ones with the best strong, clean scent. Peppermint herb tea makes a good combination with any of the following: strawberry leaves, raspberry leaves, clover, nettle, rose hips, watercress, or violet leaves. Peppermint is grown commercially on a large scale in western Oregon and Washington. The variety called *'Citrata'* or 'Orange Mint' has aromatic orange-scented foliage.

MENTZELIA DECAPETALA, Blazing Star, Evening Star. Native to eroded dry sandy areas of the Great Plains and foothills. Biennial to Zone 3.
Height: 3 feet.
Bloom: large fragrant creamy-white flowers resemble cactus flowers, dramatic golden stamens in center, open late afternoon and close by mid-morning the next day; blooms from late June to early August (long season).
Foliage: large flower size (2 to 3 inches across), velcro-textured foliage on a dramatic upright plant.
Likes: sun/semidry.

Tolerates: half-sun/dry.
Propagation: sets (transplants poorly—use peat pots) or seeds (sow in early August.)
Comments: the first year, a basal rosette of foliage emerges; the second year, a dramatic thistle-like stalk of flowers appears. The name *decapetala* refers to the flower's 'ten petals.' The petals open and close only when they are in active growth. These flowers attract large night-flying moths for pollination. There are other native species (*Mentzelia multiflora, M. nuda, M. oligosperma,* and *M. stricta*) which could be used for breeding an annual with other colors.

M. LAEVICAULIS, Small-stemmed Mentzelia. Native to rocky hillsides and road cuts in dry Great Plains areas; short-lived perennial to Zone 4.
Height: 2 feet.
Bloom: bright yellow nonfragrant flowers which open late afternoon and close mid-morning, blooms from July to frost (long season).
Likes: sun/semidry/heat.
Tolerates: half-sun/dry.
Propagation: sets (transplants poorly—use peat pots) or seeds (sow in August and winter-mulch after ground freezes).

M. LINDLEYI, Bartonia. Annual.
Height: 10 inches.
Bloom: showy clusters of fragrant yellow flowers which open late afternoon, blooms from July to frost (long season).
Likes: semidry/heat.
Tolerates: sun/dry.
Propagation: sets (transplants poorly-use peat pots).
Comments: rounded clump. This species is native to southern California and the Sierras.

MERTENSIA LONGIFLORA, Bluebells. Native to moist grassy hillsides of the foothills and Rocky Mountains. Perennial.
Height: 6 inches.
Bloom: stalk of showy nodding deep blue bell-shaped flowers, blooms from April to early June.
Foliage: small individual clumps of leathery-textured light green foliage.
Likes: half-sun/half-shade/semidry/moist/sandy soil.
Propagation: sets or seeds.
Comments: established plants have a deep root and resent transplant-

ing. This plant goes dormant and dies to the ground in mid-summer. Claude Barr mentioned selecting both a clear sapphire-blue variety as well as a white variety. A closely related species is *Mertensia paniculata,* which is native to moist forest and streambank areas of the Rocky Mountains and parklands. It has a coarsely upright habit (2 foot tall) and purplish-blue flowers from June to July (long season).

MICROBIOTA DECUSSATA, Siberian Carpet Cypress, Shade Juniper. Perennial to Zone 1-2.
Height: 1 foot.
Foliage: creeping juniper-like evergreen with a lacy arching habit, coppery-brown color in winter (some people dislike its dead-looking winter color).
Likes: half-shade/semidry/well-drained soil.
Tolerates: half-sun/shade/dry/moist.
Propagation: sets or seeds.
Comments: may need winter mulch in exposed areas. In Zone 2-3 of the chinook zone, this plant suffers much winter die-back without winter mulch. In areas with predictable snow cover, it is hardy to Zone 1-2. Originally this plant was found in the wild near Vladivostok, Siberia.

MIMULUS HYBRIDUS, Annual Monkeyflower. Annual.
Height: 6 inches.
Bloom: showy yellow tubular flowers with red or brown markings from May to frost.
Likes: half-sun/moist/humus-rich soil.
Tolerates: sun/half-shade.
Propagation: sets.
Comments: the name *Mimulus* comes from the word mimic, meaning a mime or clown. This refers to the flower's face-like markings. Varieties of note are 'Firedragon,' which has orange-red flowers with dark markings; 'Mandarin,' which has mandarin-orange colored flowers; and 'Wisley Red,' which has crimson flowers.

M. LEWISSII, Lewis' Monkeyflower. Native to the Rocky Mountains. Perennial to Zone 3.
Height: 6 inches.
Bloom: very showy rose-purple tubular flowers with yellow centers and markings, blooms from June to August.

Likes: half-sun/wet (a bog plant)/humus-rich soil.
Tolerates: sun/half-shade/moist.
Propagation: sets or seeds.
Comments: may need winter mulch in exposed areas. This plant is named for Capt. Meriwether Lewis of the Lewis and Clark Expedition. Indians ate the young foliage as a spring green.

MIRABILIS NYCTAGINEA, Heart-leafed Umbrellawort. Native to rocky areas of the Great Plains. Perennial.
Height: 3 feet.
Bloom: reddish-pink flowers.
Foliage: tall upright clump of heart-shaped leaves.
Likes: sun/half-sun/dry/semidry/moist.
Propagation: sets or seeds (tends to self-sow in favorable location).

MISCANTHUS SACCHARIFLORUS, Amur Silver Grass. Perennial to Zone 3.
Height: 7 feet.
Bloom: showy fan-like seed plumes on a long stalk, silvery-white seed plumes persist into the fall and winter.
Foliage: clump of foliage (3 feet tall) has an attractive coarse look.
Likes: moist/humus-rich soil.
Tolerates: sun/semidry/moist.
Propagation: sets or seeds.
Comments: fast-running clump habit. Very invasive by fast-spreading roots (plan ahead to plant it with water barriers or mowed strips; prefers to be at water's edge on a pond. The horticultural varieties of *Miscanthus sinensis,* a related Asian species, are also very showy and are clump forming but less hardy.

MOLINIA CAERULEA, Striped Moor Grass. Perennial to Zone 1.
Height: 1 foot.
Foliage: attractive yellow and green striped grass.
Likes: half-sun/humus-rich soil.
Tolerates: sun/semidry/moist.
Propagation: sets only.
Comments: clump habit. The variety *'Arundinacea'* is a showy 5 feet tall plant.

MONARDA DIDYMA, Monarda. Perennial to Zone 3.
Height: 2 feet.
Bloom: red, pink, white, or purple flowers from mid-June to mid-July (long season).
Foliage: aromatic.
Culture: easy.

Likes: half-sun/moist/humus-rich soil.
Tolerates: sun/half-shade/semidry/wet.
Propagation: sets or seeds.
Comments: spreading clump; mildew often makes this plant look terrible at the end of the summer. Besides being a beautiful low-maintenance garden plant, it also makes good cut flowers. Monarda flowers are also excellent for edible garnishes and in salads. Varieties of note are the following: 'Mahogany,' with brick red flowers; 'Marshall's Delight,' with deep pink flowers, light green foliage, and a high resistance to disease (this variety was developed at Morden Research Station and named for Dr. Henry Marshall); 'Melissa,' with light pink flowers; 'Prairie Night,' with rich deep purple flowers; 'Snow Queen,' with white flowers; and 'Violet Queen,' with rich purple flowers.

Lavender Monarda, *Monarda fistulosa*

M. FISTULOSA, Lavender Monarda, native to the central and northern plains and Rockies. Perennial to Zone 1.
Height: 2 feet.
Bloom: pale lavender flowers from mid-June to mid-July.
Foliage: aromatic.
Culture: easy.
Likes: half-sun/semidry.
Tolerates: sun/moist.
Propagation: sets or seeds.
Comments: for greatest attractiveness, shear stems to the ground in fall or winter. Invasive due to self-sown seeds and root spreading. This native wildflower is not as showy as *Monarda didyma,* but it is a good candidate for selective breeding of richer, brighter colors in the range from blue to dark purple. The genus was named for Nicholas Monardes, a 16th Century physician from Seville, Spain. The species name *fistulosa* means 'tubular,' referring to the flower form. These

edible flowers are very attractive in salads.

MONARDELLA ODORATISSIMA. Native to moist meadows in the Rocky Mountains. Perennial.
Height: 1 foot.
Bloom: light purple flower spikes.
Foliage: upright clump of aromatic foliage.
Likes: sun/half-sun/moist.
Propagation: sets or seeds (somewhat invasive by self-sown seeds).

MOSS. Perennial to Zone 2.
Height: 2 inches.
Foliage: fine textured carpet-like mound in varying shades of green.
Culture: easy.
Likes: half-sun/moist.
Tolerates: half-shade/shade/wet.
Comments: most species are evergreen in the winter and then go dormant in mid-summer if they dry out. Prefers to be protected from wind; can be trimmed for neatness with manicure scissors. Additionally you may wish to pick out fallen leaves and other debris occasionally. Never use chemical fertilizers near mosses—it can damage them.

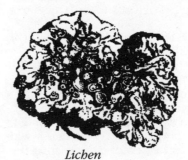
Moss

Propagate by a number of these methods:

1. Directly transplant wild plants from a site with similar light conditions. This is most successful if a small layer of soil is maintained under the clump and transplanting is done during the normal dormant period in late summer. You may wish to temporarily fasten new clumps with bobby pins to reduce damage from wind and birds.

2. The blending method: mix one part moss with one part buttermilk and crush it slightly (don't pulverize). Pour the mixture where you want it to grow and keep moist with a fine mist of water until established.

3. Encourage moss to start by itself. Moss spores are atmospheric and will start new plants wherever conditions suit them. Milk or egg white applied to a surface creates the necessary acidic pH, as well as a glue to catch the spores. Watering regularly with a fine mist will speed up the process. The advantage of this method is that it naturally establishes the moss most adapted to the conditions. Different moss species range from sun-tolerant to deep shade-tolerant and from drought-tolerant to water-tolerant. A moss suited to its conditions will be the most dependable. Some moss species are fast-growing and aggressive, while others are exceptionally refined in character and appearance. It is hoped that nurseries will sell choice mosses along with their rock garden plants. One easy-to-grow moss is the showy Pigeon Wheat Moss *(Polytricum)*. It was named for its attractive yellow-orange grain-size capsules held above the moss foliage. This moss is toler-

Lichen

ates hot, sunny areas and has creeping rhizomes which allow it to take some foot traffic.

LICHENS. Lichens are similar to mosses. The main difference is that lichens prefer more light than mosses. Some outstanding lichens developing in popularity are the brightly colored Reindeer Mosses of the Arctic Circle. As houseplants, mosses and lichens are best displayed on bare rocks or in terrariums. They demand little care except for occasional water misting and suitable light exposure. Mosses and lichens are most attractive in the garden when positioned on cracks in a rock, on Japanese lanterns, or on practically any vertical surface. However, no lichens or mosses tolerate foot traffic well.

MUSCARI, Grape Hyacinth; this flower is best displayed as a border edging for spring bulbs, or planted under early spring flowering bushes such as Forsythia or Winter Honeysuckle *(Lonicera standishii).*
Propagation: bury bulbs 3 inches deep.

Order of bloom: *M. armeniacum* (mid-April), *M. botryoides* (mid-April), *M. tubergenianum* (mid-April), *M. racemosum* (late April), *M. comosum 'Monstrosum'* (May to June).

M. ARMENIACUM, Common Grape Hyacinth. Perennial to Zone 3.
Height: 8 inches.
Bloom: fragrant blue-purple grape hyacinth flowers in mid-April.
Foliage: clump of grass-like foliage appears in late winter.
Culture: very easy.
Likes: sun/half-sun/half-shade/dry/semidry.
Propagation: bulbs (bury 2 inches deep).
Comments: this is the first *Muscari* species to bloom. An exceptional variety is 'Blue Spike,' whose large sterile flowers are extra long-blooming.

M. BOTRYOIDES, Common Grape Hyacinth. Perennial to Zone 3.
Height: 6 inches.
Bloom: fragrant blue or white flowers in mid-April.
Foliage: clump of grass-like foliage appears in mid-winter.
Culture: very easy.
Likes: half-sun.
Tolerates: sun/half-shade/dry/semidry.
Propagation: bulbs (bury 2 inches deep).
Comments: there is a showy white variety 'album,' which is also called 'Pearls of Spain.' This variety is particularly showy because it is dwarf.

M. COMOSUM 'MONSTROSUM,' Plumed Grape Hyacinth. Perennial to Zone 3-4.
Height: 8 inches.
Bloom: fragrant odd-looking blue feathery tufts in May to June.
Foliage: grass-like clump appears in late winter.
Culture: very easy.
Likes: half-sun.
Tolerates: sun/half-shade/dry/semidry.
Propagation: bulbs.
Comments: this is the last *Muscari* species to bloom. Though its flowers are attractive, they do not re-

Plum-scented Grape Hyacinth, Muscari racemosum

semble the other *Muscari* flowers.

M. RACEMOSUM, Plum-scented Grape Hyacinth. Perennial to Zone 4-5.
Height: 6 inches.
Bloom: plum-scented flowers which fade to brownish-yellow in late April.
Foliage: grass-like clump.
Culture: very easy.
Likes: semidry.
Tolerates: sun/half-sun/half-shade/dry.
Propagation: bulbs.

M. TUBERGENIANUM, Bitone Grape Hyacinth. Perennial to Zone 4.
Height: 6 inches.
Bloom: bicolor flowers are dark blue at the top and light blue at the bottom (its form resembles a tiny pineapple), blooms in mid-April.
Foliage: grass-like clump.
Culture: very easy.
Likes: half-sun/semidry.
Tolerates: sun/half-shade/dry.
Propagation: bulbs.

MUSHROOMS
Culture: the easiest method is to place edible mushroom caps in manure

Mushrooms

while it is composting and spread thickly on top of your garden. Puff-balls (*Lycoperdon*) and Meadow Mushrooms (*Agriculus*) work best for this purpose.

MUSINEON DIVARICATUM, Leafy Musineon. Native to dry exposed hillsides of the Great Plains. Perennial.
Height: 4 inches.
Bloom: yellow flower clusters from early April to end of May (one of the first natives to bloom).
Foliage: individual basal clump of smooth glossy foliage which emerges in March (winter interest).
Likes: sun/dry/semidry.
Propagation: seed germination tends to be difficult with or without pre-treatment.

Comments: the plant goes dormant and disappears in mid-summer; the taproot of this plant makes it difficult to transplant. This plant is similar to *Lomatium,* but differs by its shiny foliage. When it first greens up early in mid-winter, the foliage is relished by deer, elk, and antelope. A related species from the central Great Plains, *Musineon tenuifolius,* has a more attractive form.

MUSTARD, *Brassica juncea.* Cool-season annual vegetable.
Height: 2 feet.
Description: upright clump of foliage whose peppery taste sparks up salads or cooked greens.
Culture: easy.
Likes: half-sun/half-shade/semidry/moist.
Growing tips: produces the best flavor on well dug humus-rich soil.
Propagation: seeds (stagger seed planting every two weeks from mid-April to early August).
Comments: plants allowed to go to seed can create a weed problem. Mustard is moderately frost tolerant. Crop tends to mature in 30-40 days. Oriental varieties have the best flavor and mildness but require the coolest growing temperatures. The condiment mustard is made from the ground up seeds of a closely related plant (*Brassica nigra*).

Father Junipero Serra purposely marked his mission road from Mexico to northern California with a bag of mustard seeds. The seeds fell out of a tiny hole in the bag along the route and spread aggressively. When it bloomed in the spring, the mustard created a highly visible yellow road.

MYRRHIS ODORATA, Sweet Cicely. Annual.
Height: 2 feet.
Bloom: delicate small white flowers in late May to June.
Foliage: anise-scented finely-divided foliage that is semi-evergreen (winter interest).
Culture: easy.
Likes: half-shade/moist.
Tolerates: half-sun/shade/dry/semidry/wet.
Propagation: sets or seeds.
Comments: showy upright clump; invasive by self-sown seeds. This charming plant becomes endearing as it quickly spreads throughout the garden. Fortunately, extra plants are easily weeded.

NARCISSUS, Daffodil. Perennial to Zone 3.
Height: 1 foot.
Culture: easy.
Likes: sun/semidry/bonemeal.
Tolerates: half-sun/half-shade/dry.
Propagation: bulbs (bury in early fall so it can grow roots before the ground freezes). Bury bulbs 5 inches deep.
Comments: requires a couple years to bloom fully; in the Canadian prairie provinces, plant near the warmth of a house. For best vigor, remove spent flowers before seedhead forms. Narcissus make a showy combination with flowering fruit trees or the red spring foliage of peonies.

Daffodil, Narcissus

In Greek mythology, Narcissus was a man of such beauty that when he first saw his reflection in a pool of water, he became entranced and could not leave. The gods took pity on him and changed him into this nodding flower. All parts of this plant are extremely poisonous.

This group has been separated into the following flower types: Cyclamineus hybrids, Double Petal hybrids, Flatcup hybrids, Jonquilla hybrids, Poeticus hybrids, Triandrus hybrids, Trumpet hybrids. The common daffodil is listed under Trumpet hybrids.

CYCLAMINEUS HYBRIDS. Multiple clusters of small flowers on each stalk. 'Tete-a-tete' is a vigorous variety with clusters of golden yellow flowers.

DOUBLE PETAL HYBRIDS. Oddity-type Narcissus; odd-looking flowers in a globe-shaped cluster. 'Cheerfulness' has a rounded cluster of white flowers, heavily fragrant. 'Cheerfulness Primrose' is the same except the flowers are yellow. 'Tahiti' has large clusters of yellow flowers accented with gold and orange. It is heavily scented and blooms late in May.

FLATCUP HYBRIDS. Flowers with flaring flattened cups. They are crosses between the Poet's Narcissus and Trumpet Narcissus (these flowers resemble regular daffodils except for their small cup). 'Amor' resembles a Poet's Narcissus but has larger fragrant flowers and improved strong stems. 'Duke of Windsor' has exceptionally large white flowers with an orange cup and improved strong stems. 'Rushlight' has yellow flowers with a white cup edged with yellow. 'Salome' has off-white petals and a cup that changes from light to dark yellowish-pink.

JONQUILLA HYBRIDS. Jonquil.
Bloom: very fragrant small yellow flowers in late May to early June.
Foliage: stiff and grass-like.
Comments: its fragrance has been described as 'a scent so painfully sweet as to cause madness.' Pluto used this flower to lure Proserpine to Hades. 'Baby Moon' is a dwarf variety with profuse fragrant yellow flowers. 'Simplex' is the most fragrant variety. 'Suzy' has fragrant yellow flowers with an orange cup. 'Trevithian' has profuse fragrant yellow flowers.

POETICUS HYBRIDS. Poet's Daffodil.
Bloom: fragrant small white flowers with small orange-red cup from late May to early June.
Comments: the original species form is more fragrant than the commonly available variety *'Actea.'*

Poet's Daffodil, Narcissus poeticus

TRIANDRUS HYBRIDS. Late Narcissus.
Bloom: multiple nodding flowers on stalk with dramatic reflexed petals, all varieties are fragrant, blooms in late May long after other narcissus.
Comments: this group should be more commonly planted for their exceptional beauty and late bloom season. 'April Tears' has small delicate fragrant yellow flowers. 'Thalia' has fragrant, white, nodding flowers which are pointed in an artistic way. 'Liberty Bells' has fragrant yellow nodding flowers and closely

resembles the variety 'Thalia.'

TRUMPET HYBRIDS. Common Daffodils.
Bloom: white, pink, green or yellow flowers (many varieties are fragrant) from mid- to late April.
Foliage: appears midwinter.
Comments: Grant E. Mitsch, one of the foremost contemporary daffodil breeders, lists in his catalog those varieties that are the most fragrant. The showy white variety 'Mount Hood' is slightly fragrant. The variety 'Unsurpassable' is an improved form of the yellow 'King Alfred' with dramatically improved vigor. Other unusual varieties of interest are the 'Hibiscus-flowering' varieties which have no cup, and the 'Sunburst' varieties with their dramatic color blending. The miniature daffodils are especially cute and belong in every garden, particularly small gardens. There is an American Daffodil Society. Its address is listed in the Resource Directory.

NEMESIA STRUMOSA. Annual.
Height: 8 inches.
Bloom: flowers in every color except green, blooms from June to frost (long season).
Likes: sun/half-sun/half-shade/moist.
Propagation: sets or seeds.
Comments: rounded clump habit; pinch tips for increased bushiness. Requires mid-day shade in hot summer areas. This plant makes an excellent bulb cover, or it can be used in combination with blue lobelia. It can be used as a front edging in a garden, in containers, or as a cut flower.

NEMOPHILA MENZIESII, Baby Blue Eyes. Native to the southwestern U.S. Annual.
Height: 8 inches.
Bloom: profuse blue flowers with a white eye, blooms June to July.
Culture: easy.
Likes: half-sun/half-shade/semidry/moist.
Propagation: sets or seeds (easily sown in place in early spring).
Comments: clump habit; must have wind protection in exposed areas; self-sows in favorable location. Makes a good bulb cover. It can also be used as a front edging in a garden or in containers.

NEPETA CATARIA, Catnip. Perennial

to Zone 2.
Height: 2 feet.
Bloom: blue-green flower spikes from July to August.
Foliage: crinkly, gray-green.
Culture: easy.
Likes: half-sun.
Tolerates: sun/half-shade/dry/semidry/moist.
Propagation: sets or seeds.
Comments: fast-spreading clump; very invasive by root spreading. Cats love this plant and can rub it out of existence in the garden. 'Citriodora' has lemon-scented foliage; 'Dropmore'

Catnip, Nepeta cataria

has large blue-purple flowers; 'x faassenii' is an ornamental variety with an airy mass of mauve-colored flowers appearing for two months over a mound of grayish foliage; 'x mussii' has particularly narrow foliage. *Nepeta sibirica* is a closely related species with attractive blue flowers and gray-green foliage. *Nepeta transcaucausica* has an 8-inch-tall mat-like habit and blue flowers. In areas near water, *Nepeta* has potential for becoming a weed. Catnip makes a strong-tasting herb tea with a tranquilizing effect.

NETTLE, Urtica dioica. Perennial vegetable to Zone 1.
Height: 3 feet.
Description: upright clump of green foliage, insignificant green flowers.
Likes: sun/half-sun/half-shade/semidry/moist/manure.
Propagation: sets or seeds.
Comments: invasive by seeds and roots (this plant is best harvested from wild areas). This is a much maligned weed because of its painful sting. However, it makes an excellent compost ingredient and is shade tolerant.

It is high in nitrogen, calcium, and potassium. It can be used to make a pleasant herbal tea rich in vitamins and healing essences. The Indians used its fiber for twine, and Europeans made fine linen from it. Kim Williams in her book *Eating Wild Plants* mentioned a "rich sur-

Nature's *Garden*

LEFT: *White bog orchid*
HABENARIA DILATATA
KERRY T. NICKOU PHOTO

ABOVE: *Blue flag IRIS*
MISSOURIENSIS RICHARD FERRIES PHOTO

RIGHT: *Bunchberry CORNUS*
CANADENSIS JOHN D. FECTEAU PHOTO

BELOW: *Blue camas CAMASSIA*
QUAMASH RICHARD FERRIES PHOTO

FACING PAGE: *Harebells*
CAMPANULA ROTUNDIFOLIA on the
banks of Hyalite Reservoir in
the Gallatin Range
SALVATORE VASAPOLLI PHOTO

LEFT: *Skunk cabbage* LYSICHITUM AMERICANUM
CHUCK HANEY PHOTO

ABOVE: *Prairie sunflower* HELIANTHUS
PETIOLARIS RICHARD MOUSEL PHOTO

RIGHT: *Pearly everlasting* ANAPHALIS
MARGARITACEA D. DVORAK, JR. PHOTO

BELOW: *Sticky arnica* ARNICA DIVERSIFOLIA
CHERYL R. RICHTER PHOTO

FACING PAGE: *Oxeye daisies* CHRYSANTHEMUM
LEUCANTHEMUM *in Cut Bank Creek drainage
below Bad Marriage Mountain*
CHUCK HANEY PHOTO

Nature's *Garden*

Nature's *Garden*

ABOVE: *Lewis monkey-flowers* MIMULUS LEWISII
JOHN D. FECTEAU PHOTO

RIGHT: *Mountain lady's slipper* CYPRIPEDIUM
MONTANUM CONRAD ROWE PHOTO

BELOW: *Mountain douglasia* DOUGLASIA
MONTANA R.J. GLOVAN PHOTO

LEFT: *Glacier lily*
ERYTHRONIUM GRANDIFLORUM
RICHARD FERRIES PHOTO

FACING PAGE: *Wildflowers along Picnic Creek, below Mount Aeneas in Jewel Basin, Swan Range*
CHUCK HANEY PHOTO

The wheat's greening up, foals and calves are kicking up their heels and trying some new moves, river levels are peaking, and the meadowlarks and bluebirds are back and in full song.

Summertime in Montana—the sun shines sixteen hours a day, and you don't want to miss one minute.

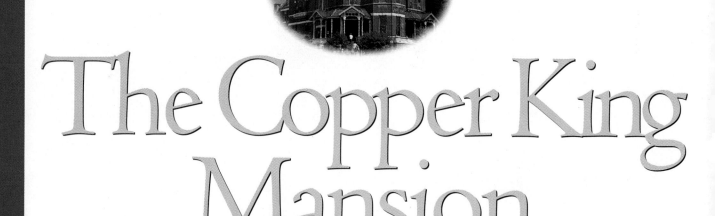

The Copper King Mansion

BY JEAN ARTHUR

THE MANSION STANDS AS MONTANA'S MOST DRAMATIC BED AND BREAKFAST. NAMED TO THE NATIONAL REGISTER OF HISTORIC Places in 1971, the structure has a tale that has intrigued visitors since the home opened for tours thirty years ago.

Riding the wave of mining riches in the 1880s, "Copper King" William Andrews Clark built a quarter-of-a-million-dollar home with the most expensive, exclusive, state-of-the art facilities and furnishings available. From 1888 until his death in 1925, Clark possessed this Butte mansion and owned a sweeping view of his town. Clark and other copper kings Marcus Daly and F. Augustus Heinze were dramatic and often ruthless figures in the war for power and wealth in Montana as the territory sought statehood.

After Clark died, leaving his vast fortunes and fabulous art collections to out-of-state recipients, the home changed hands several times until Anna Coté bought it—bare bones—in 1953. The only evidence of the original interior accouterments were two enormous picture frames in the basement. And lots of dust!

It took decades to refurbish the thirty-four rooms. Using more ingenuity and resourcefulness than income, Coté proceeded to clothe the brick and mortar skeleton. She bought some of Clark's original possessions, such as five elegant silk-screen prints, a cherry-topped table, and several unusual beer steins. Coté filled other spaces with era-appropriate antiques in an effort to recreate the style of living typical of the period between 1888 and 1930.

For Erin Sigl and John Thompson, Coté's grandchildren, growing up in a home with nine fireplaces, five frescoes, Tiffany chandeliers, and a ballroom was no more exciting than blowing blades of grass between thumbs. They moved into the run-down estate in 1957. "I was fourteen years old when we moved in with

SUMMER TRAVEL

vival stew made of young nettle shoots, ants, and a dozen minnows, heads and all." Such a mixture would sustain life for a long time in an emergency.

NICOTIANA ALATA, Flowering Tobacco. Annual.
Height: 2 feet.
Bloom: red, pink, white or lavender tubular flowers, flowers have a sweet jasmine-like fragrance but only at night, blooms from May to frost (very long season).
Culture: easy.
Likes: sun/humus-rich soil/heat.
Tolerates: half-sun/half-shade/moist.
Propagation: sets or seeds. (Seed germination: light, warm.)
Comments: this plant is showy in either a garden or a pot. Most of the vast number of powerfully fragrant Victorian varieties have been lost forever. This is a horrible tragedy that needs to be addressed. The commonly available varieties 'Lime Ice,' 'Nikki,' 'Sensation' and 'Tinkerbell' lack fragrance.

N. SYLVESTRIS. Annual.
Height: 3 feet.
Bloom: white string-like flowers on a tall upright stalk, powerfully fragrant but only at night, blooms from July to frost.
Foliage: attractive large bold leaves.
Culture: easy.
Likes: sun/humus-rich soil/heat.
Tolerates: half-sun/half-shade/moist.
Propagation: sets or seeds. (Seed germination: light, warm.)
Comments: this little-known plant is excellent either as an accent plant or for use in masses in large planters. Both the flowers and the foliage are dramatic.

NIGELLA DAMASCENA, Love-In-A-Mist. Annual.
Height: 3 feet.
Bloom: oddly attractive murky pink, murky white, or sky-blue flowers, blooms from July to frost. Oddly attractive seedpods.
Foliage: very finely-divided foliage.
Culture: easy.
Likes: sun/half-sun/semidry/moist.
Propagation: sets or seeds. (Seed germination: light.)
Comments: must have moisture in late summer to continue blooming in late summer; must be either windstaked or crowded for best appearance. 'Miss Jekyll' has flow-

ers with an improved sky-blue color. There are many other named varieties. This flower is more attractive as a cut flower or dried everlasting than in the flower bed. But if you want an unusual looking plant in your garden, this is it. Its black seeds have been used as a seasoning in eastern Mediterranean cooking since ancient times.

NUPHAR VARIEGATUM, Painted Yellow Pond Lily. Native to ponds and slow streams of the Great Plains, Rocky Mountains and boreal forest. Perennial.
Bloom: sparse green flowers with bright yellow edging and a red center from June to July.
Foliage: aquatic plant, profuse heart-shaped leaves float on the water's surface.
Propagation: roots or seeds.
Comments: the Indians ate the roots as food. The main difference between *Nuphar* and *Nymphaea* is that the sepals are the conspicuous flower in the former genus, and the petals are the conspicuous flower in the latter genus.

NYMPHAEA ODORATA, Fragrant Waterlily. Native to ponds and slow streams of the Great Plains, Rocky Mountains, and boreal forest. Perennial.
Bloom: fragrant white flowers with

Fragrant Waterlily,
Nymphaea odorata

pink edging, flowers open in the morning from June to July.
Foliage: aquatic plant, profuse heart-shaped leaves float on the water's surface.
Propagation: roots or seeds.

OCIMUM BASILICUM, Sweet Basil, culinary herb. Annual.
Height: 2 feet.

Bloom: insignificant green flower spikes.
Foliage: light green aromatic foliage.
Culture: easy.
Likes: half-sun/moist.
Tolerates: sun/semidry.
Propagation: sets or seeds.
Comments: prefers wind protection in windy areas; pinch tips for a more bushy rounded form. Lettuce Leaf Basil is a delicately flavored variety preferred for culinary use. Shepherd's Garden Seeds lists three gourmet Italian varieties. 'Dark Opal' is an ornamental variety with bronzy red-purple foliage. Other varieties are Anise Basil, Camphor Basil, Cinnamon Basil, Holy Basil, Lemon Basil, Thyme-leaved Basil, and Tree Basil. Basil is very tasty in tomato dishes, soups, eggs, and cottage cheese. Additionally, the red leaf 'Dark Opal' makes a showy red herb vinegar.

Basil can be easily grown indoors in a pot during the winter. It is native to Eurasia, and has been cultivated since ancient times. Possession of this plant was associated with witchcraft during the witch-burning eras in Europe and New England.

OENOTHERA CAESPITOSA, Tufted Evening Primrose, Gumbo-Lily, native to the dry sandy or rocky areas of the central and northern Great Plains. Perennial to Zone 2.
Height: 3 inches.
Bloom: white to pink flowers from mid-June to end of July, very fragrant in early evening (a wonderful thick sweet scent).
Foliage: basal rosette.
Culture: easy.
Likes: sun/dry/semidry/well-drained, nitrogen-poor soil.
Propagation: sets or seeds.
Comments: established plants resent transplanting. Be sure to locate this low plant near nose level to appreciate its fragrance. Claude Barr mentions a subspecies called *'montana'* with red flower tints, and gray leaf margins. A closely related species is *Oenothera albicaulis* which has pure white flowers. Any of these plants would be useful in a low aggression ground cover.

O. FRUTICOSA, Sundrops, Evening Primrose. Perennial to Zone 3.

*Sundrops,
Oenothera
fruticosa*

Height: 2 feet.
Bloom: upright stalks of bright yellow flowers from June to July.
Foliage: emerges late in the spring.
Culture: easy.
Likes: half-sun.
Tolerates: half-shade/dry/semidry.
Propagation: sets or seeds.

O. MISSOURIENSIS, Missouri Evening Primrose. Native to the central and northern Great Plains. Perennial to Zone 3.
Height: 4 inches.
Bloom: very showy large non-fragrant yellow flowers from July to frost.
Foliage: dull green.
Culture: easy.
Likes: sun/well-drained soil.
Tolerates: half-sun/dry/semidry/moist.
Propagation: sets or seeds.
Comments: floppy trailing plant. One of the three flowers nominated for the Montana state flower. The *'incana'* variety is the Western native. This dramatic-looking plant can occasionally be found growing in a city sidewalk crack. It could be used in a moderately aggressive ground cover mix.

ONION, Allium cepa. Perennial vegetable to Zone 2.
Height: 1 foot.
Description: thick upright foliage, occasional white flowers which should be removed, enlarged root used as a vegetable.
Culture: easy.
Likes: sun/half-sun/moist/humus-rich soil/evenly moist and well drained soil.
Propagation: sets (because it requires a very long season, sets are best for producing

*Onion, Allium
cepa*

large onions quickly; plant with tip of set above the ground) or seeds (seeds must be fresh for best germination). Because seeds tolerate cold soil well, you can plant them in the fall for a crop the following year. Plant seeds after the frosts start and do not water at planting. Seeds germinate slowly, so surface moisture in the spring is critical for seed germination.
Pests: root maggots. Thin to 2-3 inches apart for larger onions.
Growing tips: prefers frequent light waterings in early part of growing season, but do not water after mid-August to allow bulb to ripen and dry up. Loves regular fertilizing during the growing season with a low nitrogen fertilizer. Allowing flowers to set seed will reduce the bulb size. Shallow rooted (avoid soil compaction).
Harvest tips: can be harvested anytime as either green onions, or ripened until the leaves die to the ground in late summer and dried for storage. Harvest all onions for eating before hard frosts. Onions can survive the winter in the ground, but their cooking quality is poor after freezing.
Comments: store inside where it's cool and dry. Yellow onions tend to store the best. The mild flavored varieties 'Bermuda Red' and 'Sweet Spanish' require the longest season, and are best started as sets. The many other varieties differ in their concentrations of natural sugars and mustard oil, which gives them their hotness. Grown for so long in Europe and Asia that its origin is unknown.

ONONIS SPINOSA, Rest Harrow. Perennial to Zone 2.
Height: 2 feet.
Bloom: rounded clump with pink flowers in July, small spines.
Likes: sun/half-sun/dry/semidry.
Tolerates: poor soil/alkalinity.
Propagation: sets or seeds.
Comments: somewhat invasive due to self-sowing. This plant is an excellent choice for a low maintenance garden.

OPUNTIA FRAGILIS, Prickly Pear Cactus, the small pad species. Native to the central and northern grasslands all the way north to the boreal forest. Perennial to Zone 2.

Height: 6 inches.
Bloom: yellow flowers in June.
Foliage: spreading clump of narrowly rounded pads (these shrivel up and remain a greenish-brown color throughout the winter).
Likes: sun/very dry/well-drained nitrogen-poor soil.
Tolerates: semidry.
Propagation: sets.
Comments: the choicest variety is 'Claude Arno' which has extremely profuse pink flowers. The hybrid *'Rutila'* has very large pink flowers. The species name *fragilis* refers to this plant's ability to break off pads easily when stepped on. These pads are carried in the fur of animals and root when they hit the ground.

O. POLYACANTHA, Prickly Pear Cactus. Native to dry hillsides of the central and northern Great Plains. Perennial to Zone 3.
Height: 6 inches.
Bloom: yellow, orange, or pink flowers in June.
Foliage: low spreading clump of flat pads (these remain a greenish-brown color in winter).
Likes: sun/very dry/well-drained nitrogen-poor soil.
Tolerates: semidry.
Propagation: sets.
Comments: this plant produces tasty fruit for eating, however, you must carefully burn off the tiny spines or rub them off with a leather glove. The edible part is the layer of sweet flesh located between the skin and seeds. The cactus pads can be eaten if boiled until the skin slips off.

ORACH, German Spinach, Atriplex hortensis. Cool-season annual vegetable.
Height: 2 feet.
Description: clump of foliage, leaves are cooked like spinach, red seed clusters which resemble Curley Dock.
Likes: sun/half-sun/half-shade/semidry/moist.
Propagation: sets or seeds.
Growing tips: requires mid-day shade in hot summer areas; invasive by self-sown seeds.
Comments: this mild flavored green is cooked like spinach. It is an excellent candidate for winter cultivation in a cold frame.

ORIGANUM DICTAMNUS, Dittany of Crete, culinary herb. Annual.

Height: 10 inches.
Bloom: pinkish-purple flowerheads on stalks, blooms in July.
Foliage: woolly, gray-green, aromatic.
Culture: easy.
Likes: sun/semidry.
Tolerates: half-sun/moist.
Propagation: sets or seeds. (Seed germination: cool.)
Comments: attractive clump habit. This is a superlative cooking herb and a showy ornamental as well.

O. MAJORANA, Sweet Marjoram, culinary herb. Annual.
Height: 1 foot.
Foliage: clump of aromatic green foliage.
Culture: easy.
Likes: sun/moist.
Tolerates: half-sun/semidry.
Propagation: sets or seeds. (Seed germination: cool.)
Comments: besides being an annual in the garden, this herb can be potted up and brought inside for the winter.

O. VULGARE, Oregano, culinary herb. Perennial to Zone 3.
Height: 1 foot.
Bloom: either greenish-purple or white flowers depending on variety, blooms from late July to August.
Foliage: aromatic green.
Culture: easy.
Likes: sun/moist.
Tolerates: half-sun/semidry.
Propagation: sets or seeds. (Seed germination: cool.)
Comments: clump habit; must be protected with winter mulch for best survival in exposed areas; somewhat invasive by self-sown seeds. There is also a showy ornamental form with vivid yellow foliage. As a seasoning, use oregano in tomato dishes, lamb, beef, salads, and soups. The Greek variety, with its characteristic white flowers, has a more delicate flavor but is less hardy than the Italian variety.

The hardy Italian variety identified by its purple flowers, though less desirable as a culinary seasoning, makes an excellent winter flower display. Simply leave the dried flower stalks on the plant throughout the winter. These dried flower stalks make quite a display in the winter garden or, best of all, in a freeze-proofed old urn. The plants known as Mexican Oregano, Cuban Oregano and Puerto Rican Oregano can be used the same as this plant. However, they are not related.

OROSTACHYS SPINOSA, Spiny Hen and Chickens. Perennial to Zone 2.
Height: 1 inch.
Bloom: occasional creamy-white flower stalk in July.
Foliage: spreading clump of spiny rosettes that closely resembles Hen and Chickens.
Culture: easy.
Likes: sun.
Tolerates: half-sun/dry/semidry.
Propagation: sets or seeds.
Comments: see also *Sempervivum* (Hen and Chickens).

ORYZOPSIS HYMENOIDES, Indian Rice Grass. Native to desert dry sandy areas in the Great Plains. Perennial, short-lived.
Height: 2 feet.
Foliage: densely tufted habit, delicate airy seedheads from early June to end of July.
Likes: sun/dry/rocky or sandy soil with a minimum of competition.
Propagation: seeds (self-sows in a favorable location).
Comments: this showy plant tends to move about through its self-sowing. However, its requirements for dry sandy soil limits its appearances. In nature, many birds and animals consume its seeds. The Indians ground these seeds into flour.

OXYTROPIS, Pointvetch, Locoweed, official emblem of the Wyoming Native Plant Society. This genus is closely related to the genus *Astragalus,* Milkvetch. See *Astragalus* for additional taxonomic and cultural information on *Oxytropis.*
Comments: established plants resent transplanting. The Indians used the seeds of these plants in their sacred rattles.

O. BESSEYI. Native to dry hillsides in the Great Plains and Rocky Mountains. Perennial.
Height: 8 inches.
Bloom: reddish-purple flowers on short stalks, blooms from June to July.
Foliage: densely tufted upright clump of silver-gray woolly foliage.
Likes: sun/half-sun/dry/semidry.
Propagation: sets or seeds.
Comments: this plant closely resembles *Astragalus microcystis.*

O. LAGOPUS, Hare's Foot Pointvetch. Native to dry hillsides in the Great Plains and foothills. Perennial.
Height: 6 inches.
Bloom: medium to large size purplish-blue flowers on stalks, blooms in early May.
Foliage: multiple tuft-like crowns of densely woolly silvery-gray foliage.
Likes: sun/half-sun/dry/semidry.
Propagation: sets or seeds.
Comments: the common name refers to the rabbit's foot appearance of the basal foliage.

O. MULTICEPS. Native to the Rocky Mountains. Perennial.
Height: 3 inches.
Bloom: tiny pinkish-purple flowers on stalks.
Foliage: low-spreading clump habit, intensely woolly silver-gray foliage.
Likes: sun.
Tolerates: half-sun/dry/semidry.
Propagation: sets or seeds.
Comments: this plant is ideal for the rock garden.

O. SERICEA, Early Pointvetch. Native to grassy areas of the Great Plains and Rocky Mountains. Perennial.
Height: 10 inches.
Bloom: several whitish-yellow flower heads on stalks, blooms from early to end of June.
Foliage: upright clump habit from multiple crowns, silky fern-like gray-green foliage.
Likes: sun/half-sun/dry/semidry.
Propagation: sets or seeds.
Comments: the species name *sericea* means "silky" and refers to the foliage. There are also rare red, pink, and purple-flowering varieties.

O. SPLENDENS, Showy Pointvetch. Native to dry hillsides and open woods in the Great Plains and high mountains. Perennial.
Height: 10 inches.
Bloom: rich magenta-red flowers that fade to a purplish-blue color.
Foliage: upright clump of intensely woolly silver-gray foliage.
Likes: sun.
Tolerates: half-sun/dry/semidry.
Propagation: sets or seeds.
Comments: this is an ideal rock garden gem.

PAEONIA SPECIES, Peony. Perennial to Zone 1.
Height: 3 feet.
Bloom: red, pink, or white flowers (double and single forms, many are fragrant), blooms from mid-May to late June (long season with early, mid- and late varieties).
Culture: very easy.
Likes: half-sun/moist/bonemeal/wood ashes.
Tolerates: sun/dry/semidry.
Propagation: roots (bury in fall, but plant shallowly—2 inches deep measured from the top of the crown. Peonies will fail to bloom if planted more than 3 inches deep).
Comments: upright clump, hates fresh manure. Does not like being crowded by hungry tree roots or nearby grass and weeds. Once established, peonies resent being disturbed. New plants should be carefully winter mulched the first year after planting; requires windstaking with hoop support for best appearance. Carefully remove dead foliage in fall to reduce botrytis disease problems. In the spring, emerging new peony foliage is red and is very attractive planted near daffodils (narcissus). Ants help open flower buds by eating a sugar that the plant secretes to attract them.

Peony, Paeonia officinalis

For longest-lasting cut flowers, cut when petals just start to open. It is best to cut them early in the morning. Dried peony flowers are so dramatically beautiful that a commercial industry is being started in Alberta. Dried seed pods are attractive, though unusual-looking, in floral arrangements.

There are many kinds of peonies one can choose. The species forms themselves are also quite attractive: *Paeonia lactiflora* has moderately large leaves and fragrant pink flowers; *Paeonia mlokasewitschii* (what

a name!) has very showy gray-green foliage and yellow flowers; *Paeonia officinalis* has crimson flowers and attractive bold foliage that turns a vivid rust-red color in the fall; *Paeonia tenuifolia,* the Fernleaf Peony, has dramatic finely-divided foliage and a tendency to be slow to establish. It has varieties with red or pink flowers, either single or double form; and *Paeonia veitchii* has bright pink flowers and attractive bold foliage. Other common varieties of note are the spectacular 'bomb' type. In these flowers, the central clump of stamens and petals is exaggerated to resemble an exploding bomb. There is an American Peony Society. Its address is listed in the Resource Directory.

The following list is composed exclusively of fragrant varieties. 'early,' 'mid' and 'late' refers to bloom time. For longest bloom season, mix varieties with different bloom times in a clump planting.
'Ann Cousins'—white flowers, fragrant.
'Avalance'—mid, white flowers, fragrant.
'Baroness Schroeder'—mid to late, white flowers, fragrant.
'Blanche King'—late, deep pink flowers, fragrant.
'Chestine'—late, silvery pink flowers, fragrant.
'Diana Parks'—scarlet red flowers, fragrant.
'Doris Cooper'—late, light pink flowers, fragrant.
'Dorothy J'—late, pale salmon flowers, fragrant.
'Duchess de Nemours'—early, white flowers, soft scent.
'Edith Cavell'—early, yellow flowers, fragrant.
'Edith Scovell'—mid to late, deep pink flowers, fragrant.
'Edulus Superba'—very early, pink flowers, fragrant.
'Ella Christiansen'—mid to late, pink flowers, fragrant.
'Elsa Sass'—white flowers, fragrant.
'Festiva Maxima'—early, white flowers with red specks, fragrant.
'Florence Ellis'—pink flowers, fragrant.
'Florence Nichols'—mid to late, white to pink flowers, very fragrant.
'Golden Dawn'—mid, white flowers with a golden center, fragrant.

'Hansina Brand'—late, flesh pink flowers, fragrant.
'James Kelway'—early to mid, white flowers, heavy scent.
'Karl Rosenfield'—mid, bright crimson flowers, fragrant.
'Kelway's Glorious'—mid, white flowers with occasional red edging on the petals, rose scented.
'Kelway's Rosemary'—silvery-pink flowers, unusual spicy-herbal scent.
'Livingstone'—late, red-pink flowers, fragrant.
'Longfellow'—mid, bright crimson flowers, fragrant.
'Madame Calot'—early, white flowers with pink, heavy scent.
'Mandaleen'—mid, light pink flowers, very fragrant.
'Marie Crousse'—mid, showy shrimp-pink flowers, spicy scent.
'Martha Bullock'—mid to late, pink flowers, fragrant.
'Mary Brand'—early to mid, red flowers, fragrant.
'Marie Lemoine'—late, white flowers with crimson flecks, fragrant.
'Mattie Lafize'—mid to late, pink to white flowers, fragrant.
'Mme De Vernville'—early, white flowers, fragrant.
'Mme Jules Dessert'—mid to late, white flowers, fragrant.
'Mons Jules Elie'—very early, pink flowers, fragrant.
'Mrs A M Brand'—late, white flowers, fragrant.
'Mrs Franklin Roosevelt'—early, pink to white delicate-looking flowers, fragrant.
'Myrtle Gentry'—late, light pink flowers, very fragrant.
'Odile'—mid, light pink flowers fading to white, fragrant.
'Philippe Rivoire'—mid to late, crimson-black flowers, powerful rose scent.
'Richard Carvel'—early mid, vivid red flowers, double form, fragrant.
'Sarah Bernhardt'—early to mid, soft pink flowers, powerful scent.
'Tourangelle'—late, pink to white flowers, fragrant.
'Vivid Rose'—mid, dramatically pink flowers, fragrant.

P. SUFFRUTICOSA, Tree Peony. Perennial to Zone 4-5 (some varieties are hardier than others).
Height: 3-5 feet.
Bloom: exquisite red, pink, yellow,

or white silk-like flowers (6-8 inches across) from late May to early June.
Likes: half-sun/semidry.
Tolerates: sun/dry/moist.
Propagation: sets only. This flower has been bred for centuries in the Orient and often appears in scroll paintings. 'Roman Gold' is a fragrant Saunders hybrid bred from a cross of *Paeonia lutea* and *Paeonia suffruticosa*.

Tree peony, Paeonia suffruticosa

Comments: bushy clump with perennial stalks. Branches of less hardy varieties may need to be bent down and winter mulched; usually this plant is sold grafted, but it is more hardy and vigorous on its own roots. Prune out dead wood as soon as the buds open in the spring.

PAPAVER ALPINUM, Alpine Poppy. Perennial to Zone 1.
Height: 8 inches.
Bloom: fragrant delicate-looking orange, yellow or white flowers, blooms from May to July.
Foliage: finely-divided low basal clump.
Likes: half-sun/moist.
Tolerates: half-shade/semidry.
Propagation: sets or seeds (encourage it to self-sow in a favorable location).
Comments: requires rock garden soil; prefers cool summer areas or mid-day shade. This flower closely resembles *Papaver nudicale*, Icelandic Poppy, except that it is fragrant, less heat tolerant and requires rock garden soil. For cut flowers, cut in the bud stage and sear the cut end with a flame.

P. GLAUCUM, Tulip Poppy. Annual.
Height: 2 feet.
Bloom: scarlet tulip-like flowers from late May to late July (long season if spent flowers removed).
Foliage: showy blue-green foliage.
Culture: very easy.
Likes: sun.

Tolerates: half-sun/half-shade/semi-dry/moist.
Propagation: sets (self-sows in a favorable location).
Comments: may need windstaking with hoop support in extremely exposed areas. For cut flowers, cut in the bud stage and sear the cut end with a flame.

P. NUDICAULE, Icelandic Poppy. Perennial to Zone 1.
Height: 1 foot.
Bloom: red, pink, orange or yellow poppy flowers from April to June and September to November (long season if watered in the fall).
Foliage: attractive semi-evergreen.
Culture: easy.
Likes: half-sun/semidry.
Tolerates: dry/moist.
Propagation: sets or plant seeds very early (self-sows).
Comments: prefers cool summer areas or mid-day shade. This showy flower has naturalized all over Butte, Montana. For cut flowers, cut in the bud stage and immediately sear the cut end with a flame.

P. ORIENTALE, Oriental Poppy. Perennial to Zone 1.
Height: 2 feet.
Bloom: red, pink, orange, white or purple poppy flowers in June.
Foliage: leaves are fuzzy and finely-divided; new foliage appears in the fall and winter, then in mid-summer it goes dormant and dies to the ground (plan to hide this plant in the background).
Likes: half-sun.
Tolerates: sun/half-shade/semidry.
Propagation: sets (plant crowns 3 inches deep, crowns are best divided in late summer or fall when dormant) or seeds (can be seeded in either fall or spring).
Comments: bushy upright clump; windstake with hoop support for best appearance; winter mulch with evergreen branches to hold snowcover and protect new foliage; established plants resent being transplanted. For cut flowers, cut in bud stage and sear the cut end with a flame.
'Barr's White'—white flowers with purplish-black markings at the base.
'Black and White'—white flowers with black center markings.
'Curlilocks'—pink flowers with a fringed edge.

'Helen Elizabeth'—soft pink flowers on dwarf size plants.
'Mahogany'—mahogany-red flowers.
'Oriental'—profuse scarlet flowers with a black center.
'Pinnacle'—flowers are white in the center and shade to pink at the edges, petals have a ruffled edge.
'Spring Morn'—pink flowers with a darker pink center.

P. RHOEAS, Shirley or Corn Poppy, floral emblem for the remembrance of war dead. Annual.
Height: 2 feet.
Bloom: red or pink poppy flowers from June to frost (long season if seed planting is staggered).
Likes: half-sun.
Tolerates: sun/half-shade/semidry.
Propagation: sets or seeds.
Comments: this flower bloomed heavily in the war-torn fields of Flanders after World War I. Rev. Wilkes did selective breeding to create the

Shirley Poppy, Papaver rhoeas

spectacular variety that he named the 'Shirley Poppy' after the district of England he lived in. Now this variety is usually sold as 'Rev. Wilkes Variety.' For cut flowers, cut in the bud stage and sear the cut end with a flame.

PARADISEA LILIASTRUM, St. Bruno's Lily. Perennial to Zone 3.
Height: 3 feet.
Bloom: baby's-breath like clusters of white flowers, blooms from June to July (long season).
Foliage: grass-like.
Likes: sun/half-sun/semidry/moist/humus-rich soil.
Propagation: sets or seeds.
Comments: clump habit. Native to the Southern Alps of Europe.

PARONYCHIA SESSILIFLORA, Whitlowwort. Native to dry ridgetops in the Great Plains and Rocky Mountains. Perennial.
Height: 2 inches.

Bloom: inconspicuous stalkless yellow-green to rust-colored flowers in June.
Foliage: tufted cushion, olive-green mosslike foliage.
Likes: sun/half-sun/dry/semidry.
Propagation: sets or seeds.
Comments: when out of flower, this plant is easily confused with *Phlox hoodii.*

PARSNIP, Pastinaca sativa. Biennial vegetable usually grown as an annual.
Height: 1-2 feet.
Description: upright clump of foliage, long cream-colored taproot.
Culture: easy.
Likes: sun/half-sun/half-shade/semidry/moist/deeply dug, low nitrogen soil.
Propagation: seeds; use fresh seed for best germination and sow heavily. Because this seed tolerates cool soil, plant in the fall or early spring; seeds are very slow to germinate. If planted in the fall, plant after frosts begin, and do not water. Requires a long season, so sow

Parsnip, Pastinaca sativa

seeds only once; there is no reason to stagger sowing. For spring plantings, you can improve germination by soaking seeds overnight before planting, and using the gunny bag method mentioned in the Carrot section. Once seedlings show, thin to 3 inches apart.
Growing tips: tolerates slight shade and heavy frosts. This plant does not like manure.
Harvest tips: roots can be eaten at any time, but flavor is the sweetest after a hard frost.
Comments: roots can be winter stored in the garden if they are loosened and carefully winter-mulched before the ground freezes. Roots also store well in cool damp storage. High humidity is important for good storage. Once growth begins the second spring, the roots become too bitter to eat.

Native to northern Europe and cultivated before recorded history.

PARTHENOCISSUS QUINQUEFOLIA, Virginia Creeper Vine. Perennial to Zone 1.
Height: fast-growing vine to 30 feet.
Climbing habit: climbs with hold-fasts called aerial rootlets.
Foliage: red fall color.
Culture: very easy.
Likes: half-shade.
Tolerates: sun/half-sun/shade/very dry/semidry.
Propagation: sets.
Comments: vines grown in full sun will bear a decorative amount of black fruit. Birds love the tiny black fruit. The variety called *Engelmannii* has smaller leaves and a denser habit.

PEA, *Pisum sativum.* Cool-season annual vegetable.
Height: vine to 6 feet tall, white flowers ripen into peapods.
Likes: half-sun/light, sandy soil with humus, manure, and bonemeal.
Tolerates: sun/half-shade/moist.
Propagation: sets (buy sets for a

Pea, Pisum sativum

jump on the season) or seeds (germinate seeds inside or plant seeds outside only after frost-free date, stagger planting every 3 weeks from spring to early August).
Growing tips: prefers either east exposure or mid-day shade in hot summer areas; prefers frequent light waterings—it has heavy water requirements.

Peas are shallow rooted (avoid soil compaction around the base of the plant). Even though peas are a nitrogen-fixing legume, they still need extra nitrogen: a legume inoculant should be used the first year.

The inoculant stays in the soil year after year and does not need a re-application.

Plants produce best if allowed to climb a lattice or netting (these supports for climbing must be up before planting); this plant does not like to be crowded (give vines ample room).
Pests: rabbits and deer love to eat the vines, occasional powdery mildew.
Comments: though this plant tolerates light frosts, its seeds often get root rot if the soil is too cold for rapid germination. Therefore, it is useful to start an early planting either as sets inside or outside in a cold frame. However, seeds treated with fungicide can be planted in the ground in early to mid-April.

People who dislike cooked peas should discover the completely different sweet taste of raw peas fresh from the pod or the edible-pod peas. The edible pod peas are exceptionally sweet and tasty, especially when eaten raw in the garden. However, these varieties make a tall vine which requires staking.

Cook or eat peas immediately after picking before natural sugars are converted to starch by enzymes. Green peas and pea pods can be preserved by either freezing or canning. Vines that ripen their pods will quit producing new ones. Split peas for soup must ripen and dry on the vine. These dried peas can keep for years in dry storage.

Peas are native to Egypt where they have been grown as a dried staple since ancient times. The English bred the green peas as we know them. The variety 'Novella' has few leaves and lots of tendrils which makes picking easier, but it yields poorly. Shepherd's Garden Seeds lists two French varieties of Petit Pois: a spring type 'Precovil'; and a fall type 'Frizette.' These are described as candy sweet and tender.

PELARGONIUM, Geranium; nominated as the official floral emblem for the planet Earth. There is an International Geranium Society. Its address is listed in the Resource Directory.

P. X DOMESTICUM, Martha Washington Geranium. Annual.
Height: 1 foot.
Bloom: red, pink or white flowers (usually bicolored) from May to frost (very long season, particularly

if covered at night during early frosts).

Culture: easy.

Likes: half-sun/semidry/rich soil/humus/bonemeal.

Tolerates: half-shade/dry/moist.

Propagation: sets.

Comments: prefers regular fertilizing during the spring and summer but not with fresh manure. Does not like extreme full sun. A spectacular container plant combination is white picotee edged blackish-maroon Martha Washington Geraniums combined with blue *salvia farinacea* and white or blue lobelia.

P. X HORTORUM, Common Geranium. Annual.

Height: 1 foot.

Bloom: red, pink, or white flowers (many are bicolored), blooms from

*Common Geranium,
Pelargonium x hortorum*

May to frost (very long season into the fall if covered at night from early frosts).

Culture: easy.

Likes: half-sun/semidry/humus-rich soil/bonemeal.

Tolerates: half-shade/dry/moist.

Propagation: sets.

Comments: does not like full sun; prefers to dry out slightly between waterings; prefers regular fertilizing during the spring and summer but does not like manure. This is an excellent plant for a partially shady area.

P. PELTATUM, Ivy Geranium. Annual.

Height: 1 foot.

Bloom: red, pink, or white flowers from May to late frost (very long season, can be covered from early frosts).

Foliage: waxy, ivy-like.

Culture: easy.

Likes: semidry/humus-rich soil/bonemeal.

Tolerates: half-sun/half-shade/dry/moist.

Propagation: sets.

Comments: does not like full sun. This plant makes a dramatic edging in a container where its trailing habit can spill down the sides.

SCENTED GERANIUMS. Annual.

Height: 1 foot.

Bloom: most have insignificant flowers.

Foliage: aromatic.

Culture: easy.

Likes: half-sun/semidry/humus-rich soil.

Tolerates: half-shade/dry/moist.

Propagation: sets.

Comments: The following are a few varieties of note: apricot-scented, chocolate mint-scented, coconut-scented, lemon-scented, lime-scented, ginger-scented, mint-scented, nutmeg-scented, pine-scented, rose-scented, strawberry-scented. One of the most outstanding varieties is 'Fair Ellen.' It has dark green foliage accented by a maroon-purple midrib and a refreshingly dry scent. These plants also make good houseplants if given full sun indoors.

PENSTEMON SPECIES. A few general hints:

1. Most penstemons prefer pea-gravel or sandy soil with good drainage (exceptions are noted). Give them low-humus low-nitrogen soil and only enough water to survive; this results in longer-lived plants and the best flower color. In general, most penstemons are rather short-lived perennials.

2. In nature, these plants are nearly always found in the rocky areas. Try to include a couple of lichen-encrusted rocks for greatest attractiveness.

3. Mountain species require a light winter mulch (such as evergreen branches) in areas without snow cover. For these species, the better the basal rosette of new foliage is overwintered, the better the flower display.

4. Never mulch penstemons with organic mulches during the growing season; stone mulches, however, are very beneficial.

5. None of the penstemon species

tolerates grass or weed competition well. In nature these plants prefer uncrowded habitats.

6. Vigorous well-established penstemon species are usually not weakened from ripening seeds. You can leave seedheads on these plants to encourage self-sowing. However, seed ripening is an energy drain on less vigorous or well-adapted species.

7. Some penstemon seeds require cold treatment to germinate. In nature, winter does this. One penstemon enthusiast stated that the easiest way to seed penstemons was to put the ripened seedheads into the compost pile. This produces an abundance of penstemons sprinkled throughout the garden.

8. In gardens with lots of hybrid penstemons, seedlings will be surprises. Species penstemons, however, most always seed true to species.

9. Most penstemons make good cut flowers.

10. There is an American Penstemon Society. Its address is listed in the Resource Directory.

P. ALBERTINUS, Alberta Penstemon. Native to rocky slopes of the northern Rocky Mountains.

Height: 1 foot.

Bloom: very showy blue or pink flowers on stalks.

Foliage: low basal clump of smooth green foliage.

P. ALBIDUS, White Penstemon. Native to dry gravely slopes of the Great Plains—north to Canada and south to Texas.

Height: 1 foot.

Bloom: tubular white flowers that shade blue or pink at the edges; blooms in late May to early June; attractive hairy flower throat.

Foliage: hairy gray-green foliage.

Likes: sun/low-humus loam soil.

Comments: in areas near dirt roads, dust tends to stick to the flowers turning their color to a dingy white. Native stands of this plant are indicators of a soil rich in calcium.

P. ALPINUS. Native to the eastern edge of the central Rocky Mountains.

Height: 1 foot.

Bloom: showy large deep blue flowers at end of June.

Foliage: dark green foliage, com-

pact habit.
Propagation: seeds. (Seed germination: cold treatment and light.)
Comments: this plant's molten dark blue flower color makes it treasured by penstemon enthusiasts.

P. ANGUSTIFOLIUS, Narrowleaf Penstemon. Native to sandy areas of the central and northern Great Plains. Perennial to Zone 1.
Height: 1 foot.
Bloom: intensely beautiful sky-blue flowers (there are also varieties with lavender, pink or white flowers) at end of May.
Foliage: clump habit, narrow waxy blue-green semi-evergreen foliage.
Likes: sun/dry/gumbo or clay soil.
Tolerates: semidry.
Propagation: sets or seeds.
Comments: short-lived perennial (2-3 years). Water sparingly in clay soils. This species is considered to have one of the finest blue colors of all penstemons. But through destruction of its habitat by farming and grazing, it has become rare and should not be dug from the wild.

P. ARENICOLA. Native to sandy areas of the northern Great Plains.
Height: 1 foot.
Bloom: pink buds become sky-blue flowers.
Foliage: blue-gray foliage.

P. ARIDUS, Stiffleaf Penstemon. Native to the dry rocky slopes in the sagebrush grasslands of the Rocky Mountains.
Height: 5 inches.
Bloom: sparse deep blue flowers in June.
Foliage: attractive tidy cushion of short grass-like foliage.
Comments: Claude Barr wrote that this plant preferred a soil composed of equal parts of sand, gravel, humus and heavy clay loam.

P. ATTENUATUS. Native from mid-elevation ponderosa pine forest openings to timberline elevations in the northern Rocky Mountains.
Height: 2 feet.
Bloom: large blue, creamy-yellow, or pinkish-white flowers arranged in whorls around the stem.
Comments: this species is quite variable; some forms are garden-worthy, and others are not.

P. BARBATUS. Native to dry hillsides of the southern and central Rocky Mountains. Perennial to

Zone 4.
Height: 3 feet.
Bloom: scarlet red flowers from June to July.
Foliage: basal rosette of narrow foliage.
Likes: sun/dry.
Tolerates: semidry/moist.
Propagation: sets or seeds. (Seed germination: light.)
Comments: this species may require winter mulch. The red flowers of this plant attract hummingbirds.

P. CAESPITOSUS, Tufted Penstemon. Perennial.
Bloom: tiny blue flowers in June.
Foliage: showy moss-like clump.

P. CARYI. Native to open slopes and sagebrush grasslands in the Rocky Mountains and Great Basin. Perennial.
Bloom: rich blue flowers on stalks.
Foliage: upright, basal clump of grass-like foliage.

P. CONFERTUS, Yellow Penstemon. Native to hillsides, forest openings and meadows from eastern Oregon to central Montana and Alberta. Perennial to Zone 1.
Height: 1 foot.
Bloom: small pale yellow flowers in whorls around the stem, blooms from June to early August.
Foliage: semi-erect attractive basal clump of foliage.
Comments: there are several natural varieties with spectacular apricot and red-shaded flowers.

Yellow Penstemon, Penstemon confertus

P. CRANDALLII. Native to the foothills of the central Rocky Mountains.
Bloom: lavender-blue flowers borne singly without stalks.
Foliage: mat-forming habit that makes a good ground cover.
Tolerates: heavy clay soil.
Comments: Denver is using beds of this as a ground cover in some of its parks. The variety *atratus,* also called 'Claude Barr," is a particularly showy variety.

P. CUSICKII. Native to dry rocky sagebrush areas of the Columbia Plateau.

Height: 1 foot.
Bloom: showy intensely blue flowers from end of June to July.
Comments: this plant looks best grown in a mass planting.

P. CYANANTHUS, Wasatch Penstemon. Native to low-elevation dry sagebrush slopes and open forest areas of the central Rocky Mountains.
Height: 2 feet.
Bloom: intense bright blue flowers.
Foliage: compact upright clump.
Comments: requires windstaking for best appearance.

P. DIPHYLLUS, Late Penstemon. Native to rocky cliffs and roadcuts of the foothills and Rocky Mountains.
Height: 1 foot.
Bloom: flowers are dark gentian-blue with magenta throats and velvety texture, blooms from June to August.
Foliage: olive-green lobed foliage.
Comments: heavy taproot may interfere with transplanting. May need snow cover or light winter mulch. This was one of Butte rock gardener Clara Regan's favorite plants.

P. ERIANTHERUS, Crested Beardtongue, a widespread native from low to mid-elevation rocky hillsides of the northern and central Great Plains to the Columbia Plateau. Perennial to Zone 3.
Height: 1 foot.
Bloom: medium-large hairy lavender flowers with a fuzzy golden tongue (technically, a staminoid), blooms in mid-June.
Foliage: showy clump habit, hairy olive-green foliage.
Likes: sun/clay loam.
Tolerates: dry/semidry.
Propagation: sets or seeds.
Comments: in winter the plant is a semi-evergreen basal rosette. Will tolerate some clay in its soil. Claude Barr mentions a natural variety *saliens,* which has larger flowers.

P. FRUTICOSUS, Shrubby Penstemon. Native to rocky slopes in coniferous forests of the northern Rocky Mountains.
Height: 1 foot.
Bloom: profuse pink-purple flowers seem to nearly cover plant (also occasional blue and lavender flowering varieties).
Foliage: dense sprawling habit,

somewhat-shiny notched leaves.
Comments: prefers to grow in rocky crevices. Prefers snowcover or light winter mulch, although if unprotected, winter-burned foliage usually grows back quickly. Prune back after flowering or it gets leggy. Native varieties found at low elevations would be the most successful for plains gardeners. There is a showy pink variety called 'Charmer.' Another variety, *P. ssp serratus* 'Holly,' has attractive holly-like deep green foliage and lavender flowers.

P. GLABER, Smooth Penstemon. Native to rock upcroppings, river bluffs and roadcuts in the northern Great Plains. Perennial to Zone 4.
Height: 1 foot.
Bloom: showy blue flowers from June to mid-July.
Foliage: erect clump, glossy dark green foliage.
Likes: sun/semidry/well-drained soil.
Tolerates: half-sun/moist.
Propagation: sets or seeds.
Comments: moderately long-lived habit. Hot dry weather produces the most attractive clear blue flowers.

P. GRACILIS, Slender Penstemon. Native to moist sandy areas of the Great Plains and foothills. Perennial to Zone 1.
Height: 1½ feet.
Bloom: delicate, light blue-lavender flowers on a stalk, blooms in June.
Foliage: narrow foliage.
Likes: semidry/well-drained soil.
Tolerates: sun/half-sun/half-shade/dry.
Propagation: sets or seeds.
Comments: this penstemon is showiest used in prairie plantings in large numbers. The name *gracilis* means "slender" and refers to the foliage and overall form of this plant.

P. GRANDIFLORUS (P. bradburyi). Native to dry sandy areas of the central Great Plains. Perennial to Zone 4.
Height: 2 feet.
Bloom: very showy large lavender, white, pink, or red-purple flowers on tall flower stalks in June.
Foliage: gray-green foliage has a thick waxy appearance.
Likes: sun/semidry/well-drained sandy soil.
Tolerates: half-sun/dry.
Propagation: sets, cuttings or seeds. (Seed germination: cold treatment,

then start seed with abundant moisture.)
Comments: this is one of the easiest Penstemons to grow from seed. It has been hybridized into many attractive garden plants such as the Seeba Hybrids, Fate Hybrids, and Avalon Hybrids. However, the species form will be lost if grown in a garden with these fertile hybrids.

P. LARICIFOLIUS, Larchleaf Penstemon. Native to dry rocky Great Plains and foothills of eastern Washington and Oregon. Perennial.
Height: 6 inches.
Bloom: medium size pink-purple flowers on stalks.
Foliage: narrow almost needle-like foliage.
Comments: very delicate appearance.

P. NITIDUS, Waxleaf Penstemon. Native to dry steep hillsides of the Great Plains and foothills. Perennial to Zone 1.
Height: 1 foot.
Bloom: intense blue flowers from mid-May to early June.
Foliage: clump habit, semi-evergreen succulent gray-green foliage that leafs out very early and goes dormant in late summer.
Likes: sun/well-drained soil (in its natural habitat, it always occurs on slopes).
Tolerates: dry/semidry.
Propagation: sets (transplants relatively easily) or seeds.
Comments: this is one of the first penstemons to flower; moderately long-lived. This plant closely resembles *Penstemon angustifolius* which blooms later. Like *Penstemon angustifolius,* this plant also has one of the most prized blue colors in the entire genus of Penstemon. The name *nitidus* means "shining" and refers to the waxy leaves.

P. PENNELLIANUS. Native to mid-elevations in the Blue Mountains of eastern Oregon.
Height: 1½ feet.
Bloom: intense sky-blue flowers at end of June.

Penstemon

Foliage: a refined habit which does not require windstaking.
Comments: this species was named after Dr. Pennell, who first described it.

P. PINIFOLIUS. Native to medium to high elevations in the Rocky Mountains. Perennial to Zone 1.
Height: 4 inches.
Bloom: vivid scarlet flowers on tiny stalks, blooms from July to August.
Foliage: tuft-like clump.
Likes: half-sun/dry/semidry.
Comments: may need winter mulch in exposed areas. The name *pinifolius* means "pine-like foliage."

P. PROCERUS. Native to low- to mid-elevation meadows and open forests in the northern Rocky Mountains and adjacent areas of the Great Plains. Perennial to Zone 1.
Height: 1 foot.
Bloom: profuse small blue flowers in whorls around the stem, blooms from end of June to August (long season).
Foliage: spreading clump.
Likes: half-sun.
Tolerates: sun/semidry/moist.
Propagation: sets or seeds.
Comments: the roots of this plant are somewhat invasive. There are many natural sub-varieties of this species; selections should be made for dense flowerheads and compact growth habit. The name *procerus* means "tall."

P. SECUNDIFLORUS. Native to low- to mid-elevation open pine forests on the east side of the central Rocky Mountains.
Height: 2 feet.
Bloom: very large graceful pinkish-lavender flowers borne all on one side of the stalk.
Foliage: light gray-green waxy foliage.
Likes: half-sun/dry/semidry/rock garden soil.
Comments: will not tolerate even slight crowding by other plants. The color of this flower is described as luminous, particularly in early evening near sunset.

P. STRICTUS. Native to the Rocky Mountains. Perennial.
Bloom: blue-purple flowers from June to July (long season).
Foliage: upright clump.
Likes: sun/half-sun/semidry/moist.
Comments: may need winter mulch

in extremely exposed areas; weak stems may need windstaking.

P. VENUSTUS. Native to western Washington and Oregon. Perennial to Zone 2 (with winter protection).
Height: 1 foot.
Bloom: rosy-purple flowers from June to end of July.
Foliage: fast-growing clump, attractive light green foliage.
Likes: moist/humus-rich soil.
Tolerates: sun/half-sun/half-shade/semidry.
Propagation: sets or seeds.
Comments: self-sows in favorable location; requires winter mulch in areas without predictable snowcover.

P. VIRENS. Native to the central Rockies. Perennial to Zone 4.
Height: 8 inches.
Bloom: very showy intense blue flowers with purple throats in June.
Foliage: slow-spreading mat of attractive semi-evergreen dark green foliage.
Likes: half-sun.
Tolerates: sun/dry/semidry/moist.
Propagation: sets or seeds.
Comments: prefers some pine needles in its soil; roots where its branches touch the ground. This plant is best displayed in a mass planting.

P. VIRGATUS SSP. ASA-GRAYI (P. unilateralis). Native to low- to mid-elevation foothills on the east and west sides of the central Rocky Mountains. Perennial to Zone 4.
Height: 3 feet.
Bloom: flowers are usually blue, but there are occasionally pink, white, or purple variations; blooms from end of June to end of July (long season), and it has the characteristic of having all its flowers on same side of stalk (*unilateralis* means "one-sided").
Foliage: very showy upright plants.
Likes: sun/gravelly soil.
Tolerates: semidry/moist.
Propagation: sets or seeds. (Seed germination: light.)
Comments: prefers gravel in its soil (its natural habitat is on rocky hillsides and dry creek beds). Needs some water in August. At first glance, these showy flowers somewhat resemble delphinium hybrids. Unfortunately, this plant is short-lived.

Other species possibly useful for our area are the following: *Penstemon acuminatus, P. campanulatus, P. clutei* (pinkish flowers, bronzy foliage in winter), *P. davidsonii, P. digitalis, P. euglatapucus, P. gentianoides* (a Mexican species), *P. heterophyllus, P. hirsutus* (a nice dwarf form 'pygmaeus'), *P. kunthii* (red flowers, good ground cover), *P. neomexicanus, P. paysoniorum, P. rosinflorus* (red flowers), *P. rupicola.*

PENSTEMON HYBRIDS. Most penstemons prefer pea gravel or sandy soil with good drainage. Always give them full sun. Most are drought tolerant. These varieties tend to bloom from August to September. Besides being showy in the garden, they also produce good cut flowers.

Hybrids, these plants tend to be far easier to grow with a much longer bloom season than the species. What makes these hybrids so unusual is that for the longest time penstemon enthusiasts were completely unable to cross species to make hybrids. But then a very unusual plant was discovered—the 'Flathead Lake' Penstemon, named after its place of discovery. It had a unique characteristic; it was a natural hybrid between Penstemon barbatus and some unknown species of the Habroanthus Group and would receive pollen from any other species, resulting in the many hybrids of today. Oddly enough, this plant has spawned quite a mystery because Penstemon *barbatus* (a California species) which the Flathead Penstemon closely resembles, does not naturally occur anywhere near Flathead Lake, and no other specimen of this original plant has ever been found in Montana. From this plant, breeders have bred many new varieties. Notable for our area are the North Platte hybrids (from Nebraska), and the Saskatoon hybrids (from Saskatoon, Saskatchewan). Unfortunately, most of the varieties listed below were developed in England and are marginally hardy to Zone 4 without careful winter mulching.

'Evelyn'—old rose-pink on the outside and showy white with dark pink stripes on the inside of the throat, moderately compact habit which makes it useful in small gardens and containers.

'Garnet'—vivid tropical magenta-red flowers, profuse bloom, vigorous habit.

'Hidcote Pink'—white blending to pink on the outside, and the inside of the throat is white with pink stripes.

'Lady Alice Hindley'—dramatic light purple flowers—best described as both soothing and vibrant, tall growing habit which requires windstaking, very long bloom season.

'Midnight'—warm dark purple flowers with white stripes inside the throat.

'Prairie Fire'—bright scarlet flowers, 3 feet tall. A North Platte hybrid.

'Rose Elfe'—coral-pink flowers, a dwarf size plant useful for small gardens and containers. A Morden Research Station introduction.

'Royal Beauty'—large rich-purple flowers.

'Ruby King'—large ruby-red flowers on tall stalks.

'Sour Grape'—a strikingly beautiful lavender-blue color.

There are also Mexican Penstemon hybrids sold under the following names 'Burpee Giants,' 'Floradale Giants,' 'Rainbow' and 'Sensation.' In our area, these can be used as annuals, but they must be started early.

PEPPERS, *Capsicum annuum.* Warm-season annual fruit.
Height: 2 feet.
Description: showy upright plants which produce peppers as fruit.
Likes: sun/moist/well-drained, sandy soil with liberal additions of humus, manure, bonemeal and trace minerals.
Propagation: sets or seeds. Sets grown indoors require that their soil dries out slightly between waterings. Seeds must be fresh for best germination; start seeds inside 6-7 weeks before frost-free date.
Pests: tobacco leaf mosiac disease is spread on the hands and clothes of cigarette smokers as well as by insects; peppers, as well as eggplants and tomatoes, should be rotated to different parts of the garden each year.
Growing tips: requires maximum sun and warmth; for maximum heat retention in soil, use a clear plastic layer over a black plastic mulch; requires generous amounts of water, but prefers to dry out slightly be-

tween waterings; prefers to be fertilized regularly when flowering; for best growth, give it wind protection and moderate humidity; a lack of calcium in the soil or inconsistent watering produces the disease called blossum end rot.

Harvest tips: blossoms should be thinned at the end of summer to allow last fruit to ripen. Harvest peppers anytime once they are firm and shiny; all varieties turn red when fully ripe. Pick late peppers at the end of the season and ripen inside. Frosts will turn them black and mushy.

Comments: eaten raw or cooked, peppers are a good source of Vitamin C. Suggestions for cooking uses are stir-frys, meat stews, casseroles, and sauces. They can be preserved by freezing, canning, or pickling.

This plant is especially attractive as an ornamental and can be grown in the flower bed or in a pot. Bell peppers come in green (which turns red when ripe), yellow, or purple. The purple variety is attractive, but has a very bland flavor. Bell peppers are easier to grow in our area because they require lower temperatures to set fruit than other peppers. But they require moderate humidity to produce optimal skin quality. Chili peppers are easy to grow in hot summer areas. 'Anaheim' is one of the best for stuffing. Black and White Pepper *(Piper nigrum)* is an unrelated plant.

PERIDERIDIA GAIRDNERI, Yampa, Squawroot. Native to grassy meadows and open forest areas of the foothills and Rocky Mountains. Perennial.
Height: 2 feet.
Bloom: white flower clusters from July to August; flat-topped seedheads dry and persist until winter.
Foliage: sparse-looking upright plant that resembles Queen Anne's Lace, attractive finely-divided foliage.
Likes: semidry.
Tolerates: sun/half-sun/dry.
Propagation: seeds.
Comments: medium-size carrot-like taproot makes established plants difficult to transplant. This plant was a tremendously important foodstuff for the Indians of the Rocky Mountains. It closely resembles its cousin Queen Anne's Lace *(Daucus*

carota) from which the carrot was bred. This plant is somewhat difficult to distinguish from a number of native plants, the deadly poisonous Water Hemlock among them. The Indians beat the roots to remove the skin, then used the roots raw, boiled, or dried and pounded into flour. They contain a rich source of protein, vitamin A, vitamin C, and potassium.

PEROVSKIA ATRIPLICIFOLIA, Russian Sage. Perennial to Zone 3.
Height: 3 feet.
Bloom: airy clusters of light blue-lavender flowers, blooms from August to frost.
Foliage: aromatic, gray-green, with a finely-divided texture.
Likes: sun.
Tolerates: half-sun/very dry/semidry/moist/poor soil.
Propagation: sets or seeds.
Comments: dramatic upright clump. This late-blooming flower should be more commonly planted. Besides being an attractive low maintenance garden plant, it also produces good cut flowers. It is closely related to Garden Sage *(Salvia).* The variety 'Blue Spire' has deep blue flowers and is taller than the species. This would be a popular plant if it were better known.

PETALOSTEMON PURPUREUM, Purple Prairie Clover. Native to dry hillsides of the Great Plains and foothills. Perennial.
Height: 2 feet.
Bloom: pinkish-purple flowers with elongated dark centers, blooms from mid-June to early August.
Foliage: semi-erect upright habit, showy finely-divided foliage.
Likes: sun/half-sun/dry/semidry/moist/sand.
Tolerates: heavy clay.
Propagation: seeds.
Comments: transplants poorly, best seeded into place. Requires scarification for best germination. Two closely related species are *Petalostemon candida,* White Prairie Clover, which has less showy creamy-white flowers; and the rare native *Petalostemon villosum,* Hairy Prairie Clover, which has pinkish flowers and silky hairy foliage. These plants were used by the Indians as brooms, and their roots were chewed for their sweet taste. Wild-

life relishes the young shoots of these plants.

PETRORHAGIA SAXIFRAGA (Tunica saxifraga), Tunica Flower. Perennial to Zone 2.
Height: 6 inches.
Bloom: sparse pink or white flowers from July to frost (long season).
Foliage: rounded creeping clump, stems and foliage have an angel-hair texture.
Culture: easy.
Likes: sun/semidry.
Tolerates: half-sun/dry/semidry/moist.
Propagation: sets or seeds.
Comments: this plant does not need a winter mulch though it looks delicate; established plants resent transplanting; self-sows in a favorable location. The double flowered varieties are especially choice. Siskiyou Rare Plants lists 'Double White' (a double white variety), and 'Rosette' (a double pink variety). This plant's name is a curious misnomer because this plant isn't even in the Saxifrage family.

PETROSELINUM CRISPUM, Parsley, culinary herb. Biennial to Zone 3.
Height: 1 foot.
Bloom: attractive small greenish-yellow flowers in June.
Foliage: attractive, finely-divided (the second year's new growth emerges very early in the spring).
Culture: easy.
Likes: half-sun.
Tolerates: half-shade/semidry.
Propagation: sets (transplant carefully because of its taproot) or seeds. (Seed germination: scrape seeds with a knife or crack them with a rolling pin slightly, then cover with boiling water but do not boil. Soak overnight while the water cools, and then plant. Thus prepared, seed germinates faster. Seeds must be covered from light to germinate. Because seed tolerates cool soil, it can be planted three weeks before frost-free date.)
Comments: self-sows in favorable location; requires light winter mulch in exposed areas. If all you want are the greens, treat this plant as an annual. (The second year, it displays its showy green flowers, sets seeds, and dies.) As a salad green, this plant is an excellent source of vitamins A, C, and E, and iron. It is also tasty in soups and stews. Addition-

ally, chewing on a sprig acts as a breath freshener.

There are three main varieties of culinary parsley, each with a unique flavor: Curly Leaf, Italian, and Japanese Mitsuba. Another variety is grown for its edible root. As an ornamental, this plant is very attractive in a flower bed for its first year's green foliage and second year's 2 feet tall flower stalks. If you let this showy flower set seeds, you will have new parsley plants appearing throughout your garden. Parsley flowers attract tiny predatory wasps and lacewings; both beneficial insects. It can be easily grown indoors in a pot during the winter. It is native to Mediterranean areas. In ancient Greece, this plant was used to make wreaths for athletic awards.

PETUNIA HYBRIDA, Petunia. Annual.
Height: 10 inches.
Bloom: red, pink, yellow, white, blue, purple, or near-black flowers (double and single forms), blooms from May to frost (very long season).
Culture: very easy.
Likes: sun/heat/semidry.
Tolerates: half-shade/dry/moist/alkaline and clay soil.
Propagation: sets or seeds. (Seed germination: light.)
Comments: loves extreme full sun and heat. Plants must be pinched or they will get leggy (do this by carefully removing the tiniest green bud tip while leaving the last flower bud—it's easier than it sounds to distinguish between the leafy tip and last flower bud). *'Petun'* in Portuguese means 'tobacco,' to which both petunias and nicotianas are closely related. Nicotianas and petunias are an attractive combination requiring the same conditions. They make an especially appealing combination in a pot or container. For added interest use an accent plant, such as the white Marguerite Daisy (*Chrysanthemum frutescens*).

PHACELIA CAMPANULARIA, California Bluebells. Annual.
Height: 1 foot.
Bloom: extremely beautiful gentian-blue flowers with a one-month bloom season (longer season if seed planting is staggered).
Likes: sun/semidry/hot, sunny location/sandy soil.
Tolerates: half-sun/dry/moist/nitrogen poor soil.
Propagation: sets or seeds (stagger seed planting for longest bloom season).
Comments: this plant makes a choice display in a rock garden; use it for filling in empty spots.

P. LINERARIS, Linear-leaf Phacelia. Native to sandy hillsides and bottomlands in the Great Plains and Rocky Mountains. Annual.
Height: 1 foot.

Bloom: blue-purple flower-heads on stalks, blooms from May to June (long season).
Foliage: upright clump habit, leaves are both undivided as well as divided into linear-like sections—thus the name.

Linear-leaf Phacelia, Phacelia lineraris

Likes: semidry/sandy soil.
Tolerates: sun/half-sun/dry.
Propagation: seeds (encourage it to self-sow).
Comments: varieties should be selected for improved flower color—either true blue or true purple.

P. SERICEA, Silky Phacelia. Native from mid-elevation to high alpine slopes; usually found in disturbed areas such as roadcuts, screes, and rock walls. Perennial.
Height: 10 inches.
Bloom: dramatic woolly blue-purple flower spikes, blooms from July to mid-August (long season).
Foliage: upright clump habit, silky-woolly silvery-green fernlike foliage, strong woody stems.
Likes: half-sun/semidry/rock garden drainage.
Propagation: sets or seeds.
Comments: established plants resent transplanting; probably benefits from slight mid-day shade in low elevation areas. Search for selected natural varieties with the best pur-

ple or white flower color. The species name *sericea* means "silky." A closely related species is *Phacelia lyallii,* a true alpine with dark blue-purple flowers.

PHALARIS ARUNDINACEA 'PICTA,' Ribbon Grass—not recommended. It is an attractive but dangerous weed that spreads by both seed and roots. It should be avoided. The non-ornamental species form was planted throughout North America by the USDA's Soil Conservation Service to stop erosion. Unfortunately, it did too well and now chokes all waterway edges destroying habitat for native plants.

PHELLODENDRON AMURENSE, Amur Cork Tree. Perennial to Zone 2.
Height: 20 feet.
Shape: V-shaped tree with low branches, thick cork-like bark.
Foliage: yellow fall color.
Likes: sun.
Tolerates: semidry/moist.
Propagation: sets or seeds.
Comments: this tree is included because it is excellent for climbing and for treehouses.

PHILADELPHUS 'GALAHAD,' Mock Orange. Perennial to Zone 3.
Height: 4 feet.
Shape: bush.
Bloom: fragrant single white flowers from early to mid-June.
Culture: easy.
Likes: half-sun.
Tolerates: half-shade/semidry/moist.
Propagation: sets (softwood cuttings or hardwood cuttings in summer or winter.)
Comments:

Mock Orange, Philadelphus

For cut flowers, mash stems and remove leaves to prolong flowers. The chinook zone climate is particularly difficult for Mock Orange varieties. 'Galahad' is the most hardy for the chinook zone. Other reasonably hardy varieties for protected areas are 'Audrey,' 'Bouquet Blanc,' 'Belle Etoile,'

'Buckley's Quill,' 'Marjorie,' 'Minnesota Snowflake,' 'Patricia,' 'Purity,' 'Snowbelle,' 'Sylvia,' 'Thelma,' and 'Virginal.' Prune out oldest wood after bloom every year, remove weak twiggy stems and encourage new growth.

P. LEWISII, Mock Orange Bush; Official State Flower of Idaho. Native from California to British Columbia and east to the Continental Divide. Perennial to Zone 3.
Height: 5 feet.
Bloom: very fragrant white flowers in June; some people dislike this flower's unusual dry scent.
Culture: easy.
Likes: half-sun.
Tolerates: half-shade/dry/semidry.
Propagation: sets or seeds.
Comments: this plant is almost as showy as the hybrid varieties but is far more hardy. It is an extremely low-maintenance shrub. 'Waterton' is the hardiest variety, but it has a poor scent also. It was collected in the Waterton Parks area of southern Alberta by Augustus Griffin in 1935. The species name *lewisii* honors Capt. Lewis of the Lewis and Clark Expedition who encountered it in full bloom all along the Missouri River in Wolf Creek Canyon between Great Falls and Helena.

PHLOX DRUMMONDII. Annual.
Height: 2 feet.
Bloom: red, pink, white, lavender, or purple rounded flower clusters, blooms from late June to frost (long season if spent flowers are removed).
Likes: half-sun/humus-rich soil.
Tolerates: half-shade/moist.
Propagation: sets or seeds (best displayed in a mass planting).
Comments: windstake with brush support in exposed areas. Useful as a garden plant, a container plant, or for cut flowers. The variety called 'Twinkle' has star-like multicolored flowers.

P. HOODII, Native Rock Phlox. Native to exposed grassy ridgetops in the Great Plains and foothills. Perennial to Zone 2.
Height: 3 inches.
Bloom: white (occasionally lavender or pink) flowers, blooms in mid-April in sunny areas, and in mid-May in partially shaded areas.
Foliage: dense cushion spreading into a mat, semi-evergreen gray-green foliage.
Likes: semidry/rock garden soil.
Tolerates: half-sun/dry.
Propagation: sets or seeds. (Cuttings or offset division in fall or early spring, but it must have both full sun and protection from drying out during its vulnerable stage.)
Comments: established plants resent transplanting. When this plant blooms, it creates dramatic drifts of color. It can be mixed into a lawn for spectacular results. *Phlox kelseyi var. missouliensis* (Missoula Phlox) is a rare native species with profuse lavender flowers. There are quite a number of other native species. Unfortunately, native phloxes are relished by sheep and are threatened by livestock grazing in national forests. The genus Phlox has noticeable yellow stamens in the flower centers and can be distinguished from the similar-looking *Douglasia montana,* which lacks yellow stamens.

P. MACULATA (P. carolina or P. suffruticosa). Perennial to Zone 3.
Height: 3 feet.
Bloom: fragrant red, pink, white, blue or purple flower clusters with a rounded tip, blooms from late June to frost (long season if spent flowers removed). This plant is closely similar to *Phlox paniculata* except that this species has rounded flower spikes without a point at the tip.
Likes: half-sun/humus-rich soil.
Tolerates: half-shade/moist.
Propagation: sets or seeds.
Comments: windstake with brush support in exposed areas; may need winter mulch. Used as both a garden plant, container plant and a cut flower. 'Miss Lingard' is a common fragrant white variety. It was developed in England near the turn of the century by a Mr. Lingard.

P. PANICULATA HYBRIDS. Perennial to Zone 3.
Height: 3 feet.
Bloom: red, pink, white, blue, or purple pyramidal-shaped flower spikes from July to frost (long season if spent flowers removed).
Likes: half-sun/humus-rich soil.
Tolerates: half-shade/moist.
Propagation: sets or seeds.
Comments: windstake with brush support in exposed areas; may need winter mulch. Used as both a garden plant, container plant or cut flower. Watch for spider mite infestations that weaken plants. Spider mite problems are common near dusty roads and can be easily controlled by washing dust off plants when watering. Mildew is not normally a problem in dry plains areas, unless plants are watered at night. The species form has attractive magenta-pink flowers and is especially easy to grow.

P. SUBULATA, Moss Pink. Perennial to Zone 1.
Height: 4 inches.
Bloom: red, pink, white, or purple flowers from early to mid-May (long season).
Foliage: semi-evergreen.
Culture: easy.
Likes: half-sun/semi-dry.
Tolerates: sun/half-shade/dry.
Propagation: sets or seeds.
Comments:

Moss Pink, Phlox subulata

creeping mat habit; shear back after flowering for best appearance. The variety 'Vivid' has a rich clear pink color. Siskiyou Rare Plants Nursery lists two exceptional varieties: 'Brittonii Rosea' has tightly dense foliage and pink flowers; and 'Sneewichen' has miniature size foliage and white flowers.

PHRAGMITES COMMUNIS, Common Reed Grass, Cane Grass, native circumpolar. Perennial to Zone 1.
Height: 10 feet.
Bloom: showy pampas grass-like seedheads that stay on plant through the winter.
Likes: wet.
Tolerates: sun/half-sun/moist.
Propagation: sets or seeds.
Comments: fast-spreading coarse clump; roots are extremely invasive (similar to Running Bamboo). The flowerheads are very showy used either fresh or dried in arrangements. The name *phragmites* means 'fence-like' and refers to this plant's spreading nature. The name *communis* means 'common.' This plant is native throughout the Northern

Temperate Zone worldwide and is always seen growing at water's edge.

PHYSARIA DIDYMOCARPA, Common Twinpod. Native to rocky soil in cliffs in the foothills and Rocky Mountains. Perennial.
Height: 4 inches.
Bloom: showy yellow flowers from April to May; small creamy-white inflated seed pods in late summer and fall.
Foliage: prostrate, tufted, showy, basal clump of gray-green foliage.
Likes: sun/half-sun/dry/semidry.
Propagation: sets or seeds.
Comments: established plants resent transplanting.

P. GEYERI. Native to clay soil in cliffs of the Great Plains and foothills. Perennial.
Height: 3 inches.
Bloom: yellow flowers from April to May; bladder-like inflated seed pods in late summer and fall.
Foliage: prostrate clump habit, showy gray-green foliage.
Likes: sun/half-sun/dry/semidry.
Propagation: sets or seeds.

PHYSOCARPUS OPULIFOLIUS, 'Dart's Golden Ninebark,' native to the Rocky Mountains from New Mexico to Alberta. Perennial to Zone 1.
Height: 4 feet.
Shape: compact irregularly-shaped shrub.
Bloom: spiraea-like flowers.
Foliage: spectacular bright gold foliage from late April to May, but by mid-summer foliage becomes an attractive light green color, bark peels attractively to expose many colors from gray to brown (and thus the name ninebark).
Culture: easy.
Likes: semidry.
Tolerates: sun/half-sun/dry/moist.
Propagation: sets.
Comments: though better suited as a shrub, this plant can be pruned into a good hedge. The variety *'Lutea'* is much less attractive than the variety 'Dart's Golden.' This plant is best suited for informal areas. Some people consider the dead wood inside this plant to be offensive for formal usage. This is a low-maintenance shrub.

PHYSOSTEGIA VIRGINIANA, Obedience Plant. Perennial to Zone 4.
Height: 4 feet.
Bloom: pink, white or purple flower spikes from July to September (long season with early to late varieties).
Culture: easy.
Likes: half-sun/moist (a bog plant).
Tolerates: sun/half-shade/semidry/wet.
Propagation: sets or seeds.
Comments: upright clump; potentially invasive in areas near water. The variety 'Summer Snow' has white flowers from late July to September. *'Variegata'* has white variegated foliage, but its weak stems require careful windstaking. 'Vivid' has deep pink flowers from August to September and is the last variety to flower (fall interest). Its common name Obedience Plant refers to the way individual flowers will stay positioned when moved. Native to the eastern forests of North America.

PICEA ABIES, Norway Spruce. Perennial to Zone 1.
Foliage: green-foliaged evergreen.
Likes: sun/half-sun/semidry.
Tolerates: alkaline soil well.
Propagation: sets.
Comments: requires good drainage in winter; must be protected from winter sun and wind in exposed areas.

Dwarf Norway Spruce Varieties

'Acrocona,' large cone shape, compact habit.

'Clanbrassiliana,' showy globe shape.

'Echiniformis,' a pregnant-looking cone shape, very dense needles.

'Gregoriana,' irregular, yet graceful cascading mound.

'Inversa,' a superior cascading form, nicely irregular, never dies back at the base.

'Little Gem,' tiny dense compact green mound. Unfortunately, this variety often burns in the winter sun but soon recovers in the spring.

'Maxwellii,' flattened rounded mound.

'Nidiformis,' Bird's Nest Spruce; nondescript cupped shape that somewhat resembles a bird's nest. With age, it loses this characteristic and becomes flat-topped.

'Pendula,' a low cascading form best displayed cascading down a bank or creeping among rocks. At maturity, its large white cones are very dramatic. This variety would be very popular if better known. It is excellent for all types of gardens, including rock gardens and bonsai.

'Phylicoides,' a large size tree with very narrow foliage.

'Prostrato Esto,' a symmetrical flattened mound.

'Pygmaea,' a tiny, slow-growing pyramidal form to 2 feet tall, densely compact. This variety is showy in rock gardens and also as a bonsai.

'Reflexa,' a low cascading form. Unfortunately it tends to get bare at the base.

'Remontii,' an irregular flattened cone.

'Repens,' broadly rounded shape, moderately fast-growing.

'Virgata,' an odd-looking large size tree that closely resembles the Monkey Puzzle Tree.

'Virgata Nana,' an extremely showy semi-erect irregular form.

P. GLAUCA 'CONICA,' Dwarf Alberta Spruce. Native to the northern Rocky Mountains. Perennial to Zone 3.
Height: to 4 feet.
Shape: slow-growing pyramidal evergreen, densely compact habit.
Likes: semidry.
Tolerates: sun/half-sun/dry/moist.
Propagation: sets.
Comments: prefers one last watering before the ground freezes in winter. This plant can either be pruned into a perfectly symmetrical cone or left natural as a billowy pyramidal form.

P. PUNGENS, Colorado Blue Spruce. Native to the central Rocky Mountains extending north as far as Yellowstone National Park. Perennial to Zone 1.

Height: 60 feet.
Shape: dense pyramidal evergreen tree.
Foliage: bright silver-blue.
Likes: sun.
Tolerates: dry/semidry.
Comments:

Colorado Blue Spruce, *Picea pungens*

buy only the bluest sets because this tree's color never changes. This plant is usually grown as a tree, but with pruning can also be grown as a good hedge. Sets grafted onto Norway Spruce *(Picea abies)* understocks are less hardy on the plains. It is extremely beneficial to wash the dust off spruces in the heat of summer; this helps protect them from spruce mites.

Large Colorado Blue Spruce Varieties

'Aurea,' new growth is gold, later changing to blue-green color. Unfortunately, this variety tends to sunburn in winter and must have protection from the wind.

'Bakeri,' fast-growing variety with moderately-long blue needles.

'Fat Albert,' semi-dwarf, densely compact blue spruce. Grows to about 15 feet tall. Introduced by Wayside Gardens Nursery.

'Foxtail,' semi-dwarf blue variety with unusual foxtail-like growth pattern at the branch tips.

'Iseli Fastigate,' semi-dwarf columnar variety.

'Hoopsii,' full size tree with the bluest coloration of any variety.

'Pendula,' pendulous form which must be staked or grafted to assume a tree form, intense blue color.

'Walnut Glen,' new growth is gold, later changing to blue-green color. This variety is less hardy than the others; it sunburns in winter and requires wind protection.

Dwarf Colorado Blue Spruce Varieties

These varieties are slowly becoming better known. Once you see one, you will want one for your yard. They offer the advantages of being shrub-sized and vividly blue-colored throughout both the winter and summer.

'Blue Horizon,' semi-upright arching form, attractive blue color.

'Compacta,' attractive blue mound, becoming flat-topped with age, 3 feet tall.

'Globosa,' attractive blue mound which remains symmetrically rounded as it ages, 3 feet tall.

'Hunnewelliana,' showy irregular broad-pyramidal form, good blue color.

'Nana' on a standard; dramatic globe-like form on a tree standard. This makes a beautiful blue lolli-

pop-shaped formal tree, which has the additional advantage of being evergreen. It is best left unpruned for its showy natural shape. This plant will become wildly popular once it is better known.

'Prostrata,' low cascading form, vivid blue color. This variety may become one of the most popular plants in this garden guide. It is most showy cascading down a bank or creeping in among large rocks, but it looks just as good in a flower bed. Once you see this plant, you will want one for your garden. For care, you must occasionally remove upright shoots, or your plant will return to being a tree.

'Prostrate Blue Mist,' a broad mound-shaped plant with semi-pendulous branches and dramatic long needles.

'R H Montgomery,' slow-growing pyramidal shrub to 12 feet tall, good blue color.

'Theum,' moderately fast-growing pyramidal shrub to 12 feet tall, showy light blue color.

PIMPINELLA ANISUM, Anise, culinary herb. Annual.
Height: 2 feet.
Bloom: small yellowish-white flowers from late July to August.
Foliage: finely-divided.
Culture: easy.
Likes: sun/semidry/moist.
Propagation: seeds.
Comments: upright clump. Native to the Mediterranean area, and culti-

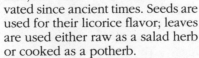

Anise, Pimpinella anisum

vated since ancient times. Seeds are used for their licorice flavor; leaves are used either raw as a salad herb or cooked as a potherb.

PLATYCODON GRANDIFLORUS, Chinese Balloonflower. Perennial to Zone 3.
Height: 2 feet.
Bloom: buds look like tiny balloons; blue or white bell-like flowers on stalks, blooms from July to August (long season).

Foliage: very late to emerge in the spring; mark its location to avoid accidentally digging it up.
Culture: easy.
Likes: half-sun/humus-rich soil.
Tolerates: sun/half-shade/semidry/moist.
Propagation: sets (transplant carefully) or seeds. (Seed germination: light.)
Comments: upright clump; windstake with hoop support in exposed areas. *'Mariessii'* is a smaller variety which does not require windstaking. Siskiyou Rare Plants lists a Japanese dwarf variety called *'Apoyama.'*

PINUS SPECIES. Various species are the official state trees of nine U.S. states (Alabama—*Pinus palustris,* Arkansas—*Pinus echinata,* Idaho—*Pinus monticola,* Maine—*Pinus strobus,* Michigan—*Pinus strobus,* Minnesota—*Pinus resinosa,* Montana—*Pinus ponderosa,* Nevada—*Pinus monophylla,* New Mexico-*Pinus edulis).*

Bristlecone Pine, Pinus aristata

P. ARISTATA, Bristlecone Pine. Native to high-elevation windswept ridges of the Sierra Nevadas. Perennial to Zone 2.
Height: 20 feet.
Shape: dense rounded form in youth becoming irregularly shaped and twisted with age.
Foliage: needles have characteristic white dots on them.
Likes: sun/half-sun/dry/semidry.
Propagation: sets or seeds.
Comments: tolerates wind well. This species has the oldest living trees on the planet.

P. CEMBRA 'SIBIRICA,' Siberian Pine. Perennial to Zone 1.
Height: 30 feet.
Shape: very slow-growing rounded-pyramidal tree.
Foliage: dark green color, attractive light colored bark.
Culture: very easy.
Likes: sun.
Tolerates: half-sun/dry/semidry.
Propagation: sets.

Siberian Pine, Pinus cembra 'siberica'

Comments: besides being an ornamental tree, this pine produces tasty edible nuts in its cones. It can also be pruned as a hedge. This plant was introduced from Manchuria by Frank Meyer.

P. CONTORTA 'SPAANS DWARF,' a very beautiful dwarf pyramidal tree. It is slow-growing and has an artistic quality to its form.

P. FLEXILIS, Limber Pine, tree. Native to central and northern Rockies. Perennial to Zone 1.
Height: 40 feet.
Shape: attractive irregular form (pyramidal in youth and round-topped in maturity), very slow-growing habit.
Culture: very easy.
Likes: sun.
Tolerates: half-sun/dry/semidry.
Propagation: sets (for best hardiness, make sure the understock is a northern strain of *Pinus flexilis)* or seeds.
Comments: the texture and form of this tree are very attractive. Besides the showy irregular shape, this species has characteristic low-to-the-ground branches that catch snow for the tree. There are a couple of particularly showy ornamental varieties. *'Fastigiata Glauca* Vanderwolf' is an irregular upright form with silvery needles. *'Glauca'* has bluish-green needles and a showy irregular form. *'Glauca Pendula'* is a vigorous prostrate form with very long blue needles. *'Reflexa Nana'* is a very attractive rounded dwarf form.

Limber Pine, Pinus flexilis

P. MUGO PUMILIO, Mugo Pine. Perennial to Zone 2.
Height: 3-5 feet.
Shape: many named varieties, nearly all are globe-like upright clumps.
Likes: sun/half-sun/dry/semidry.
Propagation: sets.
Comments: slow the growth of this plant by removing half the length of each new growth candle. An unusual variety, *'Fastigiata,'* has a narrowly upright bushy form.

P. NIGRA, Austrian Black Pine. Perennial to Zone 2.
Height: 40 feet.
Shape: dense pyramidal form in youth becoming an exceptionally beautiful flat-topped tree with an open crown.
Culture: easy.
Likes: sun/half-sun/semidry/moist.
Propagation: sets or seeds.
Comments: this dramatic tree stands out because of its distinctive characteristic shape.

P. PONDEROSA, Ponderosa Pine. Native to most of western North America. Perennial to Zone 3.
Height: 100 feet.
Shape: regal-looking pine, symmetrically pyramidal in youth; flat-topped at maturity (75-100 years); cinnamon-colored bark on trees twenty-five years and older.
Culture: very easy.
Likes: sun/well-drained soil.
Tolerates: half-sun/dry/semidry.
Propagation: sets.
Comments: this easy-to-care-for tree should be planted more commonly. However, it is best to locate it where it can shed its needles and not seem messy. The Indians used the adhesive sap of this species to seal the seams of boats and teepees. The inner bark is edible (remember all the famous Euell Gibbons TV ads?) but Indians used it only to fend off star-

Ponderosa Pine, Pinus ponderosa

vation.

P. STROBUS 'PENDULA,' Weeping White Pine. Perennial to Zone 4 (protected areas only).
Height: 10 feet.
Shape: irregularly shaped tree with drooping branches and exceptionally long blue-green down-hanging needles.
Likes: sun/moist.
Tolerates: half-sun/semidry.
Propagation: sets only.
Comments: somewhat sensitive to alkaline soil; must have wind protection in exposed areas; train tree upright with stake supports; this tree often suffers transplant shock. Because this tree will eventually arch over to the ground, it requires lots of room.

P. SYLVESTRIS, Scot's Pine. Perennial to Zone 2.
Height: 50 feet.
Shape: dramatically attractive pine with orange bark that peels with age.
Likes: sun/half-sun/semidry/moist.
Propagation: sets.
Comments: the less hardy varieties prefer wind and winter sun protection. The species form has a showy irregular form and a useful medium-large size. Low-growing novelty varieties are the following:
'Beacon Hill,' very attractive irregularly rounded clump.
'Boersma,' a dramatically beautiful prostrate form. This is my personal favorite.
'Compressa,' a narrowly pyramidal form.
'Fastigiata,' a narrowly columnar form useful for an upright accent.
'Hillside Creeper,' an irregular creeper which forms attractive multiple clumps.
'Mitsch Weeping,' a twisted weeping form. It must be staked upright to become a tree.
'Nana,' a rounded form which grows for decades to become a large compact clump. It retains its compact habit with age.
'Nana' (on a standard); a lollipop-shaped tree for a formal garden. It is surprisingly attractive.
'Viridis Compacta,' very compact irregular shape.

POA CUSICKII, Early Bluegrass. Native to dry to moist grasslands in the Great Plains and foothills. Perennial.
Height: 1 foot.

Bloom: attractive silvery-white seed-heads from end May to early June; dried seedheads become straw-colored and persist until late summer.
Foliage: individual tufted short basal clump of soft delicate foliage.
Likes: sun/half-sun/dry/semidry/moist.
Propagation: sets or seeds.
Comments: roots and seeds are not invasive. Unlike other Bluegrasses, this species is not invasive. One extremely invasive member of this genus is Kentucky Bluegrass, *Poa pratensis,* a common lawn grass. It was originally brought from Europe and planted on the Eastern Seaboard. However, this European plant moved so fast across the eastern woodlands that the first Kentucky explorers thought it was a native and mistakenly named it Kentucky Bluegrass.

POLEMONIUM CAERULEUM, Jacob's Ladder. Perennial to Zone 1.
Height: 3 feet.
Bloom: blue flowers on a very tall stalk from June to August (long season).
Foliage: graceful basal clump of fern-like foliage.
Likes: half-sun/half-shade/moist/wet.
Propagation: sets or seeds.
Comments: when out of bloom, this plant closely resembles a fern. It can be difficult to place in the garden; its fern-like clump of foliage is

Jacob's Ladder, Polemonium caeruleum

showy in the front of the garden, but its 3 feet tall flower stalk looks out of place there. Excellent companion for daylilies.

   P. PULCHERRIMUM, Showy Polemonium. Native to hillsides and open areas of the foothills and Rocky Mountains. Perennial.
Height: 6 inches.
Bloom: blue-purple flowers on stalks from April to May.
Foliage: loose clump habit, showy basal clump of fernlike foliage.
Likes: sun/half-sun/dry/semidry.
Propagation: sets or seeds.

   P. VISCOSUM, Sky Pilot, Skunk Polemonium. Native to alpine scree areas. Perennial.

Height: 5 inches.
Bloom: showy stalkless blue flowers in June.
Foliage: attractive basal clump of foliage.
Likes: half-sun.
Propagation: sets or seeds.
Comments: requires scree conditions (underground watering and good drainage). The crushed foliage has a skunk-like smell that sticks to hiker's shoes. The name *viscosum* means "sticky."

POLYGONUM AFFINE. Perennial to Zone 2.
Height: 1 foot.
Bloom: vivid red flowers that age into dry rust-colored flowers and remain on plant until midwinter.
Likes: sun/half-sun/half-shade/dry/semidry/moist/wet.
Propagation: sets.
Comments: sprawling clump; may require winter mulch in exposed locations. The variety 'Darjeeling Red' is considered the best because of its brilliant red flowers and showy display of dried flowers that remain in the winter.

   P. AUBERTII, Silver Fleece Vine. Perennial to Zone 4.
Height: rapid growing vine to 25 feet.
Bloom: fragrant white flower clusters with a lacy texture from early August to frost (long season).
Climbing habit: climbs by twining stem tips, needs a support to climb on.
Foliage: red fall color.
Culture: easy.
Likes: sun/semidry.
Tolerates: half-sun/half-shade/dry/semidry.
Propagation: sets or seeds.
Comments: dies to the ground each winter and starts from its roots (this is a real advantage with this fast-growing vine).

   P. CUSPIDATUM 'COMPACTUM' (P. reynotria), Japanese Fleeceflower. Perennial to Zone 2.
Height: 1½ feet.
Bloom: pink flowers in July, attractive red fruit in later summer.
Foliage: coarse leathery foliage that turns red in the fall.
Likes: sun.
Tolerates: half-sun/dry/semidry/moist/poor soil.
Propagation: sets.

Comments: fast-spreading clump. This plant is extremely invasive due to its spreading root. It is an attractive ground cover for areas that can tolerate its aggressive spreading.

POPCORN, *Zea mays var. praecox.* Warm-season annual grain.
Height: 6 feet.
Description: coarse leafy plant which bears ears of grain on its stalks.
Likes: sun/moist/well-drained soil.
Propagation: sets (transplants well) or seeds (plant outside after frost-free date).
Pests: Colorado potato beetle and corn borer worm; do not plant corn and popcorn near each other due to problems caused by cross-pollination.
Growing tips: must dry out in late summer; prefers a rich deeply dug soil; requires a long hot season; for best pollination from tassels, plant in clumps of 3 or more plants.
Harvest tips: popcorn ears must ripen and dry on the stalk. Then for best popping, the cobs must be dried for 2-4 months, testing regularly for popping quality. When ready, remove from cob and pack in jars for longer storage.
Comments: popcorn has been cultivated since antiquity in the Mississippi River Valley. There are also showy varieties with colored kernels.

POPULUS ALBA, White Poplar.
Height: 50 feet.
Shape: very large broad spreading form.

Foliage: dull green leaves with a white underside.
Likes: sun.
Tolerates: dry.
Propagation: sets or seeds.
Comments: the root suckering of this tree is phenome-

White Poplar, Populus alba

nal. Root suckers can be expected as much as 200 feet from the tree. Its roots are also infamous for clogging sewers.

   P. X CANESCENS, Tower Poplar. Perennial to Zone 1.

Height: 30 feet tall by 3 feet wide.
Shape: showy narrowly upright tree, extremely fast-growing habit.
Foliage: glossy green foliage with a fuzzy white underside, rich yellow fall color, attractive light gray bark.
Culture: easy.
Likes: moist.
Tolerates: sun/half-sun/semidry.
Propagation: sets (buy only sets with their terminal bud tips intact).
Comments: prefers to dry out in late summer. Some minimal root suckering; rarely needs pruning of any kind. This tree makes an attractive fast-growing screen. For best appearance, plant it in a natural grove style (not in a straight line) and mix in a few new trees every couple of years. In some situations, the abundant surface roots could be a problem. Only male trees are propagated to avoid cotton debris. This tree is an excellent substitute for the half-hardy Lombardy Poplar. The Swedish Columnar Aspen *Populus tremula 'Erecta'* was one of the parents of this tree. Introduced in 1979 by Wilbert Ronald of Morden Research Station.

P. FREMONTII, Plains Cottonwood; height 50 feet.
Shape: very large spreading tree.
Foliage: showy yellow fall color.
Likes: sun.
Tolerates: dry/semidry.
Comments: plant only named male varieties to avoid cotton debris. This showy large tree has an un-

Cottonwood, Populus fremontii

fortunate tendency to block sewers. *'Robusta'* is an excellent variety with disease resistance.

P. NIGRA 'ITALICA,' Lombardy Poplar.
Comments: this tree is at the far limits of its hardiness. A much hardier identical twin is the Tower Poplar *(Populus x canescens)*.

P. TREMULOIDES, Quaking Aspen. Perennial to Zone 2.

Quaking Aspen, Populus tremuloides

Height: 30 feet.
Shape: fast-growing small tree most attractive when grouped into a grove planting.
Foliage: leaves never seem to stop moving even when there is no breeze, vivid yellow fall color, attractive white bark (winter interest).
Propagation: sets or seeds.
Likes: sun/half-sun/half-shade/semidry/moist.
Comments: unfortunately, this tree is occasionally subject to canker disease; therefore, it is best to plant this tree in multiple groupings and not as individual trees. This showy informal tree should be more commonly planted.

PORTULACA GRANDIFLORA, Moss Rose. Annual.
Height: 3 inches.
Bloom: red, orange, yellow, white, or purple rose-like flowers from May to frost (very long season).
Foliage: trailing succulent foliage.
Culture: easy.
Likes: sun/semidry.
Tolerates: very dry.
Propagation: sets or seeds. (Seed germination: warm.)
Comments: mossy carpet-like creeper. In the garden, use this flower as a front edging. Excellent for containers because of the way it cascades over the edge. It can also be used in a rock garden to produce late summer color. It is an excellent low-maintenance plant.

POTATO, Solanum tuberosum. Annual vegetable.
Height: 3 feet.
Description: bushy clump of showy emerald-green crinkled foliage, tubers are produced underground.
Culture: easy.
Likes: sun/half-sun.
Propagation: sets (use seed potatoes; the potatoes found in most grocery stores have been treated to retard sprouting.) For an early jump on planting, start sets indoors in moist rolled-up newspaper. The vines grow straight in the rolled-up newspaper.
Pests: the very worst is the Colorado potato beetle. In the home garden these can simply be picked off by hand. It is particularly important to start looking early in the season in June. A commercial insecticide effective on this bug is Sevin. To reduce disease problems, do not walk through or touch plants when wet.
Growing tips: requires regular water in spring, then in late summer allow foliage to dry up and die: potatoes ripened this way store best; prefers fertile humus-rich, mildly acidic soil; fresh hot manure in the soil can damage plants and cause scab on the tubers; potatoes should be rotated to new soil in different parts of the garden each year.
For best growth, give wind protection and moderate humidity; hill up around plants in early to mid-summer with

Potato, Solarum tuberosum

soil or loose compost up to 3 feet tall (this encourages tuber development and prevents sun-greening).

Companion plant with lots of garlic or beans, but never plant with sunflowers. Because they tolerate cool soil, they can be planted outside several weeks before the frost-free date.

Native to the Andes Highlands of Chile, where the Incas cultivated it and called it *patata,* it was the main staple of the Inca empire. They prepared them for storage by alternately freezing and drying the tubers.
Harvest tips: potatoes can be harvested anytime during the season, but for storage allow potatoes to ripen in the ground until the plant top is fully dead. This toughens the skin on the tubers for best storage.
Comments: this vegetable is eaten cooked in a variety of methods including baking, frying, boiling, and in a multitude of casseroles. It preserves well if stored dry and cool, canned, or frozen once cooked.

However, all green parts of the plant are poisonous. (Isn't that a mystery?)

Favorite varieties are 'Batoche,' an excellent red-skinned variety with good flavor and disease resistance; 'Norland,' an early red-skinned potato; 'Russet Burbank,' a late season yellow-skinned potato; 'Yukon Gold,' a yellow-fleshed variety which keeps well; and 'Finnish Yellow,' an exceptionally tasty yellow-fleshed variety bred for cool summer areas. It grows equally well in hot summer areas. An unusual variety is 'All Blue,' which has lavender-blue flesh.

POTENTILLA CONCINNA, Elegant Cinquefoil. Native to dry grassy hills in the Great Plains and foothills. Perennial.
Height: 3 inches.
Bloom: medium large golden-yellow flowers on stalks from end of April to early June.
Foliage: spreading low basal clump of gray-green fern-like foliage with woolly white undersides.
Likes: sun/rocky or sandy soil.
Tolerates: half-sun/dry/semidry.
Propagation: sets or seeds.
Comments: a similarly showy species is *Potentilla platensis*. These plants would be useful in a moderately aggressive ground cover.

P. FRUTICOSA, Common Potentilla, native circumpolar. Perennial to Zone 1.
Bloom: yellow or white flowers from July to frost (long season).
Foliage: some varieties provide winter interest if dried flowers are left on plant.
Culture: easy.
Likes: sun/semidry.
Tolerates: half-sun/half-shade/dry.
Propagation: sets.
Comments: irregularly mounded shrub.

Practically all varieties of *Potentilla fruticosa* are extremely hardy. Here are a few particularly noteworthy varieties. Those varieties noted as having thick leaves tolerate the dry plains climate particularly well; others must be protected from dry summer wind.

'Abbotswood'—a refined spreading shape, large white flowers with a long season, showy dark green foliage.

'Abbotswood Silver'—a sport of 'Abbotswood' with white edged foliage, white flowers, and a low-growing habit to 2 feet tall. Unfortunately, it is slow to establish and bloom fully.

'Bessii'—height 1 foot, dwarf size compact clump, buttercup-yellow flowers, silvery-green foliage. This variety makes a great container plant.

'Coronation Triumph'—height 3 feet, upright mound, profuse bright yellow flowers, soft green foliage. This is the earliest and longest-bloom variety. Many consider it the best variety of all for this reason. It was introduced in 1950 by the Indian Head Forest Nursery Station in Saskatchewan.

'Dakota Sunrise'—height 3 feet, attractive mounded form, pinkish buds which open into bright yellow flowers, thick foliage.

'Elizabeth'—height 2 feet, rounded shape, yellow flowers, thick foliage. This is also considered one of the finest varieties.

'Everest'—height 3 feet, profuse white flowers, very long season, dark green foliage.

'Farrerii' (or Gold Drop)—height 2 feet, showy irregular compact mound, dwarf size, sprays of small bright yellow flowers, delicate fern-like foliage (thick foliage).

'Friedrichseii' (or 'Berlin Beauty') height 4 feet, fast-growing mound, large pale yellow flowers, gray-green foliage. This variety blooms profusely two weeks before the others start to bloom, but then sparsely later in the season.

'Goldfinger'—height 3 feet, compact rounded mound, very large vivid yellow flowers.

'Grandiflora'—height 4-5 feet, vigorous shrub habit, very large sulphur-yellow flowers (1-2 inches across).

'Katherine Dykes'—height 4 feet, graceful arching form, profuse primrose-yellow flowers, light-green

Common Potentilla, Potentilla fruticosa

delicate-looking foliage.

'Longacre'—height 2 feet, dwarf spreading clump, yellow flowers, thick foliage.

'Moonlight' (or Maanelys)—height 4 feet, rounded mound, large pale yellow flowers, gray-green semi-thick foliage. Useful for wide spreading hedges.

'Mt. Everest'—height 4 feet, compact shrub habit, white flowers, dark green foliage.

'Ochroleuca'—height 4 feet, erect shrub habit, small pale yellow flowers, light green foliage.

'Orangeman'—height 2 feet, rounded spreading habit, showy orangish-yellow flowers from early June to frost. Tolerates hot dry weather particularly well for an orange-flowering potentilla.

'Parvifolia'—height 2 feet, dwarf size clump with compact spreading habit, deep yellow flowers, showy tiny leaves.

'Pink Glow'—height 1 foot, rounded clump, a new introduction with apricot-yellow flowers edged with pink. This variety is less hardy than the other listed varieties.

'Primrose Beauty'—height 3 feet, attractive rounded mound with a compact habit, showy creamy-yellow flowers with a deep yellow center, thick gray-green foliage. This is an excellent variety that should be planted more commonly.

'Snowflake'—height 3 feet, large semi-double white flowers.

'Sundance'—height 3 feet, rounded habit, light yellow flowers with a dramatic double form.

'Sunset'—height 3 feet, yellow flowers tinged red.

'Tilford Cream'—height 1 foot, compact carpet-like habit, showy creamy-white flowers.

'Vilmoriniana'—height 2 feet, showy dwarf rounded clump, creamy-white flowers, gray-green foliage.

'White Gold'—height 1 foot, dwarf compact clump with a

spreading habit, profuse large yellow flowers, dark green foliage. This variety makes a good container plant.

P. TRIDENTATA, Wineleaf Cinquefoil, Creeping Potentilla. Perennial to Zone 2.
Height: 6 inches.
Bloom: white strawberry-like flowers from June to August.
Foliage: strawberry-like leaves turn a spectacular reddish-orange color in the fall.
Likes: sun/half-sun/half-shade/dry/semidry/moist.
Propagation: sets or seeds.
Comments: clump invades aggressively by spreading runners. Because of its fast-spreading nature, this plant is excellent for ground cover use. It should be selected for larger, more profuse flowering.

PRIMULA SPECIES. Perennial.

Order of bloom: *Primula vulgaris* (March to June), *P. auricula* (early April to June), *P. juliae* (early April to June), *P. veris* (mid-April to June), *P. polyantha* (May to June), *P. sieboldii* (May to June), *P. cortusoides* (early to mid-June), *P. japonica* (early June to July).

P. AURICULA, Auricula. Perennial to Zone 2.
Height: 6 inches.
Bloom: red, yellow or blue flowers with white or yellow centers on stalks, blooms from early April to June (long season if individual spent flowers are removed); occasional flowers from mid-August to September.
Foliage: basal clump of thick fleshy foliage.
Likes: moist/humus-rich soil.
Tolerates: half-shade.
Propagation: sets or seeds. (Seed germination: self-sows, but seedlings are very slow to come up, seeds need light to germinate.)
Comments: individual clump habit; protect from wind, full sun and heat; may need winter mulch. Plant 'garden-type' varieties instead of the less hardy 'exhibition-type' varieties. This plant is best displayed at the front of the garden or in containers. This species has been bred since the 16th century. It was brought to England by Flemish weavers escaping religious persecution in Holland. Originally, its name was *'Au-*

ricula ursi' meaning 'bear's ears' referring to the foliage.

P. CORTUSOIDES (Cortusa matthiolii). Perennial to Zone 3.
Height: 10 inches.
Bloom: showy nodding magenta-pink star-like flowers on dainty stalks, blooms from early to mid-June.
Foliage: showy, fuzzy, scalloped foliage (similar to *Primula sieboldii* to which it is closely related).
Likes: half-shade/moist/humus-rich soil.
Tolerates: half-sun/semidry.
Propagation: sets or seeds. (Seed germination: light.)
Comments: individual clump habit; requires water in late summer; protect from wind and summer heat. This flower is native to low and medium elevation birch forests in Mongolia. It grows in forest openings and on rocky slopes.

P. JAPONICA. Perennial to Zone 3.
Height: 1 foot.
Bloom: red, white or purple flowers on stalks, blooms from early June to July (long season if individual spent flowers removed).
Foliage: basal clump of foliage.
Likes: half-sun/wet/humus-rich soil (loves a bog).
Tolerates: half-shade/moist.
Propagation: sets or seeds. (Seed germination: light.)
Comments: individual clump habit; self-sows in favorable location. This plant demands a lot of water, but tolerates more sun than other Primroses. A somewhat similiar plant is the Drumstick Primrose (*Primula denticula*) from the Himalayan Mountains. *P. denticula* is cold hardy but must have an acidic soil, winter mulch, and cool shade on the north or east side of a building.

P. X JULIAE, Juliana Primrose. Perennial to Zone 3.
Height: 4 inches.
Bloom: pink, yellow or blue gem-like flowers from early April to June (long season if individual spent flowers removed).
Likes: half-shade/moist/humus-rich soil.
Propagation: sets or seeds. (Seed germination: light.)
Comments: small delicate-looking plant; must be protected from wind, full sun, and summer heat; requires

winter mulch. Plants are more tolerant to the plains climate if raised from the seed of locally-grown parents.

P. X POLYANTHA, Common Primrose. Perennial to Zone 4.
Height: 6 inches.
Bloom: red, pink, yellow, white, or blue flowers from May to June (very long season if individual spent flowers removed).
Foliage: basal clump of foliage.
Likes: half-shade/moist/humus-rich soil.
Propagation: sets or seeds. (Seed germination: light.)
Comments: protect from wind, full sun, and heat. These are the plants commonly sold in grocery stores. 'Pacific Hybrids' is the most common variety. An excellent companion plant is Wall Cress (*Arabis caucasica*). They bloom attractively together, but locate this combination in a sunnier exposure than one would otherwise.

P. SIEBOLDII. Perennial to Zone 3.
Height: 8 inches.
Bloom: showy white or pink flower clusters on stalks, blooms from May to June.
Foliage: basal clump of attractive foliage goes dormant and disappears in July.
Likes: half-sun/half-shade/moist/humus-rich soil.
Propagation: sets or seeds. (Seed germination: light.)
Comments: individual clump habit; protect from wind, full sun, and heat; requires winter mulch.

P. VERIS, Cowslip. Perennial to Zone 3.

Cowslip,
Primula veris

Height: 5 inches.
Bloom: very fragrant nodding yellow flowers on stalks, blooms from April to May (long season if individual spent flowers are removed).
Foliage: basal clump of foliage.
Likes: half-

shade/moist/humus-rich soil/manure.
Tolerates: half-sun/wet.
Propagation: sets or seeds. (Seed germination: light.)
Comments: protect from wind, full sun, and heat; needs winter mulch. Leaves and flowers are delicious in salads or tea. The species *Primula elatior* is similar enough to be confused but lacks fragrance and is more heat tolerant.

P. VULGARIS. Perennial to Zone 3.
Height: 6 inches.

Bloom: red, pink, yellow, white, blue, purple or black flowers with yellow centers, blooms from March to June (long season if individual spent flowers removed); occasional fall bloom from mid-August to late September.

Primula vulgaris

Foliage: basal clump of foliage.
Likes: half-shade/moist/humus-rich soil.
Propagation: sets or seeds. (Seed germination: light.)
Comments: individual clump habit. Protect from wind, full sun, and heat. Self-sows well, particularly the yellow varieties. The most fragrant varieties are the yellow or orange ones; the blue ones are the least fragrant. This plant is excellent for the front edging of a garden and also combined with Wall Cress (*Arabis caucasica*).

PRINSEPIA SINENSIS, Cherry Prinsepia. Perennial to Zone 1.
Height: 6 feet.
Shape: attractive arching fine-textured shrub.
Bloom: insignificant yellow flowers in early May; red cherry-like fruit which makes excellent jelly (however, birds also love this fruit).
Foliage: attractive foliage appears in very early spring.
Culture: easy.
Likes: sun/half-sun/semidry/moist.
Propagation: sets or seed.
Comments: this bush was named for Macaire Prinsep, a botanist of Geneva, Switzerland. It makes an

attractive hedge, and its small sharp spines make it useful as a barrier plant.

PRUNUS SPECIES. Perennial.

PRUNUS ARMENIACA MANDSHURICA, Manchurian Apricot. Perennial to Zone 3.
Height: 25 feet.
Shape: dramatically showy small V-shaped tree, moderately fast-growing.
Bloom: spectacular pink flowers from late April to early May, good quality apricot fruit.
Foliage: showy dark green foliage, spectacular red and yellow fall color.
Likes: sun/semidry/moist.
Propagation: sets (buy only sets with their terminal bud intact; softwood cuttings or soft-hardwood cuttings in summer).
Comments: plant two for cross-pollination or use Nanking Cherry (*Prunus tomentosa*) as a pollinator; prune only to accentuate natural shape, and prune only after bloom. A winter with temperatures below minus-35° F will eliminate that year's fruit crop but not kill the tree. Apricot trees in our area bear fruit 4 to 8 years out of ten. This is due mainly

Apricot, Prunus armeniaca

to late frosts, which damage the flowers and eliminate that year's crop. Originally, the seed for the Manchurian Apricot was sent by Mr. L. Ptitsin of Harbin, Manchuria. At Strathmore, Alberta, a large orchard of Apricots was planted. The following varieties, except those noted otherwise, were all selected from this orchard. These beautiful trees should be more commonly planted for both their fruit and their ornamental attributes.

'Brookcot,' juicy fruit with a cling stone. Tree tends to have a poor branching structure and must be pruned for strong branches. This

variety was selected by Brooks Research Station, in 1979.

'Coaldale Select,' a recent introduction by the Coaldale Nursery, Coaldale, Alberta.

'Prairie Gold,' an extra cold-hardy variety selected for its reliable annual production of delicious freestone fruit. Additionally it has showy red coloration on the foliage. Selected from William Kerr's experimental crosses in the 1930s in Saskatoon, Saskatchewan, and introduced by Lakeshore Nursery.

'Strathmore,' a variety selected by Clayton Berg, Valley Nursery in Helena, Montana.

'Sunrise,' another extra cold-hardy variety selected for its reliable yearly fruiting. It also has red-tinged leaves. Selected from William Kerr's experimental crosses in the 1930s in Saskatoon, Saskatchewan, and introduced by Lakeshore Nursery.

'Westcot,' a freestone variety selected by Mr. Les Kerr of Morden Research Station in 1982. This variety is considered the best tasting and least reliable for annual fruiting.

P. BESSEYI, Sand Cherry. Perennial to Zone 2.
Height: 3 feet.
Bloom: small white flowers which open dramatically with new leaves in early May, tart black fruit (good for jelly).
Shape: creeping shrub.
Culture: easy.
Likes: sun.
Tolerates: half-sun/dry/semidry/moist.
Propagation: sets (softwood cuttings or soft-hardwood cuttings in summer).
Comments: invasive habit; prune out oldest branches each year after flowering for best fruit production. Look for named varieties selected for their fruit.

Sand Cherry, Prunus besseyi

This native fruit is slowly becoming better known. Additionally, this plant is being researched as a hardy understock for tender varieties of peaches and sweet cherries. There is a Sand Cherry Society based in Broadus, Montana, devoted to the development of the sand cherry. Its address is listed in the Resource Directory.

P. CERASUS, Pie Cherry. Perennial to Zone 3.
Height: 10 feet.

Shape: showy small ornamental tree.
Bloom: clusters of white flowers in early May; excellent-tasting tart fruit used for pies, preserves, or freezing; ripens June to July.
Likes: sun/

Pie Cherry, Prunus cerasus

moist/humus-rich soil.
Tolerates: half-sun/semidry/moist.
Propagation: sets (buy only sets with their terminal bud tip intact; softwood cuttings or soft-hardwood cuttings in summer).
Comments: for best hardiness, soil should not be too nitrogen-rich when young tree is planted. Needs protected site and lots of water; when young, protect trunk bark from winter sunscald; it has shallow hungry roots; late frosts occasionally get the flowers and eliminate that year's crop; self pollinating; have this tree pruned professionally every ten years for best appearance. Fruit flies and birds are formidable challenges to a pie cherry harvest. The hardy variety 'Meteor' was introduced by the University of Minnesota in 1952. Another variety 'Mesabi' is similar and somewhat hardier than 'Meteor.'

P. X CISTENA, Purple-leaf Sand Cherry. Perennial to Zone 2.
Height: 7 feet.
Shape: shrubby tree.
Bloom: pinkish-white flowers open with new red leaves in early May.
Foliage: reddish-brown foliage, sparse purplish-black fruit.
Culture: easy.
Propagation: sets (softwood cuttings or soft-hardwood cuttings in summer).
Likes: sun.

Tolerates: half-sun/semidry/moist.
Comments: invasive by root spreading; prune off the weak lowest branches and oldest wood in early summer after flowering. Useful as either a showy landscaping shrub or pruned as a hedge. Selected varieties of this plant were first introduced by Dr. N. E. Hansen of the South Dakota Experimental Station in 1909. The name *'cistena'* is a Sioux word meaning baby. This plant can be used as a substitute for Japanese maple in an oriental garden.

P. DOMESTICA, Plum.
Culture: easy.
Likes: sun/moist.
Propagation: softwood cuttings or soft-hardwood cuttings in summer.
Pests: occasional black knots appear on the branches. Remove them and sterilize tools.
Comments: have this tree pruned professionally every ten years for best appearance (it will need to be drop-crotched and have any V-shaped crotches removed for greatest strength. U-shaped crotches are much stronger). For best fruit production, plant a pollinator tree nearby or graft on a pollinator branch (this can be any variety with a closely related bloom time and type). American plums (AM) form large upright rounded trees, and Japanese plums (JP) form small dramatically spreading trees. Plant only sets whose terminal bud tip is intact. Plums are eaten fresh, canned, pitted and frozen, made into jams and jellies (plums have some natural pectin), or used to make fruit leather. One possible cottage industry would be the marketing of Plum Marmalade.
FRUIT GRADING SCALE: excellent, good, fair, poor.
'Alderman' (JP). Perennial to Zone 3-4; excellent for eating or cooking; fruit color: red skin, yel-

Plum, Prunis domestica

low flesh. The variety *'Toka'* is a good pollinator. Introduced in 1985 by the University of Minnesota and named for Professor W. H. Alderman.
'Bounty' (AM). Perennial to Zone 2; good for jam; good for canning; late ripening; fruit color: dark red; orange-yellow flesh. Introduced in 1939 by Morden Research Station. It is an Assiniboine seedling.
'Brookgold' (JP). Perennial to Zone 2; good to excellent fruit for eating; fruit color: yellow and red; sweet yellow flesh; small to medium size; freestone; ripens early. For best pollination, plant an early blooming pollenizer nearby. Selected from seedlings of seed sent in 1979 by Mr. Ptitsin of Harbin, Manchuria, to Brooks Horticultural Research Station, Brooks, Alberta.
'Brookred' (JP). Perennial to Zone 2; fair to good quality for eating; good for canning; good to excellent for jam; fruit color: dull red, orange flesh; ripens mid- to late season. The tree has a large spreading form. Because it is late-flowering, it is a good pollinator for 'Pembina.' This variety was selected from open-pollinated seedlings of 'Ivanovka' by Brooks Research Station, Alberta, in 1979.
'Dandy' (AM). Perennial to Zone 2; fair for eating; poor for cooking; excellent for canning; good to excellent for jam, mid- to late ripening; fruit color: yellow skin blushed bright red, very juicy yellow-orange flesh; tends to overproduce and should be thinned early. Because of its long flowering season, this variety is a good pollinator. Introduced in 1936 from Manitoba. It is an 'Assiniboine' seedling.
'La Crescent' (AM). Perennial to Zone 4-5; fruit color: yellow; very sweet flesh; small size stone and fruit; very vigorous. Introduced in 1923 by the University of Minnesota.
'Parkside' (AM). Perennial to Zone 2; fruit color: yellow-red.
'Pembina' (AM). Perennial to Zone 3; fruit color: red with a blu-

ish bloom, flesh is bright yellow; excellent for eating; good for cooking; excellent for jam; large size fruit. Because they are both late flowering, 'Brookred' is a good pollinator for this variety. Introduced by Dr. N. E. Hansen of Brookings, South Dakota, in 1917. It is a cross between the Canada Plum (*Prunus nigra*) and 'Red June.'

'Pipestone' (JP). Perennial to Zone 3-4, excellent quality medium-large plum; fruit color: red-purple; very sweet yellow flesh; early ripening; a good pollinator for this variety is 'Toka.' Introduced in 1942 by the University of Minnesota.

'Ptitsin varieties' (JP). Perennial to Zone 3. There are several varieties denoted by number which were selected from seed sent by Mr. Ptitsin from *Prunus salicina* trees near Harbin, Manchuria. All of them bear excellent fruit early in the season (mid-August). These were introduced at Morden Research Station, Manitoba. 'Ptitsin #5' has yellow skin, juicy yellow flesh, and ripens early; 'Ptitsin #9' has greenish-yellow skin, excellent quality sweet green flesh, and is freestone; 'Ptitsin #12' has large red fruit and is freestone. The last two varieties are low shrubby trees.

'Toka' (AM). Perennial to Zone 4; fair to good for eating or jam; early ripening; medium-large size; fruit color: reddish-orange, green yellow flesh; a good pollinator for many varieties. Introduced in 1911 by Dr. N. E. Hansen of Brookings, South Dakota.

'Underwood' (AM). Perennial to Zone 4, excellent quality; fruit color: dark red, sweet yellow flesh; large size; very early ripening; needs a protected area and summer heat. Introduced by Charles Haralson of the University of Minnesota, in 1920.

'Waneta' (AM). Perennial to Zone 3-4; fair to good quality; fruit color: red-purple, yellow flesh; small size; mid-season ripening; very hardy and productive.

P. X DROPMOREANA, Dropmore Flowering Cherry. Perennial to Zone 1.
Height: 25 feet.
Bloom: profuse fragrant single white flowers from early to mid-May; small cherry fruit.

Foliage: semi-glossy foliage, yellow fall color, showy cherry-like shiny bark (winter interest).
Culture: easy.
Likes: sun/moist.
Tolerates: half-sun/semidry/moist.
Propagation: sets only (plant only sets with their terminal bud tips intact).
Comments: prefers to be protected from wind. This hybrid tree was created by Skinner's Nursery in Dropmore, Manitoba, in 1952, in a colchicine experiment which crossed Morello cherry, native chokecherry, and *Prunus maackii*. The seeds from this hybrid are fertile and will cross and graft with most of the *Prunus* genus. However, most of these seedlings resemble *Prunus maackii*. Great breeding potential exists for new varieties to be discovered from hybrids with apricots, cherries, peaches, plums, and almonds.

P. FRUTICOSA, Mongolian Cherry. Perennial to Zone 1.
Height: 5 feet.
Shape: spreading bush, shiny bark.
Bloom: white flowers in early May with new leaves; extremely flavorful sour cherries ripen from late June to mid-July.
Foliage: green.
Culture: easy.
Likes: sun/moist.
Tolerates: half-sun/semidry.
Propagation: sets or seed.
Comments: invasive due to root suckering; for best fruit harvest, prune out oldest wood every couple years after flowering; this bush makes both a good hedge and an outstanding ornamental flowering shrub, but you must control its root spread with plastic grass guard; plant two for cross pollination. This cherry makes extremely tasty preserves, wine, hard cider and pies, but it is too sour for fresh eating. With a more appealing name for this fruit, it would have a tremendous commercial potential. This fruit does not grow in the tropics, and thus offers potential for global marketing. I would like to see a local industry using this fruit for high quality chocolate-covered cherries, and cherry yogurt. The first introduced plant of this species was collected in the Ural Mountains of Russia.

P. MAACKII, Amur Cherry. Perennial to Zone 1.

Height: 30 feet.
Shape: rounded tree.
Bloom: tiny clusters of white flowers open from early to mid-May with new leaves; small bitter purplish-black fruit which the birds quickly eat.
Culture: easy.
Likes: sun/semidry.
Tolerates: half-sun/dry/moist.
Propagation: sets (buy only sets with their terminal bud tips intact).
Comments: glossy cinnamon-colored bark exfoliates attractively. Prune this tree only to accentuate its tall form and remove the weak lowest branches. Though usually grown as a tree, this plant can be pruned into a good hedge. This species was named for Richard Maack, a Russian naturalist.

P. PADUS, European Bird Cherry, May Day Tree. Perennial to Zone 1.
Height: 20 feet.
Shape: lollipop-shaped rounded tree; showy small street tree.
Bloom: 6-inch-long clusters of fragrant almond-scented white flowers from late April to early May; small bitter black fruit in July attracts birds who otherwise would be raiding domestic fruit trees.
Foliage: leafs out very early while the tree is flowering, some yellow fall color.
Culture: easy.
Likes: sun/moist.
Tolerates: half-sun/dry/semidry.
Propagation: sets (buy this plant only on its own roots; make sure its terminal bud tip is intact).
Comments: when young, this tree occasionally sunscalds in the winter. Do not plant over sidewalks which the fruit could stain. This plant is somewhat susceptible to black knot disease on its branches (simply prune off affected areas); prune after flowering to accentuate its natural form and remove interior branches and the weak lowest branches. 'Rancho' is a red-leaf variety bred by Dr. Skinner and long associated with Clayton Berg's Valley Nursery of Helena, Montana. At maturity, this variety becomes a dramatic wide-spreading tree. The variety 'Coloratus' or 'Pink Mayday' has pink flowers and red-purple foliage. 'Dropmore' is a very hardy greenleaf hybrid of *Prunus padus x*

P. virginiana with a very early bloom and especially large flower clusters. 'Purpurea,' the 'Burgundyleaf' Mayday, has purplish-green foliage and dark purple flowers.

P. PUMILA, Creeping Sand Cherry. Perennial to Zone 2.
Height: 1 foot high by 6 feet wide; fast-spreading creeper habit.
Bloom: insignificant white flowers in early May.
Foliage: grayish-green foliage.
Likes: sun/half-sun/dry/semidry/moist.
Propagation: sets or seeds.
Comments: this plant makes a good ground cover because it stays in place. Its roots do not spread sucker plants like Sand Cherry (*Prunus besseyi*).

P. X SKINNERI 'BATON ROUGE,' Muckle-Plum. Perennial to Zone 1.
Height: 6 feet.
Bloom: explosively profuse pink flowers but an extremely short bloom in early May.
Likes: sun/moist.
Tolerates: half-sun/semidry.
Propagation: sets (buy only sets with their terminal bud tip intact; softwood cuttings or soft-hardwood cuttings in summer).
Comments: prune out oldest wood after flowering to encourage new growth. For longest lasting cut flowers, crush stem ends. This hybrid of Canada Plum (*Prunus nigra*) and Russian Almond (*P. tenella*) was introduced by Frank Skinner, Dropmore, Manitoba, in 1939. The name memorializes Mr. R. M. Muckle of Clandeboye, Manitoba.

P. TENELLA, Russian Almond. Perennial to Zone 1.
Height: 3 feet.
Bloom: profuse deep pink or red flowers from mid- to late April.
Shape: upright bush.
Foliage: yellow fall color.
Culture: easy.
Likes: half-sun/moist.
Tolerates: sun/semidry.
Propagation: sets.
Comments: root suckers some; prune out oldest wood after flowering to encourage new growth. For longest lasting cut flowers, crush stem ends. The variety 'Firehill' has dark red flowers and is usually sold grafted onto Sand Cherry (*Prunus*

besseyi) rootstock to reduce root suckering.

P. TOMENTOSA, Nanking Cherry. Perennial to Zone 1.
Height: 6 feet.
Bloom: profuse pinkish-white flowers open before leaves in late April, bright red cherries with excellent sweet flavor for eating fresh off bush (this is the only sweet cherry we can grow here); fruit ripens

Nanking Cherry, Prunus tomentosa

from late June to early July.
Shape: fast-growing showy compact bush.
Foliage: attractive.
Culture: easy.
Likes: sun/moist.
Tolerates: half-sun/semidry.
Propagation: sets (softwood cuttings or soft-hardwood cuttings in summer).
Comments: plant two for cross-pollination (if you plant several bushes, there will be enough fruit for both you and the birds to feast on); for best fruit harvest, prune out oldest wood every couple years after flowering; this bush makes both a good hedge and an outstanding ornamental flowering shrub, but you must control its root spread with plastic grass guard. Frank Meyer of the USDA mailed 42,000 seeds of this plant from China to Mandan Station, North Dakota in 1913.

P. TRILOBA 'MULTIPLEX,' Double Flowering Almond. Perennial to Zone 2.
Height: 8 feet.
Bloom: showy but brief display of double pink flowers which open before foliage expands in early May.
Foliage: yellow fall color.
Culture: easy.
Likes: half-sun.

Tolerates: sun/semidry/moist.
Propagation: sets.
Comments: does not root sucker if grown on its own roots; prune out oldest wood annually after flowering. For longest lasting cut flowers, crush stem ends. The variety 'Multiplex' was selected by William Kerr of Saskatoon, Saskatchewan. In landscaping use, place this shrub in the background. It has little ornamental value after it is out of bloom.

P. VIRGINIANA SSP. MELANOCARPA, Chokecherry. Native to most of North America. Perennial to Zone 1.
Height: 25 feet.
Bloom: white flower clusters from early to mid-May with new leaves; small black cherries in July.
Shape: small multi-trunked tree.
Likes: semidry.
Tolerates: sun/half-sun/dry.
Propagation: softwood cuttings or soft-hardwood cuttings in summer.
Comments: because this species forms root suckers so abundantly, plant only named horticultural varieties, and these should be grafted onto Mayday (*Prunus padus*) rootstocks. The subspecies *Melanocarpa* is the native western form. That name means 'black-fruited.' The best red foliage variety is 'Canada Red,' a new variety with larger leaves and a superior red color. An older redleaf variety is 'Schubert.' It was introduced by Dr. George Will of Bismarck, North Dakota. 'Schubert Copper' has coppery-purple foliage and red fruit. It was selected by John Wallace of Beaverhead Nursery in Beaverhead, Alberta. 'Mini Schubert' is a densely compact small size tree with red foliage. It is an excellent candidate for formal lollipop-shaped trees. 'Boughen Yellow' has yellow fruit mild enough to eat fresh. It was selected by W. J. Boughen of Boughen Nursery in Valley River, Manitoba. 'Spearfish' is a similar yellow-fruited chokecherry introduced in 1924 by Dr. N. E. Hansen of Brookings, South Dakota.

PSORALEA ESCULENTA, Indian Breadroot, Prairie Turnip, Tipsinin (Blackfoot name); once native to a

wide area of the Great Plains, now rare and threatened. Perennial.
Height: 6 inches.
Bloom: attractive blue-purple clover-like flowerheads, blooms from mid-June to July (brief season).
Foliage: attractive woolly gray-green lupine-like foliage.
Likes: sun/half-sun/dry/semidry/moist.
Propagation: roots or seeds.
Comments: egg-sized edible root (buried about 4 inches underground); the plant goes dormant and disappears completely in mid-July. This small but attractive plant was an important foodstuff for the Indians, who harvested it in June to early July at the end of its flowering. They ate it raw or roasted. Today, it is only found on rare undisturbed prairie. Plants in their native habitat should not be disturbed. The flavor of the root is considered very good (Kim Williams described it as a cross between a potato and a turnip). During the 1880s, the French briefly experimented with growing it commercially, calling it "Picquotinae." Two closely related species *Psoralea argophylla* and *P. ceolata* are more common but less attractive.

PULMONARIA SACCHARATA, Bethlehem Sage. Perennial to Zone 2.
Height: 8 inches.
Bloom: profuse pink to blue flowers from early May to early July (long season).
Foliage: attractive white and green mottled foliage.
Likes: half-shade.
Tolerates: shade/moist.
Propagation: sets or seeds.
Comments: winter mulch in exposed areas; for greatest attractiveness, shear off flower stalks after flowering. This plant is useful for the front edging of a shady garden. A dramatically showy variety is *'Argentea,'* which has bright silvery-white foliage and blue flowers from pink buds.

Bethlehem Sage, Pulmonaria saccharata

PUMPKIN, *Cucurbita pepo.* Warm-season annual fruit.
Height: vine 1 foot tall by 6 to 10 feet wide.
Description: sprawling vine with coarse foliage and large orange fruit.
Propagation: seeds or sets. Start seed inside and plant outside after frost-free date; seed germinates easily if soaked overnight.
Likes: sun/moist/wet/deeply dug humus- and fertilizer-rich soil.
Growing tips: heavy water user; requires maximum heat and sun. For best growth, give it wind protection and maximum warmth; to increase heat retention in the soil use a clear plastic layer over a black plastic groundcover.

Pumpkin, Cucurbita pepo

Companion plant with corn; shallow rooted (avoid soil compaction); for best fruit sets, plant at least two for cross pollination and encourage bees.
Harvest tips: when harvesting fruit, cut the stem to avoid damaging the plant.
Comments: Native to tropical America, this plant requires a long hot growing season and ample space around it (radius of 4 feet per plant).

Pumpkins will store moderately well if the skin is ripened. Test with a fingernail as you would a winter squash. Store it in a dry cool area. The flesh can be preserved after it is cooked and strained, then frozen for later use.

Recommended varieties are 'Sugar Pie,' the sweetest variety for pies and bread; and 'Lady Godiva,' grown for its hull-less seeds suitable for roasting. There are a number of varieties bred for huge size, but their flavor is poor.

The either male or female flowers (female flowers have a tiny fruit attached) can be fried in butter and served as a vegetable or an appetizer. These flowers can also be used as an edible garnish.

PURSLANE, *Portulaca oleracea.* Annual vegetable.
Height: 2 inches; fast-spreading sprawling creeper.
Culture: easy.
Likes: sun/half-sun/dry/semidry/moist.
Propagation: seeds.
Tolerates: extremely poor soil.
Harvest tips: if you harvest only the plant tips, the plant can regrow quickly.
Comments: succulent stems and foliage used as a choice salad green, it has a mildly acidic flavor. Very invasive due to self-sown seeds, but unwanted plants are easily weeded out. This plant is a common weed already present in most people's gardens. Once you taste it, you will never ignorantly weed it out of your garden again.

It is a succulent, and thus uprooted plants moved into your garden will self-sow new plants into your garden. There is also a variety of this plant developed for its ornamental flowers.

In the garden, Purslane can be used both as a living mulch in among other plants or intercropped with tall sun-loving plants. Livestock relishes this plant. A closely related plant is *Portulaca grandiflora.*

In many parts of the world, this plant is sold as a cherished green. In our area, purslane has commercial potential to be sold to restaurants.

Kim Williams suggested using the greens in salads, in soups for its mucilaginous properties, or blanching and freezing it like spinach. She mentioned a casserole of purslane, eggs, and breadcrumbs. Or the black seeds can be used like buckwheat.

PUSCHKINIA SCILLOIDES. Perennial to Zone 3.
Height: 6 inches.
Bloom: grayish-blue scilla-like flowers (fragrant with violet-like scent) from late April to early May.
Foliage: narrow.
Culture: very easy.
Likes: half-shade/semidry.
Tolerates: half-sun/dry/moist.
Propagation: bulbs (bury 3 inches deep).
Comments: this plant was named for Puschkin, a Russian botanist.

PYRUS USSURIENSIS, Ussurian Pear. Perennial to Zone 1.
Height: 30 feet.
Shape: dense well-shaped rounded tree (fast-growing habit).
Bloom: showy profuse white flowers in late April; edible (but very poor textured) greenish-yellow small fruit (fruit drops to the ground hard and eventually gets messy).
Foliage: handsome glossy green foliage, showy red-or-ange fall color, spurlike thorns.
Culture: easy.
Likes: sun/moist.
Tolerates: half-sun/semidry.
Propagation: sets

*Ussurian Pear,
Pyrus ussuriensis*

(buy only sets with their terminal bud tip intact; hardwood cuttings in fall).
Comments: prune only to accentuate tall form. The variety 'Ure' named for Mr. C. R. Ure is presently considered to have the best fruit. It was introduced by Morden Research Station, Manitoba, in 1978. The commercial pear *(Pyrus communis)* has a hardy variety named 'Parker' (introduced by the University of Minnesota, 1934) which has fruited successfully in Bozeman, Montana. However, this does not mean it would also fruit successfully in plains areas. Other risky varieties include 'Goldenspice' (University of Minnesota, 1949), 'Summercrisp' (University of Minnesota), 'Luscious,' and 'Patten.' These may be foliage hardy but not predictably fruit hardy. Breeding for bud cold tolerance, delayed spring flowering, and early fruit ripening is needed.

QUERCUS SPECIES, Oak. Various species are the official state trees of seven U.S. states. The Druids derived their name from their word for this tree. In Roman and Norse mythology, oaks were considered sacred to Jupiter and Thor.

Q. BICOLOR, Swamp White Oak. Perennial to Zone 3.
Height: 40 feet.
Shape: fast-growing tree, narrow form when young but wide-spreading at maturity.
Foliage: shiny dark green foliage, some yellow-brown to red fall color.
Likes: sun/moist.
Tolerates: half-sun/wet.
Propagation: sets (buy only sets with their terminal bud tips intact).
Comments: this tree is very sensitive to alkalinity and prefers humus-rich soil; because of its taproot, it transplants poorly and often suffers transplant shock. It is best moved when very young. Prune only in winter. This plant often suffers from chlorosis (remedy with chelated iron or water leaching of the soil). Other hardy oaks are *Quercus alba* (White Oak—hardy to Zone 3), *Q. ellipsoidalis* (Northern Pin Oak—hardy to Zone 4),and *Q. rubra* (Red

*Swamp White Oak, Quercus
bicolor*

Oak—hardy to Zone 4). Unfortunately, these are even more sensitive to alkaline soil.

Q. MACROCARPA, Burr Oak. Perennial to Zone 1.
Height: 60 feet.
Shape: slow-growing tree with a strong central leader; at maturity it forms a picturesque spreading tree.
Foliage: some yellow fall color.
Likes: sun/moist/humus-rich soil.
Tolerates: half-sun/dry/semidry/moist/alkaline soil.
Propagation: sets (buy only sets with their terminal bud tips intact).
Comments: because of its taproot, it transplants poorly and often suffers transplant shock. It is best moved

when very young; prune only in winter. This eastern tree is native as far west as the lower Yellowstone River drainage in Montana and north to the Qu'Appelle Valley of Saskatchewan. It has the sweetest acorns of any oak. To use, grind up acorns and leach the bitter acids from the meal with water. Kim Williams suggested putting the acorn meal either in a bag in a stream or in a bucket placed under a dripping faucet for a couple of days. She stated that bread made from acorn flour has a pleasing sweet nut-like flavor and suggested trying it for muffins and pancakes, too.

Q. MONGOLICA, Mongolian Oak. Perennial to Zone 3.
Height: 15 feet.
Shape: moderately fast-growing multi-trunked tree.
Foliage: glossy green foliage which turns red, then brown, and attractively hangs on tree throughout the winter.
Likes: sun/moist.
Tolerates: half-sun/semidry.
Propagation: sets (buy only sets with their terminal bud tip intact).
Comments: established plants resent transplanting; prune only in winter. This attractive tree is particularly attractive in a rock garden because of its small size.

RADICCHIO, Italian Red Chicory, *Cichorium intybus.* Annual vegetable.
Height: 8 inches.
Description: round heads of small dark red leaves ribbed with white veins (some varieties have variegated red and white leaves).
Culture: difficult.
Likes: half-sun/half-shade/moist.
Growing tips: in hot summer areas give it mid-day shade; prefers a moist well drained soil; loves manure; give it a careful mulching, which holds moisture and cools the soil; it is a very frost-tolerant plant.
Propagation: sets or seeds. Because it transplants poorly, you must seed it in place in late June.
Comments: this plant is primarily used to spark up salads with its unusual strongly bitter taste and red color.

During the summer, it is a normal green color. In the fall, cut it back to the roots, and it quickly regrows its small red heads. Then it can be heavily mulched (or covered in a cold frame) to produce another crop in the very early spring.

There are two new European varieties bred for spring and summer harvest: a red one bred to be planted in the spring and harvested in mid-summer, and a green one grown in the early spring. These are both listed in Shepherd's Garden Seeds.

RADISH, *Raphanus sativus.* Cool-season annual vegetable.
Height: 6-12 inches.
Description: upright clump of coarse foliage, grown primarily for its enlarged peppery-tasting root.
Culture: easy.
Likes: sun/half-sun/half-shade/moist.
Propagation: seeds. Because seeds tolerate cold soil, plant in early April and stagger planting every two weeks for a prolonged harvest. Thin to 2 inches apart.
Pests: root maggots, white cabbage moth, flea beetle (this can be the worst pest). Besides using radishes for their roots, you can also plant radishes near brassicas (broccoli, Brussels sprouts, cabbage, cauliflower, collards, kohlrabi, parsnips, and turnips) as a trap crop for white cabbage butterfly, cutworms, and wireworms. It attracts these pests and draws them away from the more valuable crops.
Growing tips: give it mid-day shade in hot summer areas; requires an evenly cool soil; use frequent light waterings and a thick layer of mulch; prefers low nitrogen soil or else roots get pithy.
Harvest tips: taste quality is best when grown fast and harvested when marble-sized at 40 days from seeds. When they get large, they get tough, bitter, and hot. A rule of thumb: you can generally harvest radishes one month from sowing.
Comments: hot weather will cause its 3-foot-tall lavender or white flowers to bolt. It is native to Asia and grown since ancient times.

Winter radishes are grown somewhat differently. They are planted in late June to July and harvested in late fall, requiring cool growing temperatures. They can also be grown well in a coldframe or unheated greenhouse during the winter.

RANUNCULUS GLABERRINUS, Sagebrush Buttercup. Native to sagebrush areas and open ponderosa pine forests of the foothills. Perennial.
Height: 4 inches.
Bloom: showy yellow to white shiny flowers on short stalks, blooms from March to early May.
Foliage: semi-erect clump of shiny smooth semi-thick foliage.
Likes: sun/half-sun/dry/semidry/moist.
Propagation: sets or seeds (encourage it to self-sow in favorable location).
Comments: thickened fibrous roots. Plant goes dormant and disappears in late spring. This amazingly early and showy beacon of spring should be better known.

RATIBIDA COLUMNIFERA, Prairie Coneflower, native to the plains and Rocky Mountains. Perennial to Zone 2.
Height: 2 feet.
Bloom: yellow flowers with a black thimble-like center on long stalks, blooms from July to August.
Foliage: finely-divided hairy green leaves.
Likes: semidry.
Tolerates: sun/half-sun/dry/moist.
Propagation: sets or seeds.
Comments: upright clump habit. Indians made a tea from the flowerheads and leaves, and a yellow-orange dye from the roots.

RESEDA ODORATA, Mignonette. Annual.
Height: 8 inches.
Bloom: oddly colored greenish-orange flower spikes with a powerful violet-like fragrance, blooms from May to frost (long season if seed planting is staggered).
Likes: half-sun/moist/humus-rich soil.
Tolerates: sun/half-shade.
Propagation: sets (transplant carefully) or seeds.
Comments: because of its distinctive fragrance, this plant is delightful in flower beds, containers, window boxes, or for cutting; however, it is not a showy flower.

RHAMNUS FRANGULA, Glossy Buckthorn. Perennial to Zone 2.
Height: 8 feet.
Shape: upright shrub form.
Bloom: insignificant dark purple fruit held until eaten by the birds.

Glossy Buckthorn, Rhamus frangula

Foliage: glossy dark green leaves.
Culture: easy.
Likes: sun/half-sun/half-shade/dry/semidry/moist.
Tolerates: poor soil.
Propagation: sets.
Comments: a narrowly upright variety 'Columnaris,' makes an excellent hedge that does not require pruning.

RHEUM PALMATUM, Ornamental Rhubarb. Perennial to Zone 2.
Height: 2 feet.
Bloom: some varieties have showy red flower stalks.
Foliage: large green leaves come out in early spring.
Culture: very easy.
Likes: sun/moist/well-drained soil.
Tolerates: half-sun/semidry.
Propagation: sets.
Comments: bold showy plant. 'Bowle's Crimson' has red flower clusters; 'R. tanguticum' has finely-divided foliage. There are other ornamental species of this exotic looking plant.

RHODODENDRON CANADENSE, Rhododendron. Perennial to Zone 4-5 (protected areas only).
Height: 5 feet.
Bloom: showy pink flowers in mid-April.
Foliage: deciduous.
Likes: half-shade/moist/acidic soil (if possible, buy special soil for it).
Propagation: sets.
Comments: best located where protected from wind and spring warmth (north or northeast exposure). The species 'Rhododendron daurica' is a showy deciduous bush from Asia with magenta-pink flowers in mid April; 'PJM Hybrids' are bred from this line and are semi-evergreen. There is a series of ultra-hardy hybrid azaleas from the University of Minnesota—including 'Orchid Lights'—hardy to -45° F. This variety has an attractive small habit and orchid pink flowers.

RHUBARB, Rheum rhaponticum. Perennial vegetable to Zone 1.
Height: 2 feet.
Description: attractive clump of large tropical-looking poisonous leaves; red or green stems are used in pies, sauces, preserves, wine, and baked in cakes and bread.
Culture: easy.
Likes: sun/semidry/deeply dug, humus-rich soil with bonemeal added/light soil.
Tolerates: half-sun/dry/semidry/moderately heavy clay.
Propagation: sets.
Growing tips: plants need ample room and do not like competition from grass and weeds; remove flowerstalks for optimal plant vigor. *Harvest tips:* to harvest, pull stems, don't cut

Rhubarb, Rheum rhaponticum

them. Do not harvest until third year after planting. Then harvest stems up to 6 weeks until new stalks become spindly.

Varieties produce either red or green stems. The green-stemmed varieties produce an appealing soft pinkish-red color when cooked. These are 'German Wine,' 'Sutton's Seedless,' and 'Victoria'. Red-stemmed varieties maintain their vivid red color after cooking. These are 'Canada Red,' 'Crimson Wine,' 'McDonald,' 'Ruby,' and 'Valentine'.

Though the stems are edible, the leaves are very poisonous. Some nurseries keep rhubarb plants in their greenhouses to control white flies. The flies eat the leaves and die.

Originally native to Siberia, it was introduced to Europe in the 17th century.

RHUS GLABRA SSP. CISMONTANA, Creeping Sumac. This subspecies is native to the east side of the Rocky Mountains. Perennial to Zone 1.
Height: 3 feet.
Bloom: brief yellow flowers before foliage opens in late April, red fruit clusters.
Foliage: spectacular red fall color.

Culture: easy.
Likes: very dry.
Tolerates: sun/half-sun/semidry/moist/alkaline soil.
Propagation: sets or seeds or softwood cuttings in summer.
Comments: low spreading shrubby clump; invasive by root spreading. This plant grows into a low thicket, which makes it excellent for use as a ground cover. Indians dried the red autumn leaves to use as tobacco. The roots were used to obtain a yellow dye, and the inner bark and stems were used for basket weaving. The edible red fruit clusters can be used to make a drink that resembles lemonade. Kim Williams suggested adding the acidic juice from this fruit to enhance the flavor of elderberry jelly.

R. TYPHINA, Staghorn Sumac Tree. Perennial to Zone 1, low multi-trunked tree to height 20 feet.
Bloom: red fruit clusters at the branch tips; branches are covered with a distinctive velvety fuzz, which gives winter interest.
Foliage: finely-divided foliage with spectacular red fall color.
Culture: easy.
Likes: moist.
Tolerates: sun/half-sun/dry/semidry.
Propagation: sets (softwood cuttings in summer).
Comments: the red fruit clusters can be used to make a lemonade drink. This species would be more popular in landscaping if bred for dramatically large red clusters to brighten the winter garden. The variety *'Laciniata'* (Cutleaf Sumac) has very finely-divided leaves and a tropical appearance. Its form is relatively low and irregular, making it look spectacular in a planter box.

Staghorn Sumac Tree, Rhus typhina

RHYNCHELYTRUM REPENS (Tricholaena rosea), Ruby Grass. Annual.
Height: 3 feet.
Bloom: red, pink or purple airy grassheads with a silky texture from July to frost.

Likes: moist/humus-rich, sandy soil/heat.
Tolerates: sun/semidry.
Propagation: sets.
Comments: clump habit. This showy plant resembles a rosy-pink haze. It can be used either in the garden, in containers, or as a cut flower in arrangements. The variety *'Atropurpurea'* has purplish-red grass heads. Native to the Natal area of South Africa.

RIBES ALPINUM, Alpine Currant Bush. Perennial to Zone 1.
Height: 4 feet.
Bloom: profuse yellow flowers in mid-April (a hardy substitute for Forsythia).
Culture: easy.
Likes: half-sun/moist/humus-rich soil.
Tolerates: sun/half-shade/dry/semidry.
Propagation: softwood cuttings or hardwood cuttings in summer or winter.

Alpine Currant Bush, Ribes alpinum

Comments: prune to shape in the spring after flowering, prune out oldest wood in the fall; buy male sets only, females are carriers for pine blister rust. This is a good shrub for shady areas. It also makes an excellent shade-tolerant hedge.

RIBES HYBRIDS, Currants and Gooseberries; currants are smooth-stemmed and gooseberries have prickles. Perennial to Zone 1.
Height: 4 feet.
Shape: upright arching bush.
Culture: easy.
Likes: sun/moist/humus-rich soil/manure.
Tolerates: half-sun/semidry.
Propagation: sets only, best planted in early spring (layering in the spring or cuttings in the fall).
Comments: may suffer chlorosis in highly alkaline soil; for best fruit harvest, space apart 4-5 feet. Prune out all branches more than three years old every spring just before the new buds start to swell; self pollinating, but produces better with cross pollination.

Currants and Gooseberries are excellent sources of Vitamin C. Be forewarned, birds love this fruit. In fact, many people plant currants with their raspberries because both fruits ripen at about the same time, and birds seem to prefer the currants. Currants and gooseberries make an excellent forage for free run chickens.

CURRANTS. Black, red, orange, yellow, or white berries. Fruit can be used fresh, in jam, or frozen for later use. Red or white varieties are used for jellies and jams; black varieties are used for their unique flavor in jam, juice, wine or dried like raisins. Slightly unripe currants are more tart and make better jam. Nearly all known varieties are extremely hardy to Zone 1-2. Varieties of note are the following.

Currant, Ribes Hybrid

'Consort' is a large, strong-flavored black currant, late ripening. It is one of the new white pine blister rust immune varieties.

'Perfection' is a heavy bearer of high quality red fruit. It is extremely cold hardy in far northern Canada.

'Prince Albert' is a vigorous and productive variety with good quality fruit. It is resistant to aphids.

'Red Lake' has clusters of large high quality red fruit, late ripening. It was introduced by Charles Haralson, University of Minnesota, in 1933.

'Viking' is a late season red variety. It is resistant to white pine blister rust.

'White Imperial' is a heavy bearer of large high quality fruit best used to make a pale pink jelly. It is extremely cold hardy in far northern Canada.

'Willoughby,' a black currant, is a heavy bearer of excellent quality fruit. It is resistant to both white pine blister rust and mildew. Additionally, it is extremely cold hardy in far northern Canada.

GOOSEBERRIES. Gooseberries are prickly and currants are smooth-stemmed. Red, pink, yellow, or green berries; fruit can be used fresh, in jam or pies, or frozen for later use. Unripe gooseberries (hard as rocks) make the best pies and jam. Varieties of note are the following:

'Abundance' has attractive pink-purple fruit; heavy producer. Introduced by Fargo Research Station, Fargo, North Dakota, in 1932.

'Green Giant' has large, good flavored, green fruit.

'Itinnomaeki' is a red fruit variety.

'Pembina Pride' is a green-fruited variety with more vigor than 'Pixwell.'

'Pixwell' has grape-like clusters of pink fruit which hang below the plant's thorns. Mr. A. F. Yeager of North Dakota is credited with discovering this variety, introduced in 1932.

'Poorman' is an old green-fruited variety with exceptional flavor.

R. ODORATUM (R. aureum), Clove-scented Currant, Golden Currant, Buffalo Currant. Native to streambanks of the plains and foothills. Perennial to Zone 1.
Height: 5 feet.
Bloom: bright yellow flowers (fragrant only at night) in early to mid-May.
Foliage: turns a red-orange color in early fall.
Culture: very easy.
Likes: sun/half-sun/half-shade/very dry/semidry/moist.
Propagation: sets (softwood cuttings or hardwood cuttings in summer or winter).
Comments: some root suckering. Prune to shape in the spring after flowering, prune out oldest wood in the fall. Oddly enough, this plant's yellow flowers attract hummingbirds. The variety *'Abol'* was selected by Brooks Research Station for its improved fruit. This plant is known to be an alternate host for pine blister rust, but it is not a strong carrier like the notorious Black Currant (*Ribes nigra*). How-

Golden Currant, Ribes odoratum

ever, do not plant this currant within 900 feet of a five-needle pine, such as Western White Pine (*Pinus monticola*) or Limber Pine (*Pinus flexilis*). Ponderosa Pine (*Pinus ponderosa*—with 3 needles) and Mugo Pine (*Pinus mugo*—with 2 needles) are not susceptible to this disease. If in doubt about the safety of any nearby pines, count the number of needles in a bunch. Five-needle pines are the only ones affected by this problem. A distance of nine hundred feet between a currant bush and a susceptible pine is considered safe. Rust diseases are becoming much less of a problem because the affected pines are slowly developing an immunity.

RICINUS COMMUNIS, Castor Bean. Annual.
Height: 4 feet.
Bloom: tropical-looking bush with dramatically large five-lobed leaves, clusters of black seeds.
Likes: sun/moist/deeply dug humus-rich soil.
Propagation: sets or seeds. (Seed germination: plant seeds inside for an early start, or outside after the frost-free date.)
Comments: seeds are used to make castor bean oil. However, the foliage and especially the seeds are extremely poisonous.

ROCKET, Roquette, Arugula (*Eruca vesicaria*). Cool-season annual vegetable.
Culture: easy.
Likes: sun/half-sun/half-shade/moist.
Propagation: sets or seeds (stagger plantings from early spring to early fall).
Harvest tips: harvest leaves when they are 2-3 inches long. If you do not constantly harvest the young leaves, they get bitter.
Comments: this plant bolts to flower quickly, and thus the name Rocket. Fast-growing plant used for its peppery-tasting young leaves in salads and as a cooked green. The peppery-tasting flowers can also be used sprinkled into salads.

ROSA, Climbing Roses; Zone 3 with protection.
Height: 10 feet.
Climbing habit: loose.
Likes: sun/moist/humus-rich, fertilizer-rich soil.
Tolerates: half-sun.

Propagation: sets.

Comments: because these roses bloom on old wood, very few varieties can be grown, and these must be taken down in late September or early October and the entire canes carefully winter-mulched. First, the vines are laid across the ground to slowly adjust, then a week later they are weighed down and covered with straw or peat. In the spring they are uncovered in stages like hybrid tea roses. Climber roses must be tied to their support. They do not have tendrils to climb with. The hardiest choices are:

'America'—pink flowers.
'Blaze'—red flowers.
'Blossomtime'—pink flowers.
'Coral Dawn'—pink flowers.
'Elegance'—yellow flowers.
'Flame Dance'—red flowers.
'Golden Showers'—yellow flowers.
'Heidelberg'—pink flowers.
'Henry Kelsey'
Height: to 4 feet.
Climbing habit: trailing.
Bloom: very fragrant red flowers in dramatically large clusters, blooms from July to frost continuously.
Comments: resistant to mildew, susceptible to black spot. Though hardy to Zone 2, lowering branches and winter-mulching is recommended for best appearance in extreme climates.
'Illusion'—red flowers.
'Improved Blaze'—red flowers, fragrant.
'John Cabot'—arching branches to 8 feet.
Climbing habit: strong climber.
Bloom: large fragrant red flowers from June to July and sporadic rebloom in August to September.
Comments: resistant to mildew and black spot. Some winter dieback in extremely exposed areas of Zone 2, but it recovers quickly. This plant was named for the explorer who claimed North America for England. He was Genoese, like Columbus, and his real name was Giovanni Caboto. Introduced in 1978.
'John Davis'
Height: vine to 6 feet.
Climbing habit: trailing.
Bloom: profuse fragrant pink flowers from July to frost continuously.
Comments: resistant to mildew and

black spot.
'New Dawn'—pink flowers, fragrant.
'Paul's Scarlet Climber'—scarlet red variety.
'Prairie Princess'—a double pink variety, its large red hips are held attractively in the fall and winter. Developed by Dr. Griffith Buck of Iowa State University.
'Rhode Island Red'—red flowers.
'Rhonda'—pink flowers.
'Rosanna'—a fragrant variety.
'Rosarium Eutersen'—pink flowers.
'Shalom'—red flowers.
'William Baffin'—arching branches to 8 feet.
Climbing habit: strong climber.
Bloom: profuse pink flowers with yellow at the base of the petals, flowers borne in dramatically large clusters in July and rebloom in August, attractive glossy foliage.
Comments: resistant to mildew and black spot. This is the hardiest climber rose for Zone 2. It can be left unprotected throughout the winter.

ROSA SPECIES, Rose; Official Floral Emblem of Alberta, Czechoslovakia, England, Honduras, Iran, Poland, and Romania; Official State Flower of the District of Columbia, Georgia, Iowa, New York, North Dakota; this flower was selected as the official U.S. national flower.

In Europe, the rose was used as a symbol of loyalty. For centuries in England, a rose was often mentioned in the contract of a rental agreement as a symbol of loyalty to the landlord. During the War of the Roses, the color of the rose became critically important.

In deer areas, it can become a real struggle to keep hybrid tea roses from being eaten to the ground, thorns and all. For longest-lasting cut flowers, cut in the bud stage and crush stem ends. For greatest attractiveness, plant shrub roses with Baby's Breath (*Gypsophila elegans).*

Rose hips are a rich source of Vita-

min A and C, calcium, and iron. Kim Williams suggested using this fruit for jam, syrup, and tea. For best taste, mix with apple juice.

There are three main rose societies: the American Rose Society, the Canadian Rose Society, and the Heritage Rose Society (for shrub roses).

Order of bloom: *Rosa spinosissima* (late May to early June), *R. foetida bicolor* (early to mid-June), *R. cinnamomea* (early to late June), *R. eglanteria* (mid-June), *R. harrisonii* (mid-June), *R. rubrifolia* (mid- to late June), *R. alba* (late June to mid-July), *R. arkansana* (late June to late July), *R. damascena* (late June to early July), *R. gallica* (late June to mid-July), *R. nitida* (late June to mid-July), *R. virginiana* (late June to late July), *R. rugosa* (June to frost), Hybrid Teas (June to frost) and Climbers (June to frost), Portland Group (July to frost) and *R. centifolia* (July).

R. X ALBA, White Rose. Perennial to Zone 2-3.

White Rose, Rosa x alba

Height: 7 feet.
Bloom: very fragrant white flowers from late June to mid-July; showy large hips held in the fall and winter.
Shape: dense upright shrub.
Culture: easy.
Likes: sun/moist/humus-rich soil/fertilizer.
Tolerates: half-sun/semidry/moist.
Comments: This rose dates back to ancient Roman times. The variety *'Maxima'* has fragrant double white flowers; *'Semi Plena'* has fragrant semi-double white flowers with a showy gold center.
Propagation: sets.

R. ARKANSANA, Prairie Rose, official state flower of North Dakota. Native to sandy areas of the plains and foothills. Perennial to Zone 1.
Height: 2 feet.
Bloom: fragrant light pink (single or double) flowers in early June to late July (long season).
Shape: spreading clump of bramble.
Culture: easy.
Likes: moist.
Tolerates: sun/dry/semidry/moist/poor soil.

Propagation: sets or seeds.

Comments: Indians used dried rose hips as beads before trade beads became available. Two natural varieties are the following: 'Ratonensis' has pink flowers spotted with red and white flecks; 'Woodrow' has double light pink flowers. It was named after the prairie man who found it in the wild. The Parkland Series hybrids were bred from crosses with this species and others developed by Dr. H. Marshall of Morden Research Station, Manitoba. They are all rated to Zone 2 with snow cover. They die to snow level and bloom the following summer from new growth.

PARKLAND SERIES HYBRIDS

'Adelaide Hoodless,' vigorous upright shrub.

Height: 3 feet.

Bloom: profuse red double flowers in large clusters from June to frost; good red hips held in the fall and winter.

Foliage: glossy.

Comments: susceptible to blackspot. Introduced in 1973 and named after the founder of the Women's Institutes of Canada. It makes a long-lasting cut flower.

'Cuthbert Grant'

Height: 3 feet.

Bloom: large fragrant dark red flowers continuously from late June to frost.

Comments: resistant to blackspot; introduced in 1967; Manitoba's Centennial Rose and the WCSH's 'Award of Merit' in 1970.

'Morden Amorette,' a dwarf variety.

Height: 2 feet.

Bloom: extremely profuse double carmine to rose-pink flowers from July to frost; good show of red hips in the fall and winter.

Comments: resistant to mildew and rust and only partially susceptible to blackspot. Introduced in 1977.

'Morden Cardinette'

Height: 2 feet.

Bloom: double cardinal red flowers both in clusters and singly from July to frost.

Comments: this rose can also be grown outdoors in pots. Resistant to rust and blackspot. Seems to do poorly in far northern areas of the chinook zone. Introduced in 1980.

'Morden Centennial,' vigorous bush.

Height: to 5 feet.

Bloom: very large pink flowers both in clusters and singly; profuse display of red hips in the fall and winter.

Comments: fully resistant to rust and mildew. Introduced in 1980 and named for the Centennial Celebration of the town of Morden, Manitoba.

R. CENTIFOLIA, Cabbage Rose. Perennial to Zone 3.

Height: 6 feet.

Bloom: very fragrant rose-pink flowers in July.

Shape: arching shrub.

Culture: easy.

Likes: sun/moist/rich sandy soil.

Tolerates: half-sun/semidry.

Propagation: sets.

Comments: this species dates back to the early 16th century. The common name Cabbage Rose refers to the ball-like or cabbage-like appearance with many overlapping petals of the flowers. 'Cristata' has very fragrant pink flowers and the largest flowers of any rose listed here (4 inches across); 'Moscosa' (Moss Rose) has fragrant mossy-looking flowers with an unusual herbal-pine rose scent; 'Rosa de Peintres' (Rose of the Painters) has large pink flowers.

*Cabbage Rose,
Rosa centifolia*

R. CINNAMOMEA, Cinnamon Rose. Perennial to Zone 3.

Height: 10 feet tall by 8 feet wide.

Bloom: profuse fragrant single pink flowers from early to late June, bark on branches is cinnamon-colored.

Shape: wide—arching shrub (give it lots of room).

Tolerates: half-sun/semidry.

Likes: sun/moist.

Propagation: sets.

Comments: this rose dates back to the 16th century. There is a double-flowering variety named 'Plena.'

R. DAMASCENA, Damask Rose. Perennial to Zone 4 (protected areas only).

Height: 5 feet.

Bloom: extremely fragrant red, pink, or white flowers from late June to late July (long season).

Shape: shrub.

Culture: easy.

Likes: sun/moist/humus- and fertilizer-rich soil.

Tolerates: half-sun/semidry/moist.

Propagation: sets.

Comments: this rose was brought from Damascus to Europe by the Crusaders. 'Celsiana' has very large pink flowers and is one of the

*Damask Rose,
Rosa damascena*

most fragrant roses on this list. It dates back before 1750. 'Madame Hardy,' which has very fragrant white flowers dates back to 1832. 'York and Lancaster' is a very fragrant red-and-white bicolor rose. This rose, ironically, appeared shortly after the end of the thirty-year 'War of the Roses' fought for the throne of England by the House of York (whose symbol was the White Rose, *Rosa alba*) and the House of Lancaster (whose symbol was the red rose, *Rosa gallica*). Henry Tudor, a relative of Lancaster, married Elizabeth of York. This ended the war and established the house of Tudor on the throne. The official date for this rose variety's introduction is 1551.

R. EGLANTERIA, Eglantine Rose. Perennial to Zone 4 (protected areas only).

Height: 10 feet.

Bloom: fragrant single pink flowers in mid-June.

Shape: arching shrub.

Likes: sun/moist.

Tolerates: half-sun.

Propagation: sets.

Comments: prefers less fertilizer than other roses. Mainly grown for the apple-like fragrance of its foliage, which is most pronounced after a rain, often scenting the whole garden. This plant is excellent for planting under windows. It offers both fragrance and a thorny barrier to intruders. For possible breeding potential, there is a plant held by the Beaverlodge Nursery, Beaverlodge, Alberta, called 'Victoria Sweet Briar,' whose line might be used to create a hardier Eglantine Rose.

R. FOETIDA 'BICOLOR,' Austrian Copper Rose. Perennial to Zone 2.
Height: 6 feet.
Bloom: vivid orange-red flowers with a bright yellow center from early to mid-June.
Culture: easy.
Likes: sun/moist/humus- and fertilizer-rich soil.
Tolerates: half-sun/semidry.
Propagation: sets.
Comments: unfortunately, this rose is very susceptible to blackspot. A dramatically beautiful variety is 'Persiana,' the Persian Yellow Rose, which has deep yellow flowers that are fully double. This is one of the best hardy yellow shrub roses. Other hardy yellow roses are *Rosa harisonii*, *Rosa rugosa* 'Topaz Jewel,' and *Rosa spinosissima* 'Yellow Altai' and 'Hazeldean.'

R. GALLICA, Apothecary Rose, French Rose. Perennial to Zone 3-4.
Height: 3 feet.
Shape: upright shrub.
Bloom: very fragrant red, pink, or white flowers from late June to mid-July (it blooms the same time as Madonna Lily, *Lilium candidum*).
Culture: easy.
Likes: sun/moist/humus- and fertilizer-rich soil.
Tolerates: half-sun/semidry/moist.
Propagation: sets.
Comments: this species has been cultivated commercially since the Middle Ages. The varieties listed below are hardy to Zone 3.

'Camieux'
Bloom: very fragrant red-and-white striped flowers (early to late July).
Shape: showy, arching form.

Apothecary Rose, Rosa gallica

Comments: this variety dates back to 1830.

'Charles De Mills.'
Height: 5 feet.
Bloom: fragrant crimson-maroon flowers (late June to late July). This variety dates back to the early 19th century.

'Rosa Mundi'
Bloom: fragrant red-and-white striped flowers.
Comments: dates back to the 12th century.

'President De Seze.'
Height: 4 feet.
Bloom: fragrant silvery lavender-pink flowers (mid-June to mid-July).

'Tuscany'
Bloom: fragrant velvety dark maroon semi-double flowers with showy gold stamens.
Comments: 'Tuscany Superb' is a fully double-flowering variety, but not as dramatic as the original 'Tuscany.' Both Tuscany varieties date back to the Middle Ages.

R. X HARISONII, Harison's Yellow Rose. Perennial to Zone 2.
Height: 6 feet.
Shape: arching upright shrub.
Bloom: fragrant yellow rose flowers in mid-June (brief two-week season).
Culture: very easy.
Likes: sun.
Tolerates: half-sun/very dry/semidry/poor soil.
Propagation: sets or seeds.
Comments: this rose can often be found growing at old pioneer cabins. Related to the Austrian Copper Rose, it has been cultivated since 1830. For other yellow roses, see the listings under *Rosa foetida* 'Persiana,' *Rosa rugosa* 'Topaz Jewel,' *Rosa spinosissima* 'Yellow Altai,' and 'Hazeldean.'

R. NITIDA, Shining Rose. Native to the northeastern woodlands of North America. Perennial to Zone 1.
Height: 2 feet.
Bloom: clusters of pink flowers from late June to mid-July; profuse red hips held in the fall and winter.
Shape: low shrub.
Foliage: new shoots are red and densely prickly; foliage is noticeably shiny in summer, turning reddish-purple in fall.
Likes: sun/moist/acidic soil.
Tolerates: half-sun/semidry/moist.

Propagation: sets or seed.
Comments: this acid-loving plant requires peat mixed into its soil in alkaline areas. 'Metis' is an outstanding variety with double pink flowers borne in clusters and a dramatic reddish-purple fall color display. This hybrid was developed from a cross between *Rosa nitida* and 'Therese Bugnet' by Bert Hart in Manitoba, in 1966. It is very resistant to blackspot, but unfortunately very sensitive to alkalinity.

PORTLAND ROSE GROUP. Perennial to Zone 3 (with winter protection).
Height: 4 feet.
Bloom: very fragrant red, pink, or white flowers—all with button centers and double form; blooms continuously from July to frost.
Shape: bushy upright habit.
Likes: sun/semidry.
Tolerates: half-sun/dry/drought.
Propagation: sets.
Comments: requires winter mulch like a Hybrid Tea Rose. Blooms on new wood. Varieties of note:

'Blanc de Vibert,' white flowers.
'Compe de Chambord,' very profuse pink flowers.
'Duchess of Portland' (also called 'The Portland Rose'); very profuse semi-double red flowers.
'Glendora,' salmon-pink flowers.
'Panachee de Lyon,' striped red-and-pink flowers.
'Rose de Rescht,' dark red flowers.
'Rose de Roi,' red flowers. The name means 'rose of the king' in French.

R. RUBRIFOLIA, Redleaf Rose. Perennial to Zone 1.
Height: 5 feet.
Shape: upright bush.
Bloom: small sparse pink flowers from mid- to late June, good hips held in the fall and winter.
Foliage: reddish-purple with a dramatic blue cast throughout the summer.
Likes: sun.
Tolerates: half-sun/semidry/moist.
Propagation: sets or seed.

R. RUGOSA, Rugosa Rose. Perennial to Zone 1.
Height: 5 feet.
Bloom: fragrant purplish-red, pink, or white flowers from June to September (long season but flowers are sparse after the first rush of bloom);

large red rosehips in the fall and winter.
Shape: upright arching bush.
Foliage: distinctive dark green crinkled foliage, orange fall color.
Culture: easy.
Likes: sun/moist/sandy humus-rich soil.
Tolerates: half-sun/dry/semidry.
Propagation: sets.
Comments: may become chlorotic in alkaline soil. This rose is the main source for commercial rosehips. Besides being a showy garden plant, it makes an excellent hedge or barrier plant. The name *rugosa* means 'wrinkled' and refers to the foliage.

'Belle Poitevine'
Height: 5 feet.
Bloom: very fragrant large flat pink blooms with an unusual banana-clove scent.
Comments: dates back to 1894.

'Blanc Double de Coubert'
Height: 4 feet.
Bloom: very fragrant, semi-double white flowers which fade and darken.
Comments: dates back to 1892.

'Hansa'
Height: 5 feet.
Bloom: fragrant clove-scented red-purple flowers, blooms from June to frost; very large red hips held in the fall and winter.
Comments: unfortunately, this variety is sensitive to alkaline soil (mix lots of peat in its soil when first planting). This extremely hardy variety dates back to 1905.

'Therese Bugnet'
Height: 6 feet.
Bloom: large fragrant double pink flowers on attractive reddish-brown stems, blooms from mid-June to frost recurrently, blooms on old wood, sparse thorns.
Comments: developed over a twenty-five year period by Georges Bugnet of Legal, Alberta, and introduced in 1950 by Percy Wright, Saskatoon, Saskatchewan. Bugnet is a French name pronounced 'boohn-YAA' and not 'bug-net.'

'Topaz Jewel'
Bloom: soft yellow flowers (spent flowers fall off bush naturally), strong reblooming habit.
Comments: created by Ralph Moore and introduced by Wayside Gardens.

EXPLORER SERIES HYBRIDS

These plants were developed from *Rosa rugosa* and *Rosa kordesii* for Canada by Dr. Felicitas Svejda at the Central Experimental Farm in Ottawa, Ontario. All are rated to Zone 1.

'A. MacKenzie,' *(R. kordesii* hybrid).
Height: eight 6 feet.
Bloom: profuse fragrant double red flowers with a cup-like shape, blooms from July to frost continuously.

'Champlain,' *(R. kordesii* hybrid).
Height: 3 feet.
Bloom: very profuse dark red double flowers from July to frost continuously.
Comments: much winter die-back but recovers quickly. This variety closely resembles a Floribunda Rose. Resistant to mildew; susceptible to blackspot. Introduced in 1982.

'Charles Albanel,' *(R. rugosa* hybrid).
Height: 4 feet.
Bloom: large fragrant red flowers in July (long season but flowers are sparse after the first rush of bloom).
Comments: resistant to mildew and blackspot. Its vigorous and low-growing nature make it a good ground cover. Introduced in 1982.

'David Thompson,' *(R. rugosa* hybrid).
Height: 4 feet.
Bloom: profuse fragrant large red flowers from July to frost continuously.
Comments: resistant to mildew and blackspot. This variety is particularly sensitive to highly alkaline soil (dig lots of peat into its soil before planting). Introduced in 1979.

'Henry Hudson,' *(R. rugosa* hybrid).
Height: 3 feet.
Bloom: profuse fragrant white flowers with pink hue (like apple blossoms) from July to frost continuously.
Comments: resistant to mildew and blackspot. Introduced in 1977.

'Henry Kelsey,' *(R. kordesii* hybrid). See the Climber Rose section.

'Jens Munk,' *(R. rugosa* hybrid).
Height: to 5 feet.
Bloom: very fragrant pink flowers from June to July and reblooming in August.
Shape: vigorous shrub.
Comments: resistant to mildew and

blackspot; moderate tolerance to alkalinity. This is the hardiest rose for extremely cold areas (but it usually has some tip kill anyway). Introduced in 1976.

'John Cabot,' *(R. kordesii* hybrid). See the Climber Rose section.

'John Franklin,' *(R. kordesii* hybrid).
Height: 3 feet.
Bloom: profuse fragrant red flowers with a fringed edge, borne in very large clusters from July to frost continuously.
Shape: vigorous shrub.
Comments: resistant to mildew and blackspot. Expect some winter die-back in exposed areas, but it recovers quickly. Released by the Ottawa Research Station in 1980.

'Martin Frobisher,' *(R. rugosa* hybrid). Less hardy than the others, hardy only to Zone 4.
Height: 6 feet.
Bloom: profuse large fragrant soft pink flowers from July to frost continuously, attractive reddish-brown bark (most noticeable in winter).
Shape: attractive vigorous shrub.
Comments: a poor cut flower because the petals droop quickly. In exposed areas, this rose tends to die back to the snowline, but it recovers quickly. Very susceptible to the rose cucurlio insect. Introduced in 1971.

'William Baffin.' See page 154 in the Climber Rose section.

R. SPINOSISSIMA, Scotch Rose, Burnet Rose. Perennial to Zone 2.

Scotch Rose, Rosa spinosissima

Height: 3 feet.
Bloom: profuse small fragrant white or yellow flowers from late May to early June.
Shape: rambler-like habit.
Likes: sun/moist.
Tolerates: half-sun/dry/semidry/extremely poor soil.
Comments: invasive due to root spreading and stem rooting. Though this an extremely cold-hardy plant, branch tips may winterkill slightly in exposed areas. *Spinosis-*

sima means 'the spiniest' and refers to the prickles on the branches. Varieties of note are the following: *'Alba Plena'* has double white flowers and dates back to the early 19th century; *'Altaica'* has white flowers and a strikingly vigorous tall form (up to 7 feet tall). Its unusual-looking hips are nearly black; 'Hazeldean' has profuse semidouble yellow flowers in June. It is a vigorous and disease resistant shrub growing to 7 feet tall. Introduced by Percy Wright, Saskatoon, Saskatchewan in 1948; 'Kakwa,' grows to 3 feet, has very fragrant white flowers and black hips. It was introduced by John Wallace of Beaverlodge, Alberta, in 1969; 'Yellow Altai' is an ultra-hardy single yellow variety, hardy to Zone 1. It is a cross between the Altai Rose and Harison's Yellow developed by Percy Wright.

R. VIRGINIANA. Perennial to Zone 3.
Height: 5 feet.
Bloom: fragrant pink flowers from late June to late July, profuse show of red hips held throughout the fall and winter.
Shape: gracefully arching shrub.
Foliage: bright orange fall color.
Culture: easy.
Likes: sun/moist/humus-rich soil.
Tolerates: half-sun/dry/semidry.
Propagation: sets.
Comments: the wild variety has single flowers. There is a double form hybrid, called 'Rose d'Amour,' which dates back to the 17th century.

HYBRID TEA ROSES. Perennial to Zone 2 (with winter protection).
Height: 3 feet.
Bloom: flowers in every color except true blue, blooms from June to frost (very long season).
Shape: stiffly upright habit.
Likes: moist/humus- and fertilizer-rich soil.
Tolerates: sun.
Propagation: sets.
Comments: at planting time, dig a deep hole and fill it with soil, compost, manure, and bonemeal; fertilize annually with nitrogen (manure, etc.) and bone meal in the spring and mid-summer only, then fertilize in early fall with potassium for increased hardiness. Must be carefully winter mulched in layers: do first layer in October and finish in No-

vember or December, then remove mounding slowly in layers in March or April (time it with the swelling of the tree buds).

In alkaline soils, Hybrid Tea Roses tend to get chlorotic—remedy by increasing soil humus, adding iron supplements, and water leaching of the soil (unless the water is highly alkaline, of course); these roses suffer from many diseases, particularly if watering is done overhead or at night. Prune out dead wood in May but shape crown and canes in the fall before mounding (remember, the higher the canes are protected through winter the larger the bush and more flowers the following year). Carefully remove all dead leaves in the fall to reduce disease the following year. It is best to plant new roses in early spring; however, if you must plant them in the fall, winter mulch them well. In extremely cold areas, plant roots on the slant with the crown below the ground surface to additionally protect plants from a severe winter.

Hybrid Tea Roses are not easy-to-grow plants in the northern plains, but they still can be grown well by dedicated enthusiasts. Roses should be companion planted with garlic and, for greatest attractiveness, plant with a carpet of Sweet Alyssum *(Lobularia)* or beautiful blue *Lobelia.*

The following is a list of fragrant varieties of Hybrid Tea Roses; in areas with a short growing season, choose roses which bloom most profusely. All are Hybrid Tea class unless noted otherwise. These must be pruned low and are the most disease-prone. Floribunda class roses have flowers in clusters and should be pruned medium height. Grandiflora class roses have large flowers like Hybrid Tea Roses but in clusters like Floribundas and are pruned taller than the other two types.

The initials 'AARS' refers to the All American Rose Selection award given by the American Rose Society. The initials 'JAG' refers to the James Alexander Gamble award given by the American Rose Foundation to roses with outstanding fragrance.

The date listed in parentheses is the year of introduction. The hardi-

est varieties are marked 'some cold tolerance.'

'Americana' (1961); profuse red flowers; strongly fragrant.

'Angel Face' (1968); lavender flowers (floribunda type); heavy scent; AARS.

'Anna Pavlova' (1981); soft pink flowers; very fragrant.

'Antiqua' (1974); antique yellow color; slight fruit-like scent.

'Arizona' (1975); red and white bicolor flowers (grandiflora type); AARS.

'Bewitched' (1967); phlox-pink flowers; damask rose-like scent; AARS.

'Blue Moon' (1964); lavender-blue flowers; lemon-like scent.

'Candy Stripe' (1963); pink flowers with white stripes.

'Chrysler Imperial' (1952); crimson-red flowers; JAG and AARS.

'Condesa deSastago' (1932); bright red flowers with a yellow backside.

'Crimson Glory' (1935); deep crimson flowers; very fragrant; JAG. This variety was introduced by William Chords of Germany.

'Double Delight' (1977); bicolor flowers change from white to red as they age; spicy scent; AARS.

'Ena Harkness' (1949); red flowers; very fragrant.

'Etoile de Holland' (1919); very fragrant red flowers with a damask rose-like scent.

'Fragrant Cloud' (1968); flowers are an odd coral-red color; moderately cold tolerant and easy to grow; JAG.

'General MacArthur' (1950); red flowers with a damask rose-like scent; some cold tolerance.

'Golden Dawn' (1929); yellow flowers; very fragrant; attractive foliage.

'Granada' (1963); red and yellow flowers; some cold tolerance; easy to grow; JAG and AARS.

'Heirloom' (1972); purple flowers; lemony-rose scent.

'Helen Traubel' (1951); pink flowers with an apricot-yellow base; AARS.

'Honor' (1980); white flowers; slightly fragrant; a long-lasting cut flower; AARS.

'Iceberg' (1958); very profuse white flowers (floribunda type); very easy to grow and disease-free;

quick repeat-bloomer.

'**Intrigue,**' dark red-purple flowers; lemony-old rose scent; very fragrant; a good cutting flower.

'**John F Kennedy**' (1965); white flowers; very fragrant.

'**Kordes Perfecta,**' red flowers.

'**Lemon Spice**' (1966); yellow flowers; lemon-cinnamon scent.

'**Medallion**' (1973); cream yellow flowers; fruit-like scent; AARS.

'**Mirandy**' (1945); red flowers with a damask rose-like scent; AARS.

'**Mme Louis Laperriere**' (1951); dark crimson flowers; very fragrant.

'**Mr Lincoln**' (1964); profuse red flowers; some cold tolerance; AARS.

'**Oklahoma**' (1964); tropical-looking dark red flowers.

'**Papa Meilland**' (1963); dark crimson flowers; JAG.

'**Peace**' (1945); profuse yellow to pink flowers; subtle fragrance; cold tolerant; easy to grow; a good cut flower; AARS. The Meillands, the famous rose breeding family of France, bred this rose and had it airlifted to safety out of France during the Nazi invasion. At the cessation of hostilities in 1945, they named it the 'Peace' Rose.

'**Perfume Delight**' (1973); pink flowers; spicy fragrance; AARS.

'**Personality**' (1960); yellow flowers; jonquil-like scent.

'**Prominent**' (1971 Chords); orange-red flowers (grandiflora type); light fruit-like scent; AARS.

'**Red Devil**' (1970); profuse red flowers.

'**Rubaiyat**' (1946); red flowers; damask rose scent.

'**Scented Air**' (1965); deep pink flowers; fruit-like scent.

'**Seashell**' (1976); salmon pink flowers; only slightly fragrant; AARS.

'**Shot Silk**' (1924); pink flowers; very fragrant; disease-free.

'**Sterling Silver**' (1957); silvery-mauve flowers; very fragrant; considered one of the best for cut flowers.

'**Summer Sunshine**' (1962); yellow flowers; slight wild rose scent.

'**Sundowner**' (1978); golden-orange flowers (grandiflora type); very spicy scent; AARS.

'**Sunsprite,**' bright lemon-yellow flowers; JAG.

'**Sutter's Gold**' (1950); profuse golden-yellow flowers; rich jonquil-like scent; JAG and AARS.

'**Sweet Surrender**' (1983); silvery-pink flowers; damask rose-like scent; a good cutting flower; AARS.

'**Tahiti**' (1947); pink, white and gold multicolored flowers; apple-like scent; this rose is less hardy than other listed varieties.

'**Tiffany**' (1954); phlox-pink flower (1964); tropical-looking dark red flowers.

RUBUS IDAEUS, Raspberry. Perennial roots which produce biennial canes, hardy to Zone 1.
Height: 5 feet.
Bloom: tiny white flowers; delicious fruit.
Shape: arching clump of prickly canes.
Culture: easy.
Likes: half-sun/moist/humus-rich soil.
Tolerates: half-shade/semidry.
Comments: may suffer chlorosis in highly alkaline soil; mulch plants heavily to suppress weed and grass growth; often companion planted with garlic to deter insect pests; tall varieties need a wire support around them. Try to locate plants where they will be protected from

*Raspberry,
Rubus idaeus*

extreme wind exposure; protect from mid-day sun in hot summer areas; prune out two-year-old canes each fall or early spring (roots are perennial, but canes are biennial); plant roots in beds to allow root suckering to renew clump. Some people plant alternate rows and cut one row to the ground each year.

Red and yellow varieties are extremely hardy to Zone 1, but black and purple varieties are hardy only to Zones 1-2. Never plant red and black raspberries near each other because of a viral disease the red or yellow varieties give to the black or purple varieties. When first planting red or yellow varieties, cut off the top half of the canes in order to stimulate root growth the first year. Black or purple varieties fruit on the side branches, so cut to 2 feet tall in May or June to encourage side branching. Birds are less of a problem if currants, which ripen about the same time, are planted nearby. Birds prefer currants to raspberries. Fruit can be used fresh, in jams, pastries or cakes, or frozen for later use. The attractive leaves are used for medicinal teas. A cottage industry could market red raspberry vinegar. Varieties of note are the following:

'**Brandywine**' (hardy to Zone 3-4) is an excellent purple raspberry.

'**Comet**' (hardy to Zone 2) is an excellent red variety which tends to be much less thorny than other raspberries. It ripens in early mid-season and can be used fresh or preserved. Good disease resistance to mildew, anthracnose, and spur blight. Introduced in Ottawa in 1954.

'**Honey Queen**' (hardy to Zone 2) is an excellent yellow variety with a unique flavor and productive habit. It is the hardiest yellow raspberry variety. Introduced by Bert Porter of Honeywood Nursery in Parkside, Saskatchewan.

'**Madawaska**' (hardy to Zone 2) has excellent red fruit (somewhat crumbly though) and a productive habit. Ripens early in the season. Introduced in Ottawa in 1943.

'**Redbrook**' (hardy to Zone 1) is an extremely hardy red variety with good fruit quality. It is replacing 'Boyne' and 'Killarney' in the far northern areas. Introduced by Brooks Research Station in 1984.

'**Royalty**' (hardy to Zone 3-4) is an excellent purple raspberry.

'**Tahoma**' (hardy to Zone 2) is a dwarf red variety.

'**Wyoming**' (hardy to Zone 1-2) is an extremely hardy, high quality purple variety. Also, it is very productive over a long season. This variety was selected at Brooks Horticultural Station, Alberta, from seed sent from Wyoming.

RUDBECKIA HIRTA, Black-eyed Susan, Gloriosa Daisy; official state flower of Maryland, native to a wide

area of the eastern woodlands, plains and parklands. Perennial to Zone 1.
Height: 3 feet.
Bloom: yellow daisy flowers with black centers, blooms from late July to frost (long season).
Culture: easy.
Likes: sun/semidry.
Tolerates: half-sun/dry/moist.
Propagation: sets or seeds (sometimes flowers first year from seed). (Seed germination: warm.)
Comments: this plant is particularly showy in mass plantings especially if combined with Dusty Miller *(Senecio cineraria)* and Shasta Daisy *(Chrysanthemum x superbum).* This plant can also be used for cut flowers. The variety 'Gloriosa Irish Eyes' has yellow flowers with green centers.

R. LACINIATA HORTENSIA, Golden-Glow, Official City Flower of Helena, Montana. Native to open forest areas of the eastern woodlands, parklands, and boreal forest. Perennial to Zone 1.
Height: 5 feet.
Bloom: vivid yellow double flowers in clusters, blooms from August to September.
Culture: easy.
Likes: sun/semidry.
Tolerates: half-sun/half-shade/dry/moist.
Propagation: sets or seeds. (Seed germination: warm.)
Comments: invasive by root spreading. This plant makes a good garden plant as well as being useful for cut flowers. 'Gold Que' is a less invasive variety. 'Gold Drop' is a low compact plant with solid yellow flowers.

RUMEX VENOSUS, Wild Begonia. Native to sandy soil in the Great Plains and foothills. Perennial from fleshy rhizomes.
Height: 1 foot.
Bloom: dramatic pinkish-red seedpod clusters from June to August.
Foliage: upright clump of thick, fleshy, light green leaves.
Likes: sun/half-sun/dry/semidry/sandy soil.
Propagation: sets or seeds.
Comments: invasive by root spreading. This fast-spreading plant loves to grow into patches. In native prairie stands, this plant tends to grow in combina-

tion with the orangish-scarlet Globe-mallow *(Sphaeralcea coccinea).* When blooming at the same time, the effect, especially over a large area, is that of a blazing fire. The Indians used this

Wild Begonia, Rumex venosus

plant to obtain a burnt-orange dye from the peeled roots.

RUTABAGA, Swede, Brassica napus var. napobrassica. Cool-season annual vegetable.
Height: 1½ feet.
Description: upright clump of coarse blue-green foliage which tolerates heavy frosts; grown primarily for its rounded root.
Likes: half-sun/half-shade/moist/low nitrogen, deeply dug humus-rich soil.
Propagation: seeds (do not plant seed too deep).
Pests: flea beetles, root maggots, white cabbage moths.
Growing tips: in hot summer areas, plant in mid-summer for fresh use and add a later planting for a storage crop. In cool summer areas, plant only in the spring.
Harvest tips: roots are best harvested after hard frosts.
Comments: if grown in dry conditions, rutabagas become pithy. This plant was originally bred as a cross between a cabbage and a turnip. They are usually eaten cooked either by themselves or in casseroles.

The green growth tip should not be cut off until roots are used, otherwise the root dies and loses its flavor. Rutabagas last well in cold and moist storage or in the ground in loosened soil. They store much better than turnips.

SALIX SPECIES, Willow.
Willow pieces added to the water of other plant cuttings aid in their rooting by releasing growth auxins into the water.

S. ALBA 'SERICEA,' Siberian Silver Willow, tree. Perennial to Zone 1.
Height: 45 feet.
Shape: showy silvery-white strap-like leaves with a silky texture.
Culture: easy.
Likes: sun/semidry/moist/wet.
Propagation: sets.
Comments: this dramatic tree should be better known.

S. ALBA 'VITELLINA,' Golden Willow, tree. Perennial to Zone 1.
Height: 50 feet.
Shape: attractive tree. In winter its gold bark adds life to the landscape.
Culture: easy.
Likes: sun/semidry/moist/wet.
Propagation: sets.
Comments: never prune this tree in spring, shape only in fall or winter and then prune for strength and form. Its brittle wood naturally breaks in the wind. Usually grown as a tree, it can also be pruned into a hedge.

S. PENTANDRA, Laurel-leaf Willow. Perennial to Zone 1.
Height: 40 feet.
Shape: attractive multi-stemmed, round-headed tree.
Bloom: male trees produce attractive yellow catkins in late April.
Foliage: glossy leaves emerge early in the spring.
Culture: easy.
Likes: sun/semidry/moist.
Propagation: sets.

Laurel-leaf Willow, Salix pentandra

Comments: usually grown as a tree, it can also be pruned into a hedge. This tree holds its leaves until very late in the fall and then suddenly drops them all overnight. It is an excellent tree for climbing.

S. SILICICOLA, Blue Fox Willow, Polar Bear Willow. Perennial to Zone 1.
Height: 4 feet.
Shape: shrubby clump.

Culture: easy.
Likes: sun/humus-rich soil.
Tolerates: half-sun/semidry/moist.
Propagation: sets only.
Comments: may get chlorotic in alkaline soil. Non-invasive. 'Blue Fox' is a 4 feet tall, naturally symmetrical, ball-shaped shrub with striking blue-green foliage. 'Polar Bear' is a 6 feet tall shrub with densely woolly, silver-white foliage throughout the summer and large fluffy white pussy willow catkins in early April. Both are excellent for accent plants or hedges. These Arctic Willows were collected in the Canadian Northwest Territories by Dr. George Argus, a botanist with the Biosystematics Dept. of Agriculture Canada. Mr. Les Kerr, Superintendent of the Forest Tree Farm, Sutherland, Saskatchewan, named and introduced them to the horticultural trade. There are other choice willow species of unknown hardiness. Examples are *Salix fargesii, S. integra 'Albomaculata,'* and *S. nigrans.*

SALPIGLOSSIS SINUATA, Painted Tongue. Annual.
Height: 1 foot.
Bloom: vivid red, orange, yellow, or purple flowers with dramatic gold markings, blooms from July to frost.
Foliage: sticky stems and foliage catch aphids and windblown debris.
Likes: sun/half-sun/half-shade/semidry/moist/humus-rich soil.
Propagation: sets or seeds. (Seed germination: warm.)
Comments: semi-upright sprawling habit; pinching tips increases bushiness but delays blooming. In the garden, this plant makes a good companion for lilies. This plant also makes excellent cut flowers.

SALVIA AZUREA (S. pitcheri), Blue Perennial Sage, native to meadows of the southern plains. Perennial to Zone 4-5.
Height: 3 feet.
Bloom: azure-blue flower stalks from late July to frost.
Foliage: gray-green foliage (pinch for bushiness when it reaches a height of 1 foot).
Likes: half-sun.
Tolerates: sun/half-shade/moist.
Propagation: sets.

Comments: graceful clump; may need winter mulch. Variable hardiness, buy locally.

S. ELEGANS, Pineapple Sage. Annual.
Height: 2 feet.
Bloom: red tubular flowers from June to frost (long season).
Foliage: pineapple-scented.
Likes: sun/moist.
Tolerates: half-sun/semidry.
Propagation: sets.
Comments: these scarlet flowers attract hummingbirds. In the fall, this plant can be potted up and brought inside, but it needs full sun inside.

S. FARINACEA, Blue Sage. Annual.
Height: 1 foot.
Bloom: blue flower spikes from June to frost (very long season).
Culture: easy.
Likes: sun/moist/humus-rich soil.
Tolerates: half-sun/dry/semidry.
Propagation: sets or seeds. (Seed germination: warm.)
Comments: individual clump habit. This plant makes a beautiful combination with white picotee edged, blackish-maroon Martha Washington geraniums, and white or blue lobelia. It is excellent in gardens, in containers, and as a cut flower.

S. OFFICINALIS, Herb Sage, culinary herb. Perennial to Zone 3.
Height: 2 feet.
Bloom: blue flowers in July.
Foliage: gray-green aromatic foliage.
Culture: easy.
Likes: sun/moist.
Tolerates: half-sun/dry/semidry.
Propagation: sets.
Comments: somewhat invasive low spreading clump; may need winter mulch in exposed areas. There are varieties with either purple, gold or tricolor (pink, green and white) variegated foliage. These colored foliage varieties are excellent for the front of the garden. As a seasoning, use sage in cheese dishes, chicken, pork, or in stuffing.

S. PRATENSIS, Meadow Sage. Peren-

Herb Sage, Salvia officinalis

nial to Zone 2.
Height: 2 feet.
Bloom: profuse rich blue flowers on stalks, blooms from June to July.
Foliage: basal clump of foliage.
Likes: sun/half-sun/semidry/moist.
Propagation: sets or seeds.
Comments: though perennial, this plant often behaves like a biennial, so seed in a few new plants every year.

S. SCLAREA, Clary Sage. Biennial to Zone 4.
Height: 3 feet.
Bloom: showy blue flowerstalk is produced the second year; blooms from June to August.
Foliage: silvery-white basal rosette of foliage produced the first year.
Likes: semidry/deeply dug, humus-rich soil.
Tolerates: sun/half-sun/dry/moist.
Propagation: sets or seeds.
Comments: may require winter mulch in exposed areas. Give this dramatic large plant lots of room.

S. SPLENDENS, Common Scarlet Sage. Annual.
Height: 1 foot.
Bloom: clusters of red, white, purple or black flowers on stalks, blooms from May to frost (very long season).
Culture: easy.
Likes: half-sun/moist.
Tolerates: sun/half-shade/dry/semidry.
Propagation: sets or seeds. (Seed germination: warm.)
Comments: this plant can be used in the garden, in a container or for cut flowers.

S. X SUPERBA (S. nemorosa). Perennial to Zone 4-5.
Height: 3 feet.
Bloom: narrow purple spikes from July to August.
Likes: half-sun/moist.
Tolerates: sun/half-shade/semidry.
Propagation: sets or seeds.
Comments: requires winter mulch.

SAMBUCUS CANADENSIS, Purple Elderberry. Native from the eastern woodlands to the northern plains. Perennial to Zone 3.
Height: 10 feet.
Bloom: slightly fragrant white flower clusters from late June to July; blue-purple berry clusters.
Shape: spreading shrub.
Foliage: attractive new foliage

emerges in early spring.
Culture: easy.
Likes: half-sun/moist/humus-rich soil.
Tolerates: sun-half-shade/semidry/wet.
Propagation: sets or seeds (cuttings grown in summer).
Comments: may suffer chlorosis in highly alkaline soil; most varieties root sucker somewhat; birds love these berries and become formidable challenges. Prune off lower limbs and train for multiple trunks; for best fruit production, plant two or more plants for cross pollination.

Purple Elderberry, Sambucus canadensis

The old main variety for eating was 'Adams,' which has mid- to large-size fruit (early ripening). It was selected and named by William Adams of Union Springs, New York. However, it has been superseded by two of its named seedlings: 'Nova' is a heavy bearer which ripens mid-season and was discovered in Kentville, Nova Scotia, in 1959; 'York' has midsize fruit which is late ripening and has the least root suckering tendencies. It was discovered in Geneva, New York.

Fruit should be used only after it is fully ripe. Elderberries make tasty jelly when combined with acidic fruit such as apples or crabapples, lemon juice, rhubarb, or sumac fruit clusters. Fruit is easily juiced by adding fruit to boiling water, with sugar to taste, and boiling briefly. Elderberries can also be dried and stored for winter use. Kim Williams suggested using the flower clusters in pancakes or fritters, the flowers or fruit in homemade wine, and, finally, fruit dessert soup made from the berries. This fruit is excellent forage for free run chickens.

Ornamental varieties are the following: 'Aurea' to 10 feet tall, with gold-colored foliage; and 'Maxima' to 12 feet tall, with very large white flowers followed by red-purple berry clusters. Roots and stems are mildly poisonous unless dried. The Indians hollowed out the stem's pithy center and made whistles and blowguns. A cautionary note: dry them thoroughly before using.

S. NIGRA 'PURPUREA,' Black-foliage Elderberry. Perennial to Zone 4.
Height: 10 feet.
Bloom: emerging white flower clusters in May.
Foliage: purple-black foliage in the spring contrasts with bloom; in mid-summer foliage turns to green.
Likes: moist.
Tolerates: sun/half-sun/semidry/wet.
Propagation: sets only.

S. RACEMOSA, European Red Elderberry. Perennial to Zone 1.
Height: 13 feet.
Shape: spreading clump.
Bloom: white flat-topped clusters in June; red berry clusters in mid- to late summer.
Foliage: new foliage emerges in early spring.
Culture: easy.
Likes: half-sun/moist.
Tolerates: sun/half-shade/semidry/wet.
Propagation: sets.
Comments: 'Plumosa' grows to 8 feet tall, with feathery foliage. 'Plumosa-Aurea' grows to 7 feet tall, has a compact form, bright red berries in the fall, distinctive feathery gold foliage, and needs more sun than most elderberries. 'Redman' grows

Black-foliage Elderberry, Sambucus nigra

to 13 feet tall, has finely-divided foliage and profuse red fruit. This variety originated at Morden Research Station, in 1929. 'Sutherland' grows to 9 feet tall, has finely-divided yellow foliage, red berries, and needs more sun than most elderberries. Roots and stems are mildly poisonous.

SANGUISORBA MINOR (Poterium sanguisorba), Salad Burnet, culinary herb. Perennial to Zone 2.
Height: 1 foot.
Bloom: insignificant thimble-shaped green flowers on long stalks.
Foliage: attractive foliage stays green throughout the winter (winter interest).
Likes: moist.
Tolerates: sun/half-sun/half-shade/shade/semidry.
Propagation: sets or seeds. (Seed has low viability, use fresh seed and sow thickly.)
Comments: showy rounded clump; prefers wind protection in exposed locations. This plant's common name 'Salad Bur-

Salad Burnet, Sanguisorba minor

net' refers to its fresh use in salads for its cucumber-like flavor. It can also be dried and used to flavor summer beverages like wine punch, vinegar, cream cheese and cottage cheese. Its distinctive flavor is pleasing but difficult to describe. As an ornamental this plant is best used for its dramatic show of greenery during the winter. It would be most vividly displayed in a freeze-proofed pot or old urn.

S. OFFICINALIS, Rusty Pokers. Perennial to Zone 2.
Height: 4 foot.
Bloom: upright clump with reddish-brown flowers on long stalks, blooms from August to frost.
Foliage: attractive.
Likes: moist.
Tolerates: sun/half-sun/semidry.
Propagation: sets or seeds.
Comments: prefers wind protection in exposed locations. Somewhat invasive

Rusty Pokers, Sanguisorba officinalis

by self-sown seeds. Locate this large plant in the background.

SANVITALIA PROCUMBENS, Creeping Zinnia. Annual.
Height: 6 inches.
Bloom: small yellow zinnia-like flowers with a black center, blooms from late June to frost (very long season).
Culture: easy.
Likes: sun.
Tolerates: half-sun/dry/semidry.
Propagation: sets (must be transplanted carefully) or seeds. (Seed germination: light.)
Comments: semi-upright creeping habit. This low-maintenance plant is excellent in the front of the garden, as well as in containers, or best of all in hanging pots.

SATUREJA HORTENSIS, Summer Savory, culinary herb. Annual.
Height: 1 foot.
Bloom: profuse pink, white, or lavender flowers July to August (long season).
Foliage: small narrow leaves.
Culture: easy.
Likes: sun/semidry/nitrogen-poor soil.
Tolerates: half-sun/moist.
Propagation: sets or seeds. (Seed germination: light.)

Summer Savory, Satureja hortensis

Comments: shrubby plant. This culinary herb is excellent added to dried bean and pea dishes, salads, egg dishes, and all meats. It also makes a tasty herb tea.

SAXIFRAGA BRONCHIALIS, Spotted Saxifrage. Native to dry rocky areas of the foothills and Rocky Mountains. Perennial.
Height: 4 inches.
Bloom: tiny white star-like flowers with red spots, flowers are borne on low stalks, blooms in July.
Foliage: dense creeping mat; basal clump of moss-like foliage.
Likes: sun/half-sun/dry/semidry.
Propagation: sets or seeds.
Comments: a much showier, but more difficult, species is *Saxifraga oppositifolia,* native to alpine scree areas. It has spectacular rich purple

flowers in June and a moss-like habit.

Sweet Scabious, Scabiosa atropurpurea

SCABIOSA ATROPURPUREA, Sweet Scabious. Annual.
Height: 2 feet.
Bloom: fragrant red, pink, white, blue, purple or near-black pincushion-like flowers, blooms from July to frost (long season).
Culture: easy.
Likes: sun/humus-rich soil.
Tolerates: half-sun/semidry/moist.
Propagation: sets or seeds. (Seed germination: warm.)
Comments: this long-lasting cut flower was once the mainstay of Europe's florist industry. It also makes a showy garden flower. The varieties 'King of the Blacks' and 'Azure Fairy' are the most fragrant.

S. CAUCASICA, Perennial Scabious. Perennial to Zone 2.
Height: 2 feet.
Bloom: blue or white pincushion-like flowers from June to frost (long season).
Culture: easy.
Likes: sun/humus-rich soil.
Tolerates: half-sun/semidry/moist.
Propagation: sets or seeds. (Seed germination: warm.)
Comments: this plant makes both a good garden plant and cut flowers. The variety 'Blue Lady' has gentian blue flowers, and *'Perfecta'* has flowers with fringed petals.

SCHIZANTHUS PINNATUS, Butterfly Flower, Poor Man's Orchid. Annual.
Height: 2 feet.
Bloom: showy multicolored flowers in clusters, blooms from June to frost (long season).
Likes: half-sun.
Tolerates: half-shade/moist.
Propagation: sets or seeds. (Seed germination: warm.)
Comments: prefers cool summers or mid-day shade. This dramatic accent plant is showy in gardens, in containers, or as cut flowers.

SCHIZOPETALON WALKERI. Annual.
Height: 1 foot.
Bloom: fringed white flowers are

fragrant only at night (its scent resembles a combination of bitter-almond and vanilla), blooms from June to frost (very long season).
Likes: sun/moist/humus-rich soil.
Propagation: sets (transplant carefully) or seeds.
Comments: semi-erect sprawling habit. This plant is best displayed at nose level in a hanging pot.

SCILLA SIBIRICA, Squill. Perennial to Zone 1.
Height: 6 inches.
Bloom: deep blue nodding star-like flowers from late March to early May (long season); this is one of the very first flowers to appear when spring is still an illusion.
Foliage: grass-like.
Culture: very easy.
Likes: half-sun.
Tolerates: half-shade (deciduous tree shade only)/dry/semidry.
Propagation: bulbs (bury 3 inches deep) or seeds.
Comments: This is an outstandingly excellent plant for naturalizing into lawns where it spreads into spectacular drifts of cobalt blue and then disappears before the lawn starts to grow. This bulb is also excellent to plant under fruit trees. However, all parts of this plant are poisonous. The commonly available variety 'Spring Beauty' has a more profuse bloom than the species. *Scilla bifolia* is nearly identical but has lighter blue flowers.

S. TUBERGENIANA, Cluster Squill. Perennial to Zone 2.
Height: 5 inches.
Bloom: light blue hyacinth-like flowers, blooms in mid-April.
Foliage: grass-like.
Culture: very easy.
Likes: sun/half-sun/half-shade (deciduous tree shade only)/dry/semidry.
Propagation: bulbs.
Comments: All parts of this plant are poisonous.

SCORZONERA, Black Oyster Plant, Black Salsify, Vegetable Oyster *(Scorzonera hispanica).* Biennial vegetable grown as an annual.
Height: 1 foot.
Description: large yellow or purple dandelion-like flowers, coarse linear foliage, carrot-like root with black skin and white flesh.
Culture: easy.

Black Oyster Plant, Scorzonera

Likes: sun/semi-dry/moist.
Tolerates: poor soil well.
Propagation: seeds. Because this plant tolerates cool soil and heavy frosts, plant seeds outside in early April; seed must be fresh for best germination. Seeds germinate vigorously and are easy to grow.
Growing tips: in hot summer areas, mulch to keep soil cool; established plants resent transplanting. Be careful weeding young plants because they look exactly like grass.
Harvest tips: this root may be harvested at any time in late summer, but frost sweetens the flavor.
Comments: in winter, it can be stored in the ground if loosened in the soil and mulched carefully. It can be stored this way through most of the winter. In a root cellar, it stores well cool and moist.

Always leave a bit of the green growth tip on roots. After this tip is removed the root and its natural flavor dies. When cooking, leave on the black skin for its oyster-like flavor. It is best cooked breaded with bread crumbs and fried like oysters, or used in distinctive soups. Its texture is similiar to parsnips.

The related vegetable Salsify *(Tragopogon)* is more common, but has less oyster-like flavor. This plant has escaped cultivation and can be found everywhere growing as a common weed.

SCUTELLARIA GALERICULATA, Skullcap. Native to streamsides and bogs of the Great Plains and Rocky Mountains. Perennial.
Height: 2 feet.
Bloom: lavender-blue flowers from July to August.
Foliage: upright spreading clump of mint-like foliage.
Likes: half-sun/half-shade/moist/wet (a bog plant).
Propagation: sets or seeds (easily propagated from stem cuttings).
Comments: invasive due to root spreading. The related species

Scutellaria laterifolia has a more branched flower stalk. Another species of Skullcap is used as an herb for quieting the mind and inducing sleep.

S. RESINOSA. Native to dry hillsides near water in the Great Plains. Perennial.
Height: 8 inches.
Bloom: tiny blue and white flowers from June to early August.
Foliage: showy, rounded clump of fine textured aromatic foliage.
Likes: sun/semidry.
Propagation: sets or seeds.

SEDUM SPECIES. Most of these plants are excellent for the front of the garden.

Order of bloom: *Sedum acre* (May), *S. purdyii* (May), *S. hispanicum* (June), *S. hybridum* (June), *S. divergens* (June), *S. stenopetalum* (June), *S. kamtschaticum* (June to Aug), *S. album* (July), *S. telephinum* (July), *S. reflexum* (July), *S. populifolium* (July to August), *S. aizoom* (July to August), *S. anacampseros* (July to August), *S. spurium* (late July to August), *S. telephinum* (August), *S. maximum* (August), *S. spectabile* (August to September), *S. ewersii* (August to September), *S. cauticola* (mid-September).

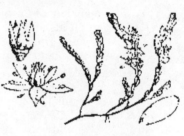

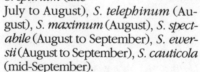
Golden Carpet Sedum, Sedum acre

S. ACRE, Golden Carpet Sedum. Perennial to Zone 1.
Height: 2 inches.
Bloom: bright yellow star-like flower clusters in May.
Foliage: evergreen succulent foliage.
Culture: very easy.
Likes: sun/semidry.
Tolerates: half-sun/dry/poor soil.
Propagation: sets or seeds (easily propagated by seed or cuttings).
Comments: mat-like habit; very invasive due to rooting stems and self-sown seeds. Kim Williams mentioned that these fat succulent leaves with a peppery taste are excellent in cole slaw. The species *Sedum sexangulare* is similar but larger than this species.

S. AIZOON. Perennial to Zone 2.
Height: 1 foot.
Bloom: yellow flower clusters from July to August.
Foliage: scalloped foliage dies to the ground in winter.
Culture: easy.
Likes: sun/semidry.
Tolerates: half-sun/dry/poor soil.
Propagation: sets or seeds.
Comments: upright clump. 'Aurantiacum' has yellowish-orange flowers with dark green leaves and red-bronze stems.

S. ALBUM. Perennial to Zone 3.
Height: 5 inches.
Bloom: pinkish-white flowers in July.
Foliage: mossy or bead-like evergreen foliage turns red in the winter.
Culture: very easy.
Likes: sun/semidry.
Tolerates: half-sun/dry/semidry.
Propagation: sets or seeds.
Comments: trailing habit. For best foliage color, give it poor soil.

S. ANACAMPSEROS, Love-Restorer Sedum. Perennial to Zone 3.
Height: 3 inches.
Bloom: light pink flowers from July to early August.
Foliage: semi-deciduous rounded blue-green foliage.
Likes: sun/semidry/poor soil.
Tolerates: dry.
Propagation: sets or seeds.
Comments: trailing habit. The common name refers to this plant's use in love potions.

S. CAUTICOLA, Cliff Dweller Sedum. Perennial to Zone 3-4.
Height: 2 inches.
Bloom: bright yellow flowers in mid-September (this is the last sedum on the list to flower).
Foliage: blue-green deciduous foliage on arching stems.
Likes: sun/semidry/well-drained soil.
Tolerates: half-sun/dry.
Propagation: sets or seeds.
Comments: trailing habit; requires a light winter mulch.

S. DIVERGENS. Perennial to Zone 3-4.
Height: 3 inches.
Bloom: yellow flowers in June.

Foliage: thick leaves on prostrate stems.
Likes: sun/half-sun/dry/semidry/moist.
Propagation: sets or seeds.
Comments: mat-like habit which spreads by stem rooting.

S. EWERSII. Perennial to Zone 2.
Height: 6 inches.
Bloom: trailing stems, purplish-pink flowers from August to September.
Foliage: deciduous blue-green foliage.
Culture: easy.
Likes: semidry.
Tolerates: half-sun/dry.
Propagation: sets or seeds.
Comments: prefers a light winter mulch.

S. HISPANICUM. Perennial to Zone 3.
Height: 2 inches.
Bloom: pinkish-white flowers in June.
Foliage: attractive moss-like tufts of blue-green deciduous foliage.
Likes: half-sun/moist.
Tolerates: half-shade/semidry.
Propagation: sets or seeds.
Comments: creeping habit; requires a light winter mulch. *'Aureum'* has gold tones in its foliage but is less hardy than the species.

S. HYBRIDUM. Perennial to Zone 2.
Height: 8 inches.
Bloom: yellow flowers that bloom on old growth in June and on new growth in August.
Foliage: glossy evergreen foliage resembles *Sedum kamtschaticum.*
Likes: sun/semidry.
Tolerates: half-sun/dry.
Comments: semi-erect creeping habit. Stems must be winter mulched in order to produce June flowers. Its name is misleading; it is a species, not a hybrid.

S. KAMTSCHATICUM. Perennial to Zone 1.
Height: 6 inches.
Bloom: bright orange flowers from June to August, attractive seed pods.
Foliage: glossy green deciduous foliage.
Culture: very easy.
Likes: sun/semidry.
Tolerates: half-sun/dry/moist/poor soil.
Propagation: sets or seeds.
Comments: sprawling upright habit; shear off old stems in late fall for

an attractive rosette of new growth in mid-winter. *'Middendorffianum'* is a compact creeping variety with yellow flowers, and *'variegatum'* has variegated foliage.

S. MAXIMUM. Perennial to Zone 3.
Height: 2 feet.
Bloom: very large creamy white flowers (up to 6 inches in diameter), blooms in August.
Foliage: large bold foliage.
Culture: easy.
Likes: sun/half-sun/dry/semidry/moist.
Propagation: sets or seeds.
Comments: floppy clump habit; requires hoop support for best appearance.

S. POPULIFOLIUM, Poplar-leaf Sedum. Perennial to Zone 3.
Height: 10 inches.
Bloom: whitish-pink flowers in July to August.
Foliage: A shrub with poplar-like leaves (semi-evergreen).
Likes: sun/half-sun/dry/semidry/moist.
Propagation: sets or seeds.
Comments: may need winter mulch in exposed locations. This shrub-like plant is quite unlike the other sedums. Native to Siberia.

S. PURDYII. Perennial to Zone 4.
Height: 1 inch.
Bloom: yellow-green flowers in May.
Foliage: dramatic foliage rosettes of rounded bright green leaves.
Likes: sun/half-sun/dry/semidry/moist.
Propagation: sets or seeds.
Comments: spreading clump; somewhat invasive by root spreading.

S. REFLEXUM. Perennial to Zone 3-4.
Height: 8 inches.
Bloom: yellow flower clusters in July.
Foliage: light blue-green foliage on stems which closely resemble spruce twigs.
Likes: sun/half-sun/dry/semidry/moist.
Propagation: sets or seeds.
Comments: semi-erect habit.

S. SPECTABILE, Showy Sedum. Perennial to Zone 2.
Height: 1 foot.
Bloom: red, pink, or white flower clusters which attract butterflies, blooms from August to September (long season).

Foliage: blue-green deciduous foliage with a fleshy texture.
Culture: easy.
Likes: half-sun/semidry.
Tolerates: sun/half-shade/dry/moist.
Propagation: sets or seeds.
Comments: upright clump habit. The variety 'Autumn Joy' (also called 'Indian Chief') has a very long season of interest. First, the flowers turn from pink to red as it blooms from August to frost, and then its showy dried flower stalks are attractive on the plant throughout the winter. The variety 'Meteor' has showy reddish-pink flowers that start blooming early. An attractive white flowering variety is 'Stardust.' The variety 'Ruby Glow' has red foliage and reddish-purple flowers. There is also a variegated variety.

S. SPURIUM. Perennial to Zone 3-4.
Height: 4 inches.
Bloom: red, pink, or white flower clusters from late July to August.
Foliage: roundish deciduous foliage.
Culture: easy.
Likes: sun/dry/semidry.
Propagation: sets or seeds.
Comments: tangled sprawling habit; may need winter mulch in exposed areas.
Varieties of Note:
  'Dragon's Blood'—red-purple foliage and dark red flowers, but it is slow-growing. This variety is hardy only to Zone 4.
  'Erdblut'—carmine flowers.
  'Purple Carpet'—pink flowers, and purple-red foliage. This one is less hardy.
  'Tricolor'—pink, yellow and green foliage.
  'Variegatum'—soft pink flowers, and white variegated foliage.

S. STENOPETALUM, native to rocky areas of the foothills and Rocky Mountains. Perennial to Zone 2.
Height: 1 foot.
Bloom: bright yellow flowers from late June to July.
Foliage: moss-like evergreen foliage.
Culture: very easy.
Likes: sun/dry/semidry.
Propagation: sets or seeds.
Comments: creeping mat habit. Indians ate the young leaves and stems in the spring. Later in the

summer, the leaves get tough and bitter.

S. TELEPHIUM 'ATROPURPUREA,' Orpine. Perennial to Zone 2.
Height: 6 inches.
Bloom: dark red-dish-purple flowers in July.
Foliage: dull purple thick fleshy foliage.
Likes: sun/semidry.
Tolerates: dry.
Propagation: sets.
Comments: sprawling clump.

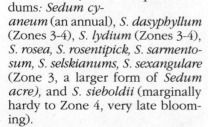

Orpine, Sedum telephium

Other hardy sedums: *Sedum cyaneum* (an annual), *S. dasyphyllum* (Zones 3-4), *S. lydium* (Zones 3-4), *S. rosea, S. rosentipick, S. sarmentosum, S. selskianums, S. sexangulare* (Zone 3, a larger form of *Sedum acre*), and *S. sieboldii* (marginally hardy to Zone 4, very late blooming).

SEMPERVIVUM ARACHNOIDEUM, Cobweb Hen and Chickens. Perennial to Zone 1.
Height: ½ inch.
Bloom: occasional pinkish-red flower stalks.
Foliage: low creeping clump of tiny evergreen rosettes, leaves are woven together with silken cobwebs.
Culture: very easy.
Likes: sun.
Tolerates: half-sun/very dry/semidry.
Propagation: sets.

S. TECTORUM, Common Hen and Chickens. Perennial to Zone 1.
Height: 2 inches.
Bloom: occasional flower stalks.
Foliage: low creeping clump of brightly colored fleshy rosettes.
Culture: very easy.
Likes: sun.
Tolerates: half-sun/dry/semidry.
Propagation: sets.

Hen and Chickens, Sempervivum tectorum

Comments: this low-maintenance plant is most attractive grown in cracks in a rock wall, on a roof, or best of all, planted in upturned masonry blocks. The colors are most vivid when plants are rootbound in a small pot and starved for nutrients. A similiar plant is the Spiny Hen and Chickens (see *Orostachys spinosa*).

Varieties of note are the following:

'Atropurpureum'—very dark purplish-green foliage (best color in the winter).

'Bella Donna'—gray-green foliage with purplish tips.

'Beta'—red-purple with silvery-gray edging.

'Blue Boy'—blue-gray foliage with dark tips.

'Cleveland Morgan'—grown for its large pink flowers.

'Edge of Night'—gray-green foliage with black tips.

'Elegans'—rich pink foliage color.

'Gama'—vivid purple foliage with silvery-gray edging (best color in spring and summer).

'Gloriosum'—vivid red foliage (best color in spring and summer).

'Icicle'—red foliage with green center and frosty-looking edging.

Jovibara heuffelii hybrids: a number of choice varieties.

'Lavender and Old Lace'—pinkish-green color with silvery-gray edging.

'Lipstick'—dark red foliage in both winter and summer. For this reason, this plant is excellent for ornamental writing in a garden bed.

'Missouri Rose'—wine-red foliage with dark tips, large size.

'Nigrum'—dark green foliage color with darker tips.

'Oddity'—showy narrow rolled leaves.

'Ohio Burgundy'—velvet-textured red foliage.

'Pink Lemonade'—pink and yellow foliage color.

'Purdy's #70-1'—attractive violet-gray color, velvety texture.

'Royal Ruby'—dark wine-red foliage color.

'Snowberger'—soft green foliage with a white sheen, attractive leaf form.

'Sunset'—striking light green foliage with orange-red tips.

'Webbianum'—maroon-red foli-

age color with an extremely fuzzy texture.

SENECIO CINERARIA, Dusty Miller. Annual.
Height: 1 foot.
Foliage: grown primarily for its finely-divided silvery-white foliage (long season of interest).
Culture: easy.
Likes: sun/half-sun/half-shade/dry/semidry/moist.
Propagation: sets.
Comments: individual clump habit. This plant tolerates light frosts and can be set out very early in the spring if hardened off. It also makes a good container plant adding a showy silvery-white accent.

SHALLOTS, *Allium cepa.* Annual vegetable.
Height: 1 foot.
Description: upright narrow foliage, occasional white flowers which should be removed, root cluster is used as a culinary seasoning and as a vegetable.
Likes: sun/moist/humus-rich, well-drained soil.
Tolerates: half-sun.
Growing tips: prefers to dry out in late summer.
Harvest tips: harvest in fall when the foliage dies.
Propagation: bulbs planted in early spring; space bulbs to 6 inches apart.
Comments: if dried carefully and stored cool and dry, bulbs can last up to a year. There is a large variety called the 'Frog's Legs' Shallots.

SILENE ACAULIS, Moss Campion. Native to alpine meadows and scree fields circumpolar. Perennial to Zone 2.

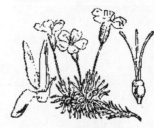

Moss Campion, Silene acaulis

Height: 2 inches.
Bloom: bright pink flowers from June to July.
Foliage: mounded creeper habit of moss-like evergreen foliage.
Culture: difficult.
Likes: half-sun/semidry/moist/slightly alkaline rocky soil.

Propagation: sets or seeds.

Comments: requires mid-day shade in hot summer areas; requires scree conditions (underground watering and good drainage). Usually found in the same areas as *Eritrichium nanum,* Alpine Forget-Me-Not.

SISYRINCHIUM MONTANUM (S. angustifolium), Blue-eyed Grass. Native to sandy moist meadows in the Great Plains and Rocky Mountains. Perennial.

Height: 8 inches.

Bloom: small blue-purple star-like flowers from early June to mid-July.

Foliage: grass-like foliage.

Likes: sun/half-sun/semidry/moist.

Propagation: roots.

Comments: though this plant closely resembles grass, it is really a member of the Iris family.

Blue-eyed Grass, Sisyrinchium montanum

SMELOWSKIA CALYCINA, Silver Rockcress. Native to alpine talus areas in the Rocky Mountains. Perennial.

Height: 4 inches.

Bloom: creamy-white flowers.

Foliage: densely compact tufted habit, showy silvery-white foliage.

Culture: difficult.

Likes: sun/half-sun/semidry/moist.

Propagation: sets or seeds.

Comments: requires mid-day shade in hot summer areas; requires scree conditions: underground watering and good drainage.

SOLIDAGO MISSOURIENSIS, Goldenrod. Native to the Great Plains. Perennial.

Height: 2 feet.

Bloom: vivid yellow sprays of flowers from end of July to August.

Likes: moist/sandy soil.

Tolerates: sun/half-sun/dry/semidry/heavy clay soil.

Propagation: sets or seeds. (Seed germination: cold.)

Comments: this plant exhausts its soil and prefers to occasionally move to new ground through self-sowing. The Indians used this plant for its edible greens and seeds, as well as an indicator to time the ripening of their corn. Other attractive species are *Solidago multiradiata* and *S. spathulata,* both native to disturbed areas in the Rocky Mountains and closely resembling *Solidago missouriensis.* However, they are smaller and more finely textured plants.

SOLIDAGO HYBRIDS, Goldenrod; official state flower of Alabama, Kentucky and Nebraska, one of the many flowers nominated for U.S. national flower. Perennial to Zone 3.

Height: 4 feet.

Bloom: showy sprays of gold flowers from August to frost (long season).

Culture: easy.

Likes: sun/moist.

Tolerates: half-sun/half-shade/dry/semidry.

Propagation: sets or seeds. (Seed germination: cold treatment.)

Comments: this plant exhausts its soil and must be moved occasionally. Varieties of note are: 'Cloth of Gold' with soft yellow flowers in a cascading flower form; 'Golden Thumb' (also called 'Queenie') a dwarf plant with a compact habit; and *'Mimosa,'* a tall compact clump with an early bloom season. Or try the unusual looking Goldenrod-Aster cross called *Solidaster.* Very few people are actually allergic to Goldenrod; the real culprit is Ragweed, which blooms at exactly the same time.

SORBUS SPECIES, Mountain Ash. This tree, also called the Rowan tree, was very sacred to the old pre-Christian religion of the northern Europeans. The red berries are edible but poor-tasting to humans. Birds, however, relish them.

S. AUCUPARIA, European Mountain Ash. Perennial to Zone 1.

Height: 35 feet.

Shape: rounded tree.

Bloom: flat white flower clusters in May; red berries in the fall and winter.

Foliage: finely-divided, showy long-lasting red fall color.

Likes: half-sun/humus-rich soil.

Tolerates: sun/half-shade/semidry/moist.

Propagation: sets.

Comments: may suffer chlorosis in highly alkaline soil. Young trees may winter scald (best prevented by painting the south side of the trunk with

Mountain Ash, Sorbus

white latex interior paint); somewhat susceptible to fire blight; best pruned to multiple trunks for wind support. 'Columnar' is a tall columnar variety. *'Fastigiata'* is a semidwarf narrow columnar variety. *'Pendula'* is a strange-looking weeping form which must be trained upright on a support. Two species, *Sorbus amurensis* and *S. rosica,* are both very similar to this species but do not suffer sunscald. Never plant this tree near buildings as birds become intoxicated from eating berries and fly into windows and walls.

S. DECORA, Showy Mountain Ash. Perennial to Zone 1.

Height: 20 feet.

Bloom: flat white flower clusters in May; red berries in the fall and winter.

Shape: rounded spreading tree.

Foliage: finely-divided with spectacular long-lasting red fall color.

Likes: semidry/moist/humus-rich soil.

Propagation: sets.

Comments: needs half-sun to develop form, but protect it from full sun and heat; may suffer chlorosis in highly alkaline soil; young trees may winter scald (best prevented by painting the south side of the trunk with white latex interior paint); somewhat susceptible to fire blight; best pruned to multiple trunks for best wind support. This

Goldenrod, Solidago missouriensis

tree suffers less from sunscald than *Sorbus aucuparia* (European Mountain Ash).

S. POHUASHANENSIS, Pohua Valley Mountain Ash. Perennial to Zone 3.
Height: 25 feet.
Shape: showy symmetrically-rounded lollipop-shaped tree.
Bloom: white flower clusters in May; red berries in the fall and winter.
Foliage: finely-divided with spectacular long-lasting red fall color.
Likes: sun/half-shade/semidry/moist/humus-rich soil.
Propagation: sets or seeds.
Comments: may suffer chlorosis in highly alkaline soil; young trees may winter scald (best prevented by painting the south side of the trunk with white latex interior paint); somewhat susceptible to fire blight. This tree should be better known for its striking natural lollipop-shape. It is suitable for use in formal gardens.

S. TIANSHANICA, Turkestan Mountain Ash Bush. Perennial to Zone 3.
Height: 12 feet.
Shape: slow-growing compact shrub.
Bloom: very large white flower clusters (4 inches across) from mid- to late May; red berries in fall and winter.
Foliage: showy glossy foliage.
Likes: sun/semidry/humus-rich soil.
Tolerates: half-sun/half-shade/dry.
Propagation: sets.
Comments: may suffer chlorosis in highly alkaline soil. This easy-to-care-for shrub should be more commonly planted. A new variety 'Red Cascade' is much faster growing and assumes a small tree form. A similar and closely related species is *Sorbus scopulina*. Native to the northern Rocky Mountains.

SORREL, FRENCH, Rumex acetosa. Perennial vegetable.
Height: 1 foot.
Description: rounded clump of arrow-shaped foliage, insignificant green flowerstalks.
Likes: sun/shade/moist/humus-rich soil.
Growing tips: for a prolonged harvest, plant some in hot sun for an early crop and some in cool shade for later usage.
Harvest tips: remove flowerstalks for

French Sorrel, Rumex acetosa

longer season of the leaves.
Propagation: sets or seeds.
Comments: this very early plant often starts greening up in March. Its sour leaves are excellent in salads, soups and casseroles.

SPHAERALCEA COCCINEA, Scarlet Globemallow. Native to the central and northern Great Plains. Perennial to Zone 2.
Height: 8 inches.
Bloom: tomato-orange-colored flowers, blooms from May to end of July.
Foliage: irregularly rounded clump habit, showy finely-divided, silvery-white foliage.
Likes: sun/dry/semidry.
Propagation: sets or seed. (Seed germination: cold.)
Comments: plant goes dormant and disappears in late summer; very invasive by root spreading. This was once the most common and memorable wildflower of the short grass prairie. Many early explorers noted seeing vast drifts of blazing color across the land. However, cattle and sheep grazing quickly made it disappear. Indians used the chewed leaves for their mucilaginous properties in treating burned skin and thickening soups. Alex Johnston, in his book *Plants and the Blackfoot* states, "Medicine Men of some tribes rubbed the chewed paste over their hands and arms. The coating that resulted protected the skin from scalding and enabled the medicine man to mystify onlookers by reaching into a pot of boiling water to retrieve a bit of meat." The name *sphaeralcea* translates to "globe mallow." The shape of the seeds are globe or sphere-like.

SPINACH—COOL SEASON, Spinachia oleracea. Cool-season annual vegetable.
Height: 8 inches.
Description: in-

Spinach, Spinachia oleracea

dividual leafy clumps, tender fleshy foliage which tolerates some winter cold and grows best during the spring and fall.
Culture: easy.
Likes: sun/half-sun/semidry/humus-rich soil/manure.
Tolerates: half-shade/moist.
Propagation: seeds. Seeds can be planted in late fall and protected in a coldframe for an early spring crop; or planted in early to mid-April for an early summer crop. Stagger spring planting 2-3 weeks apart for prolonged summer harvest, or else plant in early August for a fall crop (sow extra seed when planting in hot weather or cold-treat seed by soaking in water overnight in the refrigerator.)
Growing tips: hot summer weather and long days encourage it to bolt into flower. For best growth, refertilize when 3 inches tall. Young plants prefer to dry slightly between waterings; encourage fast growth by removing weed competition; careful mulching reduces sand in the leaves; shallow rooted (avoid soil compaction). This plant tolerates heavy frost. Spinach is excellent for intercropping between warm season vegetables such as melons, squash, cucumbers, or tomatoes.
Comments: spinach is low in calories, high in vitamins, and can be eaten either raw in spinach salads, or cooked as a green or added to casseroles. It can be preserved by freezing or canning after being lightly blanched.

Hot summer areas should grow varieties described as longstanding or heat tolerant. Shepherd's Garden Seeds lists an excellent variety called 'Italian Summer.' Frank Meyer of the USDA introduced two ultra-hardy varieties from Liaoyang and Antung, Manchuria, where they were being grown as winter crops. These varieties could be used to breed a winter hardy spinach for our area.

Originally, this plant was

native to Asia Minor. For other cool season potherbs, see also Good King Henry, mustard, orach, rocket, and Swiss chard.

SPINACH—WARM SEASON. There are three main kinds—Malabar Spinach, New Zealand Spinach, and Tampala Spinach. Of these three, New Zealand Spinach most closely resembles the taste of spinach. Tampala is considered to have the sweetest taste. However all three plants make excellent cooked greens. These heat-loving tropical plants are not related to spinach (*Spinachia oleracea*).

MALABAR SPINACH, Basella alba. Warm-season annual vegetable.
Height: vine to 6 foot.
Description: attractive fast-growing vine with glossy leaves.
Likes: sun/moist/heat/deeply dug humus- and fertilizer-rich soil.
Propagation: sets (start indoors and plant outside after frost-free date date) or seeds (because seeds tolerate cool soil, plant outside in late April).
Growing tips: give it room to spread or train it to climb a support.
Harvest tips: It can be eaten either raw in spinach salads, cooked as a green or added to casseroles. Preserve it by blanching and then freezing or canning.

NEW ZEALAND SPINACH, Tetragonia tetragonioides. Warm-season annual vegetable.
Height: upright sprawling plant to 2-3 feet.
Description: succulent green leaves used like spinach.
Likes: sun/moist/well-drained soil.
Tolerates: half-sun.
Pests: aphids (companion plant with nasturtiums to draw off the aphids).
Growing tips: give it room to spread.
Harvest tips: It can be eaten either raw in spinach salads, cooked as a green or added to casseroles. Preserve it by blanching and then freezing or canning.
Propagation: seeds only because it transplants poorly. Seed is slow to germinate, so you should either soak overnight before planting, or start it in moist paper towels and plant when roots show. Because seeds tolerate cool soil, plant outside in late April.

Comments: this plant was first discovered in New Zealand by Captain Cook.

TAMPALA, Amaranthus gangeticus. Warm-season annual vegetable.
Height: 3-4 feet.
Description: coarse upright habit, insignificant green flowerheads.
Likes: sun/semidry/moist.
Propagation: sets or seeds. Because seeds tolerate cool soil, plant outside in late April.
Growing tips: remove flowerheads for longest season; requires heat for best productivity.
Harvest tips: The moderately large leaves cook into a sweet-tasting cooked green that children prefer over regular spinach. It is extremely rich in vitamins, and can be eaten either raw in spinach salads, cooked as a green, or added to casseroles. Preserve it by blanching, and then freezing or canning.

SPIRAEA SPECIES. Prune only to maintain natural habit and shape, do not prune into box-like hedge shapes. The name *spiraea* is the ancient Greek word for 'wreath.'

S. X ARGUTA, Garland Spiraea Bush. Perennial to Zone 3.
Height: 5 feet.
Bloom: profuse white flower clusters on the ends of the branches in early May.
Shape: arched shrub.
Foliage: gray-green.
Culture: easy.
Likes: half-sun/humus-rich soil.
Tolerates: sun/half-shade/semidry/moist.
Propagation: sets.
Comments: may suffer chlorosis in highly alkaline soil. Prune only after bloom. The variety 'Grefshein' is hardier than the species. For prolonged flower display, plant together with the common *Spiraea x vanhouttei*, which this plant closely resembles. This plant can also be used as a hedge.

S. JAPONICA. Perennial to Zone 1.
Height: 3 feet.
Shape: low creeping form.
Bloom: pink flowers from mid-June to early July.
Culture: easy.
Likes: half-sun/humus-rich soil.
Tolerates: sun/half-shade/semidry/moist.

Propagation: sets.
Comments: may suffer chlorosis in highly alkaline soil. Prune out three-year-old branches in early spring before flowering. Varieties of note: 'Alpina,' commonly called the *Daphne Spiraea,* is a very interesting low dwarf form. It is 1 foot tall, has profuse pink flowers, and is excellent for a low edging; 'Coccinea' has rich red flowers; 'Crispa' has pink flower clusters from late June to mid-July and crinkled deep-green foliage tinged red in early spring; 'Froebeli' has pinkish-red flower clusters and bronze fall color; 'Goldflame' has pinkish-purple flower clusters and displays bright foliage colors of orange-red and bronze in both the spring and fall, summer foliage is green; 'Goldmound' is a compact globe-shaped variety with bright yellow foliage throughout the summer and light pink flowers in late spring.

S. PRUNIFOLIA, Bridal Wreath Spiraea. Perennial to Zone 4.
Height: 5 feet.
Bloom: small button-like flowers in clusters along the branches in mid-May.
Shape: spreading clump habit.
Foliage: glossy oval foliage, orange-red fall color.
Culture: easy.
Likes: half-sun/humus-rich soil.
Tolerates: sun/half-shade/semidry/moist.
Propagation: sets.
Comments: may suffer chlorosis in highly alkaline soil. Prune only after bloom. This plant is native to northern China and Korea.

S. TRILOBA, Three-lobed Spiraea. Perennial to Zone 1.
Height: 3 feet.
Shape: arched habit.
Bloom: profuse white flower clusters from mid- to late May.
Foliage: yellow fall color.
Culture: easy.
Likes: half-sun/semidry/humus-rich soil.
Tolerates: sun/half-shade/dry/moist.
Propagation: sets.
Comments: may suffer chlorosis in highly alkaline soil. Prune only after bloom. This plant is most attractive as a landscaping shrub, but it can also be used as a hedge. 'Fairy Queen' and 'Snow White' are pre-

ferred varieties. Both of these were bred by Frank Skinner of Dropmore, Manitoba, in 1961 and 1953, respectively. *Spiraea x vanhouttei* is a less hardy hybrid of this species but is the most commonly planted *Spiraea* in Zone 4. It is similar in appearance to *Spiraea x arguta* which blooms two weeks earlier.

SPOROBOLUS HETEROLEPIS, Prairie Dropseed. Native to the eastern and central plains. Perennial to Zone 3.
Height: 3 feet.
Bloom: delicate airy seedheads.
Foliage: showy fine foliage.
Likes: sun/dry/semidry/moist/sandy, well-drained soil.
Propagation: seeds.
Comments: clump-forming delicate-looking grass; somewhat invasive from self-sown seeds (extra plants are easily weeded out). This showy grass is most appreciated in late summer, fall and winter, a very long season of interest. It is native to the tall grass prairie.

SQUASH, *Cucurbita.* Summer squash is *Cucurbita pepo,* and winter squash and pumpkins are hybrids of *C. maxima.* Warm-season annual fruit.
Description: in general, a sprawling plant with large coarse leaves, large fruit. Bush varieties are 3 feet wide, and vine varieties are 6-10 feet wide (summer squash are more

Squash, Cucurbita

clump-like; winter squash either clump-like or long-vined; pumpkins are very long-vined).
Likes: sun/moist/well-drained, deeply dug, humus- and fertilizer-rich soil.
Propagation: sets (start seed inside and plant out after frost-free date, soak seeds overnight before planting) or seeds (very easy in hot summer areas.)
Growing tips: heavy water require-

ments; bury compost, fish emulsion and manure in planting hole; for best growth, give it wind protection and maximum warmth; to increase heat retention in the soil, use a clear plastic layer over a black plastic mulch; because it is shallow rooted, avoid soil compaction.

For best fruit set, plant two or more together for cross pollination and encourage bees. Male flowers and female flowers (the ones with a tiny fruit attached) occur on the same plants. If saving seed, note that all varieties will hybridize with each other.

This vegetable requires a long hot growing season and ample growing space (summer squash a radius of 4 feet; winter squash a radius of 6 feet). It is usually best planted on the edge of a garden.
Harvest tips: harvest summer squash anytime while skin is still soft to the touch, while young and tender. However, ripen winter squash until skin hardens (it should be hard enough to resist puncture by a fingernail), and harvest it with a good piece of stem attached.
Comments: squash stores well if cool and dry. The flowers of this plant are quite attractive and can be used either as an edible garnish or battered and fried.

Generally, summer squash is used either raw in salads or cooked. Stuff it with meat and vegetables and bake it. However, summer squash does not keep well.

Winter squash and pumpkins are used fresh in salads, for pies, baked whole, breads and soups. They are much sweeter and have a more fruit-like flavor.

Besides its easy storage in a cool and dry area, winter squash can be preserved longer by cooking it and freezing or canning. The variety called 'Hubbard,' a winter squash, keeps well and makes an outstanding pumpkin pie. The winter squash 'Tahitian' is extremely sweet and can be eaten either raw or cooked. Spaghetti Squash, a winter squash, has tasty flesh that resembles spaghetti. It is best baked, then its stringy flesh can be loosened with a fork and baked again with a mixture of hamburger, Italian seasonings, and garlic. Zucchini Squash, a summer squash, is wild-

ly prolific. It can be used raw in salads, used in a spicy Italian stew, fried in patties with potatoes, or stuffed with other vegetables, cheese, and seasonings. It also makes excellent zucchini bread which can be stored in the freezer. Shepherd's Garden Seeds lists a couple of exceptional French and Italian varieties of zucchini. See also listing for Pumpkin.

STACHYS BYZANTINA (*S. lanata or S. olympica*), Lamb's Ears. Perennial to Zone 3.
Height: 1 foot.
Bloom: insignificant purplish flowers.
Foliage: spreading clump of woolly silver-white leaves.
Culture: easy.
Likes: half-sun/semidry.
Tolerates: sun/half-shade/dry/moist.
Propagation: sets.
Comments: this plant is particularly useful for the front of the garden in partially shady areas. The advantage of planting it in partly shady areas is that it rarely blooms. In deep shade it loses its attractive silver foliage color and reverts back to green. The variety 'Primrose Heron' has yellow foliage in the spring, which turns to gray-green later in the summer.

STANLEYA PINNATA, Prince's Plume. Native to dry areas of the Great Plains. Perennial.
Height: 3 feet.
Bloom: yellow plume-like flower spikes from May to July.
Foliage: stately upright habit, dull green lance-shaped leaves.
Culture: difficult.
Likes: sun/dry/semidry/loose rocky soil/alkaline pH.
Propagation: sets or seeds.
Comments: this plant does not like being crowded; established plants resent transplanting. Closely related plants are *Stanleya viridiflora,* which has greenish-yellow flowers; and *Stanleya tomentosa,* a rare native with woolly foliage. Plants of the genus *Stanleya* are selenium indicators and may require trace amounts of it to thrive in a garden.

STIPA COMATA, Needle and Thread, Common Spear Grass. Native to dry clay areas of the Great Plains. Perennial.
Height: 2 feet.
Foliage: tufted clump of coarse

gray-green foliage.

Likes: sun/dry/semidry.

Propagation: sets or seeds (self-sows into scattered individual clumps).

Comments: unusual-looking seed-head in July that dries and persists until late fall; roots are not invasive. This plant is an important grass for use in establishing a restored prairie on dry, heavy clay soil. The common name Needle and Thread refers to the appearance of the seed and awn.

S. VIRIDULA, Green Needle Grass. Native to semi-moist fertile soils of the Great Plains. Perennial.

Height: 2 feet.

Foliage: tufted clump of green foliage.

Likes: sun/dry/semidry/moist.

Propagation: sets or seeds (self-sows into scattered clumps).

Comments: showy spike-like seed-heads in July that dry and persist until late fall. Roots are not invasive. Tolerates clay soil if given a slightly moist location. This attractive plant can be used either as an ornamental grass or for prairie restoration. The common name Needle Grass refers to the shape of the seed and awn.

STRAWBERRY, Fragaria x ananassa. Perennial fruit to Zone 1.

Height: 6 inches.

Description: small white flowers, delicious fruit.

Culture: easy.

Likes: moisture/humus-rich soil.

Tolerates: half-sun/half-shade/semi-dry.

Strawberry, Fragaria x ananassa

Growing tips: may become chlorotic in highly alkaline soil; requires some winter mulch; because the runners take lots of room, it is best planted in a large patch.

Propagation: sets.

Comments: the best varieties are the new day-neutral strawberries. They produce well the same year they are planted and are surprisingly hardy to Zone 2 if carefully winter mulched. The real advantage of day-neutral strawberries is that they start producing fruit in July or August and continue into September (a very long season). Fruit is produced over a prolonged period giving a daily harvest, quite an advantage for home gardeners.

Best winter protection comes from a layer of plastic (to protect moisture) covered with a layer of straw (to protect from sun and heat).

Two varieties of note are 'Fern,' and 'Hecker': both have superior firm sweet fruit. The Alpine Strawberry *(Fragaria alpina)* has a small, but dramatically flavored fruit. This fruit has commercial potential for our area. I would like to see high quality candy made from the pulp by a local industry and shipped around the world.

The name *fragaria* means "fragrant" and refers to the smell of the fruit. Kim Williams suggested an uncooked freezer jam to preserve the strawberry's rich aroma. She also states that "strewberry" was the original name referring to the way that the berries are strewn in among the leaves. The leaves can be used for an herbal tea rich in vitamin C.

STRAWFLOWER. See *Helichrysum bracteatum* or *Helipterum humboldtianum.* For other everlastings see *Ammobium alatum* (Winged Everlasting), *Briza major* (Quaking Grass), *Bromus briziformis* (Brome Grass), *Goniolimon tataricum* (German Statice), *Gypsophilla elegans* (Baby's Breath), *Lagurus ovatus* (Rabbit Tail Grass), *Limonium* (Statice), *Nigella damascena, Xeranthemun annuum* (Common Immortelle).

SUKSDORFIA VIOLACEA. Native to stream banks in the Rocky Mountains. Perennial.

Height: 1 foot.

Bloom: lavender flowers on a stalk.

Foliage: clump habit, kidney-shaped leaves.

Likes: sun/half-sun/moist/wet.

Propagation: sets or seeds.

Comments: a closely related species is *Suksdorfia ranunculifolia,* which has yellow flowers.

SUNFLOWER, Helianthus annuus. Official state flower of Kansas, one of the many flowers nominated for U.S. national flower. Annual.

Height: 4-8 feet (either a bush or a tall single stalk depending on variety).

Bloom: yellow or white flowers with dark centers in late July until frost (long season).

Culture: easy.

Likes: sun/moist/humus- and fertilizer-rich soil.

Tolerates: half-sun/dry/semidry.

Propagation: sets or seeds. (because seeds tolerate cool soil, plant outside in late April, seeds germinate easily).

Growing tips: cucumbers make an excellent understory companion plant for tall sunflowers; potatoes and sunflowers should not be planted with each other because they stunt each other's growth. Tall varieties are grown for their giant seedheads.

Harvest tips: harvest the head after frost and dry thoroughly indoors.

Comments: oil from the seeds is used for dry skin and for nourishing the hair.

This plant was one of the few crop plants actually cultivated by the Indians of the lower Missouri River area. Lewis and Clark recorded that the seed was dried and then pounded into a coarse gray flour. The famous ethnobotanist Melvin Gilmore recorded the following Teton Dakota saying: "When the sunflowers were tall and in full bloom, the buffalo were fat and the meat good." The original bushy North American plant was taken to Europe where it was bred into the tall seed-producing plants we are most familiar with today.

To roast seeds, mix seeds with Worcestershire sauce and salt. Roast in a shallow pan at 250° F for an hour. Seeds are rich in calories and protein, as well as Vitamins A, B, D and E, iron, and calcium. See also *Helianthus.*

SWISS CHARD, Beta vulgaris var. cicla. Cool-season annual vegetable with moderate heat tolerance.

Height: 10 inches.
Description: upright leafy clump, tender foliage is used as a cooked green, stems are red or white depending on variety.
Culture: easy.
Likes: half-sun/half-shade/moist/well-drained, moist soil.
Tolerates: moderate alkalinity.
Propagation: seeds or sets. Seeds must be fresh for best germination: planting can be staggered from early spring to late summer, or planted in fall for an early start on next year's crop. Transplants easily.
Growing tips: each seed is actually a multiple seed fruit, thus requiring that a swiss chard planting must be thinned; plants should be spaced to about 1 foot apart.
Harvest tips: regularly remove flower stalks for prolonged harvest of its leaves. Leaves must be harvested continuously during the growing season or new leaves will stop being produced. When harvesting, do not cut off leaves, pull them off. Once the plant gets leggy, it can be cut to the ground to regrow as a second harvest.
Comments: this cold hardy plant can be grown in a coldframe through the winter. It can tolerate light frosts but not heavy freezes without protection.

This plant, especially Red Swiss Chard, is very showy in the front of a flower bed or in a strip along both sides of a sidewalk. Chard was bred during the 16th century and is closely related to beets (*Beta vulgaris*).

SYMPHYTUM OFFICINALE, Comfrey. Perennial to Zone 1.
Height: 3 feet.
Bloom: murky blue flowers from late May-July.
Foliage: bold rough-textured foliage.
Culture: easy.
Likes: half-sun.
Tolerates: sun/half-shade/dry/semidry/moist.
Propagation: sets, roots or seeds.
Comments: fast-spreading large clump; this overly exuberant plant may seem invasive though it does not spread beyond its clump. If plant becomes leggy, cut it back to the ground. This plant is a powerful healing herb used internally for nutrient deficiencies and externally as a poultice to speed the mending of broken bones. Its botanical name, symphytum, translates from Latin to mean 'the leaf that mends together.' In addition, the huge quantity of foliage this plant produces makes an exceptional mineral-rich compost. (Do not forget to add grass clippings, seaweed, manure, bonemeal, and other rich components for the best compost.)

Comfrey is also excellent used in and around animal pens to dress up their appearance and catch extra nitrogen. Chickens love to forage on the leaves. There are varieties of this plant with somewhat showy murky red flowers. However, the most attractive variety is called *Symphytum x uplandicum 'variegatum,'* which has spectacular white-variegated foliage and baby-blue flowers.

SYRINGA SPECIES. Lilac, Official State Flower of New Hampshire.
Comments: Always try to buy lilacs on their own roots to reduce root suckering from *Syringa vulgaris* understocks. Propagation can be done from softwood cuttings in summer. Prune only after bloom to remove old wood, weak twiggy stems, and encourage new growth. For longest lasting cut flowers, crush stem ends and dip completely in deep water leaving them submerged overnight. Flowers must be put in water immediately after cutting. There is an International Lilac Society. Its address is listed in the Resource Directory.

Order of bloom: *hyacinthiflora* hybrids (early May), *vulgaris* (late May to June), *x chinensis* (late May to June), *patula* (late May to June), *villosa* hybrids (mid- to late June), *pekinensis* (late June to July), *reticulata* (late June to July).

S. X CHINENSIS, Rouen Lilac. Perennial to Zone 2.
Height: 8 feet.
Bloom: lavender or white flowers from late May to June.
Shape: distinctly compact graceful habit.
Foliage: delicate narrow leaves.
Culture: easy.
Likes: sun/semidry.
Tolerates: half-sun/dry/moist.
Propagation: sets only.
Comments: the species name is very confused for this hybrid (*Syringa vulgaris* and *Syringa persica*). It was first discovered in the Rouen Gardens and originally named *Syringa rothomagensis*. Later, this was changed to its present name. Two varieties of note are 'Orchid Beauty,' which has pink flowers, and a variety with bicolor white flowers with a light blue eye. This plant makes a good hedge and, since the flowers are sterile, there are no brown seedpods.

S. HYACINTHIFLORA. Perennial to Zone 1.
Height: 10 feet.
Bloom: this is the very first lilac to bloom in early May.
Shape: upright shrub.
Culture: easy.
Likes: sun/semidry.
Tolerates: half-sun/dry/moist.
Comments: it is a hybrid of *Syringa vulgaris* and *S. oblata dilatata*.
Propagation: sets.

S. Hyacinthiflora varieties
'Buffon,' soft-pink flower clusters; single form; slightly fragrant. A Lemoine hybrid, 1921. Named for Georges Louis Leclerc de Buffon, a French courtier, naturalist, and phrasemaker.
'Charles Nordine,' light blue flower clusters; single form; fragrant. A Skinner hybrid, 1960.
'Ester Staley,' magenta-pink flower clusters; fragrant. Introduced by Mr. W. B. Clarke in 1948.
'Evangeline,' deep lilac-purple flower color; double form; fragrant. A Skinner hybrid, 1934.
'Excel,' very large lavender-pink flower clusters; fragrant. A Skinner hybrid, 1935.
'Maiden's Blush,' large and loose clear-pink flower clusters; dwarf size bush (4-5 feet tall). A Skinner Hybrid, 1966.
'Pocahontas,' reddish-purple flower clusters; fragrant. A Skinner hybrid, 1935.
'Royal Purple,' near-black buds open to royal purple flower clusters; double form; very early bloom. Introduced by Skinner in 1965.
'Sunset,' red flower clusters; double form. Introduced by Mr. W. B. Clarke in 1949.

S. MICROPHYLLA 'SUPERBA,' Daphne Lilac. Perennial to Zone 4.
Height: 5 feet.
Bloom: very fragrant showy pink

flowers, occasional repeat bloom.
Likes: sun/half-sun/semidry/moist.
Propagation: sets only.

S. PATULA, Miss Kim Lilac. Perennial to Zone 1.
Height: 3 feet.
Bloom: pink buds that turn into fragrant light blue flowers from late May to June.
Shape: slow-growing spreading clump.
Foliage: small delicate foliage, attractive burgundy-red fall color.
Culture: easy.
Likes: sun.
Tolerates: alkaline soil.
Propagation: sets.
Comments: though usually grown as a shrub, this plant can also be used as a hedge. A few of the varieties, called the 'Preston Hybrids,' are included in this section. These were developed by Isabella Preston of the Central Experimental Farm in Ottawa.

Preston hybrid varieties

'Agnes Smith,' very large clusters of outstanding snow-white flowers from pink buds; large shrub. Introduced by the University of New Hampshire.

'Bellicent,' large clusters of coral-pink flowers; fragrant.

'Coral,' soft pink color; introduced by Isabella Preston in 1937.

'Donald Wyman,' deep pink to red flower clusters; non-fragrant. A Skinner hybrid, 1944.

'Isabella,' large clusters of pinkish-lilac flowers; non-fragrant. Named for Isabella Preston.

'James McFarlane,' pink flower clusters from red buds with a long bloom season; single form; showy bush habit. Introduced by the University of New Hampshire.

'Miss Canada,' flower clusters are a very clear tone of pink; non-fragrant. Introduced by Frank Skinner in 1967.

'Nocturne,' light blue flower clusters; double form. Introduced by Morden Research Station, in 1936.

'Royalty,' rich dark purple flower clusters. Named by Dr. W. R. Leslie of Morden Research Station, in 1935.

S. VULGARIS, Common Lilac; state flower of New Hampshire. Perennial to Zone 1.
Height: 10 feet.

Shape: spreading bush.
Bloom: fragrant red, pink, white, blue, or purple flowers from late May to June.
Culture: easy.
Propagation: sets.
Likes: sun/semidry.
Tolerates: half-sun/dry/moist/alkaline soil.
Pests: leaf miners create jagged edges on the leaves by mid-summer.
Comments: the common purple variety is the most fragrant and root suckers the worst; some of the white varieties get rusty-looking from the rains of early June.

The *Vulgaris* hybrids are commonly called French Hybrids, referring to the exceptional work of father and son—Victor and Emile Lemoine of Nice, France. On the following varieties, the name of the breeder and date of introduction follows the variety name.

French hybrid varieties

'Alice Harding' (Lemoine 1938); fragrant white flower clusters; dramatic double form (this is the most doubled form of any lilac variety); some difficulty of cultivation. Named for Mrs. Alice Harding, a U.S. amateur horticulturist and author of the book *Lilacs in my Garden*.

'Anabel' (Hawkins 1938); fragrant semi-double pink flowers; loose clusters.

'Boule Azuree' (Lemoine 1919); lavender-blue flower clusters; single form; enchantingly fragrant. This name translates from French to mean 'sky-blue ball or head.'

'Charm' (Havemeyer 1974); very large and showy fragrant lavender-pink flower clusters; late and long blooming season; tall shrub habit.

'Congo' (Lemoine 1896); fragrant deep purple-red flower clusters (a tropical-looking color); single form. The name refers to Congo dye, a red dye for cotton.

'De Miribel' (Lemoine 1903); fragrant violet-blue flower clusters; single form; moderately late bloom. Named for French botanist Charles Francois Brisseau De Miribel.

'Edith Cavell' (Lemoine 1916); pure ivory flower color (buds are cream-colored); fragrant; double form. Named for Edith Louisa Cavell, an English nurse executed as a spy during World War I.

'Edward J Gardner' (Gardner

1950); double pink flower clusters; considered to be the best true clear pink variety by many lilac experts.

'Etna' (Lemoine 1927); large fragrant purple flower clusters; single form; attractive shrub habit. Named for Mount Etna (or Aetna), a volcano in Sicily.

'Firmament' (Lemoine 1932); sky blue flower clusters; single form; early bloom. Name refers to the vault of heaven or the sky.

'Interlude' (Wayside Gardens Nursery); extremely large (basketball size) pinkish-red flower clusters; double form. This relatively hard to find variety should be better known.

'Katherine Havemeyer' (Lemoine 1922); showy fragrant pink flower clusters; double form. Named for the wife of Theodore Havemeyer, a U.S. amateur horticulturist and lilac breeder.

'Krasavitasa Moskvy' (Kolesmikov 1963); fragrant pink flowers which fade to white; double form. This exceptional variety's name translates from Russian to mean 'Glory of Moscow.' This variety, and also 'Znamya Lenyna,' were brought out of Russia during the Cold War in a briefcase handcuffed to a courier's arm and protected under diplomatic immunity.

'Lucy Baltet' (Lemoine pre-1888); large fragrant coral-pink flower clusters, single form, attractive low bush form which grows only to 5 feet tall. Named for the daughter of Charles Baltet, a French horticulturist.

'Ludwig Spaeth' (Spaeth 1883); fragrant flower clusters are a showy deep purple color, single form.

'Mme Lemoine' (Lemoine 1890); very fragrant snow-white flower clusters, double form. This is one of the hardiest *Vulgaris* hybrid lilacs.

'Marechal Lannes' (Lemoine 1910); fragrant blue-mauve flower clusters; a somewhat double form; a late and long blooming season. Named for Jean Lannes, Duc de Montebello and Marshall of France in 1804. He is considered to be one of the greatest engineers in French history.

'Marengo' (Lemoine 1923); extremely profuse lavender flower clusters; single form which completely cover the bush. Name refers to the Battle of Marengo in which Napoleon defeated Austria.

'Maude Notcutt' (Notcutt 1956); extremely large clear white flower clusters; single form. This variety was bred by a Dutch grower who named it 'Flora,' then the Notcutt Nursery bought the rights to it and renamed it.

'Montaigne' (Lemoine, 1926); reddish-pink flower clusters. Named for Michel Eyquem de Montaigne, a French essayist.

'Mrs. W E Marshall' (Havemeyer 1924); very large fragrant red-purple flower clusters; single form; tall shrub.

'Nadezhda' (Kolesmikov 1955); fragrant violet flower clusters; double form. The name of this variety translates from Russian to mean 'hope.'

'Night' (Havemeyer 1943); very large fragrant purple flower clusters; single form; tall shrub habit. This is one of the very last Vulgaris hybrids to bloom, often starting at the same time as the *Villosa* hybrids (Late Lilacs).

'Paul Thirion' (Lemoine 1915); fragrant magenta-red flower clusters; double form; late bloom season. Named for Paul Thirion, the famous parks horticulturist for the city of Nancy, France.

'President Grevy' (Lemoine 1886); rich lavender-blue flower clusters with pinkish buds; double form; fragrant. Named for Francois Paul Jules Grevy, president of France from 1879 to 1887.

'President Lincoln' (Dunbar 1916); fragrant lavender-blue flower clusters; moderately early. The color of the flowers closely resembles the unforgettable color of the tropical Jacaranda tree.

'Primrose' (1949); creamy-yellow flower clusters.

'Romance' (Havemeyer 1954); very large fragrant pink flower clusters; single form; tall shrub habit.

'Sensation,' a unique bicolor; fragrant red flowers with distinct white edging; single form.

'Sweetheart' (Clarke 1953); red buds which open into striking baby-pink flower clusters; double form.

'Variegated,' lavender flower clusters; leaves are mottled with yellow.

'Victor Lemoine' (Lemoine 1906); fragrant pink to blue-lavender flower clusters; double form; a late and long blooming season. Named for Victor Pierre Louis Lemoine, father of Emile Lemoine.

'Znamya Lenyna' (Kolesmikov 1963); intense red (almost cherry-red) flower clusters; single form; late-blooming season. The name of this variety translates from Russian to mean 'Banner of Lenin.'

'Zulu' (Havemeyer 1954); very large fragrant purple flower clusters; single form; tall shrub habit.

TAGETES HYBRIDS, Marigold. One of the many flowers nominated for the U.S. national flower. Annual.
Height: 6-24 inches (depending on variety).
Bloom: profuse red, orange or yellow flowers from May to late frost.
Foliage: finely-divided.
Culture: easy.
Likes: sun/semidry.
Tolerates: half-sun/half-shade/dry.
Propagation: sets or seeds. (Seed germination: can be seeded outside before the frost-free date.)
Comments: upright plants; can be pinched when young for more compact plants. This plant is excellent in gardens, in containers, and as cut flowers. The 'Marietta' varieties are showy bicolors. There is a Marigold Society of America. Its address is listed in the Resource Directory.

TAMARIX RAMOSISSIMA (T. pentandra), Tamarix. Perennial to Zone 3-4.
Height: 10 feet.
Shape: irregularly spreading bush.
Foliage: feathery branch tips which turn vivid pink in mid-July.
Culture: easy.
Likes: sun/semidry.
Tolerates: half-sun/dry/poor soil.
Propagation: sets.

Tamarix ramosissima

Comments: the improved variety 'Rubra' (or 'Summerglow') has a deep pink color and a longer season from mid-July to mid-August.

TAXUS CUSPITATA 'NANA,' Dwarf Yew. Perennial to Zone 2.
Height: 3 feet.
Bloom: occasional pinkish-red berries.
Shape: dense rounded clump.
Foliage: dark evergreen.
Likes: half-shade/moist.
Tolerates: half-sun/shade/semidry.
Propagation: sets.
Comments: requires protection from extreme wind and winter sun; prefers morning sun.

TELESONIX JAMESII (Boykinia jamesii). Native to rocky places in the foothills and high Rocky Mountains. Perennial.
Height: 4 inches.
Bloom: unforgettable nodding dull purplish-red flowers on a stalk, blooms from May to end of July (long season).
Foliage: clump habit, semi-evergreen heuchera-like foliage.
Likes: sun/half-sun/dry/semidry.
Propagation: sets or seeds.
Comments: requires mid-day shade in hot summer areas; prefers well-drained rocky soil with some organic material mixed in.

TETRADYMIA CANESCENS, Gray Horsebrush. Native to dry areas of the Great Plains and foothills. Perennial.
Height: 2 feet.
Bloom: showy yellow flowers from July to August.
Foliage: upright branching habit, showy silvery-white woolly twigs and foliage; stems have an interesting knobby surface from past leaf nodes.
Likes: sun.
Tolerates: dry/semidry.
Propagation: sets or seeds.
Comments: this plant is showy when in bloom, then in winter it makes an attractive accent as it stands above the snow. The name *tetradymia* refers to its grouping of flowers into clusters of four.

THALICTRUM AQUILEGIFOLIUM, Meadowrue. Perennial to Zone 2.
Height: 2 feet.
Bloom: showy white or pinkish-purple flower clusters from May to ear-

ly June, flower clusters resemble cotton candy.
Foliage: attractive gray-green.
Likes: half-sun.
Tolerates: half-shade/moist.
Propagation: sets or seeds.
Comments: upright clump; may need winter mulch in exposed areas; may need windstaking with brush or hoop support in exposed areas; established plants resent transplanting. The species name, *aquilegifolium,* refers to the similar appearance of the foliage of Columbine *(Aquilegia).*

T. DIPTEROCARPUM, Yunan Meadowrue. Perennial to Zone 2.
Height: 4 feet.
Bloom: spectacular pink, white, or lavender airy flowers from June to August (long season).
Foliage: attractive foliage.
Likes: half-sun.
Tolerates: half-shade/moist.
Propagation: sets or seeds.
Comments: upright clump; may need winter mulch in exposed areas; may need windstaking with brush or hoop support; established plants resent transplanting.

Yunan Meadowrue, Thalictrum dipterocarpum

When in bloom, this plant has a hazy or mist-like appearance. Lilies that bloom at the same time make a good combination. This plant was brought from China by Ernest 'Chinese' Wilson.

T. FLAVUM 'GLAUCUM,' Yellow Thalictrum. Perennial to Zone 2.
Height: 4 feet.
Bloom: showy yellow airy flowers.
Foliage: attractive blue-green.
Likes: sun/half-sun/semidry/moist.
Propagation: sets.
Comments: upright clump; requires a brush or hoop support; established plants resent transplanting; may need winter mulch in exposed areas. Be sure to hide the bottom of this top heavy plant. Plant it in the background.

THERMOPSIS CAROLINIANA, Yellow Lupine. Perennial to Zone 3.
Height: 4 feet.
Bloom: showy yellow lupine-like flower stalks from late May to June.
Foliage: lupine-like.
Culture: easy.
Likes: sun.
Tolerates: half-sun/half-shade/semidry/moist.
Propagation: sets or seeds. (Seed germination: nick seeds and soak overnight before planting.)
Comments: upright clump; may need light winter mulch; established plants resent transplanting.

Yellow Lupine, Thermopsis caroliniana

T. RHOMBIFOLIA, Yellow Lupine, Buffalo Bean, native to the grasslands and foothills of the central and northern Rockies. Perennial to Zone 3.
Height: 1 foot.
Bloom: bright yellow lupine flower stalks from early May to mid-June; attractive brown bean-like seedpods.
Foliage: lupine-like foliage.
Culture: easy.
Likes: sun.
Tolerates: half-sun/dry/semidry/clay soil.
Propagation: sets (when transplanting young plants, include extra dirt underneath for its large tap root) or seeds. (Seed germination: either cold treatment, scarification or nick seeds and soak overnight before planting.)
Comments: fast-spreading upright clump, may need light winter mulch; established plants resent transplanting; invasive by root spreading. Plant goes dormant and dies to the ground in late summer. Bean-like seeds are poisonous and have poisoned children who seem to find them appealing. For this reason, it is probably best to remove the seedpods after flowering. The other native *Thermopsis* species, *T. montana,* is poorly adapted to the plains climate, as well as being a less attractive plant. The Indian name Buffalo Flower refers to their

use of this flower's bloom time to indicate the prime time to hunt buffalo.

THUJA OCCIDENTALIS, White Cedar, Arborvitae. Perennial to Zone 1.
Height: 60 feet.
Shape: attractive cedar-like tree with red bark.
Foliage: evergreen.
Culture: easy.
Likes: half-sun/half-shade/shade/semidry/moist.
Propagation: sets (soft-hardwood cuttings or hardwood cuttings in summer or winter).
Comments: will not tolerate extreme sun exposure, especially in the winter; prefers some protection from wind; never plant this tall tree too close to a building overhang. The species form itself is very attractive. All tree size varieties can be used as a hedge. If you plant less hardy varieties, such as *'Pyramidalis'* or other grocery store varieties, they will brown out or die in a hard winter. Preferred ornamental varieties of note are the following:

Tree Size Varieties
'Brandon,' one of the hardiest tall varieties.
'Emerald Green,' 10 feet tall with a densely compact columnar form.
'Fastigata,' 20 feet tall; a narrowly upright tree with a graceful curl in its leaves.
'Holmstrup,' 15 feet tall; a smaller variety with a densely columnar, almost pyramidal shape.
'Masonic,' columnar shape; selected by Clayton Berg of Helena's Valley Nursery from an old tree on the west side of Helena's Masonic Temple.
'Techny,' 10 feet tall; an attractive semi-upright tree with a loosely spreading shape and attractive yellow seeds (in full sun).

Dwarf Size Varieties
'Danica,' 2 feet tall; globe-like form; green foliage in summer which turns bronze in winter; moderately fast rate of growth.
'Filifera,' dramatic string-like green foliage which hangs from branches; showy blue-green seeds. This variety must be grafted onto a standard.
'Globosa,' 3 feet tall; tidy globe-like shape; gray-green foliage color.
'Little Gem,' 10 inches tall; irreg-

ularly flattened mound; densely compact and slow-growing.

'Little Giant,' 3 feet tall; medium to large rounded rectangular shape. This variety was introduced by Mc-Connell Nurseries in Fort Burwell, Ontario.

'Rhinegold,' 3 feet tall; globe-like form; bright gold summer and winter coloring; very slow-growing.

'Woodwardii,' 4 feet tall; strikingly attractive globe-like shape; all branches radiate out symmetrically from the center.

THUNBERGIA ALATA, Black-eyed Susan Vine. Annual.
Height: vine to 3 feet.
Bloom: dramatic orange flowers with black centers, blooms from July to frost.
Climbing habit: loose sprawling habit; climbs by stem twining.
Culture: easy.
Likes: moist/heat.
Tolerates: sun/half-sun/semidry.
Propagation: sets or seeds. (Seed germination: warm.)
Comments: this plant is excellent in hanging pots, in window boxes, on a small lattice, or as a ground cover. Give it string or wire to twine its vine tips around.

THYMUS, Thyme. Perennial to Zone 3.
Height: 1 inch.
Bloom: red, pink, white, or lavender flowers in June or July.
Foliage: creeping mat of aromatic evergreen foliage.
Culture: easy.
Likes: sun/semidry/poor soil.
Tolerates: half-sun/very dry.
Propagation: sets.
Comments: this plant is often used as an herbal lawn mix with chamomile and yarrow. Most thyme varieties will tolerate some light foot traffic. The botanical names for this genus are in chaos—buy varieties by their common names. As a note of interest, Fox Hill Farm lists thirty-three different varieties of thyme. These plants are excellent for the front of the garden. They can also be considered low maintenance plants. Woolly Thyme is particularly dramatic in a formal garden. All thymes make good companion plants with tomatoes because they repel the tomato hornworm. There is also a lavender-scented thyme, which cats seem to love as much as catnip. As a seasoning, use thyme with any meat, fish, or vegetable. It can also be potted up and brought inside during the winter.

Apple Thyme *(T. labrescens)*

Big Thyme *(T. nummularius)*—large lilac-pink flowers, large leaves.

Caraway Thyme *(T. herba-barona)*—slow-growing habit.

Culinary Thyme *(T. vulgaris)*—lilac-purple flowers from late June to July. The variety 'Anderson's Gold' has bright yellow foliage in the fall, winter, and spring. It is marginally hardy to Zone 4.

Lemon Thyme *(T. x citriodorus)*—there are two exceptional varieties of this plant; *'Argenteus'* silver variegated (fast-growing habit), and *'Aureus'* gold variegated (fast-growing habit).

Mother of Thyme *(T. praecox subsp. arcticus)*—profuse red, pink or white flowers. 'Albus' has white flowers and dainty light green foliage. The best herbal lawn varieties are: *'Coccineus'* with deep red flowers, 'Pink Chintz' with pink flowers (fast-growing habit), and 'Snowdrift' with white flowers (slow-growing habit).

Pine-scented Thyme *(T. caespitatus)*

Woolly Thyme *(T. pseudolanuginosus)*—pink flowers, gray-green woolly foliage. This dramatic-looking plant can be used in a showy accent spot.

TILIA CORDATA, Small-Leaved Linden, tree. Perennial to Zone 3.
Height: 40 feet.
Bloom: very fragrant tiny white flowers in late June (be sure not to prune branches too far above nose level).
Shape: symmetrically shaped pyramidal tree.
Foliage: dark green.
Culture: easy.
Likes: half-sun/moist.
Tolerates: sun/semidry.
Propagation: sets or seeds (buy only sets with their terminal bud tip intact).
Comments: rarely needs pruning. A new variety of *Tilia americana,* called 'Redmond,' is creating a stir because of its classic pyramidal form. It is hardy to Zone 3-4 and was introduced in Freemont, Nebraska. For extremely harsh

Small-Leaved Linden, Tilia cordata

and exposed locations, substitute the almost as attractive 'Wascana' Linden, a seedling of the 'Dropmore' linden. Both 'Wascana' and 'Dropmore' are hybrids of *Tilia americana* and *T. cordata* with attractive intermediate size leaves and a resistance to leaf mites that curl the leaves on *T. americana.*

In European folklore, old linden trees were believed to be the favorite haunt for elves and fairies. The Indians used the inner bark of the native linden *(Tilia americana)* for twine, rope, and basket making.

T. MONGOLICA, Mongolian Linden. Perennial to Zone 2.
Height: 40 feet.
Shape: rounded tree; bark cracks attractively with age to reveal a yellow underbark.
Foliage: attractive birch-like foliage; yellow fall color.
Likes: sun.
Tolerates: semidry/moist.
Propagation: sets.
Comments: this appealing tree should be better known. Because of its low main branches, it is an excellent tree for climbing and treehouses.

TITHONIA ROTUNDIFOLIA 'GRANDIFLORA,' Mexican Sunflower. Annual.
Height: 4 feet.
Bloom: bright orange sunflowers from July to frost (long season).
Culture: easy.
Likes: sun/semidry.
Tolerates: half-sun/dry.
Propagation: sets (transplant carefully) or seeds. (Seed germination: dark.)
Comments: rounded bush habit; may need windstaking with brush support in exposed areas. This plant makes an excellent tall plant for the garden, as well as cut flowers for arrangements. 'Torch' is a more compact variety. In Greek

mythology, Tithonus was a mortal loved by Aurora, the saffron-robed, rosy-fingered goddess of the dawn. She asked Zeus to make her lover immortal but forgot to ask for eternal youth for him as well. Tithonus grew older and older until Aurora eventually turned him into a grasshopper.

TOMATILLO, Physalis ixocarpa. Warm-season annual fruit.
Height: 3 feet.
Description: sprawling tomato-like plant, showy yellow flowers which attract bees, prolific husk-covered green fruit.
Culture: easy.
Likes: sun/moist.
Propagation: sets or seeds (start seeds indoors and plant out after frost-free date).
Growing tips: prefers hot summer areas; requires windstaking just like a tomato plant; for best growth, give it wind protection and moderate humidity; remove all flowers in late summer to encourage last fruit to ripen.
Comments: tomatillos are used primarily for Mexican green sauces and chile verde because the flesh breaks down into a smooth textured sauce. They keep well in a refrigerator. Additionally, they can be preserved by freezing or canning once cooked.

TOMATO, Lycopersicon lycopersicum. Warm-season annual fruit.
Height: 4 feet.
Description: sprawling upright plant with weak stems, red, yellow or white fruit.
Culture: easy.
Likes: half-sun/moist/manure/deeply dug, humus- and fertilizer-rich soil/magnesium and calcium.
Tolerates: sun/half-shade.
Propagation: sets or seeds. Start seed inside 5-6 weeks before the frost-free date; seeds germinate easily, but require bright light indoors. The very best sets are the tall leggy ones. Plant them as deeply as possible because the long stem grows new roots. Later in the season, suckers can be removed and planted to make new plants.
Growing tips: for best growth and disease resistance, give it wind protection, moderate warmth and moderate humidity; for maximum heat

retention in the soil, use a clear plastic layer over black plastic mulch; requires a 3 foot tall hoop support to climb on; fruit set spray helps start fruit set early in the season especially on overcast or windless days (later in the summer this spray is unneccessary).

In spring and early summer, tomatoes have heavy water requirements. Give deep and frequent waterings. Then in mid-summer when

Tomato, Lycopersicon lycopersicum

fruit set becomes heavy, gradually reduce the waterings.

Loves manure, particularly aged manure, bonemeal and compost; requires trace minerals including magnesium and calcium. Two tricks for supplying these nutrients are adding poultry grit (containing calcium) and Epsom Salts (containing magnesium) to the soil near tomato roots.
Pests: cutworms, flea beetles, tomato hornworms (big ugly green worms—look for them near tattered foliage), Colorado bean beetle, and tobacco mosiac virus which spreads either from handling cigarettes or from smoke particles that catch on clothing. However, mildew is rarely a problem if water is kept off foliage at night.

Companion plant with basil and predatory wasp-attracting carrot family members (carrots, chervil, coriander, dill, fennel or lovage).
Harvest tips: when frosts start getting heavy and frequent, harvest the remaining green fruit and ripen inside. One method is to pull the entire plant, roots and all, and hang it

upside down in a cool basement to slowly ripen its fruit. A second method is to ripen fruit in a sunny window. A third method is to place green tomatoes in a paper bag with ripe bananas or apples for their ethylene gas.
Comments: this plant is intensely sensitive to cool weather; fruit does not either set or ripen if night temperature goes down to 50° F. In mid- to late August, gradually reduce watering and remove shoot tips and flowers to encourage last fruit to ripen. Protect tomato plants from early frost by covering them with blankets or tarps, otherwise frost will blacken fruit.

Tomatoes, in general, can be broken into two categories. Determinate varieties ripen all their fruit at the same time, indeteminate varieties ripen fruit over the whole season and are more vine-like in nature.

Tomatoes are eaten raw or cooked. They can be preserved by drying, or by cooking them and freezing or canning. Best tomato flavor is achieved with minimum water. Overwatering will cause the fruit to split, underwatering or a lack of calcium in the soil will cause blossom end rot—characterized by a depressed greyish area on blossom end of fruit.

Native to the Andes Mountains, tomatoes have a long history of cultivation by the Indians. They were grown in Europe as an ornamental for several centuries before anyone believed they were edible.

One of the best-flavored tomato varieties is the tiny yellow pear-shaped one called 'Yellow Pear'. Children seem to love this one best, often raiding gardens to get it. Two other outstanding small varieties are 'Sweet 100' with its extra-sweet cherry-size tomatoes, and 'Currant' with pea-sized tomatoes. Both of these two varieties form grape-like clusters of fruit. 'Persimmon' is an old variety noted for its exceptional flavor.

Full size toma-

Tomato Hornworm

toes which do well in a short season and set fruit in cool weather are 'Flier America,' 'Springset,' 'Early Cascade,' 'Ultra Boy,' and 'Ultra Girl'.

For hot summer areas, Shepherd's Garden Seeds lists five excellent varieties. They are 'Camp Joy,' a cherry tomato bred for flavor; 'Carmello,' a full size French variety bred for its flavor; 'Lorissa,' a French variety bred for its distinctive Greek-type flavor; 'Marmande,' a cold-tolerant variety bred for flavor; and 'Milano,' an early ripening Italian paste tomato. Paste tomatos have less juice, which makes them excellent for sauces and canning.

Additionally, there are varieties from Russia and Siberia that are exceptionally cold hardy, but have less quality in texture and flavor. Some of these varieties are 'Brookpact,' 'Coldset,' 'Russian Red,' and 'Siberia'.

TORENIA FOURNIERI, Torenia, Wishbone Flower. Annual.
Height: 10 inches.
Bloom: tropical-looking gloxinia-like flowers with blue, yellow and purple markings.
Foliage: bronzy-green foliage.
Culture: easy.
Likes: moist/humus-rich soil.
Tolerates: half-sun/half-shade (full sun in cool summer areas).
Propagation: sets.
Comments: upright clump; loves water. This plant is most attractive when planted in masses in a garden, or planted in a container. Native to Tropical Asia.

TOWNSENDIA EXSCAPA (*T. sericea*), Easter Daisy. Native to dry exposed ridges in the Great Plains and foothills; short-lived perennial (its over-enthusiastic seed ripening often kills it).
Height: 1 inch.
Bloom: dramatic whitish or pinkish stemless daisy flowers with yellow centers, blooms from early to end of April.
Foliage: basal clump of foliage, dramatic evergreen gray-green woolly foliage (winter interest).
Likes: sun/dry/rocky soil with humus.
Tolerates: half-sun/semidry/moderate clay soil.
Propagation: sets or seeds. (Seed germination: cold treatment.)
Comments: this plant must dry out

and go dormant in mid-summer. Grow plants in both hot sun and cool shade locations for longest flower show. Established plants resent transplanting. Its common name Easter Daisy refers to its early bloom. Indians ate the large edible root crowns.

T. INCANA. Native to alpine areas. Perennial.
Height: 1 inch.
Bloom: pinkish-purple or white stemless daisy flowers from April to May.
Foliage: tiny mounded clump, woolly gray-green foliage.
Likes: sun/half-sun/semidry/moist/well-drained rocky soil.
Propagation: sets or seeds.
Comments: established plants resent transplanting. This plant is a very rare native and should not be dug from the wild.

T. PARRYI. Native to dry grassy ridges of foothills and Rocky Mountains; short-lived perennial.
Height: 4 inches.
Bloom: profuse large lavender-blue daisy flowers on thick stalks, blooms from May to July.
Foliage: basal clump of foliage, evergreen gray-green foliage.
Likes: sun/dry/rocky soil.
Tolerates: half-sun/semidry.
Propagation: sets or seeds.
Comments: prefers to dry out slightly in summer. Established plants resent transplanting. Because this plant tends to put all its life energy into flowering and setting seed, it is a dramatic short-lived perennial. Removing spent flowers can prevent this flower from blooming itself to death. Named for Charles C. Parry (an early naturalist explorer).

TRACHYMENE COERULEA (Didiscus coeruleus), Blue Lace Flower. Annual.
Height: 2 feet.
Bloom: airy light blue flat-topped flowers (similar to Queen Anne's Lace).
Foliage: finely-divided.
Likes: sun/half-sun.
Tolerates: sun/half-shade/semidry/moist.
Propagation: sets or seeds. (Seed germination: dark.)
Comments: upright clump; prefers cool summer areas or mid-day shade; water heavily in hot weather; established plants transplant

poorly. Extreme summer heat may stop flowering and possibly kill plants. This plant is very attractive in the garden and can also be used for cut flowers. Native to Australia.

TRADESCANTIA OCCIDENTALIS, Western Spiderwort, native to moist grassy areas of the central and northern plains. Perennial.
Height: 2 feet.
Bloom: delicate pink, rich blue, or purple flowers from May to July (individual flowers last only one day).

Western Spiderwort, Tradescantia occidentalis

Foliage: unusual and grass-like.
Likes: moist/humus-rich, sandy soil.
Tolerates: sun/half-sun/half-shade/shade/semidry/wet (a bog plant).
Propagation: sets (transplants easily) or seeds.
Comments: upright clump. Soil pH affects flower color. The young stems and leaves of this plant were harvested by the Indians and eaten either raw or cooked. The taste was considered quite good. Additionally, the brightly colored flowers can be used as a garnish or added to salads. The genus was named to honor John Tradescant, the gardener to King Charles I of England. The species name *occidentalis* means 'western,' referring to this plant's range west of the Mississippi River. Horticultural varieties of this plant are 'Isis,' which has rich dark blue flowers; 'Snowcap,' which has white flowers; and 'Zwandenburg Blue,' which has very large midblue flowers.

TRITICUM AESTIVUM, Wheat. Annual.
Height: 2 feet.
Bloom: golden seedheads on stalks from July to October.
Foliage: beautiful ornamental grass.
Culture: very easy.
Likes: sun/dry/semidry.
Propagation: seeds (ordinary wheat kernels).
Comments: this common agricultural plant makes a dramatic show in the garden, and can also be used as a fresh cut flower or dried everlasting in arrangements. The bearded varieties

are particularly showy, especially the 'Black Awn Durum.' Other species with ornamental value are *Triticum monococcum* 'Eikorn,' which has a showy delicate seedhead, and *Triticum polonicum,* Polish Wheat, which has large loose seedheads produced on large, 3 feet tall, blue-green plants.

Wheat, Triticum aestivum

TROLLIUS SPECIES, Globeflower. Perennial to Zone 1.

Height: 2 feet.

Bloom: orange or yellow buttercup-like flowers from mid-May to early July (very long season).

Foliage: showy delphinium-like foliage.

Likes: wet (a bog plant).

Tolerates: half-sun/half-shade/moist.

Propagation: bulbs or sets.

Comments: clump habit; established plants resent transplanting; may need winter mulch in exposed areas. The named hybrid varieties are easiest to grow because of their combined Siberian *(Trollius ledebourii)* and European *(Trollius europaeus)* parentage. The variety 'Alabaster' has soft light yellow flowers; 'Golden Queen' has unusual-looking honey petals in its flowers; 'Lemon Queen' is an old variety with showy primrose yellow flowers; and 'Superbus' has very large orange flowers. Species of note are: *Trollius asiaticus,* which has bronzy-green foliage; *Trollius laxus,* a native white-flowered swamp plant with a low spreading habit, whose species name *laxus* means 'loose' (referring to its weak stems); and *Trollius pumilus,* which has yellow flowers and a very tidy low spreading habit.

TROPAEOLUM MAJUS, Nasturtium. Annual.

Height: 8 inches.

Bloom: slightly fragrant red, orange or yellow flowers from May to frost (very long season).

Culture: easy.

Likes: half-sun/moist.

Tolerates: sun/dry/semidry.

Propagation: sets or seeds (because they tolerate cool soil, seeds can be planted outside in mid-April).

Comments: sprawling habit; the most profuse flowers are produced in nitrogen-poor soil; established plants resent transplanting. There are both dwarf and vining type varieties. This plant is excellent for a low maintenance garden plant, a showy candidate for hanging pots, and a good cut flower. The peppery-tasting leaves and flowers are delicious in salads and sandwiches. Native to South America.

Nasturtium, Tropaeolum majus

TULIPA, Tulip. Perennial to Zone 3 (except the Kaufmania varieties which are hardy only to Zone 4).

Height: 6-30 inches.

Bloom: flowers in all colors except blue from mid-April to late May (long season with mixed early to late varieties).

Culture: very easy.

Likes: half-sun.

Tolerates: sun/half-shade/dry/semidry.

Propagation: bulbs (bury 5 inches deep).

Comments: Rembrandt or Broken Tulips are not included because of their viral infection, which can spread to healthy bulbs nearby. Bonemeal and other fertilizers must be below bulb to be utilized. Foliage must be allowed to ripen and die slowly in the heat of early summer (plan ahead to hide bulb areas either with other flowers that bloom in early summer, or best of all, hidden behind a bare rock which bakes hot in the summer sun).

For best flowering vigor, remove spent flowers before seed pods form. In gopher areas, protect bulbs by burying chicken wire mesh all around bulbs. Deer also love tulips.

A note of interest—Mrs. Eva Storm of Chugwater, Wyoming, led an unsuccessful campaign to have the entire Wyoming border planted with tulips.

Most of the tulip species are showy, hardy, and adapted to our climate. The species *Tulipa tarda* is one of the best, and is easily available. It has multiple stems of small bright yellow flowers. Other species hardy to Zone 3 are *T. batalinii, T. chrysantha, T. clusiana, T. kolpakowskiana, T. linifolia, T. pulchella, T. turkestanica* (multiple flowers on single stems), and *T. urumiensis.*

Order of bloom: *kaufmaniana* (mid-April), *greggi* (mid-April), *fosteriana* (late April), *tarda* (late April), Early (early May), Darwin hybrids (early May), Mendel and Cottage (both in mid-May), Lily-flowered (mid-May), Parrot (mid-May), Peony-flowered (mid-May), Breeder (mid-May), Darwin (mid-to late May). Plant early, midseason, and late varieties together for the longest bloom season.

The varieties listed below are known to be fragrant. Most of these have a freesia-like scent. Those commonly available are marked 'available.'

'Alaska' (Lily-flowered)—light yellow flowers, fragrant. Available.

'Alice Le Clercq' (Double Early)—orange-yellow flowers, fragrant, suitable for forcing. Available.

'Bellona' (Early)—red-orange flowers with an orange blossom scent. Available.

'Cherbourg' (Breeder)—orange flowers, fragrant.

'China Pink' (Lily-flowering)—non-fragrant soft pink flowers. Available.

'Christman Gold' (Early)—golden-yellow flowers, fragrant, suitable for forcing. Available.

'Dido' (Cottage)—reddish-pink flowers, fragrant.

'Doctor Plesman' (early)—red flowers with a Lily-of-the-Valley scent. Available.

'Ellen Willmot' (Cottage)—light yellow color, fragrant.

'Fairy Tale'—non-fragrant pastel color flowers in a mix of shades. Available.

'Fred Moore' (Early)—yellow-orange flowers with a honey-like scent.

'Fritz Kreisler'—non-fragrant soft

salmon-pink flowers. Available.

'Garden Party' (Triumph)—non-fragrant white flowers edged with pink. Available.

'General De Wet' (Early)—orange flowers with a orange-like scent. Available.

'Golden Memory' (Triumph)—yellow flowers, fragrant, suitable for forcing. Available.

'Grenadier' (Cottage)—scarlet flowers, fragrant.

'Hibernia' (Triumph)—non-fragrant white flowers delicately marked with green. Available.

'Hoangho' (Double Early)—yellow flowers. Available.

'Joan of Arc' (Darwin)—white flowers, fragrant.

'Johann Strauss'—non-fragrant yellow petals brushed with red; foliage is attractively mottled. Available.

'Mariette' (Lily-flowering)—non-fragrant hot pink flowers. Available. 'Marquette' (Early)—red flowers, fragrant. Available. 'Maytime' (Lily-flowering)—non-fragrant purple flowers with white edging and a yellow base. Available.

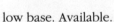

Tulip, Tulipa

'Mme Testout' (Early)—pink flowers, fragrant. Available.

'Monte Carlo' (Double Early)—yellow flowers, fragrant. Available.

'Morroccan Beauty' (Breeder)—red flowers, fragrant.

'Mrs J T Scheepers' (Cottage)—yellow flowers, fragrant. Available.

'Mrs Moon' (Cottage)—yellow flowers with an almond scent.

'Orange Elite' (Gregii)—non-fragrant yellow-orange flowers edged with orange, attractive mottled foliage. Available.

'Orange Favorite' (also called 'Orange Parrot') (Parrot)—orange-red flowers with a jasmine-like scent. Available.

'Orange Sun' (Darwin Hybrid)—orange flowers, fragrant. Available.

'President Kennedy' (Darwin Hybrid)—deep yellow flowers, fragrant. Available.

'Prince Carnival' (Early)—vivid scarlet and gold flowers, fragrant. Suitable for forcing. Available.

'Pride of Haarlem' (Late)—red. Available.

'Prince of Austria' (Early)—orange-scarlet flowers, fragrant, best tulip for forcing. Available.

'Prince of Orange' (Breeder)—orange flowers, fragrant.

'Professor Rontgen'—dramatic scarlet, yellow and green flowers with a citrus or rose-like scent.

'Queen of Sheba' (Lily-flowering)—non-fragrant red flowers edged with gold. Available.

'Red Riding Hood' (Gregii)—non-fragrant vivid scarlet flowers, attractive mottled foliage. Available.

'Schoonoord' (Early)—double white flowers, fragrant. Available.

'Tea Rose' (Early)—yellow flowers, fragrant.

'White Parrot' (Parrot)—non-fragrant white flowers, excellent for arrangements. Available.

'White Triumphator' (Lily-flowering)—non-fragrant large white flowers. Available.

TURFING CHAMOMILE, Tripleurospermum tchihatchewii (Matricaria tchihatchewii). Perennial to Zone 3.
Height: 6 inches.
Bloom: white daisy flowers with yellow center on stalks.
Foliage: finely-divided foliage.
Culture: easy.
Likes: sun/semidry.
Tolerates: half-sun/dry/poor soil.
Comments: spreading mat. This plant is used as a lawn substitute, even for hot dry areas. It can be mowed to a height of 2 inches.

TURNIP, Brassica rapa var. rapifera. Cool-season annual vegetable.
Height: 1 foot.
Description: upright clump with coarse foliage which tolerates heavy frost, large rounded root is eaten.
Likes: sun/half-sun/well-drained moist soil/low nitrogen, high phosphorus soil (give it bonemeal).
Tolerates: moderate alkalinity.
Propagation: seeds. Because it tolerates cold soil, plant in either fall or early spring; do not plant too deeply, and thin seedlings to 3 inches apart.
Pests: flea beetle, root maggot, and white cabbage moth. In far northern

Turnip, Brassica rapa

areas with severe flea beetle infestations (such as central Alberta), Kohlrabi makes an excellent alternative.
Growing tips: requires mid-day shade in hot summer areas. Do not give it fresh manure. Aged or composted manure is acceptable.
Harvest tips: This vegetable must be harvested before it gets large, tough, and fibrous.
Comments: turnips are eaten raw or cooked. They can also be preserved by cooking and freezing. Otherwise, it stores poorly. Additionally, the young foliage can be eaten as a cooked green. In fact, some people prefer the taste of the greens to the roots.

Long cultivated in northern Europe, it was brought to Canada by Jacques Cartier. Shepherd's Garden Seeds lists a French spring variety called 'De Milan,' which is described as buttery-tasting when young.

ULMUS AMERICANA, Elm tree; Official State Tree of Massachusetts, Nebraska, and North Dakota. Perennial to Zone 1.
Height: 80 feet.
Shape: spectacular tall upright tree with a cathedral-like form (no other tree forms a similarly arching canopy).
Foliage: attractive yellow fall color.
Likes: sun/semidry/moist.
Propagation: sets (varieties bred with Japanese elm are resistant to Dutch elm disease, but are less hardy).
Comments: two varieties hardy to

Zone 3 are *Jacan'* from Morden and 'Sapporo Autumn Gold' from Japan. In Greek mythology, Orpheus created this tree to make a deep green

Elm, Ulmus Americana

temple memorializing his return from Hades. In Norse mythology, the gods created the first man, 'Aske,' from an ash tree, and the first woman, 'Embla,' from an elm tree.

Dutch elm disease has been a long tragedy. Starting right after World War I, the elm trees of Europe began dying. Dutch researchers first discovered this disease and thus the name. The disease is, in fact, a fungus which is spread by elm bark beetles which bur-

Beetle Chamber of Dutch Elm Disease

row under elm bark to lay their eggs in June. By 1920, the disease had been brought to North America in wood used for furniture making. Over the last de- cades, the

disease has spread from the East Coast to the West Coast and finally to the northern plains. A permanent cure for the disease has not yet been found. However, an annual application of anti-fungal inoculant is the best treat- ment yet available. The inoculant is injected under pressure into the trees with a specially designed gouge gun. It must be reapplied annually at a cost of about $15 and a couple hours work per tree.

A recent tragedy in this story in- volves Dr. Gary Strobel, a research- er at Montana State University at Bozeman. He discovered an anti- fungal bacteria of the genus Pseudomonas. This could be inject- ed into an elm tree once and would permanently protect the tree. At

first, Dr. Strobel was given permis- sion to test his bacteria. Then an explosive scandal blew in, and he was forced to end his experiment. The reason was that he had genet- ically altered the bacteria. Dr. Stro- bel stated that the bacteria he used was a naturally occurring microor- ganism he had genetically altered to mark for identification. Local Mon- tana newspapers whipped up an ugly smear campaign of fear against Dr. Strobel. At this point, no com- promise was possible and the ex- periment was destroyed.

Fortunately in Europe, a research- er, Dr. Rud Scheffer of Baarn, The Netherlands, is conducting a similar experiment with a closely related bacteria. His inoculant should be available very soon. Besides the in- oculant treatment for already plant- ed elms, there are new disease-re- sistant elm varieties mentioned above.

When pruning, trim this tree spar- ingly and only to shape its natural form. It is important to cover wounds with dressing to reduce the unsightly weeping areas of wet- wood disease.

VALERIANA DIOICA, Marsh Valerian. Native to moist meadows and stream banks in the foothills, Rocky Mountains, and boreal forest. Pe- rennial.
Height: 1½ feet.
Bloom: slightly fragrant white flow- ers from early May to July.
Foliage: weak-stemmed upright clump, fernlike foliage on flower stalks, basal foliage is lance-shaped.
Likes: moist.
Tolerates: sun/half-sun/wet.
Propagation: sets or seeds (self- sows in favorable location).
Comments: requires windstaking in exposed areas. The closely related species *Valeriana edulis,* Edible Valerian or Tobacco Root, was eat- en by the Indians. It was baked in a pit for two days before being eat- en. White people named it Tobacco Root to describe its bitter strong smell and taste. The name of the Tobacco Root Mountains of Mon- tana came from this plant.

V. OFFICINALIS, Herb Valerian, Garden Heliotrope. Perennial to Zone 3.
Height: 4 feet.

Bloom: flat-topped clusters of fra- grant white flowers from mid-June to mid-July (long season if spent flowers removed).
Foliage: attractive, finely-divided.
Likes: half-sun/moist.
Tolerates: sun/half-shade/semidry/ wet.
Propagation: sets or seeds. (Some- what self-sowing).
Comments: upright clump. This plant is a short-lived perennial that tends to die after ripening seeds. Because of this, you should encour- age it to self sow new plants. The roots are used as a powerful seda- tive that induces sleep, yet allows a dream cycle. The drug Valium is refined from this plant. Some peo- ple enjoy the intensely strong woodsy smell of the roots.

VERBASCUM OLYMPICUM, Olympian Mullein. Annual.
Height: 6 feet.
Bloom: showy bright yellow flower spikes from July to frost (long sea- son if flower spikes are topped reg- ularly—see below).
Foliage: showy gray-green basal ro- sette.
Likes: sun/deeply dug, humus-rich soil.
Tolerates: half-sun/semidry-moist.
Propagation: sets should be planted outside in very early spring.
Comments: needs regular fertilizing during bloom season; needs wind- staking for top-heavy flower stalks. This species is non-invasive. This plant is amazingly frost tolerant if hardened off before planting. Use nursery-grown sets. If grown from seed, it acts like a biennial (which it is). Top the young plant's flower shoot in early summer to encourage it to branch out. Later, after it starts flowering, remove the tallest flower stalks on a regular basis. This en- courages numerous side shoots to bloom, lengthening its bloom sea- son, and reducing its top-heavy weight.

V. THAPSUS, Common Mullein. Bi- ennial to Zone 2.
Height: 5 feet.
Bloom: branched flower spikes of yellow from July to August (long season).
Foliage: velvety foliage is strikingly evergreen throughout the winter.
Likes: sun.

Tolerates: half-sun/dry/semidry.
Propagation: sets or seeds.
Comments: very invasive by self-sown seeds. This common roadside weed is included here for its evergreen winter foliage. In fact, early pioneer housewives potted up wild mullein plants to provide mid-winter greenery. Dried stalks can be dipped in tallow and used as torches. The fuzzy leaves can be used as footpads in shoes. This plant is used commonly as an herb to heal mucus-lined body tissue, and for sore throats. The flowers make an excellent edible garnish, and can be eaten in salads, too. Flowers used in this manner are best picked in the morning when they have a less bitter taste.

Mullein, Verbascum thapsus

VERBENA HASTATA, Blue Vervain. Perennial to Zone 4-5.
Height: 3 feet.
Bloom: narrow blue flower spikes from July to frost.
Likes: half-sun/moist/humus-rich soil.
Tolerates: sun.
Propagation: sets or seeds.
Comments: stiffly erect habit.

VERBENA HYBRIDS. Annual.
Height: 8 inches.
Bloom: fragrant red, white, blue and purple flower clusters from May to frost (very long season).
Foliage: finely-divided.
Culture: easy.
Likes: sun/semidry.
Tolerates: half-sun/dry.
Propagation: sets or seeds.
Comments: semi-erect creeping habit. This is an excellent low-maintenance garden plant, a good pot or container plant, and can be used as a cut flower. 'Snow Queen' is a fragrant white variety. Other varieties that carry parentage of *Verbena platensis* (white Evening-Scented Verbena), have the most fragrance. These fragrant varieties should be selected and bred to recreate new varieties with better fragrance.

VERONICA SPECIES. Both its flowers and foliage create texture and interest in a garden. This genus was named for Saint Veronica, the woman who wiped Christ's face on his way to Calvary. In legend, Christ's image appeared on the cloth she used. The name Veronica can be translated from two Latin words *vera* meaning 'true' and *icon* meaning 'image.'

Order of bloom: *V. repens* (May to June), *V. pectinata* (May to June), *V. teucrium* (June to July), *V. incana* (late June to July), *V. austriaca* (early to late July), *V. spuria* (July), *V. spicata* (July), *V. longifolia* (July to August).

V. AUSTRIACA. Perennial to Zone 2.
Height: 2 foot.
Bloom: large blue flowers on an elongating stalk, blooms from early to late July.
Foliage: showy, finely-divided.
Likes: half-sun/humus-rich soil.
Tolerates: sun/half-shade/semidry/moist.
Propagation: sets or seeds.
Comments: upright clump.

V. CUSICKII. Native to moist alpine meadows in the Rocky Mountains. Perennial.
Height: 4 inches.
Bloom: beautiful tiny deep blue flowers in July.
Foliage: tiny upright clump.
Culture: difficult.
Likes: half-sun/moist.
Propagation: sets or seeds.
Comments: a related species, *Veronica worskjoldii*, is also native to alpine meadows and easier to grow, but its flower color is a less attractive blue-purple.

V. INCANA, Woolly Speedwell. Perennial to Zone 1.
Height: 1 foot.
Bloom: profuse blue flower spikes from late June to July (long season).
Foliage: showy carpet-like clump of gray-woolly foliage.
Culture: easy.
Likes: sun/semidry/humus-rich soil.

Veronica worskjoldii

Tolerates: half-sun/dry/moist.
Propagation: sets or seeds.
Comments: this plant is excellent for edging the front of the garden. 'Minuet' has pink flowers; 'Saraband' has rich blue flowers.

V. LONGIFOLIA. Perennial to Zone 1.
Height: 3 feet.
Bloom: large pink, white, blue, or purple flower spikes from July to August (long season).
Foliage: low clump of dark green foliage.
Culture: easy.
Likes: half-sun/half-shade/dry/semidry/humus-rich soil.
Tolerates: sun/moist.
Propagation: sets or seeds.
Comments: upright clump; may need windstaking with hoop support in exposed areas. The shorter varieties are more wind tolerant. This species also makes good cut flowers.

V. PECTINATA. Perennial to Zone 3.
Height: 3 inches.
Bloom: tiny blue flowers from May to June (long season).
Foliage: semi-evergreen woolly gray-green creeping mat.
Culture: easy.
Likes: sun/semidry/moist/humus-rich soil.
Tolerates: half-sun/dry.
Propagation: sets or seeds.
Comments: may need a light winter mulch. This plant is excellent for the front of the garden.

V. REPENS. Perennial to Zone 2.
Height: 2 inches.
Bloom: pale blue or pink flowers from May to June (long season).
Foliage: seems almost moss-like.
Culture: easy.
Likes: half-sun/semidry/moist/humus-rich soil.
Tolerates: sun/half-shade/dry.
Propagation: sets or seeds.
Comments: may need a light winter mulch. This plant can be used as a lawn substitute and will tolerate some foot traffic. Additionally, it is an excellent cover for bulbs and edging for the front of the garden.

V. SPICATA. Perennial to Zone 1.
Height: 1 foot.
Bloom: profuse pink, white, or blue flower spikes in July.
Culture: easy.
Likes: half-sun/moist/humus-rich soil.

Tolerates: sun/half-shade/dry/semi-dry.

Propagation: sets or seeds.

Comments: upright clump. 'Barca-rolle' has dark pink flowers; 'Blue Charm' has exceptional dark blue flowers; 'Icicle' has large white flower stalks and a taller habit; 'Min-uet' has light pink flowers; *'Nana'* is a beautiful dwarf rock garden variety.

V. SPURIA. Perennial to Zone 4.

Height: 2 feet.

Bloom: branched spikes of blue flowers in July.

Foliage: hairy green foliage.

Culture: easy.

Likes: sun/semidry/moist/humus-rich soil.

Tolerates: half-sun/half-shade/dry.

Propagation: sets or seeds.

Comments: upright clump. 'Royal Blue' is an especially attractive variety.

V. TEUCRIUM (V. latifolia), Hungarian Speedwell. Perennial to Zone 2.

Height: 1½ feet.

Bloom: blue flower clusters from June to July (long season).

Culture: easy.

Likes: half-sun/semidry/moist/humus-rich soil.

Tolerates: sun-half-shade/dry.

Propagation: sets or seeds.

Comments: sprawling mound; for best appearance, windstake with hoop support; shear back after flowering for compact habit. It makes an excellent combination with Oriental Poppies. 'Crater Lake Blue' has rich gentian blue flowers, but must be windstaked. 'Trehane' has gold foliage and deep blue flowers. Its hardiness is marginal.

VIBURNUM LANTANA, Wayfaring Bush. Perennial to Zone 2.

Height: 10 feet.

Bloom: showy white flower clusters 4 inches across from mid- to late May; fruit turns from green to red to black as it ripens and then hangs on the bush all winter.

Wayfaring Bush, Viburnum lantana

Shape: irregular multi-stemmed habit.

Foliage: attractive, with red fall color.

Culture: easy.

Likes: half-sun/moist/humus-rich soil.

Tolerates: half-shade/dry/semidry.

Propagation: sets or seeds.

Comments: though usually used as a large shrub, this plant can also be used for a large size hedge. *'Rugosum'* has leathery dark green foliage. The species *Viburnum burjacticum* closely resembles *Viburnum lantana.*

V. LENTAGO, Nannyberry. Native to the eastern woodlands and boreal forest. Perennial to Zone 1.

Height: 20 feet.

Bloom: snowball-like white flower clusters in mid-May.

Shape: large arching shrub (give it lots of room).

Foliage: glossy foliage turns reddish-purple in the fall; showy edible fruit changes color from green to yellow to red to blue-black.

Likes: half-sun/moist/humus-rich soil.

Tolerates: half-shade/semidry.

Propagation: sets or seeds.

Comments: the variety 'Pink Beauty' has showy pink flowers.

V. OPULUS 'ROSEUM,' Common Snowball Bush. Perennial to Zone 2.

Height: 6-10 feet.

Shape: rounded shrub.

Bloom: snowball-like white flower clusters from early June to early July.

Foliage: red fall color.

Likes: half-sun/half-shade/moist.

Propagation: sets.

Pests: aphids attack the foliage in mid-summer and curl it unattractively. Because this variety is sterile, the flower clusters bloom longer and there are no unattractive seed clusters to remove. However, aphids turn this shrub into an unsightly mess right after its bloom is over.

Snowball Bush, Viburnum opulus

V. TRILOBUM, Highbush Cranberry. Perennial to Zone 1.

Height: 10 feet.

Bloom: white flower clusters in mid-May, edible red berries are similar to cranberries and make superb jelly (best harvested after several frosts).

Shape: arching shrub.

Foliage: red fall color.

Culture: easy.

Likes: half-sun/moist/humus-rich soil.

Tolerates: half-shade/semidry.

Propagation: sets or seeds.

Comments: plants produce more fruit if cross-pollinated (plant two). This species has fewer problems with aphids than *Viburnum opulus,* the European Highbush Cranberry. It is showy as a landscaping shrub, but can also be used as a hedge. The Indian name for this plant was Pembina. Besides using the fruit, they made blowgun toys for their children from the stems. *'Compactum'* is a non-fruiting variety which makes a densely compact hedge. 'Garry Pink' is an ornamental variety with large pink flowers. 'Pembina' has large fruit. 'Wentworth' has large fruit and particularly good fall color.

VIGUIERA MULTIFLORA, Goldeneye. Native to dry areas in the foothills and Rocky Mountains. Perennial.

Height: 2 feet.

Bloom: small yellow flowers which resemble sunflowers, blooms from July to September.

Foliage: upright clump.

Likes: sun/half-sun/dry/semidry.

Propagation: sets or seeds.

Comments: this plant resembles a dwarf sunflower.

VINCA MINOR, Periwinkle. Perennial to Zone 3.

Height: 4 inches.

Bloom: blue flowers from late April to May.

Foliage: evergreen dark green foliage.

Culture: very easy.

Likes: half-shade/semidry.

Tolerates: shade/dry/moist.

Propagation: sets.

Comments: creeping vine habit. This plant can either be grown as an aggressive ground cover or used in a container or hanging pot to show off its trailing stems and foliage. *'Alba'* has large white flowers;

Periwinkle, Vinca minor

'Bowles' is the hardiest variety; 'Gertrude Jekyll' has profuse white flowers and a dwarf habit; *'Atropurpurea'* has plum-purple flowers; *'Multiplex'* has double purple flowers; *'Variegata'* has variegated foliage.

VIOLA SPECIES, Violet. Official state flower of Illinois, New Jersey, Rhode Island and Wisconsin, one of the many flowers nominated for the U.S. national flower.

In Greek mythology, Io was a mortal woman loved by Zeus. When he was almost caught by his wife Hera, Zeus turned Io into a white heifer. When she cried for food, Zeus turned her tears into white violets for her to eat. Flowers and leaves of this plant are delicious in salads or candied. The whole plant of any viola species is edible. The dried leaves make a vitamin rich tea. Napoleon used the violet as his symbol.

V. ADUNCA, Early Blue Violet, native to moist areas and aspen forests in the Great Plains and Rocky Mountains. Perennial.
Height: 5 inches.
Bloom: large tufted clump of blue-purple flowers from late April to June (long season; occasionally this plant re-blooms in the fall if there is moisture).
Foliage: leaves grow on elongating stems.
Likes: half-sun/half-shade/semidry/moist/nitrogen-poor soil/bonemeal.
Propagation: sets or seeds. (Seed germination: cold treatment.)

Early Blue Violet, Viola

Comments: Plant elongates and gets floppy-looking by May and June. Then it prefers to dry out and go dormant by mid-summer. The flowers have a long spurlike hook on them which makes this species easy to identify. Claude Barr mentions a deep blue variety.

V. BLANDA, Sweet White Violet, native to rich soil areas in the Rocky Mountains and boreal forest. Perennial to Zone 3.
Height: 3 inches.
Bloom: very fragrant white flowers with purple markings from late April to early May.
Likes: shade/moist/humus-rich, acidic soil/cool location.
Tolerates: half-sun/half-shade/wet.
Propagation: sets or seeds (self-sows).
Comments: spreading clump; invasive by self-sown seeds. This is an eastern North American species native from Quebec to Georgia.

V. CANADENSIS, Canadian Violet, native to moist woods in the Rocky Mountains and eastern forests. Perennial to Zone 1.
Height: 10 inches.
Bloom: showy, fragrant, white or lavender flowers with yellow centers from early May to July.
Likes: half-shade/moist/humus-rich, acidic soil/cool location.
Tolerates: half-sun/shade/wet.
Propagation: sets or seeds (self-sows).
Comments: spreading clump; invasive by self sown seeds.

V. CORNUTA, Horned Violet. Perennial to Zone 1.
Height: 6 inches.
Bloom: yellow, white or purple pansy-like flowers from June to early July.
Likes: half-sun/half-shade/moist/humus-rich soil.
Propagation: sets or seeds.
Comments: grows in individual clumps.

V. MACLOSKEYI, native to swampy areas in the Rocky Mountains. Perennial.

Canadian Violet, Viola canadensis

Height: 8 inches.
Bloom: powerfully fragrant showy white flowers from May to June.
Likes: half-sun/moist/wet (a bog plant).
Propagation: sets or seeds.
Comments: clump habit. This species requires a special moist situation, but it is less weedy and more fragrant than the other species.

V. NUTTALLII, Yellow Prairie Violet, native to dry grassy ridges of the Great Plains and foothills. Perennial to Zone 1.
Height: 6 inches.
Bloom: profuse yellow flowers with purple veins from mid-April to June (long season).
Foliage: narrow lance-shaped leaves go dormant in mid-summer and disappear.
Culture: easy.
Likes: half-sun/semidry.
Tolerates: sun/dry/heavy clay soil.
Propagation: sets or seeds. (Seed germination: cold treatment.)
Comments: individual clumps; self-sows profusely. This plant is amazingly drought-tolerant. It is named for Thomas Nuttall, who first collected this species in 1811 along the Missouri River in South Dakota. This exceptionally beautiful native should be better known. It can be used in a moderately aggressive ground cover.

V. ODORATA, Sweet Violet. Perennial to Zone 4.
Height: 5 inches.
Bloom: very fragrant red, white, blue, purple or black flowers from late April to May (long season).
Likes: half-shade/moist/wet/humus-rich soil/cool location.
Tolerates: half-sun/shade/wet.
Propagation: sets or seeds.
Comments: spreading clump; may need winter mulch in exposed areas.

V. PEDATIFIDA, Purple Prairie Violet, native to exposed areas in the Great Plains. Perennial to Zone 3.
Height: 4 inches.
Bloom: large blue-purple flowers with orange centers, blooms from May to July. Foliage: finely-divided foliage is shaped like a bird's foot.
Culture: easy.
Likes: half-sun/moist/humus-rich, sandy soil.
Tolerates: sun/dry/semidry.
Propagation: sets (division of crown) or seeds.

Comments: individual clumps; prefers drier and sunnier conditions than other violets; occasionally self-sows in a favorable location. This plant has become a rare wildflower and should not be dug from the wild. Claude Barr mentions a beautiful white form.

V. TRICOLOR, Viola or Johnny-Jump-Up. Annual.
Height: 6 inches.
Bloom: multicolored flowers from March to June and October to December (very long season if watered in early spring and fall).
Culture: easy.

*Johnny-Jump-Up,
Viola tricolor*

Likes: half-sun/moist/humus-rich soil/cool location. *Tolerates:* half-shade/dry/semidry. *Propagation:* sets or seeds. *Comments:* individual clump habit. Can be used either in the garden or in containers. This plant self-sows so freely that most people already have it in their gardens. If you learn to recognize its foliage and avoid weeding it out, it can become a colorful living mulch in your yard. Unfortunately, its leaf shape closely resembles that of Rapacious Bellflower (*Campanula rapunculoides*), a viciously dangerous weed.

V. X WITTROCKIANA (V. tricolor 'Hortensis'), Pansy. Annual.
Height: 6 inches.
Bloom: red, orange, yellow, white, blue, purple, or black flowers from April to June and October to December (very long season if spent flowers removed).
Culture: easy.
Likes: half-shade/moist/humus-rich soil/cool location.
Tolerates: half-sun/shade/semidry.
Propagation: sets or seeds.
Comments: individual clump habit; be sure to water pansies in the fall. Sets of this plant can be hardened-off and planted outside in mid- to late April (a month before the frost-free date). It can be used either in the garden or in pots.

VITIS AMURENSIS, Amur Grape, Ornamental Grape Vine. Perennial to Zone 2.
Height: dense vine to 20 feet.
Bloom: small black berries are poor tasting.
Climbing habit: climbs with tendrils.
Foliage: grown for its canopy of large bright green leaves and its bright red-purple fall color.
Culture: very easy.

*Ornamental Grape
Vine, Vitis amurensis*

Likes sun/semidry.
Tolerates: half-sun/dry/semidry.
Propagation: sets or seeds.
Comments: less winter dieback if planted in a protected site. In harsher areas, *Vitis riparia,* the native Riverbank Grape, is an attractive substitute with yellow fall color. Breeding work needs to be done to select the most colorful *Vitis riparia* and crossbreed them with *Vitis amurensis* and *Vitis coignetiae* (Glorybower).

VITIS HYBRIDS, Grapes.
Height: dense vine to 20 feet.
Bloom: delicious fruit.
Climbing habit: train vines on lattice or 3-wire horizontal support (the lowest wire near the ground ensures that at least some of the vine will survive a harsh winter); climbs with tendrils.
Foliage: attractive large leaves with plain yellow fall color.
Culture: very easy.
Likes: sun/semidry/heat/low nitrogen soil.
Tolerates: half-sun/dry.
Propagation: sets.
Comments: needs heat to ripen fruit and mature the vines; give it less water in late fall to harden off the vine. In short-season areas, grow grapes in a protected southern exposure next to the foundation of a heated building. Grapes can be eaten fresh, made into preserves or jelly, or best of all, made into a soft candy.

'Beta'—Perennial to Zone 3, this grape is being replaced by the improved variety 'Valiant.'

'Bluebelle'—Perennial to Zone 4, large blue grape with good quality for dessert, wine or jelly. Developed in Minnesota.

'Canadice'—Perennial to Zone 4-5, seedless red dessert grape, medium-large size.

'Fredonia'—Perennial to Zone 3, a reliably cold-hardy variety with showy large black grapes, poor to medium fruit quality for eating or wine. The leaves of this variety are particularly good for making dolmas, stuffed grape leaves. To make, briefly submerge leaves in boiling water, fill with stuffing, and roll up.

'Price'—Perennial to Zone 4-5, a high quality blue grape, medium size, useful for eating, some keeping quality.

'Swenson Red'—Perennial to Zone 4, a high quality red dessert and wine grape, medium-large size.

'Valiant'—Perennial to Zone 3, a small blue grape with a good to excellent quality for dessert, wine, and jelly. Though this grape is rather tart for fresh eating, it has a wonderful grape flavor. I can see a cottage industry using this grape in candy confections. It is an improved variety of 'Beta' developed by South Dakota State University.

'Van Buren'—Perennial to Zone 3-4, a blue-black grape for juice and jam.

WATERCRESS, Nasturtium officinale. Perennial vegetable to Zone 1.
Height: 1 foot.
Description: bright green foliage and tiny white flowers.
Likes: half-sun/half-shade/wet (a bog plant).
Propagation: sets (a cutting stuck in wet soil will quickly root—wild plants or stems from grocery store plants work equally well).
Growing tips: prefers light shade for mildest flavor; can be grown in either a bog, flooded planter or water bucket, but has the mildest flavor if grown in moving fresh water.
Harvest tips: these greens can be used throughout the winter as long as the water is not frozen solid. In

the summer, harvest continuously to slow flowering. Once flowers appear, the leaves get bitter.
Comments: its tender stems and leaves are used for their peppery flavor in sandwiches, quiche, casse-

Watercress, Nasturtium officinale

roles, flavoring for soups, salads or as a garnish. Kim Williams suggested putting it in scrambled eggs, potato salad, creamed soups, and cottage cheese. She also suggested adding the cooking water to soup stocks, gravies and sauces.

This plant has been cultivated since ancient times. The Persians believed that eating this plant made children extra strong and healthy. It is rich in vitamins A, B, C, E, calcium, potassium, and sulfur. Originally native to Europe, it is now an introduced weed in all of North America. When gathering wild plants, try to make sure they are not contaminated by man-made poisons, most commonly from agricultural land runoff.

WEIGELA FLORIDA. Perennial to Zone 4-5 (protected areas only).
Height: 3 feet.
Bloom: pink flowers with yellow centers, blooms in mid-May.
Shape: broadly rounded shrub.
Foliage: light green foliage which becomes purple-tinged in late summer.
Likes: moist.
Tolerates: sun/half-sun/semidry.
Propagation: sets (hardwood cuttings in summer).
Comments: this low shrub can be used as a ground cover. The variety 'Rumba' has purple foliage and red flowers. It is a hybrid of the varieties *'Purpurea'* and 'Dropmore Pink' developed by Felicitas Svejda of Agriculture Canada's Ottawa Research Station. A similar variety is 'Minuet,' which is more compact

and has bicolor pink and red flowers. 'Tango' has showy red flowers and a symmetrical form. 'Centennial' is the hardiest variety, good to Zone 3.

WONDERBERRY, Edible Nightshade, *Solanum nigrum.* Annual fruit.
Height: 1½ feet.
Description: attractive purple flowers, green berries turn red, then black.
Likes: moist.
Tolerates: half-sun/half-shade/dry/semidry.
Harvest tips: harvest berries only when fully black.
Propagation: sets or seeds.
Comments: The variety 'Garden Huckleberry' was developed by Luther Burbank. It has a 3 foot tall bushy habit. Another variety, 'Mrs B's,' was developed for its flavor. Cooking makes the berries fully edible. Use them for pies, jellies and jams, canning or freezing.

XERANTHEMUM ANNUUM, Common Immortelle. Annual.
Height: 2 feet.
Bloom: pink or purple papery strawflowers from August to September (long season).
Foliage: upright grayish foliage with a woolly texture.
Likes: semidry.
Tolerates: sun/dry/moist.
Propagation: sets (transplant carefully) or seeds. (Seed germination: light.)
Comments: windstake with brush support; established plants transplant poorly. These long-lasting flowers are showy in the garden left on plant, used as fresh cut flowers, or dried like strawflowers. Cut for use only when fully open. There should be work done to breed a good white variety. When this occurs, there will be a large commercial market for this everlasting. Sheperd's lists the variety 'Choice Mixed Colors,' which they describe as having a color range of deep rose pink, creamy white, and violet-purple.

YUCCA FILAMENTOSA, Adam's Needle, official state flower of New Mexico. Perennial to Zone 4.
Height: 4 feet.
Bloom: candle-like stalk of showy white flowers that open fully only at night, blooms in June.

Foliage: rosette of evergreen bayonet-like leaves.
Culture: very easy.
Likes: sun/dry/semidry.
Propagation: sets. (Seed germination: cold.)
Comments: 'Bright Edge' and 'Golden Sword' are yellow-edged variegated varieties (unfortunately, these varieties are less hardy than the species); 'Rosea' is a rare pink-flowering form. The flowers are edible and relished by livestock. The immature fruit is edible, but bitter.

Y. GLAUCA. Native Yucca. Perennial to Zone 3.
Height: 2 feet.
Bloom: cluster of greenish-white flowers in June.

Foliage: rosette of evergreen bayonet-like leaves.
Culture: very easy.
Likes: very dry.
Tolerates: sun/semidry.
Propagation: sets. (Seed germination: cold.)

Adam's Needle, Yucca filamentosa

Comments: the variety 'Pink Brilliance' has flowers edged with pink. Breeding work needs to be done to select better varieties with tall well-branched stalks and improved flower color. There is also potential for selecting varieties with variegated foliage. Claude Barr mentions a red flowering variety, as well as a selection with gracefully opened petals.

The Indians used the root for soap, particularly for hair and clothing. Additionally, the fiber of the leaves was beaten out and used in weaving, twine and rope. The flowers and immature seedpods are edible. Cattle seem to relish eating this flower. This plant provides shelter for many reptiles and small mammals. Seeds are an important food source for small rodents. The name yucca is a misnomer applied by the 16th century herbalist Gerard, who thought this plant was the manioc plant of the tropics.

ZINNIA ELEGANS, Common Zinnia, official state flower of Indiana. Annual.
Height: 6-30 inches.
Bloom: every color except blue, flowers from June to frost (very long season if spent flowers removed).
Culture: easy.
Likes: sun/semidry.
Tolerates: half-sun/dry.
Propagation: sets (transplants well) or seeds. (Seed germination: warm, do not plant seeds outside until after frost-free date.)
Comments: do not water overhead or this plant will get powdery mildew; can be pinched when young for bushier plants. This plant is excellent used in the garden, in containers, or as a cut flower. Luther Burbank created the commonly available Dahlia-flowering Zinnias. For cut flowers, cut when flowers are open.

Z. AAGEANA, Mexican Zinnia. Annual.
Height: 2 feet.
Bloom: marigold-like red and yellow bicolored flowers from June to frost (very long season if spent flowers removed).
Culture: easy.
Likes: sun/semidry.
Tolerates: half-sun/dry.
Propagation: sets or seeds (plant seeds outside only after the frost-free date).

Comments: can be pinched for bushier plants. At first glance, this plant closely resembles a bicolor marigold.

ZIZIA APTERA, Heart-leaf Alexanders. Native to moist meadows and open woods in the Great Plains and foothills. Perennial.
Height: 1½ feet.
Bloom: bright yellow flower clusters from June to July.
Foliage: basal clump of heart-shaped leaves.
Likes: sun/half-sun/semidry/moist.
Tolerates: mildly alkaline soil.
Propagation: sets (division in spring or fall).
Comments: established plants resent transplanting.

ZYGADENUS ELEGANS, White Camas, Death Camas. Native to moist grassy areas of the Great Plains and Rocky Mountains. Perennial to Zone 1.
Height: 1 foot.
Bloom: compact spike of white flowers with a green center, blooms from early June to July.
Foliage: gray-green grass-like foliage greens up very early in the spring.
Culture: easy.
Likes: moist.
Tolerates: sun/half-sun/dry/semidry/clay soil.

Death Camas, Zygadenus elegans

Propagation: sets or seeds.
Comments: This plant is a good candidate for selective breeding for larger, more pure white flowers. When out of bloom, this deadly poisonous plant is difficult to distinguish from *Allium cernuum,* Nodding Onion (lavender flowers), *Brodiaea grandiflora* (deep blue flowers), *Calochortus,* Mariposa Lily (tulip-like whitish flowers), *Fritillaria* (nodding yellow or brown flowers), or *Camassia,* Camas (light blue flowers)—all of which have tasty edible bulbs. Death Camas's three distinguishing characteristics are the white flowers on a stalk, the distinctive white seeds, and the black covering on the bulb. Furthermore, this plant tends to poison large numbers of sheep in the early spring because it greens up so early.

LANDSCAPING PLANTS NATIVE TO THE CHINOOK ZONE AND NORTHERN GREAT PLAINS

Plants

Abronia fragrans, Sand Verbena
Achillea millefolium, Yarrow
Agastache foeniculum, Anise Hyssop
Allium cernuum, Nodding Purple Onion
Allium textile, Prairie Onion
Andromeda polifolia 'nana,' Dwarf Bog Rosemary
Anemone canadensis
   A. multifida, Ball Anemone
   A. occidentalis, White Pasque Flower, Chalice Flower
   A. patens, (Pulsatilla patens), Pasque Flower, Prairie Crocus
Angelica arguta, Lyall's Angelica
Antennaria, Pussytoes
   A. anaphaloides
   A. aromatica
   A. corymbosa
   A. dimorpha, Dwarf Pussytoes
   A. parvifolia
   A. rosea
Aquilegia flavescens, Yellow Columbine
   A. jonesii
Arabis nuttallii, Nuttall's Rockcress
Arctostaphylos uva-ursi, Kinnikinnick, Bearberry
Argemone polyanthemos (A. intermedia), Prickly Poppy
   A. ericoides, Many-Flowered Aster
   A. laevis (A. geyeri)
   A. scopulorum, Rock Aster
   A. stenomeres
Aster alpinue, Alpine Aster
   A. conspicuus, Showy Aster
   A. ericoides, Many-Flowered Aster
   A. iaevis
   A. novae-belgii, New York Aster, Michaelmas Daisy
   A. scopulorum, Rock Aster
   A. stenomeres
Astragalus, Milkvetch
   A. aboriginum, Indian Milkvetch
   A. adsurgens, Standing Milkvetch
   A. agrestis, Purple Field Milkvetch
   A. aretioides, Sweetwater Milkvetch
   A. argophyllus, Silverleaf Milkvetch
   A. barrii, Barr's Milkvetch
   A. bisulcatus, Two-Grooved Milkvetch
   A. ceramicus, Painted Milkvetch
   A. crassicarpus, Buffalo Ground Plum
   A. drummondii, Drummond Milkvetch
   A. gilviflorus (A. triphyllus), Threeleaved Milkvetch
   A. glareosus
   A. hyalinus
   A. inflexus
   A. kentrophyta, Prickly Milkvetch
   A. microcystis
   A. missouriensis, Missouri Milkvetch
   A. pectinatus, Narrowleaf Milkvetch
   A. purshii, Woolly Pod Milkvetch
   A. spatulatus, Draba Milkvetch
   A. vexilliflexus, Bent-flowered Milkvetch
Balsamorhiza incana, Hoary Balsamroot
   B. sagittata, Arrowleaf Balsamroot, Vaseline-root
Besseya wyomingensis (B. cinerea), Kittentails
Boltonia asteroides, Prairie Aster
Brodiaea grandiflora
Bupleurum americanum, Thorough-wax
Callirhoe involucrata, Purple Mallow
Calochortus gunnisoni, Prairie Mariposa Lily, Sego Lily
Camassia cusickii, Camas
Campanula rotundifolia, Harebell, Bluebell of Scotland
Ceratoides lanata (Eurotia lanata), Winterfat
Cheilanthes gracillima, Rock Fern
Chrysopsis villosa (Heterotheca villosa), Golden Aster
Claytonia lanceolata, Springbeauty, Groundnut, Fairy Spud
Cleome serrulata, Prairie Cleome, Rocky Mountain Beeplant
Coryphantha missouriensis (Neobesseya missouriensis), Ball Cactus
   C. vivipara, Cushion Cactus
Cryptantha interrupta, Miner's Candle
Deschampsia caespitosa, Tufted Hair Grass
Delphinium bicolor, Low Larkspur
Dicentra formosa, Bleeding Heart
Dodecatheon conjugens, Shooting Star
Douglasia montana
Draba incerta, Yellowstone Draba
   D. paysonii
Dracocephalum nuttallii, False Dragonhead
Dryas drummondii
Echinacea purpurea, Purple Coneflower
Equisetum scirpoides, Horsetail
Erigeron, Daisy Fleabane
   E. caespitosus
   E. filifolius
   E. glabellus
   E. ochroleucus, Bluff Fleabane
   E. pumilus, Shaggy Fleabane
   E. tweedyi
Eriogonum acaule, Stemless Eriogonum
   E. annum, Annual Eriogonum
   E. caespitosum, Tufted Eriogonum
   E. flavum, Yellow Eriogonum
   E. mancum
   E. ovalifolium, Oval-leaf Eriogonum
   E. umbellatum, Sulphur Flower

Eriophyllum lanatum, Woolly
Yellow Daisy, Oregon Sunshine
Eritrichium howardii, Foothills
Forget-Me-Not
E. nanum, Alpine Forget-Me-Not
Erysimum asperum, Western
Wallflower, Siberian Wallflower
Fragaria virginiana, Wild Straw-
berry
Fritillaria atropurpurea, Leopard
Lily
F. pudica, Yellow Bells, Yellow
Snowdrops
Gaillardia aristata, Blanketflower
Gentiana affinis, Prairie Gentian
Geum triflorum, Prairie Smoke
Gilia rubra, Scarlet Gilia
Godetia amoena, Farewell to
Spring
Gutierrezia sarothrae
(Xanthocephalum sarothrae),
Broom Snakeweed
Haplopappus lanuginosus,
Goldenweed
H. spinulosus, Spiny
Goldenweed
E. subfruticosus, Woody
Goldenweed
Helenium autumnale, Sneezeweed
Helianthus petiolaris, Sunflower
Heracleum lanatum, Cow Parsnip
Holly Grape. See Mahonia repens
Horsetail. See Equisetum
Huechera sanguinea, Coral Bells
Hymenoxys acaulis, Butte Mari-
gold
H. richardsonii, Colorado
Rubber Plant
Iliamna rivularis, Streambank
Mallow
Impatiens biflora, Jewel Weed
Iris havessima, Goldbeard Iris
I. missouriensis (I. montana),
Rocky Mountain Iris
Kelseya uniflora
Lesquerella alpina, Alkaline
Bladderpod
Leucocrinum montanum, Prairie
Star Lily
Lewisia pygmaea, Pygmy Bitter-
root
L. rediviva. Native Bitterroot
Liatris punctata, Liatris
Lilium philadelphicum, Western
Orange Cup, Prairie Lily
Linanthus septentrionalis
Linum perenne ssp. lewisii, Blue
Flax
Lithophragma tenella, Prairie Star
Lomatium dissectum, Desert
Parsley

L. macrocarpum, Long-fruited
Prairie Parsley
L. villosum (L. foeniculaceum),
Yellow Prairie Parsley, Biscuit
Root, Parsley Dill
Lupinus lepidus, Mountain Dwarf
Lupine
Lychnis alpina (Viscaria alpina),
Arctic Campion
Lygodesmia juncea, Rush
Skeletonweed, Prairie Pink
Machaeranthera tanacetifolia,
Tahoka Daisy
Mahonia repens, Oregon Grape,
Holly Grape
Matteuccia struthiopteris, Ostrich
Fern
Mentha aquatica, River Mint
Mentzelia decapetala, Blazing Star,
Evening Star
M. laevicaulis, Small-stemmed
Mentzelia
Mertensia longiflora, Bluebells
M. particulata
Mimulus lewissi, Lewis'
Monkeyflower
Mirabilis nyctaginea, Heart-leafed
Umbrellawort
Monarda fistulosa, Lavender
Monarda
Monardella odoratissima
Musineon divaricatum, Leafy
Musineon
Nuphar variegatum, Painted
Yellow Pond Lily
Nymphaea odorata, Fragrant
Waterlily
Oenothera caespitosa, Tufted
Evening Primrose
O. missouriensis, Missouri
Evening Primrose
Opuntia fragilis, Prickly Pear
Cactus
O. polyacantha, Prickly Pear
Cactus
Oregon Grape. See Mahonia
repens
Oxytropis, Pointvetch, Locoweed
O. besseyi
O. lagopus, Hare's Foot
Pointvetch
O. multiceps
O. sericea, Early Pointvetch
O. splendens, Showy Pointvetch
Paronychia sessiliflora, Whitlow-
wort
Penstemon species
P. albertinus, Alberta Penstemon
P. albidus, White Penstemon
P. alpinus

P. angustifolius, Narrowleaf
Penstemon
P. arenicola
P. aridus, Stiffleaf Penstemon
P. attenuatus
P. barbatus
P. caespitosus, Tufted Penste-
mon
P. caryi
P. confertus, Yellow Penstemon
P. crandallii
P. cusickii
P. cyananthus, Wasatch Penste-
mon
P. diphyllus, Late Penstemon
P. eriantherus, Crested Beard-
tongue
P. fruticosus, Shrubby Penste-
mon
P. glaber, Smooth Penstemon
P. gracilis, Slender Penstemon
P. grandiflorus (P. bradburyi)
P. laricifolius, Larchleaf Penste-
mon
P. nitidus, Waxleaf Penstemon
P. pennellianus
P. pinifolius
P. procerus
P. secundiflorus
P. strictus
P. venustus
P. virens
P. virgatus ssp asa-grayi (P.
unilateralis)
Perideridia gairdneri, Yampa,
Squawroot
Petalostemon purpureum, Purple
Prairie Clover
Phacelia lineraris, Linear-leaf
Phacelia
P. sericea, Silky Phacelia
Phlox hoodii. Native Rock Phlox
Physaria didymocarpa, Common
Twinpod
P. geyeri
Polemonium pulcherrimum,
Showy Polemonium
P. viscosum, Sky Pilot, Skunk
Polemonium
Potentilla concinna, Elegant
Cinquefoil
Psoralea esculenta, Indian
Breadroot, Prairie Turnip,
Tipsinin (Blackfoot name)
Ranunculus glaberrinus, Sage-
brush Buttercup
Ratibida columnifera, Coneflower
Rhus glabbra ssp. cismontana,
Creeping Sumac
Ribes odoratum, Buffalo Currant,
Clove-Scented Currant, Golden
Currant

Rosa arkansana, Prairie Rose
Rumex venosus, Wild Begonia
Saxifraga bronchialis, Spotted
Saxifrage
S. oppositifolia
Scutellaria galericulata, Skullcap
S. resinosa
Sedum stenopetalum
Silene acaulis, Moss Campion
Smelowskia calycina, Silver
Rockcress
Solidago missouriensis, Goldenrod
Sphaeralcea coccinea, Scarlet
Globemallow
Spiderwort. See Tradescantia
occidentalis
Stanleya pinnata, Prince's Plume
Suksdorfia violacea
Telesonix jamesii (Boykinia
jamesii)
Tetradymia canescens, Gray
Horsebrush
Thermopsis rhombifolia, Yellow
Lupine, Buffalo Bean
Townsendia exscapa (T. sericea),
Easter Daisy
T. incana
T. parryi
Tradescantia occidentalis, Western
Spiderwort
Trollius laxus, Native Globeflower
Valeriana dioica, Marsh Valerian
Veronica cusickii
Viguiera multiflora, Goldeneye
Viola adunca, Early Blue Violet
V. blanda, Sweet White Violet
V. canadensis, Canadian Violet
V. macloskeyi
V. nuttalli, Yellow Prairie Violet
V. pedatifida, Purple Prairie
Violet

Grasses

Agropyron spicatum, Bluebunch
Wheat Grass
Andropogon scoparius
(Schizachyrium scoparium),
Little Bluestem

Bouteloua curtipendula, Sideoats
Grama Grass
B. gracilis, Blue Grama Grass
Buchloe dactyloides, Buffalo
Grass
Calamagrostis canadensis,
Bluejoint, Marsh Reed Grass
Deschampsia caespitosa, Tufted
Hair Grass
Eriophorum angustifolium,
Northern Cotton Grass
Koeleria cristata, June Grass
Linum perenne ssp. lewisii, Blue
Flax
L. rigidum
Melica spectabilis, Purple Onion
Grass
Oryzopsis hymenoides, Indian
Rice Grass
Phragmites communis, Common
Reed Grass, Cane Grass
Poa cusickii, Early Bluegrass
Sisyrinchium montanum (S.
angustifolium), Blue-eyed Grass
Sporobolus heterolepis, Prairie
Dropseed
Stipa comata, Needle and Thread,
Common Spear Grass
S. viridula, Green Needle Grass
Yucca glauca. Native Yucca
Zizia aptera, Heart-leaf Alexanders
Zygadenus elegans, White Camas,
Death Camas

Shrubs

Artemisia arbuscula
A. frigida, Fringed Sage, Woman
Sage
A. longifolium, Longleaf Sage-
brush
A. ludoviciana, Cudweed Sage,
Man Sage
Cercocarpus ledifolius, Curl-leaf
Mountain Mahogany
Chrysothamnus nauseosus,
Rubber Rabbit Bush
Holodiscus discolor, Mountain
Spray Bush

Ocean Spray
Juniperus communis
J. horizontalis, Carpet Juniper
J. sabina
J. scopulorum, Rocky Mountain
Juniper
Philadelphus lewisii, Mock
Orange Bush
Physocarpus opulifolius, Dart's
Golden Ninebark
Picea glauca 'conica,' Dwarf
Alberta Spruce
P. pungens, Colorado Blue
Spruce
Prunus besseyi, Sand Cherry
Sambucus canadensis, Purple
Elderberry
Sorbus tianshanica, Turkestan
Mountain Ash Bush
Viburnum dentago, Nannyberry

Trees

Abie lasiocarpa, Alpine Fir
Amelanchier alnifolia, Saskatoon,
Serviceberry
Betula occidentalis, Water Birch
Corylus hybrids, Hazelnut
Pinus flexilis, Limber Pine
P. ponderosa, Ponderosa Pine
Prunus virginiana ssp. melano
carpa, Chokecherry
Quercus macrocarpa, Burr Oak
Tilia americana, Native Linden

Vines

Clematis hirsutissima, Vase
Flower, Sugar Bowls
C. columbiana, Rocky Mountain
Clematis
C. ilgusticifolis, Traveler's Joy
C. occidentale, Native Blue
Clematis
Vitis riparia, Riverbank Grape

RESOURCE DIRECTORY

BOOKS

These books are the best ones I've ever found. Most are available on interlibrary loan at your local library.

My Favorites
Earthly Delights, Rosalind Creasy, Sierra Club Pub., 1985—good sections on prairie and pleasure gardening.
Easy Gardens, Donald Wyman and Curtis Prendergast, Time/Life Books, 1978.
The Easy Garden, Alec Bristow, Thomas Y. Crowell Pub., 1977.
The Fragrant Year: Scented Plants for Your Garden and Your House, Helen Wilson and Bell, M. Barrows and Co, Inc, 1967
The Heirloom Gardener, Carolyn Jabs, Sierra Club Pub., 1984.
Perennial Garden: Color Harmonies Through the Seasons, Jeff and Marilyn Cox, Rodale Press, 1985.
Landscaping with Wildflowers and Native Plants, William H. W. Wilson, Ortho Books, 1984.
Lawn Beauty The Organic Way, Glen F. Johns, Rodale Press, 1970.
Perennials, Frederick McGourty and Pamela Harper, HP Books Pub., 1985.
Perennials for the Western Garden, The Amateur Gardener's Fieldbook for the Growing of Perennials, Biennials and Bulbs, Margaret Klipstein Coates, Pruett Pub., 1976—a tremendous book written for Wyoming, but it never got the recognition it deserved.
Scented Flora of the World, Roy Genders, St. Martin's Press, 1977.
The Scented Garden, Rosemary Verey, Van Nostrum and Reinhold Co., 1981.
Sunset's New Western Garden Book, Sunset Books and Magazine, Lane Pub.—though criticized for ignoring the whole area east of the Cascades, it is still the definitive horticultural guide for North America.
The Well-Chosen Garden, Christopher Lloyd, Harper and Row Pub., 1984—a fun design book with great photos.
The Wild Garden: Making Natural Gardens Using Wild and Native Plants, Violet Stevenson, Penguin Books, 1985.

Canadian Agriculture Publications
Alberta Horticulture Guide—an exceptional guidebook of flowers, fruit and trees for the chinook zone. It is available at Alberta Agriculture offices in the province.
Nursery Propagation of Woody and Herbaceous Perennials for the Prairie Provinces, Agriculture Canada, pub #1733E—this publication is best for someone involved with propagation.
Preserving Flowers with Silica Gel, Agriculture Canada, pub #1649 1978—a fun book.
Tree Fruits for the Prairie Provinces, Agriculture Canada, pub #1672.

Fruit and Vegetable Guides
The Beautiful Food Garden: Encyclopedia of Attractive Food Plants, Kate Rogers Gessert, Van Nostrand Reinhold, Co, 1983.
The Complete Book of Edible Landscaping, Rosalind Creasy, Sierra Club Books, 1982.
Fruits and Berries for the Home Garden, Lewis Hill, Garden Way Pub., 1980.
Intensive Gardening Round the Year, Paul Doscher, Stephen Greene Press, 1981—good section on season extenders.
Potted Orchards: Growing Fruit in Small Spaces, Alan Simmons, David and Charles Pub., 1975—essential for Montana peaches and blueberries.
Unusual Vegetables: Something New For This Year's Garden, Rodale Press, 1978.

Prairie Books
Alpines of the Americas: The Report of the First Interim International Rock Plant Conference, American Rock Garden Society, 1976.
The Audubon Society Nature Guides: Grasslands, Lauren Brown, Alfred A. Knopf, Inc.
Directory to Resources on Wildflower Propagation, Missouri Botanic Garden, Box 299, St. Louis, MO 63166, $5 plus 4% for postage and handling. Has a number of regional sections.
Flora of Montana, Parts I and II, William Edwin Booth, Montana State University, 1950.
Flora of the Prairies and Plains of Central North America, Per. A. Ryberg, Hafner Pub., 1965.
Prairie Wildflowers: Showy Wildflowers of the Plains, Valleys, and Foothills in the Northern Rocky Mountain States, Dr. Dee Strickler, Falcon Press, 1986.
Jewels of the Plains, Wildflowers of the Great Plains, Grasslands and Hills, Claude A. Barr, Univ. of Minnesota, 1983—a famous and much loved book and author.
The Prairie Garden: 70 Native Plants You Can Grow in Town or Country, J. Robert and Beatrice Smith, Univ. of Wisconsin Press, Madison, WI, 1980.
Prairie Wildflowers—An Illustrated Manual of Species Suitable for Cultivation and Grassland Restoration, R. Currah, A. Smreciu and M. Van Dyk, published in 1983 by Friends of the Devonian Botanic Garden, Univ. of Alberta (Edmonton, Alta. T6G 1E9).
The Prairie World, David Costello, Thomas Crowell Pub., 1969—excellent, fun to read, highly recommended.
The Short Grass Prairie, Ruth Carol Cushman and Stephen R. Jones, Pruett Publishing Co., 1988.

Native Wildflowers and Wildlife
Alpine Wildflowers of the Rocky Mountains, Joseph F. Duft and Robert K. Moseley, Mountain Press Publishing, 1989.
The Arctic and the Rockies as Seen by a Botanist Pictorial, In-Cho Chung, Samhwa Printing, Seoul Korea, 1984—lots of color pictures. This book is worth any price!
Budd's Flora of the Canadian Prairie Provinces, revised by J. Looman and K. F. Best, published by Agriculture Canada, 1987.
Butterflies of North America, William Howe, Doubleday, 1976—color pictures.
Butterflies of the Rocky Mountain States, C. D. Ferris and F.M. Brown, Univ. of Oklahoma Press, 1981—black and white pictures.
Eating Wild Plants, Kim Williams, Mountain Press Publishers, 1977.
Flora of the Prairie Provinces, Bernard Boivin, Dept of Agriculture, Ottawa, Canada, 1969.
Gardening with Wildlife: A Complete Guide to Attracting and Enjoying the Fascinating Creatures in Your Yard, National Wildlife Federation, 1974—an illustrated how-to book, very enjoyable.
Sagebrush Country: Wildflowers 2, Ronald Taylor and Rolf Valum, Touchstone Press, 1974.

Vascular Plants of Montana, Robert Dorn, Mountain West Pub., Box 1471, Cheyenne WY, 1984.

Wildflowers of the Northern Great Plains, F.R. Vance, Univ. of Minn Press, 1984.

Wildflowers of the Pacific Northwest, Lewis J. Clark, Gray's Pub., Sidney, British Columbia, 1976—the very best book on wildflowers of the Northern Rocky Mountains, with lots of color pictures.

Wildlife in Your Garden, or, Dealing with Deer, Rabbits, Raccoons, Moles, Crows, Sparrows and Other of Nature's Creatures in Ways That Keep Them Around but Away from Your Fruits and Vegetables, Gene Logsdon, Rodale Press, 1983.

Design and Theme Books

All About Rock Gardens and Plants, Walter Kolaga, Doubleday and Co, 1966—an excellent book for mountain areas and central and northern Alberta.

The Art of Zen Gardens, A Guide to their Creation and Enjoyment, A. K. Davidson, J P Tarcher, Inc., 1983—a great how-to book on Japanese Gardens.

Decorative Gardening in Containers, Elvin McDonald, Doubleday, 1978.

Earthly Paradise: Garden and Courtyard in Islam, Jonas Lehrman, University of CA Press, 1980—exceptional book on the Persian garden.

The Garden: An Illustrated History, Julia Berrall, Viking Press, 1966.

Garden Design, Sylvia Crowe, Packard Publishing Ltd., 1981.

Garden Design: History, Principles, Elements, and Practice, Douglas, Frey, Johnson, Littlefield, and Von Valkenburgh, Simon and Schuster, 1987.

The Gardens of Japan, Teiji Itoh, Kodansha International, 1984—the very very best book on Japanese gardens.

Great Gardens of Britain, Peter Coates, G. P. Putnam's Sons, 1967.

Great Gardens of the Western World, Peter Coates, Spring Books, 1963.

Hedges, Screens and Espaliers, Susan Chamgerlin, H P Books, 1983

A History of Garden Art, Marie Luise Gothein, J. M. Dent and Sons, 1928.

How to Plan, Establish and Maintain Rock Gardens, George Schenk, Sunset Books-Lane Pub., 1964.

Ideas for Hanging Gardens, Sunset Books-Lane Pub., 1974.

Ideas for Entry Ways and Front Gardens, Sunset Books- Lane Pub., 1961.

Japanese Garden and Flora Art, Viola Kincaid, Hearthside Press, 1966—about Japanese gardens, the tea ceremony, and bonsai.

Japanese Gardens for Today, David H.

Engel, CE Tuttle Pub., 1959—great pictures.

Landscape Gardening in Japan, Josiah Conder, Dover Publishing, 1964.

Magic of Trees and Stones: Secrets of Japanese Gardening, Katsuo Saito and Sadaji Wada, Japan Publications Trading Co, 1964—excellent.

Medieval English Gardens, Teresa McLean, Viking Press, 1980.

Natural Landscaping, Designing with Native Plant Communities, John Diekelmann and Robert Schuster, McGraw Hill, 1982.

Right Plant, Right Place, Nicola Ferguson, Summit Books, 1984.

Theme Gardens, Barbara Damrosch, Workman Pub., 1982—an exceptionally beautiful illustrated book; this is one of my favorites.

A Thousand Years of Japanese Gardens, Samuel Newson, Tokyo News Service Ltd, 1953—exceptional book on the history and meaning of Japanese gardens, mostly in pictures and captions.

Victorian Gardens, John Highstone, Harper and Row Publishers, 1982.

What Makes the Crops Rejoice: An Introduction to Gardening, Robert Howard and Eric Skjei, Little, Brown and Co., 1986.

Miscellaneous Garden Books

Better Ways to Successful Gardening In Western Canada, Charles and Isabelle Young, 1970.

Bizarre Plants: Magical, Monstrous and Mythical, William A. Emboden, Macmillan Pub., 1974—a really fun book.

The Butterfly Garden, Michael Tekulsky, Harvard Common Press, Doubleday Co, 1980.

The Butterfly Gardener, Rothschild and Farrel, Rainbird Pub., London England, 1983—exceptional book including a section on creating a special greenhouse for butterflies.

Gardening by Mail: A Source Book, Barbara J. Barton, Tusker Press, 1986.

Gardening on the Prairies, A Guide to Canadian Home Gardening, Roger Vick, Western Producer Prairie Books, 1987.

Gardening Under the Arch, Millarville Horticultural Club, 1983—a very well written book on gardening in the chinook zone; particularly recommended is the section on birds.

Green Immigrants: The Plants that Transformed America, Claire Haughton, HarBrace, 1980.

Green Magic: Flowers, Plants and Herbs in Lore and Legend, Lesley Gordon, Webb and Bower Books, Exeter England, 1977—excellent section on Flower Lanquage.

Grow Native: Landscaping with Native and Apt Plants of the Rocky

Mountains, S. Huddleston and M. Hussey, Heddleston and Hussey, Denver Co, 1981.

The Low Maintenance Garden, A Complete Illustrated Guide to Designing, Planting and Keeping an Easy-to-Care-for Garden, NY Botanical Garden Institute of Urban Horticulture, Viking Press, 1983.

Making a Cottage Garden, Faith and Geoff Whiten, Salem House Pub., Salem England, 1985—a fun book on English gardening.

My Book of Flowers, Princess Grace of Monaco, Doubleday Pub., 1980—great ideas for parks for the handicapped, and wonderful stories about famous people, music, poetry and history.

The Natural Way to Pest-Free Gardening, Jack Kramer, Scribner Pub., 1972.

Nature's Design: A Practical Guide to Natural Landscaping, Carol Smyser, Rodale Press, 1982.

Park's Success with Seeds, Ann Reilly, Geo Park Seed Co, 1978.

Park's Success with Herbs, Foster and Louden, Geo Park Seed Co, 1980.

Park's Success with Bulbs, Alfred Scheider, Geo Park Seed Co, 1981.

Permaculture I and II, Bill Mollison, Internation Tree Crops Pub., 1979—the first volume is very rare, both volumes are excellent.

The Prairie Gardener, H.F. Harp, Hurtig Pub., Edmonton Alberta, 1970—a garden book written for the prairie provinces of Canada.

Reference Guide to Ornamental Plant Cultivars, Laurence C Hatch, Taxonomic Computer Research, PO Box 5747, Raleigh, NC, 27650—this is an on-going reference to plant variety names.

Rhetoric and Roses: A History of Canadian Gardening, Edwinna Von Baeyer, Fitzhenry and Whiteside Pub., 1984—an incredible book on Canada.

"Rx for Alkalinity," Richard and Shirley Flint, *Rodale's Organic Gardening Magazine*, Jan. 1986, pp. 73-77.

The Self-Sufficient Gardener, John Seymour, Doubleday and Co, Inc, 1979.

Trees and Shrubs for the Northern Plains, Donald Hoag, North Dakota Institute For Regional Studies, 1965.

University of Alberta Woody Ornamentals for the Prairies, Hugh Knowles, University of Alberta, 1989.

The Weatherwise Gardener: a Guide to Understanding, Predicting and Working with the Weather, Calvin Simonds, Rodale Press, 1983.

Wyman's Gardening Encyclopedia, Donald Wyman, Macmillan Pub., 1977.

Individual Plant Subject Books

The Bulb Book: A Photographic Guide to over 800 Hardy Bulbs, Martyn Rix, Toger Phillips, Pan Books Ltd, London England, 1981.

Bulbs: How to Select, Grow and Enjoy, George Harmon Scott, HP Books, 1982.

Gourds: Decorative and Edible, for Garden, Craftwork and Table, John Organ, Charles T Banford Co, 1963—everything there is to know about gourds.

A Handbook of Garden Irises, W. R. Dykes, Martin, Hopkinson and Co, 1924.

Making the Most of Clematis, Raymond J Evisosn, Flora Print Ltd, Nottingham England, 1979.

Manual of Dwarf Conifers, Humphrey Welch, Theophrastrus Press, 1979—good key for identification, but black and white pictures.

Modern Roses: The International Checklist of Roses, The McFarland Co, Harrisburg PA.

Ornamental Conifers, Charles R. Harrison, Hafner Press, 1975—extensively illustrated with color pictures.

Roses: How to Select, Grow and Enjoy, Richard Ray and Michael MacCaskey, HP Books, 1981.

The Water Garden, Anthony Paul and Yvonne Rees, Penguin Press.

Trees

Arboriculture: Care of Trees, Shrubs, and Vines in the Landscape, Richard W. Harris, Prentice-Hall, 1983—the best book on tree care that exists today.

How to Prune Almost Everything, John P Baumgardt, W. Barrows Pub., 1968.

"How to Hire a Tree-Care Pro", Steve Sandfort and Edwin Butcher, *American Forests Magazine*, Oct 1985.

Pruning Handbook, Sunset Editors, Sunset-Lane Pub., 1983.

Pruning: A How-to Guide for Gardeners, Michael MacCaskey and Robert Stebbins, HP Books, 1982.

Tree Ecology and Preservation, A Dernatzky, Elsevier Pub., 1978.

Trees in the Landscape, Graham Stuart Thomas, Jonathan Cape Ltd., 1983.

Urban Forestry, Gene W. Gray and Frederick Peneke, Wiley Pub., 1978.

Parks and Playgrounds

Design for Play, Richard Dattner AIA, MIT Press, 1969.

Environmental Planning for Children's Play, Arvid Bengtsson, Praeger Pub., 1970—a world view of playgrounds.

Especially for Great Falls: A Beautification Guide, by the Community Beautification Association—an excellent booklet of ideas for Great Falls, I hope they republish it.

Parks for our City-A Primer for Great Falls, Andy Beck, WICHE (Western Interstate Commission for Higher Education), P.O. Drawer P, Boulder CO—available for $4.00.

A Plan: Parks, Recreation, Open Space, Byron Stienerson, WICHE (Western Interstate Commission for Higher Education), P.O. Drawer P, Boulder, CO—this plan was written for Great Falls, Montana. Available for $4.00.

Play and Interplay, M. Paul Friedberg and Ellen Perry Berkeley, Macmillan Co, 1970—very thought provoking and insightful.

The Politics of Park Design: A History of Urban Parks in America, Galen Cranz, MIT Press, 1982.

Struggle for Space: The Greening of New York City, Tom Fox, Ian Koeppel and Susan Kellan, Neighborhood Open Space Coalition, 1985—an excellent book on how to find space for new parks and community gardens in a compressed city; very inspiring.

Urban Open Spaces, Cooper-Hewitt Museum, Smithsonian Institution Pub., 1981—fascinating ideas for waterfronts, plazas, park furniture, handicapped accessibility, and excellent reading list at end.

A Visual Approach to Park Design, Albert J. Rutledge, Garland STPM Press, 1981—fun to read.

Water in Landscape Architecture, Craig S. Campbell, Van Nostrand Reinhold Co., 1978—great ideas on waterfalls, presented with beautiful pictures.

The Really Miscellaneous Category

Birth Without Violence, Frederick Leboyer, Knopf Pub., 1975—a very important book, I wish every pregnant woman and her family could read this book.

Foundations of Findhorn, Eileen Caddy, Findhorn Foundation, 1976—my copy has been reread so many times it has become a clump of pages bunched together.

Gaia: An Atlas of Planetary Management, Dr Norman Myers, Anchor Books, 1984.

Living Poor with Style, Ernest Callenbach, Bantam Book—out of print; I hope they re-release it.

My Life, My Trees, Richard St. Barbe Baker, Lutterworth Press, London UK, 1970—an autobiography of a modern saint.

To Hear The Angels Sing, Dorothy Maclean, Lorian Press, 1980—a much beloved spiritual book on gardening.

2150 AD, Thea Alexander, Macro Books, 1971—you will read this book and start buying copies for all your friends. It is set in the year 2150 AD, and is partially a science fiction book. But mainly it is a joyous guide to what life is all about—this is the book you've been waiting for.

Vagabonding in the USA, Ed Buryn, Ed Buryn Pub., 1983—this is my all-time favorite book.

What to Do After You Turn the TV Off: Fresh Ideas for Enjoying Leisure Time with Children, Francis M. Lappe, Ballantine Books, 1985.

Wishcraft, How to Get What You Really Want, Barbara Sher, Ballantine Books, 1979—this book should be required reading for every man, woman and child on the planet, a great gift for new parents, high school students, burned-out employees, and anyone looking for a meaningful career and life. The best part about this book is that it's very, very fun to read and reread.

Work Your Way Around the World, Susan Griffith, Writer's Digest Books, 1983.

CATALOGS AND SOCIETIES

Organized as follows:
1. My Favorites
2. Iris Catalogs
3. Peonies, Daylilies and Hostas
4. Assorted Plant Catalogs
5. Garden Furnishings
6. Plant Societies
7. Canadian Addresses
8. Magazines
9. Book Sources
10. Miscellaneous Addresses
11. Semi-Political, Human Interest Organizations

My Favorites

Thompson and Morgan
PO Box 1308
Jackson, NJ 08527
    The oldest and biggest seed company in the world, free illustrated catalog that gives information on seeds. Send for this catalog first. Free.

Four Winds Nursery
Jerry Berner
P O Box 971
Polson, MT 59860
    One of the best ever.

Valley Nursery
Clayton Berg
PO Box 4845
Helena, MT 59601
    The best tree and shrub nursery in the chinook zone. Visit his nursery in Helena or Great Falls before buying plants anywhere else, but avoid buying topped trees from this or any other nursery.

Honeywood Lilies
Burt Porter and Allan Daku
Box 63
Parkside, Sask. S0J 2A0
  Much more than just lilies.

Shepherd's Garden Seeds
7389 W Zayante Rd
Felton, CA 95018
  The best vegetable catalog I've ever seen.

Andre Viette Farm and Nursery
Route 1, Box 16
Fishersville, VA 22939
  Sells perennial plants; great selection on Oriental poppy. Cost: $1.50

Garden City Seeds
1324 Red Crow Rd
Victor, MT 59875-9713
  A Down Home Project; exceptional vegetable seeds (some flower seeds). Cost: $1.

Seeds Blum
Idaho City Stage
Boise, ID 83706
  This is more than a heirloom seed company, it is like discovering a whole new bunch of friends. Cost: $1.

Lamb Nurseries
E. 101 Sharp Ave
Spokane, WA 99202
  Exceptional source for hard-to-find perennial and rock garden plants, sells plants. Free.

Lost Prairie Herb Farm
805 Kienas Rd
Kalispell, MT 59901
  A Rocky Mountain herb nursery. Cost: $2

G Seed Co
PO Box 702
Tonasket, WA 98855
  Mostly old-time vegetables selected for flavor, some flowers. "G" stands for Good. Cost: $1

Bear Creek Farms
PO Box 411
Northport, WA 99157
  Excellent source for fruit trees, specializong in old varieties selected for flavor. Cost: 2 stamps.

Friends of the Trees Society
P O Box 1466
Chelan, WA 98816
  An information source on permaculture, and tree and earth awareness—very highly recommended. Current yearbook is $4.

Abundant Life Seed Foundation
PO Box 772
Port Townsend, WA 98368
  Pretty good selection of vegetable and flower seed, excellent collection of books. Cost: $1.

Parks Seed Co.
Hwy. 254 N
Greenwood, SC 29647
  Send for this illustrated catalog even if you send for no others; sells both seed and plants. Free.

P. de Jager and Sons, Inc.
PO Box 100
Brewster, NY 10509
  One of the best illustrated bulb catalogs; specializes in bulbs. Free.

Rocknoll Nursery
9210 U.S. 50
Hillsboro, OH 45133-8546
  Everything in perennials. Free.

Siskiyou Rare Plant Nursery
2825 Cummings Rd
Medford, OR 97501
  The ultimate rare plant catalog. Free.

Chiltern Seeds
Bortree Stile
Ulverston, Cumbria, LA12 7PB, UK
  The ultimate British seed catalog.

Seed Savers Exchange
Kent Whealy, Director
PO Box 70
Decorah, IA 52101
  Not a seed company, but a group of dedicated people saving vegetable varieties; publishes both a Fall Harvest Book and an Annual Seed Yearbook. Membership: $10.00 (and well worth it!).

The Olde Thyme Flower and Herb
  Seed Exchange
Barbara Bond
RFD 1, Box 124A
Nebraska City, NE 68410
  Similar to the Seed Savers Exchange, except preserving flowers and herbs instead of vegetables.

Smith and Hawken
25 Corte Madera
Mill Valley, CA 94941
  The best tool and supply catalog in the world today, published quarterly; illustrated.

The Fragrant Path
PO Box 328
Fort Calhoun, NE 68023
  What else?—fragrant flowers. Cost: $1.

Wayside Gardens
Hodges, SC 29695
  The most spectacular illustrated garden catalog around, sells plants. Cost: $1.

Garden Place
6780 Heisley Rd
PO Box 83
Mentor, OH 44060
  A good selection of perennials: sells plants. Cost: $1.

White Flower Farm
Litchfield, CT 06759
  More like a garden book than a catalog; sold in most bookstores.

Siberia Seeds
Box 2026
Sweet Grass, MT 59484

Big Sky Wholesale Seeds
Box 852
Shelby, MT 59474
  Prairie grass and wildflowers. Free.

Iris Catalogs
Jayne K Ritchie
1713 Camas Ave. N.E.
Renton, WA 98056
  Dwarf and median iris. Free.

Kirkland Iris Garden
Carol and George Lankow
725 20th Ave. West
Kirkland, WA 98033
  Dwarf and median Iris. Free.

Riverdale Iris Gardens
7124 Riverdale Rd
Minneapolis, MN 55430
  An extremely large collection of dwarf and median iris. Free.

Cooper's Garden
212 W. Co. Rd C
Roseville, MN 55113
  The best collection of irises—period. Emphasis on species. Free.

Laurie's Garden
41886 McKenzie Hwy.
Springfield, OR 97478
  Large selection of Japanese iris, also many species and Siberian iris. Free

Chehalem Gardens
Tom and Ellen Abrego
PO Box 693
Newberg, OR 97132
  Great collection of Siberians and spurias. Free.
Tranquil Lake Nursery
45 River St.
Rehoboth, MA 02769
  Great collection of Siberians; also Japanese iris and daylilies. Free.

Melrose Gardens
The Connoisseur's Catalog
309 Best Rd S.
Stockton, CA 95205
  Very large collection of all kinds of iris. Cost: $1.

Maryott's Gardens
1678 Andover Lane
San Jose, CA 95124
  Mostly tall bearded iris; catalog with a few illustrations; listed because of their emphasis on fragrance in their catalog. Cost: $1.

Iris Test Gardens
Austin and Ione Morgan
1010 Highland Park Drive
College Place, WA 99324
   Price list from a noteworthy hybridizer of tall bearded iris. Free.

Schreiner's
3625 Quinaby Rd
Salem, OR 97303
   A profusely illustrated catalog of tall bearded iris. Cost: $2.

Cooley's Gardens
PO Box 126
Silverton, OR 97381
   Another illustrated wish book of tall bearded iris. Cost: $2.

Peonies, Daylilies and Hostas
Borbeleta Gardens
15974 Canby Ave—Route 5
Faribault, MN 55021
   A tremendous illustrated catalog of lilies, daylilies, Siberian iris and median iris. Cost: $3.

Busse Gardens
635 E 7th St., Rt. 2, Box 13
Cokato, MN 55321
   A great nursery with hardy perennials of all kinds. Cost: $1.

Gilbert H. Wild and Son, Inc.
Sarcoxie, MO 64862
   An illustrated wish book of peonies, iris and daylilies. Cost: $2.

Klehm Nursery
2 East Algonquin Rd
Arlington Heights, IL 60005
   A connoisseur's catalog of peonies, daylilies, iris, and hosta from a long-time hybridizer. Cost: $2.

Caprice Farm Nursery
15425 SW Pleasant Hill Rd
Sherwood, OR 97140
   Lots of peonies and iris. Cost: $1.

Greenwood Nursery
2 El Camino Ratel
Goleta, CA 93117
   A daylily collection included because of their emphasis on fragrant varieties. Cost: $1.

Tischler Peony Garden
1021 E Division St.
Faribault, MN 55021
   The best, most reliable source for peonies. Free.

Reath's Nursery
PO Box 521, 100 Central Blvd.
Vulcan, MI 49892
   A reliable source of peony hybrids. Cost: $1.

Englerth Gardens
2461 22nd St., Rt. 2
Hopkins, MI 49328
   Great collection of low-priced hosta and daylilies; not illustrated. Free.

Savory's Gardens
5300 Whiting Ave
Edina, MN 55435
   Large collection of hosta, no illustrations cost: $1.

Lenington-Long Gardens
7007 Manchester Ave.
Kansas City, MO 64133
   Large collection of daylilies. Cost: 2 stamps.

Assorted Plant Catalogs
Huff's Gardens
PO Box 187
Burlington, KS 66839
   Large selection with bloom date information, no illustrations. Free.

Dooley Gardens
Rt. 1
Hutchinson, MN 55350
   A small collection with bloom date information. Free.

King's
PO Box 368
Clements, CA 95227
   Very large collection of chrysanthemums with bloom date info, some illustrations. Free.

B and D Lilies
Bob and Dianna Gibson
330 "P" St.
Port Townsend, WA 98368
   Exceptional collection of lilies, illustrated catalog. Cost: $1.

Borbeleta Gardens, Inc.
15974 Canby Ave, Rt. 5
Faribault, MN 55021
   A great source for hardy lilies; illustrated catalog. Cost: $3.

McClure and Zimmerman
1422 W Thorndale
Chicago, IL 60660
   Amazing bulb seller. Free.

International Growers Exchange, Inc.
17142 Lahser Rd.
Detroit, MI 48219
   Tremendous catalog of bulbs now selling retail as well as wholesale; illustrated catalog. Cost: $3 (well worth twice this price)

John D. Lyon
143 Alewife Brook Parkway
Cambridge, MA 02140
   Species bulbs. Free.

John Scheepers, Inc.
63 Wall St.
New York, NY 10005
   High-quality bulbs. Free.

Grant E. Mitsch Daffodils
PO Box 218
Hubbard, OR 97032
   Connoisseur's collection and prices, illustrated catalog. Cost: $3.

Nancy R. Wilson
Species and Miniature Narcissus
571 Woodmont Ave
Berkeley, CA 94708
   Free.

Intermountain Cactus
2344 S. Redwood Rd
Salt Lake City, UT 84119
   Where else can you buy hardy cactus? Free.

Clifford's Perennial and Vine
Rt. 2, Box 320
East Troy, WI 53120
   Best noted for their clematis collection. Free.

The D. S. George Nurseries
2515 Penfield Rd
Fairport, NY 13350
   Clematis only.

Steffen Clematis
1259 Fairport Rd
Box 184
Fairport, NY 13350
Blackthorne Gardens
48 Quincy St.
Holbrook, MA 02343
   Best noted for their clematis collection. Cost: $1.

Le Marche Seeds International
PO Box 566
Dixon, CA 95620
   Gourmet collection of vegetable seeds. Cost: $3.

Vermont Bean Seed Co.
Garden Lane
Fair Haven, VT 05743
   Vegetable seeds.

Tsang and Ma
PO Box 294
Belmont, CA 94002
   Extensive catalog of Oriental vegetables and kitchenware. Free.

Graces Garden
10 Bay street
Westport, CT
   Truly bizarre vegetables—like square tomatoes. Free.

Rakestraw's Perennial Gardens and
   Nursery
3094 S Term St.
Burton, MI 48529
   Sedums and rock garden plants. Cost: $1.

Alpine Gardens
15920 SW Oberst Lane
Sherwood, OR 97140
   Sedums (stonecrop) and sempervivums (hen and chickens) cost: 50 cents.

Squaw Mountain Gardens
36212 SE Squaw Mtn. Rd
Estacada, OR 97023
   Sedums and sempervivums.

Van Ness Water Gardens
2460 N Euclid Ave
Upland, CA 91786
  Everything you need for a pond; great illustrated catalog. Cost: $2.

Heritage Rose Gardens
40350 Wilderness Rd
Branscomb, CA 95417
  It is best to buy shrub roses locally, but this is such a good company it is listed for connoisseurs. Cost: $1.

Pickering Nurseries, Inc.
670 Kingston Rd
Pickering, Ont. L1V 1A6
  Some say this is the best old-rose nursery. Cost: $1.

Heard Gardens
5355 Merle Hay Rd
Johnston, IA 50131
  A fantastic catalog; sells only lilacs.

Nichols Garden Nursery
1190 N Pacific Hwy.
Albany, OR 97321
  A tremendous catalog of herbs. Free.
Kurt Bluemel, Inc.
2740 Greene Lane
Baldwin, MD 21013
  Best known for his ornamental grasses. Cost: $1.

Joel W Spingarn
1535 Forest Ave
Baldwin, NY 11510
  It is best to buy dwarf conifers locally, but this catalog is listed for those connoisseurs who know what they want. Cost: $1.

Robin Parer
122 Hillcrest Ave
Kentfield, CA 94904
  Sells only hardy geraniums. Free.

Far North Gardens
16785 Harrison
Livonia, MI 48154
  For primrose connoisseurs. Cost: $2.

Cook's Geranium Nursery
712 North Grand
Lyons, KS 67554
  After this catalog, there will never again be such a thing a basic geranium. Cost: $1.

Wilson Plants
202 S Indiana
Roachdale, IN 46172
  Geraniums, African violets, and houseplants, illustrated. Free.

Native Plants, Inc.
1697 West 2100 North
PO Box 177
Lehi, UT 84043
  This company is a leader in the field of wildflower gardening.

Northplan Seed Producers
Box 9107
Moscow, ID 83843
  Seeds for native trees and wildflowers. Free.

Applewood Seed Co.
833 Parfet St.
Lakewood, CO 80215
  Wildflower seed mixes.

Dutch Mountain Nursery
7984 N. 48th St.
Augusta, MI 49012
  Trees and shrubs for attracting birds. Cost: 50 cents.

Kester's Wild Game Food
Nurseries, Inc.
PO Box V
Omro, WI 54963
  The name says it all—seed for wildlife cover and food—an exceptional catalog. Cost: $2.

Dorothy Biddle Service
Greeley, PA 18425
  A catalog of flower arrangement supplies. Free.

Ringer Research
6880 Flying Cloud Dr.
Eden Prairie, MN 55344
  Hi-tech organic supplies and fertilizers. Free.

Wild Westerners
McLaughlin's Seeds
Buttercup's Acre
Mead, WA 99021
  Native plants for gardeners in the mountains. Free.

Forest Farm
990 Tetherow Rd
Williams, OR 97544
  Same as above. Cost: $1.50.

High Altitude Gardens
P O Box 4238
Ketchum, ID 83340
  An exceptional and informative catalog of flowers and vegetables for mountain gardeners. Cost: $2.

Mushroom Supplies
Fungi Perfecti
P O Box 7634
Olympia, WA 98507
  An illustrated catalog of supplies and books. Cost: $2.50.

Full Moon Fungi
PO Box 6138
Olympia, WA 98502
  Cultures and spawn mix.

The Kinoko Company
P O Box 6425
Oakland, CA 94621
  A fascinating catalog of growing supplies for some very exotic mushrooms, as well as for dried mushrooms.

Mushroompeople
P O Box 158
Inverness, CA 94937
  The very best mushroom supplies and books catalog; includes a computer hook-up for more information. Cost: $2.

Prairie Ridge Nursery
RR2, 9738 Overland Rd
Mt. Horeb, WI 53572
  One of the most inspiring midwestern prairie nurseries. Free.

Stock Seed Farms, Inc.
R R 1, Box 112
Murdock, NE 68407
  Grass seed and prairie forbs. Free.

Organic Pest Management
Box 55267
Seattle, WA 98155
  Supplies and live bugs.

North Star Seed and Plant Search
Sandy Olsen
Box 1655 A, RFD 1
Burnham, ME 04922
  A computerized international search service for all hardy plants.

Garden Furnishings
Country Casual
17317 Germantown Rd
Germantown, MD 20874
  Hand-crafted garden furniture, including swings. Cost: $1

American Sundials, Inc.
300 Main St.
Point Arena, CA 95468
  Sundials of sorts. Free.

Clapper's
1125 Washington St.
West Newton, MA 02165
  European-style outdoor furniture. Free.

Erkins Studios
604 Thames St.
Newport, RI 02840
  Statuary and fountains. Cost: $4.

Florentine Craftsmen
46-24 28th St.
Long Island, NY 11101
  Statuary, urns, and flower boxes. Cost: $3.

Garden Concepts Collection
P O Box 241233
Memphis, TN 38124
  Essential hedonistic items for affluent gardeners, cost: $2.

Imagineering, Inc.
P O Box 648
Rockland, ME 04841
  Extremely high-quality garden furniture. Cost: $2.

Kenneth Lynch and Sons, Inc.
P O Box 488
Wilton, CT 06897
  An amazing illustrated catalog of European garden ornaments. Cost: $7.50.

Robinson Iron
Robinson Rd
Alexander City, AL 35010
   An ancient urn and vase company.
Cost: $3.

Seahorse Trading Co.
P O Box 677
Berryville, VA 22611
   Essential stonework for an English
garden. Cost: $3.50.

Vixen Hill Gazebos
Route 2
Phoenixville, PA 19460
   Victorian gazebos. Free.

Wind and Weather
P O Box 1012
Mendocino, CA 95460
   A great catalog of wind toys, weather
vanes, and many other things. Free.

Plant Societies
   All publish a newsletter or journal,
many have seed exchanges, field trips,
and annual get-togethers. Requests for
information are always welcome.

African Violet Society of America
P O Box 3609
Beaumont, TX 77704

Agri-Source Software Library
3815 Adams St
Lincoln, NE 68504
   Computer software for farmers and
gardeners.

American Daffodil Society
Miss Leslie Anderson
Route 3, 2302 Byhalia Rd
Hernando, MS 38632

American Gourd Society
Box 274
Mount Gilead, OH 43338

American Hemerocallis Society
Aine Busse
Rt. 2, Box 13
Cokato, MN 55321

American Herb Association
P O Box 353
Rescue, CA 95672

American Horticultural Society
Box 0105
Mount Vernon, VA 22121
   This is becoming the best garden society in the world. I support this organization above all others. Wait till you see all
they do. But their publication is the best
reason to join.

The American Hosta Society
Jack Freedman
3103 Heatherhill Dr.
Huntsville, AL 35802

American Penstemon Society
Mr. Orville M Steward
PO Box 33
Plymouth, VT 05056

American Peony Society
Greta Kessenich
250 Interlachen Rd
Hopkins, MN 55343

American Primrose Society
Candy Strickland
2722 E. 84th
Tacoma, WA 98445

American Rock Garden Society
Buffy Parker
15 Fairmead Rd
Darien, CT 06820
   A very active society.

American Rose Society
Box 30000
Shreveport, LA 71130

Bio-Dynamic Literature
Box 253
Wyoming, RI 02898

Brooklyn Botanic Gardens
1000 Washington Ave
Brooklyn, NY 11225

The Cactus and Succulent Society of
   America
Dept. of Zoology
San Diego State Univ.
San Diego, CA 92182

Canadian Prairie Lily Society
Dept. of Horticulture Science
Univ. of Saskatchewan
Saskatoon, Sask.
S7N 0W0
   The prairie lily (*Lilium philadelphi-
cum*) is Saskatchewan's floral em-
blem.
Coalition for Scenic Beauty
44 East Front St
Media, PA 19063
   Fights to control billboards.

The Cottage Garden Society
Mrs.Philippa Carr
15 Faenol Ave.
Abergele, Clwyd.
England, LL22 7HT

Devonian Botanic Garden
University of Alberta
Edmonton, Alta. T6G 2E9
   This is the best horticultural informa-
tion source for our area.

Denver Botanic Gardens
909 York Street
Denver, CO 80206
   This is the best resource in the chinook
zone, and they publish a fantastic newlet-
ter.

Elm Research Institute
Harrisville,NH 03450
   They love sending info for school
projects!

Greater Yellowstone Coalition
Box 1874
Bozeman, MT 59771

Heritage Rose Society
Mary Rae Mattix
120 N Barner Dr.
Centralia, WA 98531
   Heritage roses are shrub and old vari-
eties of roses.

Home Orchard Society
P O Box 776
Clackamas, OR 97015
   A really great organization.

Idaho Native Plant Society
Pahove Chapter
Box 9451
Boise, ID 83707

International Bee Research Associa-
tion
Hill House
Gerrards Cross, Bucks
England SL9 0NR
   An international center for informa-
tion on bees.

The International Delphinium Society
Mrs. Shirley Basset
Takakkaw, Ice House Wood
Oxted, Surrey
England RH8 9DW

The International Clematis Society
Mrs. Hildegard Widmann-Evison
Burford House
Tenbury Wells
Worcestershire
England WR15 8HQ

International Geranium Society
Mrs. Robin Schultz
5871 Walnut Dr.
Eureka, CA 95501
International Lilac Society
Walter Oakes
Box 315
Rumford, ME 04276

International Ornamental Crabapple
 Society
c/o T L Green
The Morton Arboretum
Lisle, IL 60532

Marigold Society of America
National Headquarters
Box 112
New Britain, PA 18901

Median Iris Society
Mrs. George Lankow
725 20th Ave. W.
Kirkland, WA 98033

Missouri Botanical Garden
P O Box 299
St Louis, MO 63166

Montana Land Reliance
Box 355
Helena, MT 59624

Montana Native Plant Society
P O Box 992
Bozeman, MT 59771-0992

National Center for Appropriate Technology
3040 Continental Dr.
Butte, MT 5959701
  Research in greenhouse and aquaculture techniques, in addition to solar energy. A tremendous library.

National Chrysanthemum Society
Galen Goss
5012 Kingston Dr.
Annandale, VA 22003

National Council for Therapy and Rehabilitation through Horticulture
9220 Wrightman Rd., Suite 300
Gaithersburg, MD 20879

National Sweet Pea Society
L. H. O. Williams
Acacia Cottage, Down Ampney
Nr. Cirencester, Glos., England
GL7 5QW

National Wildflower Research Center
2600 FM 973 North
Austin, TX 78725
  This is one of my favorites of all the listed plant societies.

National Xeriscape Council, Inc.
8080 South Holly
Littleton, CO 80122
  A great organization that encourages people to plant drought-tolerant landscapes.

The Nature Company
Box 2310
Berkeley, CA 94702
  Lots of fun stuff.

North American Fruit Explorers
Mary Kurle
10 S. 055 Madison St.
Hinsdale, IL 60521

The North American Lily Society, Inc.
Mrs. Dorothy Schaefer
P O Box 476
Waukee, IA 50263

Northern Nut Growers Assoc.
John English
R R 3, Box 167
Bloomington, IL

Perennial Plant Association
217 Howlett Hall
2001 Fyffe Court
Columbus, OH 43210
The Royal Horticultural Society
Wisley, Woking, Surrey
England GU23 6QB
  This is the granddaddy of them all.

Sempervivum Fanciers Assoc.
C. William Nixon
37 Ox Bow Lane
Randolph, MA 02368
  Sempervivums are "chickens and hens"

The Society for Siberian Irises
Mr. Gunther Stark
Rt. 1, Box 7
Norwalk, IA 50211

Society of Municipal Arborists
7447 Old Dayton Rd
Dayton, OH 45427

Species Iris Society
Mrs. J A Witt
16516 25th N.E.
Seattle, WA 98155

State Arboretum of Utah
University of Utah
Salt Lake City, UT 84112
(801) 581-4969
  Write or call for wildflower information (weekly reports).

The Terrarium Association
57 Wolfpit Ave
Norwalk, CT 06851

Tilth Association
4649 Sunnyside N.
Seattle, WA 98103
  Groups like this one give me hope for the future. The name refers to the quality of the soil, and they stress small-scale garden projects.

U S National Arboretum
24th and R Streets N.E.
Washington, DC 20002

Waterlily Society
PO Box 104
Buckeystown, MD 21717

Western Agricultural Research Center
531 Quast Lane
Corvallis, MT 59828
  Best known for Nancy Callan's work with fruit trees.

Western Sand Cherry Society
Don Birkholz
Broadus, MT 59317
  This group is involved with breeding fruits for extreme hardiness. If you like cherries, peaches, plums or apples—then get involved with this group.

Wyoming Native Plant Society
Box 1471
Cheyenne, WY 82003

Wyoming Outdoor Council
Box 1449
201 Main
Lander, WY 82520

The Xerces Society
10 SW Ash St
Portland, OR 97204
Protects butterfly habitat.

Canadian Addresses
  Canadian specialist plant societies list compiled by Trevor Cole; write to:

Plant Research Centre
Central Experimental Farm
Research Branch Bldg # 50
Ottawa, Ont. K1A 0C6
  A tremendous list of Canadian plant societies.

Alberta League for Environmentally Responsible Tourism
Box 1288
Rocky Mountain House, Alta. T0M 1T0

Alberta Nurseries and Seeds Ltd.
Box 20
Bowden, Alta. T0M 0K0

Alberta Regional Lily Society
Jim Annett
Devonian Botanic Garden
Univ. of Alberta
Edmonton, Alberta
T6G 2E1

Alberta Wilderness Assoc.
Box 6398, Stn D
Calgary, Alberta
T2P 2E1

Beaverlodge Nursery
Box 127
Beaverlodge, Alta. T0H 0L0

Calgary Dahlia Society
Mrs. F. Van Gastel
2310 Morrison St SW
Calgary, Alta. T2J 3J3

Calgary Garden Club
Mr Bill Henderson
2436 25th St SW
Calgary, Alta. T3E 1X6.

Calgary Horticultural Society
Mrs. Gerda White
2004 27th Ave. SW
Calgary, Alta. T3E 1X6

Calgary Rose Society
Mrs. Eric Whiteside
#419, 3131 63rd Ave. SW
Calgary, Alta.

Canadian Chrysanthemum and Dahlia Society
G. H. Lawrence
83 Aramaman Dr
Agincourt, Ont. M1T 2PM

Canadian Geranium and Pelargonium Society
B. van Assum
254 W Kings Rd
North Vancouver, BC V7N 2L9

Canadian Gladiolus Society
P. Q. Drysdale
3770 Hardy Rd—RR1
Agassiz, BC

Canadian Iris Society
V. Laurin
199 Florence Ave
Willowdale, Ont. M2N 1G5

Canadian Orchid Journal Society
Charlotte M Ball
PO Box 9472, Station B
St John's, NF A1A 2Y4

Canadian Organic Growers
Lida Martin
146 Elvaston Dr
Toronto, Ont. M4A 1N6

Canadian Parks and Wilderness Society
#200, 11044 - 82 Ave.
Edmonton, Alta. T6G 0T2

Canadian Prairie Lily Society
—listed with Plant Societies (above)

Canadian Rose Society
B. Hunter
20 Portico Dr
Scarborough, Ont. M1G 3R3

The Canadian Wildflower Society
35 Bauer Crescent
Unionville, Ont. L3R 4H3

Coaldale Nurseries
Box 1267
Coaldale, Alta. T0K 0L0

Eagle Lake Nurseries, Ltd.
Box 819
Strathmore, Alta. T0J 3H0

Edmonton Horticultural Society
Mrs.Arlene Smith
11707 150th Ave
Edmonton, Alta. T5X 1C1

Federation of Alberta Naturalists
Box 1472
Edmonton, Alta. T5J 2N5

Friends of the Earth—Canada
53 Queen St, Room 16
Ottawa, Ont. K1P 5C5

Golden Acre Garden Centres, Ltd.
620 Goddard Ave. N.E.
Calgary, Alta. T2K 5S6

Lacombe Nurseries, Ltd.
Box 1480
Lacombe, Alta. T0C 1S0

Lethbridge Horticultural Society
Miss Sue Black
623 18th St S.
Lethbridge, Alta. T1J 3E9

Prairie Seeds, Ltd.
R.R. 1
S. Edmonton, Alta. V3T 4N6

Rocky Mountain Seed Service
Box 215
Golden, BC V0A 1H0

Sanctuary Seeds
2388 West 4th St.
Vancouver, BC V6K 1P1

Saskatchewan Natural History Society
Box 1784
Saskatoon, Sask. S7K 3S1

Shearer Properties, Ltd.
9515 49th Ave.
Edmonton, Alta. T6E 5Z5
Sierra Club of Western Canada
620 View St
Victoria, BC V8W 1J6

Southern Alberta Environmental
Group
2302 20th Ave. S
Lethbridge, Alta. T1K 1G5

Tansy Farm
R.R. 1-D
Agassiz, BC V0M 1A0
Large selection of herbs. Cost: $1.50
Western Canadian Society for Horti-
culture
Lewis Lenz
Plant Science Dept.
Univ. of Manitoba
Winnepeg, Man. R3T 2N2
The Wildlife Society of Canada (Alber-
ta Chapter)
c/o IEC—Beak Consultants
5925 - 3 St
Calgary, Alta. T2H 1K3

Wild Rose College of Natural Healing,
Ltd.
302, 1220 Kensington Rd NW
Calgary, Alta. T2N 3P3

Magazines
I encourage people to donate sub-
scriptions to their local libraries.

The Bu$iness of Herbs
P O Box 559
Madison, VA 22727
A really great magazine for people
who make money from their plant hob-
bies.

Garden Design
1733 Connecticut Ave. N W
Washington, DC 20009
Expensive, but worth its weight in
gold.

Gardens For All
180 Flynn Ave
Burlington, VT 05401
An excellent magazine.

Horticulture
755 Boylston St
Boston, MA 02116
You can buy this in any garden store;
try there first.

Hort Ideas
Route 1
Gravel Switch, KY 40328
This newsletter has all the latest news
for gardeners and is wonderfully humorous, also. You'll wonder how you
ever made it without it.

Mushroom
The Journal of Wild Mushrooming
Box 3156, Univ. Station
Moscow, ID 83843

Book Sources
Carol Barnett—Books
3128 SE Alder Ct
Portland, OR 97214
A seller of rare gardening books.

The Book Nest
National Audubon Society
Richardson Bay Audubon Center
376 Greenwood Beach Rd
Tiburon, CA 94920
They carry books on wildlife.

The Greater Spiral
P O Box 12515
Portland, OR 97212
New Age tapes and books—wonder-
ful!

Ian Jackson
P O Box 9075
Berkeley, CA 94709
Another seller of rare gardening books

Looking Glass Bookstore
318 SW Taylor
Portland, OR 97204
The best bookstore in Portland; now
they send a Christmas catalog.

Miscellaneous Addresses
American Kitefliers Association
113 W. Franklin St.
Baltimore, MD 21201
The national organization of kitefliers,
and publisher of a lively magazine.

Center For Urban Horticulture
University of Washington
Seattle, WA 98195

Cheweka Graphics
Rice, WA 99167
They make beautiful Tibetan prayer
flags. The Tibetans believed that the
wind carried along the messages on the
flags and imbued the local area with
their special magic.

Duncraft
Penacook, NH 03303
A catalog of bird feeders, and other
supplies, guaranteed to warm anybody's
heart. Free.

The Farallones Institute
15290 Coleman Valley Rd
Occidental, CA 95465
A network for appropriate technology
and small-scale agriculture.

Flower Essence Society
PO Box 586
Nevada City, CA 95959
This organization continues the work
of Dr. Bach, famous for his flower
remedies. Send $2.50 for a copy of their
journal.

Gnome News
Gnomes Anonymous
Alexion
224 Kingston Rd
New Malden, Surrey, England
A club for the little folk (elves, gnomes,
and fairies) and for big folk with a sense
of humor.

Herb-Pharm
P O Box 116
Williams, OR 97544
A very reputable, and established, healing herb source; sells mostly tinctures. Cost: $1.

The International Permaculture Seed
  Yearbook
P O Box 202
Orange, MA 01364
An important source for publications on permaculture.

Into The Wind
2047 Broadway
Boulder, CO 80302
I can't say enough good things about this catalog. If you're not interested in kites, then send for it to look at the pictures. A hint: kites make great multi-colored decorations. If you do send for kites, then ask which kites do best in the gusty Chinook winds. Cost: $1.

Kitelines
7106 Campfield Rd
Baltimore, MD 21207
The premier kite fliers' magazine; ask around town in the bookstores for it.

New Alchemy Institute
237 Hatchville Rd
East Falmouth, MA 02536
Similiar to Farallones only much more dynamic.

Permaculture Institute of North America
6488 S. Maxwelton Rd.
Clinton, WA 98236
This is in the forefront of the permaculture movement in North America.

Plant Database Library
Taxonomic Computer Research
Box 5747
Raleigh, NC 27650
Horticultural information on computer disks. They also sell plant markers with the same information printed on them—this would be of interest to nurseries and landscapers.

Semi-Political Human Interest Organizations
Children of the Green Earth
P.O. Box 95219
Seattle, WA 98145
Their spiritual-political focus is on the importance of tree planting, especially by children.

Circle Magazine
Box 1682
Helena, MT 59624
This is a magazine of new age classes and happenings around the state. It is closely tied to the Feathered Pipe Ranch near Helena.

Earth First!
P.O. Box 235
Ely, NV 89301
A group of people whose number-one concern is the protection of the earth.

Great Bear Foundation
P.O. Box 2699
Missoula, MT 59806
They are concerned about the protection of bears and publish a newsletter called *The Bear News*.

Heartland
P.O. Box 7282
Missoula, MT 59807
An excellent new age magazine, perhaps the most important magazine in Montana.

Holyearth Foundation
P.O. Box 399
Monte Rio, CA 95462
Earth Stewards Network: their name says it all.

In Context
A Quarterly of Human Sustainable
Culture
P.O. Box 2107
Sequim, WA 98382
A very informative magazine devoted to a different topic each issue, such as education, friendships, economics, and restoring the North American dream.

The Montana Environmental Information Center
P.O. Box 1184
Helena, MT 59624-1184
A political organization that fights to protect the land.

Montana Wilderness Association
P.O. Box 635
Helena, MT 59624

Planet Drum Foundation
P.O. Box 31251
San Francisco, CA 94131
Their focus is on creating an awareness of bioregional identification.

Pueblo to People
5218 Chenevert #1013
Houston, TX
A catalog of choice hand-crafted goods from Central America. They merchandise crafts of the common people in hopes of breaking the poverty cycle. Besides their altruistic purpose, these goods are of exceptional quality and are very cheaply priced.

Sunbow Quilt Project
14812 S.E. 368th
Auburn, WA 98002
A peace organization which organizes the sending of quilts to paired cities of the US and USSR.

INDEX

ACKNOWLEDGMENTS

Closing is a time for thanking the readers (thank you), and adding the stories of the other people involved in this guide. First there is Dr. Homer Metcalf, retired Professor of Ornamental Horticulture at Montana State University. Joining his fine company are Duncan Himmelman, Buck Godwin, Thom Rypien and the exceptionally generous staff of the Department of Plant Science, Olds College, Alberta. Much heartfelt gratitude for the patient help of Brendan Casement and Paul Regan, Brooks, Alberta, and the kind staff at Morden Research Station (Lynn Collicott, Bert Chubey, and Campbell Davidson). Finally there is the ever-patient librarian, Jane Gates, at the Strybing Arboretum, San Francisco.

For the Clematis and Rose section, I am forever indebted to Stanley Zubrowski of Prairie River, Sasketchewan. Many other inspired gardeners offered their knowledge. Most notable among these wonderful people are Jamie Sagmiller of Ronan, Montana; Mrs. Betty Enns and Bill Metzlaff, both of Calgary, Alberta; Dr. Dale Herman at NDSU, Fargo, North Dakota; Klaus Lackschewitz, Missoula, Montana; Jan Nixon of Bozeman, Montana; Louis Hagener, Havre, Montana; Phyllis Pierrepont, Bowsman, Manitoba; Pat Heally, Belmont, Manitoba; Panyoti and Gwen Kelaidais of Denver, Colorado; Jean Witt of Seattle, Washington; Arthur Lee Jacobson also of Seattle, Walter Oakes (of the International Lilac Society); Cliff Lewis (of the Penstemon Society); and Roy Davidson (plantsman extraordinaire). And not to be forgotten are Jim Annett, Rodger Vick, and Peter Odynski of the Devonian Botanic Gardens at Edmonton, Alberta, and dear old Clayton Berg of Valley Nursery, Helena, Montana (a legend in his own time). These people are the wellspring of my inspiration.

And then to complete the process, my friend Tyler Preston and his amazing computer system did the layout and page setting [of the original edition] entirely in WordPerfect and DrawPerfect using a Hewlett Packard LaserJet printer and ScanJet scanner.

Perhaps at this point I should introduce myself. I am 32 years old and seemingly rather young and inexperienced to be doing such a project. Furthermore, I must state that my qualifications for doing this guide are an exceptional memory for plant names and a determination to finish this creation. It's kind of like having a baby. For several years now, the driving madness of artistic pursuit has precluded all other areas of interest. Needless to say, most of my friends are very tired of my talking about plants, local history, print options and marketing. But all would agree that it's been quite an adventure.

Now I search for words to thank someone who is nearest and dearest to my heart. With tears and a great lump in my throat, I can say only that this person is my friend. She is my grandmother, Helen S. Maberry.

James D. Searles released the original edition of The Garden of Joy *in 1990 under his Medicine River Publishing imprint. He also was the author and publisher of* What To Do on a Boring Day in Great Falls: A Winter/Summer Adventure Guide, *about his chinook-zone hometown of Great Falls, Montana. He died in 1991.*

Cover art by Kevin Nicolay.

The author gathered the illustrations in this volume from a variety of rare 19th and early 20th century gardening and botany books from the United States and Europe.